# The Norton Book of

# American Autobiography

# THE NORTON BOOK OF

# AMERICAN AUTOBIOGRAPHY

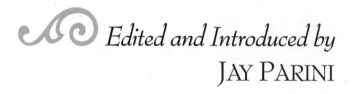

*Edited and Introduced by*
JAY PARINI

*and with a preface by*
GORE VIDAL

W · W · NORTON & COMPANY · NEW YORK · LONDON

Copyright © 1999 by Jay Parini

All rights reserved
Printed in the United States of America
First Edition

The text of this book is composed in Avanta with the display set in Bernhard Modern
Composition and manufacturing by the Haddon Craftsmen, Inc.
Book design by Antonina Krass

Since this page cannot legibly accommodate all the copyright notices, pages 709–711
constitute an extension of the copyright page.

Library of Congress Cataloging-in-Publication Data
The Norton book of American autobiography / edited and introduced by Jay Parini and
with a preface by Gore Vidal.
p. cm.
Includes bibliographical references.
ISBN 0-393-04677-X
1. Autobiographies—United States. 2. United States—Biography.
I. Parini, Jay.
CT211.N67   1999
920.073—dc21                                                                    98-43398
                                                                                    CIP

W. W. Norton & Company, Inc., 500 Fifth Avenue, New York, N.Y. 10110
http://www.wwnorton.com

W. W. Norton & Company Ltd., 10 Coptic Street, London WC1A 1PU

1  2  3  4  5  6  7  8  9  0

# CONTENTS

# PREFACE

BY GORE VIDAL

When one considers that Jay Parini's generous collection is only the tip of an iceberg—a whole Antarctica of American memoir-writing—one is duly awed by his bravery at what he includes and excludes. If American memoir-writing has a specific genesis it is the dour Puritanism of the first British settlers, with their conviction that each of us must bear witness to God directly for his life and deeds. Hence, the self-mortification of seventeenth- and eighteenth-century writers, with Ben Franklin as the sly joker who had all life every which way, to the chagrin of Jefferson, the *bon viveur* Virginian, and John Adams, New England's stern moralist. With later arrivals from other lands, our original Protestantism has been heavily diluted; new voices clamor to be heard. Meanwhile, at the start of the twentieth century, Henry Adams put *finis* to the founders' world: *The Education of Henry Adams* slyly celebrates in a third-person autobiography the failure of his life and mind in a masterpiece of overwrought irony, making possible the modern world's self-flagellaters like Fitzgerald and spacious reporters of man's condition like the great Theodore Dreiser.

There are interesting, if unlikely, connections between some of the writers here on display. Gertrude Stein thought (as I do) that Ulysses S. Grant's memoir was the best American prose, proof that genius is innate since West Point's English department, in his day, did not dazzle. The enthusiasm of Emerson for Whitman is well known and does two totally dissimilar writers considerable credit. James Baldwin's agon with Malcolm X still reverberates. But then writers are often at their most interesting when writing against other selves, as contemporaries of the same rank tend to be—same but other. Henry James once noted, somewhat wearily, "The historian, essentially, wants more documents than he can really use; the dramatist only wants more liberties than he can really take." So what does the memoirist want? Proof that he was there, that wherever he was, is. Is this vanity? Perhaps. Perhaps in vain, too. But then as the French writer Jules Renard noted: "I find that when I do not think of myself I do not think at all."

9

# INTRODUCTION

## BY JAY PARINI

Autobiography could easily be called the essential American genre, a form of writing closely allied to our national self-consciousness. Any shortlist of classic American texts, for example, would have to include Benjamin Franklin's *Autobiography*, Henry David Thoreau's *Walden*, Mark Twain's *Life on the Mississippi*, Frederick Douglass's *Narrative of the Life of Frederick Douglass*, and *The Education of Henry Adams*. These are all works that would muscle aside most American novels or volumes of poetry of the same period.

It should perhaps have come as no surprise that autobiography would become a central, even dominant, form of writing in a society devoted, at least in principle, to the notion of radical equality: democracy presupposes a social context in which the individual is not only valued but preeminent and also representative. That is, the individual member (in literature as in politics) *stands in* for the group, suggesting that his or her experience is general. When Emerson prophesied that autobiography would become the central form of American literature, enabling each author (thus self-authorized) to acquire power in the world through writing, he went so far as to suggest (in "Experience") that "the true romance which the world exists to realize will be the transformation of genius into practical power."

That sense of genius translating itself into practical power already existed in *The Autobiography of Benjamin Franklin*, which is not only the first major autobiography by an American but one in which the revolutionary nature of the American character becomes, in effect, the subject of the work itself. Franklin had access to two models for writing his life: the "confession" and the "memoir." In the former, as in the *Confessions of Saint Augustine* or Rousseau's *Confessions*, the writer reveals his inner torments or moments of ecstasy—an account of private experience. In the memoir, the writer offers a chronicle of external events: wars, political battles, business ventures; the role of the individual on the great stage of history becomes the subject.

Franklin originally resorted to the title *Memoirs* for his account of his life; the term "autobiography" did not yet exist. A revolutionary genre, autobiography came of age in the wake of the American and French revolutions—political movements that, whatever else they did, released the energies of the modern self. (According to the *Oxford English Dictionary*, the term "autobiography" was first used by Robert Southey, the English poet, in a review published in 1809.) Franklin's account of his own life certainly broke the generic boundaries suggested by "memoir" and "confession," combining both and moving beyond both as he narrates his rise from obscurity, his steady progress from desire to fulfillment, from conflict to resolution. He was writing an "exemplary life" of himself.

In the past, "exemplary lives" of saints were often written to suggest ways to live in the world. Indeed, the Gospels were the first great example of this genre in the West; one was quite literally meant to imitate Christ. In the Middle Ages, the lives of saints were popular in the same vein. But Franklin made a radical move in putting himself forward as a model, composing a New World gospel of self-reliance, self-proficiency, and self-realization.

Franklin writes specifically about the period between 1771 and 1788—the years when the Revolution led to confederation and the former colonies were organized under the Constitution. These events (in which he played a key role) are nevertheless displaced by the story of his own progress and development; Franklin becomes, in effect, the incarnation of radical democracy. How he moved from powerlessness in the world to purchase, from nowhere to somewhere, directly parallels the American story: its self-removal from colony to independent power.

This remarkable work is both history and fiction, although the events it describes are factual. Yet one must come to terms with Franklin's astonishing exclusion of the major historical events of his times, events in which he actually played a part. Fiction, as it were, means "shaping," from the Latin *fictio*. The facts of any life are too overwhelming, too detailed, too confusing to constitute a narrative; all narrative works by exclusion. The autobiographer cancels in order to clarify, shaping experience to make it readable, using techniques normally found in fiction, such as foreshadowing or scene setting. It is not surprising that novelists have often been important autobiographers as well.

Like the novelist, the autobiographer creates a parallel world, a linguistic fabric that somehow corresponds to the "real" world of what happened. But the reader, like the writer, knows that only a part of what happened is being told. A vast range of experience (much of it inarticulate, mute) is left out, left to challenge and subvert the text that appears on the printed page. Every sentence of every autobiography at once nails down and excludes something, and that sense of a vast, inaccessible world of "life" that the autobiography draws from is part of the fascination of the form, for both reader and writer.

American literature begins with Benjamin Franklin. Before that, there was colonial literature. And though we have earlier memoirs, such as Mary Rowlandson's astonishing account of her captivity in 1675 or Jonathan Edwards's account of his religious awakening, the genre of autobiography does not properly begin until Franklin writes the history of a self-created life, represented here by the chapter in which (with more than a touch of irony) he describes his "bold and arduous Project of arriving at Moral Perfection," an enterprise well suited to the New World, where citizens become their own Adams or Eves, summoning Paradise on their own terms.

Franklin set the standard for American autobiography, and future writers would work with or against his grain. That he wrote in a revolutionary, or transitional, time is worth noting; it may be that autobiographical writing tends to peak during periods of upheaval, when the drama of daily political life seems to outstrip the possibilities of fiction; the next great period of crisis in American culture culminated in the Civil War, and the major autobiographical text of this period was Henry David Thoreau's *Walden*. Though Thoreau wrote well before the war broke out, issues of slavery and abolition weighed heavily on his mind as he wrote. He was, in effect, laying down the gauntlet. Part of the force of his work lies in its moral challenge to the reader. The author seems to be saying: this is how to front the essentials of life, how to strip existence to its bare elements, how to discover what is important and what is not.

More so than Franklin by far, Thoreau draws on the techniques of fiction, turning his two years into one for the sake of economy, allowing the cycle of four seasons to stand in for the cycle of life. The book moves toward an end point, toward the dissolving ice on the pond in spring, toward a "Conclusion," something most autobiographers resist, not wanting to complete their own life and kill their fictive selves. Yet the optimism of America, so evident in all of Emerson, who was Thoreau's mentor and friend in Concord, radiates in the "Conclusion" of *Walden*: "I learned this, at least, by my experiment; that if one advances confidently in the direction of his dreams, and endeavors to live the life which he has imagined, he will meet with a success unexpected in common hours."

This is the democratic hope—a vision of fulfillment that is self-constructed, that comes not by fiat from above (signaling the favors of a God or some royal patron) but from within. Thoreau's revolutionary notion is that the instruments of our liberation lie at hand, as near as the neighboring pond. Writing just before the cataclysm of the Civil War, he envisions a kind of freedom that entails a liberation from the machinery of production, from the soiled world of industrialism, from the human depredations of slavery, from the growing din of mass culture, which was already threatening to overwhelm the quiet and calm inner voice, the last retreat of the self.

*Walden* is also, of course, a founding text in the tradition of nature writing—a genre that has been essential to American literature since the mid-nineteenth century. Much of the best nature writing is also autobiographical, since the forms closely overlap, and both involve the production of self-consciousness. One sees this autobiographical motive at work in many of our finest current nature writers, such as Annie Dillard, Edward Hoagland, Edward Abbey, John Elder, Scott Russell Sanders, and others. (Dillard, Sanders, and Elder are represented in this collection by pieces where encounter with the natural world is central to a process of self-discovery.)

Many autobiographies fall into a category often called "conversion narratives," stories about self-transformation. Religious conversion as autobiographical focus reaches back to Saint Augustine, who transmogrified sexual energies into spiritual energies through repentance and redirection: the Pauline story redescribed. Countless religious autobiographies followed this example, which still manages to inspire a good number of contemporary autobiographies. In the mode of confessions, Jean-Jacques Rousseau created a modern prototype, describing his secular conversion to a life governed by deep feeling and inspired by the powers of imagination; his work thus became a founding text in the Romantic tradition. In poetry, the tradition of personal growth or transformation finds its archetype in Wordsworth's *Prelude*, a book-length poem on "the growth of the poet's mind." But in prose, in America, it is Franklin and Thoreau who offered autobiographical modes that later writers would imitate and extend.

One of the most widely read autobiographies of the nineteenth century was the *Memoirs of U. S. Grant*. In keeping with the traditional notion of memoir, Grant wrote mostly about the external events of his life in the realms of war and politics. There was, of course, much to relate about his career as leader of the Union's military forces during the Civil War and, later, as president of the United States. A heroic one beyond doubt, on many fronts, Grant's life not only had a public aspect; it was shaped by history. On the other hand, his *Memoirs* begin with his "private" history, tracing his rise from obscurity to prominence as vividly as in any autobiography. We learn of his early soldiering in the Mexican war, his famous Civil War battles, his views of war in general. For the most part, Grant saw himself as a military man, not a politician, and his memoirs fall in a tradition of memoirs by military men going back to Julius Caesar and running through Napoleon, who dictated his memoirs to four assistants from exile on St. Helena, referring to himself (like Caesar) in the third person, as befitted a man who was not so much a recorder of history as history itself.

Grant, wisely, writes in the first person. He is the American self in progress, self-realizing, increasing in influence as the chronology proceeds, modestly enjoying his accomplishments, such as the campaign against Vicksburg—the account included here, one of the most arresting scenes depicted in his *Memoirs*. It is interesting to note that these memoirs were in themselves the author's last battlefield: he was bankrupt at the end of his life and desperate to make enough money to salvage his finances and leave something for his family to live on. Although he did not live to see his book published, it was immensely popular, and his goal of financial security for his family was attained, his last battle won.

Grant's publisher was Mark Twain, who offered liberal royalties and knew exactly how to promote Grant, as he had over the years promoted himself. This was the same Twain who had written to his wife, Olivia Langdon Clemens, that he would never touch a project "if there wasn't money in it." The commercial value of literary work—the swift translation of imagination into hard capital—was part of the age, and Twain represents the entrepreneurial author in the extreme. He spent his life mining his own experience relentlessly, always managing to find another fresh vein, as in *Life on the Mississippi* (1883), where he writes about his years as a pilot on a riverboat. "When I was a boy," Twain says (in one of several chapters included here), "there was but one permanent ambition among my comrades in our village on the west bank of the Mississippi River. That was, to be a steamboatman." Thus the reader is led to share the author's young ambition and to join him on the river. Twain would rewrite his life many times, publishing a formal *Autobiography* at the end of his career, but his finest moments as an autobiographer will be found in *Life on the Mississippi*.

Twain's is a particularly important kind of autobiographical book—one that takes a discrete period in an author's life, circles it, and sets it apart as a fiction, a shaped thing. The ideal model for this was Richard Henry Dana's remarkable *Two Years before the Mast* (1840), the story of a nineteen-year-old Harvard boy who went to sea on a two-year voyage around Cape Horn to California. The title alone sets the parameters of the journey: its romance, its adventurousness. The work is written in diary form, and the content breaks upon the reader as the experience broke upon the author. The sharpness of observation seen throughout Dana's book impressed readers at the time, and it appealed to later critics, including D. H. Lawrence, who in his *Studies in Classic American Literature* (1922) selected this as one of the classics (this good opinion of Dana was also held by Herman Melville, another seafaring author).

Dana represents a type of American, one still harking back to England, to the idea of the English gentleman, one who goes into the wild but retains a basic coolness, an aloofness. There is a fastidiousness about Dana's prose that seems characteristic of the man, who was shaping a version of himself for public consumption. Dana is not, like Franklin, telling us about his rise in the world; nor is he, like Thoreau, offering a covert critique of the body politic; rather, he is always the detached observer, writing in a prose stripped of emotional freight, even when the scene (as in part of the excerpt here) concerns a flogging. His manner anticipates the later prose styles of Stephen Crane, Ernest Hemingway, and a vast trail of cool recorders of experience. Dana also establishes the mode of travelogue-as-autobiography, a form used in different ways by such writers as Mark Twain (in *The Innocents Abroad*) and Theodore Dreiser (as in *A Hoosier Holiday*, excerpted here). In Dana's book, the hero is the author himself, who follows the mode of what Joseph Campbell has called the "heroic journey," a journey wherein the hero breaks away from his customary world (Harvard, upper-middle-class Boston) and goes off in search of some boon (adventure, sexual experience, self-knowledge). The hero returns a changed person, a grown man.

Among the oddest, and finest, examples of American autobiography is *The Education of Henry Adams* (1918), which was conceived and written between 1905 and 1907. Adams's book marked a kind of watershed for American autobiography, a work that both summarized all that went before and commented, ironically, on the form itself. It becomes a kind of end point for autobiography: a book that future autobiographers must ignore or go around. Unlike Franklin and Thoreau, Adams did not offer much of a generative model; himself a historian (he wrote a nine-volume history of the administrations of Jefferson and Madison), he offered his own history as a definitive history of a man who was representative by default, being an Adams—the great-grandson and grandson of presidents.

Like Caesar and Napoleon (and Gertrude Stein after him), Adams wrote about himself in the third person. This makes for peculiar reading. Autobiography is (unlike biography) open-ended by definition; the author cannot be dead, although he can (like Grant) be dying. But Henry Adams wanted to achieve a kind of finality here, especially in the climactic chapter ("The Virgin and the Dynamo," included here). But the irony of Adams's choice of the third person is obvious: his account is that of a man who failed to live up to his name. At the center of this chronological account of his life is a twenty-year gap: a period in which Adams taught history (at Harvard), wrote history, and was married (to a woman who committed suicide, thus ending the emotional life of Henry Adams). These central facts of his life are more or less ignored.

Adams sees himself in his former incarnations as a representative of an old order, a world now subjected to fierce critique. Here one might find some resemblance to Thoreau; but whereas Thoreau stood outside the world he criticized, Adams was at the center of his. A transitional work, *The Education* is a book about the transformation of the static Old World into the dynamic New World, symbolized by the great Paris Exposition of 1900. "The Virgin and the Dynamo" describes a liminal moment in American literature and history: the point where the world of electricity, of technology, of Einsteinian relativity, comes into being.

That electricity as a force became the symbolic agent of transformation in the life of Henry Adams, and the history of our time links Adams back to Franklin, an early experimenter with electricity. Both wrote in times of obvious transition, and their autobiographies become vehicles of self-transformation as well as representative volumes that embody the changes occurring in the larger world.

Autobiography inherently involves a challenge to social and personal norms; writers put themselves forward as exemplary, with the implication that they are doing something different from their fellow citizens. There is, at a minimum, the fact that the writer can write: the book itself becomes a challenge to all who remain silent. Furthermore, the "I" of the poem creates a fiction of separateness, even wholeness. Ben Franklin, for example, appears quietly superior to his countrymen: more inventive, firmer in his moral stance, more democratic than thou. Thoreau will not deign to mix with the mob, repudiating slavery, foreign wars, capitalist greed, and the degrading culture of consumption. Henry Adams is the writer-as-historian: a lofty figure whose objectivity is so refined that he critiques himself, as a stand-in, for American culture and civilization. Dana and Twain, and countless others like them, set themselves above, or apart from, the mob by their adventurousness, their fine sense of themselves.

This challenge to society is most visible, however, in the autobiographies of those who do not see themselves as belonging to the mainstream. Outsiders (minorities, women, political activists) often resort to autobiography as a weapon in their struggle, as in the prison memoirs of Alexander Berkman, a political radical, or those of his lover, Emma Goldman—a major force in various liberation movements. In a more nuanced way, autobiography attracts the outsider as a means of self-definition; the power to articulate a form of experience becomes an agent of self-liberation. For this reason, women have often been attracted to the form. From colonial days onward, women (who were often banished from public life) have been assiduous keepers of diaries and journals, recorders of daily life. In this writing, they have been able to recall, reimagine, and reconstitute their lives. A quick perusal of the contents of this volume will suggest the range of writing by American women in the autobiographical mode, ranging from Elizabeth Ashbridge to Mary Karr and Elizabeth Wurtzel.

Perhaps the most technically interesting, and innovative, of modern autobiographies is *The Autobiography of Alice B. Toklas*, by Gertrude Stein, a writer who inhabited the role of outsider in an extraordinary way, writing about herself in the third person by becoming Toklas, her companion of many decades. This allowed her to combine biography and autobiography, offering the completeness of the former with the interiority of the latter. The oddness of this work is part of its success: as a member of the modernist movement, Stein was devoted to making the familiar strange: the familiar being *herself* in this case. She was, somewhat like Henry Adams, an insider, having come from a wealthy Pennsylvania family. In response, she first removed herself into the world of medicine, studying to become a doctor, then exiled herself to Paris, the so-called City of Art, where she hammered her life into a work of art.

Like her friends Hemingway and Fitzgerald, Stein saw the materials of her life as the raw material from which art could be fashioned. Indeed, Hemingway and Fitzgerald, like Stein, also wrote about themselves with a kind of clinical detachment. Fitzgerald, in particular, mercilessly used his own experience as primary material—in his novels and short stories as well as in "The Crack-Up," one of the most witheringly honest self-portraits of an artist written in this century.

For African Americans, autobiography has been crucial as a means of protest and liberation, of self-discovery and societal critique. The nineteenth century is rich with affecting slave narratives, such as Harriet Jacobs's autobiography, *Incidents in the Life of a Slave Girl* (1863), or, most famously, the three autobiographies by Frederick Douglass, whose first autobiography—*The Narrative of the Life of Frederick Douglass, an American Slave, Written by Himself* (1845)—was a galvanizing text in the fight against slavery, followed ten years later by *My Bondage and My Freedom*—a vivid reexamination of his life after fifteen years of freedom. His third autobiography, *Life and Times of Frederick Douglass*, appeared in 1881 and was expanded and revised in 1892.

Douglass uses language with full command of all traditional rhetoric to declare, like Ben Franklin, his independence, his transportation from nowhere to somewhere; in addition, he offers a bitter critique of a society burdened by the inhuman institution of slavery. Not surprisingly, his work stunned readers, and became a model for later African American writers, including Booker T. Washington, W. E. B. Du Bois, Zora Neale Hurston, Richard Wright, James Baldwin, Malcolm X, and bell hooks, each of whom is represented in this collection.

That autobiography occupies a central place in African American writing has long been obvious. Among the most complex of these is *The Autobiography of Malcolm X*. This is an "as told to" book, a collaboration; Malcolm's Boswell, Alex Haley, has something in common with Alice B. Toklas as imagined narrator, although Haley quite literally wrote the book in this case, basing it on Malcolm's oral and written recollections. For all of Haley's input, the book is deeply formed by the mind of Malcolm, who covered Haley's draft with his own revisions and annotations. The narrative swirls around a fixed point: the religion of Elijah Muhammad; it derives energy from Malcolm's second conversion, which takes place at Mecca. Malcolm's book is at once a conversion narrative, an exemplary life, and a social tract, a polemic of huge force and fury written by a man aware that his time was running out.

In all, the range of tone, focus, and form in American autobiography is dizzying. In recent years, the genre has yielded an extraordinary crop of important and popular works, such as Frank McCourt's *Angela's Ashes* (which I excluded only because it largely involves his life in Ireland). The immense interest in this form of writing owes something to a moment when our culture as a whole has turned introspective, interested in (some might say obsessed by) self-definition. Many of our current autobiographers struggle to find a sense of their place in the world, to connect with a particular community defined by sexual and ethnic identity. Others focus on a particular problem, such as alcoholism or drug addiction. Partisan politics often come into play, and one sees many memoirs describing the rise of a subject's commitment to a specific ideology.

In an essay published in 1961 called "Writing American Fiction," Philip Roth shrewdly anticipated the rise of memoir. He observed that "the American writer in the middle of the twentieth century has his hands full in trying to understand, describe, and then make credible much of American reality. It stupefies, it sickens, it infuriates, and finally it is even a kind of embarrassment to one's meager imagination. The actuality is continually outdoing our talents, and the culture tosses up figures almost daily that are the envy of any novelist." As this daily actuality has grown increasingly bizarre, the temptation to fictionalize has often been less intense; merely to describe the reality at hand is, indeed, a sufficient challenge.

Many of our best contemporary writers, from Gore Vidal and Maxine Hong Kingston to Mary Karr and Julia Alvarez, have met that challenge, and the work presented here will, I hope, suggest the range and nature of that accomplishment. One must also be struck by certain continuities in American autobiography. Thoreau, for example, was an obvious model and inspiration for such contemporaries as Scott Russell Sanders, John Elder, and Terry Tempest Williams. Indeed, autobiography often shades over into what is loosely called "nature writing," and one could have included excerpts here from a wide range of articulate voices in praise of the natural world. (I would simply mention a few sadly excluded here: Aldo Leopold, Barry Lopez, Gretel Ehrlich, and Vicki Hearne.)

The regionalism seen in early writers such as Lucy Larcom, Mark Twain, and Theodore Dreiser emerges again in, say, Wallace Stegner and Harry Crews. The spiritual questing of Elizabeth Ashbridge is continuously present in American autobiographical writing, comprising a major vein of our literature. The revolutionary tang of Emma Goldman and Alexander Berkman echoes in the writings of Malcolm X and others. The voices of American women are heard strongly from the beginning, with writers such as Mary Rowlandson; the woman's movement, of course, has inspired writers from Emma Goldman and Gertrude Stein through Erica Jong and a wide range of current writers. Needless to say, these categories are rarely exclusive, and one often encounters a memoir that explores a complex terrain of psychological and political areas.

Not surprisingly, a sense of vertigo overwhelmed me as I came to choose particular texts for this book. Readers will inevitably note that a great deal of important work in the field is simply not here, mostly for reasons of space. I have made a gesture in the direction of inclusiveness, but this is perhaps necessarily a failed gesture—something that must be said of every anthology. The original manuscript of this collection was three times its current size, and cutting has often felt arbitrary. The realm of very contemporary work, in any anthology, is exceptionally tricky. My decision—the only one possible—was always to go with my heart, and I can say frankly that all the pieces included here have moved me personally. (I should here especially thank my research assistant, Pauls Toutonghi, who gave me invaluable help in assembling this collection.)

*The Norton Book of American Autobiography*, as a whole, offers a testament to a tradition quintessentially American in its forms and performance. The autobiographical mode has been crucial to our culture from the outset, allowing the nation to see itself evolving in the lives of distinct individuals, to hear itself in myriad voices that celebrate the self and, in doing so, celebrate a union of selves.

# The Norton Book of
# American Autobiography

# MARY ROWLANDSON

## (ca. 1635–1711)

Relatively little is known about Mary Rowlandson, who was born in England and migrated to the New World with her father, John White. She married Joseph Rowlandson, a minister, in 1656. But her life changed on February 10, 1676, when she and her three children were captured by the Wampanoag Indian leader, Matocomet. The story of her captivity by Indians was issued in 1682, entitled *The Sovereignty and Goodness of God . . . Being a Narrative of the Captivity and Restauration of Mrs. Mary Rowlandson.* This memoir is governed by a deeply religious sensibility; indeed, Rowlandson underwent a profound transformation during the eleven weeks of her captivity. Rowlandson's sorrow is evident here: she deeply misses her husband and the two of three children who were taken away from her during the captivity period. Through the negotiations of her husband, Rowlandson and her two surviving children (one died in captivity) were released.

Rowlandson's story offers the first detailed account of a woman's experience of being captured by Indians. A tough-minded, independent woman, she never lost her faith in God while dwelling in a "lively semblance of hell." Her voice is singular—one of the first strong voices of a woman writing about her experience in North America—and her memoir became a model for later writers, who often wrote about periods of crisis that were also times of spiritual transformation.

## FROM *The True History of the Captivity and Deliverance of Mary Rowlandson*

On the tenth of February came the Indians with great numbers upon Lancaster: Their first coming was about sunrise; hearing the noise of some guns, we looked out; several houses were burning, and the smoke ascending to Heaven. There were five persons taken in one house, the father, and the mother, and one sucking child they knocked on the head; the other two they took and carried away, and there were two others, who being out of the garrison upon some occasion, were set upon, one was knocked on the head, the other escaped, another there was who run-

23

ning along was shot and wounded, and fell down; he begged of them his
life, promising them money, (as they told me) but they would not hear-
ken to him, but knocked him in head, striped him naked, and split open
his bowels. Another seeing many of the Indians about his barn, ventured
and went out, but was quickly shot down. There were three others belonging to the same garrison who were killed; the Indians getting up
upon the roof of the barn, had advantage to shoot down upon them over
their fortification. Thus these murderous wretches went on burning and
destroying before them.

At length they came and beset our own house, and quickly it was the
dolefullest day that ever mine eyes saw. The house stood upon the edge
of a hill; some of the Indians got behind the hill, others in the barn, and
others behind any thing that would shelter them; from all which places
they shot against the house, so that the bullets seemed to fly like hail; and
quickly they wounded one man among us, then another, and then a
third. About two hours (according to my observation in that amazing
time) they had been about the house before they prevailed to fire it,
(which they did with flax and hemp which they brought out of the barn,
and there being no defence about the house, only two flankers at two opposite corners, and one of them not finished) they fired it once and one
ventured out and quenched it, but they quickly fired it again, and that
took. Now is that dreadful hour come, that I have often heard of, (in the
time of the war, as it was the case of others) but now mine eyes see it.
Some in our house were fighting for their lives, others wallowing in their
blood, the house on fire over our heads, and the bloody heathen ready
to knock us on the head if we stirred out. Now might we hear mothers
and children crying out for themselves, and one another, *Lord what shall
we do!* Then I took my children (and one of my sisters heirs) to go forth
and leave the house: But as soon as we came to the door, and appeared,
the Indians shot so thick that the bullets rattled against the house, as if
one had taken a handful of stones and threw them so that we were forced
to give back. We had six stout dogs belonging to our garrison, but none
of them would stir, though another time, if an Indian had come to the
door, they were ready to fly upon him and tear him down. The Lord
hereby would make us the more to acknowledge his hand, and to see that
our help is always in him. But out we must go, the fire increasing, and
coming along behind us, roaring, and the Indians gaping before us with
their guns, spears, and hatchets to devour us. No sooner were we out of
the house, but my brother in law (being before wounded in defending
the house, in or near the throat) fell down dead, whereat the Indians
scornfully shouted, and halloed, and were presently upon him, stripping
off his cloaths. The bullets flying thick, one went through my side, and
the same (as would seem) through the bowels and hand of my poor child

in my arms. One of my elder sisters children (named *William*) had then his leg broke, which the Indians perceiving, they knocked him on head. Thus were we butchered by those merciless heathens, standing amazed, with the blood running down to our heels. My elder sister being yet in the house, and seeing those woful sights, the infidels hauling mothers one way, and children another, and some wallowing in their blood: And her eldest son telling her that her son *William* was dead, and myself was wounded, she said, and Lord let me die with them: Which was no sooner said, but she was struck with a bullet, and fell down dead over the threshold. I hope she is reaping the fruit of her good labors, being faithful to the service of God in her place. In her younger years she lay under much trouble upon spiritual accounts, till it pleased God to make that precious scripture take hold of her heart, 2 *Cor.* 12, 9. *And he said unto me, my grace is sufficient for thee.* More than twenty years after I have heard her tell how sweet and comfortable that place was to her. But to return; The Indians laid hold of us, pulling me one way, and the children another, and said, come go along with us. I told them they would kill me; they answered, if I were willing to go along with them they would not hurt me.

Oh! the doleful sight that now was to behold at this house! come, behold the works of the Lord, what desolations he has made in the earth. Of thirty seven persons who were in this one house, none escaped either present death, or a bitter captivity, save only one, who might say as he, *Job,* 1. 15. *And I only am escaped alone to tell the news.* There were twelve killed, some shot, some stabbed with their spears, some knocked down with their hatchets. When we are in prosperity, Oh the little that we think of such dreadful sights, to see our dear friends and relations lie bleeding out their hearts blood upon the ground. There was one who was choped into the head with a hatchet, and striped naked and yet was crawling up and down. It is a solemn sight to see so many Christians lying in their blood, some here and some there, like a company of sheep torn by wolves. All of them striped naked by a company of hell hounds, roaring, singing, ranting and insulting, as if they would have torn our very hearts out; yet the Lord by his Almighty Power, preserved a number of us from death, for there were twentyfour of us taken alive and carried captive.

I had often before this said, that if the Indians should come, I should chuse rather to be killed by them, than taken alive: But when it came to a trial, my mind changed; their glittering weapons so daunted my spirit, that I chose rather to go along with those (as I may say) ravenous bears, than that moment to end my days. And that I may the better declare what happened to me during that grievous captivity, I shall particularly speak of the several removes we had up and down the wilderness.

## The First Remove

Now away we must go with those barbarous creatures, with our bodies wounded and bleeding, and our hearts no less than our bodies. About a mile we went that night, up upon a hill within sight of the town, where they intended to lodge. There was hard by a vacant house, deserted by the English before, for fear of the Indians, I asked them whether I might not lodge in that house that night? to which they answered, what will you love Englishmen still? This was the dolefulest night that ever my eyes saw. Oh the roaring, singing, dancing, and yelling of those black creatures in the night, which made the place a lively resemblance of hell: And as miserable was the waste that was there made, of horses, cattle, sheep, swine, calves, lambs, roasting pigs, and fowls, (which they had plundered in the town) some roasting, some frying and burning, and some boyling, to feed our merciless enemies; who were joyful enough, though we were disconsolate. To add to the dolefulness of the former day, and the dismalness of the present night, my thoughts ran upon my losses and sad bereaved condition. All was gone, my husband gone, (at least separated from me, he being in the bay; and to add to my grief, the Indians told me they would kill him as he came homeward) my children gone, my relations and friends gone, our house and home, and all our comforts within door and without, all was gone, (except my life) and I knew not but the next moment that might go too.

There remained nothing to me but one poor wounded babe, and it seemed at present worse than death, that it was in such a pitiful condition, bespeaking compassion, and I had no refreshing for it, nor suitable things to revive it. Little do many think, what is the savageness and brutishness of this barbarous enemy, even those that seem to profess more than others among them, when the English have fallen into their hands.

Those seven that were killed at Lancaster the summer before upon a Sabbath day, and the one that was afterwards killed upon a week day, were slain and mangled in a barbarous manner, by one eyed John and Marlborough's praying Indians, which Capt. Mosely brought to Boston, as the Indians told me.

## The Second Remove

But now (the next morning) I must turn my back upon the town, and travel with them into the vast and desolate wilderness, I know now whither. It is not my tongue or pen can express the sorrows of my heart, and bitterness of my spirit, that I had at this departure: But God was with me in a wonderful manner, carrying me along, and bearing up my spirit, that it did not quite fail. One of the Indians carried my poor wounded babe upon a horse; it went moaning all along, I shall die, I shall die. I went on foot after it, with sorrow that cannot be exprest. At length I took it off the horse, and carried it in my arms, till my strength failed, and I fell down with it. Then they set me upon a horse, with my wounded child in my lap, and there being no furniture upon the horses back, as we were going down a steep hill, we both fell over the horses head, at which they like inhuman creatures laughed, and rejoiced to see it, though I thought we should there have ended our days, as overcome with so many difficulties. But the Lord renewed my strength still, and carried me along that I might see more of his Power, yea, so much that I could never have thought of, had I not experienced it.

After this it quickly began to snow, and when night came on, they stoped: And now down I must sit in the snow, by a little fire, and a few boughs behind me, with my sick child in my lap, and calling much for water, being now (through the wound) fallen into a violent Fever. My own wound also growing so stiff, that I could scarce sit down or rise up, yet so it must be, that I must sit all this cold winter night, upon the cold snowy ground, with my sick child in my arms, looking that every hour would be the last of its life; and having no Christian friend near me, either to comfort or help me. Oh I may see the wonderful power of God, that my spirit did not utterly sink under my afflictions; still the Lord upheld me with his gracious and merciful spirit, and we were both alive to see the light of the next morning.

## THE THIRD REMOVE

The morning being come, they prepared to go on their way: One of the Indians got up upon a horse, and they set me up behind him, with my poor sick babe in my lap. A very wearisome and tedious day I had of it; what with my own wound, and my child being so exceeding sick, and in a lamentable condition with her wound, it might easily be judged what a poor feeble condition we were in, there being not the least crumb of refreshing that came within either of our mouths from Wednesday night to Saturday night, except only a little cold water. This day in the afternoon, about an hour by sun, we came to the place where they intended, viz. an Indian town called Wenimesset, northward of Quabaug. When we were come, Oh the number of Pagans (now merciless enemies) that there came about me, that I may say as *David*, Psal. 27. 13. *I had fainted, unless I had believed*, &c. The next day was the Sabbath: I then remembered how careless I had been of God's holy time; how many sabbaths I had lost and misspent, and how evilly I had walked in God's sight; which lay so close upon my spirit, that it was easier for me to see how righteous it was with God to cut off the thread of my life, and cast me out of his presence for ever. Yet the Lord still shewed mercy to me, and helped me; and as he wounded me with one hand, so he healed me with the other. This day there came to me one Robert Pepper, (a man belonging to Roxbury,) who was taken at Capt. Beer's fight; and had been now a considerable time with the Indians, and up with them almost as far as Albany, to see King Philip, as he told me, and was now very lately come with them into these parts. Hearing I say, that I was in this Indian town he obtained leave to come and see me. He told me he himself was wounded in the leg at Capt. Beer's fight; and was not able sometimes to go but as they carried him, and that he took oak leaves and laid to his wound, and by the blessing of God, he was able to travel again. Then I took oak leaves and laid to my side, and with the blessing of God, it cured me also; yet before the cure was wrought, I may say as it is in *Psal.* 38. 5, 6. *My wounds stink and are corrupt, I am troubled, I am bowed down greatly, I go mourning all the day long.* I sat much alone with my poor wounded child in my lap, which moaned night and day, having nothing to revive the body, or cheer the spirits of her; but instead of that, one Indian would come and tell me one hour, your master will knock your child on the head, and then a second, and then a third, your master will quickly knock your child on the head.

This was the comfort I had from them; miserable comforters were they all. Thus nine days I sat upon my knees, with my babe in my lap, till my flesh was raw again. My child being even ready to depart this sorrowful world, they bid me carry it out to another wigwam; (I suppose because they would not be troubled with such spectacles) whither I went with a very heavy heart, and down I sat with the picture of death in my lap. About two hours in the night, my sweet babe like a lamb departed this life, on Feb. 18. 1675. it being about six years and five months old. It was nine days from the first wounding, in this miserable condition, without any refreshing of one nature or other, except a little cold water. I cannot but take notice how at another time I could not bear to be in the room where any dead person was, but now the case is changed; I must, and could lie down by my dead babe all the night after. I have thought since of the wonderful goodness of God to me, in preserving me so in the use of my reason and senses, in that distressed time, that I did not use wicked and violent means to end my own miserable life. In the morning, when they understood that my child was dead, they sent for me home to my masters wigwam: (By my master in this writing, must be understood

*Qunnaopin*, who was a saggamore, and married K. Philip's wives sister; not that he first took me, but I was sold to him by a Narraganset Indian, who took me when I first came out of the garrison) I went to take up my dead child in my arms to carry it with me, but they bid me let it alone: There was no resisting, but go I must and leave it. When I had been a while at my masters wigwam, I took the first opportunity I could get, to go look after my dead child: When I came, I asked them what they had done with it? they told me it was upon the hill; then they went and shewed me where it was, where I saw the ground was newly digged, and where they told me they had buried it; there I left that child in the wilderness, and, and must commit it and myself also in this wilderness condition, to him who is above all. God having taken away this dear child, I went to see my daughter *Mary*, who was at this same Indian town, at a wigwam not very far off, though we had little liberty or opportunity to see one another; she was about ten years old, and taken from the door at first by a praying Indian, and afterward sold for a gun. When I came in sight, she would fall a weeping, at which they were provoked, and would not let me come near her, but bid me be gone; which was a heart cutting word to me. I had one child dead, another in the wilderness, I knew not where, the third they would not let me come near to; *Me* (as he said) *have ye bereaved of my children, Joseph is not, and Simeon is not, and ye will take Benjamin also, all these things are against me.* I could not sit still in this condition, but kept walking from one place to another. And as I was going along, my heart was even overwhelmed with the thoughts of my condition, and that I should have children, and a nation that I knew not, ruled over them. Whereupon I earnestly intreated the Lord that he would consider my low estate, and shew me a token for good, and if it were his blessed will, some sign and hope of some relief. And indeed quickly the Lord answered, in some measure, my poor prayer: For as I was going up and down mourning and lamenting my condition, my son came to me, and asked me how I did? I had not seen him before, since the destruction of the town; and I knew not where he was, till I was informed by himself, that he was amongst a smaller parcel of Indians, whose place was about six miles off, with tears in his eyes, he asked me whether his sister Sarah was dead? and told me he had seen his sister Mary; and prayed me, that I would not be troubled in reference to himself. The occasion of his coming to see me at this time was this: There was, as I said, about six miles from us, a small plantation of Indians, where it seems he had been, during his captivity; and at this time, there were some forces of the Indians gathered out of our company, and some also from them, (amongst whom was my sons master) to go to assault and burn Medfield: In this time of his masters absence, his dame brought him to see me. I took this to be some gracious answer to my earnest and

unfeigned desire. The next day the Indians returned from Medfield: (all
the company, for those that belonged to the other smaller company,
came through the town that now we were at) but before they came to us,
oh the outrageous roaring and hooping that there was! they began their
din about a mile before they came to us. By their noise and hooping
they signified how many they had destroyed (which was at that time
twenty three) those that were with us at home, were gathered together as
soon as they heard the hooping, and every time that the other went over
their number, these at home gave a shout, that the very earth rang again.
And thus they continued till those that had been upon the expedition
were come up to the Saggamor's wigwam; and then, oh the hideous, insulting and triumphing that there was over some English mens scalps,
that they had taken (as their manner is) and brought with them. I cannot but take notice of the wonderful mercy of God to me in those afflictions, in sending me a bible: One of the Indians that came from Medfield
fight, and had brought some plunder, came to me, and asked me if I
would have a bible, he had got one in his basket, I was glad of it, and
asked him if he thought the Indians would let me read? he answered yes?
so I took the bible, and in that melancholy time it came into my mind
to read first the 28th, Chap. of *Deuteronomy*, which I did, and when I had
read it, my dark heart wrought on this manner, that there was no mercy
for me, that the blessings were gone, and the curses came in their room,
and that I had lost my opportunity. But the Lord helped me still to go on
reading, till I came to chap. 30. the seven first verses; where I found there
was mercy promised again, if we would return to him, by repentance;
and though we were scattered from one end of the earth to the other, yet
the Lord would gather us together, and turn all those curses upon our enemies. I do not desire to live to forget this scripture, and what comfort it
was to me.

Now the Indians began to talk of removing from this place, some one
way, and some another. There were now besides myself nine English cap-
tives in this place, (all of them children except one woman) I got an opportunity to go and take my leave of them; they being to go one way, and
I another. I asked them whether they were earnest with God for deliverance, they all told me they did as they were able, and it was some comfort to me, that the Lord stirred up children to look to him. The woman,
viz good wife Joslin, told me, she should never see me again, and that she
could find in her heart to run away: I desired her not to run away by any
means, for we were near thirty miles from any English town, and she very
big with child, having but one week to reckon; and another child in her
arms two years old, and bad rivers there were to go over, and we were feeble with our poor and coarse entertainment. I had my bible with me, I
pulled it out, and asked her whether she would read; we opened the

bible, and lighted on *Psal.* 27. in which psalm we especially took notice of that verse, *Wait on the Lord, be of good courage, and he shall strengthen thine heart, wait I say on the Lord.*

## THE FOURTH REMOVE

And now must I part with that little company that I had. Here I parted from my daughter Mary, (whom I never saw again till I saw her in Dorchester, returned from captivity) and from four little cousins and neighbors, some of which I never saw afterward, the Lord only knows the end of them. Among them also was that poor woman before mentioned, who came to a sad end, as some of the company told me in my travel: She having much grief upon her Spirits, about her miserable condition, being so near her time, she would be often asking the Indians to let her go home; they not being willing to that, and yet vexed with her importunity, gathered a great company together about her, and striped her naked, and set her in the midst of them; and when they had sung and danced about her (in their hellish manner) as long as they pleased, they knocked her on the head, and the child in her arms with her: When they had done that, they made a fire and put them both into it, and told the other children that were with them, that if they attempted to go home, they would serve them in like manner. The children said she did not shed one tear, but prayed all the while. But to return to my own journey: We travelled about half a day or a little more, and came to a desolate place in the wilderness, where there were no wigwams or inhabitants before: We came about the middle of the afternoon to this place; cold, wet, snowy, hungry, and weary, and no refreshing (for man) but the cold ground to sit on, and our poor Indian cheer.

Heart acheing thoughts here I had about my poor children, who were scattered up and down among the wild beasts of the forest: My head was light and dissy, (either through hunger or hard lodging, or trouble, or altogether) my knees feeble, my body raw by sitting double night and day, that I cannot express to man, the affliction that lay upon my spirit, but the Lord helped me at that time to express it to himself. I opened my bible to read, and the Lord brought that precious scripture to me, *Jer.* 31. 16. *Thus saith the Lord, refrain thy voice from weeping, and thine eyes from tears, for thy work shall be rewarded, and they shall come again from the land of the enemy.* This was a sweet cordial to me, when I was ready to faint, many and many a time have I sat down, and wept sweetly over this scripture. At this place we continued about four days.

## The Fifth Remove

The occasion (as I thought) of their moving at this time, was the English Army's being near and following them: For they went as if they had
gone for their lives, for some considerable way; and then they made a
stop, and chose out some of their stoutest men, and sent them back to
hold the English Army in play whilst the rest escaped; and then like
Jehu they marched on furiously, with their old and young: Some carried
their old decriped mothers, some carried one and some another. Four of
them carried a great Indian upon a bier; but going through a thick wood
with him, they were hindered, and could make no haste; whereupon they
took him upon their backs, and carried him one at a time, till we came
to Bacquag River. Upon a Friday a little after noon we came to this river:
When all the company was come up, and were gathered together, I
thought to count the number of them, but they were so many, and being
somewhat in motion, it was beyond my skill. In this travel, because of my
wound, I was somewhat favored in my load: I carried only my knitting-
work, and two quarts of parched meal: Being very faint, I asked my mistress to give me one spoonful of the meal, but she would not give me a
taste. They quickly fell to cutting dry trees, to make rafts to carry them
over the river, and soon my turn came to go over. By the advantage of
some brush which they had laid upon the raft to sit on, I did not wet my
foot, (which many of themselves at the other end were mid leg deep)
which cannot but be acknolwedged as a favor of God to my weakened
Body, it being a very cold time. I was not before acquainted with such
kind of doings, or dangers. *When thou passeth through the waters I will
be with thee, and through the rivers they shall not overflow thee.* Isai. 43.
2. A certain number of us got over the river that night, but it was the night
after the Sabbath before all the company was got over. On the Saturday
they boiled an old horse's Leg (which they had got) and so we drank of
the broth, as soon as they thought it was ready, and when it was almost
all gone, they filled it up again.

The first week of my being among them, I hardly eat any thing: The
second week I found my stomach grew very faint for want of something;
and yet it was very hard to get down their filthy trash; but the third week
(though I could think how formerly my stomach would turn against this
or that, and I could starve and die before I could eat such things,) yet they
were pleasant and savory to my taste. I was at this time knitting a pair of
white cotten stockings for my mistress, and I had not yet wrought upon
the Sabbath Day: when the Sabbath came, they bid me go to work; I told
them it was Sabbath day, and desired them to let me rest, and told them

I would do as much more tomorrow; to which they answered me, they would break my face. And here I cannot but take notice of the strange Providence of God in preserving the heathen: They were many hundreds, old and young, some sick and some lame, many had papooses at their backs, the greatest number (at this time with us) were Squaws, and they travelled with all they had, bag and baggage, and yet they got over this river aforesaid; and on Monday they set their wigwams on fire, and away they went; on that very day came the English Army after them to this river, and saw the smoak of their wigwams, and yet this river put a stop to them. God did not give them courage or activity to go over after us; we were not ready for so great a mercy as victory and deliverance; if we had been, God would have found out a way for the English to have passed this River, as well as for the Indians with their Squaws and children, and all their luggage. *Oh that my people had hearkened to me, and Israel had walked in my ways, I should soon have subdued their enemies, and turned my hand against their adversaries.* Psal. 81. 13, 14.

## THE SIXTH REMOVE

On Monday (as I said) they set their wigwams on fire, and went away. It was a cold morning, and before us there was a great brook with ice on it: Some waded through it, up to the knees and higher, but others went till they came to a beaver dam, and I amongst them, where through the good providence of God, I did not wet my foot. I went along that day, mourning and lamenting (leaving farther my own country, and travelling farther into the vast and howling wilderness) and I understood something of Lot's wife's temptation, when she looked back: We came that day to a great swamp, by the side of which we took up our lodging that night. When we came to the brow of the hill that looked toward the swamp, I thought we had come to a great Indian town. (Though there were none but our own company) the Indians were as thick as the trees; it seemed as if there had been a thousand hatchets going at once: If one looked before one, there was nothing but Indians, and behind one, nothing but Indians; and so on either hand: And I myself in the midst, and no christian soul near me, and yet how hath the Lord preserved me in safety! Oh the experience that I have had of the goodness of God to me and mine!

## THE SEVENTH REMOVE

After a restless and hungry night there, we had a wearisome time of it the next day. The swamp by which we lay, was as it were a deep dungeon, and an exceeding high and steep hill before it. Before I got to the top of the hill, I thought my heart and legs and all would have broken, and failed me. What through faintness and soreness of body, it was a grievous day of travel to me. As we went along, I saw a place where English cattle had been, that was comfort to me, such as it was; quickly after that we came to an English path, which so took with me, that I thought I could there have freely lain down and died. That day, a little after noon, we came to Squauheag, where the Indians quickly spread themselves over the deserted English fields, gleaning what they could find; some picked up ears of wheat, that were crinckled down, some found ears of Indian corn, some found ground nuts, and others sheaves of wheat that were frozen together in the shock, and went to threshing of them out. Myself got two ears of Indian corn, and whilst I did but turn my back, one of them was stolen from me, which much troubled me. There came an Indian to them at that time, with a basket of horse liver; I asked him to give me a piece: What (says he) can you eat horse liver? I told him I would try if he would give me a piece, which he did; and I laid it on the coals to roast, but before it was half ready, they got half of it away from me; so that I was forced to take the rest and eat it as it was, with the blood about my mouth, and yet a savory bit it was to me; for to the hungry soul every bitter thing is sweet. A solemn sight me thought it was, to see whole fields of wheat and Indian corn forsaken and spoiled, and the remainder of them to be food for our merciless Enemies. That night we had a mess of wheat for our supper.

## THE EIGHTH REMOVE

On the morrow morning we must go over Connecticut river to meet with King Philip; two canoes full they had carried over, the next turn myself was to go; but as my foot was upon the canoe to step in, there was a sudden outcry among them, and I must step back; and instead of going over the river, I must go four or five miles up the river farther Northward. Some of the Indians ran one way, and some another. The cause of this rout was, as I thought, their espying some English scouts, who were thereabouts. In this travel up the river, about noon the company made a stop, and sat down, some to eat, and others to rest them. As I sat amongst them, musing on things past, my son Joseph unexpectedly came to me: We asked of each others welfare, bemoaning our doleful condition, and the change that had come upon us: We had husband, and father, and children, and sisters, and friends, and relations, and house, and home, and many comforts of this life; but now we might say as *Job, naked came I out of my mothers womb, and naked shall I return: The Lord gave, and the Lord hath taken away, blessed be the name of the Lord.* I asked him whether he would read? he told me, he earnestly desired it. I gave him my bible, and he lighted upon that comfortable scripture, *Psal. 118. 17, 18. I shall not die, but live, and declare the works of the Lord: The Lord hath chastened me sore, yet he hath not given me over to death.* Look here mother (says he) did you read this? And here I may take occasion to ⌊mention one principal ground of my setting forth these few lines, even as the psalmist says, to declare the works of the Lord, and his wonderful power in carrying us along, preserving us in the wilderness, while under the enemies hand, and returning of us in safety again; and his goodness in bringing to my hand so many comfortable and suitable scriptures in my distress.

But to return: We travelled on till night, and in the morning we must go over the river to Philip's crew. When I was in the canoe, I could not but be amazed at the numerous crew of Pagans that were on the bank on the other side. When I came ashore, they gathered all about me, I sitting alone in the midst: I observed they asked one another questions, and laughed, and rejoiced over their gains and victories. Then my heart began to fail, and I fell a weeping; which was the first time, to my re-membrance, that I wept before them; although I had met with so much affliction, and my heart was many times ready to break, yet could I not shed one tear in their sight, but rather had been all this while in a maze, and like one astonished; but now I may say as *Psal. 137. 1. By the rivers of Babylon, there we sat down, yea, we wept, when we remembered Zion.* There one of them asked me, why I wept? I could hardly tell what to say; yet I answered, they would kill me: No, said he, none will hurt you. Then came one of them, and gave me two spoonfuls of meal (to comfort me) and another gave me half a pint of pease, which was more worth than many bushels at another time. Then I went to see King Philip; he bid me come in, and sit down; and asked me whether I would smoke it? (a usual complement now a days, among Saints and Sinners) but this no way suited me. For though I had formerly used tobacco, yet I had left it ever since I was first taken. It seems to be a bait, the devil lays to make men lose their precious time. I remember with shame, how formerly, when I had taken two or three pipes, I was presently ready for another; such a bewitching thing it is:⌊But I thank God, he has now given me power over it; surely there are many who may be better employed, than to sit sucking a stinking tobacco pipe.

Now the Indians gather their Forces to go against Northampton: Over night one went about yelling and hooting to give notice of the design. Whereupon they went to boiling of ground nuts, and parching of corn (as many as had it) for their provision; and in the Morning away they went. During my abode in this place, Philip spake to me to make a shirt for his boy, which I did; for which he gave me a shilling; I offered the money to my master, but he bid me keep it, and with it I bought a piece of horse flesh. Afterward he asked me to make a cap for his boy, for which he invited me to dinner: I went, and he gave me a pancake, about as big as two fingers; it was made of parched wheat, beaten, and fryed in bears grease, but I thought I never tasted pleasanter meat in my life. There was a Squaw who spake to me to make a shirt for her sannup; for which she gave me a piece of bear. Another asked me to knit a pair of stockings, for which she gave me a quart of pease. I boiled my pease and bear together, and invited my master and mistress to dinner; but the proud gossip, because I served them both in one dish, would eat nothing, except one bit that he gave her upon the point of his knife. Hearing that my son was come to this place, I went to see him, and found him lying flat upon the ground; I asked him how he could sleep so? he answered me, that he was not asleep, but at prayer; and that he lay so, that they might not observe what he was doing. I pray God he may remember these things now he is returned in safety. At this place, (the Sun now getting higher) what with the beams and heat of the Sun, and the smoke of the wigwams, I thought I should have been blind. I could scarce discern one wigwam from another. There was here one Mary Thurston of Medfield, who seeing how it was with me, lent me a hat to wear; but as soon as I was gone, the Squaw who owned that Mary Thurston, came running after me, and got it away again. Here was a Squaw who gave me a spoonful of meal, I put it in my pocket to keep it safe, yet notwithstanding somebody stole it, but put five Indian corns in the room of it; which corns were the greatest provision I had in my travel for one day.

## The Ninth Remove

But instead of going either to Albany or homeward we must go five miles up the river, and then go over it. Here we abode a while. Here lived a sorry Indian, who spake to me to make him a shirt, when I had done it, he would pay me nothing for it. But he living by the river side, where I often went to fetch water, I would often be putting of him in mind, and calling for my pay; at last he told me, if I would make another shirt for a papoos not yet born, he would give me a knife, which he did, when I had done it. I carried the knife in, and my master asked me to give it him, and I was not a little glad that I had any thing that they would accept of, and be pleased with. When we were at this place, my master's maid came home; she had been gone three weeks into the Narraganset country to fetch corn, where they had stored up some in the ground: She brought home about a peck and a half of corn. This was about the time that their great captain *(Naananto)* was killed in the Narraganset country.

My son being now about a mile from me, I asked liberty to go and see him, they bid me go, and away I went; but quickly lost myself, travelling over hills and through swamps, and could not find the way to him. And I cannot but admire at the wonderful power and goodness of God to me, in that though I was gone from home, and met with all sorts of Indians, and those I had no knowledge of, and there being no christian soul near me, yet not one of them offered the least imaginable miscarriage to me. I turned homeward again, and met with my master, and he shewed me the way to my son. When I came to him, I found him, not well; and with-all he had a bile on his side, which much troubled him: We bemoaned one another a while, as the Lord helped us, and then I returned, again. When I was returned I found myself as unsatisfied as I was before. I went up and down mourning and lamenting, and my spirit was ready to sink, with the thoughts of my poor children; my son was ill, and I could not but think of his mournful looks, having no christian friend near him, to do any office of love for him, either for soul or body. And my poor girl, I knew not where she was, nor whether she was sick, or well, or alive or dead. I repaired under these thoughts to my bible, (my great comforter in that time) and that scripture came to my hand, *Cast thy burden upon the Lord, and he shall sustain thee,* Psal. 55. 22.

But I was fain to go and look after something to satisfy my hunger: And going among the wigwams, I went into one, and there found a Squaw who shewed herself very kind to me, and gave me a piece of bear. I put it into my pocket, and came home; but could not find an opportunity to broil it, for fear they should get it from me; and there it lay all that day and night in my stinking pocket. In the morning I went again to the same Squaw, who had a kettle of ground nuts boiling: I asked her to let me boil my piece of bear in her kettle, which she did, and gave me some ground nuts to eat with it, and I cannot but think how pleasant it was to me. I have sometimes seen bear baked handsomely amongst the English, and some liked it, but the thoughts that it was bear, made me tremble: But now that was savory to me that one would think was enough to turn the stomach of a brute creature.

One bitter cold day, I could find no room to sit down before the fire: I went out, and could not tell what to do, but I went into another wig-wam, where they were also sitting round the fire; but the Squaw laid a skin for me, and bid me sit down, and gave me some ground nuts, and bid me come again; and told me they would buy me, if they were able; and yet these were strangers to me that I never knew before.

### The Tenth Remove

That day a small part of the company removed about three quarters of a mile, intending farther the next day. When they came to the place where they intended to lodge, and had pitched their wigwams, being hungry I went again back to the place we were before at, to get something to eat; being encouraged by the Squaw's kindness, who bid me come again. When I was there, there came an Indian to look after me; who when he had found me, kicked me all along. I went home and found venison roasting that night, but they would not give me one bit of it. Sometimes I met with favors, and sometimes with nothing but frowns.

### The Eleventh Remove

The nex day in the morning, they took their travel, intending a days Journey up the river; I took my load at my back, and quickly we came to wade over a river, and passed over tiresome and wearisome hills. One hill was so steep, that I was fain to creep up upon my knees, and to hold by the twigs and bushes to keep myself from falling backward. My head also was so light that I usually reeled as I went, but, I hope all those wearisome steps that I have taken, are but a forwarding of me to the heavenly rest. *I know O Lord, that thy Judgments are right and that thou in faithfulness hast afflicted me*, Psal. 119.75.

### The Twelfth Remove

It was upon a Sabbath day morning, that they prepared for their travel. This morning I asked my master whether he would sell me to my husband? he answered nux; which did much rejoice my spirit. My mistress, before we went, was gone to the burial of a papoos, and returning, she found me sitting, and reading in my bible: She snatched it hastily out of my hand, and threw it out of doors; I ran out and catched it up, and put it in my pocket, and never let her see it afterward. Then they packed up their things to be gone, and gave me my load: I complained it was too heavy, whereupon she gave me a slap on the face, and bid me be gone. I lifted up my heart to God, hoping that redemption was not far off; and the rather because their insolency grew worse and worse.

# JONATHAN EDWARDS
## (1703–1758)

Born in East Windsor, Connecticut, Edwards was the son of a Puritan minister, who encouraged his son to study for the ministry at Yale College. His mother's father, Solomon Stoddard, was among the best-known clergymen in New England. Edwards himself assumed his grandfather's pulpit in Northampton, Massachusetts, in 1729. After twenty-one years of preaching, however, Edwards's congregation turned against him, and he was removed from his position by a majority vote. This was a blow for a man whose name had been closely connected with the Great Awakening of the 1730s, a period of intense religious revival.

Edwards later became the third president of the College of New Jersey (now Princeton University). By this time, he was a well-known and highly regarded theologian, perhaps best remembered for a sermon entitled "Sinners in the Hands of an Angry God," first delivered in 1741 and often associated with the "fire and brimstone" style of preaching. In *The Life and Character of the Late Rev. Mr. Jonathan Edwards* (written about 1740 but not published until 1765), one sees a very different Edwards: a man deeply concerned about his inner life, a theologian whose speculative energies were immense.

As autobiography, Edwards's narrative stands in contrast to that of his more secular contemporary Benjamin Franklin. Indeed, Edwards might well be considered a founding father in the realm of American spiritual autobiography.

## FROM *The Life and Character of the Late Rev. Mr. Jonathan Edwards*

I had a variety of concerns and exercises about my soul from my childhood, but had two more remarkable seasons of awakening before I met with that change by which I was brought to those new dispositions and that new sense of things that I have since had. The first time was when I was a boy, some years before I went to college, at a time of remarkable awakening in my father's congregation. I was then very much affected for many months and concerned about the things of religion and my soul's salvation and was abundant in duties. I used to pray five times a day in secret, and to spend much time in religious talk with other boys and used to meet with them to pray together. I experienced I know not what kind of delight in religion. My mind was much engaged in it, and had much self-righteous pleasure; and it was my delight to abound in religious duties. I, with some of my schoolmates, joined together and built a booth in a swamp, in a very secret and retired place, for a place of prayer. And besides, I had particular secret places of my own in the woods, where I used to retire by myself, and used to be from time to time much affected. My affections seemed to be lively and easily moved, and I seemed to be in my element, when engaged in religious duties. And I am ready to think, many are deceived with such affections and such a kind of delight, as I then had in religion, and mistake it for grace.

But in process of time, my convictions and affections wore off; and I entirely lost all those affections and delights, and left off secret prayer, at least as to any constant performance of it, and returned like a dog to his vomit, and went on in ways of sin.

Indeed, I was at some times very uneasy, especially towards the latter part of the time of my being at college. 'Til it pleased God, in my last year at college, at a time when I was in the midst of many uneasy thoughts about the state of my soul, to seize me with a pleurisy; in which he brought me nigh to the grave, and shook me over the pit of hell.

But yet, it was not long after my recovery before I fell again into my old ways of sin. But God would not suffer me to go on with any quietness; but I had great and violent inward struggles: 'til after many conflicts with wicked inclinations and repeated resolutions and bonds that I laid myself under by a kind of vows to God, I was brought wholly to break off all former wicked ways and all ways of known outward sin, and to apply myself to seek my salvation and practice the duties of religion, but without that kind of affection and delight that I had formerly experienced. My concern now wrought more by inward struggles and conflicts and self-reflections. I made seeking my salvation the main business of my life. But yet it seems to me I sought after a miserable manner, which has made me sometimes since to question whether ever it issued in that which was saving, being ready to doubt, whether such miserable seeking was ever succeeded. But yet I was brought to seek salvation in a manner that I never was before. I felt a spirit to part with all things in the world for an interest in Christ. My concern continued and prevailed, with many exercising thoughts and inward struggles; but yet it never seemed to be proper to express my concern that I had, by the name of terror.

From my childhood up, my mind had been wont to be full of objections against the doctrine of God's sovereignty, in choosing whom he would to eternal life and rejecting whom he pleased, leaving them eternally to perish and be everlastingly tormented in hell. It used to appear like a horrible doctrine to me. But I remember the time very well when

I seemed to be convinced, and fully satisfied, as to this sovereignty of God and his justice in thus eternally disposing of men according to his sovereign pleasure. But never could give an account how or by what means I was thus convinced; not in the least imagining, in the time of it nor a long time after, that there was any extraordinary influence of God's spirit in it; but only that now I saw further, and my reason apprehended the justice and reasonableness of it. However, my mind rested in it; and it put an end to all those cavils and objections, that had 'til then abode with me, all the proceeding part of my life. And there has been a wonderful alteration in my mind, with respect to the doctrine of God's sovereignty, from that day to this; so that I scarce ever have found so much as the rising of an objection against God's sovereignty, in the most absolute sense, in showing mercy to whom he will show mercy and hardening and eternally damning whom he will. God's absolute sovereignty and justice, with respect to salvation and damnation, is what my mind seems to rest assured of, as much as of anything that I see with my eyes; at least it is so at times. But I have oftentimes since that first conviction had quite another kind of sense of God's sovereignty than I had then. I have often since not only had a conviction, but a delightful conviction. The doctrine of God's sovereignty has very often appeared an exceeding pleasant, bright and sweet doctrine to me; and absolute sovereignty is what I love to ascribe to God. By my first conviction was not with this.

The first that I remember that ever I found anything of that sort of inward, sweet delight in God and divine things, that I have lived much in since, was on reading those words, 1 Timothy 1:17, "Now unto the king eternal, immortal, invisible, the only wise God, be honor and glory for ever and ever, Amen." As I read the words, there came into my soul, and was as it were diffused through it, a sense of the glory of the Divine Being, a new sense, quite different from anything I ever experienced before. Never any words of scripture seemed to me as these words did. I thought with myself, how excellent a being that was, and how happy I should be if I might enjoy that God and be rapt up to God in Heaven, and be as it were swallowed up in him. I kept saying, and as it were singing over these words of scripture to myself; and went to prayer to pray to God that I might enjoy him; and prayed in a manner quite different from what I used to do, with a new sort of affection. But it never came into my thought that there was anything spiritual or of a saving nature in this.

From about that time I began to have a new kind of apprehensions and ideas of Christ, and the work of redemption, and the glorious way of salvation by him. I had an inward, sweet sense of these things, that at times came into my heart; and my soul was led away in pleasant views and contemplations of them. And my mind was greatly engaged to spend my time in reading and meditating on Christ, and the beauty and excellency of his person, and the lovely way of salvation, by free grace in him. I found no books so delightful to me as those that treated of these subjects. Those words Canticles 2:1, used to be abundantly with me: "I am the Rose of Sharon, the lily of the valleys." The words seemed to me, sweetly to represent the loveliness and beauty of Jesus Christ. And the whole book of Canticles used to be pleasant to me; and I used to be much in reading it, about that time. And found, from time to time, an inward sweetness that used, as it were, to carry me away in my contemplations, in what I know not how to express otherwise, than by a calm, sweet abstraction of soul from all the concerns of this world, and a kind of vision, or fixed ideas and imaginations, of being alone in the mountains or some solitary wilderness, far from all mankind, sweetly conversing with Christ, and rapt and swallowed up in God. The sense I had of divine things would often of a sudden as it were, kindle up a sweet burning in my heart, an ardor of my soul, that I know not how to express.

Not long after I first began to experience these things, I gave an account to my father of some things that had passed in my mind. I was pretty much affected by the discourse we had together. And when the discourse was ended, I walked abroad alone, in a solitary place in my father's pasture, for contemplation. And as I was walking there, and looked up on the sky and clouds; there came into my mind a sweet sense of the glorious majesty and grace of God that I know not how to express. I seemed to see them both in a sweet conjunction, majesty and meekness joined together. It was a sweet and gentle, and holy majesty; and also a majestic meekness; an awful sweetness; a high, and great, and holy gentleness.

After this my sense of divine things gradually increased, and became more and more lively, and had more of that inward sweetness. The appearance of everything was altered: there seemed to be, as it were, a calm, sweet cast, or appearance of divine glory, in almost everything. God's excellency, his wisdom, his purity and love, seemed to appear in everything: in the sun, moon and stars; in the clouds, and blue sky; in the grass, flowers, trees; in the water, and all nature; which used greatly to fix my mind. I often used to sit and view the moon for a long time, and so in the daytime spent much time in viewing the clouds and sky to behold the sweet glory of God in these things, in the meantime, singing forth with a low voice my contemplations of the Creator and Redeemer. And scarce anything, among all the works of nature, was so sweet to me as thunder and lightning. Formerly, nothing had been so terrible to me. I used to be a person uncommonly terrified with thunder, and it used to strike me with terror when I saw a thunderstorm rising. But now, on the contrary, it rejoiced me. I felt God at the first appearance of a thunderstorm. And used to take the opportunity at such times to fix myself to view the clouds, and see the lightnings play, and hear the majestic and awful voice of God's thunder, which often times was exceeding entertaining, leading me to sweet contemplations of my great and glorious God. And while I viewed, used to spend my time, as it always seemed natural to me, to sing or chant forth my meditations, to speak my thoughts in soliloquies, and speak with a singing voice.

I felt then a great satisfaction as to my good estate. But that did not content me. I had vehement longings of soul after God and Christ, and after more holiness, wherewith my heart seemed to be full and ready to break: which often brought to mind the words of the psalmist, Psalm 119:28: "My soul breaketh for the longing it hath." I often felt a mourning and lamenting in my heart that I had not turned to God sooner, that I might have had more time to grow in grace. My mind was greatly fixed on divine things; I was almost perpetually in the contemplation of them. Spent most of my time in thinking of divine things, year after year. And used to spend abundance of my time in walking alone in the woods and solitary places for meditation, soliloquy and prayer, and converse with God. And it was always my manner, at such times, to sing forth my contemplations. And was almost constantly in ejaculatory prayer, wherever I was. Prayer seemed to be natural to me, as the breath by which the inward burnings of my heart had vent.

The delights which I now felt in things of religion were of an exceeding different kind from those forementioned, that I had when I was a boy. They were totally of another kind; and what I then had no more notion or idea of, than one born blind has of pleasant and beautiful colors. They were of a more inward, pure, soul-animating and refreshing nature. Those former delights never reached the heart, and did not arise from any sight of the divine excellency of the things of God or any taste of the soul-satisfying and life-giving good there is in them.

My sense of divine things seemed gradually to increase, 'til I went to preach at New York, which was about a year and a half after they began. While I was there, I felt them, very sensibly, in a much higher degree, than I had done before. My longings after God and holiness, were much increased. Pure and humble, holy and heavenly Christianity appeared exceeding amiable to me. I felt in me a burning desire to be in everything a complete Christian, and conformed to the blessed image of Christ, and that I might live in all things, according to the pure, sweet and blessed rules of the gospel. I had an eager thirsting after progress in these things. My longings after it put me upon pursuing and pressing after them. It was my continual strife day and night, and constant inquiry, how I should be more holy, and live more holily, and more becoming a child of God, and disciple of Christ. I sought an increase of grace and holiness, and that I might live an holy life with vastly more earnestness than ever I sought grace, before I had it. I used to be continually examining myself, and studying and contriving for likely ways and means how I should live holily with far greater diligence and earnestness than ever I pursued anything in my life; but with too great a dependence on my own strength, which afterwards proved a great damage to me. My experience had not then taught me, as it has done since, my extreme feebleness and impotence, every manner of way, and the innumerable and bottomless depths of secret corruption and deceit that there was in my heart. However, I went on with my eager pursuit after more holiness, and sweet conformity to Christ.

The Heaven I desired was a heaven of holiness, to be with God, and to spend my eternity in divine love, and holy communion with Christ. My mind was very much taken up with contemplations on heaven, and the enjoyments of those there, and living there in perfect holiness, humility and love. And it used at that time to appear a great part of the happiness of heaven that there the saints could express their love to Christ. It appeared to me a great clog and hindrance and burden to me that what I felt within I could not express to God and give vent to as I desired. The inward ardor of my soul seemed to be hindered and pent up, and could not freely flame out as it would. I used often to think how in heaven this sweet principle should freely and fully vent and express itself. Heaven appeared to me exceeding delightful as a world of love. It appeared to me that all happiness consisted in living in pure, humble, heavenly, divine love.

I remember the thoughts I used then to have of holiness. I remember I then said sometimes to myself, "I do certainly know that I love holiness such as the gospel prescribes." It appeared to me there was nothing in it but what was ravishingly lovely. It appeared to me to be the highest beauty and amiableness, above all other beauties, that it was a divine beauty, far purer than anything here upon earth; and that everything else, was like mire, filth and defilement in comparison of it.

Holiness, as I then wrote down some of my contemplations on it, appeared to me to be of a sweet, pleasant, charming, serene, calm nature. It seemed to me it brought an inexpressible purity, brightness, peacefulness and ravishment to the soul, and that it made the soul like a field or garden of God, with all manner of pleasant flowers; that is, all pleasant, delightful and undisturbed, enjoying a sweet calm, and the gently vivifying beams of the sun. The soul of a true Christian, as I then wrote my meditations, appeared like such a little white flower as we see in the spring of the year, low and humble on the ground, opening its bosom, to receive the pleasant beams of the sun's glory, rejoicing as it were, in a calm rapture, diffusing around a sweet fragrancy, standing peacefully and lovingly in the midst of other flowers round about, all in like manner opening their bosoms, to drink in the light of the sun.

There was no part of creature holiness that I then, and at other times, had so great a sense of the loveliness of, as humility, brokenness of heart and poverty of spirit, and there was nothing that I had such a spirit to long for. My heart, as it were, panted after this to lie low before God, and in the dust; that I might be nothing, and that God might be all; that I might become as a little child.

While I was there at New York, I sometimes was much affected with reflections on my past life, considering how late it was, before I began to be truly religious and how wickedly I had lived 'til then; and once so as to weep abundantly, and for a considerable time together.

On January 12, [1723,] I made a solemn dedication of myself to God, and wrote it down; giving up myself, and all that I had to God; to be for the future in no respect my own; to act as one that had no right to himself, in any respect. And solemnly vowed to take God for my whole portion and felicity, looking on nothing else as any part of my happiness, nor acting as if it were: and his law for the constant rule of my obedience, engaging to fight with all my might against the world, the flesh and the devil, to the end of my life. But have reason to be infinitely humbled, when I consider, how much I have failed of answering my obligation.

I had then abundance of sweet religious conversation in the family where I lived, with Mr. John Smith, and his pious mother. My heart was knit in affection to those in whom were appearances of true piety, and I could bear the thoughts of no other companions but such as were holy, and the disciples of the blessed Jesus.

I had great longings for the advancement of Christ's kingdom in the world. My secret prayer used to be in great part taken up in praying for it. If I heard the least hint of anything that happened in any part of the world that appeared to me in some respect or other, to have a favorable aspect on the interest of Christ's kingdom, my soul eagerly catched at it; and it would much animate and refresh me. I used to be earnest to read public newsletters, mainly for that end, to see if I could not find some news favorable to the interest of religion in the world.

I very frequently used to retire into a solitary place, on the banks of Hudson's river, at some distance from the city, for contemplation on divine things and secret converse with God, and had many sweet hours there. Sometimes Mr. Smith and I walked there together to converse of the things of God, and our conversation used much to turn on the advancement of Christ's kingdom in the world, and the glorious things that God would accomplish for his church in the latter days.

I had then, and at other times, the greatest delight in the holy Scriptures, of any book whatsoever. Oftentimes in reading it, every word seemed to touch my heart. I felt an harmony between something in my heart, and those sweet and powerful words. I seemed often to see so much light exhibited by every sentence, and such a refreshing ravishing food communicated, that I could not get along in reading. Used oftentimes to dwell long on one sentence, to see the wonders contained in it; and yet almost every sentence seemed to be full of wonders.

I came away from New York in the month of April, 1723, and had a most bitter parting with Madam Smith and her son. My heart seemed to sink within me, at leaving the family and city, where I had enjoyed so many sweet and pleasant days. I went from New York to Weathersfield [Connecticut] by water. As I sailed away, I kept sight of the city as long as I could; and when I was out of sight of it, it would affect me much to look that way, with a kind of melancholy mixed with sweetness. However, that night after this sorrowful parting, I was greatly comforted in God at Westchester, where we went ashore to lodge, and had a pleasant time of it all the voyage to Saybrook. It was sweet to me to think of meeting dear Christians in heaven, where we should never part more. At Saybrook we went ashore to lodge on Saturday, and there kept sabbath where I had a sweet and refreshing season, walking alone in the fields.

After I came home to Windsor [Connecticut], remained much in a like frame of my mind as I had been in at New York, but only sometimes felt my heart ready to sink with the thoughts of my friends at New York. And my refuge and support was in contemplations on the heavenly state, as I find in my diary of May 1, 1723. It was my comfort to think of that state where there is fulness of joy; where reigns heavenly, sweet, calm and delightful love, without alloy; where there are continually the dearest expressions of this love; where is the enjoyment of the persons loved without ever parting; where these persons that appear so lovely in this world will really be inexpressibly more lovely, and full of love to us. And how sweetly will the mutual lovers join together to sing the praises of God and the Lamb! How full will it fill us with joy to think that this enjoyment, these sweet exercises will never cease or come to an end, but will last to all eternity!

Continued much in the same frame in the general that I had been in at New York, 'til I went to New Haven to live there as tutor of the college, having some special seasons of uncommon sweetness; particularly once at Bolton [Connecticut] in a journey from Boston, walking out alone in the fields. After I went to New Haven, I sunk in religion, my mind being diverted from my eager and violent pursuits after holiness by some affairs that greatly perplexed and distracted my mind.

In September, 1725, was taken ill at New Haven, and endeavoring to go home to Windsor, was so ill at the North Village that I could go no further where I lay sick for about a quarter of a year. And in this sickness, God was pleased to visit me again with the sweet influences of his spirit. My mind was greatly engaged there on divine, pleasant contemplations and longings of soul. I observed that those who watched with me would often by looking out for the morning, and seemed to wish for it. Which brought to my mind those words of the psalmist, which my soul with sweetness made its own language: "My soul waitest for the Lord, more than they that watch for the morning, I say, more than they that watch for the morning." And when the light of the morning came, and the beams of the sun came in at the windows, it refreshed my soul from one morning to another. It seemed to me to be some image of the sweet light of God's glory.

I remember, about that time, I used greatly to long for the conversion of some that I was concerned with. It seemed to me I could gladly honor them, and with delight be a servant to them, and lie at their feet, if they were but truly holy.

But sometime after this, I was again greatly diverted in my mind with some temporal concerns that exceedingly took up my thoughts, greatly to the wounding of my soul, and went on through various exercises, that it would be tedious to relate, that gave me much more experience of my own heart than ever I had before.

Since I came to this town [Northampton], I have often had sweet complacency in God, in views of his glorious perfections and the excellency of Jesus Christ. God has appeared to me a glorious and lovely Being, chiefly on the account of his holiness. The holiness of God has always appeared to me the most lovely of all his attributes. The doctrines of God's absolute sovereignty and free grace in showing mercy to whom he would show mercy, and man's absolute dependence on the operations of God's Holy Spirit, have very often appeared to me as sweet and glorious doctrines. These doctrines have been much my delight. God's sovereignty has ever appeared to me as great part of his glory. It has often been sweet to me to go to God and adore him as a sovereign God, and ask sovereign mercy of him.

I have loved the doctrines of the gospel; they have been to my soul like green pastures. The gospel has seemed to me to be the richest treasure, the treasure that I have most desired and longed that it might dwell richly in me. The way of salvation by Christ has appeared in a general way glorious and excellent, and most pleasant and beautiful. It has often seemed to me that it would in a great measure spoil heaven to receive it in any other way. That text has often been affecting and delightful to me, Isaiah 32:2: "A man shall be an hiding place from the wind, and a covert from the tempest," etc.

It has often appeared sweet to me to be united to Christ; to have him for my head, and to be a member of his body; and also to have Christ for my teacher and prophet. I very often think with sweetness and longings and pantings of soul, of being a little child, taking hold of Christ, to be led by him through the wilderness of this world. That text, Matthew 18:3 at the beginning, has often been sweet to me, "Except ye be converted, and become as little children, etc." I love to think of coming to Christ, to receive salvation of him, poor in spirit, and quite empty of self; humbly exalting him alone; cut entirely off from my own root, and to grow into and out of Christ; to have God in Christ to be all in all; and to live by faith on the Son of God, a life of humble, unfeigned confidence in him. That Scripture has often been sweet to me, Psalm 115:1: "Not unto us, O Lord, not unto us, but unto Thy name give glory, for Thy mercy, and for Thy truth's sake." And those words of Christ, Luke 10:21: "In that hour Jesus rejoiced in spirit, and said, I thank thee, O Father, Lord of heaven and earth, that Thou hast hid these things from the wise and prudent, and hast revealed them unto babes: Even so Father, for so it seemed good in Thy sight." That sovereignty of God that Christ rejoiced in seemed to me to be worthy to be rejoiced in, and that rejoicing of Christ seemed to me to show the excellency of Christ, and the spirit that he was of.

Sometimes only mentioning a single word causes my heart to burn within me, or only seeing the name of Christ or the name of some attribute of God. And God has appeared glorious to me on account of the Trinity. It has made me have exalting thoughts of God, that he subsists in three persons: Father, Son, and Holy Ghost.

The sweetest joys and delights I have experienced have not been those that have arisen from a hope of my own good estate, but in a direct view of the glorious things of the gospel. When I enjoy this sweetness it seems to carry me above the thoughts of my own safe estate. It seems at such times a loss that I cannot bear, to take off my eye from the glorious, pleasant object I behold without me, to turn my eye in upon myself, and my own good estate.

My heart has been much on the advancement of Christ's kingdom in the world. The histories of the past advancement of Christ's kingdom have been sweet to me. When I have read histories of past ages, the pleasantest thing in all my reading has been to read of the kingdom of Christ being promoted. And when I have expected in my reading to come to any such thing, I have lotted [delighted] upon it all the way as I read. And my mind has been much entertained and delighted with the Scripture promises and prophecies of the future glorious advancement of Christ's kingdom on earth.

I have sometimes had a sense of the excellent fullness of Christ, and his meetness and suitableness as a Savior; whereby he has appeared to me, far above all, the chief of ten thousands. And His blood and atonement has appeared sweet, and His righteousness sweet; which is always accompanied with an ardency of spirit, and inward strugglings and breathings and groanings, that cannot be uttered, to be emptied of myself and swallowed up in Christ.

Once, as I rid out into the woods for my health, Anno 1737, and having lit from my horse in a retired place, as my manner commonly has been, to walk for divine contemplation and prayer, I had a view, that for me was extraordinary, of the glory of the Son of God, as mediator between God and man, and his wonderful, great, full, pure and sweet grace and love, and meek and gentle condescension. This grace, that appeared to me so calm and sweet, appeared great above the heavens. The person of Christ appeared ineffably excellent, with an excellency great enough to swallow up all thought and conception, which continued, as near as I can judge, about an hour, which kept me, the bigger part of the time, in a flood of tears, and weeping aloud. I felt withal an ardency of soul to be, what I know not otherwise how to express, than to be emptied and annihilated; to lie in the dust, and to be full of Christ alone; to love him with a holy and pure love; to trust in him; to live upon him; to serve and follow him, and to be totally wrapt up in the fullness of Christ; and to be perfectly sanctified and made pure with a divine and heavenly purity. I have several other times had views very much of the same nature and that have had the same effects.

I have many times had a sense of the glory of the third person in the Trinity in his office of sanctifier; in his holy operations communicating divine light and life to the soul. God in the communications of his Holy Spirit has appeared as an infinite fountain of divine glory and sweetness, being full and sufficient to fill and satisfy the soul, pouring forth itself in sweet communications, like the sun in its glory, sweetly and pleasantly diffusing light and life.

I have sometimes had an affecting sense of the excellency of the Word of God, as a word of life; as the light of life; a sweet, excellent, life-giving word, accompanied with a thirsting after that word, that it might dwell richly in my heart.

I have often, since I lived in this town, had very affecting views of my own sinfulness and vileness; very frequently so as to hold me in a kind of loud weeping, sometimes for a considerable time together, so that I have often been forced to shut myself up. I have had a vastly greater sense of my wickedness, and the badness of my heart, since my conversion, than ever I had before. It has often appeared to me, that if God should mark iniquity against me, I should appear the very worst of all mankind, of all that have been since the beginning of the world of this time, and that I should have by far the lowest place in hell. When others that have come to talk with me about their soul concerns have expressed the sense they have had of their own wickedness by saying that it seemed to them that they were as bad as the devil himself, I thought their expressions seemed

exceeding faint and feeble to represent my wickedness. I thought I should
wonder that they should content themselves with such expressions as
these, if I had any reason to imagine that their sin bore any proportion to
mine. It seemed to me I should wonder at myself if I should express my
wickedness in such feeble terms as they did.

My wickedness, as I am in myself, has long appeared to me perfectly
ineffable and infinitely swallowing up all thought and imagination, like
an infinite deluge or infinite mountains over my head. I know not how
to express better what my sins appear to me to be than by heaping infinite upon infinite, and multiplying infinite by infinite. I go about very
often, for this many years, with these expressions in my mind and in my
mouth, "Infinite upon infinite. Infinite upon infinite!" When I look into
my heart and take a view of my wickedness, it looks like an abyss infinitely deeper than hell. And it appears to me that were it not for free
grace, exalted and raised up to the infinite height of all the fullness and
glory of the great Jehovah, and the arm of his power and grace stretched
forth, in all the majesty of his power and in all the glory of his sovereignty,
I should appear sunk down in my sins infinitely below hell itself, far beyond sight of everything but the piercing eye of God's grace, that can
pierce even down to such a depth and to the bottom of such an abyss.

And yet I be not in the least inclined to think that I have a greater conviction of sin than ordinary. It seems to me my conviction of sin is exceeding small and faint. It appears to me enough to amaze me that I have
no more sense of my sin. I know certainly that I have very little sense of
my sinfulness. That my sins appear to me so great don't seem to me to
be because I have so much more conviction of sin than other Christians, but because I am so much worse and have so much more wickedness to be convinced of. When I have had these turns of weeping and
crying for my sins, I thought I knew in the time of it that my repentance
was nothing to my sin.

I have greatly longed of late for a broken heart and to lie low before
God. And when I ask for humility of God, I can't bear the thoughts of
being no more humble than other Christians. It seems to me that though
their degrees of humility may be suitable for them, yet it would be a vile
self-exaltation in me not to be the lowest in humility of all mankind.
Others speak of their longing to be humbled to the dust. Though that
may be a proper expression for them I always think for myself that I
ought to be humbled down below hell. 'Tis an expression that it has long
been natural for me to use in prayer to God. I ought to lie infinitely low
before God.

It is affecting to me to think how ignorant I was, when I was a young
Christian, of the bottomless, infinite depths of wickedness, pride,
hypocrisy and deceit left in my heart.

I have vastly a greater sense of my universal, exceeding dependence on God's grace and strength and mere good pleasure, of late, than I used formerly to have, and have experienced more of an abhorrence of my own righteousness. The thought of any comfort or job, arising in me, on any consideration or reflection on my own amiableness, or any of my performances or experiences, or any goodness of heart or life is nauseous and detestable to me. And yet I am greatly afflicted with a proud and self-righteous spirit, much more sensibly than I used to be formerly. I see that serpent rising and putting forth its head, continually, everywhere, all around me.

Though it seems to me that in some respects I was a far better Christian for two or three years after my first conversion than I am now, and lived in a more constant delight and pleasure, yet of late years I have had a more full and constant sense of the absolute sovereignty of God and a delight in that sovereignty, and have had more of a sense of the glory of Christ as a mediator as revealed in the gospel. On one Saturday night in particular, had a particular discovery of the excellency of the gospel of Christ, above all other doctrines, so that I could not but say to myself, "This is my chosen light, my chosen doctrine," and of Christ, "This is my chosen prophet." It appeared to me to be sweet beyond all expression to follow Christ and to be taught and enlightened and instructed by him, to learn of him, and live to him.

Another Saturday night, January, [1739], had such a sense how sweet and blessed a thing it was to walk in the way of duty, to do that which was right and meet to be done and agreeable to the holy mind of God, that it caused me to break forth into a kind of a loud weeping, which held me some time, so that I was forced to shut myself up, and fasten the doors. I could not but as it were cry out, "How happy are they which do that which is right in the sight of God! They are blessed indeed, they are the happy ones!" I had at the same time, a very affecting sense how meet and suitable it was that God should govern the world, and order all things according to his own pleasure, and I rejoiced in it, and God reigned, and that his will was done.

# BENJAMIN FRANKLIN
## (1706–1790)

Benjamin Franklin might be considered the model for the self-invented American. He was a statesman, an author, an inventor, and a printer—among many other things. In 1723, he moved to Philadelphia from Boston, where he set up a newspaper, published *Poor Richard's Almanack*, and established a subscription library, a philosophical society, a hospital, a militia, and a fire company. Among his many inventions were bifocal lenses, the Franklin stove, and the lightning rod. An important voice during the American Revolution, he was a signer of the Declaration of Independence, which he helped to draft. He also served as the American ambassador to France, where he was immensely popular. His *Autobiography* (1791) is a classic of the genre, one that establishes a particular mode of memoir focused on the self-invention of the narrator. Indeed, Franklin broke fiercely with the previous models in this genre and, in doing so, helped a young nation to imagine ways of thinking about itself. In its secular aspect, his book also represents a shift away from spiritual introspection, the sort of book one might imagine the Enlightenment period to have produced: clear-eyed, commonsensical, matter-of-fact. It would be hard to overestimate the degree to which the American character was shaped by Franklin in this seminal work.

## FROM *The Autobiography of Benjamin Franklin*

At the time I establish'd my self in Pensylvania, there was not a good Bookseller's Shop in any of the Colonies to the Southward of Boston. In New-York & Philad the Printers were indeed Stationers, they sold only Paper, &c. Almanacks, Ballads, and a few common School Books. Those who lov'd Reading were oblig'd to send for their Books from England.— The Members of the Junto had each a few. We had left the Alehouse where we first met, and hired a Room to hold our Club in. I propos'd that we should all of us bring our Books to that Room, where they would not only be ready to consult in our Conferences, but become a common Benefit, each of us being at Liberty to borrow such as he wish'd to read at home. This was accordingly done, and for some time contented us. Finding the Advantage of this little Collection, I propos'd to render the Benefit from Books more common by commencing a Public Subscription Library. I drew a Sketch of the Plan and Rules that would be necessary, and got a skilful Conveyancer Mr Charles Brockden to put the whole in Form of Articles of Agreement to be subscribed, by which each Subscriber engag'd to pay a certain Sum down for the first Purchase of Books and an annual Contribution for encreasing them.—So few were the Readers at that time in Philadelphia, and the Majority of us so poor, that I was not able with great Industry to find more than Fifty Persons, mostly young Tradesmen, willing to pay down for this purpose Forty shillings each, & Ten Shillings per Annum. On this little Fund we began. The Books were imported. The Library was open one Day in the Week for lending them to the Subscribers, on their Promisory Notes to pay Double the Value if not duly returned. The Institution soon manifested its Utility, was imitated by other Towns and in other Provinces, the Librarys were augmented by Donations, Reading became fashionable, and our People having no publick Amusements to divert their Attention from Study became better acquainted with Books, and in a few Years were observ'd by Strangers to be better instructed & more intelligent than People of the same Rank generally are in other Countries.—

When we were about to sign the above-mentioned Articles, which were to be binding on us, our Heirs, &c for fifty Years, Mr Brockden, the Scrivener, said to us, "You are young Men, but it is scarce probable that any of you will live to see the Expiration of the Term fix'd in this Instrument." A Number of us, however, are yet living: But the Instrument was after a few Years rendered null by a Charter that incorporated & gave Perpetuity to the Company.—

The Objections, & Reluctances I met with in Soliciting the Subscriptions, made me soon feel the Impropriety of presenting one's self as the Proposer of any useful Project that might be suppos'd to raise one's Reputation in the smallest degree above that of one's Neighbours, when one has need of their Assistance to accomplish that Project. I therefore put my self as much as I could out of sight, and stated it as a Scheme of *a Number of Friends*, who had requested me to go about and propose it to such as they thought Lovers of Reading. In this way my Affair went on more smoothly, and I ever after practis'd it on such Occasions; and from my frequent Successes, can heartily recommend it. The present little Sacrifice of your Vanity will afterwards be amply repaid. If it remains a while uncertain to whom the Merit belongs, some one more vain than yourself will be encourag'd to claim it, and then even Envy will be dispos'd to do you Justice, by plucking those assum'd Feathers, & restoring them to their right Owner.

This Library afforded me the Means of Improvement by constant Study, for which I set apart an Hour or two each Day; and thus repair'd in some Degree the Loss of the Learned Education my Father once intended for me. Reading was the only Amusement I allow'd my self. I spent no time in Taverns, Games, or Frolicks of any kind. And my Industry in my Business continu'd as indefatigable as it was necessary. I was in debt for my Printing-house, I had a young Family coming on to be educated, and I had to contend with for Business two Printers who were establish'd in the Place before me. My Circumstances however grew daily easier: my original Habits of Frugality continuing. And My Father having among his Instructions to me when a Boy, frequently repeated a Proverb of Solomon, *"Seest thou a Man diligent in his Calling, he shall stand before Kings, he shall not stand before mean Men."* I from thence consider'd Industry as a Means of obtaining Wealth and Distinction, which encourag'd me; tho' I did not think that I should ever literally stand before Kings, which however has since happened. — for I have stood before five, & even had the honour of sitting down with one, the King of Denmark, to Dinner.

We have an English Proverb that says,

> He that would thrive
> Must ask his Wife;

it was lucky for me that I had one as much dispos'd to Industry & Frugality as my self. She assisted me chearfully in my Business, folding & stitching Pamphlets, tending Shop, purchasing old Linen Rags for the Paper-makers, &c &c. We kept no idle Servants, our Table was plain & simple, our Furniture of the cheapest. For instance my Breakfast was a long time Bread & Milk, (no Tea,) and I ate it out of a twopenny earthen Porringer with a Pewter Spoon. But mark how Luxury will enter Families, and make a Progress, in Spite of Principle. Being Call'd one Morning to Breakfast, I found it in a China Bowl with a Spoon of Silver. They had been bought for me without my Knowledge by my Wife, and had cost her the enormous Sum of three and twenty Shillings, for which she had no other Excuse or Apology to make, but that she thought *her* Husband deserv'd a Silver Spoon & China Bowl as well as any of his Neighbours. This was the first Appearance of Plate & China in our House, which afterwards in a Course of Years as our Wealth encreas'd, augmented gradually to several Hundred Pounds in Value. —

I had been religiously educated as a Presbyterian; and tho' some of the Dogmas of that Persuasion, such as the Eternal Decrees of God, Election, Reprobation, &c. appear'd to me unintelligible, others doubtful, & I early absented myself from the Public Assemblies of the Sect, Sunday being my Studying-Day, I never was without some religious Principles; I never doubted, for instance, the Existance of the Deity, that he made the World, & govern'd it by his Providence; that the most acceptable Service of God was the doing Good to Man; that our Souls are immortal; and that all Crime will be punished & Virtue rewarded either here or hereafter; these I esteem'd the Essentials of every Religion, and being to be found in all the Religions we had in our Country I respected them all, tho' with different degrees of Respect as I found them more or less mix'd with other Articles which without any Tendency to inspire, promote or confirm Morality, serv'd principally to divide us & make us unfriendly to one another.—This Respect to all, with an Opinion that the worst had some good Effects, induc'd me to avoid all Discourse that might tend to lessen the good Opinion another might have of his own Religion; and as our Province increas'd in People and new Places of worship were continually wanted, & generally erected by voluntary Contribution, my Mite for such purpose, whatever might be the Sect, was never refused.—

Tho' I seldom attended any Public Worship, I had still an Opinion of its Propriety, and of its Utility when rightly conducted, and I regularly paid my annual Subscription for the Support of the only Presbyterian Minister or Meeting we had in Philadelphia. He us'd to visit me sometimes as a Friend, and admonish me to attend his Administrations, and I was now and then prevail'd on to do so, once for five Sundays successively. Had he been, *in my Opinion,* a good Preacher perhaps I might have continued, notwithstanding the occasion I had for the Sunday's Leisure in my Course of Study: But his Discourses were chiefly either polemic Arguments, or Explications of the peculiar Doctrines of our Sect, and were all to me very dry, uninteresting and unedifying, since not a single moral Principle was inculcated or enforc'd, their Aim seeming to be rather to make us Presbyterians than good Citizens. At length he took for his Text that Verse of the 4th Chapter of Philippians, *Finally, Brethren, Whatsoever Things are true, honest, just, pure, lovely, or of good report, if there be any virtue, or any praise, think on these Things;* & I imagin'd in a Sermon on such a Text, we could not miss of having some Morality: But he confin'd himself to five Points only as meant by the Apostle, viz. 1. Keeping holy the Sabbath Day. 2. Being diligent in Reading the Holy Scriptures. 3. Attending duly the Publick Worship. 4. Partaking of the Sacrament. 5. Paying a due Respect to God's Ministers.—These might be all good Things, but as they were not the kind of good Things that I expected from that Text, I despaired of ever meeting with them from any other, was disgusted, and attended his Preaching no more.—I had some Years before compos'd a little Liturgy or Form of Prayer for my own private Use, viz, in 1728. entitled, *Articles of Belief & Acts of Religion.* I return'd to the Use of this, and went no more to the public Assemblies.—My Conduct might be blameable, but I leave it without attempting farther to excuse it, my present purpose being to relate Facts, and not to make Apologies for them.—

It was about this time that I conceiv'd the bold and arduous Project of arriving at moral Perfection. I wish'd to live without committing any Fault at any time; I would conquer all that either Natural Inclination, Custom, or Company might lead me into. As I knew, or thought I knew, what was right and wrong, I did not see why I might not *always* do the one and avoid the other. But I soon found I had undertaken a Task of more Difficulty than I had imagined: While my Care was employ'd in guarding against one Fault, I was often surpriz'd by another. Habit took the Advantage of Inattention. Inclination was sometimes too strong for Reason. I concluded at length, that the mere speculative Conviction that it was our Interest to be compleatly virtuous, was not sufficient to prevent our Slipping, and that the contrary Habits must be broken and good Ones acquired and established, before we can have any Dependance on a steady uniform Rectitude of Conduct. For this purpose I therefore contriv'd the following Method. —

In the various Enumerations of the moral Virtues I had met with in my Reading, I found the Catalogue more or less numerous, as different Writers included more or fewer ideas under the same Name. Temperance, for Example, was by some confin'd to Eating & Drinking, while by others it was extended to mean the moderating every other Pleasure, Appetite, Inclination or Passion, bodily or mental, even to our Avarice & Ambition. I propos'd to myself, for the sake of Clearness, to use rather more Names with fewer Ideas annex'd to each, than a few Names with more Ideas; and I included under Thirteen Names of Virtues all that at that time occurr'd to me as necessary or desirable, and annex'd to each a short Precept, which fully express'd the Extent I gave to its Meaning. —

These Names of Virtues with their Precepts were

1. TEMPERANCE.

Eat not to Dulness

Drink not to Elevation.

2. SILENCE.

Speak not but what may benefit others or your self. Avoid trifling Conversation.

3. ORDER.

Let all your Things have their Places. Let each Part of your Business have its Time.

4. RESOLUTION.

Resolve to perform what you ought. Perform without fail what you resolve.

5. FRUGALITY.

Make no Expence but to do good to others or yourself: i.e. Waste nothing.

6. Industry.
Lose no Time.—Be always employ'd in something useful.—Cut off all unnecessary Actions.—
7. Sincerity.
Use no hurtful Deceit.
Think innocently and justly; and, if you speak; speak accordingly.
8. Justice.
Wrong none, by doing Injuries or omitting the Benefits that are your Duty.
9. Moderation.
Avoid Extreams. Forbear resenting Injuries so much as you think they deserve.
10. Cleanliness.
Tolerate no Uncleanness in Body, Cloaths or Habitation.—
11. Tranquility
Be not disturbed at Trifles, or at Accidents common or unavoidable.
12. Chastity.
Rarely use Venery but for Health or Offspring; Never to Dulness, Weakness, or the Injury of your own or another's Peace or Reputation.—
13. Humility.
Imitate Jesus and Socrates.—

My intention being to acquire the *Habitude* of all these Virtues, I judg'd it would be well not to distract my Attention by attempting the whole at once, but to fix it on one of them at a time, and when I should be Master of that, then to proceed to another, and so on till I should have gone thro' the thirteen. And as the previous Acquisition of some might facilitate the Acquisition of certain others, I arrang'd them with that View as they stand above. *Temperance* first, as it tends to procure that Coolness & Clearness of Head, which is so necessary where constant Vigilance was to be kept up, and Guard maintained, against the unremitting Attraction of ancient Habits, and the Force of perpetual Temptations. This being acquir'd & establish'd, *Silence* would be more easy, and my Desire being to gain Knowledge at the same time that I improv'd in Virtue, and considering that in Conversation it was obtain'd rather by the Use of the Ears than of the Tongue, & therefore wishing to break a Habit I was getting into of Prattling, Punning & Joking, which only made me acceptable to trifling Company, I gave *Silence* the second Place. This, and the next, *Order*, I expected would allow me more Time for attending to my Project and my Studies; Resolution once become habitual, would keep me firm in my Endeavours to obtain all the subsequent Virtues; *Frugality &Industry*, by freeing me from my remaining Debt, & producing Affluence & Independance would make more easy the Practice of *Sincerity* and *Jus-*

*tice*, &c. &c.. Conceiving then that agreeable to the Advice of Pythagoras in his Golden Verses,* daily Examination would be necessary, I contriv'd the following Method for conducting that Examination.

I made a little Book in which I allotted a Page for each of the Virtues. I rul'd each Page with red Ink so as to have seven Columns, one for each Day of the Week, marking each Column with a Letter for the Day. I cross'd these Columns with thirteen red Lines, marking the Beginning of each Line with the first Letter of one of the Virtues, on which Line & in its proper Column I might mark by a little black Spot every Fault I found upon Examination, to have been committed respecting that Virtue upon that Day.

FORM OF THE PAGES

| TEMPERANCE | | | | | | |
|---|---|---|---|---|---|---|
| *Eat not to Dulness.* *Drink not to Elevation.* | | | | | | |
| S | M | T | W | T | F | S |
| T | | | | | | |
| S ● ● | ● | | ● | | ● | |
| O ● | ● | ● | | ● | ● | ● |
| R | | ● | | | ● | |
| F | ● | | | ● | | |
| I | | ● | | | | |
| S | | | | | | |
| J | | | | | | |
| M | | | | | | |
| Cl. | | | | | | |
| T | | | | | | |
| Ch | | | | | | |
| H | | | | | | |

*Let not the stealing God of Sleep surprize,*
*Nor creep in Slumbers on thy weary Eyes,*
*Ere ev'ry Action of the former Day,*

I determined to give a Week's strict Attention to each of the Virtues successively. Thus in the first Week my great Guard was to avoid every the least Offence against Temperance, leaving the other Virtues to their ordinary Chance, only marking every Evening the Faults of the Day. Thus if in the first Week I could keep my first Line marked T clear of Spots, I suppos'd the Habit of that Virtue so much strengthen'd and its opposite weaken'd, that I might venture extending my Attention to include the next, and for the following Week keep both Lines clear of Spots. Proceeding thus to the last. I could go thro' a Course compleat in Thirteen Weeks, and four Courses in a Year. — And like him who having a Garden to weed, does not attempt to eradicate all the bad Herbs at once, which would exceed his Reach and his Strength, but works on one of the Beds at a time, & having accomplish'd the first proceeds to a second; so I should have, (I hoped) the encouraging Pleasure of seeing on my Pages the Progress I made in Virtue, by clearing successively my Lines of their Spots, till in the End by a Number of Courses, I should be happy in viewing a clean Book after a thirteen Weeks daily Examination.

This my little Book had for its Motto these Lines from *Addison's Cato;*

> *Here will I hold: If there is a Pow'r above us,*
> *(And that there is, all Nature cries aloud*
> *Thro' all her Works) he must delight in Virtue,*
> *And that which he delights in must be happy.*

Another from *Cicero.*

---

Strictly *thou dost, and* righteously *survey.*
With rev'rence at thy own Tribunal stand,
And answer justly to thy own Demand
Where have I been? In what have I trangrest?
What Good or Ill has this Day's Life exprest?
Where have I fail'd in what I ought to do?
In what to GOD, to Man, or to myself I owe?
Inquire severe whate'er from first to last,
From Morning's Dawn till Ev'nings Gloom has past.
If Evil were thy Deeds, repenting mourn,
And let thy Soul with strong Remorse be torn:
If Good, the Good with Peace of Mind repay, ⎫
And to thy secret Self with Pleasure say,     ⎬
Rejoice, my Heart, for all went well to Day. ⎭

[Franklin's note]

*O Vitae Philosophia Dux! O Virtutum indagatrix, expultrixque vitiorum! Unus dies bene, & ex preceptis tuis actus, peccanti immortalitati est anteponendus.* \*

Another from the Proverbs of Solomon speaking of Wisdom or Virtue;

Length of Days is in her right hand, and in her Left Hand Riches and Honours; Her Ways are Ways of Pleasantness, and all her Paths are Peace. III, 16, 17.

And conceiving God to be the Fountain of Wisdom, I thought it right and necessary to solicit his Assistance for obtaining it; to this End I form'd the following little Prayer, which was prefix'd to my Tables of Examination; for daily Use.

O Powerful Goodness! bountiful Father! merciful Guide! Increase in me that Wisdom which discovers my truest Interests; Strengthen my Resolutions to perform what that Wisdom dictates. Accept my kind Offices to thy other Children, as the only Return in my Power for thy continual Favours to me.

I us'd also sometimes a little Prayer which I took from *Thomson's* Poems. viz

Father of Light and Life, thou Good supreme,
O teach me what is good, teach me thy self!
Save me from Folly, Vanity and Vice,
From every low Pursuit, and fill my Soul
With Knowledge, conscious Peace, & Virtue pure,
Sacred, substantial, neverfading Bliss!

The Precept of *Order* requiring that *every Part of my Business should have its allotted Time,* one Page in my little Book contain'd the following Scheme of Employment for the Twenty-four Hours of a natural Day.

I enter'd upon the Execution of this Plan for Self Examination, and continu'd it with occasional Intermissions for some time. I was surpriz'd to find myself so much fuller of Faults than I had imagined, but I had the Satisfaction of seeing them diminish. To avoid the Trouble of renewing now & then my little Book, which by scraping out the Marks on the Paper of old Faults to make room for new Ones in a new Course, became full of Holes: I transferr'd my Tables & Precepts to the Ivory Leaves of a Memorandum Book, on which the Lines were drawn with red Ink that

---

\*"O Philosophy, leader of life! O seeker of virtue, and critic of vice! From your teachings, a single day of good is preferred to an eternity of sin."

| The Morning Question, | 5 | Rise, wash, and address *Powerful* |
| What Good Shall | 6 | *Goodness*; contrive Day's Business and |
| I do this Day? | 7 | take the Resolution of the Day; prosecute |
| | 8 | the present Study: and breakfast?— |
| | 9 | Work. |
| | 10 | |
| | 11 | |
| | 12 | Read, or overlook my Accounts, |
| | 1 | and dine. |
| | 2 | |
| | 3 | Work. |
| | 4 | |
| | 5 | |
| | 6 | |
| Evening Question, | 7 | Put Things in their Places, Supper, |
| What Good have I | 8 | Musick or Diversion, or Conversation, |
| done to day? | 9 | Examination of the Day. |
| | 10 | |
| | 11 | |
| | 12 | |
| | 1 | Sleep— |
| | 2 | |
| | 3 | |
| | 4 | |

made a durable Stain, and on those Lines I mark'd my Faults with a black Lead Pencil, which Marks I could easily wipe out with a wet Sponge. After a while I went thro' one Course only in a Year, and afterwards only one in several Years; till at length I omitted them entirely, being employ'd in Voyages & Business abroad with a Multiplicity of Affairs, that interfered. But I always carried my little Book with me. My Scheme of ORDER, gave me the most Trouble, and I found, that tho' it might be practicable where a Man's Business was such as to leave him the Disposition of his Time, that of a Journey-man Printer for instance, it was not possible to be exactly observ'd by a Master, who must mix with the World, and often receive People of Business at their own Hours.— *Order* too, with regard to Places for Things, Papers, &c. I found extreamly difficult to acquire. I had not been early accustomed to it, & having an exceeding good Memory, I was not so sensible of the Inconvenience attending Want of Method. This Article therefore cost me so much painful Attention & my Faults in it vex'd me so much, and I made so little Progress in Amendment, & had such frequent Relapses, that I was almost ready to give up the Attempt, and content my self with a faulty Character in that respect. Like the Man who in buying an Ax of a Smith my Neighbour, desired to have the whole of its Surface as bright as the Edge; the Smith consented to grind it bright for him if he would turn the Wheel. He turn'd while the Smith press'd the broad Face of the Ax hard & heavily on the Stone, which made the Turning of it very fatiguing. The Man came every now & then from the Wheel to see how the Work went on; and at length would take his Ax as it was without farther Grinding. No, says the Smith, Turn on, turn on; we shall have it bright by and by; as yet 'tis only speckled. Yes, says the Man; but—*I think I like a speckled Ax best.*—And I believe this may have been the Case with many who having for want of some such Means as I employ'd found the Difficulty of obtaining good, & breaking bad Habits, in other Points of Vice & Virtue, have given up the Struggle, & concluded that *a speckled Ax was best.* For something that pretended to be Reason was every now and then suggesting to me, that such extream Nicety as I exacted of my self might be a kind of Foppery in Morals, which if it were known would make me ridiculous; that a perfect Character might be attended with the Inconvenience of being envied and hated; and that a benevolent Man should allow a few Faults in himself, to keep his Friends in Countenance. In Truth I found myself incorrigible with respect to *Order;* and now I am grown old, and my Memory bad, I feel very sensibly the want of it. But on the whole, tho' I never arrived at the Perfection I had been so ambitious of obtaining, but fell far short of it, yet I was by the Endeavour made a better and a happier Man than I otherwise should have been, if I had not attempted it; As those who aim at perfect Writing by imitating the engraved Copies, tho' they never reach the wish'd for Excellence of those Copies, their Hand is mended by the Endeavour, and is tolerable while it continues fair & legible.—

# ELIZABETH ASHBRIDGE
## (1713–1755)

One of the most enduring forms of memoir is the spiritual autobiography, and one of the earliest (and finest) examples of this genre in the New World was Elizabeth Ashbridge's *Some Account of the Fore-Part of the Life of Elizabeth Ashbridge* (1774). As we learn from her account, the author was born in 1713 in Middlewich, England. Her father was a doctor who often served as a ship's surgeon at sea, and he was often away from home. Ashbridge was herself an unruly child, and she ran away from home with a much older man at the age of fourteen. He died soon thereafter, and she wandered to Ireland (where she had Quaker relatives) and America. After several tempestuous, adventurous years, she married a man called Sullivan (not mentioned in her account) in 1735. This marriage failed, but eventually she settled down with a man called Aaron Ashbridge in New Jersey in 1746. She was by this time a successful Quaker preacher. She returned to Ireland and England to preach, in 1753, and died two years later. Her posthumously published account offers a striking portrait of the New World in the eighteenth century: its poverty and narrow-mindedness, its refusal to acknowledge or help the downtrodden.

## FROM *Some Account of the Fore-Part of the Life of Elizabeth Ashbridge*

My life being attended with many uncommon occurrences, some of which I brought upon myself, which I believe were for my good, I have therefore thought proper to make some remarks on the dealings of Divine Goodness with me, having often had cause with David, to say, "It is good for me that I have been afflicted"; and I most earnestly desire that whosoever reads the following lines may take warning and shun the evils that through the deceitfulness of Satan I have been drawn into.

I was born in Middlewich, in Cheshire, in the year 1713, of honest parents. My father's name was Thomas Sampson, he was a surgeon; my mother's name was Mary. My father was a man that bore a good character, but not so strictly religious as my mother, who was a pattern of virtue to me. I was the only child of my father, but my mother had a son and a daughter by a former husband. Soon after my birth my father took to the sea, and followed his profession on board a ship many long voyages, till I was twelve years old, about which time he settled at home; so that my education lay mostly on my mother, in which she discharged her duty by endeavoring to instill into me the principles of virtue during my tender age, for which I have since had cause to be thankful to the Lord, that He blessed me with such a parent, tho' her good advice and counsel have been as cast upon the water, etc. In short, she was a good example to all about her, and beloved by most that knew her, tho' not of the same religious persuasion I am now of. But oh! alas, when the time came that she might reasonably have expected the benefit of her labor, and have had comfort from me, I left her, of which I shall mention in its proper place.

In my very infancy I had an awful regard for religion and a great love for religious people, particularly the ministers, and sometimes grieved at my not being a boy and therefore could not be one, as I thought they were good men, and beloved of God. I also had a great love for the poor, remembering I had read they were blessed of the Lord; this I took to mean such as were poor in this world, and often went to their poor cottages to see them, and if I had any money or other things, I used to give them some, remembering that saying, that they that give to the poor lend to the Lord, and I had when very young an earnest desire to be beloved of Him. I used also to make remarks on those called gentlemen, and when I heard them swear it would grieve me much; for my mother had informed me that if I used any naughty words, God would not love me. As I grew up I took notice that there were several different religious societies, wherefore I often went alone and wept, desiring that I might be directed to the right. Thus my young years were attended with such like tender desires, tho' I was sometimes guilty of those things incident to children, but then I always found something in me that made me sorry for what I did amiss. Till I arrived at the age of fourteen years, I was as innocent as most children, about which time my sorrows began, and have continued most part of my life, through my giving way to a foolish passion, in setting my affections on a young man, who became a suitor to me, without my parents' consent, till I suffered myself (I may say with sorrow of heart) to be carried off in the night, and to be married before my parents found me; altho' as soon as they missed me all possible search was made after me, but all in vain, till too late to recover me.

This precipitate act plunged me into a vast scene of sorrow, for I was soon smote with remorse for thus leaving my parents, who had a right to have disposed of me, or at least their approbation ought to have been consulted in the affair, for I was soon chastised for my disobedience. Divine Providence let me see my error, and in five months I was stripped of the darling of my soul, and left a young and disconsolate widow.

I had then no home to fly to. My father was so displeased that he would do nothing for me, but my dear mother had some compassion towards me, and kept me amongst the neighbors for some time, till by her advice I went to Dublin, to a relation of hers, in hopes that absence would help to regain my father's affection. But he continued inflexible and would not send for me, and I dared not to return without his permission. — This relation with whom I lived was one of the people called Quakers. His conduct was so different from the manner of my education, which was in the way of the Church of England, that it made my situation disagreeable; for tho', as I said, I had a religious education, yet I was allowed to sing and dance, which my cousins were against, and I having a great vivacity in my natural disposition could not bear to give way to the gloomy scene of sorrow, and conviction gave it the wrong effect, and made me more wild and airy than before, for which I was often reproved. But I then thought, as a great many do now, that it was the effect of singularity and therefore would not be subject to it.

I having at that time a distant relation in the west of Ireland, I left Dublin, and went there, where I was entertained, and what rendered me disagreeable in the former place was quite pleasing to the latter. Between these two relations I spent 3 years and 2 months. While I was in Ireland I contracted an intimacy with a widow and her daughter, who were Papists, with whom I used to discourse about religion, they in defense of their faith, and I of mine; and altho' I was then very wild, it made me very thoughtful. The old woman would tell me of such mighty miracles done by their priests that I began to be disturbed in my mind, and thought that if those things were so, they must be the Apostle's successors. The old woman perceiving it one day, said in rapture, that if I, under God, can be instrumental to convert you to the holy Catholic faith, all the sins that ever I committed will be forgiven me. In a while it got so far that the priests came to converse with me, and I being young and my judgment weak was ready to believe what they said. And tho' wild as I was, it cost me many a tear with desires that I might be rightly directed. For some time I frequented their place of worship, but none of my relations knew I had any intention of going with them. At length I concluded never to be led darkly into their belief, and thought to myself — if their articles of faith are good, they will not be against my knowing them. Therefore the next time I had an opportunity with the priest, I told him I had some thoughts of becoming one of his flock, but I did not like to join with them till I knew all I was to agree to, and therefore desired to see their principles. He answered I must first confess my sins to him, and gave me till next day to consider of them. I was not much against that, having done nothing that any person could hurt me, and if, thought I, what the man says be true, it will be for my good. So when he came again, I told him all I could remember, which I thought bad enough; but he thought me, as he said, the most innocent creature that ever made confession to him. When he had done he took a book out of his pocket, and read all which I was to swear to, if I joined with them.

Tho' I was but young, I made my remarks as he went on, but I do not think it worth my writing, nor the reader's hearing. It was a great deal of ridiculous stuff. But what made me sick of my new intention was (I believe I should have swallowed the rest), I was to swear "I believed the Pretender to be the true heir to the crown of England, and that he was King James' son, and also, that whosoever died out of the pale of the church were damned." As to the first, I did not believe it essential to salvation, whether I believed it or not, and to take an oath to any such thing would be very unsafe; and the second I saw struck directly against charity, which the Apostles preferred before all other Graces. And besides, I had a religious mother who was out of that opinion. I therefore thought it would be wicked in me to believe she was damned. I therefore concluded to consider about it, but before I saw him again a sudden turn took hold of me, which put a final end to it.

My father still keeping me at so great a distance, I thought myself quite shut out of his affections, and therefore concluded, since my absence was most agreeable he should have it, and getting acquaintance with a gentlewoman lately come from Pennsylvania, who was going back again, where I had an uncle, my mother's brother, I soon agreed with her for my passage, and being ignorant in the nature of an indenture consented to be bound. As soon as this was over, she invited me to go and see the vessel we was to sail in, [to] which I readily consented, not knowing what would follow. When I came on board I found a young woman, who I afterwards understood was of a good family and had been deluded away by this creature. I was extremely glad to think I should have such an agreeable companion, but while we were in discourse, our kidnapper left us, and went ashore, and when I wanted to go was not permitted. I was kept there near three weeks, in which time the young woman's friends found her and fetched her away, by which means my friends found me, and went to the water bailiff, who brought me on shore, and our gentlewoman was obliged to conceal herself, or she would have been laid fast. My friends kept me close for two weeks, but at last I found means to get away, for my thoughts being full of going to America, I was determined to proceed with my intention, and one day meeting with the captain, I inquired of him when they sailed, and entered on board the same ship that I was on board before, and I have since thought there was [a] Providential hand in it.

There was sixty Irish servants on board, and several English passengers, but none of the English, excepting myself, understood a word of the

Irish language. As for me, I had been at no small pains to learn it, by which I had acquired so much as to discover anything they discoursed upon in Irish, which was of service to us all. There was on board the aforesaid gentlewoman and her husband's brother. While we were on the coast of Ireland, for the wind kept us there some time, I overheard the servants contriving how they should get their liberty when they came to America. To accomplish which they concluded to rise and kill the ship's crew, and all the English passengers on board, and the above mentioned young man was to navigate the ship. I took a private opportunity of informing the captain with their wicked intentions, and he let the English know of it. The next day they bore for the shore, and at a small distance from the Cove of Cork they lowered sail and cast anchor, under pretense of the wind not being fair to stand their course, then hoisted out their boat and invited the passengers to go on shore to divert themselves. And among the rest this young man that was to be this rabble's captain went, by which our end was answered. And as soon as he was on shore the rest left him and came on board, and our captain immediately ordered to weigh anchor and hoist sail. At this there was a great outcry for the young man on shore, but the captain told them the wind was fresh up, and he would not stay, [even] if it was for his own son. So their treachery was betrayed in good time, and in a manner they did not mistrust; for it was thought most advisable to keep it private least any of them should do me a mischief. But at length they found out that I understood Irish by my smiling at a story that they were telling in that language, and from that time they devised many ways to do me hurt, for which several of them were put in irons.

In nine weeks from the time I left Dublin we arrived at New York, viz., on the 15 of the 7th month, 1732. Now those to whom I had been instrumental to preserve life proved treacherous to me. — I was a stranger in a strange land.

The captain got an indenture and demanded of me to sign it, at the same time threatening me if I refused it. I told him I could find means to satisfy him for my passage without being bound, but he told me I might take my choice: either to sign that or have the other in force which I signed in Ireland. By this time I had learned the character of the beforementioned woman, by which she appeared to be a vile person, and I feared if ever I was in her power she would use me ill on her brother's account. I therefore in a fright signed the latter, and tho' there was no magistrate present it proved sufficient to make me a servant for four years. In two weeks time I was sold, and were it possible to convey in characters a scene of the sufferings of my servitude, it would affect the most stony heart with pity for a young creature who had been so tenderly brought up. For tho' my father had no great estate yet he lived well, and I had been used to little but the school, tho' it had been better for me now if I had been brought up to greater hardships.

For a while I was pretty well used, but in a little time the scale turned, which was occasioned by a difference between my master and me, wherein I was innocent; but from that time he set himself against me, and was so inhuman that he would not suffer me to have clothes to be decent in, making me to go barefoot in the snowy weather, and to be employed in the meanest drudgery, wherein I suffered the utmost hardships that my body was able to bear, and which the rest of my troubles had like to have been my ruin to all eternity, had not Almighty God interposed. My master would seem to be a religious man, often taking the Sacrament, so called, and used to pray every night in his family, except when his prayer book was lost, for he never prayed without it as I remember, but the difference was of such a kind, that I was sick of his religion. For tho' I had but little myself, I had an idea what sort of people they should be who professed much. But at length the enemy by his insinuations made me believe there was no such a thing as religion, and that the convictions I had felt in my youth were nothing more than the prejudice of education, which convictions were at times so strong that I have gone and fallen on the ground, crying for mercy. But now I began to be hardened and for some months don't remember I felt any such thing, so that I was ready to conclude there was no God, and that all was priestcraft, I having a different opinion of those sort of men than what I had in my youth. And what corroborated with my atheistical opinion was this: my master's house used to be a place of great resort for the clergy, which gave me an opportunity of making my remarks on them; for sometimes those that came out of the country used to lodge there, and their evening diversions often was playing at cards and singing, and in a few moments after, praying and singing psalms to Almighty God. But I thought, if there be a God, He must be a Pure Being and will not hear the prayers of polluted lips; for He hath in an abundant manner shown mercy to me as will be shown in the sequel, which did not suffer me to doubt in this manner any longer. For when my feet were near the bottomless pit, He plucked me back.

I had to one woman and no other discovered the occasion of this difference, and the nature of it, which two years before had happened betwixt my master and me, and by that means he heard of it, and tho' he knew it to be true, he sent for the town whipper to correct me for it, and upon his appearing, I was called in and ordered to strip, without asking whether I deserved it or not, at which my heart was ready to burst, for I could as freely have given up my life, as suffer such ignominy. And I then said, "If there be a God, be graciously pleased to look down on one of the most unhappy creatures, and plead my cause, for Thou knowest what I have said is the truth, and had it not been from a principle more noble than he was capable of, I would have told it before his wife." Then fixing my eyes on the barbarous man, in a flood of tears, I said to him, "Sir, if you have no pity on me, yet for my father's sake spare me from this shame" (for before this he had heard of my father several ways), "and if you think I deserve such punishment do it yourself." He then took a turn about the room and bid the whipper go about his business, so I came off without a blow, which I thought something remarkable.

I now began to think my credit was gone, for they said several things of me, which (I bless God) were not true; and here I suffered so much cruelty that I knew not how to bear it, and the enemy immediately came in and put me in a way how to get rid of it all, by tempting me to end my miserable life, which I joined with, and for that purpose went into the garret in order to hang myself, at which time I was convinced there was a God, for as my feet entered the place, horror seized me to that degree that I trembled much, and while I stood in amazement, it seemed as tho' I heard a voice say, "There is a hell beyond the grave," at which I was greatly astonished and convinced of an Almighty Power, to whom I prayed, saying "God be merciful and enable me to bear whatsoever Thou of Thy Providence shall bring or suffer to come upon me for my disobedience." I then went downstairs but let none know what I had been about.

Soon after this I had a dream, and tho' some may ridicule dreams, yet this seems very significant to me, therefore I shall mention it.—I thought somebody knocked at the door, which when I had opened there stood a grave woman, holding in her right hand an oil lamp burning, who with a solid countenance fixed her eyes on me, and said, "I am sent to tell thee, that if thou wilt return to the Lord they God, He will have mercy on thee, and thy lamp shall not be put out in obscure darkness"; upon which the light flamed from the lamp in a very radiant manner and the vision left me. But oh! alas, I did not give up to join with the heavenly vision, as I think I may call it; for, after all this, I was near being caught in another snare, which if I had, would probably have been my ruin, from which I was also preferred.

I was accounted a fine singer and dancer, in which I took great delight, and once falling in company with some of the stage players, then at New York, they took a great fancy to me, as they said, and persuaded me to become an actress amongst them, and they would find means to get me from my servitude, and that I should live like a lady. The proposal took with me, and I used much pains to qualify myself for the stage, by reading plays, even when I should have slept, but after all this I found a stop in my mind, when I came to consider what my father would think when he heard of it, who had not only forgiven my disobedience in marriage, but had sent for me home, tho' my proud heart would not suffer me to return in so mean a condition I was then in, but rather chose bondage.

When I had served three years I bought the remainder of my time, and got a genteel maintenance by my needle, but alas! I was not sufficiently punished by my former servitude but got into another, and that for life; for a few months after this, I married a young man, who fell in love with me for my dancing—a poor motive for a man to choose a wife, or a woman to choose a husband.

As to my part I fell in love for nothing I saw in him, and it seems unaccountable, that I, who had refused several offers, both in this country and in Ireland, should at last marry a man I had no value for.

In a week after we were married, my husband, who was a schoolmaster, removed from New York, and took me along with him to New England, and settled at a place called Westerley, in Rhode Island government. With respect to religion, he was much like myself, without any; for when he was in drink he would use the worst of oaths. I don't mention this to expose my husband, but to show the effect it had upon me, for I now saw myself ruined, as I thought, being joined to a man I had no love for, and who was a pattern of no good to me. I therefore began to think we were like two joining hands and going to destruction, which made me conclude that if I was not forsaken of God, to alter my course of life. But to love the Divine Being, and not to love my husband, I saw was an inconfidency, and seemed impossible; therefore I requested, with tears, that my affections might increase towards my husband, and I can say in truth that my love was sincere to him. I now resolved to do my duty towards God, and expecting that I must come to the knowledge of it by reading the Scriptures, I read them with a strong resolution of following their directions, but the more I read the more uneasy I grew, especially about baptism, for altho' I had reason to believe I was sprinkled in my infancy, because at the age of fourteen I passed under the bishop's hands for confirmation, as it is called, yet I could not find any precedent for that practice, and upon reading where it is said, "he that believes and is baptized, etc.," I observed that belief went before baptism, which I was not capable of when I was sprinkled, at which I grew very uneasy, and living in a neighborhood that were mostly Seventh Day Baptists, I conversed with them, and at length thinking it to be really my duty, I was baptized by one of their teachers, but did not join strictly with them, tho' I began to think the seventh-day the true sabbath, and for some time kept it as such. My husband did not yet oppose me, for he saw I grew more affectionate to him, but I did not yet leave off singing and dancing so much, but I could divert him whenever he desired it.

Soon after this my husband and I concluded to go to England, and for that purpose went to Boston, where we found a ship bound for Liverpool, and agreed for our passage, expecting to sail in two weeks. But my time was not yet come, for there came one called a gentleman, who hired the ship to carry him and his attendants to Philadelphia, and to take no other passengers. There being no other ship near sailing, we for that time gave it over.

We stayed several weeks at Boston, and I remained still dissatisfied as to religion, tho' I had reformed my conduct so as to be accounted by those that knew me a sober woman. But that was not sufficient; for even then I expected to find the sweets of such a change, and though several thought me religious, I dared not to think myself so, and what to do to be so, I seemed still an utter stranger to. I used to converse with people of all societies, as opportunity offered, and, like many others, had got a deal of head knowledge, and several societies thought me of their opinion, but I joined strictly with none, resolving never to leave searching till I found the TRUTH. This was in the 22d year of my age.

While we were at Boston, I went one day to the Quakers' meeting, not expecting to find what I wanted, but from a motive of curiosity. At this meeting there was a woman spoke, at which I was a little surprised, for I had never heard one before. I looked on her with pity for her ignorance, and in contempt of her practice said to myself, "I am sure you're a fool, for if ever I should turn Quaker, which will never be, I could not be a preacher." In these and such like thoughts I sat while she was speaking. After she had done, there stood up a man, which I could better bear; he spoke well, as I thought, from good Joshua's resolutions, viz., "As for me and my house we will serve the Lord." After a time of silence he went to prayer, which was attended with something so awful and affecting that I was reduced to tears, yet a stranger to the cause.

Soon after this we left Boston, for my husband was given to ramble, which was very disagreeable to me, but I must submit. We went to Rhode Island, where he hired a place to keep a school. This place was mostly inhabited with Presbyterians, where I soon got acquainted with some of the most religious amongst them; for tho' I was poor, I was favored with respect amongst people of the best credit, and had frequent discourses with them, but the more I was acquainted with their principles, the worse I liked them, so that I remained dissatisfied, and the old enemy of my happiness, knowing I was resolved to abandon him, assaulted me afresh, and laid a bait with which I had like to have been caught. For one day having been abroad, at my return home, I found the people, at whose house we had taken a room, had left some flax in an apartment through which I went to my own, at sight of which I was tempted to steal some to make some thread, and I went and took a small bunch in my hand, at which I was smote with remorse, and immediately laid it down, saying, "Lord help me from such a vile act as this." But the twisting serpent did not leave me yet, his assaults were so strong and prevalent that I took it into my room; when I came there horror seized me, and bursting into tears, I cried, "O God of mercy, enable me to resist this temptation," which He of His mercy did, and gave me power to say, "I will regard thy convictions." So I carried it back, and returning to my room, I was so filled with thanksgiving to God, and wrapped into such a frame as I have not words to express, neither can any guess but those who have resisted temptation, and tasted of the same sweet peace by experience.

Soon after this my husband hired a place further up the island, where we were nearer a Church of England, to which place I used to go, for tho' I disliked some of their ways, yet I approved of them the best.

At this time a new exercise fell upon me, and of such a sort as I had never heard of before, and while I was under it I thought myself alone. — It was in the 2d month of the year. I was sitting by a fire in company with several persons, amongst whom my husband was one; there arose a thunder gust and with the noise that struck my ear, a voice attending, even as the sound of a mighty trumpet piercing through me with these words: "Oh, eternity! eternity! the endless term of long eternity!" at which I was exceedingly surprised and sat speechless as in a trance, and in a moment saw myself in such a state as made me despair of ever being happy. I seemed to behold a roll, wrote in black characters, at sight of which I heard a voice say, "These are thy sins"; and immediately followed another saying: "The Blood of Christ is not sufficient to wash them away, and this is shown thee that thou mayst confess thy damnation is just, and not in order that they should be forgiven thee."

All this while I sat speechless, but at last I got up trembling, and threw myself upon a bed. The company thought my indisposition proceeded only from the fright of the thunder, but oh! alas, it was of another kind, and from that time for several months I was in the utmost despair, for if I at any time did endeavor to hope or lay hold of a gracious promise, the old accuser would come in telling me it was now too late, that I had withstood the day of mercy, and that I should add to my sins by praying for pardon and provoke the Divine Vengeance to make a monument of wrath of me.

I now was like one already in torment. My sleep departed from me, I ate little, became extremely melancholy, and took no delight in anything. Had this world been mine and the glory of it, I would gladly have given it for a glimpse of hope. My husband was shocked to see me so changed. I that once could divert him with a song, in which he took great delight, nay after I grew religious as to the outward form, and till I could do it no longer. But now my singing was turned into mourning, and my dancing into lamentations; for my nights and days were one continual scene of sorrow. I let none know my desperate condition. My husband used all means to divert my melancholy state, but all in vain; the wound was too deep to be healed with anything short of the true Balm of Gilead. I durst not go much alone for fear of evil spirits, but if I would, my husband would not suffer it, and if I took the Bible he would take it from me, saying, "How you are altered; you used to be agreeable company, but now I have no comfort of you." I endeavored to bear all with patience, expecting soon to bear more than man could inflict upon me.

At length I went to a priest to see if he could relieve me, but he was a stranger to my condition, and advised me to take the Sacrament, and to use some innocent diversions, and sent me a book of prayers which he said was for my condition. But all was in vain. As to the Sacrament, I thought myself in a state very unfit to receive it worthily, and I then could not use my prayers, for I thought that if ever my prayers should be acceptable, I should be enabled to pray without a book, and diversions were burdensome, for as I said, my husband used all means tending that way to no purpose. Yet he with some others once persuaded me to the raising of a building, where much people were got, in hopes of diverting my grief. But instead of relief, it added to my sorrow; for to this place came an officer to summon a jury to inquire concerning the body of a man that had hanged himself, which as soon as I understood, it seemed to be attended with a voice, saying, "Thou shalt be the next monument of wrath, for thou art not worthy to die a natural death."

For two months after this I was daily tempted to destroy myself, and sometimes the temptation was so strong I could scarce resist, through fear of which, when I went alone I used to throw off my apron and garters, and if I had a knife, to cast it from me, crying, "Lord keep me from taking away that life Thou gave me, and which Thou wouldst have made happy, if I had joined with the offers of Thy grace, and had regarded the convictions I've had from my youth—the fault is my own, Thou, O Lord, [art] clear." And yet so great was my agony that I desired death, that I might know the worst of my torments; all this while I was so hardened that I could not shed a tear. But God in His own good time delivered my soul out of this thralldom.

For one night as I lay in my bed, my husband by me asleep, bemoaning my miserable condition, I had strength to cry, "O my God, hast Thou no mercy left? Look down I beseech Thee for Christ's sake, who has promised that all manner of sin and blasphemy shall be forgiven. Therefore Lord, if Thou wilt graciously please to extend this promise to me, an unworthy creature, trembling before Thee, there is nothing Thou shalt command, but I will obey." In an instant my heart tendered and dissolved into a flood of tears, abhorring my past offenses, and admiring the mercies of God; for I was made to hope in Christ my redeemer, and enabled to look upon Him with an eye of faith, and saw fulfilled what I believed when the priest lent me his book, that if ever my prayers would be acceptable to God, I should be enabled to pray without form, and so used it no more. Nevertheless I thought to join with some religious society, but met with none that I liked in everything. Yet the Church of England seemed nearest, upon which I joined with them and received the Sacrament, so called, and can say in truth that I did it with reverence and fear.

Being thus released from deep distress, I seemed like another creature, and went often alone without fear and tears flowed abundantly from my eyes; and once as I was abhorring myself, in great humility of mind, I heard a gracious voice say, "I will not forsake thee, only obey what I shall make known unto thee." I then entered into covenant, saying, "My soul doth magnify Thee the God of mercy; if Thou will vouchsafe Thy Grace, the rest of my days shall be devoted to Thee, and if it be Thy will that I beg my bread, I will be content and submit to Thy Providence."

I now began to think of my relations in Pennsylvania, whom I had not yet seen, and having a great desire to see them, I got leave of my husband to go, and also a certificate from the priest, in order that if I made any stay, I might be received as a member wherever I came. Then setting out, my husband bore me company to the Blazing Star Ferry, saw me safe over, and then returned. In the way near a place called Maidenhead, I fell from my horse and was disabled from traveling for some time, and abode at the house of an honest Dutchman, who with his wife was very kind to me—and tho' they had much trouble in going to the doctor and waiting upon me, for I was several days unable to help myself—yet would have nothing for it, which I thought very kind, and charged me if ever I came that way again to call and lodge there.—I mention this because I shall have occasion to remark this place again.

I arrived next at Trent town Ferry, where I met with no small mortification upon hearing that my relations were Quakers, and what was worst of all, my aunt was a preacher. I was sorry to hear of it, for I was exceedingly prejudiced against those people, and have often wondered with what face they could call themselves Christians; and I began to repent my coming, sometimes having a mind to return back without seeing them. At last I concluded to go see them, since I was so far on my journey, tho' I expected little comfort from my visit. But see how God brings unforeseen things to pass, for by my going there I was brought to the knowledge of the TRUTH.

I went from Trent town Ferry to Philadelphia by water, and thence to my uncle's on horseback, where I met with a very kind reception; for tho' my own uncle was dead and my aunt married again, yet both she and her husband received me in a very kind manner. I had not been there 3 hours before I met with a shock, and my opinion began to alter with respect to these people; for seeing a book lie on the table, and being much given to reading, I took it up, which my aunt observing, said, "Cousin, that is a Quaker's book, Samuel Crisp's *Two Letters*," and I suppose she thought I should not like it, at perceiving that I was not one. I made her no answer, but thought to myself, "What can these people write about, for I have heard that they deny the Scripture, and have no other bible but George Foxe's *Journal*, and that they deny all the holy Ordinances"; for I resolved to read a little, and had not read two pages before my very heart burned within me, and tears came into my eyes, which I was afraid would be seen. I therefore walked with the book into the garden, and the piece being small, read it through before I went in, and sometimes uttering these involuntary expressions: "My God, if ever I come to the true knowledge of the truth, must I be of this man's opinion, who has fought Thee as I have done, and join with these people that I preferred the Papists to, but a [few] hours ago. Oh! Thou the God of my salvation and of my life, who hast in an abundant manner manifested Thy long-suffering and tender mercy in redeeming me as from the lowest hell, a monument of Thy grace. Lord my soul beseeches Thee to direct me in the right way, and keep me from error; and then according to my covenant, I'll think nothing too near to part with for Thy name's sake, if these things be so. Oh! happy people thus beloved of God."

After I came a little to myself I washed my face, lest any in the house should perceive I had been weeping. At night I got very little sleep, for the old enemy began to suggest that I was one of those that wavered and was not steadfast in the faith, advancing several texts of Scripture against me and them that mention in the latter days there shall be those that will deceive the very elect, and these people were them, and that I was in danger of being deluded. Here the subtle serpent transformed himself so hiddenly that I verily thought this to be a timely caution from a good angel, so resolved to beware of these deceivers, and for some weeks did not touch any of their books.

The next day being the first of the week, I wanted to have gone to church, which was distant about four miles, but being a stranger and having nobody to go with me, was forced to give it up, and as most of the family was going to meeting, I went with them. But with this conclusion: not to like them. And so it was; for as they sat in silence, I looked over the meeting, thinking within myself, how like fools these people sit, how much better were it to stay at home and read the Bible, or some good book, than to come here and go to sleep; for I being very sleepy thought they were no better than me. Indeed, at length I fell asleep and had like to have fallen down, but this was the last time I ever fell asleep in a meeting, tho' often assaulted with it.

I now began to be lifted up with spiritual pride, and thought myself better than they, but through mercy this did not last long, for in a little time I was brought low, and saw that they were the people to whom I must join. It may seem strange that I, who had lived so long with one of this society in Dublin, should yet be so great a stranger to them. In answer, let it be considered, that during the time I was there, I never read one of their books or went to one meeting, and besides, I had heard such ridiculous stories of them as made me think they were the worst of any society of people. But God that knew the sincerity of my heart, looked with pity on my weakness, and soon let me see my error; for in a few weeks there was an afternoon's meeting held at my uncle's to which came that servant of the Lord, William Hammons, who was then made instrumental in convincing me of the TRUTH more perfectly, and helping me over some great doubts, tho' I believe no one did ever sit in greater opposition than I did when he first stood up. But I was soon brought down, for he preached the Gospel with such power that I was forced to give up and confess it was the TRUTH.

As soon as meeting was ended, I endeavored to get alone, for I was not fit to be seen, being so broken; yet afterwards the restless adversary assaulted me again in the manner following. The morning before this meeting I had been disputing with my uncle about Baptism, which was the subject this good man dwelt upon and which he handled so clearly as to answer all my scruples beyond objection. Yet the crooked serpent farther alleged that the sermon I had heard did not proceed from Divine Revelation, but that my uncle and aunt had acquainted the Friend of me, which being strongly suggested, I fell to accusing them of it, and of which they both cleared themselves, saying they had not seen him since my coming to these parts until he came to the meeting.

I then concluded he was a messenger sent from God to me, and with fervent cries desired I might be directed right. And now I laid aside all prejudice and set my heart to receive TRUTH, and the Lord in His own good time revealed to my soul not only the beauty there is in it, and that those should shine who continued faithful to it, but also the emptiness of all shadows, which in their way were glorious, but now the Son of Glory was come to put an end to them all and establish everlasting righteousness in the room thereof, which is a work in the soul. He likewise let me see that all I had gone through was to prepare me for this day, and that the time was near that He would require me to go forth and declare to others what the God of mercy had done for my soul; at which I was surprised and desired I might be excused, for fear I should bring dishonor to the TRUTH, and cause His holy Name to be evil spoken of.

All this while I did not let anybody know the condition I was in, nor did appear like a Friend, and feared a discovery. I now began to think of returning to my husband, but found a restraint to stay where I was. I then hired a place to keep a school, and hearing of a place for him wrote desiring him to come to me, but let him know nothing how it was with me.

I loved to go to meetings, but did not like to be seen to go on week days, and therefore to shun it used to go from my school through the woods to them. But notwithstanding all my care, the neighbors that were not Friends soon began to revile, calling me Quaker, saying they supposed I intended to be a fool and turn preacher. I then received the same censure that I, a little above a year before, had passed on one of the handmaids of the Lord at Boston, and so weak was I, alas, I could not bear the reproach, and in order to change their opinions got in to greater excess in apparel than I had freedom to wear for some time before I became acquainted with Friends. In this condition I continued till my husband came, and then began the trial of my faith. Before he reached me he heard I was turned Quaker, at which he stamped, saying, I had rather have heard she had been dead, well as I love her, for if so all my comfort is gone; he then came to me, and had not seen me for four months; I got up and met him, saying, "My dear, I am glad to see thee," at which he fell in a great passion, and said, "The devil THEE thee, don't THEE me." I used all the mild means I could to pacify him, and at length got him fit to go and speak to my relations, but he was alarmed, and as soon as he got alone he said, "So I see your Quaker relations have made you one." I told him they had not, which was true, nor had I ever told them how it was with me. But he would have it that I was one, and therefore should not stay amongst them, and having found a place to his mind, hired it, and came directly back to fetch me, and in one afternoon walked near thirty miles to keep me from meeting, the next day being the first-day, and on the morrow took me to the aforesaid place, hired lodgings at a Church-man's house, who was one of the wardens, and a bitter enemy to Friends, and would tell me a great deal of ridiculous stuff. But my judgment was too clearly convinced to believe. I still did not appear like a Friend, but they all believed I was one. When my husband and him used to be making their diversions and revilings, I used to sit in silence, but now and then an involuntary sigh would break from me, at which he would say to my husband, "There, did not I tell you your wife was a Quaker, and she will be a preacher soon," upon which my husband once in a great rage came up to me, and shaking his hand over me said, "You had better be hanged on that day." I then, Peter like, in a panic denied my being a Quaker, at which great horror seized upon me, and continued for near three months, so that I again feared that by denying the Lord who bought me the heavens were shut against me; for great darkness surrounded me, and I was again plunged in despair.

I used to walk much alone in the woods, where no eye saw, or ear heard me, and there lamented my miserable condition, and have often gone from morning till night without breaking my fast, with which I was brought so low that my life was a burden to me. The devil seemed to vaunt [that although] the sins [of] my youth were forgiven, yet now he was sure of me, for that I had committed the unpardonable sin, and hell would inevitably be my portion, and my torments would be greater than if I had hanged myself at the first.

In this doleful condition I had now to bewail my misery, and even in the night, when I could not sleep, under the painful distress of my mind. And if my husband perceived me weeping he used to revile me for it. At last, when he and his friends thought themselves too weak to overset me, tho' I feared it was already done, he went to the priest at Chester to advise what to do with me. This man knew I was a member of the Church, for I had shown him my certificate. His advice was to take me out of Pennsylvania, and find some place where there was no Quakers, and there my opinion would wear off. To this my husband agreed, saying he did not care where he went, if he could but restore me to that liveliness of temper I was naturally of, and to that Church of which I was a member. I, on my part, had no spirit to oppose their proposals, neither much cared where I was; for I seemed to have nothing to hope for, but daily expected to be made a spectacle of Divine Wrath, and I was possessed it would be by thunder.

The time of removal came and I was not suffered to bid my relations farewell. My husband was poor and kept no horse, so I must travel on foot. We came to Wilmington, 15 miles thence to Philadelphia, by water; here he took me to a tavern, where I soon became a spectacle and discourse of the company. My husband told them his wife was turned Quaker, and that he designed, if possible, to find out some place where there was none. Oh, thought I, I was once in condition of deserving that name, but now it was over with me. Oh, that I might, from a true hope, once more have an opportunity to confess to the TRUTH, tho' sure of all manner of cruelties yet I would not regard it. These were my concerns while he was entertaining the company with my story, in which he told them that I had been a good dancer, but now he could neither get me to dance nor sing; upon which one of the company starts up, saying, "I'll go fetch my fiddle and we'll have a dance," at which my husband was pleased. The fiddle came, the sight of which put me in a sad condition, for fear, if I refused, my husband would be in a great passion. However I took up this resolution not to comply whatever might be the consequence. He came to me and took me by the hand, saying, "Come my dear, shake off that gloom, let's have a civil dance, you would now and then, when you were a good Church-woman and that is better than a stiff Quaker." I, trembling, desired to be excused. But he insisted on it, and knowing his temper to be exceeding choleric, I durst not say much, but would not consent. He then pulled me round the room till tears affected my eyes, at sight of which the musician stopped, and said, "I'll play no more, let your wife alone," of which I was glad. There was also a man in [this] company who came from Freehold, in West Jersey, who said, "I see your wife is a Quaker, but if you'll take my advice, you need not go so far (for my husband designed to go to Staten Island), come and live amongst us and we'll soon cure her from her Quakerism, and we want both a school-master and mistress." To which he agreed, and a happy turn it was for me as will be seen by and by, and the wonderful turn of Providence, who had not yet abandoned me, but raised a glimmering hope and afforded the answer of peace in refusing to dance, for which I was more rejoiced than if I were made a mistress of much riches, and in floods of tears, said, "Lord, I dread to ask, and yet without Thy gracious pardon I am miserable, I therefore fall down before Thy throne, imploring mercy at Thy hand. O Lord, once more I beseech Thee try my obedience, and then whatsoever Thou commands, I will obey, and not fear to confess Thee before men." Thus was my soul engaged before God in sincerity, and He of His tender mercy heard my cries, and in me has shewn that He delights not in the death of a sinner, for He again set my soul at liberty and I could praise Him.

# BLACK HAWK
## (1767–1838)

Though Black Hawk's autobiography was told to Antoine LeClair, and then subsequently reorganized by a second editor, it remains an accurate and verifiable account of the interactions between the U.S. government and the Sauk people during the Black Hawk War of 1832. The narrator recounts the destruction of a Native American people by the U.S. Army and volunteer groups acting in their behalf, motivated chiefly by land speculators and merchants and by a desire to secure the safety of white settlers, who felt threatened by the Sauk presence. Very much in contrast to the picture of Indians one gets in, say, Mary Rowlandson's account of her captivity, Black Hawk suggests that his people are highly moral, tolerant, and resourceful in the face of a terrible onslaught by settlers who do not live up to what any decent community would recognize as common standards of morality.

By the end of his life, Black Hawk had become something of a cult hero among Americans. Defeated in battle, the stoic general became an icon in Burlington, Iowa, where he circulated peacefully, attending lectures and speeches though he understood only limited English. He was used as a figurehead by the tribal leader Keokuk—an unscrupulous man who "sold" millions of acres of Sauk land and embezzled what little money he was given in return for the deeds. Because of Keokuk's schemes, the Sauk people were forced to leave their ancestral homeland and relocate to a reservation near the headwaters of the Osage River in Kansas. To the end, Black Hawk argued against Keokuk, saying, "My reason teaches me that land cannot be sold."

## FROM *An Autobiography*

Our village was situate[d] on the north side of Rock river, at the foot of its rapids, and on the point of land between Rock river and the Mississippi. In its front, a prairie extended to the bank of the Mississippi; and in our rear, a continued bluff, gently ascending from the prairie. On the side of this bluff we had our corn-fields, extending about two miles up, running parallel with the Mississippi; where we joined those of the Foxes whose village was on the bank of the Mississippi, opposite the lower end of Rock island, and three miles distant from ours. We had about eight hundred acres in cultivation, including what we had on the islands of Rock river. The land around our village, uncultivated, was covered with blue-grass, which made excellent pasture for our horses. Several fine springs broke out of the bluff, near by, from which we were supplied with good water. The rapids of Rock river furnished us with an abundance of excellent fish, and the land, being good, never failed to produce good crops of corn, beans, pumpkins, and squashes. We always had plenty—our children never cried with hunger, nor our people were never in want. Here our village had stood for more than a hundred years, during all which time we were the undisputed possessors of the valley of the Mississippi, from the Ouisconsin to the Portage des Sioux, near the mouth of the Missouri, being about seven hundred miles in length.

At this time we had very little intercourse with the whites, except our traders. Our village was healthy, and there was no place in the country possessing such advantages, nor no hunting grounds better than those we had in possession. If another prophet had come to our village in those days, and told us what has since taken place, none of our people would have believed him. What! to be driven from our village and hunting grounds, and not even permitted to visit the graves of our forefathers, our relations, and friends?

This hardship is not known to the whites. With us it is a custom to visit the graves of our friends, and keep them in repair for many years. The mother will go alone to weep over the grave of her child! The brave, with pleasure, visits the grave of his father, after he has been successful in war, and re-paints the post that shows where he lies! There is no place like that where the bones of our forefathers lie, to go to when in grief. Here the Great Spirit will take pity on us!

But, how different is our situation now, from what it was in those days! Then we were as happy as the buffalo on the plains—but now, we are as miserable as the hungry, howling wolf in the prairie! But I am digressing from my story. Bitter reflection crowds upon my mind, and must find utterance.

When we returned to our village in the spring, from our wintering grounds, we would finish trading with our traders, who always followed us to our village. We purposely kept some of our fine furs for this trade; and, as there was great opposition among them, who should get these skins, we always got our goods cheap. After this trade was over, the traders would give us a few kegs of rum, which was generally promised in the fall, to encourage us to make a good hunt, and not go to war. They would then start with their furs and peltries for their homes. Our old men would take a frolic, (at this time our young men never drank.) When this was ended, the next thing to be done was to bury our dead, (such as had died during the year.) This is a great *medicine feast.* The relations of those who have died, give all the goods they have purchased, as presents to their friends—thereby reducing themselves to poverty, to show the Great Spirit that they are humble, so that he will take pity on them. We would next open the cashes, and take out corn and other provisions, which had been put up in the fall,—and then commence repairing our lodges. As soon as this is accomplished, we repair the fences around our fields, and clean them off, ready for planting corn. This work is done by our women. The men, during this time, are feasting on dried venison, bear's meat, wild fowl, and corn, prepared in different ways; and recounting to each other what took place during the winter.

Our women plant the corn, and as soon as they get done, we make a feast, and dance the *crane* dance, in which they join us, dressed in their best, and decorated with feathers. At this feast our young braves select the young woman they wish to have for a wife. He then informs his mother, who calls on the mother of the girl, when the arrangement is made, and the time appointed for him to come. He goes to the lodge when all are asleep, (or pretend to be,) lights his matches, which have been provided for the purpose, and soon finds where his intended sleeps. He then awakens her, and holds the light to his face that she may know him—after which he places the light close to her. If she blows it out, the ceremony is ended, and he appears in the lodge the next morning, as one of the family. If she does not blow out the light, but leaves it to burn out, he retires from the lodge. The next day he places himself in full view of it, and plays his flute. The young women go out, one by one, to see who he is playing for. The tune changes, to let them know that he is not playing for them. When his intended makes her appearance at the door, he continues his *courting* tune, until she returns to the lodge. He then gives over playing, and makes another trial at night, which generally turns out favorable. During the first year they ascertain whether they can agree with each other, and can be happy—if not, they part, and each looks out again. If we were to live together and disagree, we should be as foolish as the whites. No indiscretion can banish a woman from her parental lodge—no difference how many children she may bring home, she is always welcome—the kettle is over the fire to feed them.

The crane dance often lasts two or three days. When this is over, we feast again, and have our *national* dance. The large square in the village is swept and prepared for the purpose. The chiefs and old warriors, take seats on mats which have been spread at the upper end of the square—the drummers and singers come next, and the braves and women form the sides, leaving a large space in the middle. The drums beat, and the singers commence. A warrior enters the square, keeping time with the music. He shows the manner he started on a war party—how he approached the enemy—he strikes, and describes the way he killed him. All join in applause. He then leaves the square, and another enters and takes his place. Such of our young men as have not been out in war parties, and killed an enemy, stand back ashamed—not being able to enter the square. I remember that I was ashamed to look where our young women stood, before I could take my stand in the square as a warrior.

What pleasure it is to an old warrior, to see his son come forward and relate his exploits—it makes him feel young, and induces him to enter the square, and "fight his battles o'er again."

This national dance makes our warriors. When I was travelling last summer, on a steam boat, on a large river, going from New York to Albany, I was shown the place where the Americans dance their national dance [West Point]; where the old warriors recount to their young men, what they have done, to stimulate them to go and do likewise. This surprised me, as I did not think the whites understood our way of making braves.

When our national dance is over—our corn-fields hoed, and every weed dug up, and our corn about knee-high, all our young men would start in a direction towards sun-down, to hunt deer and buffalo—being prepared, also, to kill Sioux, if any are found on our hunting grounds—a part of our old men and women to the lead mines to make lead—and the remainder of our people start to fish, and get mat stuff. Every one leaves the village, and remains about forty days. They then return: the hunting party bringing in dried buffalo and deer meat, and sometimes *Sioux scalps*, when they are found trespassing on our hunting grounds. At other times they are met by a party of Sioux too strong for them, and are driven in. If the Sioux have killed the Sacs last, they expect to be retaliated upon, and will fly before them, and vice versa. Each party knows that the other has a right to retaliate, which induces those who have killed last, to give way before their enemy—as neither wish to strike, except to avenge the death of their relatives. All our wars are predicated by the relatives of those killed; or by aggressions upon our hunting grounds.

The party from the lead mines bring lead, and the others dried fish, and mats for our winter lodges. Presents are now made by each party; the first, giving to the others dried buffalo and deer, and they, in exchange, presenting them with lead, dried fish and mats.

This is a happy season of the year—having plenty of provisions, such as beans, squashes, and other produce, with our dried meat and fish, we continue to make feasts and visit each other, until our corn is ripe. Some lodge in the village makes a feast daily, to the Great Spirit. I cannot explain this so that the white people would comprehend me, as we have no regular standard among us. Every one makes his feast as he thinks best, to please the Great Spirit, who has the care of all beings created. Others believe in two Spirits: one good and one bad, and make feasts for the Bad Spirit, *to keep him quiet*! If they can make peace with him, the Good Spirit will not hurt them! For my part, I am of opinion, that so far as we have *reason*, we have a right to use it, in determining what is right or wrong; and should pursue that path which we believe to be right—believing, that "whatever is, is right." If the Great and Good Spirit wished us to believe and do as the whites, he could easily change our opinions, so that we would see, and think, and act as they do. We are *nothing* compared to His power, and we feel and know it. We have men among us, like the whites, who pretend to know the right path, but will not consent to show it without *pay*! I have no faith in their paths—but believe that every man must make his own path!

When our corn is getting ripe, our young people watch with anxiety for the signal to pull roasting-ears—as none dare touch them until the proper time. When the corn is fit to use, another great ceremony takes place, with feasting, and returning thanks to the Great Spirit for giving us corn.

I will here relate the manner in which corn first came. According to tradition, handed down to our people, a beautiful woman was seen to descend from the clouds, and alight upon the earth, by two of our ancestors, who had killed a deer, and were sitting by a fire, roasting a part of it to eat. They were astonished at seeing her, and concluded that she must be hungry, and had smelt the meat—and immediately went to her, taking with them a piece of the roasted venison. They presented it to her, and she eat—and told them to return to the spot where she was sitting, at the end of one year, and they would find a reward for their kindness and generosity. She then ascended to the clouds, and disappeared. The two men returned to their village, and explained to the nation what they had seen, done, and heard—but were laughed at by their people. When the period arrived, for them to visit this consecrated ground, where they were to find a reward for their attention to the beautiful woman of the clouds, they went with a large party, and found, where her right hand had rested on the ground, *corn* growing—and where the left hand had rested, *beans*—and immediately where she had been seated, *tobacco*.

The two first have, ever since, been cultivated by our people, as our principal provisions—and the last used for smoking. The white people have since found out the latter, and seem to relish it as much as we do—as they use it in different ways, viz. smoking, snuffing and eating!

We thank the Great Spirit for all the benefits he has conferred upon us. For myself, I never take a drink of water from a spring, without being mindful of his goodness.

We next have our great ball play—from three to five hundred on a side, play this game. We play for horses, guns, blankets, or any other kind of property we have. The successful party take the stakes, and all retire to our lodges in peace and friendship.

We next commence horse-racing, and continue our sport and feasting, until the corn is all secured. We then prepare to leave our village for our hunting grounds. The traders arrive, and give us credit for such articles as we want to clothe our families, and enable us to hunt. We first, however, hold a council with them, to ascertain the price they will give us for our skins, and what they will charge us for goods. We inform them where we intend hunting—and tell them where to build their houses. At this place, we deposit part of our corn, and leave our old people. The traders have always been kind to them, and relieved them when in want. They were always much respected by our people—and never since we have been a nation, has one of them been killed by any of our people.

We disperse, in small parties, to make our hunt, and as soon as it is over, we return to our traders' establishment, with our skins, and remain feasting, playing cards and other pastimes, until near the close of the winter. Our young men then start on the beaver hunt; others to hunt raccoons and muskrats—and the remainder of our people go to the sugar camps to make sugar. All leave our encampment, and appoint a place to meet on the Mississippi, so that we may return to our village together, in the spring. We always spent our time pleasantly at the sugar camp. It being the season for wild fowl, we lived well, and always had plenty, when the hunters came in, that we might make a feast for them. After this is over, we return to our village, accompanied, sometimes, by our traders. In this way, the year rolled round happily. But these are times that were!

On returning, in the spring, from our hunting ground, I had the pleasure of meeting our old friend, the trader of Peoria, at Rock Island. He came up in a boat from St. Louis, not as a trader, as in times past, but as our *agent*. We were all pleased to see him. He told us, that he narrowly escaped falling into the hands of Dixon. He remained with us a short time, gave us good advice, and then returned to St. Louis.

The Sioux having committed depredations on our people, we sent out war parties that summer, who succeeded in killing *fourteen*. I paid several visits to fort Armstrong during the summer, and was always well treated. We were not as happy then in our village as formerly. Our people got more liquor than customary. I used all my influence to prevent drunkenness, but without effect. As the settlements progressed towards us, we became worse off, and more unhappy. Many of our people, instead of going to their old hunting grounds, where game was plenty, would go near to the settlements to hunt—and, instead of saving their skins to pay the trader for goods furnished them in the fall, would sell them to the settlers for whisky! and return in the spring with their families, almost naked, and without the means of getting any thing for them.

About this time my eldest son was taken sick and died. He had always been a dutiful child, and had just grown to manhood. Soon after, my youngest daughter, an interesting and affectionate child, died also. This was a hard stroke, because I loved my children. In my distress, I left the noise of the village, and built my lodge on a mound in my corn-field, and enclosed it with a fence, around which I planted corn and beans. Here I was with my family alone. I gave every thing I had away, and reduced myself to poverty. The only covering I retained, was a piece of buffalo robe. I resolved on blacking my face and fasting, for two years, for the loss of my two children—drinking only of water in the middle of the day, and eating sparingly of boiled corn at sunset. I fulfilled my promise, hoping that the Great Spirit would take pity on me.

My nation had now some difficulty with the Ioways, with whom we wished to be at peace. Our young men had repeatedly killed some of the Ioways; and these breaches had always been made up by giving presents to the relations of those killed. But the last council we had with them, we promised that, in case any more of their people were killed by ours, instead of presents, we would give up the person, or persons, that had done the injury. We made this determination known to our people; but, notwithstanding, one of our young men killed an Ioway the following winter.

A party of our people were about starting for the Ioway village to give the young man up. I agreed to accompany them. When we were ready to start, I called at the lodge for the young man to go with us. He was sick, but willing to go. His brother, however, prevented him, and insisted on going to die in his place, as he was unable to travel. We started, and on the seventh day arrived in sight of the Ioway village, and when within a short distance of it, halted and dismounted. We all bid farewell to our young brave, who entered the village alone, singing his *death-song,* and sat down in the square in the middle of the village. One of the Ioway chiefs came out to us. We told him that we had fulfilled our promise— that we had brought the brother of the young man who had killed one of their people—that he had volunteered to come in his place, in consequence of his brother being unable to travel from sickness. We had no further conversation, but mounted our horses and rode off. As we started, I cast my eye towards the village, and observed the Ioways coming out of their lodges with spears and war clubs. We took our trail back, and travelled until dark—then encamped and made a fire. We had not been here long, before we heard the sound of horses coming towards us. We seized our arms; but instead of an enemy, it was our young brave with two horses. He told me that after we had left him, they menaced him with death for some time—then gave him something to eat—smoked the pipe with him—and made him a present of the two horses and some goods, and started him after us. When we arrived at our village, our people were much pleased; and for the noble and generous conduct of the Ioways, on this occasion, not one of their people has been killed since by any of our nation.

That fall I visited Malden* with several of my band, and were well treated by our British father, who gave us a variety of presents. He also gave me a medal, and told me there never would be war between England and America again; but, for my fidelity to the British during the war that had terminated sometime before, requested me to come with my band every year and get presents, as Col. Dixon had promised me.

I returned, and hunted that winter on the Two-Rivers. The whites were now settling the country fast. I was out one day hunting in a bottom, and met three white men. They accused me of killing their hogs; I denied it; but they would not listen to me. One of them took my gun out of my hand and fired it off—then took out the flint, gave back my gun, and commenced beating me with sticks, and ordered me off. I was so much bruised that I could not sleep for several nights.

Some time after this occurrence, one of my camp cut a bee-tree, and carried the honey to his lodge. A party of white men soon followed, and told him that the bee-tree was theirs, and that he had no right to cut it. He pointed to the honey, and told them to take it; they were not satisfied with this, but took all the packs of skins that he had collected during the winter, to pay his trader and clothe his family with in the spring, and carried them off!

How could we like such people, who treated us so unjustly? We determined to break up our camp, for fear that they would do worse—and when we joined our people in the spring, a great many of them complained of similar treatment.

This summer our agent came to live at Rock Island. He treated us well, and gave us good advice. I visited him and the trader† very often during the summer, and, for the first time, heard talk of our having to leave my village. The trader explained to me the terms of the treaty that had been made, and said we would be obliged to leave the Illinois side of the Mississippi, and advised us to select a good place for our village, and remove to it in the spring. He pointed out the difficulties we would have to encounter, if we remained at our village on Rock river. He had great influence with the principal Fox chief, (his adopted brother,) and persuaded him to leave his village, and to go to the west side of the Mis-

---

*Fort Malden, a British stronghold at Amherstburg, Ontario, commanding the entrance to the Detroit River.

†George Davenport (1783–1845), who traded with the Indians after 1816, both independently and as a representative of the American Fur Company.

sissippi river, and build another—which he did the spring following.

Nothing was now talked of but leaving our village. Ke-o-kuck had been persuaded to consent to go; and was using all his influence, backed by the war chief at fort Armstrong, and our agent and trader at Rock Island, to induce others to go with him. He sent the crier through the village to inform our people that it was the wish of our Great Father that we should remove to the west side of the Mississippi—and recommended the Ioway river as a good place for the new village—and wished his party to make such arrangements, before they started out on their winter's hunt, as to preclude the necessity of their returning to the village in the spring.

The party opposed to removing, called upon me for my opinion. I gave it freely—and after questioning Quàsh-quà-me about the sale of the lands, he assured me that he "never had consented to the sale of our village." I now promised this party to be their leader, and raised the standard of opposition to Ke-o-kuck, with a full determination not to leave my village. I had an interview with Ke-o-kuck, to see if this difficulty could not be settled with our Great Father—and told him to propose to give other land, (any that our Great Father might choose, even our *lead mines*,) to be peaceably permitted to keep the small point of land on which our village and fields were situate. I was of opinion that the white people had plenty of land, and would never take our village from us, Ke-o-kuck promised to make an exchange if possible; and applied to our agent, and the great chief at St. Louis, (who has charge of all the agent, and the great chief at St. Louis, (who has charge of all the agents), for permission to go to Washington to see our Great Father for that purpose. This satisfied us for some time. We started to our hunting grounds, in good hopes that something would be done for us. During the winter, I received information that three families of whites had arrived at our village, and destroyed some of our lodges, and were making fences and dividing our corn-fields for their own use—*and were quarreling among themselves about their lines, in the division!* I immediately started for Rock river, a distance of ten days' travel, and on my arrival, found the report to be true. I went to my lodge, and saw a family occupying it. I wished to talk with them, but they could not understand me. I then went to Rock Island, and (the agent being absent,) told the interpreter what I wanted to say to those people, viz: "Not to settle on our lands—nor trouble our lodges or fences—that there was plenty of land in the country for them to settle upon—and they must leave our village, as we were coming back to it in the spring." The interpreter wrote me a paper, and I went back to the village, and showed it to the intruders, but could not understand their reply. I expected, however, that they would remove, as I requested them. I returned to Rock Island, passed the night there, and had a long conversation with the trader. He again advised me to give up, and make my village with Ke-o-kuck, on the Ioway river. I told him that I would not. The next morning I crossed the Mississippi, on very bad ice—but the Great Spirit made it strong, that I might pass over safe. I travelled three days farther to see the Winnebago sub-agent, and converse with him on the subject of our difficulties. He gave me no better news than the trader had done. I started then, by way of Rock river, to see the prophet, believing that he was a man of great knowledge. When we met, I explained to him every thing as it was. He at once agreed that I was right, and advised me never to give up our village, for the whites to plough up the bones of our people. He said, that if we remained at our village, the whites would not trouble us—and advised me to get Ke-o-kuck, and the party that had consented to go with him to the Ioway in the spring, to return, and remain at our village.

I returned to my hunting ground, after an absence of one moon, and related what I had done. In a short time we came up to our village, and found that the whites had not left it—but that others had come, and that the greater part of our corn-fields had been enclosed. When we landed, the whites appeared displeased because we had come back. We repaired the lodges that had been left standing, and built others. Ke-o-kuck came to the village; but his object was to persuade others to follow him to the Ioway. He had accomplished nothing towards making arrangements for us to remain, or to exchange other lands for our village. There was no more friendship existing between us. I looked upon him as a coward, and no brave, to abandon his village to be occupied by strangers. What *right* had these people to our village, and our fields, which the Great Spirit had given us to live upon?

My reason teaches me that *land cannot be sold.* The Great Spirit gave it to his children to live upon, and cultivate, as far as is necessary for their subsistence; and so long as they occupy and cultivate it, they have the right to the soil—but if they voluntarily leave it, then any other people have a right to settle upon it. Nothing can be sold, but such things as can be carried away.

In consequence of the improvements of the intruders on our fields, we found considerable difficulty to get ground to plant a little corn. Some of the whites permitted us to plant small patches in the fields they had fenced, keeping all the best ground for themselves. Our women had great difficulty in climbing their fences, (being unaccustomed to the kind,) and were ill-treated if they left a rail down.

One of my old friends thought he was safe. His corn-field was on a small island of Rock river. He planted his corn; it came up well—but the white man saw it!—he wanted the island, and took his team over, ploughed up the corn, and re-planted it for himself! The old man shed tears; not for himself, but the distress his family would be in if they raised no corn.

The white people brought whisky into our village, made our people drunk, and cheated them out of their horses, guns, and traps! This fraudulent system was carried to such an extent that I apprehended serious difficulties might take place, unless a stop was put to it. Consequently, I visited all the whites and begged them not to sell whisky to my people. One of them continued the practice openly. I took a party of my young men, went to his house, and took out his barrel and broke in the head and turned out the whisky. I did this for fear some of the whites might be killed by my people when drunk.

Our people were treated badly by the whites on many occasions. At one time, a white man beat one of our women cruelly, for pulling a few suckers of corn out of his field, to suck, when hungry! At another time, one of our young men was beat with clubs by two white men for opening a fence which crossed our road, to take his horse through. His shoulder blade was broken, and his body badly bruised, from which he soon after *died*!

Bad, and cruel, as our people were treated by the whites, not one of them was hurt or molested by any of my band. I hope this will prove that we are a peaceable people—having permitted ten men to take possession of our corn-fields; prevent us from planting corn; burn and destroy our lodges; ill-treat our women; and *beat to death* our men, without offering resistance to their barbarous cruelties. This is a lesson worthy for the white man to learn: to use forbearance when injured.

We acquainted our agent daily with our situation, and through him, the great chief at St. Louis—and hoped that something would be done for us. The whites were *complaining* at the same time that *we* were *intruding* upon *their rights*! THEY made themselves out the *injured* party, and *we* the *intruders*! and called loudly to the great war chief to protect *their* property!

How smooth must be the language of the whites, when they can make right look like wrong, and wrong like right.

During this summer, I happened at Rock Island, when a great chief arrived, (whom I had known as the great chief of Illinois, [governor Cole]), in company with another chief, who, I have been told, is a great writer, [judge Jas. Hall]. I called upon them and begged to explain to them the grievances under which me and my people were laboring, hoping that they could do something for us. The great chief, however, did not seem disposed to council with me. He said he was no longer the great chief of Illinois—that his children had selected another father in his stead, and that he now only ranked as they did. I was surprised at this talk, as I had always heard that he was a good, brave, and great chief. But the white people never appear to be satisfied. When they get a good father, they hold councils, (at the suggestion of some bad, ambitious man, who wants the place himself,) and conclude, among themselves, that this man, or some other equally ambitious, would make a better father than they have, and nine times out of ten they don't get as good as one again.

I insisted on explaining to these two chiefs the true situation of my people. They gave their assent: I rose and made a speech, in which I explained to them the treaty made by Quàsh-quà-me, and three of our braves, according to the manner the trader and others had explained it to me. I then told them that Quàsh-quà-me and his party *denied*, positively, having ever sold my village; and that, as I had never known them to *lie*, I was determined to keep it in possession.

I told them that the white people had already entered our village, *burnt our lodges, destroyed our fences, ploughed up our corn, and beat our people:* that they had brought *whisky* into our country, *made our people drunk*, and taken from them their *horses, guns*, and *traps*; and that I had borne all this injury, without suffering any of my braves to raise a hand against the whites.

My object in holding this council, was to get the opinion of these two chiefs, as to the best course for me to pursue. I had appealed in vain, time after time, to our agent, who regularly represented our situation to the great chief at St. Louis, whose duty it was to call upon our Great Father to have justice done to us; but instead of this, we are told *that the white people want our country, and we must leave it to them*!

I did not think it possible that our Great Father wished us to leave our village, where we had lived so long, and where the bones of so many of our people had been laid. The great chief said that, as he was no longer a chief, he could do nothing for us; and felt sorry that it was not in his power to aid us—nor did he know how to advise us. Neither of them could do any thing for us; but both evidently appeared very sorry. It would give me great pleasure, at all times, to take these two chiefs by the hand.

That fall I paid a visit to the agent, before we started to our hunting grounds, to hear if he had any good news for me. He had news! He said that the land on which our village stood was now ordered to be sold to individuals; and that, when sold, *our right* to remain, by treaty, would be at an end, and that if we returned next spring, we would be *forced* to remove!

We learned during the winter, that *part* of the lands where our village stood had been sold to individuals, and that the *trader* at Rock Island had bought the greater part that had been sold. The reason was now plain to me, why *he* urged us to remove. His object, we thought, was to get our lands. We held several councils that winter to determine what we should do, and resolved, in one of them, to return to our village in the spring, as usual; and concluded, that if we were removed by force, that the *trader*, agent, and others, must be the cause; and that, if found guilty of having us driven from our village, they should be *killed!* The trader stood foremost on this list. He had purchased the land on which my lodge stood, and that of our *grave yard* also! Ne-a-pope promised to kill him, the agent, interpreter, the great chief at St. Louis, the war chief at fort Armstrong, Rock Island, and Ke-o-kuck—these being the principal persons to blame for endeavoring to remove us.

Our women received bad accounts from the women that had been raising corn at the new village—the difficulty of breaking the new prairie with hoes—and the small quantity of corn raised. We were nearly in the same situation in regard to the latter, it being the first time I ever knew our people to be in want of provision.

I prevailed upon some of Ke-o-kuck's band to return this spring to the Rock river village. Ke-o-kuck would not return with us. I hoped that we would get permission to go to Washington to settle our affairs with our Great Father. I visited the agent at Rock Island. He was displeased because we had returned to our village, and told me that we *must* remove to the west of the Mississippi. I told him plainly that we *would not!* I visited the interpreter at his house, who advised me to do as the agent had directed me. I then went to see the trader, and upbraided him for buying our lands. He said that if he had not purchased them, some person else would, and that if our Great Father would make an exchange with us, he would willingly give up the land he had purchased to the government. This I thought was fair, and began to think that he had not acted as badly as I had suspected. We again repaired our lodges, and built others, as most of our village had been burnt and destroyed. Our women selected small patches to plant corn, (where the whites had not taken them within their fences,) and worked hard to raise something for our children to subsist upon.

I was told that, according to the treaty, we had no *right* to remain upon the lands *sold*, and that the government would *force* us to leave them. There was but a small portion, however, that *had been sold*; the balance remaining in the hands of the government, we claimed the right (if we had no other) to "live and hunt upon, as long as it remained the property of the government," by a stipulation in the same treaty that required us to evacuate it *after* it had been sold. This was the land that we wished to inhabit, and thought we had the best right to occupy.

I heard that there was a great chief on the Wabash, and sent a party to get his advice. They informed him that we had not sold our village. He assured them then, that if we had not sold the land on which our village stood, our Great Father would not take it from us.

I started early to Malden to see the chief of my British Father, and told him my story. He gave the same reply that the chief on the Wabash had given; and in justice to him, I must say, that he never gave me any bad advice: but advised me to apply to our American Father, who, he said, would do us justice. I next called on the great chief at Detroit,* and made the same statement to him that I had to the chief of our British Father. He gave the same reply. He said, if we had not sold our lands, and would remain peaceably on them, that we would not be disturbed. This assured me that I was right, and determined me to hold out, as I had promised my people.

I returned from Malden late in the fall. My people were gone to their hunting ground, whither I followed. Here I learned that they had been badly treated all summer by the whites; and that a treaty had been held at Prairie du Chien. Ke-o-kuck and some of our people attended it, and found out that our Great Father had exchanged a small strip of the land that was ceded by Quàsh-quà-me and his party, with the Pottowatomies, for a portion of their land, near Chicago; and that the object of this treaty was to get it back again; and that the United States had agreed to give them *sixteen thousand dollars a year forever*, for this small strip of land— it being less than the twentieth part of that taken from our nation, for *one thousand dollars a year*! This bears evidence of something I cannot explain. This land, they say, belonged to the United States. What reason, then, could have induced them to exchange it with the Pottowatomies, if it was so valuable? Why not keep it? Or, if they found that they had made a bad bargain with the Pottowatomies, why not take back their land at a fair proportion of what they gave our nation for it? If this small portion of the land that they took from us for *one thousand dollars* a year, be worth *sixteen thousand dollars a year forever*, to the Pottowatomies, then the whole tract of country taken from us ought to be worth, to our nation, *twenty times* as much as this small fraction.

Here I was again puzzled to find out how the white people reasoned; and began to doubt whether they had any standard of right and wrong!

---

*Lewis Cass, who was to become secretary of war the following year.

# HARRIET JACOBS

## (ca. 1813–1897)

At the start of the seventh section of Harriet Jacobs's richly textured and affecting autobiography, *Incidents in the Life of a Slave Girl* (1861), she asks, "Why does the slave ever love?" This remark begins a sad story of love frustrated and ultimately destroyed by the institution of slavery. In this remarkable book, Jacobs describes her struggles to avoid the sexual advances of her master and, eventually, to evade his rule altogether. Fleeing to an unheated shed on her grandmother's land with her two children, she went on to spend seven years in hiding. It was during this period that she wrote her account of her life. The power of her intellect shines through her work, which moves well beyond a personal account of her own painful life to paint a colorful and detailed picture of plantation life in the Old South. Perhaps more important is Jacobs's account of her resistance to the special injustices that were heaped upon women slaves. While many male authors of slave narratives, such as Frederick Douglass and William Wells Brown, had pointed out that women were abused sexually during slavery, Jacobs gave the first account by a woman of this suffering; she detailed her efforts to resist this exploitation and in doing so sent shock waves throughout the nation. In 1842, she escaped to the North, where she eventually settled in Washington, D.C., and helped to found the National Association of Colored Women. The influence of Jacobs can be seen in many later autobiographies by African American women, and in the fiction of writers as diverse as Toni Morrison and Alice Walker.

## FROM *Incidents in the Life of a Slave Girl*

### THE LOVER

Why does the slave ever love? Why allow the tendrils of the heart to twine around objects which may at any moment be wrenched away by the hand of violence? When separations come by the hand of death, the pious soul can bow in resignation, and say, "Not my will, but thine be done, O Lord!" But when the ruthless hand of man strikes the blow, regardless of the misery he causes, it is hard to be submissive. I did not reason thus when I was a young girl. Youth will be youth. I loved, and I indulged the hope that the dark clouds around me would turn out a bright lining. I forgot that in the land of my birth the shadows are too dense for light to penetrate. A land

> "Where laughter is not mirth; nor thought the mind;
> Nor words a language; nor e'en men mankind.
> Where cries reply to curses, shrieks to blows,
> And each is tortured in his separate hell."

There was in the neighborhood a young colored carpenter; a free born man. We had been well acquainted in childhood, and frequently met together afterwards. We became mutually attached, and he proposed to marry me. I loved him with all the ardor of a young girl's first love. But when I reflected that I was a slave, and that the laws gave no sanction to the marriage of such, my heart sank within me. My lover wanted to buy me; but I knew that Dr. Flint was too wilful and arbitrary a man to consent to that arrangement. From him, I was sure of experiencing all sorts of opposition, and I had nothing to hope from my mistress. She would have been delighted to have got rid of me, but not in that way. It would have relieved her mind of a burden if she could have seen me sold to some distant state, but if I was married near home I should be just as much in her husband's power as I had previously been, — for the husband of a slave has no power to protect her. Moreover, my mistress, like many others, seemed to think that slaves had no right to any family ties of their own; that they were created merely to wait upon the family of the mistress. I once heard her abuse a young slave girl, who told her that a colored man wanted to make her his wife. "I will have you peeled and picked, my lady," said she, "if I ever hear you mention that subject again. Do you suppose that I will have you tending *my* children with the children of that nigger?" The girl to whom she said this had a mulatto child, of course not acknowledged by its father. The poor black man who loved her would have been proud to acknowledge his helpless offspring.

Many and anxious were the thoughts I revolved in my mind. I was at a loss what to do. Above all things, I was desirous to spare my lover the insults that had cut so deeply into my own soul. I talked with my grandmother about it, and partly told her my fears. I did not dare to tell her the worst. She had long suspected all was not right, and if I confirmed her suspicions I knew a storm would rise that would prove the overthrow of all my hopes.

This love-dream had been my support through many trials; and I could not bear to run the risk of having it suddenly dissipated. There was a lady in the neighborhood, a particular friend of Dr. Flint's, who often visited the house. I had a great respect for her, and she had always manifested a friendly interest in me. Grandmother thought she would have great influence with the doctor. I went to this lady, and told her my story. I told her I was aware that my lover's being a free-born man would prove a great objection; but he wanted to buy me; and if Dr. Flint would consent to that arrangement, I felt sure he would be willing to pay any reasonable price. She knew that Mrs. Flint disliked me; therefore, I ventured to suggest that perhaps my mistress would approve of my being sold, as that would rid her of me. The lady listened with kindly sympathy, and promised to do her utmost to promote my wishes. She had an interview with the doctor, and I believe she pleaded my cause earnestly; but it was all to no purpose.

How I dreaded my master now! Every minute I expected to be summoned to his presence; but the day passed, and I heard nothing from him. The next morning, a message was brought to me: "Master wants you in his study." I found the door ajar, and I stood a moment gazing at the hateful man who claimed a right to rule me, body and soul. I entered, and tried to appear calm. I did not want him to know how my heart was bleeding. He looked fixedly at me, with an expression which seemed to say, "I have half a mind to kill you on the spot." At last he broke the silence, and that was a relief to both of us.

"So you want to be married, do you?" said he, "and to a free nigger."

"Yes, sir."

"Well, I'll soon convince you whether I am your master, or the nigger fellow you honor so highly. If you *must* have a husband, you may take up with one of my slaves."

What a situation I should be in, as the wife of one of *his* slaves, even if my heart had been interested!

I replied, "Don't you suppose, sir, that a slave can have some preference about marrying? Do you suppose that all men are alike to her?"

"Do you love this nigger?" said he, abruptly.

"Yes, sir."

"How dare you tell me so!" he exclaimed, in great wrath. After a slight pause, he added, "I supposed you thought more of yourself; that you felt above the insults of such puppies."

I replied, "If he is a puppy I am a puppy, for we are both of the negro race. It is right and honorable for us to love each other. The man you call a puppy never insulted me, sir; and he would not love me if he did not believe me to be a virtuous woman."

He sprang upon me like a tiger, and gave me a stunning blow. It was the first time he had ever struck me; and fear did not enable me to control my anger. When I had recovered a little from the effects, I exclaimed,

"You have struck me for answering you honestly. How I despise you!"

There was silence for some minutes. Perhaps he was deciding what should be my punishment; or, perhaps, he wanted to give me time to reflect on what I had said, and to whom I had said it. Finally, he asked, "Do you know what you have said?"

"Yes, sir; but your treatment drove me to it."

"Do you know that I have a right to do as I like with you,—that I can kill you, if I please?"

"You have tried to kill me, and I wish you had; but you have no right to do as you like with me."

"Silence!" he exclaimed, in a thundering voice. "By heavens, girl, you forget yourself too far! Are you mad? If you are, I will soon bring you to your senses. Do you think any other master would bear what I have borne from you this morning? Many masters would have killed you on the spot. How would you like to be sent to jail for your insolence?"

"I know I have been disrespectful, sir," I replied; "but you drove me to it; I couldn't help it. As for the jail, there would be more peace for me there than there is here."

"You deserve to go there," said he, "and to be under such treatment, that you would forget the meaning of the word *peace*. It would do you good. It would take some of your high notions out of you. But I am not ready to send you there yet, notwithstanding your ingratitude for all my kindness and forbearance. You have been the plague of my life. I have wanted to make you happy, and I have been repaid with the basest ingratitude; but though you have proved yourself incapable of appreciating my kindness, I will be lenient towards you, Linda. I will give you one more chance to redeem your character. If you behave yourself and do as I require, I will forgive you and treat you as I always have done; but if you disobey me, I will punish you as I would the meanest slave on my plantation. Never let me hear that fellow's name mentioned again. If I ever know of your speaking to him, I will cowhide you both; and if I catch him lurking about my premises, I will shoot him as soon as I would a dog. Do you hear what I say? I'll teach you a lesson about marriage and free niggers! Now go, and let this be the last time I have occasion to speak to you on this subject."

Reader, did you ever hate? I hope not. I never did but once; and I trust I never shall again. Somebody has called it "the atmosphere of hell"; and I believe it is so.

For a fortnight the doctor did not speak to me. He thought to mortify me; to make me feel that I had disgraced myself by receiving the honorable addresses of a respectable colored man, in preference to the base proposals of a white man. But though his lips disdained to address me, his eyes were very loquacious. No animal ever watched its prey more narrowly than he watched me. He knew that I could write, though he had failed to make me read his letters; and he was now troubled lest I should exchange letters with another man. After a while he became weary of silence; and I was sorry for it. One morning, as he passed through the hall, to leave the house, he contrived to thrust a note into my hand. I thought I had better read it, and spare myself the vexation of having him read it to me. It expressed regret for the blow he had given me, and reminded me that I myself was wholly to blame for it. He hoped I had become convinced of the injury I was doing myself by incurring his displeasure. He wrote that he had made up his mind to go to Louisiana; that he should take several slaves with him, and intended I should be one of the number. My mistress would remain where she was; therefore I should have nothing to fear from that quarter. If I merited kindness from him, he assured me that it would be lavishly bestowed. He begged me to think over the matter, and answer the following day.

The next morning I was called to carry a pair of scissors to his room. I laid them on the table, with the letter beside them. He thought it was my answer, and did not call me back. I went as usual to attend my young mistress to and from school. He met me in the street, and ordered me to stop at his office on my way back. When I entered, he showed me his letter, and asked me why I had not answered it. I replied, "I am your daughter's property, and it is in your power to send me, or take me, wherever you please." He said he was very glad to find me so willing to go, and that we should start early in the autumn. He had a large practice in the town, and I rather thought he had made up the story merely to frighten me. However that might be, I was determined that I would never go to Louisiana with him.

Summer passed away, and early in the autumn Dr. Flint's eldest son was sent to Louisiana to examine the country, with a view to emigrating. That news did not disturb me. I knew very well that I should not be sent with *him*. That I had not been taken to the plantation before this time, was owing to the fact that his son was there. He was jealous of his son; and jealousy of the overseer had kept him from punishing me by sending me into the fields to work. Is it strange that I was not proud of these protectors? As for the overseer, he was a man for whom I had less respect than I had for a bloodhound.

Young Mr. Flint did not bring back a favorable report of Louisiana, and I heard no more of that scheme. Soon after this, my lover met me at the corner of the street, and I stopped to speak to him. Looking up, I saw my master watching us from his window. I hurried home, trembling with fear. I was sent for, immediately, to go to his room. He met me with a blow. "When is mistress to be married?" said he, in a sneering tone. A shower of oaths and imprecations followed. How thankful I was that my lover was a free man! that my tyrant had no power to flog him for speaking to me in the street!

Again and again I revolved in my mind how all this would end. There was no hope that the doctor would consent to sell me on any terms. He had an iron will, and was determined to keep me, and to conquer me. My lover was an intelligent and religious man. Even if he could have obtained permission to marry me while I was a slave, the marriage would give him no power to protect me from my master. It would have made him miserable to witness the insults I should have been subjected to. And then, if we had children, I knew they must "follow the condition of the mother." What a terrible blight that would be on the heart of a free, intelligent father! For *his* sake, I felt that I ought not to link his fate with my own unhappy destiny. He was going to Savannah to see about a little property left him by an uncle; and hard as it was to bring my feelings to it, I earnestly entreated him not to come back. I advised him to go to the Free States, where his tongue would not be tied, and where his intelligence would be of more avail to him. He left me, still hoping the day would come when I could be bought. With me the lamp of hope had gone out. The dream of my girlhood was over. I felt lonely and desolate.

Still I was not stripped of all. I still had my good grandmother, and my affectionate brother. When he put his arms round my neck, and looked into my eyes, as if to read there the troubles I dared not tell, I felt that I still had something to love. But even that pleasant emotion was chilled by the reflection that he might be torn from me at any moment, by some sudden freak of my master. If he had known how we love each other, I think he would have exulted in separating us. We often planned together how we could get to the north. But, as William remarked, such things are easier said than done. My movements were very closely watched, and we had no means of getting any money to defray our expenses. As for grandmother, she was strongly opposed to her children's undertaking any such project. She had not forgotten poor Benjamin's sufferings, and she was afraid that if another child tried to escape, he would have a similar or a worse fate. To me, nothing seemed more dreadful than my present life. I said to myself, "William *must* be free. He shall go to the north, and I will follow him." Many a slave sister has formed the same plans.

# ELIZABETH CADY STANTON

## (1815–1902)

Stanton published her memoirs with the intention of giving depth to her public persona. As an advocate of women's suffrage, she was a pioneer, playing the most prominent role in the Seneca Falls Woman's Rights Convention of 1848. Yet she wanted to be known as a private person as well, a wife and mother who kept house, cared deeply for her husband of nearly fifty years, and lavished attention on her seven children. Through observations on these aspects of her life, Stanton hoped that perhaps readers would take her political activism more seriously. Despite these intentions, *Eighty Years and More* (1898) argues persuasively for women's rights, and focuses dramatically on Stanton's political accomplishments. Stanton's writing is both witty and insightful, and offers an intimate account of the life of a pioneer in the women's movement. Indeed, her autobiography anticipates work by many writers in the women's movement, such as Emma Goldman, Erica Jong, and others.

## FROM *Eighty Years and More: Reminiscences, 1815–1897*

### REFORMS AND MOBS

There was one bright woman among the many in our Seneca Falls literary circle to whom I would give more than a passing notice—Mrs. Amelia Bloomer, who represented three novel phases of woman's life. She was assistant postmistress; an editor of a reform paper advocating temperance and woman's rights; and an advocate of the new costume which bore her name!

In 1849 her husband was appointed postmaster, and she became his deputy, was duly sworn in, and, during the administration of Taylor and Fillmore, served in that capacity. When she assumed her duties the improvement in the appearance and conduct of the office was generally acknowledged. A neat little room adjoining the public office became a

kind of ladies' exchange, where those coming from different parts of the town could meet to talk over the news of the day and read the papers and magazines that came to Mrs. Bloomer as editor of the *Lily*. Those who enjoyed the brief reign of a woman in the post office can readily testify to the void felt by the ladies of the village when Mrs. Bloomer's term expired and a man once more reigned in her stead. However, she still edited the *Lily*, and her office remained a fashionable center for several years. Although she wore the bloomer dress, its originator was Elizabeth Smith Miller, the only daughter of Gerrit Smith. In the winter of 1852 Mrs. Miller came to visit me in Seneca Falls, dressed somewhat in the Turkish style—short skirt, full trousers of fine black broadcloth; a Spanish cloak, of the same material, reaching to the knee; beaver hat and feathers and dark furs; altogether a most becoming costume and exceedingly convenient for walking in all kinds of weather. To see my cousin, with a lamp in one hand and a baby in the other, walk upstairs with ease and grace, while, with flowing robes, I pulled myself up with difficulty, lamp and baby out of the question, readily convinced me that there was sore need of reform in woman's dress, and I promptly donned a similar attire. What incredible freedom I enjoyed for two years! Like a captive set free from his ball and chain, I was always ready for a brisk walk through sleet and snow and rain, to climb a mountain, jump over a fence, work in the garden, and, in fact, for any necessary locomotion.

Bloomer is now a recognized word in the English language. Mrs. Bloomer, having the *Lily* in which to discuss the merits of the new dress, the press generally took up the question, and much valuable information was elicited on the physiological results of woman's fashionable attire; the crippling effect of tight waists and long skirts, the heavy weight on the hips, and high heels, all combined to throw the spine out of plumb and lay the foundation for all manner of nervous diseases. But, while all agreed that some change was absolutely necessary for the health of women, the press stoutly ridiculed those who were ready to make the experiment.

A few sensible women, in different parts of the country, adopted the costume, and farmers' wives especially proved its convenience. It was also worn by skaters, gymnasts, tourists, and in sanitariums. But, while the few realized its advantages, the many laughed it to scorn, and heaped such ridicule on its wearers that they soon found that the physical freedom enjoyed did not compensate for the persistent persecution and petty annoyances suffered at every turn. To be rudely gazed at in public and private, to be the conscious subjects of criticism, and to be followed by crowds of boys in the streets, were all, to the very last degree, exasperating. A favorite doggerel that our tormentors chanted, when we appeared in public places, ran thus:

> "Heigh! ho! in rain and snow,
> The bloomer now is all the go.
> Twenty tailors take the stitches,
> Twenty women wear the breeches.
> Heigh! ho! in rain or snow,
> The bloomer now is all the go."

The singers were generally invisible behind some fence or attic window. Those who wore the dress can recall countless amusing and annoying experiences. The patience of most of us was exhausted in about two years; but our leader, Mrs. Miller, bravely adhered to the costume for nearly seven years, under the most trying circumstances. While her father was in Congress, she wore it at many fashionable dinners and receptions in Washington. She was bravely sustained, however, by her husband, Colonel Miller, who never flinched in escorting his wife and her coadjutors, however inartistic their costumes might be. To tall, gaunt women with large feet and to those who were short and stout, it was equally trying. Mrs. Miller was also encouraged by the intense feeling of her father on the question of woman's dress. To him the whole revolution in woman's position turned on her dress. The long skirt was the symbol of her degradation.

The names of those who wore the bloomer costume, besides those already mentioned, were Paulina Wright Davis, Lucy Stone, Susan B. Anthony, Sarah and Angelina Grimke, Mrs. William Burleigh, Celia Burleigh, Charlotte Beebe Wilbour, Helen Jarvis, Lydia Jenkins, Amelia Willard, Dr. Harriet N. Austin, and many patients in sanitariums, whose names I cannot recall. Looking back to this experiment, I am not surprised at the hostility of men in general to the dress, as it made it very uncomfortable for them to go anywhere with those who wore it. People would stare, many men and women make rude remarks, boys followed in crowds, with jeers and laughter, so that gentlemen in attendance would feel it their duty to show fight, unless they had sufficient self-control to pursue the even tenor of their way, as the ladies themselves did, without taking the slightest notice of the commotion they created. But Colonel Miller went through the ordeal with coolness and dogged determination, to the vexation of his acquaintances, who thought one of his duties as a husband was to prescribe his wife's costume.

Though we did not realize the success we hoped for by making the dress popular, yet the effort was not lost. We were well aware that the dress was not artistic, and though we made many changes, our own good taste was never satisfied until we threw aside the loose trousers and adopted buttoned leggins. After giving up the experiment, we found that the costume in which Diana the Huntress is represented, and that worn on the stage by Ellen Tree in the play of "Ion," would have been more artistic and convenient. But we, who had made the experiment, were too happy to move about unnoticed and unknown, to risk, again, the happiness of ourselves and our friends by any further experiments. I have never wondered since that the Chinese women allow their daughters' feet to be encased in iron shoes, nor that the Hindoo widows walk calmly to the funeral pyre; for great are the penalties of those who dare resist the behests of the tyrant Custom.

Nevertheless the agitation has been kept up, in a mild form, both in England and America. Lady Harberton, in 1885, was at the head of an organized movement in London to introduce the bifurcated skirt; Mrs. Jenness Miller, in this country, is making an entire revolution in every garment that belongs to a woman's toilet; and common-sense shoemakers have vouchsafed to us, at last, a low, square heel to our boots and a broad sole in which the five toes can spread themselves at pleasure. Evidently a new day of physical freedom is at last dawning for the most cribbed and crippled of Eve's unhappy daughters.

It was while living in Seneca Falls, and at one of the most despairing periods of my young life, that one of the best gifts of the gods came to me in the form of a good, faithful housekeeper. She was indeed a treasure, a friend and comforter, a second mother to my children, and understood all life's duties and gladly bore its burdens. She could fill any department in domestic life, and for thirty years was the joy of our household. But for this noble, self-sacrificing woman, much of my public work would have been quite impossible. If by word or deed I have made the journey of life easier for any struggling soul, I must in justice share the meed of praise accorded me with my little Quaker friend Amelia Willard.

There are two classes of housekeepers—one that will get what they want, if in the range of human possibilities, and then accept the inevitable inconveniences with cheerfulness and heroism; the other, from a kind of chronic inertia and a fear of taking responsibility, accept everything as they find it, though with gentle, continuous complainings. The latter are called amiable women. Such a woman was our congressman's wife in 1854, and, as I was the reservoir of all her sorrows, great and small, I became very weary of her amiable non-resistance. Among other domestic trials, she had a kitchen stove that smoked and leaked, which could neither bake nor broil,—a worthless thing,—and too small for any purpose. Consequently half their viands were spoiled in the cooking, and the cooks left in disgust, one after another.

In telling me, one day, of these kitchen misadventures, she actually shed tears, which so roused my sympathies that, with surprise, I exclaimed: "Why do you not buy a new stove?" To my unassisted common sense that seemed the most practical thing to do. "Why," she replied, "I have never purchased a darning needle, to put the case strongly, without consulting Mr. S., and he does not think a new stove necessary." "What, pray," said I, "does he know about stoves, sitting in his easy-chair in Washington? If he had a dull old knife with broken blades, he would soon get a new one with which to sharpen his pens and pencils, and, if he attempted to cook a meal—granting he knew how—on your old stove, he would set it out of doors the next hour. Now my advice to you is to buy a new one this very day!"

"Bless me!" she said, "that would make him furious; he would blow me sky-high." "Well," I replied, "suppose he did go into a regular tantrum and use all the most startling expletives in the vocabulary for fifteen minutes! What is that compared with a good stove 365 days in the year? Just put all he could say on one side, and all the advantages you would enjoy on the other, and you must readily see that his wrath would kick the beam." As my logic was irresistible, she said, "Well, if you will go with me, and help select a stove, I think I will take the responsibility."

Accordingly we went to the hardware store and selected the most approved, largest-sized stove, with all the best cooking utensils, best Russian pipe, etc. "Now," said she, "I am in equal need of a good stove in my sitting room, and I would like the pipes of both stoves to lead into dumb stoves above, and thus heat two or three rooms upstairs for my children to play in, as they have no place except the sitting room, where they must be always with me; but I suppose it is not best to do too much at one time." "On the contrary," I replied, "as your husband is wealthy, you had better get all you really need now. Mr. S. will probably be no more surprised with two stoves than with one, and, as you expect a hot scene over the matter, the more you get out of it the better."

So the stoves and pipes were ordered, holes cut through the ceiling, and all were in working order next day. The cook was delighted over her splendid stove and shining tins, copper-bottomed tea kettle and boiler, and warm sleeping room upstairs; the children were delighted with their large playrooms, and madam jubilant with her added comforts and that newborn feeling of independence one has in assuming responsibility.

She was expecting Mr. S. home in the holidays, and occasionally weakened at the prospect of what she feared might be a disagreeable encounter. At such times she came to consult with me, as to what she would say and do when the crisis arrived. Having studied the *genus homo* alike on the divine heights of exaltation and in the valleys of humiliation, I was able to make some valuable suggestions.

"Now," said I, "when your husband explodes, as you think he will, neither say nor do anything; sit and gaze out of the window with that faraway, sad look women know so well how to affect. If you can summon tears at pleasure, a few would not be amiss; a gentle shower, not enough to make the nose and eyes red or to detract from your beauty. Men cannot resist beauty and tears. Never mar their effect with anything bordering on sobs and hysteria; such violent manifestations being neither refined nor artistic. A scene in which one person does the talking must be limited in time. No ordinary man can keep at white heat fifteen minutes; if his victim says nothing, he will soon exhaust himself. Remember every time you speak in the way of defense, you give him a new text on which to branch out again. If silence is ever golden, it is when a husband is in a tantrum."

In due time Mr. S. arrived, laden with Christmas presents, and Charlotte came over to tell me that she had passed through the ordeal. I will give the scene in her own words as nearly as possible. "My husband came yesterday, just before dinner, and, as I expected him, I had all things in order. He seemed very happy to see me and the children, and we had a gay time looking at our presents and chatting about Washington and all that had happened since we parted. It made me sad, in the midst of our happiness, to think how soon the current of his feelings would change, and I wished in my soul that I had not bought the stoves. But, at last, dinner was announced, and I knew that the hour had come. He ran upstairs to give a few touches to his toilet, when lo! the shining stoves and pipes caught his eyes. He explored the upper apartments and came down the back stairs, glanced at the kitchen stove, then into the dining room, and stood confounded, for a moment, before the nickel-plated 'Morning Glory.' Then he exclaimed, 'Heavens and earth! Charlotte, what have you been doing?' I remembered what you told me and said nothing, but looked steadily out of the window. I summoned no tears, however, for I felt more like laughing than crying; he looked so ridiculous flying round spasmodically, like popcorn on a hot griddle, and talking as if making a stump speech on the corruptions of the Democrats. The first time he paused to take breath I said, in my softest tones: 'William, dinner is waiting; I fear the soup will be cold.' Fortunately he was hungry, and that great central organ of life and happiness asserted its claims on his attention, and he took his seat at the table. I broke what might have been an awkward silence, chatting with the older children about their school lessons. Fortunately they were late, and did not know what had happened, so they talked to their father and gradually restored his equilibrium. We had a very good dinner, and I have not heard a word about the stoves since. I suppose we shall have another scene when the bill is presented."

A few years later, Horace Greeley came to Seneca Falls to lecture on temperance. As he stayed with us, we invited Mr. S., among others, to dinner. The chief topic at the table was the idiosyncrasies of women. Mr.

Greeley told many amusing things about his wife, of her erratic movements and sudden decisions to do and dare what seemed most impracticable. Perhaps, on rising some morning, she would say: "I think I'll go
to Europe by the next steamer, Horace. Will you get tickets to-day for me,
the nurse, and children?" "Well," said Mr. S., "she must be something
like our hostess. Every time her husband goes away she cuts a door or
window. They have only ten doors to lock every night, now."

"Yes," I said, "and your own wife, too, Mrs. S., has the credit of some
high-handed measures when you are in Washington." Then I told the
whole story, amid peals of laughter, just as related above. The dinner
table scene fairly convulsed the Congressman. The thought that he had
made such a fool of himself in the eyes of Charlotte that she could not
even summon a tear in her defense, particularly pleased him. When sufficiently recovered to speak, he said: "Well, I never could understand how
it was that Charlotte suddenly emerged from her thraldom and manifested such rare executive ability. Now I see to whom I am indebted for
the most comfortable part of my married life. I am a thousand times
obliged to you; you did just right and so did she, and she has been a happier woman ever since. She now gets what she needs, and frets no more,
to me, about ten thousand little things. How can a man know what
implements are necessary for the work he never does? Of all agencies for
upsetting the equanimity of family life, none can surpass an old, broken-
down kitchen stove!"

In the winter of 1861, just after the election of Lincoln, the abolitionists decided to hold a series of conventions in the chief cities of the North.
All their available speakers were pledged for active service. The Republican party, having absorbed the political abolitionists within its ranks by
its declared hostility to the extension of slavery, had come into power with
overwhelming majorities. Hence the Garrisonian abolitionists, opposed
to all compromises, felt that this was the opportune moment to rouse the
people to the necessity of holding that party to its declared principles, and
pushing it, if possible, a step or two forward.

I was invited to accompany Miss Anthony and Beriah Green to a few
points in Central New York. But we soon found, by the concerted action
of Republicans all over the country, that anti-slavery conventions would
not be tolerated. Thus Republicans and Democrats made common
cause against the abolitionists. The John Brown raid, the year before, had
intimidated Northern politicians as much as Southern slaveholders, and
the general feeling was that the discussion of the question at the North
should be altogether suppressed.

From Buffalo to Albany our experience was the same, varied only by
the fertile resources of the actors and their surroundings. Thirty years of
education had somewhat changed the character of Northern mobs. They

no longer dragged men through the streets with ropes around their necks, nor broke up women's prayer meetings; they no longer threw eggs and brickbats at the apostles of reform, nor dipped them in barrels of tar and feathers, they simply crowded the halls, and, with laughing, groaning, clapping, and cheering, effectually interrupted the proceedings. Such was our experience during the two days we attempted to hold a convention in St. James' Hall, Buffalo. As we paid for the hall, the mob enjoyed themselves, at our expense, in more ways than one. Every session, at the appointed time, we took our places on the platform, making, at various intervals of silence, renewed efforts to speak. Not succeeding, we sat and conversed with each other and the many friends who crowded the platform and anterooms. Thus, among ourselves, we had a pleasant reception and a discussion of many phases of the question that brought us together. The mob not only vouchsafed to us the privilege of talking to our friends without interruption, but delegations of their own came behind the scenes, from time to time, to discuss with us the right of free speech and the constitutionality of slavery.

These Buffalo rowdies were headed by ex-Justice Hinson, aided by younger members of the Fillmore and Seymour families, and the chief of police and fifty subordinates, who were admitted to the hall free, for the express purpose of protecting our right of free speech, but who, in defiance of the mayor's orders, made not the slightest effort in our defense. At Lockport there was a feeble attempt in the same direction. At Albion neither hall, church, nor schoolhouse could be obtained, so we held small meetings in the dining room of the hotel. At Rochester, Corinthian Hall was packed long before the hour advertised. This was a delicately appreciative, jocose mob. At this point Aaron Powell joined us. As he had just risen from a bed of sickness, looking pale and emaciated, he slowly mounted the platform. The mob at once took in his look of exhaustion, and, as he seated himself, they gave an audible simultaneous sigh, as if to say, what a relief it is to be seated! So completely did the tender manifestation reflect Mr. Powell's apparent condition that the whole audience burst into a roar of laughter. Here, too, all attempts to speak were futile. At Port Byron a generous sprinkling of cayenne pepper on the stove soon cut short all constitutional arguments and pæans to liberty.

And so it was all the way to Albany. The whole State was aflame with the mob spirit, and from Boston and various points in other States the same news reached us. As the legislature was in session, and we were advertised in Albany, a radical member sarcastically moved "That as Mrs. Stanton and Miss Anthony were about to move on Albany, the militia be ordered out for the protection of the city." Happily, Albany could then boast of a Democratic mayor, a man of courage and conscience, who said the right of free speech should never be trodden under foot where he had the right to prevent it. And grandly did that one determined man maintain order in his jurisdiction. Through all the sessions of the convention Mayor Thatcher sat on the platform, his police stationed in different parts of the hall and outside the building, to disperse the crowd as fast as it collected. If a man or boy hissed or made the slightest interruption, he was immediately ejected. And not only did the mayor preserve order in the meetings, but, with a company of armed police, he escorted us, every time, to and from the Delevan House. The last night Gerrit Smith addressed the mob from the steps of the hotel, after which they gave him three cheers and dispersed in good order.

When proposing for the Mayor a vote of thanks, at the close of the convention, Mr. Smith expressed his fears that it had been a severe ordeal for him to listen to these prolonged anti-slavery discussions. He smiled, and said: "I have really been deeply interested and instructed. I rather congratulate myself that a convention of this character has, at last, come in the line of my business; otherwise I should have probably remained in ignorance of many important facts and opinions I now understand and appreciate."

While all this was going on publicly, an equally trying experience was progressing, day by day, behind the scenes. Miss Anthony had been instrumental in helping a much abused mother, with her child, to escape from a husband who had immured her in an insane asylum. The wife belonged to one of the first families of New York, her brother being a United States senator, and the husband, also, a man of position; a large circle of friends and acquaintances was interested in the result. Though she was incarcerated in an insane asylum for eighteen months, yet members of her own family again and again testified that she was not insane. Miss Anthony, knowing that she was not, and believing fully that the unhappy mother was the victim of a conspiracy, would not reveal her hiding place.

Knowing the confidence Miss Anthony felt in the wisdom of Mr. Garrison and Mr. Phillips, they were implored to use their influence with her to give up the fugitives. Letters and telegrams, persuasions, arguments, and warnings from Mr. Garrison, Mr. Phillips, and the Senator on the one side, and from Lydia Mott, Mrs. Elizabeth F. Ellet, and Abby Hopper Gibbons, on the other, poured in upon her, day after day; but Miss Anthony remained immovable, although she knew that she was defying and violating the law and might be arrested any moment on the platform. We had known so many aggravated cases of this kind that, in daily counsel, we resolved that this woman should not be recaptured if it were possible to prevent it. To us it looked as imperative a duty to shield a sane mother, who had been torn from a family of little children and doomed to the companionship of lunatics, and to aid her in fleeing to a place of safety, as to help a fugitive from slavery to Canada. In both cases an unjust law was violated; in both cases the supposed owners of the victims were defied; hence, in point of law and morals, the act was the same in both cases. The result proved the wisdom of Miss Anthony's decision, as all with whom Mrs. P. came in contact for years afterward, expressed the opinion that she was, and always had been, perfectly sane. Could the dark secrets of insane asylums be brought to light we should be shocked to know the great number of rebellious wives, sisters, and daughters who are thus sacrificed to false customs and barbarous laws made by men for women.

# RICHARD HENRY DANA

## (1815–1882)

"All the books professing to give life at sea," writes Dana, "have been written by persons who have gained their experience as naval officers, or passengers, and of these, there are very few which are intended to be taken as narratives of facts." A factual account, then, is what he seeks to establish in *Two Years before the Mast* (1840), which records his experience as a deckhand aboard a ship engaged in a two-year voyage around Cape Horn to California. The details of his journey are drawn with a bold pen. By the time of his death from pleurisy in Rome in 1882, *Two Years before the Mast* had been installed as standard reading material on the ships of the British Admiralty.

Born into a wealthy Boston family, Dana attended Harvard, where he was suspended for voicing his solidarity with a fellow student who was undergoing punishment for an infraction; upon returning from this suspension, he was struck by the measles and rendered too weak to study. Once he recovered fully, he decided that the university did not provide the best path for his life, and prevailed upon his father to book him passage as a deckhand on the *Pilgrim*. Eventually, he would become a prominent Boston lawyer and work tirelessly to defend the victims of the Fugitive Slave Law of 1850. Indeed, his antislavery stance would cost him the support of many influential friends, sabotage his attempts at gaining public office, and render him a political failure.

Dana's memoir of his time at sea remains a fine example of the travelogue-as-autobiography, a form of writing often used by later writers, including Ossa Johnson (*I Married Adventure*) and Paul Theroux (*The Great Railway Bazaar*).

## FROM *Two Years before the Mast*

### DEPARTURE

The fourteenth of August was the day fixed upon for the sailing of the brig *Pilgrim* on her voyage from Boston round Cape Horn to the western coast of North America. As she was to get under weigh early in the afternoon, I made my appearance on board at twelve o'clock, in full sea-rig, and with my chest, containing an outfit for a two or three years' voyage, which I had undertaken from a determination to cure, if possible, by an entire change of life, and by a long absence from books and study, a weakness of the eyes, which had obliged me to give up my pursuits, and which no medical aid seemed likely to cure.

The change from the tight dress coat, silk cap, and kid gloves of an undergraduate at Cambridge, to the loose duck trowsers, checked shirt and tarpaulin hat of a sailor, though somewhat of a transformation, was soon made, and I supposed that I should pass very well for a jack tar. But it is impossible to deceive the practised eye in these matters; and while I supposed myself to be looking as salt as Neptune himself, I was, no doubt, known for a landsman by every one on board as soon as I hove in sight. A sailor has a peculiar cut to his clothes, and a way of wearing them which a green hand can never get. The trowsers, tight round the hips, and thence hanging long and loose round the feet, a superabundance of checked shirt, a low-crowned, well varnished black hat, worn on the back of the head, with half a fathom of black ribbon hanging over the left eye, and a peculiar tie to the black silk neckerchief, with sundry other minutiæ, are signs, the want of which betray the beginner, at once. Beside the points in my dress which were out of the way, doubtless my complexion and hands were enough to distinguish me from the regular *salt*, who, with a sun-burnt cheek, wide step, and rolling gait, swings his bronzed and toughened hands athwart-ships, half open, as though just ready to grasp a rope.

"With all my imperfections on my head," I joined the crew, and we hauled out into the stream, and came to anchor for the night. The next day we were employed in preparations for sea, reeving studding-sail gear, crossing royal yards, putting on chafing gear, and taking on board our powder. On the following night, I stood my first watch. I remained awake nearly all the first part of the night from fear that I might not hear when I was called; and when I went on deck, so great were my ideas of the importance of my trust, that I walked regularly fore and aft the whole length of the vessel, looking out over the bows and taffrail at each turn, and was not a little surprised at the coolness of the old salt whom I called to take my place, in stowing himself snugly away under the long boat, for a nap. That was a sufficient lookout, he thought, for a fine night, at anchor in a safe harbor.

The next morning was Saturday, and a breeze having sprung up from the southward, we took a pilot on board, hove up our anchor, and began beating down the bay. I took leave of those of my friends who came to see me off, and had barely opportunity to take a last look at the city, and well-known objects, as no time is allowed on board ship for sentiment. As we drew down into the lower harbor, we found the wind ahead in the bay, and were obliged to come to anchor in the roads. We remained there through the day and a part of the night. My watch began at eleven o'clock at night, and I received orders to call the captain if the wind came out from the westward. About midnight the wind became fair, and having called the captain, I was ordered to call all hands. How I accomplished this I do not know, but I am quite sure that I did not give the true hoarse, boatswain call of "A-a-ll ha-a-a-nds! up anchor, a-ho-oy!" In a short time every one was in motion, the sails loosed, the yards braced, and we began to heave up the anchor, which was our last hold upon Yankee land. I could take but little part in all these preparations. My little knowledge of a vessel was all at fault. Unintelligible orders were so rapidly given and so immediately executed; there was such a hurrying about, and such an intermingling of strange cries and stranger actions, that I was completely bewildered. There is not so helpless and pitiable an object in the world as a landsman beginning a sailor's life. At length those peculiar, long-drawn sounds, which denote that the crew are heaving at the windlass, began, and in a few moments we were under weigh. The noise of the water thrown from the bows began to be heard, the vessel leaned over from the damp night breeze, and rolled with the heavy ground swell, and we had actually begun our long, long journey. This was literally bidding "good night" to my native land. . . .

## FLOGGING

For several days the captain seemed very much out of humour. Nothing went right or fast enough for him. He quarrelled with the cook, and threatened to flog him for throwing wood on deck, and had a dispute with the mate about reeving a Spanish burton; the mate saying that he was right, and had been taught how to do it by a man *who was a sailor*! This the captain took in dudgeon and they were at swords' points at once. But his displeasure was chiefly turned against a large, heavy-moulded fellow from the Middle States, who was called Sam. This man hesitated in his speech, was rather slow in his motions, and was only a tolerably good sailor, but usually seemed to do his best; yet the captain took a dislike to him, thought he was surly and lazy, and "if you once give a dog a bad name"—as the sailor-phrase is—"he may as well jump overboard." The captain found fault with everything this man did, and hazed him for dropping a marline-spike from the mainyard, where he was at work. This, of course, was an accident, but it was set down against him. The captain was on board all day Friday, and everything went on hard and disagreeably. "The more you drive a man, the less he will do," was as true with us as with any other people. We worked late Friday night, and were turned-to early Saturday morning. About ten o'clock the captain ordered our new officer, Russell, who by this time had become thoroughly disliked by all the crew, to get the gig ready to take him ashore. John, the Swede, was sitting in the boat alongside, and Mr. Russell and I were standing by the main hatchway, waiting for the captain, who was down in the hold, where the crew were at work, when we heard his voice raised in violent dispute with somebody, whether it was with the mate or one of the crew I could not tell, and then came blows and scuffling. I ran to the side and beckoned to John, who came aboard, and we leaned down the hatchway, and though we could see no one, yet we knew that the captain had the advantage, for his voice was loud and clear—

"You see your condition! You see your condition! Will you ever give me any more of your *jaw?*" No answer; and then came wrestling and heaving, as though the man was trying to turn him. "You may as well keep still, for I have got you," said the captain. Then came the question, "Will you ever give me any more of your jaw?"

"I never gave you any, sir," said Sam; for it was his voice that we heard, though low and half choked.

"That's not what I ask you. Will you ever be impudent to me again?"

"I never have been, sir," said Sam.

"Answer my question, or I'll make a spread eagle of you! I'll flog you, by G——d."

"I'm no negro slave," said Sam.

"Then I'll make you one," said the captain; and he came to the hatchway, and sprang on deck, threw off his coat, and, rolling up his sleeves, called out to the mate: "Seize that man up, Mr. Amerzene! Seize him up! Make a spread eagle of him! I'll teach you all who is master aboard!"

The crew and officers followed the captain up the hatchway; but it was not until after repeated orders that the mate laid hold of Sam, who made no resistance, and carried him to the gangway.

"What are you going to flog that man for, sir?" said John, the Swede, to the captain.

Upon hearing this, the captain turned upon John; but, knowing him to be quick and resolute, he ordered the steward to bring the irons, and, calling upon Russell to help him, went up to John.

"Let me alone," said John. "I'm willing to be put in irons. You need not use any force"; and, putting out his hands, the captain slipped the irons on, and sent him aft to the quarter-deck. Sam, by this time, was *seized up,* as it is called; that is placed against the shrouds, with his wrists made fast to them, his jacket off, and his back exposed. The captain stood on the break of the deck, a few feet from him, and a little raised, so as to have a good swing at him, and held in his hand the end of a thick, strong rope. The officers stood round, and the crew grouped together in the waist. All these preparations made me feel sick and almost faint, angry and excited as I was. A man—a human being, made in God's likeness—fastened up and flogged like a beast! A man, too, whom I had lived with, eaten with, and stood watch with for months, and knew so well! If a thought of resistance crossed the minds of any of the men, what was to be done? Their time for it had gone by. Two men were fast, and there were left only two men besides Stimson and myself, and a small boy of ten or twelve years of age; and Stimson and I would not have joined the men in a mutiny, as they knew. And then, on the other side, there were (besides the captain) three officers, steward, agent, and clerk, and the cabin supplied with weapons. But besides the numbers, what is there for sailors to do? If they resist, it is mutiny; and if they succeed, and take the vessel, it is piracy. If they ever yield again, their punishment must come; and if they do not yield, what are they to be for the rest of their lives? If a sailor resist his commander, he resists the law, and piracy or submission is his only alternative. Bad as it was, they saw it must be borne. It is what a sailor ships for. Swinging the rope over his head, and bending his body so as to give it full force, the captain brought it down upon the poor fellow's back. Once, twice,—six times. "Will you ever give me any more of your jaw?" The man writhed with pain, but said not a word. Three times more. This was too much, and he muttered something which I could not hear; this brought as many more as the man could stand, when the captain ordered him to be cut down.

"Now for you," said the captain, making up to John, and taking his irons off. As soon as John was loose, he ran forward to the forecastle. "Bring that man aft!" shouted the captain. The second mate, who had been in the forecastle with these men the early part of the voyage, stood still in the waist, and the mate walked slowly forward; but our third officer, anxious to show his zeal, sprang forward over the windlass, and laid hold of John; but John soon threw him from him. The captain stood on the quarter-deck, bareheaded, his eyes flashing with rage, and his face as red as blood, swinging the rope, and calling out to his officers, "Drag him aft! Lay hold of him! I'll *sweeten him!*" etc., etc. The mate now went forward, and told John quietly to go aft; and he, seeing resistance vain, threw the blackguard third mate from him, said he would go aft of himself, that they should not drag him, and went up to the gangway and held out his hands; but as soon as the captain began to make him fast, the indignity was too much, and he struggled; but, the mate and Russell holding him, he was soon seized up. When he was made fast, he turned to the captain, who stood rolling up his sleeves, getting ready for the blow, and asked him what he was to be flogged for. "Have I ever refused my duty, sir? Have you ever known me to hang back or to be insolent, or not to know my work?"

"No," said the captain, "it is not that that I flog you for; I flog you for your interference, for asking questions."

"Can't a man ask a question here without being flogged?"

"No," shouted the captain; "nobody shall open his mouth aboard this vessel but myself;" and he began laying the blows upon his back, swinging half round between each blow, to give it full effect. As he went on his passion increased, and he danced about the deck, calling out, as he swung the rope, "If you want to know what I flog you for, I'll tell you. It's because I like to do it! because I like to do it! It suits me! That's what I do it for!"

The man writhed under the pain until he could endure it no longer, when he called out, with an exclamation more common among foreigners than with us: "O Jesus Christ! O Jesus Christ!"

"Don't call on Jesus Christ," shouted the captain; "*He can't help you. Call on Frank Thompson!* He's the man! He can help you! Jesus Christ can't help you now!"

At these words, which I never shall forget, my blood ran cold. I could look on no longer. Disgusted, sick, I turned away, and leaned over the rail, and looked down into the water. A few rapid thoughts, I don't know what—our situation, a resolution to see the captain punished when we got home—crossed my mind; but the falling of the blows and the cries of the man called me back once more. At length they ceased, and, turning round, I found that the mate, at a signal from the captain, had cast him loose. Almost doubled up with pain, the man walked slowly forward, and went down into the forecastle. Every one else stood still at his post, while the captain, swelling with rage and with the importance of his achievement, walked the quarter-deck, and at each turn, as he came forward, calling out to us: "You see your condition! You see where I've got you all, and you know what to expect! You've been mistaken in me! You didn't know what I was! Now you know what I am! I'll make you toe the mark, every soul of you, or I'll flog you all, fore and aft, from the boy up! You've got a driver over you! Yes, a *slave-driver—a nigger-driver!* I'll see who'll tell me he isn't a NIGGER slave!" With this and the like matter, equally calculated to quiet us, and to allay any apprehensions of future trouble, he entertained us for about ten minutes, when he went below. Soon after, John came aft, with his bare back covered with stripes and wales in every direction, and dreadfully swollen, and asked the steward to ask the captain to let him have some salve, or balsam, to put upon it. "No," said the captain, who heard him from below; "tell him to put his shirt on; that's the best thing for him, and pull me ashore in the boat. Nobody is going to lay-up on board this vessel." He then called to Mr. Russell to take those two men and two others in the boat, and pull him ashore. I went for one. The two men could hardly bend their backs, and the captain called to them to "give way!" but finding they did their best, he let them alone. The agent was in the stern sheets, but during the

whole pull—a league or more—not a word was spokoen. We landed; the
captain, agent, and officer went up to the house, and left us with the boat.
I and the man with me stayed near the boat, while John and Sam walked
slowly away, and sat down on the rocks. They talked some time together,
but at length separated, each sitting alone. I had some fears of John. He
was a foreigner, and violently tempered, and under suffering; and he
had his knife with him, and the captain was to come down alone to the
boat. But nothing happened; and we went quietly on board. The captain
was probably armed, and if either of them had lifted a hand against him,
they would have had nothing before them but flight, and starvation in the
woods of California, or capture by the soldiers and Indians, whom the
offer of twenty dollars would have set upon them.

After the day's work was done we went down into the forecastle and ate
our plain supper; but not a word was spoken. It was Saturday night; but,
there was no song—no "sweethearts and wives." A gloom was over everything. The two men lay in their berths, groaning with pain, and we all
turned in, but, for myself, not to sleep. A sound coming now and then
from the berths of the two men showed that they were awake, as awake
they must have been, for they could hardly lie in one posture long; the
dim swinging lamp shed its light over the dark hole in which we lived,
and many and various reflections and purposes coursed through my
mind. I had no real apprehension that the captain would lay a hand on
me; but our situation, living under a tyranny, with an ungoverned, swag-
gering fellow administering it; of the character of the country we were in;
the length of the voyage; the uncertainty attending our return to America; and then, if we should return, the prospect of obtaining justice and
satisfaction for these poor men; and I vowed that, if God should ever give
me the means, I would do something to redress the grievances and relieve the sufferings of that class of beings with whom my lot had so long
been cast.

The next day was Sunday. We worked, as usual, washing decks, etc.,
until breakfast-time. After breakfast we pulled the captain ashore, and,
finding some hides there which had been brought down the night before,
he ordered me to stay ashore and watch them, saying that the boat would
come again before night. They left me, and I spent a quiet day on the hill,
eating dinner with three men at the little house. Unfortunatley they had
no books; and, after talking with them, and walking about, I began to
grow tired of doing nothing. The little brig, the home of so much hardship and suffering, lay in the offing, almost as far as one could see, and
the only other thing which broke the surface of the great bay was a small,
dreary-looking island, steep and conical, of a clayey soil, and without the
sign of vegetable life upon it, yet which had a peculiar and melancholy
interest, for on the top of it were buried the remains of an Englishman,

the commander of a small merchant brig, who died while lying in this port. It was always a solemn and affecting spot to me. There it stood desolate, and in the midst of desolation; and there were the remains of one who died and was buried alone and friendless. Had it been a common burying-place, it would have been nothing. The single body corresponded well with the solitary character of everything around. It was the only spot in California that impressed me with anything like poetic interest. Then, too, the man died far from home, without a friend near him—by poison, it was suspected, and no one to inquire into it—and without funeral rites; the mate (as I was told), glad to have him out of the way, hurrying him up the hill and into the ground, without a word or a prayer.

I looked anxiously for a boat during the latter part of the afternoon, but none came until toward sundown, when I saw a speck on the water, and as it drew near I found it was the gig, with the captain. The hides, then, were not to go off. The captain came up the hill, with a man, bringing my monkey-jacket and a blanket. He looked pretty black, but inquired whether I had enough to eat; told me to make a house out of the hides, and keep myself warm, as I should have to sleep there among them, and to keep good watch over them. I got a moment to speak to the man who brought my jacket.

"How do things go aboard?" said I.

"Bad enough," said he; "hard work and not a kind word spoken."

"What!" said I, "have you been at work all day?"

"Yes! no more Sunday for us. Everything has been moved in the hold, from stem to stern, and from the water-ways to the keelson."

I went up to the house to supper. We had frijoles (the perpetual food of the Californians, but which, when well cooked, are the best bean in the world), coffee made of burnt wheat, and hard bread. After our meal, the three men sat down by the light of a tallow candle, with a pack of greasy Spanish cards, to the favourite game of "treintay uno," a sort of Spanish "everlasting." I left them and went out to take up my bivouac among the hides. It was now dark; the vessel was hidden from sight, and except the three men in the house there was not a living soul within a league. The coyotes (a wild animal of a nature and appearance between that of the fox and the wolf) set up their sharp, quick bark, and two owls, at the end of two distant points running out into the bay, on different sides of the hill where I lay, kept up their alternate dismal notes. I had heard the sound before at night, but did not know what it was, until one of the men, who came down to look at my quarters, told me it was the owl. Mellowed by the distance, and heard alone, at night, it was a most melancholy and boding sound. Through nearly all the night they kept it up, answering one another slowly at regular intervals. This was relieved by the noisy coyotes, some of which came quite near to my quarters, and were not very pleasant neighbours. The next morning, before sunrise, the long-boat came ashore, and the hides were taken off.

We lay at San Pedro about a week, engaged in taking off hides and in other labours, which had now become our regular duties. I spent one more day on the hill, watching a quantity of hides and goods, and this time succeeded in finding a part of a volume of Scott's *Pirate* in a corner of the house; but it failed me at a most interesting moment, and I betook myself to my acquaintances on shore, and from them learned a good deal about the customs of the country, the harbours, etc. This, they told me, was a worse harbour than Santa Barbara for south-easters, the bearing of the headland being a point and a half more to windward, and it being so shallow that the sea broke often as far out as where we lay at anchor. The gale for which we slipped at Santa Barbara had been so bad a one here, that the whole bay, for a league out, was filled with the foam of the breakers, and seas actually broke over the Dead Man's Island. The *Lagoda* was lying there, and slipped at the first alarm, and in such haste that she was obliged to leave her launch behind her at anchor. The little boat rode it out for several hours, pitching at her anchor, and standing with her stern up almost perpendicularly. The men told me that they watched her till towards night, when she snapped her cable and drove up over the breakers high and dry upon the beach.

On board the *Pilgrim* everything went on regularly, each one trying to get along as smoothly as possible; but the comfort of the voyage was evidently at an end. "That is a long lane which has no turning." "Every dog must have his day, and mine will come by and by," and the like proverbs, were occasionally quoted; but no one spoke of any probable end to the voyage, or of Boston, or anything of the kind; or, if he did, it was only to draw out the perpetual surly reply from his shipmate: "Boston, is it? You may thank your stars if you ever see that place. You had better have your back sheathed, and your head coppered, and your feet shod, and make out your log for California for life!" or else something of this kind: "Before you get to Boston the hides will wear all the hair off your head, and you'll take up all your wages in clothes, and won't have enough left to buy a wig with!"

The flogging was seldom, if ever, alluded to by us in the forecastle. If any one was inclined to talk about it, the others, with a delicacy which I hardly expected to find among them, always stopped him, or turned the subject. But the behaviour of the two men who were flogged toward one another showed a consideration which would have been worthy of admiration in the highest walks of life. Sam knew John had suffered solely on his account; and in all his complaints he said that, if he alone had been flogged, it would have been nothing; but he never could see him without thinking that he had been the means of bringing this disgrace upon him; and John never, by word or deed, let anything escape him to remind the other that it was by interfering to save his shipmate that he had suffered. Neither made it a secret that they thought the Dutchman Bill and Foster might have helped them; but they did not expect it of Stimson or me. While we showed our sympathy for their suffering, and our indignation at the captain's violence, we did not feel sure that there was only one side to the beginning of the difficulty, and we kept clear of any engagement with them, except our promise to help them when they got home.*

Having got all our spare room filled with hides, we hove up our anchor, and made sail for San Diego. In no operation can the disposition of a crew be better discovered than in getting under way. Where things are done "with a will," every one is like a cat aloft; sails are loosed in an instant; each one lays out his strength on his handspike, and the windlass goes briskly round with the loud cry of "Yo heave ho! Heave and pawl! Heave hearty, ho!" and the chorus of "Cheerly, men!" cats the anchor. But with us, at this time, it was all dragging work. No one went aloft beyond his ordinary gait, and the chain came slowly in over the windlass. The mate, between the knight-heads, exhausted all his official rhetoric in calls of "Heave with a will!" "Heave hearty, men! heave hearty!" "Heave, and raise the dead!" "Heave, and away!" etc., etc., but it would not do. Nobody broke his back or his hand-spike by his efforts. And when the cat-tackle-fall was strung along, and all hands, cook, steward, and all, laid hold, to cat the anchor, instead of the lively song of "Cheerly, men!"

*Owing to the change of vessels that afterwards took place, Captain Thompson arrived in Boston nearly a year before the *Pilgrim*, and was off on another voyage, and beyond the reach of these men. Soon after the publication of the first edition of this book, in 1841, I received a letter from Stimson, dated at Detroit, Michigan, where he had re-entered mercantile life, from which I make this extract: — "As to your account of the flogging scene, I think you have given a fair history of it, and, if anything, been too lenient towards Captain Thompson for his brutal, cowardly treatment of those men. As I was in the hold at the time the affray commenced, I will give you a short history of it as near as I can recollect. We were breaking out goods in the fore-hold, and, in order to get at them, we had to shift our hides from forward to aft. After having removed part of them, we came to the boxes, and attempted to get them out without moving any more of the hides. While doing so, Sam accidentally hurt his hand, and, as usual, began swearing about it, and was not sparing of his oaths, although I think he was not aware that Captain Thompson was so near him at the time. Captain Thompson asked him, in no moderate way, what was the matter with him. Sam, on account of the impediment in his speech, could not answer immediately, although he endeavoured to, but as soon as possible answered in a matter that almost any one would, under the like circumstances, yet, I believe, not with the intention of giving a short answer; but being provoked, and suffering pain from the injured hand, he perhaps answered rather short, or sullenly. Thus commenced the scene you have so vividly described, and which seems to me exactly the history of the whole affair without any exaggeration."

in which all hands join in the chorus, we pulled a long, heavy, silent pull, and, as sailors say a song is as good as ten men, the anchor came to the cat-head pretty slowly. "Give us 'Cheerly!' " said the mate; but there was no "cheerly" for us and we did without it. The captain walked the quarter-deck, and said not a word. He must have seen the change, but there was nothing which he could notice officially.

We sailed leisurely down the coast before a light fair wind, keeping the land well abroad, and saw two other missions, looking like blocks of white plaster, shining in the distance; one of which, situated on the top of a high hill, was San Juan Capistrano, under which vessels sometimes come to anchor, in the summer season, and take off hides. At sunset on the second day we had a large and well-wooded headland directly before us, behind which lay the little harbour of San Diego. We were becalmed off this point all night; but the next morning, which was Saturday, the 14th of March, having a good breeze, we stood round the point, and, hauling our wind, brought the little harbour, which is rather the outlet of a small river, right before us. Every one was desirous to get a view of the new place. A chain of high hills, beginning at the point (which was on our larboard hand coming in), protected the harbour on the north and west, and ran off into the interior, as far as the eye could reach. On the other sides the land was low and green, but without trees. The entrance is so narrow as to admit but one vessel at a time, the current swift, and the channel runs so near to a low stony point that the ship's sides appeared almost to touch it. There was no town in sight, but on the smooth sand beach, abreast, and within a cable's length of which three vessels lay moored, were four large houses, built of rough boards and looking like the great barns in which ice is stored on the borders of the large ponds near Boston, with piles of hides standing round them, and men in red shirts and large straw hats walking in and out of the doors. These were the hide-houses. Of the vessels; one, a short, clumsy little hermaphrodite brig, we recognised as our old acquaintance, the *Loriotte*; another, with sharp bows and raking masts, newly painted and tarred, and glittering in the morning sun, with the blood-red banner and cross of St. George at her peak, was the handsome *Ayacucho*. The third was a large ship, with topgallant-masts housed and sails unbent, and looking as rusty and worn as two years' "hide droghing" could make her. This was the *Lagoda*. As we drew near, carried rapidly along by the current, we overhauled our chain, and clewed up the topsails. "Let go the anchor!" said the captain; but either there was not chain enough forward of the windlass, or the anchor went down foul, or we had too much headway on, for it did not bring us up. "Pay out chain!" shouted the captain; and we gave it to her; but it would not do. Before the other anchor could be let go we drifted down, broadside on, and went smash into the *Lagoda*. Her crew were at breakfast in the forecastle, and her cook, seeing us coming, rushed out of his galley, and called up the officers and men.

Fortunately, no great harm was done. Her jib-boom passed between our fore and mainmasts, carrying away some of our rigging, and breaking down the rail. She lost her martingale. This brought us up, and as they paid out chain, we swung clear of them and let go the other anchor; but this had as bad luck as the first, for, before any one perceived it, we were drifting down upon the *Loriotte*. The captain now gave out his orders rapidly and fiercely, sheeting home the topsails, and backing and filling the sails, in hope of starting or clearing the anchors; but it was all in vain, and he sat down on the rail, taking it very leisurely, and calling out to Captain Nye that he was coming to pay him a visit. We drifted fairly into the *Loriotte*, her larboard bow into our starboard quarter, carrying away a part of our starboard quarter railing, and breaking off her larboard bumpkin and one or two stanchions above the deck. We saw our handsome sailor, Jackson, on the forecastle, with the Sandwich-Islanders, working away to get us clear. After paying out chain, we swung clear, but our anchors were, no doubt, afoul of hers. We manned the windlass, and hove, and hove away, but to no purpose. Sometimes we got a little upon the cable, but a good surge would take it all back again. We now began to drift down toward the *Ayacucho*; when her boat put off, and brought her commander, Captain Wilson, on board. He was a short, active, well-built man, about fifty years of age; and being some twenty years older than our captain, and a thorough seaman, he did not hesitate to give his advice, and from giving advice he gradually came to taking the command; ordering us when to heave and when to pawl, and backing and filling the topsails, setting and taking in jib and trysail, whenever he thought best. Our captain gave a few orders, but as Wilson generally countermanded them, saying, in an easy, fatherly kind of way, "Oh, no! Captain Thompson, you don't want the jib on her," or "It isn't time yet to heave!" he soon gave it up. We had no objections to this state of things, for Wilson was a kind man, and had an encouraging and pleasant way of speaking to us, which made everything go easily. After two or three hours of constant labour at the windlass, heaving and yo-ho-ing with all our might, we brought up an anchor, with the *Loriotte*'s small bower fast to it. Having cleared this, and let it go, and cleared our hawse, we got our other anchor, which had dragged half over the harbour. "Now," said Wilson, "I'll find you a good berth"; and, setting both the topsails, he carried us down, and brought us to anchor, in handsome style, directly abreast of the hide-house which we were to use. Having done this, he took his leave, while we furled the sails and got our breakfast, which was welcome to us, for we had worked hard and eaten nothing since yesterday afternoon, and it was nearly twelve o'clock. After breakfast, and until night, we were employed in getting out the boats and mooring ship.

After supper two of us took the captain on board the *Lagoda.* As he came alongside he gave his name, and the mate, in the gangway, called out to Captain Bradshaw, down the companion-way, "Captain Thompson has come aboard, sir!" "Has he brought his brig with him?" asked the rough old fellow, in a tone which made itself heard fore and aft. This mortified our captain not a little, and it became a standing joke among us, and, indeed, over the coast, for the rest of the voyage. The captain went down into the cabin, and we walked forward and put our heads down the forecastle, where we found the men at supper. "Come down, shipmates!* come down!" said they, as soon as they saw us; and we went down, and found a large, high forecastle, well lighted, and a crew of twelve or fourteen men eating out of their kids and pans, and drinking their tea, and talking and laughing, all as independent and easy as so many "woodsawyer's clerks." This looked like comfort and enjoyment, compared with the dark little forecastle, and scanty, discontented crew of the brig. It was Saturday night; they had got through their work for the week, and being snugly moored, had nothing to do until Monday again. After two years' hard service they had seen the worst, and all, of California; had got their cargo nearly stowed, and expected to sail in a week or two for Boston.

We spent an hour or more with them, talking over California matters, until the word was passed—"Pilgrims, away!" and we went back to our brig. The Lagodas were a hardy, intelligent set, a little roughened, and their clothes patched and old, from California wear; all able seamen, and between the ages of twenty and thirty-five or forty. They inquired about our vessel, the usage on board, etc., and were not a little surprised at the story of the flogging. They said there were often difficulties in vessels on the coast, and sometimes knock-downs and fightings, but they had never heard before of a regular seizing-up and flogging. "Spread eagles" were a new kind of bird in California.

Sunday, they said, was always given in San Diego, both at the hidehouses and on board the vessels, a large number usually going up to the town, on liberty. We learned a good deal from them about the curing and stowing of hides, etc., and they were desirous to have the latest news (seven months old) from Boston. One of their first inquiries was for Father Taylor, the seamen's preacher in Boston. Then followed the usual strain of conversation, inquiries, stories, and jokes, which one must always hear in a ship's forecastle, but which are, perhaps, after all, no worse, though more gross and coarse, than those one may chance to hear from some well-dressed gentlemen around their tables.

---

*"Shipmate" is the term by which sailors address one another when not acquainted.

# HENRY DAVID THOREAU
## (1817–1862)

A graduate of Harvard, Thoreau worked as a schoolteacher, pencil maker, surveyor, and occasional lecturer. He spent much of his life in Concord, Massachusetts, where his neighbor, close friend, and mentor was Ralph Waldo Emerson, the Transcendentalist poet-philosopher. Although he published several nonfiction books in his lifetime, and wrote voluminously in his journals, *Walden* (1854) lies at the center of both his work and the American tradition in autobiographical writing. It records the author's "experiment" of living alone in a small cabin on Walden Pond, in Concord, Massachusetts, from 1845 to 1847. His goal was to "front only the essential facts of life," removing himself bodily and mentally from the materialism of American life. Thoreau observes the course of the seasons in concrete, concise prose and maintains a sense of high moral principles, learned by close observation of life and the natural world. His work has influenced readers and writers throughout the world, from Tolstoy to Gandhi. Indeed, a good deal of the best nature writing (which often has a strong autobiographical component) may be traced back to the example of Thoreau. Among the most notable of his contemporary inheritors are John Elder, Annie Dillard, Terry Tempest Williams, and Scott Russell Sanders.

## FROM *Walden*

### THE BEAN-FIELD

Meanwhile my beans, the length of whose rows, added together, was seven miles already planted, were impatient to be hoed, for the earliest had grown considerably before the latest were in the ground; indeed they were not easily to be put off. What was the meaning of this so steady and self-respecting, this small Herculean labor, I knew not. I came to love my rows, my beans, though so many more than I wanted. They attached me to the earth, and so I got strength like Antæus. But why should I raise them? Only Heaven knows. This was my curious labor all summer,—to make this portion of the earth's surface, which had yielded only cinque-foil, blackberries, johnswort, and the like, before, sweet wild fruits and pleasant flowers, produce instead this pulse. What shall I learn of beans or beans of me? I cherish them, I hoe them, early and late I have an eye to them; and this is my day's work. It is a fine broad leaf to look on. My auxiliaries are the dews and rains which water this dry soil, and what fertility is in the soil itself, which for the most part is lean and effete. My enemies are worms, cool days, and most of all woodchucks. The last have nibbled for me a quarter of an acre clean. But what right had I to oust johnswort and the rest, and break up their ancient herb garden? Soon, however, the remaining beans will be too tough for them, and go forward to meet new foes.

When I was four years old, as I well remember, I was brought from Boston to this my native town, through these very woods and this field, to the pond. It is one of the oldest scenes stamped on my memory. And now to-night my flute has waked the echoes over that very water. The pines still stand here older than I; or, if some have fallen, I have cooked my supper with their stumps, and a new growth is rising all around, preparing another aspect for new infant eyes. Almost the same johnswort springs from the same perennial root in this pasture, and even I have at length helped to clothe that fabulous landscape of my infant dreams, and one of the results of my presence and influence is seen in these bean leaves, corn blades, and potato vines.

I planted about two acres and a half of upland; and as it was only about fifteen years since the land was cleared, and I myself had got out two or three cords of stumps, I did not give it any manure; but in the course of the summer it appeared by the arrow-heads which I turned up in hoeing, that an extinct nation had anciently dwelt here and planted corn and beans ere white men came to clear the land, and so, to some extent, had exhausted the soil for this very crop.

Before yet any woodchuck or squirrel had run across the road, or the sun had got above the shrub-oaks, while all the dew was on, though the farmers warned me against it,—I would advise you to do all your work if possible while the dew is on,—I began to level the ranks of haughty weeds in my bean-field and throw dust upon their heads. Early in the morning I worked barefooted, dabbling like a plastic artist in the dewy and crumbling sand, but later in the day the sun blistered my feet. There the sun lighted me to hoe beans, pacing slowly backward and forward over that yellow gravelly upland, between the long green rows, fifteen rods, the one end terminating in a shrub oak copse where I could rest in the shade, the other in a blackberry field where the green berries deepened their tints by the time I had made another bout. Removing the weeds, putting fresh soil about the bean stems, and encouraging this weed which I had sown, making the yellow soil express its summer thought in bean leaves and blossoms rather than in wormwood and piper and millet grass, making the earth say beans instead of grass,—this was my daily work. As I had little aid from horses or cattle, or hired men or boys, or improved implements of husbandry, I was much slower, and became much more intimate with my beans than usual. But labor of the hands, even when pursued to the verge of drudgery, is perhaps never the worst form of idleness. It has a constant and imperishable moral, and to the scholar it yields a classic result. A very *agricola laboriosus* was I to travellers bound westward through Lincoln and Wayland to nobody knows where; they sitting at their ease in gigs, with elbows on knees, and reins loosely hanging in festoons; I the home-staying, laborious native of the soil. But soon my homestead was out of their sight and thought. It was the only open and cultivated field for a great distance on either side of the road; so they made the most of it; and sometimes the man in the field heard more of travellers' gossip and comment than was meant for his ear: "Beans so late! peas so late!"—for I continued to plant when others had began to hoe,—the ministerial husbandman had not suspected it. "Corn, my boy, for fodder; corn for fodder." "Does he *live* there?" asks the black bonnet of the gray coat; and the hard-featured farmer reins up his grateful dobbin to inquire what you are doing where he sees no manure in the furrow, and recommends a little chip dirt, or any little waste stuff, or it may be ashes or plaster. But here were two acres and a half of furrows, and only a hoe for cart and two hands to draw it,—there being an aversion to other carts and horses,—and chip dirt far away. Fellow-travellers as they rattled by compared it aloud with the fields which they had passed, so that I came to know how I stood in the agricultural world. This was one field not in Mr. Coleman's report. And, by the way, who estimates the value of the crop which Nature yields in the still wilder fields unimproved by man? The crop of *English* hay is carefully weighed, the moisture calculated, the silicates and potash; but in all dells and pond holes in the woods and pastures and swamps grows a rich and various crop only un-reaped by man. Mine was, as it were, the connecting link between wild and cultivated fields; as some states are civilized, and others half-civilized, and others savage or barbarous, so my field was, though not in a bad sense, a half-cultivated field. They were beans cheerfully returning to their wild and primitive state that I cultivated, and my hoe played the *Rans des Vaches* for them.

Near at hand, upon the topmost spray of a birch, sings the brown-thrasher—or red mavis, as some love to call him—all the morning, glad of your society, that would find out another farmer's field if yours were not here. While you are planting the seed, he cries—"Drop it, drop it,—cover it up,—pull it up, pull it up, pull it up." But this was not corn, and

so it was safe from such enemies as he. You may wonder what his rig-
marole, his amateur Paganini performances on one string or on twenty,
have to do with your planting, and yet prefer it to leached ashes or plaster. It was a cheap sort of top dressing in which I had entire faith.

As I drew a still fresher soil about the rows with my hoe, I disturbed the
ashes of unchronicled nations who in primeval years lived under these
heavens, and their small implements of war and hunting were brought
to the light of this modern day. They lay mingled with other natural
stones, some of which bore the marks of having been burned by Indian
fires, and some by the sun, and also bits of pottery and glass brought
hither by the recent cultivators of the soil. When my hoe tinkled against
the stones, that music echoed to the woods and the sky, and was an accompaniment to my labor which yielded an instant and immeasurable
crop. It was no longer beans that I hoed, nor I that hoed beans; and I remembered with as much pity as pride, if I remembered at all, my acquaintances who had gone to the city to attend the oratorios. The
night-hawk circled overhead in the sunny afternoons—for I sometimes
made a day of it—like a mote in the eye, or in heaven's eye, falling from
time to time with a swoop and a sound as if the heavens were rent, torn
at last to very rags and tatters, and yet a seamless cope remained; small
imps that fill the air and lay their eggs on the ground on bare sand or
rocks on the tops of hills, where few have found them; graceful and slender like ripples caught up from the pond, as leaves are raised by the wind
to float in the heavens; such kindredship is in Nature. The hawk is aer-
ial brother of the wave which he sails over and surveys, those his perfect
air-inflated wings answering to the elemental unfledged pinions of the
sea. Or sometimes I watched a pair of hen-hawks circling high in the sky,
alternately soaring and descending, approaching and leaving one another, as if they were the imbodiment of my own thoughts. Or I was attracted by the passage of wild pigeons from this wood to that, with a
slight quivering winnowing sound and carrier haste; or from under a rotten stump my hoe turned up a sluggish portentous and outlandish spotted salamander, a trace of Egypt and the Nile, yet our contemporary.
When I paused to lean on my hoe, these sounds and sights I heard and
saw any where in the row, a part of the inexhaustible entertainment
which the country offers.

On gala days the town fires its great guns, which echo like popguns to
these woods, and some waifs of martial music occasionally penetrate
thus far. To me, away there in my bean-field at the other end of the town,
the big guns sounded as if a puff ball had burst; and when there was a
military turnout of which I was ignorant, I have sometimes had a vague
sense all the day of some sort of itching and disease in the horizon, as if
some eruption would break out there soon, either scarlatina or canker-

rash, until at length some more favorable puff of wind, making haste over the fields and up the Wayland road, brought me information of the "trainers." It seemed by the distant hum as if somebody's bees had swarmed, and that the neighbors, according to Virgil's advice, by a faint *tintinnabulum* upon the most sonorous of their domestic utensils, were endeavoring to call them down into the hive again. And when the sound died quite away, and the hum had ceased, and the most favorable breezes told no tale, I knew that they had got the last drone of them all safely into the Middlesex hive, and that now their minds were bent on the honey with which it was smeared.

I felt proud to know that the liberties of Massachusetts and of our fatherland were in such safe keeping; and as I turned to my hoeing again I was filled with an inexpressible confidence, and pursued my labor cheerfully with a calm trust in the future.

When there were several bands of musicians, it sounded as if all the village was a vast bellows, and all the buildings expanded and collapsed alternately with a din. But sometimes it was a really noble and inspiring strain that reached these woods, and the trumpet that sings of fame, and I felt as if I could spit a Mexican with a good relish,—for why should we always stand for trifles?—and looked round for a woodchuck or a skunk to exercise my chivalry upon. These martial strains seemed as far away as Palestine, and reminded me of a march of crusaders in the horizon, with a slight tantivy and tremulous motion of the elm-tree tops which overhang the village. This was one of the *great* days; though the sky had from my clearing only the same everlastingly great look that it wears daily, and I saw no difference in it.

It was a singular experience that long acquaintance which I cultivated with beans, what with planting, and hoeing, and harvesting, and threshing, and picking over, and selling them,—the last was the hardest of all,—I might add eating, for I did taste. I was determined to know beans. When they were growing, I used to hoe from five o'clock in the morning till noon, and commonly spent the rest of the day about other affairs. Consider the intimate and curious acquaintance one makes with various kinds of weeds,—it will bear some iteration in the account, for there was no little iteration in the labor,—disturbing their delicate organization so ruthlessly, and making such invidious distinctions with his hoe, levelling whole ranks of one species, and sedulously cultivating another. That's Roman wormwood,—that's pigweed,—that's sorrel,—that's pipergrass,—have at him, chop him up, turn his roots upward to the sun, don't let him have a fibre in the shade, if you do he'll turn himself t'other side up and be as green as a leek in two days. A long war, not with cranes, but with weeds, those Trojans who had sun and rain and dews on their side. Daily the beans saw me come to their rescue armed with a hoe, and thin the ranks of their enemies, filling up the trenches with weedy dead. Many a lusty crest-waving Hector, that towered a whole foot above his crowding comrades, fell before my weapon and rolled in the dust.

Those summer days which some of my contemporaries devoted to the fine arts in Boston or Rome, and others to contemplation in India, and others to trade in London or New York, I thus, with the other farmers of New England, devoted to husbandry. Not that I wanted beans to eat, for I am by nature a Pythagorean, so far as beans are concerned, whether they mean porridge or voting, and exchanged them for rice; but, perchance, as some must work in fields if only for the sake of tropes and expression, to serve a parable-maker one day. It was on the whole a rare amusement, which, continued too long, might have become a dissipation. Though I gave them no manure, and did not hoe them all once, I hoed them unusually well as far as I went, and was paid for it in the end, "there being in truth," as Evelyn says, "no compost or lætation whatsoever comparable to this continual motion, repastination, and turning of the mould with the spade." "The earth," he adds elsewhere, "especially if fresh, has a certain magnetism in it, by which it attracts the salt, power, or virtue (call it either) which gives it life, and is the logic of all the labor and stir we keep about it, to sustain us; all dungings and other sordid temperings being but the vicars succedaneous to this improvement." Morever, this being one of those "worn-out and exhausted lay fields which enjoy their sabbath," had perchance, as Sir Kenelm Digby thinks likely, attracted "vital spirits" from the air. I harvested twelve bushels of beans.

But to be more particular, for it is complained that Mr. Coleman has reported chiefly the expensive experiments of gentlemen farmers, my outgoes were,—

| | | | |
|---|---|---|---|
| For a hoe, . . . . . . . . . . . . | .$ | 0 | 54 |
| Ploughing, harrowing, and furrowing, . . . . . . | | 7 | 50, Too much. |
| Beans for seed, . . . . . . . . . . . . | | 3 | 12½ |
| Potatoes " . . . . . . . . . . . . | | 1 | 33 |
| Peas " . . . . . . . . . . . . | | 0 | 40 |
| Turnip seed, . . . . . . . . . . . . | | 0 | 06 |
| White line for crow fence, . . . . . . . . | | 0 | 02 |
| Horse cultivator and boy three hours, . . . . . . | | 1 | 00 |
| Horse and cart to get crop, . . . . . . . . | | 0 | 75 |
| In all, . . . . . . . . . . . . . . | .$14 | | 72½ |

My income was, (patrem familias vendacem, non emacem esse oportet,) from

| | | | |
|---|---|---|---|
| Nine bushels and twelve quarts of beans sold, . . . . . . | .$16 | 94 |
| Five " large potatoes, . . . . . . . . . . . | . 2 | 50 |
| Nine " small, . . . . . . . . . . . . . . | . 2 | 25 |
| Grass, . . . . . . . . . . . . . . . . . . | . 1 | 00 |
| Stalks, . . . . . . . . . . . . . . . . . . | . 0 | 75 |
| In all, . . . . . . . . . . . . . . . | .$23 | 44 |
| Leaving a pecuniary profit, as I have elsewhere said, of . . . . . . . . . | $8 | 71½ |

This is the result of my experience in raising beans. Plant the common small white bush bean about the first of June, in rows three feet by eighteen inches apart, being careful to select fresh round and unmixed seed. First look out for worms, and supply vacancies by planting anew. Then look out for woodchucks, if it is an exposed place, for they will nibble off the earliest tender leaves almost clean as they go; and again, when the young tendrils make their appearance, they have notice of it, and will shear them off with both buds and young pods, sitting erect like a squirrel. But above all harvest as early as possible, if you would escape frosts and have a fair and salable crop; you may save much loss by this means.

This further experience also I gained. I said to myself, I will not plant beans and corn with so much industry another summer, but such seeds, if the seed is not lost, as sincerity, truth, simplicity, faith, innocence, and the like, and see if they will not grow in this soil, even with less toil and manurance, and sustain me, for surely it has not been exhausted for these crops. Alas! I said this to myself; but now another summer is gone, and another, and another, and I am obliged to say to you, Reader, that the seeds which I planted, if indeed they *were* the seeds of virtues, were wormeaten or had lost their vitality, and so did not come up. Commonly men will only be brave as their fathers were brave, or timid. This generation is very sure to plant corn and beans each new year precisely as the Indians did centuries ago and taught the first settlers to do, as if there were a fate in it. I saw an old man the other day, to my astonishment, making the holes with a hoe for the seventieth time at least, and not for himself to lie down in! But why should not the New Englander try new adventures, and not lay so much stress on his grain, his potato and grass crop, and his orchards, — raise other crops than these? Why concern ourselves so much about our beans for seed, and not be concerned at all about a new generation of men? We should really be fed and cheered if when we met a man we were sure to see that some of the qualities which I have named, which we all prize more than those other productions, but which are for the most part broadcast and floating in the air, had taken root and grown in him. Here comes such a subtile and ineffable quality, for instance, as truth or justice, though the slightest amount or new variety of it, along the road. Our ambassadors should be instructed to send home such seeds as these, and Congress help to distribute them over all the land. We should never stand upon ceremony with sincerity. We should never cheat and insult and banish one another by our meanness, if there were present the kernel of worth and friendliness. We should not meet thus in haste. Most men I do not meet at all, for they seem not to have time; they are busy about their beans. We would not deal with a man thus plodding ever, leaning on a hoe or a spade as a staff between his work, not as a mushroom, but partially risen out of the earth, something more than erect, like swallows alighted and walking on the ground: —

> "And as he spake, his wings would now and then
> Spread, as he meant to fly, then close again,"

so that we should suspect that we might be conversing with an angel. Bread may not always nourish us; but it always does us good, it even takes stiffness out of our joints, and makes us supple and buoyant, when we knew not what ailed us, to recognize any generosity in man or Nature, to share any unmixed and heroic joy.

Ancient poetry and mythology suggest, at least, that husbandry was once a sacred art; but it is pursued with irreverent haste and heedlessness by us, our object being to have large farms and large crops merely. We have no festival, nor procession, nor ceremony, not excepting our Cattle-shows and so called Thanksgivings, by which the farmer expresses a sense of the sacredness of his calling, or is reminded of its sacred origin. It is the premium and the feast which tempt him. He sacrifices not to Ceres and the Terrestrial Jove, but to the infernal Plutus rather. By avarice and self-ishness, and a grovelling habit, from which none of us is free, of regard-ing the soil as property, or the means of acquiring property chiefly, the landscape is deformed, husbandry is degraded with us, and the farmer leads the meanest of lives. He knows Nature but as a robber. Cato says that the profits of agriculture are particularly pious or just, *(maximeque pius quaestus,)* and according to Varro the old Romans "called the same earth Mother and Ceres, and thought that they who cultivated it led a pious and useful life, and that they alone were left of the race of King Saturn."

We are wont to forget that the sun looks on our cultivated fields and on the prairies and forests without distinction. They all reflect and absorb his rays alike, and the former make but a small part of the glorious pic-ture which he beholds in his daily course. In his view the earth is all equally cultivated like a garden. Therefore we should receive the bene-fit of his light and heat with a corresponding trust and magnanimity. What though I value the seed of these beans, and harvest that in the fall of the year? This broad field which I have looked at so long looks not to me as the principal cultivator, but away from me to influences more genial to it, which water and make it green. These beans have results which are not harvested by me. Do they not grow for woodchucks partly? The ear of wheat, (in Latin *spica*, obsoletely *speca*, from *spe*, hope,) should not be the only hope of the husbandman; its kernel or grain (*granum*, from *gerendo*, bearing,) is not all that it bears. How, then, can our harvest fail? Shall I not rejoice also at the abundance of the weeds whose seeds are the granary of the birds? It matters little comparatively whether the fields fill the farmer's barns. The true husbandman will cease from anxiety, as the squirrels manifest no concern whether the woods will bear chestnuts this year or not, and finish his labor with every day, relinquishing all claim to the produce of his fields, and sacrificing in his mind not only his first but his last fruits also.

## THE VILLAGE

After hoeing, or perhaps reading and writing, in the forenoon, I usually bathed again in the pond, swimming across one of its coves for a stint, and washed the dust of labor from my person, or smoothed out the last wrinkle which study had made, and for the afternoon was absolutely free. Every day or two I strolled to the village to hear some of the gossip which is incessantly going on there, circulating either from mouth to mouth, or from newspaper to newspaper, and which, taken in homœopathic doses, was really as refreshing in its way as the rustle of leaves and the peeping of frogs. As I walked in the woods to see the birds and squirrels, so I walked in the village to see the men and boys; instead of the wind among the pines I heard the carts rattle. In one direction from my house there was a colony of muskrats in the river meadows; under the grove of elms and buttonwoods in the other horizon was a village of busy men, as curious to me as if they had been prairie dogs, each sitting at the mouth of its burrow, or running over to a neighbor's to gossip. I went there frequently to observe their habits. The village appeared to me a great news room; and on one side, to support it, as once at Redding & Company's on State Street, they kept nuts and raisins, or salt and meal and other groceries. Some have such a vast appetite for the former commodity, that is, the news, and such sound digestive organs, that they can sit forever in public avenues without stirring, and let it simmer and whisper through them like the Etesian winds, or as if inhaling ether, it only producing numbness and insensibility to pain,—otherwise it would often be painful to hear,—without affecting the consciousness. I hardly ever failed, when I rambled through the village, to see a row of such worthies, either sitting on a ladder sunning themselves, with their bodies inclined forward and their eyes glancing along the line this way and that, from time to time, with a voluptuous expression, or else leaning against a barn with their hands in their pockets, like caryatides, as if to prop it up. They, being commonly out of doors, heard whatever was in the wind. These are the coarsest mills, in which all gossip is first rudely digested or cracked up before it is emptied into finer and more delicate hoppers within doors. I observed that the vitals of the village were the grocery, the bar-room, the post-office, and the bank; and, as a necessary part of the machinery, they kept a bell, a big gun, and a fire-engine, at convenient places; and the houses were so arranged as to make the most of mankind, in lanes and fronting one another, so that every traveller had to run the gantlet, and every man, woman, and child might get a lick at him. Of course, those who were stationed nearest to the head of the line, where they could most see and be seen, and have the first blow at him, paid the highest price for their places; and the few straggling inhabitants in the outskirts, where long gaps in the line began to occur, and the traveller could get over walls or turn aside into cow paths, and so escape, paid a very slight ground or window tax. Signs were hung out on all sides to allure him; some to catch him by the appetite, as the tavern and victualling cellar; some by the fancy, as the dry goods store and the jeweller's; and others by the hair or the feet or the skirts, as the barber, the shoemaker, or the tailor. Besides, there was a still more terrible standing invitation to call at every one of these houses, and company expected about these times. For the most part I escaped wonderfully from these dangers, either by proceeding at once boldly and without deliberation to the goal, as is recommended to those who run the gantlet, or by keeping my thoughts on high things, like Orpheus, who, "loudly singing the praises of the gods to his lyre, drowned the voices of the Sirens, and kept out of danger." Sometimes I bolted suddenly, and nobody could tell my whereabouts, for I did not stand much about gracefulness, and never hesitated at a gap in a fence. I was even accustomed to make an irruption into some houses, where I was well entertained, and after learning the kernels and very last sieve-ful of news, what had subsided, the prospects of war and peace, and whether the world was likely to hold together much longer, I was let out through the rear avenues, and so escaped to the woods again.

It was very pleasant, when I staid late in town, to launch myself into the night, especially if it was dark and tempestuous, and set sail from some bright village parlor or lecture room, with a bag of rye or Indian meal upon my shoulder, for my snug harbor in the woods, having made all tight without and withdrawn under hatches with a merry crew of thoughts, leaving only my outer man at the helm, or even tying up the helm when it was plain sailing. I had many a genial thought by the cabin fire "as I sailed." I was never cast away nor distressed in any weather, though I encountered some severe storms. It is darker in the woods, even in common nights, than most suppose. I frequently had to look up at the opening between the trees above the path in order to learn my route, and, where there was no cart-path, to feel with my feet the faint track which I had worn, or steer by the known relation of particular trees which I felt with my hands, passing between two pines for instance, not more than eighteen inches apart, in the midst of the woods, invariably in the darkest night. Sometimes, after coming home thus late in a dark and muggy night, when my feet felt the path which my eyes could not see, dreaming and absent-minded all the way, until I was aroused by having to raise my hand to lift the latch, I have not been able to recall a single step of my walk, and I have thought that perhaps my body would find its way home if its master should forsake it, as the hand finds its way to the mouth without assistance. Several times, when a visitor chanced to stay into evening, and it proved a dark night, I was obliged to conduct him to the cart-path in the rear of the house, and then point out to him the direction he was to pursue, and in keeping which he was to be guided rather by his feet than his eyes. One very dark night I directed thus on their way two young men who had been fishing in the pond. They lived about a mile off through the woods, and were quite used to the route. A day or two after one of them told me that they wandered about the greater part of the night, close by their own premises, and did not get home till toward morning, by which time, as there had been several heavy showers in the mean while, and the leaves were very wet, they were drenched to their skins. I have heard of many going astray even in the village streets, when the darkness was so thick that you could cut it with a knife, as the saying is. Some who live in the outskirts, having come to town a-shopping in their wagons, have been obliged to put up for the night; and gentlemen and ladies making a call have gone half a mile out of their way, feeling the sidewalk only with their feet, and not knowing when they turned. It is a surprising and memorable, as well as valuable experience, to be lost in the woods any time. Often in a snow storm, even by day, one will come out upon a well-known road and yet find it impossible to tell which way leads to the village. Though he knows that he has travelled it a thousand times, he cannot recognize a feature in it, but it is as strange to him as if it were a road in Siberia. By night, of course, the perplexity is infinitely greater. In our most trivial walks, we are constantly, though unconsciously, steering like pilots by certain well-known beacons and headlands, and if we go beyond our usual course we still carry in our minds the bearing of some neighboring cape; and not till we are completely lost, or turned round, — for a man needs only to be turned round once with his eyes shut in this world to be lost, — do we appreciate the vastness and strangeness of Nature. Every man has to learn the points of compass again as often as he awakes, whether from sleep or any abstraction. Not till we are lost, in other words, not till we have lost the world, do we begin to find ourselves, and realize where we are and the infinite extent of our relations.

One afternoon, near the end of the first summer, when I went to the village to get a shoe from the cobbler's, I was seized and put into jail, because, as I have elsewhere related, I did not pay a tax to, or recognize the authority of, the state which buys and sells men, women, and children, like cattle at the door of its senate-house. I had gone down to the woods for other purposes. But, wherever a man goes, men will pursue and paw him with their dirty institutions, and, if they can, constrain him to belong to their desperate odd-fellow society. It is true, I might have resisted forcibly with more or less effect, might have run "amok" against society; but I preferred that society should run "amok" against me, it being the desperate party. However, I was released the next day, obtained my mended shoe, and returned to the woods in season to get my dinner of huckleberries on Fair-Haven Hill. I was never molested by any person but those who represented the state. I had no lock nor bolt but for the desk which held my papers, not even a nail to put over my latch or windows. I never fastened my door night or day, though I was to be absent several days; not even when the next fall I spent a fortnight in the woods of Maine. And yet my house was more respected than if it had been surrounded by a file of soldiers. The tired rambler could rest and warm himself by my fire, the literary amuse himself with the few books on my table, or the curious, by opening my closet door, see what was left of my dinner, and what prospect I had of a supper. Yet, though many people of every class came this way to the pond, I suffered no serious inconvenience from these sources, and I never missed any thing but one small book, a volume of Homer, which perhaps was improperly gilded, and this I trust a soldier of our camp has found by this time. I am convinced, that if all men were to live as simply as I then did, thieving and robbery would be unknown. These take place only in communities where some have got more than is sufficient while others have not enough. The Pope's Homers would soon get properly distributed. —

> "Nec bella fuerunt,
> Faginus astabat dum scyphus ante dapes."
> "Nor wars did men molest,
> When only beechen bowls were in request."

"You who govern public affairs, what need have you to employ punishments? Love virtue, and the people will be virtuous. The virtues of a superior man are like the wind; the virtues of a common man are like the grass; the grass, when the wind passes over it, bends."

# FREDERICK DOUGLASS
## (1817–1895)

"Behold the practical operation of this internal slave trade—the American slave trade sustained by American politics and American religion! Here you will see men and women reared like swine for the market. You know what is a swine drover? I will show you a man-drover. . . . You will see one of these human-flesh-jobbers, armed with pistol, whip, and bowie-knife, driving a company of a hundred men, women, and children, from the Potomac to the slave market at New Orleans. . . ."

This fragment from a Fredrick Douglass speech—delivered on July 5, 1852, in Rochester, New York—is not atypical. Douglass often spoke like one whose heart was touched with fire. He spent his first two decades in slavery. Upon escaping to freedom in 1838, he began to lecture on the abolitionist circuit, spreading word of slavery's inherent moral bankruptcy. Upon publishing his first autobiography *(The Narrative of the Life of Frederick Douglass, an American Slave, Written by Himself)* in 1845, Douglass saw his personal liberty as endangered because he identified the owner from which he had fled. He traveled undercover by boat to England, where a group of abolitionists arranged to provide him with the money he required to buy his freedom.

*My Bondage and My Freedom*, a revised autobiography, appeared in 1855. A final version of his life came out in 1881 and was expanded in 1892.

## FROM *My Bondage and My Freedom*

### GRADUAL INITIATION INTO THE MYSTERIES OF SLAVERY

Although my old master—Capt. Anthony—gave me at first, (as the reader will have already seen,) very little attention, and although that little was of a remarkably mild and gentle description, a few months only were sufficient to convince me that mildness and gentleness were not the prevailing or governing traits of his character. These excellent qualities were displayed only occasionally. He could, when it suited him, appear to be literally insensible to the claims of humanity, when appealed to by the helpless against an aggressor, and he could himself commit outrages, deep, dark and nameless. Yet he was not by nature worse than other men. Had he been brought up in a free state, surrounded by the just restraints of free society—restraints which are necessary to the freedom of all its members, alike and equally—Capt. Anthony might have been as humane a man, and every way as respectable, as many who now oppose the slave system; certainly as humane and respectable as are members of society generally. The slaveholder, as well as the slave, is the victim of the slave system. A man's character greatly takes its hue and shape from the form and color of things about him. Under the whole heavens there is no relation more unfavorable to the development of honorable character, than that sustained by the slaveholder to the slave. Reason is imprisoned here, and passions run wild. Like the fires of the prairie, once lighted, they are at the mercy of every wind, and must burn, till they have consumed all that is combustible within their remorseless grasp. Capt. Anthony could be kind, and, at times, he even showed an affectionate disposition. Could the reader have seen him gently leading me by the hand—as he sometimes did—patting me on the head, speaking to me in soft, caressing tones and calling me his "little Indian boy," he would have deemed him a kind old man, and, really, almost fatherly. But the pleasant moods of a slaveholder are remarkably brittle; they are easily snapped; they neither come often, nor remain long. His temper is subjected to perpetual trials; but, since these trials are never borne patiently, they add nothing to his natural stock of patience.

Old master very early impressed me with the idea that he was an unhappy man. Even to my child's eye, he wore a troubled, and at times, a haggard aspect. His strange movements excited my curiosity, and awakened my compassion. He seldom walked alone without muttering to himself; and he occasionally stormed about, as if defying an army of invisible foes. "He would do this, that, and the other; he'd be d——d if he did not,"—was the usual form of his threats. Most of his leisure was spent in walking, cursing and gesticulating, like one possessed by a demon. Most evidently, he was a wretched man, at war with his own soul, and with all the world around him. To be overheard by the children, disturbed him very little. He made no more of *our* presence, than of that of the ducks and geese which he met on the green. He little thought that the little black urchins around him, could see, through those vocal crevices, the very secrets of his heart. Slaveholders ever underrate the intelligence with which they have to grapple. I really understood the old man's mutterings, attitudes and gestures, about as well as he did himself. But slaveholders never encourage that kind of communication, with the slaves, by which they might learn to measure the depths of his knowledge. Ignorance is a high virtue in a human chattel; and as the master studies to keep the slave ignorant, the slave is cunning enough to make the master think he succeeds. The slave fully appreciates the saying, "where ignorance is bliss, 'tis folly to be wise." When old master's gestures were violent, ending with a threatening shake of the head, and a sharp snap of his middle finger and thumb, I deemed it wise to keep at a respectable distance from him; for, at such times, trifling faults stood, in his eyes, as momentous offenses; and, having both the power and the disposition, the victim had only to be near him to catch the punishment, deserved or undeserved.

One of the first circumstances that opened my eyes to the cruelty and wickedness of slavery, and the heartlessness of my old master, was the refusal of the latter to interpose his authority, to protect and shield a young woman, who had been most cruelly abused and beaten by his overseer in Tuckahoe. This overseer—a Mr. Plummer—was a man like most of his class, little better than a human brute; and, in addition to his general profligacy and repulsive coarseness, the creature was a miserable drunkard. He was, probably, employed by my old master, less on account of the excellence of his services, than for the cheap rate at which they could be obtained. He was not fit to have the management of a drove of mules. In a fit of drunken madness, he committed the outrage which brought the young woman in question down to my old master's for protection. This young woman was the daughter of Milly, an aunt of mine. The poor girl, on arriving at our house, presented a pitiable appearance. She had left in haste, and without preparation; and, probably, without the knowledge of Mr. Plummer. She had traveled twelve miles, bare-footed, bare-necked and bare-headed. Her neck and shoulders were covered with scars, newly made; and, not content with marring her neck and shoulders, with the cowhide, the cowardly brute had dealt her a blow on the head with a hickory club, which cut a horrible gash, and left her face literally covered with blood. In this condition, the poor young woman came down, to implore protection at the hands of my old master. I expected to see him boil over with rage at the revolting deed, and to hear him fill the air with curses upon the brutal Plummer; but I was disappointed. He sternly told her, in an angry tone, he "believed she deserved every bit of it," and, if she did not go home instantly, he would himself take the remaining skin from her neck and back. Thus was the poor girl compelled to return, without redress, and perhaps to receive an additional flogging for daring to appeal to old master against the overseer.

Old master seemed furious at the thought of being troubled by such complaints. I did not, at that time, understand the philosophy of his treatment of my cousin. It was stern, unnatural, violent. Had the man no bowels of compassion? Was he dead to all sense of humanity? No. I think

I now understand it. This treatment is a part of the system, rather than a part of the man. Were slaveholders to listen to complaints of this sort against the overseers, the luxury of owning large numbers of slaves, would be impossible. It would do away with the office of overseer, entirely; or, in other words, it would convert the master himself into an overseer. It would occasion great loss of time and labor, leaving the overseer in fetters, and without the necessary power to secure obedience to his orders. A privilege so dangerous as that of appeal, is, therefore, strictly prohibited; and any one exercising it, runs a fearful hazard. Nevertheless, when a slave has nerve enough to exercise it, and boldly approaches his master, with a well-founded complaint against an overseer, though he may be repulsed, and may even have that of which he complains repeated at the time, and, though he may be beaten by his master, as well as by the overseer, for his temerity, in the end the policy of complaining is, generally, vindicated by the relaxed rigor of the overseer's treatment. The latter becomes more careful, and less disposed to use the lash upon such slaves thereafter. It is with this final result in view, rather than with any expectation of immediate good, that the outraged slave is induced to meet his master with a complaint. The overseer very naturally dislikes to have the ear of the master disturbed by complaints; and, either upon this consideration, or upon advice and warning privately given him by his employers, he generally modifies the rigor of his rule, after an outbreak of the kind to which I have been referring.

Howsoever the slaveholder may allow himself to act toward his slave, and, whatever cruelty he may deem it wise, for example's sake, or for the gratification of his humor, to inflict, he cannot, in the absence of all provocation, look with pleasure upon the bleeding wounds of a defenseless slave-woman. When he drives her from his presence without redress, or the hope of redress, he acts, generally, from motives of policy, rather than from a hardened nature, or from innate brutality. Yet, let but his own temper be stirred, his own passions get loose, and the slave-owner will go *far beyond* the overseer in cruelty. He will convince the slave that his wrath is far more terrible and boundless, and vastly more to be dreaded, than that of the underling overseer. What may have been mechanically and heartlessly done by the overseer, is now done with a will. The man who now wields the lash is irresponsible. He may, if he pleases, cripple or kill, without fear of consequences; except in so far as it may concern profit or loss. To a man of violent temper—as my old master was—this was but a very slender and inefficient restraint. I have seen him in a tempest of passion, such as I have just described—a passion into which entered all the bitter ingredients of pride, hatred, envy, jealousy, and the thirst for revenge.

The circumstances which I am about to narrate, and which gave rise to this fearful tempest of passion, are not singular nor isolated in slave life, but are common in every slaveholding community in which I have lived. They are incidental to the relation of master and slave, and exist in all sections of slaveholding countries.

The reader will have noticed that, in enumerating the names of the slaves who lived with my old master, *Esther* is mentioned. This was a young woman who possessed that which is ever a curse to the slave-girl; namely,—personal beauty. She was tall, well formed, and made a fine appearance. The daughters of Col. Lloyd could scarcely surpass her in personal charms. Esther was courted by Ned Roberts, and he was as fine looking a young man, as she was a woman. He was the son of a favorite slave of Col. Lloyd. Some slaveholders would have been glad to promote the marriage of two such persons; but, for some reason or other, my old master took it upon him to break up the growing intimacy between Esther and Edward. He strictly ordered her to quit the company of said Roberts, telling her that he would punish her severely if he ever found her again in Edward's company. This unnatural and heartless order was, of course, broken. A woman's love is not to be annihilated by the peremptory command of any one, whose breath is in his nostrils. It was impossible to keep Edward and Esther apart. Meet they would, and meet they did. Had old master been a man of honor and purity, his motives, in this matter, might have been viewed more favorably. As it was, his motives were as abhorrent, as his methods were foolish and contemptible. It was too evident that he was not concerned for the girl's welfare. It is one of the damning characteristics of the slave system, that it robs its victims of every earthly incentive to a holy life. The fear of God, and the hope of heaven, are found sufficient to sustain many slave-women, amidst the snares and dangers of their strange lot; but, this side of God and heaven, a slave-woman is at the mercy of the power, caprice and passion of her owner. Slavery provides no means for the honorable continuance of the race. Marriage—as imposing obligations on the parties to it—has no existence here, except in such hearts as are purer and higher than the standard morality around them. It is one of the consolations of my life, that I know of many honorable instances of persons who maintained their honor, where all around was corrupt.

Esther was evidently much attached to Edward, and abhorred—as she had reason to do—the tyrannical and base behavior of old master. Edward was young, and fine looking, and he loved and courted her. He might have been her husband, in the high sense just alluded to; but WHO and *what* was this old master? His attentions were plainly brutal and selfish, and it was as natural that Esther should loathe him, as that she should love Edward. Abhorred and circumvented as he was, old master, having the power, very easily took revenge. I happened to see this exhibition of his rage and cruelty toward Esther. The time selected was singular. It was early in the morning, when all besides was still, and before any of the family, in the house or kitchen, had left their beds. I saw but few of the shocking preliminaries, for the cruel work had begun before I awoke. I was probably awakened by the shrieks and piteous cries of poor Esther. My sleeping place was on the floor of a little, rough closet, which opened into the kitchen; and through the cracks of its unplaned boards, I could distinctly see and hear what was going on, without being seen by old master. Esther's wrists were firmly tied, and the twisted rope was fastened to a strong staple in a heavy wooden joist above, near the fireplace. Here she stood, on a bench, her arms tightly drawn over her breast. Her back and shoulders were bare to the waist. Behind her stood old master, with cowskin in hand, preparing his barbarous work with all manner of harsh, coarse, and tantalizing epithets. The screams of his victim were most piercing. He was cruelly deliberate, and protracted the torture, as one who was delighted with the scene. Again and again he drew the hateful whip through his hand, adjusting it with a view of dealing the most pain-giving blow. Poor Esther had never yet been severely whipped, and her shoulders were plump and tender. Each blow, vigorously laid on, brought screams as well as blood. *"Have mercy; Oh! have mercy"* she cried; *"I won't do so no more"*; but her piercing cries seemed only to increase his fury. His answers to them are too coarse and blasphemous to be produced here. The whole scene, with all its attendants, was revolting and shocking, to the last degree; and when the motives of this brutal castigation are considered, language has no power to convey a just sense of its awful criminality. After laying on some thirty or forty stripes, old master untied his suffering victim, and let her get down. She could scarcely stand, when untied. From my heart I pitied her, and—child though I was—the outrage kindled in me a feeling far from peaceful; but I was hushed, terrified, stunned, and could do nothing, and the fate of Esther might be mine next. The scene here described was often repeated in the case of poor Esther, and her life, as I knew it, was one of wretchedness.

## TREATMENT OF SLAVES ON LLOYD'S PLANTATION

The heart-rending incidents, related in the foregoing chapter, led me, thus early, to inquire into the nature and history of slavery. *Why am I a slave? Why are some people slaves, and others masters? Was there ever a time when this was not so? How did the relation commence?* These were the perplexing questions which began now to claim my thoughts, and to exercise the weak powers of my mind, for I was still but a child, and knew less than children of the same age in the free states. As my questions concerning these things were only put to children a little older, and little better informed than myself, I was not rapid in reaching a solid footing. By some means I learned from these inquiries, that "*God, up in the sky*," made every body; and that he made *white* people to be masters and mistresses, and *black* people to be slaves. This did not satisfy me, nor lessen my interest in the subject. I was told, too, that God was good, and that He knew what was best for me, and best for everybody. This was less satisfactory than the first statement; because it came, point blank, against all my notions of goodness. It was not good to let old master cut the flesh off Esther, and make her cry so. Besides, how did people know that God made black people to be slaves? Did they go up in the sky and learn it? or, did He come down and tell them so? All was dark here. It was some relief to my hard notions of the goodness of God, that, although he made white men to be slaveholders, he did not make them to be *bad* slaveholders, and that, in due time, he would punish the bad slaveholders; that he would, when they died, send them to the bad place, where they would be "burnt up." Nevertheless, I could not reconcile the relation of slavery with my crude notions of goodness.

Then, too, I found that there were puzzling exceptions to this theory of slavery on both sides, and in the middle. I knew of blacks who were *not* slaves; I knew of whites who were *not* slaveholders; and I knew of persons who were *nearly* white, who were slaves. *Color,* therefore, was a very unsatisfactory basis for slavery.

Once, however, engaged in the inquiry, I was not very long in finding out the true solution of the matter. It was not *color,* but *crime,* not *God,* but *man,* that afforded the true explanation of the existence of slavery; nor was I long in finding out another important truth, viz: what man can make, man can unmake. The appalling darkness faded away, and I was master of the subject. There were slaves here, direct from Guinea; and there were many who could say that their fathers and mothers were stolen from Africa—forced from their homes, and compelled to serve as slaves. This, to me, was knowledge; but it was a kind of knowledge which filled me with a burning hatred of slavery, increased my suffering, and left me without the means of breaking away from my bondage. Yet it was knowledge quite worth possessing. I could not have been more than seven or eight years old, when I began to make this subject my study. It was with me in the woods and fields; along the shore of the river, and wherever my boyish wanderings led me; and though I was, at that time, quite ignorant of the existence of the free states, I distinctly remember being, *even then,* most strongly impressed with the idea of being a freeman some day. This cheering assurance was an inborn dream of my human nature—a constant menace to slavery—and one which all the powers of slavery were unable to silence or extinguish.

Up to the time of the brutal flogging of my Aunt Esther—for she was my own aunt—and the horrid plight in which I had seen my cousin from Tuckahoe, who had been so badly beaten by the cruel Mr. Plummer, my attention had not been called, especially, to the gross features of slavery. I had, of course, heard of whippings, and of savage *rencontres* between overseers and slaves, but I had always been out of the way at the times and places of their occurrence. My plays and sports, most of the time, took me from the corn and tobacco fields, where the great body of the hands were at work, and where scenes of cruelty were enacted and witnessed. But, after the whipping of Aunt Esther, I saw many cases of the same shocking nature, not only in my master's house, but on Col. Lloyd's plantation. One of the first which I saw, and which greatly agitated me, was the whipping of a woman belonging to Col. Lloyd, named Nelly. The offense alleged against Nelly, was one of the commonest and most indefinite in the whole catalogue of offenses usually laid to the charge of slaves, viz: "impudence." This may mean almost anything, or nothing at all, just according to the caprice of the master overseer, at the moment. But, whatever it is, or is not, if it gets the name of "impudence," the party charged with it is sure of a flogging. This offense may be committed in various ways; in the tone of an answer; in answering at all; in not answering; in the expression of countenance; in the motion of the head; in the gait, manner and bearing of the slave. In the case under consideration, I can easily believe that, according to all slaveholding standards, here was a genuine instance of impudence. In Nelly there were all the necessary conditions for committing the offense. She was a bright mulatto, the recognized wife of a favorite "hand" on board Col. Lloyd's sloop, and the mother of five sprightly children. She was a vigorous and spirited woman, and one of the most likely, on the plantation, to be guilty of impudence. My attention was called to the scene, by the noise, curses and screams that proceeded from it; and, on going a little in that direction, I came upon the parties engaged in the skirmish. Mr. Sevier, the overseer, had hold of Nelly, when I caught sight of them; he was endeavoring to drag her toward a tree, which endeavor Nelly was sternly resisting; but to no purpose, except to retard the progress of the overseer's plans. Nelly—as I have said—was the mother of five children; three of them were present, and though quite small, (from seven to ten years old, I should think,) they gallantly came to their mother's defense, and gave the overseer an excellent pelting with stones. One of the little fellows ran up, seized the overseer by the leg and bit him; but the monster was too busily engaged with Nelly, to pay any attention to the assaults of the children. There were numerous bloody marks on Mr. Sevier's face, when I first saw him, and they increased as the struggle went on. The imprints of Nelly's fingers were visible, and I was glad to see them. Amidst the wild

screams of the children—*"Let my mammy go"*—*"let my mammy go"*—
there escaped, from between the teeth of the bullet-headed overseer, a
few bitter curses, mingled with threats, that "he would teach the d——d
b——h how to give a white man impudence." There is no doubt that
Nelly felt herself superior, in some respects, to the slaves around her. She
was a wife and a mother; her husband was a valued and favorite slave. Besides, he was one of the first hands on board of the sloop, and the sloop
hands—since they had to represent the plantation abroad—were generally treated tenderly. The overseer never was allowed to whip Harry; why
then should he be allowed to whip Harry's wife? Thoughts of this kind,
no doubt, influenced her; but, for whatever reason, she nobly resisted,
and, unlike most of the slaves, seemed determined to make her whipping
cost Mr. Sevier as much as possible. The blood on his (and her) face, at-
tested her skill, as well as her courage and dexterity in using her nails.
Maddened by her resistance, I expected to see Mr. Sevier level her to the
ground by a stunning blow; but no; like a savage bull-dog—which he resembled both in temper and appearance—he maintained his grip, and
steadily dragged his victim toward the tree, disregarding alike her blows,
and the cries of the children for their mother's release. He would, doubtless, have knocked her down with his hickory stick, but that such act
might have cost him his place. It is often deemed advisable to knock a
*man* slave down, in order to tie him, but it is considered cowardly and in-
excusable, in an overseer, thus to deal with a *woman*. He is expected to
tie her up, and to give her what is called, in southern parlance, a "genteel flogging," without any very great outlay of strength or skill. I watched,
with palpitating interest, the course of the preliminary struggle, and was
saddened by every new advantage gained over her by the ruffian. There
were times when she seemed likely to get the better of the brute, but he
finally overpowered her, and succeeded in getting his rope around her
arms, and in firmly tying her to the tree, at which he had been aiming.
This done, and Nelly was at the mercy of his merciless lash; and now,
what followed, I have no heart to describe. The cowardly creature made
good his every threat; and wielded the lash with all the hot zest of furious revenge. The cries of the woman, while undergoing the terrible in-
fliction, were mingled with those of the children, sounds which I hope
the reader may never be called upon to hear. When Nelly was tied, her
back was covered with blood. The red stripes were all over her shoulders.
She was whipped—severely whipped; but she was not subdued, for she
continued to denounce the overseer, and to call him every vile name. He
had bruised her flesh, but had left her invincible spirit undaunted. Such
floggings are seldom repeated by the same overseer. They prefer to whip
those who are most easily whipped. The old doctrine that submission is
the best cure for outrage and wrong, does not hold good on the slave

plantation. He is whipped oftenest, who is whipped easiest; and that slave who has the courage to stand up for himself against the overseer, although he may have many hard stripes at the first, becomes, in the end, a freeman, even though he sustain the formal relation of a slave. "You can shoot me but you can't whip me," said a slave to Rigby Hopkins; and the result was that he was neither whipped nor shot. If the latter had been his fate, it would have been less deplorable than the living and lingering death to which cowardly and slavish souls are subjected. I do not know that Mr. Sevier ever undertook to whip Nelly again. He probably never did, for it was not long after his attempt to subdue her, that he was taken sick, and died. The wretched man died as he had lived, unrepentant; and it was said—with how much truth I know not—that in the very last hours of his life, his ruling passion showed itself, and that when wrestling with death, he was uttering horrid oaths, and flourishing the cowskin, as though he was tearing the flesh off some helpless slave. One thing is certain, that when he was in health, it was enough to chill the blood, and to stiffen the hair of an ordinary man, to hear Mr. Sevier talk. Nature, or his cruel habits, had given to his face an expression of unusual savageness, even for a slave-driver. Tobacco and rage had worn his teeth short, and nearly every sentence that escaped their compressed grating, was commenced or concluded with some outburst of profanity. His presence made the field alike the field of blood, and of blasphemy. Hated for his cruelty, despised for his cowardice, his death was deplored by no one outside his own house—if indeed it was deplored there; it was regarded by the slaves as a merciful interposition of Providence. Never went there a man to the grave loaded with heavier curses. Mr. Sevier's place was promptly taken by a Mr. Hopkins, and the change was quite a relief, he being a very different man. He was, in all respects, a better man than his predecessor; as good as any man can be, and yet be an overseer. His course was characterized by no extraordinary cruelty; and when he whipped a slave, as he sometimes did, he seemed to take no especial pleasure in it, but, on the contrary, acted as though he felt it to be a mean business. Mr. Hopkins stayed but a short time; his place—much to the regret of the slaves generally—was taken by a Mr. Gore, of whom more will be said hereafter. It is enough, for the present, to say, that he was no improvement on Mr. Sevier, except that he was less noisy and less profane.

I have already referred to the business-like aspect of Col. Lloyd's plantation. This business-like appearance was much increased on the two days at the end of each month, when the slaves from the different farms came to get their monthly allowance of meal and meat. These were gala days for the slaves, and there was much rivalry among them as to *who* should be elected to go up to the great house farm for the allowance, and, indeed, to attend to any business at this, (for them,) the capital. The beauty and grandeur of the place, its numerous slave population, and the fact that Harry, Peter and Jake—the sailors of the sloop—almost always kept, privately, little trinkets which they bought at Baltimore, to sell, made it a privilege to come to the great house farm. Being selected, too, for this office, was deemed a high honor. It was taken as a proof of confidence and favor; but, probably, the chief motive of the competitors for the place, was, a desire to break the dull monotony of the field, and to get beyond the overseer's eye and lash. Once on the road with an ox team, and seated on the tongue of his cart, with no overseer to look after him, the slave was comparatively free; and, if thoughtful, he had time to think. Slaves are generally expected to sing as well as to work. A silent slave is not liked by masters or overseers. "*Make a noise,*" "*make a noise,*" and "*bear a hand,*" are the words usually addressed to the slaves when there is silence amongst them. This may account for the almost constant singing heard in the southern states. There was, generally, more or less singing among the teamsters, as it was one means of letting the overseer know where they were, and that they were moving on with the work. But, on allowance day, those who visited the great house farm were peculiarly excited and noisy. While on their way, they would make the dense old woods for miles around, reverberate with their wild notes. These were not always merry because they were wild. On the contrary, they were mostly of a plaintive cast, and told a tale of grief and sorrow. In the most boisterous outbursts of rapturous sentiment, there was ever a tinge of deep melancholy. I hade never heard any songs like those anywhere since I left slavery, except when in Ireland. There I heard the same *wailing notes,* and was much affected by them. It was during the famine of 1845–6. In all the songs of the slaves, there was ever some expression in praise of the great house farm; something which would flatter the pride of the owner, and, possibly, draw a favorable glance from him.

> "I am going away to the great house farm,
> O yea! O yea! O yea!
> My old master is a good old master,
> Oh yea! O yea! O yea!"

This they would sing, with other words of their own improvising—jargon to others, but full of meaning to themselves. I have sometimes thought, that the mere hearing of those songs would do more to impress truly spiritual-minded men and women with the soul-crushing and death-dealing character of slavery, than the reading of whole volumes of its mere physical cruelties. They speak to the heart and to the soul of the thoughtful. I cannot better express my sense of them now, than ten years ago, when, in sketching my life, I thus spoke of this feature of my plantation experience:

> "I did not, when a slave, understand the deep meanings of those rude, and apparently incoherent songs. I was myself within the circle, so that I neither saw nor heard as those without might see and hear. They told a tale which was then altogether beyond my feeble comprehension; they were tones, loud, long and deep, breathing the prayer and complaint of souls boiling over with the bitterest anguish. Every tone was a testimony against slavery, and a prayer to God for deliverance from chains. The hearing of those wild notes always depressed my spirits, and filled my heart with ineffable sadness. The mere recurrence, even now, afflicts my spirit, and while I am writing these lines, my tears are falling. To those songs I trace my first glimmering conceptions of the dehumanizing character of slavery. I can never get rid of that conception. Those songs still follow me, to deepen my hatred of slavery, and quicken my sympathies for my brethren in bonds. If any one wishes to be impressed with a sense of the soul-killing power of slavery, let him go to Col. Lloyd's plantation, and on allowance day, place himself in the deep, pine woods, and there let him, in silence, thoughtfully analyze the sounds that shall pass through the chambers of his soul, and if he is not thus impressed, it will only be because 'there is no flesh in his obdurate heart.' "*

The remark is not unfrequently made, that slaves are the most contented and happy laborers in the world. They dance and sing, and make all manner of joyful noises—so they do; but it is a great mistake to suppose them happy because they sing. The songs of the slave represent the sorrows, rather than the joys, of his heart; and he is relieved by them, only as an aching heart is relieved by its tears. Such is the constitution of the human mind, that, when pressed to extremes, it often avails itself of the most opposite methods. Extremes meet in mind as in matter. When the slaves on board of the "Pearl" were overtaken, arrested, and carried to prison—their hopes for freedom blasted—as they marched in chains they sang, and found (as Emily Edmunson tells us) a melancholy relief in singing.† The singing of a man cast away on a desolate island, might be as appropriately considered an evidence of his contentment and happiness, as the singing of a slave. Sorrow and desolation have their songs,

---

*From "The Time-Piece," book 2, line 8, in William Cowper, *The Task* (1785): "There is no flesh in man's obdurate heart."

†On April 15, 1848, seventy-seven slaves from Washington, D.C., hid themselves aboard the schooner *Pearl* and set sail for freedom in the North. They were apprehended the next day near the mouth of the Potomac River. Among the fugitives were two mulatto teenagers, Emily and Mary Edmondson, the purchase of whose freedom became a cause célèbre in Boston. After their liberation, Emily told her story to Harriet Beecher Stowe, who recorded the details of their ordeal, including a description of the singing of the *Pearl* fugitives as they were marched in a coffle, in her *Key to Uncle Tom's Cabin* (1853).

as well as joy and peace. Slaves sing more to *make* themselves happy, than to express their happiness.

It is the boast of slaveholders, that their slaves enjoy more of the physical comforts of life than the peasantry of any country in the world. My experience contradicts this. The men and the women slaves on Col. Lloyd's farm, received, as their monthly allowance of food, eight pounds of pickled pork, or their equivalent in fish. The pork was often tainted, and the fish was of the poorest quality—herrings, which would bring very little if offered for sale in any northern market. With their pork or fish, they had one bushel of Indian meal—unbolted—of which quite fifteen per cent was fit only to feed pigs. With this, one pint of salt was given; and this was the entire monthly allowance of a full grown slave, working constantly in the open field, from morning until night, every day in the month except Sunday, and living on a fraction more than a quarter of a pound of meat per day, and less than a peck of corn-meal per week. There is no kind of work that a man can do which requires a better supply of food to prevent physical exhaustion, than the fieldwork of a slave. So much for the slave's allowance of food; now for his raiment. The yearly allowance of clothing for the slaves on this plantation, consisted of two tow-linen shirts—such linen as the coarsest crash towels are made of; one pair of trowsers of the same material, for summer, and a pair of trowsers and a jacket of woolen, most slazily put together, for winter; one pair of yarn stockings, and one pair of shoes of the coarsest description. The slave's entire apparel could not have cost more than eight dollars per year. The allowance of food and clothing for the little children, was committed to their mothers, or to the older slave-women having the care of them. Children who were unable to work in the field, had neither shoes, stockings, jackets nor trowsers given them. Their clothing consisted of two coarse tow-linen shirts—already described—per year; and when these failed them, as they often did, they went naked until the next allowance day. Flocks of little children from five to ten years old, might be seen on Col. Lloyd's plantation, as destitute of clothing as any little heathen on the west coast of Africa; and this, not merely during the summer months, but during the frosty weather of March. The little girls were no better off than the boys; all were nearly in a state of nudity.

As to beds to sleep on, they were known to none of the field hands; nothing but a coarse blanket—not so good as those used in the north to cover horses—was given them, and this only to the men and women. The children stuck themselves in holes and corners, about the quarters; often in the corner of the huge chimneys, with their feet in the ashes to keep them warm. The want of beds, however, was not considered a very great privation. Time to sleep was of far greater importance, for, when the day's work is done, most of the slaves have their washing, mending and cooking to do; and, having few or none of the ordinary facilities for doing such things, very many of their sleeping hours are consumed in necessary preparations for the duties of the coming day.

The sleeping apartments—if they may be called such—have little regard to comfort or decency. Old and young, male and female, married and single, drop down upon the common clay floor, each covering up with his or her blanket,—the only protection they have from cold or exposure. The night, however, is shortened at both ends. The slaves work often as long as they can see, and are late in cooking and mending for the coming day; and, at the first gray streak of morning, they are summoned to the field by the driver's horn.

More slaves are whipped for oversleeping than for any other fault. Neither age nor sex finds any favor. The overseer stands at the quarter door, armed with stick and cowskin, ready to whip any who may be a few minutes behind time. When the horn is blown, there is a rush for the door, and the hindermost one is sure to get a blow from the overseer. Young mothers who worked in the field, were allowed an hour, about ten o'clock in the morning, to go home to nurse their children. Sometimes they were compelled to take their children with them, and to leave them in the corner of the fences, to prevent loss of time in nursing them. The overseer generally rides about the field on horseback. A cowskin and a hickory stick are his constant companions. The cowskin is a kind of whip seldom seen in the northern states. It is made entirely of untanned, but dried, ox hide, and is about as hard as a piece of well-seasoned live oak. It is made of various sizes, but the usual length is about three feet. The part held in the hand is nearly an inch in thickness; and, from the extreme end of the butt or handle, the cowskin tapers its whole length to a point. This makes it quite elastic and springy. A blow with it, on the hardest back, will gash the flesh, and make the blood start. Cowskins are painted red, blue and green, and are the favorite slave whip. I think this whip worse than the "cat-o'-nine-tails." It condenses the whole strength of the arm to a single point, and comes with a spring that makes the air whistle. It is a terrible instrument, and is so handy, that the overseer can always have it on his person, and ready for use. The temptation to use it is ever strong; and an overseer can, if disposed, always have cause for using it. With him, it is literally a word and a blow, and, in most cases, the blow comes first. As a general rule, slaves do not come to the quarters for either breakfast or dinner, but take their "ash cake" with them, and eat it in the field. This was so on the home plantation; probably, because the distance from the quarter to the field, was sometimes two, and even three miles.

The dinner of the slaves consisted of a huge piece of ash cake, and a small piece of pork, or two salt herrings. Not having ovens, nor any suitable cooking utensils, the slaves mixed their meal with a little water, to such thickness that a spoon would stand erect in it; and, after the wood had burned away to coals and ashes, they would place the dough between oak leaves and lay it carefully in the ashes, completely covering it; hence, the bread is called ash cake. The surface of this peculiar bread is covered with ashes, to the depth of a sixteenth part of an inch, and the ashes, certainly, do not make it very grateful to the teeth, nor render it very palatable. The bran, or coarse part of the meal, is baked with the fine, and bright scales run through the bread. This bread, with its ashes and bran, would disgust and choke a northern man, but it is quite liked by the slaves. They eat it with avidity, and are more concerned about the quantity than about the quality. They are far too scantily provided for, and are worked too steadily, to be much concerned for the quality of their food. The few minutes allowed them at dinner time, after partaking of their coarse repast, are variously spent. Some lie down on the "turning row," and go to sleep; others draw together, and talk; and others are at work with needle and thread, mending their tattered garments. Sometimes you may hear a wild, hoarse laugh arise from a circle, and often a song. Soon, however, the overseer comes dashing through the field. *"Tumble up! Tumble up,* and to *work, work,"* is the cry; and, now, from twelve o'-clock (mid-day) till dark, the human cattle are in motion, wielding their clumsy hoes; hurried on by no hope of reward, no sense of gratitude, no love of children, no prospect of bettering their condition; nothing, save the dread and terror of the slave-driver's lash. So goes one day, and so comes and goes another.

But, let us now leave the rough usage of the field, where vulgar coarseness and brutal cruelty spread themselves and flourish, rank as weeds in the tropics; where a vile wretch, in the shape of a man, rides, walks, or struts about, dealing blows, and leaving gashes on broken-spirited men and helpless women, for thirty dollars per month—a business so horrible, hardening, and disgraceful, that, rather than engage in it, a decent man would blow his own brains out—and let the reader view with me the equally wicked, but less repulsive aspects of slave life; where pride and pomp roll luxuriously at ease; where the toil of a thousand men supports a single family in easy idleness and sin. This is the great house; it is the home of the LLOYDS! Some idea of its splendor has already been given—and, it is here that we shall find that height of luxury which is the opposite of that depth of poverty and physical wretchedness that we have just now been contemplating. But, there is this difference in the two extremes; viz: that in the case of the slave, the miseries and hardships of his lot are imposed by others, and, in the master's case, they are imposed by himself. The slave is a subject, subjected by others; the slaveholder is a subject, but he is the author of his own subjection. There is more truth in the saying, that slavery is a greater evil to the master than to the slave, than many, who utter it, suppose. The self-executing laws of eternal justice follow close on the heels of the evil-doer here, as well as elsewhere; making escape from all its penalties impossible. But, let others philosophize; it is my province here to relate and describe; only allowing myself a word or two, occasionally, to assist the reader in the proper understanding of the facts narrated.

# WALT WHITMAN
## (1819–1892)

Scented herbage of my breast,
Leaves from you I glean, I write, to be perused best afterwards,
Tomb-leaves, body-leaves growing up above me above death,
Perennial roots, tall leaves, O the winter shall not freeze you,
    delicate leaves,
Every year you shall bloom again. . . .

— Walt Whitman, *Scented Herbage of My Breast*

Whitman's career as a poet and prose writer began late in his life; he self-published the first edition of *Leaves of Grass* when he was thirty-six years old. This seminal volume of American poetry met with critical disdain and was a financial failure. Whitman did, however, send one copy to Ralph Waldo Emerson, who replied, "I find it the most extraordinary piece of wit and wisdom that America has yet contributed. I am very happy in reading it, as great power makes us happy."

He lived as a vagabond for much of his early life, sleeping in flophouses and doing editing work for newspapers in the New York area. He was fired from several papers for openly expressing his views regarding sexuality, slavery, and abortion. He was a vocal lover of both men and women, and one who praised the human body in all of its forms.

Whitman's writing was almost exclusively autobiographical. His famous *Song of Myself* evoked his personality with great care. Much of his prose focused on his experiences as a nurse in the Civil War, where he cared for the wounded and the dying. *Specimen Days in America* (1882), which covers these events, is drawn from his diary entries for the last three years of the war—a war whose brutality shocked him horribly. Nevertheless, his belief in the Union cause held firm, and he hoped that democractic good will would triumph over the obvious evils of war.

## FROM *Specimen Days in America*

### DOWN AT THE FRONT

CULPEPPER, VA., *Feb.*, '64. Here I am pretty well down toward the extreme front. Three or four days ago General S., who is now in chief command, (I believe Meade is absent, sick,) moved a strong force southward from camp as if intending business. They went to the Rapidan; there has since been some manœuvring and a little fighting, but nothing of consequence. The telegraphic accounts given Monday morning last, make entirely too much of it, I should say. What General S. intended we here know not, but we trust in that competent commander. We were somewhat excited, (but not so very much either,) on Sunday, during the day and night, as orders were sent out to pack up and harness, and be ready to evacuate, to fall back towards Washington. But I was very sleepy and went to bed. Some tremendous shouts arousing me during the night, I went forth and found it was from the men above mention'd, who were returning. I talk'd with some of the men; as usual I found them full of gaiety, endurance, and many fine little outshows, the signs of the most excellent good manliness of the world. It was a curious sight to see those shadowy columns moving through the night. I stood unobserv'd in the darkness and watch'd them long. The mud was very deep. The men had their usual burdens, overcoats, knapsacks, guns and blankets. Along and along they filed by me, with often a laugh, a song, a cheerful word, but never once a murmur. It may have been odd, but I never before so realized the majesty and reality of the American people *en masse.* It fell upon me like a great awe. The strong ranks moved neither fast nor slow. They had march'd seven or eight miles already through the slipping unctuous mud. The brave First corps stopped here. The equally brave Third corps moved on to Brandy station. The famous Brooklyn 14th are here, guarding the town. You see their red legs actively moving everywhere. Then they have a theatre of their own here. They give musical performances, nearly everything done capitally. Of course the audience is a jam. It is good sport to attend one of these entertainments of the 14th. I like to look around at the soldiers, and the general collection in front of the curtain, more than the scene on the stage.

### Paying the Bounties

One of the things to note here now is the arrival of the paymaster with his strong box, and the payment of bounties to veterans re-enlisting. Major H. is here to-day, with a small mountain of greenbacks, rejoicing the hearts of the 2nd division of the First corps. In the midst of a rickety shanty, behind a little table, sit the major and clerk Eldridge, with the rolls before them, and much money. A re-enlisted man gets in cash about $200 down, (and heavy instalments following, as the pay-days arrive, one after another.) The show of the men crowding around is quite exhilarating; I like to stand and look. They feel elated, their pockets full, and the ensuing furlough, the visit home. It is a scene of sparkling eyes and flush'd cheeks. The soldier has many gloomy and harsh experiences, and this makes up for some of them. Major H. is order'd to pay first all the re-enlisted men of the First corps their bounties and back pay, and then the rest. You hear the peculiar sound of the rustling of the new and crisp greenbacks by the hour, through the nimble fingers of the major and my friend clerk E.

### RUMOURS, CHANGES, ETC.

About the excitement of Sunday, and the orders to be ready to start, I have heard since that the said orders came from some cautious minor commander, and that the high principalities knew not and thought not of any such move; which is likely. The rumour and fear here intimated a long circuit by Lee, and flank attack on our right. But I cast my eyes at the mud, which was then at its deepest and palmiest condition, and re-tired composedly to rest. Still it is about time for Culpepper to have a change. Authorities have chased each other here like clouds in a stormy sky. Before the first Bull Run this was the rendezvous and camp of in-struction of the secession troops. I am stopping at the house of a lady who has witness'd all the eventful changes of the war, along this route of con-tending armies. She is a widow, with a family of young children, and lives here with her sister in a large handsome house. A number of army offi-cers board with them.

### VIRGINIA

Dilapidated, fenceless, and trodden with war as Virginia is, wherever I move across her surface, I find myself rous'd to surprise and admiration. What capacity for products, improvements, human life, nourishment and expansion. Everywhere that I have been in the old Dominion, (the subtle mockery of that title now!) such thoughts have fill'd me. The soil is yet far above the average of any of the northern States. And how full of breadth the scenery, everywhere distant mountains, everywhere conve-nient rivers. Even yet prodigal in forest woods, and surely eligible for all the fruits, orchards, and flowers. The skies and atmosphere most lus-cious, as I feel certain, from more than a year's residence in the State, and movements hither and yon. I should say very healthy, as a general thing. Then a rich and elastic quality, by night and by day. The sun rejoices in his strength, dazzling and burning, and yet, to me, never unpleasantly weakening. It is not the panting tropical heat, but invigorates. The north tempers it. The nights are often unsurpassable. Last evening (Feb. 8,) I saw the first of the new moon, the outlined old moon clear along with it; the sky and air so clear, such transparent hues of colour, it seem'd to me I had never really seen the new moon before. It was the thinnest cut crescent possible. It hung delicate just above the sulky shadow of the Blue mountains. Ah, if it might prove an omen and good prophecy for this unhappy State.

### SUMMER OF 1864

I am back again in Washington, on my regular daily and nightly rounds. Of course there are many specialities. Dotting a ward here and there are always cases of poor fellows, long-suffering under obstinate wounds, or weak and dishearten'd from typhoid fever, or the like; mark'd cases, needing special and sympathetic nourishment. These I sit down and either talk to, or silently cheer them up. They always like it hugely, (and so do I.) Each case has its peculiarities, and needs some new adaptation. I have learnt to thus conform—learnt a good deal of hospital wisdom. Some of the poor young chaps, away from home for the first time in their lives, hunger and thirst for affection; this is sometimes the only thing that will reach their condition. The men like to have a pencil, and something to write in. I have given them cheap pocket-diaries, and almanacs for 1864, interleav'd with blank paper. For reading I generally have some old pictorial magazines or story papers—they are always acceptable. Also the morning or evening papers of the day. The best books I do not give, but lend to read through the wards, and then take them to others, and so on; they are very punctual about returning the books. In these wards, or on the field, as I thus continue to go round, I have come to adapt myself to each emergency, after its kind or call, however trivial, however solemn, every one justified and made real under its circumstances—not only visits and cheering talk and little gifts—not only washing and dressing wounds, (I have some cases where the patient is unwilling any one should do this but me)—but passages from the Bible, expounding them, prayer at the bedside, explanations of doctrine, etc. (I think I see my friends smiling at this confession, but I was never more in earnest in my life.) In camp and everywhere, I was in the habit of reading or giving recitations to the men. They were very fond of it, and liked declamatory poetical pieces. We would gather in a large group by ourselves, after supper, and spend the time in such readings, or in talking, and occasionally by an amusing game called the game of twenty questions.

### A New Army Organization Fit for America

It is plain to me out of the events of the war, north and south, and out of all considerations, that the current military theory, practice, rules, and organization, (adopted from Europe from the feudal institutes, with, of course, the "modern improvements" largely from the French,) though tacitly follow'd, and believ'd in by the officers generally, are not at all consonant with the United States, nor our people, nor our days. What it will be I know not—but I know that as entire an abnegation of the present military system, and the naval too, and a building up from radically different root-bases and centres appropriate to us, must eventually result, as that our political system has resulted and become establish'd, different from feudal Europe, and built up on itself from original, perennial, democratic premisses. We have undoubtedly in the United States the greatest military power—an exhaustless, intelligent, brave and reliable rank and file—in the world, any land, perhaps all lands. The problem is to organize this in the manner fully appropriate to it, to the principles of the republic, and to get the best service out of it. In the present struggle, as already seen and review'd, probably three-fourths of the losses, men, lives, etc., have been sheer superfluity, extravagance, waste.

### Death of a Hero

I wonder if I could ever convey to another—to you, for instance, reader dear—the tender and terrible realities of such cases, (many, many happen'd,) as the one I am now going to mention. Steward C. Glover, company E, 5th Wisconsin—was wounded May 5, in one of those fierce tussels of the Wilderness—died May 21—aged about 20. He was a small and beardless young man—a splendid soldier—in fact almost an ideal American, of his age. He had serv'd nearly three years, and would have been entitled to his discharge in a few days. He was in Hancock's corps. The fighting had about ceas'd for the day, and the general commanding the brigade rode by and call'd for volunteers to bring in the wounded. Glover responded among the first—went out gaily—but while in the act of bearing in a wounded sergeant to our lines, was shot in the knee by a rebel sharpshooter; consequence, amputation and death. He had resided with his father, John Glover, an aged and feeble man, in Batavia, Genesee county, N. Y., but was at school in Wisconsin, after the war broke out, and there enlisted—soon took to soldier-life, liked it, was very manly, was belov'd by officers and comrades. He kept a little diary, like so many of the soldiers. On the day of his death he wrote the following in it, "To-day the doctor says I must die—all is over with me—ah, so young to die." On another blank leaf he pencill'd to his brother, "Dear brother Thomas, I have been brave but wicked—pray for me."

## HOSPITAL SCENES—INCIDENTS

It is Sunday afternoon, middle of summer, hot and oppressive, and very silent through the ward. I am taking care of a critical case, now lying in a half lethargy. Near where I sit is a suffering rebel, from the 8th Lousiana; his name is Irving. He has been here a long time, badly wounded, and lately had his leg amputated; it is not doing very well. Right opposite me is a sick soldier-boy, laid down with his clothes on, sleeping, looking much wasted, his pallid face on his arm. I see by the yellow trimming on his jacket that he is a cavalry boy. I step softly over and find by his card that he is named William Cone, of the 1st Maine cavalry, and his folks live in Skowhegan.

*Ice Cream Treat.* One hot day toward the middle of June, I gave the inmates of Carver hospital a general ice cream treat, purchasing a large quantity, and, under convoy of the doctor or head nurse, going around personally through the wards to see to its distribution.

*An Incident.* In one of the fights before Atlanta, a rebel soldier, of large size, evidently a young man, was mortally wounded top of the head, so that the brains partially exuded. He lived three days, lying on his back on the spot where he first dropt. He dug with his heel in the ground during that time a hole big enough to put in a couple of ordinary knapsacks. He just lay there in the open air, and with little intermission kept his heel going night and day. Some of our soldiers then moved him to a house, but he died in a few minutes.

*Another.* After the battles at Columbia, Tennessee, where we repuls'd about a score of vehement rebel charges, they left a great many wounded on the ground, mostly within our range. Whenever any of these wounded attempted to move away by any means, generally by crawling off, our men without exception brought them down by a bullet. They let none crawl away, no matter what his condition.

## A YANKEE SOLDIER

As I turn'd off the Avenue one cool October evening into Thirteenth street, a soldier with knapsack and overcoat stood at the corner inquiring his way. I found he wanted to go part of the road in my direction, so we walk'd on together. We soon fell into conversation. He was small, and not very young, and a tough little fellow, as I judged in the evening light, catching glimpses by the lamps we pass'd. His answers were short, but clear. His name was Charles Carroll; he belong'd to one of the Massachusetts regiments, and was born in or near Lynn. His parents were living, but were very old. There were four sons, and all had enlisted. Two had died of starvation and misery in the prison at Andersonville, and one had been kill'd in the west. He only was left. He was now going home, and by the way he talk'd I inferr'd that his time was nearly out. He made great calculations on being with his parents to comfort them the rest of their days.

## UNION PRISONERS SOUTH

Michael Stansbury, 48 years of age, a seafaring man, a southerner by birth and raising, formerly captain of U. S. light ship *Long Shoal*, station'd at Long Shoal point, Pamlico sound—though a southerner, a firm Union man—was captur'd Feb. 17, 1863, and has been nearly two years in the Confederate prisons; was at one time order'd releas'd by Governor Vance, but a rebel officer re-arrested him; then sent on to Richmond for exchange—but instead of being exchanged was sent down (as a southern citizen, not a soldier,) to Salisbury, N.C., where he remain'd until lately, when he escap'd among the exchang'd by assuming the name of a dead soldier, and coming up via Wilmington with the rest. Was about sixteen months in Salisbury. Subsequent to October, '64, there were about 11,000 Union prisoners in the stockade; about 100 of them southern unionists, 200 U. S. deserters. During the past winter 1,500 of the prisoners, to save their lives, join'd the confederacy, on condition of being assign'd merely to guard duty. Out of the 11,000 not more than 2,500 came out; 500 of these were pitiable, helpless wretches—the rest were in a condition to travel. There were often 60 dead bodies to be buried in the morning; the daily average would be about 40. The regular food was a meal of corn, the cob and husk ground together, and sometimes once a week a ration of sorghum molasses. A diminutive ration of meat might possibly come once a month, not oftener. In the stockade, containing the 11,000 men, there was a partial show of tents, not enough for 2,000. A large proportion of the men lived in holes in the ground, in the utmost wretchedness. Some froze to death, others had their hands and feet frozen. The rebel guards would occasionally, and on the least pretence, fire into the prison from mere demonism and wantonness. All the horrors that can be named, starvation, lassitude, filth, vermin, despair, swift loss of self-respect, idiocy, insanity, and frequent

murder, were there. Stansbury has a wife and child living in Newbern—
has written to them from here—is in the U.S. lighthouse employ still—
(had been home to Newbern to see his family, and on his return to the
ship was captured in his boat.) Has seen men brought there to Salisbury
as hearty as you ever see in your life—in a few weeks completely dead
gone, much of it from thinking on their condition—hope all gone. Has
himself a hard, sad, strangely deaden'd kind of look, as of one chill'd for
years in the cold and dark, where his good manly nature had no room to
exercise itself.

## Deserters

*Oct.* 24. Saw a large squad of our own deserters, (over 300) surrounded
with a cordon of arm'd guards, marching along Pennsylvania avenue.
The most motley collection I ever saw, all sorts of rig, all sorts of hats and
caps, many fine-looking young fellows, some of them shame-faced, some
sickly, most of them dirty, shirts very dirty and long worn, etc. They
tramp'd along without order, a huge huddling mass, not in ranks. I saw
some of the spectators laughing, but I felt like anything else but laughing. These deserters are far more numerous than would be thought. Almost every day I see squads of them, sometimes two or three at a time,
with a small guard; sometimes ten or twelve, under a larger one. (I hear
that desertions from the army now in the field have often averaged 10,000
a month. One of the commonest sights in Washington is a squad of deserters.)

## A Glimpse of War's Hell-Scenes

In one of the late movements of our troops in the valley, (near Up-
perville, I think,) a strong force of Moseby's mounted guerillas attack'd
a train of wounded, and the guard of cavalry convoying them. The ambulances contain'd about 60 wounded, quite a number of them officers
of rank. The rebels were in strength, and the capture of the train and its
partial guard after a short snap was effectually accomplish'd. No sooner
had our men surrender'd, the rebels instantly commenced robbing the
train and murdering their prisoners, even the wounded. Here is the scene
or a sample of it, ten minutes after. Among the wounded officers in the
ambulances were one, a lieutenant of regulars, and another of higher
rank. These two were dragg'd out on the ground on their backs, and were
now surrounded by the guerillas, a demoniac crowd, each member of
which was stabbing them in different parts of their bodies. One of the of-

ficers had his feet pinn'd firmly to the ground by bayonets stuck through them and thrust into the ground. These two officers, as afterwards found on examination, had receiv'd about twenty such thrusts, some of them through the mouth, face, etc. The wounded had all been dragg'd (to give a better chance also for plunder,) out of their wagons; some had been effectually dispatch'd, and their bodies were lying there lifeless and bloody. Others, not yet dead, but horribly mutilated, were moaning or groaning. Of our men who surrender'd, most had been thus maim'd or slaughter'd.

At this instant a force of our cavalry, who had been following the train at some interval, charged suddenly upon the secesh captors, who proceeded at once to make the best escape they could. Most of them got away, but we gobbled two officers and seventeen men, in the very acts just described. The sight was one which admitted of little discussion, as may be imagined. The seventeen captur'd men and two officers were put under guard for the night, but it was decided there and then that they should die. The next morning the two officers were taken in the town, separate places, put in the centre of the street, and shot. The seventeen men were taken to an open ground, a little one side. They were placed in a hollow square, half-encompass'd by two of our cavalry regiments, one of which regiments had three days before found the bloody corpses of three of their men hamstrung and hung up by the heels to limbs of trees by Moseby's guerillas, and the other had not long before had twelve men, after surrendering, shot and then hung by the neck to limbs of trees, and jeering inscriptions pinn'd to the breast of one of the corpses, who had been a sergeant. Those three, and those twelve, had been found, I say, by these environing regiments. Now, with revolvers, they form'd the grim cordon of the seventeen prisoners. The latter were placed in the midst of the hollow square, unfasten'd, and the ironical remark made to them that they were now to be given "a chance for themselves." A few ran for it. But what use? From every side the deadly pills came. In a few minutes the seventeen corpses strew'd the hollow square. I was curious to know whether some of the Union soldiers, some few, (some one or two at least of the youngsters,) did not abstain from shooting on the helpless men. Not one. There was no exultation, very little said, almost nothing, yet every man there contributed his shot.

Multiply the above by scores, aye hundreds—verify it in all the forms that different circumstances, individuals, places, could afford—light it with every lurid passion, the wolf, the lion's lapping thirst for blood—the passionate boiling volcanoes of human revenge for comrades, brothers slain—with the light of burning farms, and heaps of smutting, smouldering black embers—and in the human heart everywhere black, worse embers—and you have an inkling of this war. . . .

## SOUTHERN ESCAPEES

*Feb.* 23, '65. I saw a large procession of young men from the rebel army, (deserters they are call'd, but the usual meaning of the word does not apply to them,) passing the Avenue to-day. There were nearly 200, come up yesterday by boat from James river. I stood and watch'd them as they shuffled along, in a slow, tired, worn sort of way; a large proportion of light-hair'd, blonde, light grey-eyed young men among them. Their costumes had a dirt-stain'd uniformity; most had been originally grey; some had articles of our uniform, pants on one, vest or coat on another; I think they were mostly Georgia and North Carolina boys. They excited little or no attention. As I stood quite close to them, several good looking enough youths, (but oh what a tale of misery their appearance told,) nodded or just spoke to me, without doubt divining pity and fatherliness out of my face, for my heart was full enough of it. Several of the couples trudg'd along with their arms about each other, some probably brothers, as if they were afraid they might somehow get separated. They nearly all look'd what one might call simple, yet intelligent, too. Some had pieces of old carpet, some blankets, and others old bags around their shoulders. Some of them here and there had fine faces, still it was a procession of misery. The two hundred had with them about half a dozen arm'd guards. Along this week I saw some such procession, more or less in numbers, every day, as they were brought up by the boat. The government does what it can for them, and sends them north and west.

*Feb.* 27. Some three or four hundred more escapees from the confederate army came up on the boat. As the day has been very pleasant indeed, (after a long spell of bad weather,) I have been wandering around a good deal, without any other object than to be out-doors and enjoy it; have met these escaped men in all directions. Their apparel is the same ragged, long-worn motley as before described. I talk'd with a number of the men. Some are quite bright and stylish, for all their poor clothes — walking with an air, wearing their old head-coverings on one side, quite saucily. I find the old, unquestionable proofs, as all along the past four years, of the unscrupulous tyranny exercised by the secession government in conscripting the common people by absolute force everywhere, and paying no attention whatever to the men's time being up — keeping them in military service just the same. One gigantic young fellow, a Georgian, at least six feet three inches high, broad-sized in proportion, attired in the dirtiest, drab, well-smear'd rags, tied with strings, his trousers at the knees all strips and streamers, was complacently standing eating some bread and meat. He appear'd contented enough. Then a few minutes after I saw him slowly walking along. It was plain he did not take anything to heart.

*Feb.* 28. As I pass'd the military headquarters of the city, not far from the President's house, I stopped to interview some of the crowd of escapees who were lounging there. In appearance they were the same as previously mention'd. Two of them, one about 17, and the other perhaps 25 or 26, I talk'd with some time. They were from North Carolina, born and rais'd there, and had folks there. The elder had been in the rebel service four years. He was first conscripted for two years. He was then kept arbitrarily in the ranks. This is the case with a large proportion of the secession army. There was nothing downcast in these young men's manners; the younger had been soldiering about a year; he was conscripted; there were six brothers (all the boys of the family) in the army, part of them as conscripts, part as volunteers; three had been kill'd; one had escaped about four months ago, and now this one had got away; he was a pleasant and well-talking lad, with the peculiar North Carolina idiom (not at all disagreeable to my ears.) He and the elder one were of the same company, and escaped together—and wish'd to remain together. They thought of getting transportation away to Missouri, and working there; but were not sure it was judicious. I advised them rather to go to some of the directly northern States, and get farm work for the present. The younger had made six dollars on the boat, with some tobacco he brought; he had three and a half left. The elder had nothing; I gave him a trifle. Soon after, met John Wormley, 9th Alabama, a West Tennessee rais'd boy, parents both dead—had the look of one for a long time on short allowance—said very little—chew'd tobacco at a fearful rate, spitting in proportion—large clear dark-brown eyes, very fine—didn't know what to make of me—told me at last he wanted much to get some clean underclothes, and a pair of decent pants. Didn't care about coat or hat fixings. Wanted a chance to wash himself well, and put on the underclothes. I had the very great pleasure of helping him to accomplish all those wholesome designs.

*March* 1. Plenty more butternut or clay-color'd escapees every day. About 160 came in to-day, a large portion South Carolinians. They generally take the oath of allegiance, and are sent north, west, or extreme south-west if they wish. Several of them told me that the desertions in their army, of men going home, leave or no leave, are far more numerous than their desertions to our side. I saw a very forlorn looking squad of about a hundred, late this afternoon, on their way to the Baltimore depôt.

## THE CAPITOL BY GASLIGHT

To-night I have been wandering awhile in the capitol which is all lit up. The illuminated rotunda looks fine. I like to stand aside and look a long, long while, up at the dome; it comforts me somehow. The House and Senate were both in session till very late. I look'd in upon them, but only a few moments; they were hard at work on tax and appropriation bills. I wander'd through the long and rich corridors and apartments under the Senate; an old habit of mine, former winters, and now more satisfaction than ever. Not many persons down there, occasionally a flitting figure in the distance.

## THE INAUGURATION

*March* 4. The President very quietly rode down to the capitol in his own carriage, by himself, on a sharp trot, about noon, either because he wish'd to be on hand to sign bills, or to get rid of marching in line with the absurd procession, the muslin temple of liberty, and pasteboard monitor. I saw him on his return, at three o'clock, after the performance was over. He was in his plain two-horse barouche, and look'd very much worn and tired; the lines, indeed, of vast responsibilities, intricate questions, and demands of life and death, cut deeper than ever upon his dark brown face; yet all the old goodness, tenderness, sadness, and canny shrewdness, underneath the furrows. (I never see that man without feeling that he is one to become personally attach'd to, for his combination of purest, heartiest tenderness, and native western form of manliness.) By his side sat his little boy, of ten years. There were no soldiers, only a lot of civilians on horse-back, with huge yellow scarfs over their shoulders, riding around the carriage. (At the inauguration four years ago, he rode down and back again surrounded by a dense mass of arm'd cavalrymen eight deep, with drawn sabres; and there were sharp-shooters station'd at every corner on the route.) I ought to make mention of the closing levée of Saturday night last. Never before was such a compact jam in front of the White House—all the grounds fill'd, and away out to the spacious sidewalks. I was there, as I took a notion to go—was in the rush inside with the crowd—surged along the passage-ways, the blue and other rooms, and through the great east room. Crowds of country people, some very funny. Fine music from the Marine band, off in a side place. I saw Mr. Lincoln, drest all in black, with white kid gloves and a claw-hammer coat, receiving, as in duty bound, shaking hands, looking very disconsolate, and as if he would give anything to be somewhere else.

### ATTITUDE OF FOREIGN GOVERNMENTS DURING THE WAR

Looking over my scraps, I find I wrote the following during 1864. The happening to our America, abroad as well as at home, these years, is indeed most strange. The democratic republic has paid her to-day the terrible and resplendent compliment of the united wish of all the nations of the world that her union should be broken, her future cut off, and that she should be compell'd to descend to the level of kingdoms and empires ordinarily great. There is certainly not one government in Europe but is now watching the war in this country, with the ardent prayer that the United States may be effectually split, crippled, and dismember'd by it. There is not one but would help toward that dismemberment, if it dared. I say such is the ardent wish to-day of England and of France, as governments, and of all the nations of Europe, as governments. I think indeed it is to-day the real, heartfelt wish of all the nations of the world, with the single exception of Mexico—Mexico, the only one to whom we have ever really done wrong, and now the only one who prays for us and for our triumph, with genuine prayer. Is it not indeed strange? America, made up of all, cheerfully from the beginning opening her arms to all, the result and justifier of all, of Britain, Germany, France and Spain— all here—the accepter, the friend, hope, last resource and general house of all—she who has harm'd none, but been bounteous to so many, to millions, the mother of strangers and exiles, all nations—should now, I say, be paid this dread compliment of general governmental fear and hatred. Are we indignant, alarm'd? Do we feel jeopardized? No; help'd, braced, concentrated, rather. We are all too prone to wander from ourselves, to affect Europe, and watch her frowns and smiles. We need this hot lesson of general hatred, and henceforth must never forget it. Never again will we trust the moral sense nor abstract friendliness of a single *government* of the old world.

### THE WEATHER—DOES IT SYMPATHIZE WITH THESE TIMES?

Whether the rains, the heat and cold, and what underlies them all, are affected with what affects man in masses, and follow his play of passionate action, strain'd stronger than usual, and on a larger scale than usual— whether this, or no, it is certain that there is now, and has been for twenty months or more, on this North, American continent many a remarkable, many an unprecedented expression of the subtile world of air above us and around us. There, since this war, and the wide and deep national agitation, strange analogies, different combinations, a different sunlight, or absence of it; different products even out of the ground. After every great battle, a great storm. Even civic events the same. On Saturday last, a forenoon like whirling demons dark, with slanting rain, full of rage; and then the afternoon, so calm, so bathed with flooding splendour from heaven's most excellent sun, with atmosphere of sweetness; so clear, it show'd the stars, long, long before they were due. As the President came out on the capitol portico, a curious little white cloud, the only one in that part of the sky, appear'd like a hovering bird, right over him.

Indeed, the heavens, the elements, all the meteorological influences, have run riot for weeks past. Such caprices, abruptest alternation of frowns and beauty, I never knew. It is a common remark that (as last summer was different in its spells of intense heat from any preceding it,) the winter just completed has been without parallel. It has remain'd so down to the hour I am writing. Much of the daytime of the past month was sulky, with leaden heaviness, fog, interstices of bitter cold, and some insane storms. But there have been samples of another description. Nor earth nor sky ever knew spectacles of superber beauty than some of the nights lately here. The western star, Venus, in the earlier hours of evening, has never been so large, so clear; it seems as if it told something, as if it held rapport indulgent with humanity, with us Americans. Five or six nights since, it hung close by the moon, then a little past its first quarter. The star was wonderful, the moon like a young mother. The sky, dark blue, the transparent night, the planets, the moderate west wind, the elastic temperature, the miracle of that great star, and the young and swelling moon swimming in the west, suffused the soul. Then I heard, slow and clear, the deliberate notes of a bugle come up out of the silence, sounding so good through the night's mystery, no hurry, but firm and faithful, floating along, rising, falling leisurely, with here and there a long-drawn note; the bugle, well play'd, sounding tattoo, in one of the army hospitals near here, where the wounded (some of them personally so dear to me,) are lying in their cots, and many a sick boy come down to the war from Illinois, Michigan, Wisconsin, Iowa, and the rest.

# U. S. GRANT
## (1822–1885)

Ulysses S. Grant, the eighteenth president of the United States, was educated at West Point and rose to command the Union forces during the Civil War. He won the attention of President Lincoln after capturing Forts Henry and Donelson, in Tennessee, and was promoted to major general. He led the Union army at Shiloh and captured Vicksburg in a crucial battle (1863). In 1864, as commander in chief of all Union forces, he invaded the Confederate capital of Richmond, Virginia. It was a slow, but ultimately devastating, victory that led to the surrender of General Robert E. Lee at Appomattox Courthouse. After the Civil War, he parlayed his reputation as a warrior into two terms as president.

In the White House, Grant operated in a manner friendly to business, and also campaigned strongly against the Ku Klux Klan. However, Grant's presidency was marked by scandal as well. In his second term, the infamous Whiskey Ring affair led to the downfall of Grant's personal secretary and friend, Orville E. Babcock. After Grant completed his second term, in 1877, he failed at several business ventures, plunging his family into debt.

Upon the suggestion that he write his memoirs as a means of regaining lost money and stature, Grant composed the account even as he was dying of throat cancer. The proceeds from the *Personal Memoirs of U. S. Grant* (1885) would be nearly $500,000 dollars and would ensure the financial solvency of his family. Grant did not live to see this, however; he died on July 23, 1885.

## FROM *Memoirs*

The real work of the campaign and siege of Vicksburg now began. The problem was to secure a footing upon dry ground on the east side of the river from which the troops could operate against Vicksburg. The Mississippi River, from Cairo south, runs through a rich alluvial valley of many miles in width, bound on the east by land running from eighty up to two or more hundred feet above the river. On the west side the highest land, except in a few places, is but little above the highest water. Through this valley the river meanders in the most tortuous way, varying in direction to all points of the compass. At places it runs to the very foot of the bluffs. After leaving Memphis, there are no such highlands coming to the water's edge on the east shore until Vicksburg is reached.

The intervening land is cut up by bayous filled from the river in high water—many of them navigable for steamers. All of them would be, except for overhanging trees, narrowness and tortuous course, making it impossible to turn the bends with vessels of any considerable length. Marching across this country in the face of an enemy was impossible; navigating it proved equally impracticable. The strategical way according to the rule, therefore, would have been to go back to Memphis; establish that as a base of supplies; fortify it so that the storehouses could be held by a small garrison, and move from there along the line of railroad, repairing as we advanced, to the Yallabusha, or to Jackson, Mississippi. At this time the North had become very much discouraged. Many strong Union men believed that the war must prove a failure. The elections of 1862 had gone against the party which was for the prosecution of the war to save the Union if it took the last man and the last dollar. Voluntary enlistments had ceased throughout the greater part of the North, and the draft had been resorted to to fill up our ranks. It was my judgment at the time that to make a backward movement as long as that from Vicksburg to Memphis, would be interpreted, by many of those yet full of hope for the preservation of the Union, as a defeat, and that the draft would be resisted, desertions ensue and the power to capture and punish deserters lost. There was nothing left to be done but to *go forward to a decisive victory*. This was in my mind from the moment I took command in person at Young's Point.

The winter of 1862–3 was a noted one for continuous high water in the Mississippi and for heavy rains along the lower river. To get dry land, or rather land above the water, to encamp the troops upon, took many miles of river front. We had to occupy the levees and the ground immediately behind. This was so limited that one corps, the 17th, under General McPherson, was at Lake Providence, seventy miles above Vicksburg.

It was in January the troops took their position opposite Vicksburg. The water was very high and the rains were incessant. There seemed no possibility of a land movement before the end of March or later, and it would not do to lie idle all this time. The effect would be demoralizing to the troops and injurious to their health. Friends in the North would have grown more and more discouraged, and enemies in the same section more and more insolent in their gibes and denunciation of the cause and those engaged in it.

I always admired the South, as bad as I thought their cause, for the boldness with which they silenced all opposition and all croaking, by press or by individuals, within their control. War at all times, whether a civil war between sections of a common country or between nations, ought to be avoided, if possible with honor. But, once entered into, it is too much for human nature to tolerate an enemy within their ranks to give aid and comfort to the armies of the opposing section or nation.

Vicksburg, as stated before, is on the first high land coming to the river's edge, below that on which Memphis stands. The bluff, or high land, follows the left bank of the Yazoo for some distance and continues in a southerly direction to the Mississippi River, thence it runs along the Mississippi to Warrenton, six miles below. The Yazoo River leaves the high land a short distance below Haines' Bluff and empties into the Mississippi nine miles above Vicksburg. Vicksburg is built on this high land where the Mississippi washes the base of the hill. Haines' Bluff, eleven miles from Vicksburg, on the Yazoo River, was strongly fortified. The whole distance from there to Vicksburg and thence to Warrenton was also intrenched, with batteries at suitable distances and rifle-pits connecting them.

From Young's Point the Mississippi turns in a north-easterly direction to a point just above the city, when it again turns and runs south-westerly, leaving vessels, which might attempt to run the blockade, exposed to the fire of batteries six miles below the city before they were in range of the upper batteries. Since then the river has made a cut-off, leaving what was the peninsula in front of the city, an island. North of the Yazoo was all a marsh, heavily timbered, cut up with bayous, and much overflowed. A front attack was therefore impossible, and was never contemplated; certainly not by me. The problem then became, how to secure a landing on high ground east of the Mississippi without an apparent retreat. Then commenced a series of experiments to consume time, and to divert the attention of the enemy, of my troops and of the public generally. I, myself, never felt great confidence that any of the experiments resorted to would prove successful. Nevertheless I was always prepared to take advantage of them in case they did.

In 1862 General Thomas Williams had come up from New Orleans and cut a ditch ten or twelve feet wide and about as deep, straight across from Young's Point to the river below. The distance across was a little over a mile. It was Williams' expectation that when the river rose it would cut a navigable channel through; but the canal started in an eddy from both ends, and, of course, it only filled up with water on the rise without doing any execution in the way of cutting. Mr. Lincoln had navigated the Mississippi in his younger days and understood well its tendency to change its channel, in places, from time to time. He set much store accordingly by this canal. General McClernand had been, therefore, directed before I went to Young's Point to push the work of widening and deepening this canal. After my arrival the work was diligently pushed with about 4,000 men—as many as could be used to advantage—until interrupted by a sudden rise in the river that broke a dam at the upper end, which had been put there to keep the water out until the excavation was completed. This was on the 8th of March [March 7].

Even if the canal had proven a success, so far as to be navigable for steamers, it could not have been of much advantage to us. It runs in a direction almost perpendicular to the line of bluffs on the opposite side, or east bank, of the river. As soon as the enemy discovered what we were doing he established a battery commanding the canal throughout its length. This battery soon drove out our dredges, two in number, which were doing the work of thousands of men. Had the canal been completed it might have proven of some use in running transports through, under the cover of night, to use below; but they would yet have to run batteries, though for a much shorter distance.

While this work was progressing we were busy in other directions, trying to find an available landing on high ground on the east bank of the river, or to make water-ways to get below the city, avoiding the batteries.

On the 30th of January, the day after my arrival at the front, I ordered General McPherson, stationed with his corps at Lake Providence, to cut the levee at that point. If successful in opening a channel for navigation by this route, it would carry us to the Mississippi River through the mouth of the Red River, just above Port Hudson and four hundred miles below Vicksburg by the river.

Lake Providence is a part of the old bed of the Mississippi, about a mile from the present channel. It is six miles long and has its outlet through Bayou Baxter, Bayou Macon, and the Tensas, Washita and Red Rivers. The last three are navigable streams at all seasons. Bayous Baxter and Macon are narrow and tortuous, and the banks are covered with dense forests overhanging the channel. They were also filled with fallen timber, the accumulation of years. The land along the Mississippi River, from Memphis down, is in all instances highest next to the river, except where the river washes the bluffs which form the boundary of the valley through which it winds. Bayou Baxter, as it reaches lower land, begins to spread out and disappears entirely in a cypress swamp before it reaches the Macon. There was about two feet of water in this swamp at the time. To get through it, even with vessels of the lightest draft, it was necessary to clear off a belt of heavy timber wide enough to make a passage way. As the trees would have to be cut close to the bottom—under water—it was an undertaking of great magnitude.

On the 4th of February I visited General McPherson, and remained with him several days. The work had not progressed so far as to admit the water from the river into the lake, but the troops had succeeded in drawing a small steamer, of probably not over thirty tons' capacity, from the river into the lake. With this we were able to explore the lake and bayou as far as cleared. I saw then that there was scarcely a chance of this ever becoming a practicable route for moving troops through an enemy's country. The distance from Lake Providence to the point where vessels going by that route would enter the Mississippi again, is about four hundred and seventy miles by the main river. The distance would probably be greater by the tortuous bayous through which this new route would carry us. The enemy held Port Hudson, below where the Red River debouches, and all the Mississippi above to Vicksburg. The Red River, Washita and Tensas were, as has been said, all navigable streams, on which the enemy could throw small bodies of men to obstruct our passage and pick off our troops with their sharpshooters. I let the work go on, believing employment was better than idleness for the men. Then, too, it served as a cover for other efforts which gave a better prospect of success. This work was abandoned after the canal proved a failure.

Lieutenant-Colonel [J. H.] Wilson of my staff was sent to Helena, Arkansas, to examine and open a way through Moon Lake and the Yazoo Pass if possible. Formerly there was a route by way of an inlet from the Mississippi River into Moon Lake, a mile east of the river, thence east through Yazoo Pass to Coldwater, along the latter to the Tallahatchie, which joins the Yallabusha about two hundred and fifty miles below Moon Lake and forms the Yazoo River. These were formerly navigated by steamers trading with the rich plantations along their banks; but the State of Mississippi had built a strong levee across the inlet some years before, leaving the only entrance for vessels into this rich region the one by way of the mouth of the Yazoo several hundreds of miles below.

On the 2d of February [February 3] this dam, or levee, was cut. The river being high the rush of water through the cut was so great that in a very short time the entire obstruction was washed away. The bayous were soon filled and much of the country was overflowed. This pass leaves the Mississippi River but a few miles below Helena. On the 24th General Ross, with his brigade of about 4,500 men on transports, moved into this new water-way. The rebels had obstructed the navigation of Yazoo Pass and the Coldwater by felling trees into them. Much of the timber in this region being of greater specific gravity than water, and being of great size, their removal was a matter of great labor; but it was finally accomplished, and on the 11th of March Ross found himself, accompanied by two gunboats under the command of Lieutenant-Commander Watson Smith, confronting a fortification at Greenwood, where the Tallahatchie and Yallabusha unite and the Yazoo begins. The bends of the rivers are such at this point as to almost form an island, scarcely above water at that stage of the river. This island was fortified and manned. It was named Fort Pemberton after the commander at Vicksburg. No land approach was accessible. The troops, therefore, could render no assistance towards an assault further than to establish a battery on a little piece of ground which was discovered above water. The gunboats, however, attacked on the 11th and again on the 13th of March. Both efforts were failures and were not renewed. One gunboat was disabled and we lost six men killed and twenty-five wounded. The loss of the enemy was less.

Fort Pemberton was so little above the water than it was thought that a rise of two feet would drive the enemy out. In hope of enlisting the elements on our side, which had been so much against us up to this time, a second cut was made in the Mississippi levee, this time directly opposite Helena, or six miles above the former cut. It did not accomplish the desired result, and Ross, with his fleet, started back. On the 22d he met [General Isaac F.] Quinby with a brigade at Yazoo Pass. Quinby was the senior of Ross, and assumed command. He was not satisfied with returning to his former position without seeing for himself whether anything could be accomplished. Accordingly Fort Pemberton was revisited by our troops; but an inspection was sufficient this time without an attack. Quinby, with his command, returned with but little delay. In the meantime I was much exercised for the safety of Ross, not knowing that Quinby had been able to join him. Reinforcements were of no use in a country covered with water, as they would have to remain on board of their transports. Relief had to come from another quarter. So I determined to get into the Yazoo below Fort Pemberton.

Steel's Bayou empties into the Yazoo River between Haines' Bluff and its mouth. It is narrow, very tortuous, and fringed with a very heavy growth of timber, but it is deep. It approaches to within one mile of the Mississippi at Eagle Bend, thirty miles above Young's Point. Steel's Bayou connects with Black Bayou, Black Bayou with Deer Creek, Deer Creek with Rolling Fork, Rolling Fork with the Big Sunflower River, and the Big Sunflower with the Yazoo River about ten miles above Haines' Bluff in a right line but probably twenty or twenty-five miles by the winding of the river. All these waterways are of about the same nature so far as navigation is concerned, until the Sunflower is reached; this affords free navigation.

Admiral Porter explored this waterway as far as Deer Creek on the 14th of March, and reported it navigable. On the next day he started with five gunboats and four mortar-boats. I went with him for some distance. The heavy, overhanging timber retarded progress very much, as did also the short turns in so narrow a stream. The gunboats, however, ploughed their way through without other damage than to their appearance. The transports did not fare so well although they followed behind. The road was somewhat cleared for them by the gunboats. In the evening I returned to headquarters to hurry up reinforcements. Sherman went in person on the 16th, taking with him Stuart's division of the 15th corps.

They took large river transports to Eagle Bend on the Mississippi, where they debarked and marched across to Steel's Bayou, where they re-embarked on the transports. The river steamers, with their tall smoke-stacks and light guards extending out, were so much impeded that the gunboats got far ahead. Porter, with his fleet, got within a few hundred yards of where the sailing would have been clear and free from the obstructions caused by felling trees into the water, when he encountered rebel sharpshooters, and his progress was delayed by obstructions in his front. He could do nothing with gunboats against sharp-shooters. The rebels, learning his route, had sent in about 4,000 men—many more than there were sailors in the fleet.

Sherman went back, at the request of the admiral, to clear out Black Bayou and to hurry up reinforcements, which were far behind. On the night of the 19th he received notice from the admiral that he had been attacked by sharp-shooters and was in imminent peril. Sherman at once returned through Black Bayou in a canoe, and passed on until he met a steamer, with the last of the reinforcements he had, coming up. They tried to force their way through Black Bayou with their steamer, but, finding it slow and tedious work, debarked and pushed forward on foot. It was night when they landed, and intensely dark. There was but a narrow strip of land above water, and that was grown up with underbrush or cane. The troops lighted their way through this with candles carried in their hands for a mile and a half, when they came to an open plantation. Here the troops rested until morning. They made twenty-one miles from this resting-place by noon the next day, and were in time to rescue the fleet. Porter had fully made up his mind to blow up the gunboats rather than have them fall into the hands of the enemy. More welcome visitors he probably never met than the "boys in blue" on this occasion. The vessels were backed out and returned to their rendezvous on the Mississippi; and thus ended in failure the fourth attempt to get in rear of Vicksburg.

*　　*　　*

The original canal scheme was also abandoned on the 27th of March. The effort to make a waterway through Lake Providence and the connecting bayous was abandoned as wholly impracticable about the same time.

At Milliken's Bend, and also at Young's Point, bayous or channels start, which connecting with other bayous passing Richmond, Louisiana, enter the Mississippi at Carthage twenty-five or thirty miles above Grand Gulf. The Mississippi levee cuts the supply of water off from these bayous or channels, but all the rainfall behind the levee, at these points, is carried through these same channels to the river below. In case of a crevasse in this vicinity, the water escaping would find its outlet through the same channels. The dredges and laborers from the canal having been driven out by overflow and the enemy's batteries, I determined to open these other channels, if possible. If successful the effort would afford a route, away from the enemy's batteries, for our transports. There was a good road back of the levees, along these bayous, to carry the troops, artillery and wagon trains over whenever the water receded a little, and after a few days of dry weather. Accordingly, with the abandonment of all the other plans for reaching a base heretofore described, this new one was undertaken.

As early as the 4th of February I had written to Halleck about this route, stating that I thought it much more practicable than the other undertaking (the Lake Providence route), and that it would have been accomplished with much less labor if commenced before the water had got all over the country.

The upper end of these bayous being cut off from a water supply, further than the rainfall back of the levees, was grown up with dense timber for a distance of several miles from their source. It was necessary, therefore, to clear this out before letting in the water from the river. This work was continued until the waters of the river began to recede and the road to Richmond, Louisiana, emerged from the water. One small steamer and some barges were got through this channel, but no further use could be made of it because of the fall in the river. Beyond this it was no more successful than the other experiments with which the winter was whiled away. All these failures would have been very discouraging if I had expected much from the efforts; but I had not. From the first the most I hoped to accomplish was the passage of transports, to be used below Vicksburg, without exposure to the long line of batteries defending that city.

This long, dreary and, for heavy and continuous rains and high water, unprecedented winter was one of great hardship to all engaged about Vicksburg. The river was higher than its natural banks from December, 1862, to the following April. The war had suspended peaceful pursuits in the South, further than the production of army supplies, and in consequence the levees were neglected and broken in many places and the whole country was covered with water. Troops could scarcely find dry ground on which to pitch their tents. Malarial fevers broke out among the men. Measles and small-pox also attacked them. The hospital arrangements and medical attendance were so perfect, however, that the loss of life was much less than might have been expected. Visitors to the camps went home with dismal stories to relate; Northern papers came back to the soldiers with these stories exaggerated. Because I would not divulge my ultimate plans to visitors, they pronounced me idle, incompetent and unfit to command men in an emergency, and clamored for my removal. They were not to be satisfied, many of them, with my simple removal, but named who my successor should be. McClernand, Fremont, Hunter and McClellan were all mentioned in this connection. I took no steps to answer these complaints, but continued to do my duty, as I understood it, to the best of my ability. Every one has his superstitions. One of mine is that in positions of great responsibility every one should do his duty to the best of his ability where assigned by competent authority, without application or the use of influence to change his position. While at Cairo I had watched with very great interest the operations of the Army of the Potomac, looking upon that as the main field of the war. I had no idea, myself, of ever having any large command, nor did I suppose that I was equal to one; but I had the vanity to think that as a cavalry officer I might succeed very well in the command of a brigade. On one occasion, in talking about this to my staff officers, all of whom were civilians without any military education whatever, I said that I would give anything if I were commanding a brigade of cavalry in the Army of the Potomac and I believed I could do some good. Captain Hillyer spoke up and suggested that I make application to be transferred there to command the cavalry. I then told him that I would cut my right arm off first, and mentioned this superstition.

In time of war the President, being by the Constitution Commander-in-chief of the Army and Navy, is responsible for the selection of commanders. He should not be embarrassed in making his selections. I having been selected, my responsibility ended with my doing the best I knew how. If I had sought the place, or obtained it through personal or political influence, my belief is that I would have feared to undertake any plan of my own conception, and would probably have awaited direct orders from my distant superiors. Persons obtaining important commands by application or political influence are apt to keep a written record of complaints and predictions of defeat, which are shown in case of disaster. Somebody must be responsible for their failures.

With all the pressure brought to bear upon them, both President Lincoln and General Halleck stood by me to the end of the campaign. I had never met Mr. Lincoln, but his support was constant.

At last the waters began to recede; the roads crossing the peninsula behind the levees of the bayous, were emerging from the waters; the troops were all concentrated from distant points at Milliken's Bend preparatory to a final move which was to crown the long, tedious and discouraging labors with success.

# ELIZABETH HOBBS KECKLEY
### (1824–1907)

"As one of the victims of slavery," writes Keckley, "I drank of the bitter water." The water gushed from every pump and well in the Virginia of Keckley's childhood. She endured frequent beatings, blows conferred upon her for such offenses as "excessive pride."

Keckley passed from owner to owner, witnessing numerous painful scenes that only the institution of slavery could have produced. She eventually came to St. Louis, where her owner allowed her, with the help of members of the local community, to buy her freedom. But even emancipation proved difficult. Her marriage fell apart, and she fled St. Louis in the spring of 1860, taking a train to Washington, D.C., where she planned to start afresh.

In Washington, Keckley was confronted by the financial burdens of independence—debts and bills filled her life with a new, bitter water. Hoping to utilize her strongest skill in a profitable way, she turned to making dresses and doing alterations as a way of supporting herself.

This work proved her salvation. Word of her skill spread, and she was soon making dresses for the wives of leading politicians, including Jefferson Davis (future president of the Confederacy) and Abraham Lincoln. These figures both make appearances in her autobiography, *Behind the Scenes; or, Thirty Years a Slave, and Four Years in the White House* (1868).

## FROM *Behind the Scenes; or, Thirty Years a Slave, and Four Years in the White House*

Ever since arriving in Washington I had a great desire to work for the ladies of the White House, and to accomplish this end I was ready to make almost any sacrifice consistent with propriety. Work came in slowly, and I was beginning to feel very much embarrassed, for I did not know how I was to meet the bills staring me in the face. It is true, the bills were small, but then they were formidable to me, who had little or nothing to pay them with. While in this situation I called at the Ringolds, where I met Mrs. Captain Lee. Mrs. L. was in a state bordering on excitement, as the great event of the season, the dinner-party given in honor of the Prince of Wales, was soon to come off, and she must have a dress suitable for the occasion. The silk had been purchased, but a dress-maker had not yet been found. Miss Ringold recommended me, and I received the order to make the dress. When I called on Mrs. Lee the next day, her husband was in the room, and handing me a roll of bank bills, amounting to one hundred dollars, he requested me to purchase the trimmings, and to spare no expense in making a selection. With the money in my pocket I went out in the street, entered the store of Harper & Mitchell, and asked to look at their laces. Mr. Harper waited on me himself, and was polite and kind. When I asked permission to carry the laces to Mrs. Lee, in order to learn whether she could approve my selection or not, he gave a ready assent. When I reminded him that I was a stranger, and that the goods were valuable, he remarked that he was not afraid to trust me—that he believed my face was the index to an honest heart. It was pleasant to be spoken to thus, and I shall never forget the kind words of Mr. Harper. I often recall them, for they are associated with the dawn of a brighter period in my dark life. I purchased the trimmings, and Mr. Harper allowed me a commission of twenty-five dollars on the purchase. The dress was done in time, and it gave complete satisfaction. Mrs. Lee attracted great attention at the dinner-party, and her elegant dress proved a good card for me. I received numerous orders, and was relieved from all pecuniary embarrassments. One of my patrons was Mrs. Gen. McClean, a daughter of Gen. Sumner. One day when I was very busy, Mrs. McC. drove up to my apartments, came in where I was engaged with my needle, and in her emphatic way said:

"Lizzie, I am invited to dine at Willard's on next Sunday, and positively I have not a dress fit to wear on the occasion. I have just purchased material, and you must commence work on it right away."

"But Mrs. McClean," I replied, "I have more work now promised than I can do. It is impossible for me to make a dress for you to wear on Sunday next."

"Pshaw! Nothing is impossible. I must have the dress made by Sunday"; and she spoke with some impatience.

"I am sorry," I began, but she interrupted me.

"Now don't say no again. I tell you that you must make the dress. I have often heard you say that you would like to work for the ladies of the White House. Well, I have it in my power to obtain you this privilege. I know Mrs. Lincoln well, and you shall make a dress for her provided you finish mine in time to wear at dinner on Sunday."

The inducement was the best that could have been offered. I would undertake the dress if I should have to sit up all night—every night, to make my pledge good. I sent out and employed assistants, and, after much worry and trouble, the dress was completed to the satisfaction of Mrs. McClean. It appears that Mrs. Lincoln had upset a cup of coffee on the dress she designed wearing on the evening of the reception after the inauguration of Abraham Lincoln as President of the United States, which rendered it necessary that she should have a new one for the occasion. On asking Mrs. McClean who her dress-maker was, that lady promptly informed her,

"Lizzie Keckley."

"Lizzie Keckley? The name is familiar to me. She used to work for some of my lady friends in St. Louis, and they spoke well of her. Can you recommend her to me?"

"With confidence. Shall I send her to you?"

"If you please. I shall feel under many obligations for your kindness."

The next Sunday Mrs. McClean sent me a message to call at her house at four o'clock P.M., that day. As she did not state why I was to call, I determined to wait till Monday morning. Monday morning came, and nine o'clock found me at Mrs. McC.'s house. The streets of the capital were thronged with people, for this was Inauguration day. A new President, a man of the people from the broad prairies of the West, was to accept the solemn oath of office, was to assume the responsibilities attached to the high position of Chief Magistrate of the United States. Never was such deep interest felt in the inauguration proceedings as was felt today; for threats of assassination had been made, and every breeze from the South came heavily laden with the rumors of war. Around Willard's hotel swayed an excited crowd, and it was with the utmost difficulty that I worked my way to the house on the opposite side of the street, occupied by the McCleans. Mrs. McClean was out, but presently an aide on General McClean's staff called, and informed me that I was wanted at Willard's. I crossed the street, and on entering the hotel was met by Mrs. McClean, who greeted me:

"Lizzie, why did you not come yesterday, as I requested? Mrs. Lincoln wanted to see you, but I fear that now you are too late."

"I am sorry, Mrs. McClean. You did not say what you wanted with me yesterday, so I judged that this morning would do as well."

"You should have come yesterday," she insisted. "Go up to Mrs. Lincoln's room"—giving me the number—"she may find use for you yet."

With a nervous step I passed on, and knocked at Mrs. Lincoln's door. A cheery voice bade me come in, and a lady, inclined to stoutness, about forty years of age, stood before me.

"You are Lizzie Keckley, I believe."

I bowed assent.

"The dress-maker that Mrs. McClean recommended?"

"Yes, madam."

"Very well; I have not time to talk to you now, but would like to have you call at the White House, at eight o'clock to-morrow morning, where I shall then be."

I bowed myself out of the room, and returned to my apartments. The day passed slowly, for I could not help but speculate in relation to the appointed interview for the morrow. My long-cherished hope was about to be realized, and I could not rest.

Tuesday morning, at eight o'clock, I crossed the threshold of the White House for the first time. I was shown into a waiting-room, and informed that Mrs. Lincoln was at breakfast. In the waiting-room I found no less than three mantua-makers waiting for an interview with the wife of the new President. It seems that Mrs. Lincoln had told several of her lady friends that she had urgent need for a dress-maker, and that each of these friends had sent her mantua-maker to the White House. Hope fell at once. With so many rivals for the position sought after, I regarded my chances for success as extremely doubtful. I was the last one summoned to Mrs. Lincoln's presence. All the others had a hearing, and were dismissed. I went up-stairs timidly, and entering the room with nervous step, discovered the wife of the President standing by a window, looking out, and engaged in lively conversation with a lady, Mrs. Grimsly, as I afterwards learned. Mrs. L. came forward, and greeted me warmly.

"You have come at last. Mrs. Keckley, who have you worked for in the city?"

"Among others, Mrs. Senator Davis has been one of my best patrons," was my reply.

"Mrs. Davis! So you have worked for her, have you? Of course you gave satisfaction; so far, good. Can you do my work?"

"Yes, Mrs. Lincoln. Will you have much work for me to do?"

"That, Mrs. Keckley, will depend altogether upon your prices. I trust that your terms are reasonable. I cannot afford to be extravagant. We are just from the West, and are poor. If you do not charge too much, I shall be able to give you all my work."

"I do not think there will be any difficulty about charges, Mrs. Lincoln; my terms are reasonable."

"Well, if you will work cheap, you shall have plenty to do. I can't afford to pay big prices, so I frankly tell you so in the beginning."

The terms were satisfactorily arranged, and I measured Mrs. Lincoln, took the dress with me, a bright rose-colored moire-antique, and returned the next day to fit it on her. A number of ladies were in the room, all making prepartions for the levee to come off on Friday night. These ladies, I learned, were relatives of Mrs. L's,—Mrs. Edwards and Mrs. Kellogg, her own sisters, and Elizabeth Edwards and Julia Baker, her nieces. Mrs. Lincoln this morning was dressed in a cashmere wrapper, quilted down the front; and she wore a simple head-dress. The other ladies wore morning robes.

I was hard at work on the dress, when I was informed that the levee had been postponed from Friday night till Tuesday night. This, of course, gave me more time to complete my task. Mrs. Lincoln sent for me, and suggested some alteration in style, which was made. She also requested that I make a waist of blue watered silk for Mrs. Grimsly, as work on the dress would not require all my time.

Tuesday evening came, and I had taken the last stitches on the dress. I folded it and carried it to the White House, with the waist for Mrs. Grimsly. When I went up-stairs, I found the ladies in a terrible state of excitement. Mrs. Lincoln was protesting that she could not go down, for the reason that she had nothing to wear.

"Mrs. Keckley, you have disappointed me—deceived me. Why do you bring my dress at this late hour?"

"Because I have just finished it, and I thought I should be in time."

"But you are not in time, Mrs. Keckley; you have bitterly disappointed me. I have no time now to dress, and, what is more, I will not dress, and go down-stairs."

"I am sorry if I have disappointed you, Mrs. Lincoln, for I intended to be in time. Will you let me dress you? I can have you ready in a few minutes."

"No, I won't be dressed. I will stay in my room. Mr. Lincoln can go down with the other ladies."

"But there is plenty of time for you to dress, Mary," joined in Mrs. Grimsly and Mrs. Edwards. "Let Mrs. Keckley assist you, and she will soon have you ready."

Thus urged, she consented. I dressed her hair, and arranged the dress on her. It fitted nicely, and she was pleased. Mr. Lincoln came in, threw himself on the sofa, laughed with Willie and little Tad, and then commenced pulling on his gloves, quoting poetry all the while.

"You seem to be in a poetical mood to-night," said his wife.

"Yes, mother, these are poetical times," was his pleasant reply. "I declare, you look charming in that dress. Mrs. Keckley has met with great success." And then he proceeded to compliment the other ladies.

Mrs. Lincoln looked elegant in her rose-colored moire-antique. She wore a pearl necklace, pearl ear-rings, pearl bracelets, and red roses in her hair. Mrs. Baker was dressed in lemon-colored silk; Mrs. Kellogg in a drab silk, ashes of rose; Mrs. Edwards in a brown and black silk; Miss Edwards in crimson, and Mrs. Grimsly in blue watered silk. Just before starting down-stairs, Mrs. Lincoln's lace handkerchief was the object of search. It had been displaced by Tad, who was mischievous, and hard to restrain. The handkerchief found, all became serene. Mrs. Lincoln took

the President's arm, and with smiling face led the train below. I was surprised at her grace and composure. I had heard so much, in current and
malicious report, of her low life, of her ignorance and vulgarity, that I expected to see her embarrassed on this occasion. Report, I soon saw, was
wrong. No queen, accustomed to the usages of royalty all her life, could
have comported herself with more calmness and dignity than did the
wife of the President. She was confident and self-possessed, and confidence always gives grace.

This levee was a brilliant one, and the only one of the season. I became
the regular modiste of Mrs. Lincoln. I made fifteen or sixteen dresses for
her during the spring and early part of the summer, when she left Washington; spending the hot weather at Saratoga, Long Branch, and other
places. In the mean time I was employed by Mrs. Senator Douglas, one
of the loveliest ladies that I ever met, Mrs. Secretary Wells, Mrs. Secretary Stanton, and others. Mrs. Douglas always dressed in deep mourning,
with excellent taste, and several of the leading ladies of Washington society were extremely jealous of her superior attractions. . . .

✻    ✻    ✻

Mr. Lincoln was fond of pets. He had two goats that knew the sound of
his voice, and when he called them they would come bounding to his
side. In the warm bright days, he and Tad would sometimes play in the
yard with these goats, for an hour at a time. One Saturday afternoon I
went to the White House to dress Mrs. Lincoln. I had nearly completed
my task when the President came in. It was a bright day, and walking to
the window, he looked down into the yard, smiled, and, turning to me,
asked:

"Madam Elizabeth, you are fond of pets, are you not?"

"O yes, sir," I answered.

"Well, come here and look at my two goats. I believe they are the
kindest and best goats in the world. See how they sniff the clear air, and
skip and play in the sunshine. Whew! what a jump," he exclaimed as one
of the goats made a lofty spring. "Madam Elizabeth, did you ever before
see such an active goat?" Musing a moment, he continued: "He feeds on
my bounty, and jumps with joy. Do you think we could call him a
bounty-jumper? But I flatter the bounty-jumper. My goat is far above
him. I would rather wear his horns and hairy coat through life, than de-
mean myself to the level of the man who plunders the national treasury
in the name of patriotism. The man who enlists into the service for a consideration, and deserts the moment he receives his money but to repeat
the play, is bad enough; but the men who manipulate the grand machine
and who simply make the bounty-jumper their agent in an outrageous

fraud are far worse. They are beneath the worms that crawl in the dark hidden places of earth."

His lips curled with haughty scorn, and a cloud was gathering on his brow. Only a moment the shadow rested on his face. Just then both goats looked up at the window and shook their heads as if they would say "How d'ye do, old friend?"

"See, Madam Elizabeth," exclaimed the President in a tone of enthusiasm, "my pets recognize me. How earnestly they look! There they go again; what jolly fun!" and he laughed outright as the goats bounded swiftly to the other side of the yard. Just then Mrs. Lincoln called out, "Come, Lizabeth; if I get ready to go down this evening I must finish dressing myself, or you must stop staring at those silly goats."

Mrs. Lincoln was not fond of pets, and she could not understand how Mr. Lincoln could take so much delight in his goats. After Willie's death, she could not bear the sight of anything he loved, not even a flower. Costly bouquets were presented to her, but she turned from them with a shudder, and either placed them in a room where she could not see them, or threw them out of the window. She gave all of Willie's toys—everything connected with him—away, as she said she could not look upon them without thinking of her poor dead boy, and to think of him, in his white shroud and cold grave, was maddening. I never in my life saw a more peculiarly constituted woman. Search the world over, and you will not find her counterpart. After Mr. Lincoln's death, the goats that he loved so well were given away—I believe to Mrs. Lee, *née* Miss Blair, one of the few ladies with whom Mrs. Lincoln was on intimate terms in Washington.

During my residence in the Capital I made my home with Mr. and Mrs. Walker Lewis, people of my own race, and friends in the truest sense of the word.

The days passed without any incident of particular note disturbing the current of life. On Friday morning, April 14th—alas! what American does not remember the day—I saw Mrs. Lincoln but for a moment. She told me that she was to attend the theatre that night with the President, but I was not summoned to assist her in making her toilette. Sherman had swept from the northern border of Georgia through the heart of the Confederacy down to the sea, striking the death-blow to the rebellion. Grant had pursued General Lee beyond Richmond, and the army of Virginia, that had made such stubborn resistance, was crumbling to pieces. Fort Sumter had fallen;—the stronghold first wrenched from the Union, and which had braved the fury of Federal guns for so many years, was restored to the Union; the end of the war was near at hand, and the great pulse of the loyal North thrilled with joy. The dark war-cloud was fading, and a white-robed angel seemed to hover in the sky, whispering "Peace—peace on earth, good-will toward men!" Sons, brothers, fathers, friends, sweethearts were coming home. Soon the white tents would be folded, the volunteer army be disbanded, and tranquillity again reign. Happy, happy day!—happy at least to those who fought under the banner of the Union. There was great rejoicing throughout the North. From the Atlantic to the Pacific, flags were gayly thrown to the breeze, and at night every city blazed with its tens of thousand lights. But scarcely had the fireworks ceased to play, and the lights been taken down from the windows, when the lightning flashed the most appalling news over the magnetic wires. "The President has been murdered!" spoke the swift-winged messenger, and the loud huzza died upon the lips. A nation suddenly paused in the midst of festivity, and stood paralyzed with horror—transfixed with awe.

Oh, memorable day! Oh, memorable night! Never before was joy so violently contrasted with sorrow.

At 11 o'clock at night I was awakened by an old friend and neighbor, Miss M. Brown, with the startling intelligence that the entire Cabinet had been assassinated, and Mr. Lincoln shot, but not mortally wounded. When I heard the words I felt as if the blood had been frozen in my veins, and that my lungs must collapse for the want of air. Mr. Lincoln shot! the Cabinet assassinated! What could it mean? The streets were alive with wondering, awe-stricken people. Rumors flew thick and fast, and the wildest reports came with every new arrival. The words were repeated with blanched cheeks and quivering lips. I waked Mr. and Mrs. Lewis, and told them that the President was shot, and that I must go to the White House. I could not remain in a state of uncertainty. I felt that the house would not hold me. They tried to quiet me, but gentle words could not calm the wild tempest. They quickly dressed themselves, and we sallied out into the street to drift with the excited throng. We walked rapidly towards the White House, and on our way passed the residence of Secretary Seward, which was surrounded by armed soldiers, keeping back all intruders with the point of the bayonet. We hurried on, and as we approached the White House, saw that it too was surrounded with soldiers. Every entrance was strongly guarded, and no one was permitted to pass. The guard at the gate told us that Mr. Lincoln had not been brought home, but refused to give any other information. More excited than ever, we wandered down the street. Grief and anxiety were making me weak, and as we joined the outskirts of a large crowd, I began to feel as meek and humble as a penitent child. A gray-haired old man was passing. I caught a glimpse of his face, and it seemed so full of kindness and sorrow that I gently touched his arm, and imploringly asked:

"Will you please, sir, to tell me whether Mr. Lincoln is dead or not?"

"Not dead," he replied, "but dying. God help us!" and with a heavy step he passed on.

"Not dead, but dying! then indeed God help us!"

We learned that the President was mortally wounded—that he had been shot down in his box at the theatre, and that he was not expected to live till morning; when we returned home with heavy hearts. I could not sleep. I wanted to go to Mrs. Lincoln, as I pictured her wild with grief; but then I did not know where to find her, and I must wait till morning. Never did the hours drag so slowly. Every moment seemed an age, and I could do nothing but walk about and hold my arms in mental agony.

Morning came at last, and a sad morning was it. The flags that floated so gayly yesterday now were draped in black, and hung in silent folds at half-mast. The President was dead, and a nation was mourning for him. Every house was draped in black, and every face wore a solemn look. People spoke in subdued tones, and glided whisperingly, wonderingly, silently about the streets.

About eleven o'clock on Saturday morning a carriage drove up to the door, and a messenger asked for "Elizabeth Keckley."

"Who wants her?" I asked.

"I come from Mrs. Lincoln. If you are Mrs. Keckley, come with me immediately to the White House."

I hastily put on my shawl and bonnet, and was driven at a rapid rate to the White House. Everything about the building was sad and solemn. I was quickly shown to Mrs. Lincoln's room, and on entering, saw Mrs. L. tossing uneasily about upon a bed. The room was darkened, and the only person in it besides the widow of the President was Mrs. Secretary Welles, who had spent the night with her. Bowing to Mrs. Welles, I went to the bedside.

"Why did you not come to me last night, Elizabeth—I sent for you?" Mrs. Lincoln asked in a low whisper.

"I did try to come to you, but I could not find you," I answered, as I laid my hand upon her hot brow.

I afterwards learned, that when she had partially recovered from the first shock of the terrible tragedy in the theatre, Mrs. Welles asked:

"Is there no one, Mrs. Lincoln, that you desire to have with you in this terrible affliction?"

"Yes, send for Elizabeth Keckley. I want her just as soon as she can be brought here."

Three messengers, it appears, were successively despatched for me, but all of them mistook the number and failed to find me.

Shortly after entering the room on Saturday morning, Mrs. Welles excused herself, as she said she must go to her own family, and I was left alone with Mrs. Lincoln.

She was nearly exhausted with grief, and when she became a little quiet, I asked and received permission to go into the Guests' Room, where the body of the President lay in state. When I crossed the threshold of the room, I could not help recalling the day on which I had seen little Willie lying in his coffin where the body of his father now lay. I remembered how the President had wept over the pale beautiful face of his gifted boy, and now the President himself was dead. The last time I saw him he spoke kindly to me, but alas! the lips would never move again. The light had faded from his eyes, and when the light went out the soul went with it. What a noble soul was his—noble in all the noble attributes of God! Never did I enter the solemn chamber of death with such palpitating heart and trembling footsteps as I entered it that day. No common mortal had died. The Moses of my people had fallen in the hour of his triumph. Fame had woven her choicest chaplet for his brow. Though the brow was cold and pale in death, the chaplet should not fade, for God had studded it with the glory of the eternal stars.

When I entered the room, the members of the Cabinet and many distinguished officers of the army were grouped around the body of their fallen chief. They made room for me, and, approaching the body, I lifted the white cloth from the white face of the man that I had worshipped as an idol—looked upon as a demi-god. Notwithstanding the violence of the death of the President, there was something beautiful as well as grandly solemn in the expression of the placid face. There lurked the sweetness and gentleness of childhood, and the stately grandeur of god-like intellect. I gazed long at the face, and turned away with tears in my eyes and a choking sensation in my throat. Ah! never was man so widely mourned before. The whole world bowed their heads in grief when Abraham Lincoln died.

Returning to Mrs. Lincoln's room, I found her in a new paroxysm of grief. Robert was bending over his mother with tender affection, and little Tad was crouched at the foot of the bed with a world of agony in his young face. I shall never forget the scene—the wails of a broken heart, the unearthly shrieks, the terrible convulsions, the wild, tempestuous outbursts of grief from the soul. I bathed Mrs. Lincoln's head with cold water, and soothed the terrible tornado as best I could. Tad's grief at his father's death was as great as the grief of his mother, but her terrible outbursts awed the boy into silence. Sometimes he would throw his arms around her neck, and exclaim, between his broken sobs, "Don't cry so, Mamma! don't cry, or you will make me cry, too! You will break my heart."

Mrs. Lincoln could not bear to hear Tad cry, and when he would plead to her not to break his heart, she would calm herself with a great effort, and clasp her child in her arms.

Every room in the White House was darkened, and every one spoke in subdued tones, and moved about with muffled tread. The very atmosphere breathed of the great sorrow which weighed heavily upon each heart. Mrs. Lincoln never left her room, and while the body of her husband was being borne in solemn state from the Atlantic to the broad prairies of the West, she was weeping with her fatherless children in her private chamber. She denied admittance to almost every one, and I was her only companion, except her children, in the days of her great sorrow.

# LUCY LARCOM
## (1824–1893)

In a biography of Lucy Larcom, Shirley Marchalonis concludes that "Larcom's own assessment of her life and achievements would undoubtedly stress . . . her struggle towards a secure faith and her ability to use her writing to share that faith and to comfort and inspire others." Larcom was an exceptionally popular writer in the late nineteenth century. Her partial autobiography, *A New England Girlhood*, was published four years before her death in 1893; she declares it was written "for women who have not forgotten their girlhood." In many ways, her work foreshadows that of a host of later recorders of childhood—including Mark Twain, Henry James, and, among contemporaries, Mary Karr and bell hooks.

Larcom was primarily a poet, deemed the "best of America's minor poets" by the *Boston Globe*. Her verse follows strict metrical convention and often approaches the world as an idyllic, wonder-filled place. In her autobiography, however, her time working in the Lowell mills seems of equal importance to her time spent writing verse; she portrays herself as a restless and searching New England girl, conjuring her world with swift, bold strokes.

## FROM *A New England Girlhood*

### GLIMPSES OF POETRY

Our close relationship to Old England was sometimes a little misleading to us juveniles. The conditions of our life were entirely different, but we read her descriptive stories and sang her songs as if they were true for us, too. One of the first things I learned to repeat—I think it was in the spelling-book—began with the verse:—

> "I thank the goodness and the grace
> That on my birth has smiled,
> And made me, in these latter days,
> A happy *English* child."

And some lines of a very familiar hymn by Dr. Watts ran thus:—

> "Whene'er I take my walks abroad,
>    How many poor I see.
> . . . . . . . . . . . . . . . . . . . . . . . . . .
> "How many children in the street
>    Half naked I behold;
> While I am clothed from head to feet,
>    And sheltered from the cold."

Now a ragged, half-clothed child, or one that could really be called poor, in the extreme sense of the word, was the rarest of all sights in a thrifty New England town fifty years ago. I used to look sharply for those children, but I never could see one. And a beggar! Oh, if a real beggar would come along, like the one described in

> "Pity the sorrows of a poor old man,"

what a wonderful event that would be! I believe I had more curiosity about a beggar, and more ignorance, too, than about a king. The poem read:—

> "A pampered menial drove me from the door."

What sort of creature could a "pampered menial" be? Nothing that had ever come under our observation corresponded to the words. Nor was it easy for us to attach any meaning to the word "servant." There were women who came in occasionally to do the washing, or to help about extra work. But they were decently clothed, and had homes of their own, more or less comfortable, and their quaint talk and free-and-easy ways were often as much of a lift to the household as the actual assistance they rendered.

I settled down upon the conclusion that "rich" and "poor" were book-words only, describing something far off, and having nothing to do with our every-day experience. My mental definition of "rich people," from home observation, was something like this: People who live in three-story houses, and keep their green blinds closed, and hardly ever come out and talk with the folks in the street. There were a few such houses in Beverly, and a great many in Salem, where my mother sometimes took me for a shopping walk. But I did not suppose that any of the people who lived near us were *very* rich, like those in books.

Everybody about us worked, and we expected to take hold of our part while young. I think we were rather eager to begin, for we believed that work would make men and women of us.

I, however, was not naturally an industrious child, but quite the reverse. When my father sent us down to weed his vegetable-garden at the foot of the lane, I, the youngest of his weeders, liked to go with the rest, but not for the sake of the work or the pay. I generally gave it up before I had weeded half a bed. It made me so warm! and my back did ache so! I stole off into the shade of the great apple-trees, and let the west wind fan my hot cheeks, and looked up into the boughs, and listened to the many, many birds that seemed chattering to each other in a language of their own. What was it they were saying? and why could not I understand it? Perhaps I should, sometime. I had read of people who did, in fairy tales.

When the others started homeward, I followed. I did not mind their calling me lazy, nor that my father gave me only one tarnished copper cent, while Lida received two or three bright ones. I had had what I wanted most. I would rather sit under the apple-trees and hear the birds sing than have a whole handful of bright copper pennies. It was well for my father and his garden that his other children were not like me.

The work which I was born to, but had not begun to do, was sometimes a serious weight upon my small, forecasting brain.

One of my hymns ended with the lines,—

> "With books, and work, and healthful play,
>  May my first years be passed,
> That I may give, for every day,
>  Some good account at last."

I knew all about the books and the play; but the work,—how should I ever learn to do it?

My father had always strongly emphasized his wish that all his children, girls as well as boys, should have some independent means of self-support by the labor of their hands; that every one should, as was the general custom, "learn a trade." Tailor's work—the finishing of men's outside garments—was the "trade" learned most frequently by women in those days, and one or more of my older sisters worked at it; I think it must have been at home, for I somehow or somewhere got the idea, while I was a small child, that the chief end of woman was to make clothing for mankind.

This thought came over me with a sudden dread one Sabbath morning when I was a toddling thing, led along by my sister, behind my father and mother. As they walked arm in arm before me, I lifted my eyes from my father's heels to his head, and mused: "How tall he is! and how long his coat looks! and how many thousand, thousand stitches there must be in his coat and pantaloons! And I suppose I have got to grow up and have a husband, and put all those little stitches into *his* coats and pantaloons.

Oh, I never, never can do it!" A shiver of utter discouragement went through me. With that ask before me, it hardly seemed to me as if life were worth living. I went on to meeting, and I suppose I forgot my trouble in a hymn, but for the moment it was real. It was not the only time in my life that I have tired myself out with crossing bridges to which I never came.

Another trial confronted me in the shape of an ideal but impossible patchwork quilt. We learned to sew patchwork at school, while we were learning the alphabet; and almost every girl, large or small, had a bed-quilt of her own begun, with an eye to future house furnishing. I was not over fond of sewing, but I thought it best to begin mine early.

So I collected a few squares of calico, and undertook to put them together in my usual independent way, without asking direction. I liked assorting those little figured bits of cotton cloth, for they were scraps of gowns I had seen worn, and they reminded me of the persons who wore them. One fragment, in particular, was like a picture to me. It was a delicate pink and brown sea-moss pattern, on a white ground, a piece of a dress belonging to my married sister, who was to me bride and angel in one. I always saw her face before me when I unfolded this scrap, — a face with an expression truly heavenly in its loveliness. Heaven claimed her before my childhood was ended. Her beautiful form was laid to rest in mid-ocean, too deep to be pillowed among the soft sea-mosses. But she lived long enough to make a heaven of my childhood whenever she came home.

One of the sweetest of our familiar hymns I always think of as belonging to her, and as a still unbroken bond between her spirit and mine. She had come back to us for a brief visit, soon after her marriage, with some deep, new experience of spiritual realities which I, a child of four or five years, felt in the very tones of her voice, and in the expression of her eyes.

My mother told her of my fondness for the hymn-book, and she turned to me with a smile and said, "Won't you learn one hymn for me — one hymn that I love very much?"

Would I not? She could not guess how happy she made me by wishing me to do anything for her sake. The hymn was, —

"Whilst Thee I seek, protecting Power."

In a few minutes I repeated the whole to her; and its own beauty, pervaded with the tenderness of her love for me, fixed it at once indelibly in my memory. Perhaps I shall repeat it to her again, deepened with a lifetime's meaning, beyond the sea, and beyond the stars.

I could dream over my patchwork, but I could not bring it into conventional shape. My sisters, whose fingers had been educated, called my sewing "gobblings." I grew disgusted with it myself, and gave away all my pieces except the pretty sea-moss pattern, which I was not willing to see patched up with common calico. It was evident that I should never conquer fate with my needle.

Among other domestic traditions of the old times was the saying that every girl must have a pillow-case full of stockings of her own knitting before she was married. Here was another mountain before me, for I took it for granted that marrying was inevitable — one of the things that everybody must do, like learning to read, or going to meeting.

I began to knit my own stockings when I was six or seven years old, and kept on, until home-made stockings went out of fashion. The pillow-case full, however, was never attempted, any more than the patchwork quilt. I heard somebody say one day that there must always be one "old maid" in every family of girls, and I accepted the prophecy of some of my elders, that I was to be that one. I was rather glad to know that freedom of choice in the matter was possible.

One day, when we younger ones were hanging about my golden-haired and golden-hearted sister Emilie, teasing her with wondering questions about our future, she announced to us (she had reached the mature age of fifteen years) that she intended to be an old maid, and that we might all come and live with her. Some one listening reproved her, but she said, "Why, if they fit themselves to be good, helpful, cheerful old maids, they will certainly be better wives, if they ever are married," and that maxim I laid by in my memory for future contingencies, for I believed in every word she ever uttered. She herself, however, did not carry out her girlish intention. "Her children arise up and call her blessed; her husband also; and he praiseth her." But the little sisters she used to fondle as her "babies" have never allowed their own years nor her changed relations to cancel their claim upon her motherly sympathies.

I regard it as a great privilege to have been one of a large family, and nearly the youngest. We had strong family resemblances, and yet no two seemed at all alike. It was like rehearsing in a small world each our own part in the great one awaiting us. If we little ones occasionally had some severe snubbing mixed with the petting and praising and loving, that was wholesome for us, and not at all to be regretted.

Almost every one of my sisters had some distinctive aptitude with her fingers. One worked exquisite lace-embroidery; another had a knack at cutting and fitting her doll's clothing so perfectly that the wooden lady was always a typical specimen of the genteel doll-world; and another was an expert at fine stitching, so delicately done that it was a pleasure to see or to wear anything her needle had touched. I had none of these gifts. I looked on and admired, and sometimes tried to imitate, but my efforts usually ended in defeat and mortification.

I did like to knit, however, and I could shape a stocking tolerably well. My fondness for this kind of work was chiefly because it did not require much thought. Except when there was "widening" or "narrowing" to be done, I did not need to keep my eyes upon it at all. So I took a book upon my lap and read, and read, while the needles clicked on, comforting me with the reminder that I was not absolutely unemployed, while yet I was having a good time reading.

I began to know that I liked poetry, and to think a good deal about it at my childish work. Outside of the hymn-book, the first rhymes I committed to memory were in the "Old Farmer's Almanac," files of which hung in the chimney corner, and were an inexhaustible source of entertainment to us younger ones.

My father kept his newspapers also carefully filed away in the garret, but we made sad havoc among the "Palladiums" and other journals that we ought to have kept as antiquarian treasures. We valued the anecdote column and the poet's corner only; these we clipped unsparingly for our scrap-books.

A tattered copy of Johnson's large Dictionary was a great delight to me, on account of the specimens of English versification which I found in the Introduction. I learned them as if they were so many poems. I used to keep this old volume close to my pillow; and I amused myself when I awoke in the morning by reciting its jingling contrasts of iambic and trochaic and dactylic metre, and thinking what a charming occupation it must be to "make up" verses.

I made my first rhymes when I was about seven years old. My brother John proposed "writing poetry" as a rainy-day amusement, one afternoon when we two were sent up into the garret to entertain ourselves without disturbing the family. He soon grew tired of his unavailing attempts, but I produced two stanzas, the first of which read thus:—

> One summer day, said little Jane,
> We were walking down a shady lane,
> When suddenly the wind blew high,
> And the red lightning flashed in the sky.

The second stanza descended in a dreadfully abrupt anti-climax; but I was blissfully ignorant of rhetoricians' rules, and supposed that the rhyme was the only important thing. It may amuse my child-readers if I give them this verse too:—

> The peals of thunder, how they rolled!
> *And I felt myself a little cooled;*
> *For I before had been quite warm;*
> But now around me was a storm.

My brother was surprised at my success, and I believe I thought my verses quite fine, too. But I was rather sorry that I had written them, for I had to say them over to the family, and then they sounded silly. The habit was formed, however, and I went on writing little books of ballads, which I illustrated with colors from my toy paint-box, and then squeezed down into the cracks of the garret floor, for fear that somebody would find them.

My fame crept out among the neighbors, nevertheless. I was even invited to write some verses in a young lady's album; and Aunt Hannah asked me to repeat my verses to her. I considered myself greatly honored by both requests.

My fondness for books began very early. At the age of four I had formed the plan of collecting a library. Not of limp, paper-covered picture-books, such as people give to babies; no! I wanted books with stiff covers, that could stand up side by side on a shelf, and maintain their own character as books. But I did not know how to make a beginning, for mine were all of the kind manufactured for infancy, and I thought they deserved no better fate than to be tossed about among my rag-babies and playthings.

One day, however, I found among some rubbish in a corner a volume with one good stiff cover; the other was missing. It did not look so very old, nor as if it had been much read; neither did it look very inviting to me as I turned its leaves. On its title-page I read: "The Life of John Calvin." I did not know who he was, but a book was a book to me, and this would do as well as any to begin my library with. I looked upon it as a treasure, and to make sure of my claim, I took it down to my mother and timidly asked if I might have it for my own. She gave me in reply a rather amused "Yes," and I ran back happy, and began my library by setting John Calvin upright on a beam under the garret eaves, my "make-believe" book-case shelf.

I was proud of my literary property, and filled out the shelf in fancy with a row of books, every one of which should have two stiff covers. But I found no more neglected volumes that I could adopt. John Calvin was left to a lonely fate, and I am afraid that at last the mice devoured him. Before I had quite forgotten him, however, I did pick up one other book of about his size, and in the same one-covered condition; and this attracted me more, because it was in verse. Rhyme had always a sort of magnetic power over me, whether I caught at any idea it contained or not. . . .

## BEGINNING TO WORK

. . . We helped a little about the housework, before and after school, making beds, trimming lamps, and washing dishes. The heaviest work was done by a strong Irish girl, my mother always attending to the cooking herself. She was, however, a better caterer than the circumstances required or permitted. She liked to make nice things for the table, and, having been accustomed to an abundant supply, could never learn to economize. At a dollar and a quarter a week for board, (the price allowed for mill-girls by the corporations) great care in expenditure was necessary. It was not in my mother's nature closely to calculate costs, and in this way there came to be a continually increasing leak in the family purse. The older members of the family did everything they could, but it was not enough. I heard it said one day, in a distressed tone, "The children will have to leave school and go into the mill."

There were many pros and cons between my mother and sisters before this was positively decided. The mill-agent did not want to take us two little girls, but consented on condition we should be sure to attend school the full number of months prescribed each year. I, the younger one, was then between eleven and twelve years old.

I listened to all that was said about it, very much fearing that I should not be permitted to do the coveted work. For the feeling had already frequently come to me, that I was the one too many in the overcrowded family nest. Once, before we left our old home, I had heard a neighbor condoling with my mother because there were so many of us, and her emphatic reply had been a great relief to my mind:—

"There is n't one more than I want. I could not spare a single one of my children."

But her difficulties were increasing, and I thought it would be a pleasure to feel that I was not a trouble or burden or expense to anybody. So I went to my first day's work in the mill with a light heart. The novelty of it made it seem easy, and it really was not hard, just to change the bobbins on the spinning-frames every three quarters of an hour or so, with half a dozen other little girls who were doing the same thing. When I came back at night, the family began to pity me for my long, tiresome day's work, but I laughed and said,—

"Why, it is nothing but fun. It is just like play."

And for a little while it was only a new amusement; I liked it better than going to school and "making believe" I was learning when I was not. And there was a great deal of play mixed with it. We were not occupied more than half the time. The intervals were spent frolicking around among the spinning-frames, teasing and talking to the older girls, or entertaining ourselves with games and stories in a corner, or exploring, with the overseer's permission, the mysteries of the carding-room, the dressing-room, and the weaving-room.

I never cared much for machinery. The buzzing and hissing and whizzing of pulleys and rollers and spindles and flyers around me often grew tiresome. I could not see into their complications, or feel interested in them. But in a room below us we were sometimes allowed to peer in through a sort of blind door at the great water-wheel that carried the works of the whole mill. It was so huge that we could only watch a few of its spokes at a time, and part of its dripping rim, moving with a slow, measured strength through the darkness that shut it in. It impressed me with something of the awe which comes to us in thinking of the great Power which keeps the mechanism of the universe in motion. Even now, the remembrance of its large, mysterious movement, in which every little motion of every noisy little wheel was involved, brings back to me a verse from one of my favorite hymns: —

> "Our lives through various scenes are drawn,
>     And vexed by trifling cares,
> While Thine eternal thought moves on
>     Thy undisturbed affairs."

There were compensations for being shut in to daily toil so early. The mill itself had its lessons for us. But it was not, and could not be, the right sort of life for a child, and we were happy in the knowledge that, at the longest, our employment was only to be temporary.

When I took my next three months at the grammar school, everything there was changed, and I too was changed. The teachers were kind, and thorough in their instruction; and my mind seemed to have been ploughed up during that year of work, so that knowledge took root in it easily. It was a great delight to me to study, and at the end of the three months the master told me that I was prepared for the high school.

But alas! I could not go. The little money I could earn — one dollar a week, besides the price of my board — was needed in the family, and I must return to the mill. It was a severe disappointment to me, though I did not say so at home. I did not at all accept the conclusion of a neighbor whom I heard talking about it with my mother. His daughter was going to the high school, and my mother was telling him how sorry she was that I could not.

"Oh," he said, in a soothing tone, "my girl has n't got any such head-piece as yours has. Your girl does n't need to go."

Of course I knew that whatever sort of a "head-piece" I had, I did need and want just that very opportunity to study. I think the resolution was then formed, inwardly, that I *would* go to school again, some time, whatever happened. I went back to my work, but now without enthusiasm. I had looked through an open door that I was not willing to see shut upon me.

I began to reflect upon life rather seriously for a girl of twelve or thirteen. What was I here for? What could I make of myself? Must I submit to be carried along with the current, and do just what everybody else did? No: I knew I should not do that, for there was a certain Myself who was always starting up with her own original plan or aspiration before me, and who was quite indifferent as to what people generally thought.

Well, I would find out what this Myself was good for, and that she should be!

It was but the presumption of extreme youth. How gladly would I know now, after these long years, just why I was sent into the world, and whether I have in any degree fulfilled the purpose of my being!

In the older times it was seldom said to little girls, as it always has been said to boys, that they ought to have some definite plan, while they were children, what to be and do when they were grown up. There was usually but one path open before them, to become good wives and house-keepers. And the ambition of most girls was to follow their mothers' footsteps in this direction; a natural and laudable ambition. But girls, as well as boys, must often have been conscious of their own peculiar capabilities,—must have desired to cultivate and make use of their individual powers. When I was growing up, they had already begun to be encouraged to do so. We were often told that it was our duty to develop any talent we might possess, or at least to learn how to do some one thing which the world needed, or which would make it a pleasanter world.

When I thought what I should best like to do, my first dream—almost a baby's dream—about it was that it would be a fine thing to be a school-teacher, like Aunt Hannah. Afterward, when I heard that there were artists, I wished I could some time be one. A slate and pencil, to draw pictures, was my first request whenever a day's ailment kept me at home from school; and I rather enjoyed being a little ill, for the sake of amusing myself in that way. The wish grew up with me; but there were no good drawing-teachers in those days, and if there had been, the cost of instruction would have been beyond the family means. My sister Emilie, however, who saw my taste and shared it herself, did her best to assist me, furnishing me with pencil and paper and paint-box.

If I could only make a rose bloom on paper, I thought I should be happy! or if I could at last succeed in drawing the outline of winter-stripped boughs as I saw them against the sky, it seemed to me that I should be willing to spend years in trying. I did try a little, and very often. Jack Frost was my most inspiring teacher. His sketches on the bedroom window-pane in cold mornings were my ideal studies of Swiss scenery, crags and peaks and chalets and fir-trees,—and graceful tracery of ferns, like those that grew in the woods where we went huckleberrying, all blended together by his touch of enchantment. I wondered whether human fingers ever succeeded in imitating that lovely work.

The taste has followed me all my life through, but I could never indulge it except as a recreation. I was not to be an artist, and I am rather glad that I was hindered, for I had even stronger inclinations in other directions; and art, really noble art, requires the entire devotion of a lifetime.

I seldom thought seriously of becoming an author, although it seemed to me that anybody who had written a book would have a right to feel very proud. But I believed that a person must be exceedingly wise, before presuming to attempt it: although now and then I thought I could feel ideas growing in my mind that it might be worth while to put into a book,—if I lived and studied until I was forty or fifty years old.

I wrote my little verses, to be sure, but that was nothing; they just grew. They were the same as breathing or singing. I could not help writing them, and I thought and dreamed a great many that never were put on paper. They seemed to fly into my mind and away again, like birds going with a carol through the air. It seemed strange to me that people should notice them, or should think my writing verses anything peculiar; for I supposed that they were in everybody's mind, just as they were in mine, and that anybody could write them who chose.

One day I heard a relative say to my mother,—

"Keep what she writes till she grows up, and perhaps she will get money for it. I have heard of somebody who earned a thousand dollars by writing poetry."

It sounded so absurd to me. Money for writing verses! One dollar would be as ridiculous as a thousand. I should as soon have thought of being paid for thinking! My mother, fortunately, was sensible enough never to flatter me or let me be flattered about my scribbling. It never was allowed to hinder any work I had to do. I crept away into a corner to write what came into my head, just as I ran away to play; and I looked upon it only as my most agreeable amusement, never thinking of preserving anything which did not of itself stay in my memory. This too was well, for the time did not come when I could afford to look upon verse-writing as an occupation. Through my life, it has only been permitted to me as an aside from other more pressing employments. Whether I should have written better verses had circumstances left me free to do what I chose, it is impossible now to know.

All my thoughts about my future sent me back to Aunt Hannah and my first infantile idea of being a teacher. I foresaw that I should be that before I could be or do anything else. It had been impressed upon me that I must make myself useful in the world, and certainly one could be useful who could "keep school" as Aunt Hannah did. I did not see anything else for a girl to do who wanted to use her brains as well as her hands. So the plan of preparing myself to be a teacher gradually and almost unconsciously shaped itself in my mind as the only practicable one. I could earn my living in that way, — an all-important consideration.

I liked the thought of self-support, but I would have chosen some artistic or beautiful work if I could. I had no especial aptitude for teaching, and no absorbing wish to be a teacher, but it seemed to me that I might succeed if I tried. What I did like about it was that one must know something first. I must acquire knowledge before I could impart it, and that was just what I wanted. I could be a student, wherever I was and whatever else I had to be or do, and I would!

I knew I should write; I could not help doing that, for my hand seemed instinctively to move towards pen and paper in moments of leisure. But to write anything worth while, I must have mental cultivation; so, in preparing myself to teach, I could also be preparing myself to write.

This was the plan that indefinitely shaped itself in my mind as I returned to my work in the spinning-room, and which I followed out, not without many breaks and hindrances and neglects, during the next six or seven years, — to learn all I could, so that I should be fit to teach or to write, as the way opened. And it turned out that fifteen or twenty of my best years were given to teaching.

# MARK TWAIN
## (1835–1910)

Mark Twain was born Samuel Langhorne Clemens in 1835, and raised in Hannibal, Missouri. His boyhood in this small town on the banks of the Mississippi would inspire much of his best work. His formal schooling ended early, but he apprenticed himself to a printer—whose trade led him naturally into journalism. He soon became a successful journalist, humorist, and lecturer, traveling the globe in search of fame and fortune.

In 1857, having spent years away from the Mississippi that he loved, he became a pilot on a riverboat, thus fulfilling a boyhood dream. This is the period he wrote about in *Life on the Mississippi* (1883), where the vividness of his writing equals that of his masterpiece, *Huckleberry Finn* (1884); indeed, it established Twain as one of America's consummate autobiographers. Yet it could easily be said there is hardly a story, novel, or travelogue by Twain that cannot be considered a further installment in his autobiography.

In his last years, he fought his way out of bankruptcy (brought on by ill-considered speculation in a typesetting machine) by lecturing around the world. His later writings were often bitter and cynical, but the whole of his work constitutes one of the most buoyant, varied, and entertaining oeuvres in American literature.

## FROM *Life on the Mississippi*

### THE BOYS' AMBITION

When I was a boy, there was but one permanent ambition among my comrades in our village* on the west bank of the Mississippi River. That was, to be a steamboatman. We had transient ambitions of other sorts, but they were only transient. When a circus came and went, it left us all burning to become clowns; the first negro minstrel show that came to our

*Hannibal, Missouri.

section left us all suffering to try that kind of life; now and then we had
a hope that if we lived and were good, God would permit us to be pirates.
These ambitions faded out, each in its turn; but the ambition to be a
steamboatman always remained.

Once a day a cheap, gaudy packet arrived upward from St. Louis, and
another downward from Keokuk. Before these events, the day was glorious with expectancy; after them, the day was a dead and empty thing.
Not only the boys, but the whole village, felt this. After all these years I
can picture that old time to myself now, just as it was then: the white town
drowsing in the sunshine of a summer's morning; the streets empty, or
pretty nearly so; one or two clerks sitting in front of the Water Street
stores, with their splint-bottomed chairs tilted back against the wall, chins
on breasts, hats slouched over their faces, asleep—with shingle-shavings
enough around to show what broke them down; a sow and a litter of pigs
loafing along the sidewalk, doing a good business in watermelon rinds
and seeds; two or three lonely little freight piles scattered about the
"levee"; a pile of "skids" on the slope of the stone-paved wharf, and the
fragrant town drunkard asleep in the shadow of them; two or three wood
flats at the head of the wharf, but nobody to listen to the peaceful lapping
of the wavelets against them; the great Mississippi, the majestic, the magnificent Mississippi, rolling its mile-wide tide along, shining in the sun;
the dense forest away on the other side; the "point" above the town, and
the "point" below, bounding the river-glimpse and turning it into a sort
of sea, and withal a very still and brilliant and lonely one. Presently a film
of dark smoke appears above one of those remote "points"; instantly a
negro drayman, famous for his quick eye and prodigious voice, lifts up
the cry, "S-t-e-a-m-boat a-comin'!" and the scene changes! The town
drunkard stirs, the clerks wake up, a furious clatter of drays follows, every
house and store pours out a human contribution, and all in a twinkling
the dead town is alive and moving. Drays, carts, men, boys, all go hurrying from many quarters to a common centre, the wharf. Assembled there,
the people fasten their eyes upon the coming boat as upon a wonder
they are seeing for the first time. And the boat *is* rather a handsome sight,
too. She is long and sharp and trim and pretty; she has two tall, fancy-
topped chimneys, with a gilded device of some kind swung between
them; a fanciful pilot-house, all glass and "gingerbread," perched on top
of the "texas" deck behind them; the paddle-boxes are gorgeous with a
picture or with gilded rays above the boat's name; the boiler deck, the
hurricane deck, and the texas deck are fenced and ornamented with
clean white railings; there is a flag gallantly flying from the jack-staff; the
furnace doors are open and the fires glaring bravely; the upper decks are
black with passengers; the captain stands by the big bell, calm, imposing,
the envy of all; great volumes of the blackest smoke are rolling and tum-

bling out of the chimneys—a husbanded grandeur created with a bit of pitch pine just before arriving at a town; the crew are grouped on the forecastle; the broad stage is run far out over the port bow, and an envied deck-hand stands picturesquely on the end of it with a coil of rope in his hand; the pent steam is screaming through the gauge-cocks; the captain lifts his hand, a bell rings, the wheels stop; then they turn back, churning the water to foam, and the steamer is at rest. Then such a scramble as there is to get aboard, and to get ashore, and to take in freight and to discharge freight, all at one and the same time; and such a yelling and cursing as the mates facilitate it all with! Ten minutes later the steamer is under way again, with no flag on the jack-staff and no black smoke issuing from the chimneys. After ten more minutes the town is dead again, and the town drunkard asleep by the skids once more.

My father was a justice of the peace, and I supposed he possessed the power of life and death over all men and could hang anybody that offended him. This was distinction enough for me as a general thing; but the desire to be a steamboatman kept intruding, nevertheless. I first wanted to be a cabin-boy, so that I could come out with a white apron on and shake a table-cloth over the side, where all my old comrades could see me; later I thought I would rather be the deck-hand who stood on the end of the stage-plank with the coil of rope in his hand, because he was particularly conspicuous. But these were only day-dreams,—they were too heavenly to be contemplated as real possibilities. By and by one of our boys went away. He was not heard of for a long time. At last he turned up as apprentice engineer or "striker" on a steamboat. This thing shook the bottom out of all my Sunday-school teachings. That boy had been notoriously worldly, and I just the reverse; yet he was exalted to this eminence, and I left in obscurity and misery. There was nothing generous about this fellow in his greatness. He would always manage to have a rusty bolt to scrub while his boat tarried at our town, and he would sit on the inside guard and scrub it, where we could all see him and envy him and loathe him. And whenever his boat was laid up he would come home and swell around the town in his blackest and greasiest clothes, so that nobody could help remembering that he was a steamboatman; and he used all sorts of steamboat technicalities in his talk, as if he were so used to them that he forgot common people could not understand them. He would speak of the "labboard" side of a horse in an easy, natural way that would make one wish he was dead. And he was always talking about "St. Looy" like an old citizen; he would refer casually to occasions when he "was coming down Fourth Street," or when he was "passing by the Planter's House," or when there was a fire and he took a turn on the brakes of "the old Big Missouri"; and then he would go on and lie about how many towns the size of ours were burned down there that day. Two or three of the boys had long been persons of consideration among us because they had been to St. Louis once and had a vague general knowledge of its wonders, but the day of their glory was over now. They lapsed into a humble silence, and learned to disappear when the ruthless "cub"-engineer approached. This fellow had money, too, and hair oil. Also an ignorant silver watch and a showy brass watch chain. He wore a leather belt and used no suspenders. If ever a youth was cordially admired and hated by his comrades, this one was. No girl could withstand his charms. He "cut out" every boy in the village. When his boat blew up at last, it diffused a tranquil contentment among us such as we had not known for months. But when he came home the next week, alive, renowned, and appeared in church all battered up and bandaged, a shining hero, stared at and wondered over by everybody, it seemed to us that the partiality of Providence for an undeserving reptile had reached a point where it was open to criticism.

This creature's career could produce but one result, and it speedily followed. Boy after boy managed to get on the river. The minister's son became an engineer. The doctor's and the post-master's sons became "mud clerks"; the wholesale liquor dealer's son became a bar-keeper on a boat; four sons of the chief merchant, and two sons of the county judge, became pilots. Pilot was the grandest position of all. The pilot, even in those days of trivial wages, had a princely salary—from a hundred and fifty to two hundred and fifty dollars a month, and no board to pay. Two months of his wages would pay a preacher's salary for a year. Now some of us were left disconsolate. We could not get on the river—at least our parents would not let us.

So by and by I ran away. I said I never would come home again till I was a pilot and could come in glory. But somehow I could not manage it. I went meekly aboard a few of the boats that lay packed together like sardines at the long St. Louis wharf, and very humbly inquired for the pilots, but got only a cold shoulder and short words from mates and clerks. I had to make the best of this sort of treatment for the time being, but I had comforting day-dreams of a future when I should be a great and honored pilot, with plenty of money, and could kill some of these mates and clerks and pay for them.

### I WANT TO BE A CUB-PILOT

Months afterward the hope within me struggled to a reluctant death, and I found myself without an ambition. But I was ashamed to go home. I was in Cincinnati, and I set to work to map out a new career. I had been reading about the recent exploration of the river Amazon by an expedition sent out by our government. It was said that the expedition, owing to difficulties, had not thoroughly explored a part of the country lying about the head-waters, some four thousand miles from the mouth of the river. It was only about fifteen hundred miles from Cincinnati to New Orleans, where I could doubtless get a ship. I had thirty dollars left; I would go and complete the exploration of the Amazon. This was all the thought I gave to the subject. I never was great in matters of detail. I packed my valise, and took passage on an ancient tub called the "Paul Jones," for New Orleans. For the sum of sixteen dollars I had the scarred and tarnished splendors of "her" main saloon principally to myself, for she was not a creature to attract the eye of wiser travellers.

When we presently got under way and went poking down the broad Ohio, I became a new being, and the subject of my own admiration. I was a traveller! A word never had tasted so good in my mouth before. I had an exultant sense of being bound for mysterious lands and distant climes which I never have felt in so uplifting a degree since. I was in such a glorified condition that all ignoble feelings departed out of me, and I was able to look down and pity the untravelled with a compassion that had hardly a trace of contempt in it. Still, when we stopped at villages and wood-yards, I could not help lolling carelessly upon the railings of the boiler deck to enjoy the envy of the country boys on the bank. If they did not seem to discover me, I presently sneezed to attract their attention, or moved to a position where they could not help seeing me. And as soon as I knew they saw me I gaped and stretched, and gave other signs of being mightily bored with travelling.

I kept my hat off all the time, and stayed where the wind and the sun could strike me, because I wanted to get the bronzed and weather-beaten look of an old traveller. Before the second day was half gone, I experienced a joy which filled me with the purest gratitude; for I saw that the skin had begun to blister and peel off my face and neck. I wished that the boys and girls at home could see me now.

We reached Louisville in time—at least the neighborhood of it. We stuck hard and fast on the rocks in the middle of the river, and lay there four days. I was now beginning to feel a strong sense of being a part of the boat's family, a sort of infant son to the captain and younger brother to the officers. There is no estimating the pride I took in this grandeur, or the affection that began to swell and grow in me for those people. I could not know how the lordly steamboatman scorns that sort of presumption in a mere landsman. I particularly longed to acquire the least trifle of notice from the big stormy mate, and I was on the alert for an opportunity to do him a service to that end. It came at last. The riotous powwow of setting a spar was going on down on the forecastle, and I went down there and stood around in the way—or mostly skipping out of it—till the mate suddenly roared a general order for somebody to bring him a capstan bar. I sprang to his side and said: "Tell me where it is—I'll fetch it!"

If a rag-picker had offered to do a diplomatic service for the Emperor of Russia, the monarch could not have been more astounded than the mate was. He even stopped swearing. He stood and stared down at me. It took him ten seconds to scrape his disjointed remains together again. Then he said impressively: "Well, if this don't beat hell!" and turned to his work with the air of a man who had been confronted with a problem too abstruse for solution.

I crept away, and courted solitude for the rest of the day. I did not go to dinner; I stayed away from supper until everybody else had finished. I did not feel so much like a member of the boat's family now as before. However, my spirits returned, in instalments, as we pursued our way down the river. I was sorry I hated the mate so, because it was not in (young) human nature not to admire him. He was huge and muscular, his face was bearded and whiskered all over; he had a red woman and a blue woman tattooed on his right arm,—one on each side of a blue anchor with a red rope to it; and in the matter of profanity he was sublime. When he was getting out cargo at a landing, I was always where I could see and hear. He felt all the majesty of his great position, and made the world feel it, too. When he gave even the simplest order, he discharged it like a blast of lightning, and sent a long, reverberating peal of profanity thundering after it. I could not help contrasting the way in which the average landsman would give an order, with the mate's way of doing it.

If the landsman should wish the gang-plank moved a foot farther forward, he would probably say: "James, or William, one of you push that plank forward, please"; but put the mate in his place, and he would roar out: "Here, now, start that gang-plank for'ard! Lively, now! *What*'re you about! Snatch it! *snatch* it! There! there! Aft again! aft again! Don't you hear me? Dash it to dash! are you going to *sleep* over it! 'Vast heaving. 'Vast heaving, I tell you! Going to heave it clear astern? WHERE're you going with that barrel! *for'ard* with it 'fore I make you swallow it, you dash-dash-dash-*dashed* split between a tired mud-turtle and a crippled hearse-horse!"

I wished I could talk like that.

When the soreness of my adventure with the mate had somewhat worn off, I began timidly to make up to the humblest official connected with the boat—the night watchman. He snubbed my advances at first, but I presently ventured to offer him a new chalk pipe, and that softened him. So he allowed me to sit with him by the big bell on the hurricane deck, and in time he melted into conversation. He could not well have helped it, I hung with such homage on his words and so plainly showed that I felt honored by his notice. He told me the names of dim capes and shadowy islands as we glided by them in the solemnity of the night, under the winking stars, and by and by got to talking about himself. He seemed over-sentimental for a man whose salary was six dollars a week — or rather he might have seemed so to an older person than I. But I drank in his words hungrily, and with a faith that might have moved mountains if it had been applied judiciously. What was it to me that he was soiled and seedy and fragrant with gin? What was it to me that his grammar was bad, his construction worse, and his profanity so void of art that it was an element of weakness rather than strength in his conversation? He was a wronged man, a man who had seen trouble, and that was enough for me. As he mellowed into his plaintive history his tears dripped upon the lantern in his lap, and I cried, too, from sympathy. He said he was the son of an English nobleman — either an earl or an alderman, he could not remember which, but believed was both; his father, the nobleman, loved him, but his mother hated him from the cradle; and so while he was still a little boy he was sent to "one of them old, ancient colleges" — he couldn't remember which; and by and by his father died and his mother seized the property and "shook" him, as he phrased it. After his mother shook him, members of the nobility with whom he was acquainted used their influence to get him the position of "loblolly-boy in a ship"; and from that point my watchman threw off all trammels of date and locality and branched out into a narrative that bristled all along with incredible adventures; a narrative that was so reeking with bloodshed and so crammed with hair-breadth escapes and the most engaging and unconscious personal villanies, that I sat speechless, enjoying, shuddering, wondering, worshipping.

It was a sore blight to find out afterwards that he was a low, vulgar, ignorant, sentimental, half-witted humbug, an untravelled native of the wilds of Illinois, who had absorbed wildcat literature and appropriated its marvels, until in time he had woven odds and ends of the mess into this yarn, and then gone on telling it to fledglings like me, until he had come to believe it himself.

## Perplexing Lessons

At the end of what seemed a tedious while, I had managed to pack my head full of islands, towns, bars, "points," and bends; and a curiously inanimate mass of lumber it was, too. However, inasmuch as I could shut my eyes and reel off a good long string of these names without leaving out more than ten miles of river in every fifty, I began to feel that I

could take a boat down to New Orleans if I could make her skip those little gaps. But of course my complacency could hardly get start enough to
lift my nose a trifle into the air, before Mr. Bixby would think of something to fetch it down again. One day he turned on me suddenly with this
settler: —

"What is the shape of Walnut Bend?"

He might as well have asked me my grandmother's opinion of proto-
plasm. I reflected respectfully, and then said I didn't know it had any particular shape. My gunpowdery chief went off with a bang, of course, and
then went on loading and firing until he was out of adjectives.

I had learned long ago that he only carried just so many rounds of ammunition, and was sure to subside into a very placable and even re-
morseful old smooth-bore as soon as they were all gone. That word "old"
is merely affectionate; he was not more than thirty-four. I waited. By and
by he said, —

"My boy, you've got to know the *shape* of the river perfectly. It is all
there is left to steer by on a very dark night. Everything else is blotted out
and gone. But mind you, it hasn't the same shape in the night that it has
in the day-time."

"How on earth am I ever going to learn it, then?"

"How do you follow a hall at home in the dark? Because you know the
shape of it. You can't see it."

"Do you mean to say that I've got to know all the million trifling variations of shape in the banks of this interminable river as well as I know
the shape of the front hall at home?"

"On my honor, you've got to know them *better* than any man ever did
know the shapes of the halls in his own house."

"I wish I was dead!"

"Now I don't want to discourage you, but" —

"Well, pile it on me; I might as well have it now as another time."

"You see, this has got to be learned; there isn't any getting around it.
A clear starlight night throws such heavy shadows that if you didn't know
the shape of a shore perfectly you would claw away from every bunch of
timber, because you would take the black shadow of it for a solid cape;
and you see you would be getting scared to death every fifteen minutes
by the watch. You would be fifty yards from shore all the time when you
ought to be within fifty feet of it. You can't see a snag in one of those shadows, but you know exactly where it is, and the shape of the river tells you
when you are coming to it. Then there's your pitch-dark night; the river
is a very different shape on a pitch-dark night from what it is on a starlight
night. All shores seem to be straight lines, then, and mighty dim ones,
too; and you'd *run* them for straight lines only you know better. You
boldly drive your boat right into what seems to be a solid, straight wall

(you knowing very well that in reality there is a curve there), and that wall falls back and makes way for you. Then there's your gray mist. You take a night when there's one of these grisly, drizzly, gray mists, and then there isn't *any* particular shape to a shore. A gray mist would tangle the head of the oldest man that ever lived. Well, then, different kinds of *moonlight* change the shape of the river in different ways. You see"—

"Oh, don't say any more, please! Have I got to learn the shape of the river according to all these five hundred thousand different ways? If I tried to carry all that cargo in my head it would make me stoop-shouldered."

"*No!* you only learn *the* shape of the river; and you learn it with such absolute certainty that you can always steer by the shape that's *in your head*, and never mind the one that's before your eyes."

"Very well, I'll try it; but after I have learned it can I depend on it? Will it keep the same form and not go fooling around?"

Before Mr. Bixby could answer, Mr. W—— came in to take the watch, and he said,—

"Bixby, you'll have to look out for President's Island and all that country clear away up above the Old Hen and Chickens. The banks are caving and the shape of the shores changing like everything. Why, you wouldn't know the point above 40. You can go up inside the old sycamore snag, now."*

So that question was answered. Here were leagues of shore changing shape. My spirits were down in the mud again. Two things seemed pretty apparent to me. One was, that in order to be a pilot a man had got to learn more than any one man ought to be allowed to know; and the other was, that he must learn it all over again in a different way every twenty-four hours.

That night we had the watch until twelve. Now it was an ancient river custom for the two pilots to chat a bit when the watch changed. While the relieving pilot put on his gloves and lit his cigar, his partner, the retiring pilot, would say something like this:—

"I judge the upper bar is making down a little at Hale's Point; had quarter twain with the lower lead and mark twain† with the other."

"Yes, I thought it was making down a little, last trip. Meet any boats?"

"Met one abreast the head of 21, but she was away over hugging the bar, and I couldn't make her out entirely. I took her for the 'Sunny South'—hadn't any skylights forward of the chimneys."

And so on. And as the relieving pilot took the wheel his partner**

---

*It may not be necessary, but still it can do no harm to explain that "inside" means between the snag and the shore.—M. T.

†Two fathoms. Quarter twain is 2 ¼ fathoms, 13 ½ feet. Mark three is three fathoms.

**"Partner" is technical for "the other pilot."

would mention that we were in such-and-such a bend, and say we were abreast of such-and-such a man's wood-yard or plantation. This was courtesy; I supposed it was *necessity*. But Mr. W—— came on watch full twelve minutes late on this particular night,—a tremendous breach of etiquette; in fact, it is the unpardonable sin among pilots. So Mr. Bixby gave him no greeting whatever, but simply surrendered the wheel and marched out of the pilot-house without a word. I was appalled; it was a villanous night for blackness, we were in a particularly wide and blind part of the river, where there was no shape or substance to anything, and it seemed incredible that Mr. Bixby should have left that poor fellow to kill the boat trying to find out where he was. But I resolved that I would stand by him any way. He should find that he was not wholly friendless. So I stood around, and waited to be asked where we were. But Mr. W—— plunged on serenely through the solid firmament of black cats that stood for an atmosphere, and never opened his mouth. Here is a proud devil, thought I; here is a limb of Satan that would rather send us all to destruction than put himself under obligations to me, because I am not yet one of the salt of the earth and privileged to snub captains and lord it over everything dead and alive in a steamboat. I presently climbed up on the bench; I did not think it was safe to go to sleep while this lunatic was on watch.

However, I must have gone to sleep in the course of time, because the next thing I was aware of was the fact that day was breaking, Mr. W—— gone, and Mr. Bixby at the wheel again. So it was four o'clock and all well—but me; I felt like a skinful of dry bones and all of them trying to ache at once.

Mr. Bixby asked me what I had stayed up there for. I confessed that it was to do Mr. W—— a benevolence,—tell him where he was. It took five minutes for the entire preposterousness of the thing to filter into Mr. Bixby's system, and then I judge it filled him nearly up to the chin; because he paid me a compliment—and not much of a one either. He said,—

"Well, taking you by-and-large, you do seem to be more different kinds of an ass than any creature I ever saw before. What did you suppose he wanted to know for?"

I said I thought it might be a convenience to him.

"Convenience! D—nation! Didn't I tell you that a man's got to know the river in the night the same as he'd know his own front hall?"

"Well, I can follow the front hall in the dark if I know it *is* the front hall; but suppose you set me down in the middle of it in the dark and not tell me which hall it is; how am *I* to know?"

"Well, you've *got* to, on the river!"

"All right. Then I'm glad I never said anything to Mr. W——"

"I should say so. Why, he'd have slammed you through the window and utterly ruined a hundred dollars' worth of window-sash and stuff."

I was glad this damage had been saved, for it would have made me unpopular with the owners. They always hated anybody who had the name of being careless, and injuring things.

I went to work now to learn the shape of the river; and of all the eluding and ungraspable objects that ever I tried to get mind or hands on, that was the chief. I would fasten my eyes upon a sharp, wooded point that projected far into the river some miles ahead of me, and go to laboriously photographing its shape upon my brain; and just as I was beginning to succeed to my satisfaction, we would draw up toward it and the exasperating thing would begin to melt away and fold back into the bank! If there had been a conspicuous dead tree standing upon the very point of the cape, I would find that tree inconspicuously merged into the general forest, and occupying the middle of a straight shore, when I got abreast of it! No prominent hill would stick to its shape long enough for me to make up my mind what its form really was, but it was as dissolving and changeful as if it had been a mountain of butter in the hottest corner of the tropics. Nothing ever had the same shape when I was coming downstream that it had borne when I went up. I mentioned these little difficulties to Mr. Bixby. He said, —

"That's the very main virtue of the thing. If the shapes didn't change every three seconds they wouldn't be of any use. Take this place where we are now, for instance. As long as that hill over yonder is only one hill, I can boom right along the way I'm going; but the moment it splits at the top and forms a V, I know I've got to scratch to starboard in a hurry, or I'll bang this boat's brains out against a rock; and then the moment one of the prongs of the V swings behind the other, I've got to waltz to larboard again, or I'll have a misunderstanding with a snag that would snatch the keelson out of this steamboat as neatly as if it were a sliver in your hand. If that hill didn't change its shape on bad nights there would be an awful steamboat grave-yard around here inside of a year."

It was plain that I had got to learn the shape of the river in all the different ways that could be thought of, — upside down, wrong end first, inside out, fore-and-aft, and "thortships," — and then know what to do on gray nights when it hadn't any shape at all. So I set about it. In the course of time I began to get the best of this knotty lesson, and my self-complacency moved to the front once more. Mr. Bixby was all fixed, and ready to start it to the rear again. He opened on me after this fashion: —

"How much water did we have in the middle crossing at Hole-in-the-Wall, trip before last?"

I considered this an outrage. I said: —

"Every trip, down and up, the leadsmen are singing through that tangled place for three quarters of an hour on a stretch. How do you reckon I can remember such a mess as that?"

"My boy, you've got to remember it. You've got to remember the exact spot and the exact marks the boat lay in when we had the shoalest water, in every one of the five hundred shoal places between St. Louis and New Orleans; and you mustn't get the shoal soundings and marks of one trip mixed up with the shaol soundings and marks of another, either, for they're not often twice alike. You must keep them separate."

When I came to myself again, I said, —

"When I get so that I can do that, I'll be able to raise the dead, and then I won't have to pilot a steamboat to make a living. I want to retire from this business. I want a slush-bucket and a brush; I'm only fit for a roustabout. I haven't got brains enough to be a pilot; and if I had I wouldn't have strength enough to carry them around, unless I went on crutches."

"Now drop that! When I say I'll learn* a man the river, I mean it. And you can depend on it, I'll learn him or kill him."

## Continued Perplexities

There was no use in arguing with a person like this. I promptly put such a strain on my memory that by and by even the shoal water and the countless crossing-marks began to stay with me. But the result was just the same. I never could more than get one knotty thing learned before another presented itself. Now I had often seen pilots gazing at the water and pretending to read it as if it were a book; but it was a book that told me nothing. A time came at last, however, when Mr. Bixby seemed to think me far enough advanced to bear a lesson on water-reading. So he began: —

"Do you see that long slanting line on the face of the water? Now, that's a reef. Moreover, it's a bluff reef. There is a solid sand-bar under it that is nearly as straight up and down as the side of a house. There is plenty of water close up to it, but mighty little on top of it. If you were to hit it you would knock the boat's brains out. Do you see where the line fringes out at the upper end and begins to fade away?"

"Yes, sir."

"Well, that is a low place; that is the head of the reef. You can climb over there, and not hurt anything. Cross over, now, and follow along close under the reef—easy water there—not much current."

---

*"Teach" is not in the river vocabulary.

I followed the reef along till I approached the fringed end. Then Mr. Bixby said,—

"Now get ready. Wait till I give the word. She won't want to mount the reef; a boat hates shoal water. Stand by—wait—*wait*—keep her well in hand. *Now* cramp her down! Snatch her! snatch her!"

He seized the other side of the wheel and helped to spin it around until it was hard down, and then we held it so. The boat resisted, and refused to answer for a while, and next she came surging to starboard, mounted the reef, and sent a long, angry ridge of water foaming away from her bows.

"Now watch her; watch her like a cat, or she'll get away from you. When she fights strong and the tiller slips a little, in a jerky, greasy sort of way, let up on her a trifle; it is the way she tells you at night that the water is too shoal; but keep edging her up, little by little, toward the point. You are well up on the bar, now; there is a bar under every point, because the water that comes down around it forms an eddy and allows the sediment to sink. Do you see those fine lines on the face of the water that branch out like the ribs of a fan? Well, those are little reefs; you want to just miss the ends of them, but run them pretty close. Now look out—look out! Don't you crowd that slick, greasy-looking place; there ain't nine feet there; she won't stand it. She begins to smell it; look sharp, I tell you! Oh blazes, there you go! Stop the starboard wheel! Quick! Ship up to back! Set her back!"

The engine bells jingled and the engines answered promptly, shooting white columns of steam far aloft out of the 'scape pipes, but it was too late. The boat had "smelt" the bar in good earnest; the foamy ridges that radiated from her bows suddenly disappeared, a great dead swell came rolling forward and swept ahead of her, she careened far over to larboard, and went tearing away toward the other shore as if she were about scared to death. We were a good mile from where we ought to have been, when we finally got the upper hand of her again.

During the afternoon watch the next day, Mr. Bixby asked me if I knew how to run the next few miles. I said:—

"Go inside the first snag above the point, outside the next one, start out from the lower end of Higgins's wood-yard, make a square crossing and"—

"That's all right. I'll be back before you close up on the next point."

But he wasn't. He was still below when I rounded it and entered upon a piece of river which I had some misgivings about. I did not know that he was hiding behind a chimney to see how I would perform. I went gayly along, getting prouder and prouder, for he had never left the boat in my sole charge such a length of time before. I even got to "setting" her and letting the wheel go, entirely, while I vaingloriously turned my back and inspected the stern marks and hummed a tune, a sort of easy indifference which I had prodigiously admired in Bixby and other great pilots. Once I inspected rather long, and when I faced to the front again my heart flew into my mouth so suddenly that if I hadn't clapped my teeth together I should have lost it. One of those frightful bluff reefs was stretching its deadly length right across our bows! My head was gone in a moment; I did not know which end I stood on; I gasped and could not get my breath; I spun the wheel down with such rapidity that it wove itself together like a spider's web; the boat answered and turned square away from the reef, but the reef followed her! I fled, and still it followed still it kept—right across my bows! I never looked to see where I was going, I only fled. The awful crash was imminent—why didn't that villain come! If I committed the crime of ringing a bell, I might get thrown overboard. But better that than kill the boat. So in blind desperation I started such a rattling "shivaree" down below as never had astounded an engineer in this world before, I fancy. Amidst the frenzy of the bells the engines began to back and fill in a furious way, and my reason forsook its throne—we were about to crash into the woods on the other side of the river. Just then Mr. Bixby stepped calmly into view on the hurricane deck. My soul went out to him in gratitude. My distress vanished; I would have felt safe on the brink of Niagara, with Mr. Bixby on the hurricane deck. He blandly and sweetly took his tooth-pick out of his mouth between his fingers, as if it were a cigar,—we were just in the act of climbing an overhanging big tree, and the passengers were scudding astern like rats,—and lifted up these commands to me ever so gently:—

"Stop the starboard. Stop the larboard. Set her back on both."

The boat hesitated, halted, pressed her nose among the boughs a critical instant, then reluctantly began to back away.

"Stop the larboard. Come ahead on it. Stop the starboard. Come ahead on it. Point her for the bar."

I sailed away as serenely as a summer's morning. Mr. Bixby came in and said, with mock simplicity,—

"When you have a hail, my boy, you ought to tap the big bell three times before you land, so that the engineers can get ready."

I blushed under the sarcasm, and said I hadn't had any hail.

"Ah! Then it was for wood, I suppose. The officer of the watch will tell you when he wants to wood up."

I went on consuming, and said I wasn't after wood.

"Indeed? Why, what could you want over here in the bend, then? Did you ever know of a boat following a bend up-stream at this stage of the river?"

"No, sir,—and *I* wasn't trying to follow it. I was getting away from a bluff reef."

"No, it wasn't a bluff reef; there isn't one within three miles of where you were."

"But I saw it. It was as bluff as that one yonder."

"Just about. Run over it!"

"Do you give it as an order?"

"Yes. Run over it."

"If I don't, I wish I may die."

"All right; I am taking the responsibility."

I was just as anxious to kill the boat, now, as I had been to save her before. I impressed my orders upon my memory, to be used at the inquest, and made a straight break for the reef. As it disappeared under our bows I held my breath; but we slid over it like oil.

"Now don't you see the difference? It wasn't anything but a *wind* reef. The wind does that."

"So I see. But it is exactly like a bluff reef. How am I ever going to tell them apart?"

"I can't tell you. It is an instinct. By and by you will just naturally *know* one from the other, but you never will be able to explain why or how you know them apart."

It turned out to be true. The face of the water, in time, became a wonderful book—a book that was a dead language to the uneducated passenger, but which told its mind to me without reserve, delivering its most cherished secrets as clearly as if it uttered them with a voice. And it was not a book to be read once and thrown aside, for it had a new story to tell every day. Throughout the long twelve hundred miles there was never a page that was void of interest, never one that you could leave unread without loss, never one that you would want to skip, thinking you could find higher enjoyment in some other thing. There never was so wonderful a book written by man; never one whose interest was so absorbing, so unflagging, so sparklingly renewed with every re-perusal. The passenger who could not read it was charmed with a peculiar sort of faint dimple on its surface (on the rare occasions when he did not overlook it altogether); but to the pilot that was an *italicized* passage; indeed, it was more than that, it was a legend of the largest capitals, with a string of shouting exclamation points at the end of it; for it meant that a wreck or a rock was buried there that could tear the life out of the strongest vessel that ever floated. It is the faintest and simplest expression the water ever makes, and the most hideous to a pilot's eye. In truth, the passenger who could not read this book saw nothing but all manner of pretty pictures in it, painted by the sun and shaded by the clouds, whereas to the trained eye these were not pictures at all, but the grimmest and most dead-earnest of reading-matter.

Now when I had mastered the language of this water and had come to know every trifling feature that bordered the great river as familiarly as I knew the letters of the alphabet, I had made a valuable acquisition. But I had lost something, too. I had lost something which could never be restored to me while I lived. All the grace, the beauty, the poetry had gone out of the majestic river! I still keep in mind a certain wonderful sunset which I witnessed when steamboating was new to me. A broad expanse of the river was turned to blood; in the middle distance the red hue brightened into gold, through which a solitary log came floating, black and conspicuous; in one place a long, slanting mark lay sparkling upon the water; in another the surface was broken by boiling, tumbling rings, that were as many-tinted as an opal; where the ruddy flush was faintest, was a smooth spot that was covered with graceful circles and radiating lines, ever so delicately traced; the shore on our left was densely wooded, and the sombre shadow that fell from this forest was broken in one place by a long, ruffled trail that shone like silver; and high above the forest wall a clean-stemmed dead tree waved a single leafy bough that glowed like a flame in the unobstructed splendor that was flowing from the sun. There were graceful curves, reflected images, woody heights, soft distances; and over the whole scene, far and near, the dissolving lights drifted steadily, enriching it, every passing moment, with new marvels of coloring.

I stood like one bewitched. I drank it in, in a speechless rapture. The world was new to me, and I had never seen anything like this at home. But as I have said, a day came when I began to cease from noting the glories and the charms which the moon and the sun and the twilight wrought upon the river's face; another day came when I ceased altogether to note them. Then, if that sunset scene had been repeated, I should have looked upon it without rapture, and should have commented upon it, inwardly, after this fashion: This sun means that we are going to have wind to-morrow; that floating log means that the river is rising, small thanks to it; that slanting mark on the water refers to a bluff reef which is going to kill somebody's steamboat one of these nights, if it keeps on stretching out like that; those tumbling "boils" show a dissolving bar and a changing channel there; the lines and circles in the slick water over yonder are a warning that that troublesome place is shoaling up dangerously; that silver streak in the shadow of the forest is the "break" from a new snag, and he has located himself in the very best place he could have found to fish for steamboats; that tall dead tree, with a single living branch, is not going to last long, and then how is a body ever going to get through this blind place at night without the friendly old land-mark?

No, the romance and the beauty were all gone from the river. All the value any feature of it had for me now was the amount of usefulness it could furnish toward compassing the safe piloting of a steamboat. Since those days, I have pitied doctors from my heart. What does the lovely flush in a beauty's cheek mean to a doctor but a "break" that ripples above some deadly disease? Are not all her visible charms sown thick with what are to him the signs and symbols of hidden decay? Does he ever see her beauty at all, or doesn't he simply view her professionally, and comment upon her unwholesome condition all to himself? And doesn't he sometimes wonder whether he has gained most or lost most by learning his trade?

# MARY ANN WEBSTER
# LOUGHBOROUGH
## (1836–1887)

"War is a species of passionate insanity," writes Loughborough in her introduction to *My Cave Life in Vicksburg* (1864), a book that chronicles the three years of devastation she endured as the wife of a Southern officer during the Civil War. Her account documents the struggles of a woman of the privileged classes whose sheltered life was shattered by the advent of war.

Loughborough has a hugely empathetic imagination, and she can easily imagine the pain of Northern mothers whose sons die in battle or agonize over the death of the animals that might have fed her family. When Vicksburg does eventually fall to federal troops, forcing her to leave the cave in which she and her family have been living for several months, she overcomes her strong personal feelings of prejudice and tries to help her personal servant defect to the Union Army. Her account of her experience offers a lively and insightful glimpse of the Southern side of the Civil War.

## FROM *My Cave Life in Vicksburg*

It has been said that the peasants of the Campagna, in their semi-annual visits to the Pontine marshes, arrive piping and dancing; but it is seldom they return in the same merry mood, the malaria fever being sure to affect them more or less. Although I did not leave Jackson on the night of the 15th piping and dancing, yet it was with a very happy heart and very little foreboding of evil that I set off with a party of friends for a pleasant visit to Vicksburg. Like the peasants, I returned more serious and with a dismal experience. How little do we know with what rapidity our feelings may change! We had been planning a visit to Vicksburg for some weeks, and anticipating pleasure in meeting our friends. How gladly, in a few days, we left it, with the explosions of bombs still sounding in our ears! How beautiful was this evening: the sun glowed and warmed into mellow tints over the rough forest trees; over the long moss that swung in slow and stately dignity, like old-time dancers, scorning the quick and tripping movements of the present day! Glowing and warming over all, this evening sun, this mellow, pleasant light, breaking in warm tints over the rugged ground of the plantation, showing us the home scenes as we passed; the sober and motherly cows going home for the evening's milking through the long lanes between the fields, where the fences threw shadows across the road; making strange, weird figures of the young colts' shadows, lean and long-limbed and distorted; the mothers, tired of eating the grass that grew so profusely, were standing in quiet contentment, or drank from the clear runs of water. And so we passed on by the houses, where the planter sat on his veranda, listening to the voice of his daughter reading the latest paper, while round her fair head, like a halo, the lingering beams of the sun played.

And on to Black River, "Big Black," with its slow, sluggish tide! Dark, like the Stygian stream, it flowed in the mist of the evening, the twilight. And soon we see Vicksburg, classic ground forever in America. The Hudson must now yield the palm to the Father of Waters. Our interest will centre around spots hallowed by the deeds of our countrymen. I had thought, during the first bombardment of Vicksburg, that the town must have been a ruin; yet very little damage has been done, though very few houses are without evidence of the first trial of metal. One, I saw, with a hole through the window; behind was one of corresponding size through the panel of the door, which happened to be open. The corner of the piano had been taken off, and on through the wall the shot passed; one, also, passed through another house, making a huge gap through the chimney. And yet the inhabitants live in their homes (those who have not lost some loved one) happy and contented, not knowing what moment the house may be rent over their heads by the explosion of a shell.

"Ah!" said I to a friend, "how is it possible you live here?" "After one is accustomed to the change," she answered, "we do not mind it; but becoming accustomed, that is the trial." I was reminded of the poor man in an infected district who was met by a traveller and asked, "How do you live here?" "Sir, we die," was the laconic reply. And this is becoming accustomed. I looked over this beautiful landscape, and in the distance plainly saw the Federal transports lying quietly at their anchorage. Was it a dream? Could I believe that over this smiling scene, in the bright April morning, the blight of civil warfare lay like a pall?—lay over the fearful homesteads—some, even now, jarred by the shock of former conflicts—lay by the hearthstones, making moan in many a bereaved heart looking forward with vague fears to the coming summer!

What soul in the land but has felt and witnessed this grief—this unavailing sorrow for the brave and untimely dead? I thought of the letter from the sorrowing one in Iowa, whose son, a prisoner, I had nursed, receiving with the last breath words for the distant, unconscious mother; of her sorrow in writing of him in his distant grave; of her pride in him, her only son. How many in the land could take her hand and weep over a mutual sorrow! And in the hospital wards, men, who still hold the name of Americans, together were talking of battles, prisoners, and captors, when each told the other of acts of bravery performed on hostile fields, and took out pictures of innocent babes, little children, and wives, to show each other, all feeling a sympathy and interest in the unknown faces. Verily, war is a species of passionate insanity. While standing and thinking thus, the loud booming of the guns in the water batteries startled me, the smoke showing that it was the battery just below me, that opened, I was told, on what was thought to be a masked battery on the opposite shore. No reply was elicited, however; and on looking through the glass, we saw in the line of levee, between the river and the Federal canal, a spot where new earth seemed to have been thrown up, and branches of trees to have been laid quite regularly in one place. This was all. General Lee, however, had ordered the spot to be fired on, and the firing continued some little time. Our ride that evening had been delightful. We sat long on the veranda in the pleasant air, with the soft melody and rich swell of music from the band floating around us, while ever and anon my eye sought the bend of the river, two miles beyond, where the Federal transports, brought out in bold relief by the waning, crimson light of the evening, lay in seeming quiet. Still, resting in Vicksburg seemed like resting near a volcano.

✻     ✻     ✻

At night I was sleeping profoundly, when the deep boom of the signal cannon startled and awoke me. Another followed, and I sprang from my bed, drew on my slippers and robe, and went out on the veranda. Our friends were already there. The river was illuminated by large fires on the bank, and we could discern plainly the huge, black masses floating down with the current, now and then belching forth fire from their sides, followed by the loud report, and we could hear the shells exploding in the upper part of town. The night was one of pitchy darkness; and as they neared the glare thrown upon the river from the large fires, the gunboats could be plainly seen. Each one, on passing the track of the brilliant light on the water, became a target for the land batteries. We could hear the gallop, in the darkness, of couriers upon the paved streets; we could hear the voices of the soldiers on the riverside. The rapid firing from the boats, the roar of the Confederate batteries, and, above all, the screaming, booming sound of the shells, as they exploded in the air and around the city, made at once a new and fearful scene to me. The boats were rapidly nearing the lower batteries, and the shells were beginning to fly unpleasantly near. My heart beat quickly as the flashes of light from the port-holes seemed facing us. Some of the gentlemen urged the ladies to go down into the cave at the back of the house: M—— insisted on my going, if alone. While I hesitated, fearing to remain, yet wishing still to witness the termination of the engagement, a shell exploded near the side of the house. Fear instantly decided me, and I ran, guided by one of the ladies, who pointed down the steep slope of the hill, and left me to run back for a shawl. While I was considering the best way of descending the hill, another shell exploded near the foot, and, ceasing to hesitate, I flew down, half sliding and running. Before I had reached the mouth of the cave, two more exploded on the side of the hill near me. Breathless and terrified, I found the entrance and ran in, having left one of my slippers on the hill-side.

I found two or three of our friends had already sought refuge under the earth; and we had not been there long before we were joined by the remainder of the party, who reported the boats opposite the house. As I had again become perfectly calm and collected, I was sorry to find myself slightly fluttered and in a state of rapid heart-beatings, as shell after shell fell in the valley below us, exploding with a loud, rumbling noise, perfectly deafening. The cave was an excavation in the earth the size of a large room, high enough for the tallest person to stand perfectly erect, provided with comfortable seats, and altogether quite a large and habitable abode (compared with some of the caves in the city), were it not for the dampness and the constant contact with the soft earthy walls. We had remained but a short time, when one of the gentlemen came down to tell us that all danger was over, and that we might witness a beautiful sight by going upon the hill, as one of the transports had been fired by a shell, and was slowly floating down as it burned.

We returned to the house, and from the veranda looked on the burning boat, the only one, so far as we could ascertain, that had been injured, the other boats having all passed successfully by the city. We remained on the veranda an hour or more, the gentlemen speculating on the result of the successful run by the batteries. All were astonished and chagrined. It was found that very few of the Confederate guns had been discharged at all. Several reasons had been assigned; the real one was supposed to have been the quality of the fuses that were recently sent from Richmond, and had not been tried since their arrival. This night of all others they were found to be defective. The lurid glare from the burning boat fell in red and amber light upon the house, the veranda, and the animated faces turned toward the river—lighting the white magnolias, paling the pink crape myrtles, and bringing out in bright distinctness the railing of the terrace, where drooped in fragrant wreaths the clustering passion vine: fair and beautiful, but false, the crimson, wavering light.

I sat and gazed upon the burning wreck of what an hour ago had thronged with human life; with men whose mothers had this very night prayed for them; with men whose wives tearfully hovered over little beds, kissing each tender, sleeping lid for the absent one. Had this night made them orphans? Did this smooth, deceitful current of the glowing waters glide over forms loved and lost to the faithful ones at home? O mother and wife! ye will pray and smile on, until the terrible tidings come: "Lost at Vicksburg!" Lost at Vicksburg! In how many a heart the name for years will lie like a brand!—lie until the warm heart and tried soul shall be at peace forever.

# HENRY ADAMS
## (1838–1918)

A descendant of John Adams, one of the Founding Fathers, Henry Adams worked as a journalist for a while, editing the *North American Review*; he was also a professor at Harvard, where he taught European and American history. His densely allusive autobiography describes his long spiritual quest for order in a world that seemed, to him, on the brink of chaos. His subject, analyzed with strange detachment, is himself: "Adams," always referred to in the third person.

With visionary intensity, Henry Adams saw that the twentieth century posed a turning point in world history, a transitional moment equal to that of the building of the cathedral at Chartres. Its embodiment, he believed, was found in the Great Exposition of 1900.

Although not published until 1918, *The Education of Henry Adams* was actually conceived and written between 1905 and 1907. During this period, Adams believed he could see the mechanical era transmogrifying before his eyes into something more awesome and frightening than anything that had gone before—the world of the dynamo. The fate of the West is another major theme in this book, culminating in the author's speculation that were he to live to be a hundred, in 1938, he might well live long enough to "see the silly bubble explode" as technology consumed the world.

FROM *The Education of Henry Adams*

### THE DYNAMO AND THE VIRGIN (1900)

Until the Great Exposition of 1900 closed its doors in November, Adams haunted it, aching to absorb knowledge, and helpless to find it. He would have liked to know how much of it could have been grasped by the best-informed man in the world. While he was thus meditating chaos, Langley came by, and showed it to him. At Langley's behest, the Exhibition dropped its superfluous rags and stripped itself to the skin, for Langley knew what to study, and why, and how; while Adams might as well have stood outside in the night, staring at the Milky Way. Yet Langley said nothing new, and taught nothing that one might not have learned from Lord Bacon, three hundred years before; but though one should have known the "Advancement of Science" as well as one knew the "Comedy of Errors," the literary knowledge counted for nothing until some teacher should show how to apply it. Bacon took a vast deal of trouble in teaching King James I and his subjects, American or other, towards the year 1620, that true science was the development or economy of forces; yet an elderly American in 1900 knew neither the formula nor the forces; or even so much as to say to himself that his historical business in the Exposition concerned only the economies or developments of force since 1893, when he began the study at Chicago.

Nothing in education is so astonishing as the amount of ignorance it accumulates in the form of inert facts. Adams had looked at most of the accumulations of art in the storehouses called Art Museums; yet he did not know how to look at the art exhibits of 1900. He had studied Karl Marx and his doctrines of history with profound attention, yet he could not apply them at Paris. Langley, with the ease of a great master of experiment, threw out of the field every exhibit that did not reveal a new application of force, and naturally threw out, to begin with, almost the whole art exhibit. Equally, he ignored almost the whole industrial exhibit. He led his pupil directly to the forces. His chief interest was in new motors to make his airship feasible, and he taught Adams the astonishing complexities of the new Daimler motor, and of the automobile, which, since 1893, had become a nightmare at a hundred kilometres an hour, almost as destructive as the electric tram which was only ten years older; and threatening to become as terrible as the locomotive steam-engine itself, which was almost exactly Adams's own age.

Then he showed his scholar the great hall of dynamos, and explained how little he knew about electricity or force of any kind, even of his own special sun, which spouted heat in inconceivable volume, but which, as far as he knew, might spout less or more, at any time, for all the certainty he felt in it. To him, the dynamo itself was but an ingenious channel for conveying somewhere the heat latent in a few tons of poor coal hidden in a dirty engine-house carefully kept out of sight; but to Adams the dynamo became a symbol of infinity. As he grew accustomed to the great gallery of machines, he began to feel the forty-foot dynamos as a moral force, much as the early Christians felt the Cross. The planet itself seemed less impressive, in its old-fashioned, deliberate, annual or daily revolution, than this huge wheel, revolving within arm's-length at some vertiginous speed, and barely murmuring—scarcely humming an audible warning to stand a hair's-breadth further for respect of power—while it would not wake the baby lying close against its frame. Before the end, one began to pray to it; inherited instinct taught the natural expression of man before silent and infinite force. Among the thousand symbols of ultimate energy, the dynamo was not so human as some, but it was the most expressive.

Yet the dynamo, next to the steam-engine, was the most familiar of exhibits. For Adams's objects its value lay chiefly in its occult mechanism. Between the dynamo in the gallery of machines and the engine-house outside, the break of continuity amounted to abysmal fracture for a historian's objects. No more relation could he discover between the steam and the electric current than between the Cross and the cathedral. The forces were interchangeable if not reversible, but he could see only an absolute *fiat* in electricity as in faith. Langley could not help him. Indeed, Langley seemed to be worried by the same trouble, for he constantly repeated that the new forces were anarchical, and especially that he was not responsible for the new rays, that were little short of parricidal in their wicked spirit towards science. His own rays, with which he had doubled the solar spectrum, were altogether harmless and beneficent; but Radium denied its God—or, what was to Langley the same thing, denied the truths of his Science. The force was wholly new.

A historian who asked only to learn enough to be as futile as Langley or Kelvin, made rapid progress under this teaching, and mixed himself up in the tangle of ideas until he achieved a sort of Paradise of ignorance vastly consoling to his fatigued senses. He wrapped himself in vibrations and rays which were new, and he would have hugged Marconi and Branly had he met them, as he hugged the dynamo; while he lost his arithmetic in trying to figure out the equation between the discoveries and the economies of force. The economies, like the discoveries, were absolute, supersensual, occult; incapable of expression in horse-power. What mathematical equivalent could he suggest as the value of a Branly coherer? Frozen air, or the electric furnace, had some scale of measurement, no doubt, if somebody could invent a thermometer adequate to the purpose; but X-rays had played no part whatever in man's consciousness, and the atom itself had figured only as a fiction of thought. In these seven years man had translated himself into a new universe which had no common scale of measurement with the old. He had entered a supersensual world, in which he could measure nothing except by chance collisions of movements imperceptible to his senses, perhaps even imperceptible to his instruments, but perceptible to each other, and so to some known ray at the end of the scale. Langley seemed prepared for anything, even for an indeterminable number of universes interfused—physics stark mad in metaphysics.

Historians undertake to arrange sequences,—called stories, or histories—assuming in silence a relation of cause and effect. These assumptions, hidden in the depths of dusty libraries, have been astounding, but commonly unconscious and childlike; so much so, that if any captious critic were to drag them to light, historians would probably reply, with one voice, that they had never supposed themselves required to know what they were talking about. Adams, for one, had toiled in vain to find out what he meant. He had even published a dozen volumes of American history for no other purpose than to satisfy himself whether, by the severest process of stating, with the least possible comment, such facts as seemed sure, in such order as seemed rigorously consequent, he could fix for a familiar moment a necessary sequence of human movement. The result had satisfied him as little as at Harvard College. Where he saw sequence, other men saw something quite different, and no one saw the same unit of measure. He cared little about his experiments and less about his statesmen, who seemed to him quite as ignorant as himself and, as a rule, no more honest; but he insisted on a relation of sequence, and if he could not reach it by one method, he would try as many methods as science knew. Satisfied that the sequence of men led to nothing and that the sequence of their society could lead no further, while the mere sequence of time was artificial, and the sequence of thought was chaos, he turned at last to the sequence of force; and thus it happened that, after ten years' pursuit, he found himself lying in the Gallery of Machines at the Great Exposition of 1900, with his historical neck broken by the sudden irruption of forces totally new.

Since no one else showed much concern, an elderly person without other cares had no need to betray alarm. The year 1900 was not the first to upset schoolmasters. Copernicus and Galileo had broken many professorial necks about 1600; Columbus had stood the world on its head towards 1500; but the nearest approach to the revolution of 1900 was that of 310, when Constantine set up the Cross. The rays that Langley disowned, as well as those which he fathered, were occult, supersensual, irrational; they were a revelation of mysterious energy like that of the Cross; they were what, in terms of mediæval science, were called immediate modes of the divine substance.

The historian was thus reduced to his last resources. Clearly if he was bound to reduce all these forces to a common value, this common value could have no measure but that of their attraction on his own mind. He must treat them as they had been felt; as convertible, reversible, interchangeable attractions on thought. He made up his mind to venture it; he would risk translating rays into faith. Such a reversible process would vastly amuse a chemist, but the chemist could not deny that he, or some of his fellow physicists, could feel the force of both. When Adams was a boy in Boston, the best chemist in the place had probably never heard of Venus except by way of scandal, or of the Virgin except as idolatry; neither had he heard of dynamos or automobiles or radium; yet his mind was ready to feel the force of all, though the rays were unborn and the women were dead.

Here opened another totally new education, which promised to be by far the most hazardous of all. The knife-edge along which he must crawl, like Sir Lancelot in the twelfth century, divided two kingdoms of force which had nothing in common but attraction. They were as different as a magnet is from gravitation, supposing one knew what a magnet was, or gravitation, or love. The force of the Virgin was still felt at Lourdes, and seemed to be as potent as X-rays; but in America neither Venus nor Virgin ever had value as force—at most as sentiment. No American had ever been truly afraid of either.

This problem in dynamics gravely perplexed an American historian. The Woman had once been supreme; in France she still seemed potent, not merely as a sentiment, but as a force. Why was she unknown in America? For evidently America was ashamed of her, and she was ashamed of herself, otherwise they would not have strewn fig-leaves so profusely all over her. When she was a true force, she was ignorant of fig-leaves, but the monthly-magazine-made American female had not a feature that would have been recognized by Adam. The trait was notorious, and often humorous, but anyone brought up among Puritans knew that sex was sin. In any previous age, sex was strength. Neither art nor beauty was needed. Everyone, even among Puritans, knew that neither Diana of the Ephesians nor any of the Oriental goddesses was worshipped for her beauty. She was goddess because of her force; she was the animated dynamo; she was reproduction—the greatest and most mysterious of all energies; all she needed was to be fecund. Singularly enough, not one of Adams's many schools of education had ever drawn his attention to the opening lines of Lucretius, though they were perhaps the finest in all Latin literature, where the poet invoked Venus exactly as Dante invoked the Virgin:—

"Quae quoniam rerum naturam *sola* gubernas."

The Venus of Epicurean philosophy survived in the Virgin of the Schools:—

"Donna, sei tanto grande, e tanto vali,
Che qual vuol grazia, e a te non ricorre,
Sua disianza vuol volar senz' ali."

All this was to American thought as though it had never existed. The true American knew something of the facts, but nothing of the feelings; he read the letter, but he never felt the law. Before this historical chasm, a mind like that of Adams felt itself helpless; he turned from the Virgin to the Dynamo as though he were a Branly coherer. On one side, at the Louvre and at Chartres, as he knew by the record of work actually done and still before his eyes, was the highest energy ever known to man, the creator of four-fifths of his noblest art, exercising vastly more attraction over the human mind than all the steam-engines and dynamos ever dreamed of; and yet this energy was unknown to the American mind. An American Virgin would never dare command; an American Venus would never dare exist.

The question, which to any plain American of the nineteenth century seemed as remote as it did to Adams, drew him almost violently to study, once it was posed; and on this point Langleys were as useless as though they were Herbert Spencers or dynamos. The idea survived only as art. There one turned as naturally as though the artist were himself a woman. Adams began to ponder, asking himself whether he knew of any American artist who had ever insisted on the power of sex, as every classic had always done; but he could think only of Walt Whitman; Bret Harte, as far as the magazines would let him venture; and one or two painters, for the flesh-tones. All the rest had used sex for sentiment, never for force; to them, Eve was a tender flower, and Herodias an unfeminine horror. American art, like the American language and American education, was as far as possible sexless. Society regarded this victory over sex as its greatest triumph, and the historian readily admitted it, since the moral issue, for the moment, did not concern one who was studying the relations of unmoral force. He cared nothing for the sex of the dynamo until he could measure its energy.

Vaguely seeking a clue, he wandered through the art exhibit, and, in his stroll, stopped almost every day before St. Gaudens's General Sherman, which had been given the central post of honor. St. Gaudens himself was in Paris, putting on the work his usual interminable last touches, and listening to the usual contradictory suggestions of brother sculptors. Of all the American artists who gave to American art whatever life it breathed in the seventies, St. Gaudens was perhaps the most sympathetic, but certainly the most inarticulate. General Grant or Don Cameron had scarcely less instinct of rhetoric than he. All the others — the Hunts, Richardson, John La Farge, Stanford White — were exuberant; only St. Gaudens could never discuss or dilate on an emotion, or suggest artistic arguments for giving to his work the forms that he felt. He never laid down the law, or affected the despot, or became brutalized like Whistler by the brutalities of his world. He required no incense; he was no egoist; his simplicity of thought was excessive; he could not imitate, or give any form but his own to the creations of his hand. No one felt more strongly than he the strength of other men, but the idea that they could affect him never stirred an image in his mind.

This summer his health was poor and his spirits were low. For such a temper, Adams was not the best companion, since his own gaiety was not *folle*; but he risked going now and then to the studio on Mont Parnasse to draw him out for a stroll in the Bois de Boulogne, or dinner as pleased his moods, and in return St. Gaudens sometimes let Adams go about in his company.

Once St. Gaudens took him down to Amiens, with a party of Frenchmen, to see the cathedral. Not until they found themselves actually studying the sculpture of the western portal, did it dawn on Adams's mind that, for his purposes, St. Gaudens on that spot had more interest to him than the cathedral itself. Great men before great monuments express great truths, provided they are not taken too solemnly. Adams never tired of quoting the supreme phrase of his idol Gibbon, before the Gothic cathedrals: "I darted a contemptuous look on the stately monuments of superstition." Even in the footnotes of his history, Gibbon had never inserted a bit of humor more human than this, and one would have paid largely for a photograph of the fat little historian, on the background of Notre Dame of Amiens, trying to persuade his readers—perhaps himself—that he was darting a contemptuous look on the stately monument, for which he felt in fact the respect which every man of his vast study and active mind always feels before objects worthy of it; but besides the humor, one felt also the relation. Gibbon ignored the Virgin, because in 1789 religious monuments were out of fashion. In 1900 his remark sounded fresh and simple as the green fields to ears that had heard a hundred years of other remarks, mostly no more fresh and certainly less simple. Without malice, one might find it more instructive than a whole lecture of Ruskin. One sees what one brings, and at that moment Gibbon brought the French Revolution. Ruskin brought reaction against the Revolution. St. Gaudens had passed beyond all. He liked the stately monuments much more than he liked Gibbon or Ruskin; he loved their dignity; their unity; their scale; their lines; their lights and shadows; their decorative sculpture; but he was even less conscious than they of the force that created it all—the Virgin, the Woman—by whose genius "the stately monuments of superstition" were built, through which she was expressed. He would have seen more meaning in Isis with the cow's horns, at Edfoo, who expressed the same thought. The art remained, but the energy was lost even upon the artist.

Yet in mind and person St. Gaudens was a survival of the 1500's; he bore the stamp of the Renaissance, and should have carried an image of the Virgin round his neck, or stuck in his hat, like Louis XI. In mere time he was a lost soul that had strayed by chance into the twentieth century,

and forgotten where it came from. He writhed and cursed at his ignorance, much as Adams did at his own, but in the opposite sense. St. Gaudens was a child of Benvenuto Cellini, smothered in an American cradle.
Adams was a quintessence of Boston, devoured by curiosity to think like
Benvenuto. St. Gaudens's art was starved from birth, and Adams's instinct was blighted from babyhood. Each had but half of a nature, and
when they came together before the Virgin of Amiens they ought both
to have felt in her the force that made them one; but it was not so. To
Adams she became more than ever a channel of force; to St. Gaudens
she remained as before a channel of taste.

For a symbol of power, St. Gaudens instinctively preferred the horse,
as was plain in his horse and Victory of the Sherman monument. Doubtless Sherman also felt it so. The attitude was so American that, for at least
forty years, Adams had never realized that any other could be in sound
taste. How many years had he taken to admit a notion of what Michael
Angelo and Rubens were driving at? He could not say; but he knew that
only since 1895 had he begun to feel the Virgin or Venus as force, and not
everywhere even so. At Chartres—perhaps at Lourdes—possibly at
Cnidos if one could still find there the divinely naked Aphrodite of Prax-
iteles—but otherwise one must look for force to the goddesses of Indian
mythology. The idea died out long ago in the German and English stock.
St. Gaudens at Amiens was hardly less sensitive to the force of the female
energy than Matthew Arnold at the Grande Chartreuse. Neither of them
felt goddesses as power—only as reflected emotion, human expression,
beauty, purity, taste, scarcely even as sympathy. They felt a railway train
as power; yet they, and all other artists, constantly complained that the
power embodied in a railway train could never be embodied in art. All
the steam in the world could not, like the Virgin, build Chartres.

Yet in mechanics, whatever the mechanicians might think, both energies acted as interchangeable forces on man, and by action on man all
known force may be measured. Indeed, few men of science measured
force in any other way. After once admitting that a straight line was the
shortest distance between two points, no serious mathematician cared to
deny anything that suited his convenience, and rejected no symbol, un-
proved or unprovable, that helped him to accomplish work. The symbol was force, as a compass-needle or a triangle was force, as the
mechanist might prove by losing it, and nothing could be gained by ignoring their value. Symbol or energy, the Virgin had acted as the greatest force the Western world ever felt, and had drawn man's activities to
herself more strongly than any other power, natural or supernatural, had
ever done; the historian's business was to follow the track of the energy;
to find where it came from and where it went to; its complex source and
shifting channels; its values, equivalents, conversions. It could scarcely be

more complex than radium; it could hardly be deflected, diverted, po-
larized, absorbed more perplexingly than other radiant matter. Adams
knew nothing about any of them, but as a mathematical problem of influence on human progress, though all were occult, all reacted on his
mind, and he rather inclined to think the Virgin easiest to handle.

The pursuit turned out to be long and tortuous, leading at last into the
vast forests of scholastic science. From Zeno to Descartes, hand in hand
with Thomas Aquinas, Montaigne, and Pascal, one stumbled as stupidly
as though one were still a German student of 1860. Only with the instinct
of despair could one force one's self into this old thicket of ignorance
after having been repulsed at a score of entrances more promising and
more popular. Thus far, no path had led anywhere, unless perhaps to an
exceedingly modest living. Forty-five years of study had proved to be
quite futile for the pursuit of power; one controlled no more force in 1900
than in 1850, although the amount of force controlled by society had
enormously increased. The secret of education still hid itself somewhere
behind ignorance, and one fumbled over it as feebly as ever. In such
labyrinths, the staff is a force almost more necessary than the legs; the pen
becomes a sort of blind-man's dog, to keep him from falling into the gutters. The pen works for itself, and acts like a hand, modelling the plastic
material over and over again to the form that suits it best. The form is
never arbitrary, but is a sort of growth like crystallization, as any artist
knows too well; for often the pencil or pen runs into side-paths and shape-
lessness, loses its relations, stops or is bogged. Then it has to return on its
trail, and recover, if it can, its line of force. The result of a year's work depends more on what is struck out than on what is left in; on the sequence
of the main lines of thought, than on their play or variety. Compelled
once more to lean heavily on this support, Adams covered more thousands of pages with figures as formal as though they were algebra, laboriously striking out, altering, burning, experimenting, until the year had
expired, the Exposition had long been closed, and winter drawing to its
end, before he sailed from Cherbourg, on January 19, 1901, for home.

# HENRY JAMES
## (1843–1916)

James spent his childhood traveling the world with his wealthy parents, and these youthful journeys became the foundation for the international themes that marked his writing. Most of the great protagonists of his fiction are Americans, and they are often studied in a European context. Among his earliest novels was *The American* (1877), which dealt with the problems of an American in Paris.

James's novels, while always posing some difficulties because of the author's naturally periphrastic style, became even more difficult toward the end of his career, when he began to dictate to a typist. Nonetheless, these later works, including *The Ambassadors* (1903) and *The Golden Bowl* (1904), have won him immense acclaim.

After the death of his brother, William (the philosopher), in 1910, Henry turned to writing his autobiography, which eventually spread out over three volumes: *A Small Boy and Others* (1913), *Notes of a Son and Brother* (1914), and *The Middle Years* (1917). The same qualities of mind that make his fiction compelling are also found in these often ignored volumes.

## FROM *Notes of a Son and Brother*

I went up from Newport to Cambridge early in the autumn of '62, and on one of the oddest errands, I think, that, given the several circumstances, I could possibly have undertaken. I was nineteen years old, and it had seemed to me for some time past that some such step as my entering for instance the Harvard Law School more or less urgently concerned what I could but try to help myself out by still putting forward as my indispensable education—I am not sure indeed that the claim didn't explicitly figure, or at least successfully dangle, as that of my possibly graceful mere "culture." I had somehow—by which I mean for reasons quite sufficient—to fall back on the merciful "mere" for any statement of my pretensions even to myself: so little they seemed to fit into any scheme of the conventional maximum as compared with those I saw so variously and strongly asserted about me, especially since the outbreak of the War. I am not sure whether I yet made bold to say it, but I should surely be good for nothing, all my days, if not for projecting into the concrete, by hook or by crook—that is my imagination shamelessly aiding—some show of (again) mere life. This impression was not in the least the flag I publicly brandished; in fact I must have come as near as possible to brandishing none whatever, a sound instinct always hinting to me, I gather, that the time for such a performance was much more after than before—before the perfect place had been found for the real planting of the standard and the giving of its folds to the air. No such happy spot had been marked, decidedly, at that period, to my inquiring eye; in consequence of which the emblazoned morsel (hoisted sooner or later by all of us, I think, somehow and somewhere) might have passed for the hour as a light extravagant bandanna rolled into the tight ball that fits it for hiding in the pocket. There it considerably stayed, so far as I was concerned; and all the more easily as I can but have felt how little any particular thing I might meanwhile "do" would matter—save for some specious appearance in it. This last, I recognise, had for me a virtue—principally that of somehow gaining time; though I hasten to add that my approach to the Law School can scarcely, as a means to this end, in the air of it that comes back to me, have been in the least deceptive. By which I mean that my appearance of intentions, qualifications, possibilities, or whatever else, in the connection, hadn't surely so much as the grace of the specious. I spoke above of the assumed "indispensability" of some show of my being further subject to the "education" theory, but this was for the moment only under failure to ask to whom, or for what, such a tribute *was* indispensable. The interest to myself would seem to have been, as I recover the sense of the time, that of all the impossibilities of action my proceeding to Cambridge on the very vaguest grounds that probably ever determined a residence there might pass for the least flagrant; as I breathe over again at any rate the comparative confidence in which I so moved I feel it as a confidence in the positive saving virtue of vagueness. Could I but work that force as an ideal I felt it must see me through, for the beauty of it in that form was that it should absolutely superabound. I wouldn't have allowed, either, that it was vaguer to do nothing; for in the first place just staying at home when everyone was on the move couldn't in any degree show the right mark: to be properly and perfectly vague one had to be vague *about* something; mere inaction quite lacked the note—it was nothing but definite and dull. I thought of the Law School experiment, I remember, in all sorts of conceivable connections, but in the connection of dulness surely never for an hour. I thought of it under the head of "life"—by which term at the same time, I blush to confess, I didn't in the least mean free evening access to Boston in a jangling horse-car, with whatever extension this might give to the joy of the liberated senses. I simply meant—well, what was monstrously to happen; which I shall be better inspired here to deal with as a demonstration made in its course than as a premonition relatively crude and at the time still to be verified. Marked in the whole matter, however these things might be, was that irony of fate under the ugly grin of which I found my father reply in the most offhand and liberal manner to my remark that the step in question—my joining, in a sense, my brother at Cambridge—wouldn't be wholly unpracticable. It might have been, from his large assent to it, a masterstroke of high policy. A certain inconsequence in this left me wondering why then if the matter was now so natural it hadn't been to his mind a year before equally simple that I should go to college, and to *that* College, after a more showy, even though I see it would have been at the same time a less presumptuous, fashion. To have deprecated the "college course" with such emphasis only so soon afterwards to forswear all emphasis and practically smile, in mild oblivion, on *any* Harvard connection I might find it in me to take up, was to bring it home, I well recall, that the case might originally have been much better managed.

All of which would seem to kick up more dust than need quite have hung about so simple a matter as my setting forth to the Cambridge scene with no design that I could honourably exhibit. A superficial account of the matter would have been that my father had a year or two earlier appeared to think so ill of it as to reduce me, given the "delicacy," the inward, not then the outward, which I have glanced at, to mild renunciation—mild I say because I remember in fact, rather to my mystification now, no great pang of disappointment, no soreness of submission. I didn't want anything so much as I wanted a certain good (or wanted thus supremely *to* want it, if I may say so), with which a conventional going to college wouldn't have so tremendously much to do as for the giving it up to break my heart—or an unconventional not-going so tremendously much either. What I "wanted to want" to be was, all intimately, just *literary*: a decent respect for the standard hadn't yet made my approach so straight that there weren't still difficulties that might seem to meet it, questions it would have to depend on. Passing the Harvard portal positively failed in fact to strike me as the shorter cut to literature; the sounds that rose from the scene as I caught them appeared on the contrary the most detached from any such interest that had ever reached my ear. Merely to open the door of the big square closet, the ample American closet, to the like of which Europe had never treated us, on the shelves and round the walls of which the pink Revues sat with the air, row upon row, of a choir of breathing angels, was to take up that particular, that sacred connection in a way that put the coarser process to shame. The drop of the Harvard question had of a truth really meant, as I recover it, a renewed consecration of the rites of that chapel where the taper always twinkled—which circumstance I mention as not only qualifying my sense of loss, but as symbolising, after a queer fashion, the independence, blest vision (to the extent, that is, of its being a closer compact with the life of the imagination), that I should thus both luckily come in for and designingly cultivate: cultivate in other words under the rich cover of obscurity. I have already noted how the independence was, ever so few months later, by so quaint a turn, another mere shake of the tree, to drop into my lap in the form of a great golden apple—a value not a simple windfall only through the fact that my father's hand had after all just lightly loosened it. This accession pointed the moral that there was no difficulty about anything, no intrinsic difficulty; so that, to re-emphasise the sweet bewilderment, I was to "go" where I liked in the Harvard direction and do what I liked in the Harvard relation. Such was the situation as offered me; though as I had to take it and use it I found in it no little difference. Two things and more had come up—the biggest of which, and very wondrous as bearing on any circumstance of mine, as having a grain of weight to spare for it, was the breaking out of the War. The other, the infinitely small affair in comparison, was a passage of personal history the most entirely personal, but between which, as a private catastrophe or difficulty, bristling with embarrassments, and the great public convulsion that announced itself in bigger terms each day, I felt from the very first an association of the closest, yet withal, I fear, almost of the least clearly expressible. Scarce at all to be stated, to begin with, the queer fusion or confusion established in my consciousness during the soft spring of '61 by the firing on Fort Sumter, Mr. Lincoln's instant first call for volunteers and a physical mishap, already referred to as having overtaken me at the same dark hour, and the effects of which were to draw themselves out incalculably and intolerably. Beyond all present notation the interlaced, undivided way in which what had happened to me, by a turn of fortune's hand, in twenty odious minutes, kept company of the most unnatural—I can call it nothing less—with my view of what was happening, with the question of what might still happen, to everyone about me, to the country at large: it so made of these marked disparities a single vast visitation. One had the sense, I mean, of a huge comprehensive ache, and there were hours at which one could scarce have told whether it came most from one's own poor organism, still so young and so meant for better things, but which had suffered particular wrong, or from the enclosing social body, a body rent with a thousand wounds and that thus treated one to the honour of a sort of tragic fellowship. The twenty minutes had sufficed, at all events, to establish a relation—a relation to everything occurring round me not only for the next four years but for long afterward—that was at once extraordinarily intimate and quite awkwardly irrelevant. I must have felt in some befooled way in presence of a crisis—the smoke of Charleston Bay still so acrid in the air—at which the likely young should be up and doing or, as familiarly put, lend a hand much wanted; the willing youths, all round, were mostly starting to their feet, and to have trumped up a lameness at such a juncture could be made to pass in no light for graceful. Jammed into the acute angle between two high fences, where the rhythmic play of my arms, in tune with that of several other pairs, but at a dire disadvantage of position, induced a rural, a rusty, a quasi-extemporised old engine to work and a saving stream to flow, I had done myself, in face of a shabby conflagration, a horrid even if an obscure hurt; and what was interesting from the first was my not doubting in the least its duration—though what seemed equally clear was that I needn't as a matter of course adopt and appropriate it, so to speak, or place it for increase of interest on exhibition. The interest of it, I very presently knew, would certainly be of the greatest, would even in conditions kept as simple as I might make them become little less than absorbing. The shortest account of what was to follow for a long time after is therefore to plead that the interest never did fail. It was naturally what is called a painful one, but it consistently declined, as an influence at play, to drop for a single instant. Circumstances, by a wonderful chance, overwhelmingly favoured it—*as* an interest, an inexhaustible, I mean; since I also felt in the whole enveloping tonic atmosphere a force promoting its growth. Interest, the interest of life and of death, of our national existence, of the fate of those, the vastly numerous, whom it closely concerned, the interest of the extending War, in fine, the hurrying troops, the transfigured scene, formed a cover for every sort of intensity, made tension itself in fact contagious—so that almost any tension would do, would serve for one's share.

I have here, I allow, not a little to foreshorten—have to skip sundry particulars, certain of the steps by which I came to think of my relation to my injury as a *modus vivendi* workable for the time. These steps had after the first flush of reaction inevitably *had* to be communications of my state, recognitions and admissions; which had the effect, I hasten to add, of producing sympathies, supports and reassurances. I gladly took these things, I perfectly remember, at that value; distinct to me as it still is nevertheless that the indulgence they conveyed lost part of its balm by involving a degree of publication. Direfully distinct have remained to me the conditions of a pilgrimage to Boston made that summer under my father's care for consultation of a great surgeon, the head of his profession there; whose opinion and advice—the more that he was a guaranteed friend of my father's—had seemed the best light to invoke on the less and less bearable affliction with which I had been for three or four months seeking to strike some sort of bargain: mainly, up to that time, under protection of a theory of temporary supine "rest" against which everything inward and outward tended equally to conspire. Agitated scraps of rest, snatched, to my consciousness, by the liveliest violence, were to show for futile almost to the degree in which the effort of our interview with the high expert was afterwards so to show; the truth being that this interview settled my sad business, settled it just in that saddest sense, for ever so long to come. This was so much the case that, as the mere scene of our main appeal, the house from which we had after its making dejectedly emerged put forth to me as I passed it in many a subsequent season an ironic smug symbolism of its action on my fate. That action had come from the complete failure of our approached oracle either to warn, to comfort or to command—to do anything but make quite unassistingly light of the bewilderment exposed to him. In default of other attention or suggestion he might by a mere warning as to gravities only too possible, and already well advanced, have made such a difference; but I have little forgotten how I felt myself, the warning absent, treated but to a comparative pooh-pooh—an impression I long looked back to as a sharp parting of the ways, with an adoption of the wrong one distinctly determined. It was not simply small comfort, it was only a mystification the more, that the inconvenience of my state had to reckon with the strange fact of there being nothing to speak of the matter with me. The graceful course, on the whole ground again (and where moreover was delicacy, the proposed, the intended, without grace?), was to behave accordingly, in good set terms, as if the assurance were true; since the time left no margin at all for one's gainsaying with the right confidence so high an authority. There were a hundred ways to behave—in the general sense so freely suggested, I mean; and I think of the second half of that summer of '62 as my attempt at selection of the best. The best still remained, under closer comparisons, very much what it had at first seemed, and there was in fact this charm in it that to prepare for an ordeal essentially intellectual, as I surmised, might justly involve, in the public eye, a season of some retirement. The beauty was—I can fairly see it now, through the haze of time, even as beauty!—that studious retirement and preparatory hours did after all supply the supine attitude, did invest the ruefulness, did deck out the cynicism of lying down book in hand with a certain fine plausibility. This was at least a negative of combat, an organised, not a loose and empty one, something definitely and firmly parallel to action in the tented field; and I well recall, for that matter, how, when early in the autumn I had in fact become the queerest of forensic recruits, the bristling horde of my Law School comrades fairly produced the illusion of a mustered army. The Cambridge campus was tented field enough for a conscript starting so compromised; and I can scarce say moreover how easily it let me down that when it came to the point one had still fine fierce young men, in great numbers, for company, there being at the worst so many such who hadn't flown to arms. I was to find my fancy of the merely relative right in any way to figure, or even on such terms just to exist, I was to find it in due course quite drop from me as the Cambridge year played itself out, leaving me all aware that, full though the air might be of stiffer realities, one had yet a rare handful of one's own to face and deal with.

At Cambridge of course, when I got there, I was further to find my brother on the scene and already at a stage of possession of its contents that I was resigned in advance never to reach; so thoroughly I seemed to feel a sort of quickening savoury meal in any cold scrap of his own experience that he might pass on to my palate. This figure has definite truth, that is, but for association at the board literally yielding us nourishment—the happiest as to social composition and freedom of supply of all the *tables d'hôte* of those days, a veritable haunt of conversation ruled by that gently fatuous Miss Upham something of whose angular grace and antique attitude has lived again for us in William's letters. I place him, if not at the moment of my to that extent joining him then at least from a short time afterwards, in quarters that he occupied for the next two or three years—quiet cloistered rooms, as they almost appeared to me, in the comparatively sequestered Divinity Hall of that still virtually rustic age; which, though mainly affected to the use of post-graduates and others, of a Unitarian colour, enrolled under Harvard's theological Faculty, offered chance accommodation, much appreciated for a certain supposedly separate charm, not to say a finer dignity, by the more maturely studious in other branches as well. The superstition or aftertaste of Europe had then neither left me nor hinted that it ever might; yet I recall as a distinct source of interest, to be desperately dealt with, and dealt with somehow to my inward advantage, the special force of the circumstance that I was now for the first time in presence of matters normally, entirely, consistently American, and that more particularly I found myself sniff up straight from the sources, such as they unmistakably were, the sense of that New England which had been to me till then but a name. This from the first instant was what I most took in, and quite apart from the question of what one was going to make of it, of whether one was going, in the simple formula, to like it, and of what would come, could the impression so triumph, of such monstrous assimilations. Clear to me in the light thus kindled that my American consciousness had hitherto been after all and at the best singularly starved, and that Newport for instance, during the couple of years, had fed it but with sips of an adulterated strain. Newport, with its opera-glass turned for ever across the sea—for Newport, or at least *our* Newport, even during the War, lived mainly, and quite visibly, by the opera-glass—was comparatively, and in its degree incurably, cosmopolite; and though on our first alighting there I had more or less successfully, as I fancied, invited the local historic sense to vibrate, it was at present left me to feel myself a poor uninitiated creature. However, an initiation, at least by the intelligence, into some given thing—almost anything really given would do—was essentially what I was, as we nowadays say, after; the fault with my previous data in the American kind had been that they weren't sufficiently given; so that here would be Boston and Cambridge giving as with absolute authority. The War had by itself of course, on the ground I speak of, communicated something of the quality, or rather of the quantity, otherwise deficient; only this was for my case, of which alone I speak, an apprehension without a language or a channel—a revelation as sublime as one would like to feel it, but spreading abroad as a whole and not, alas, by any practice of mine, reducible to parts. What I promptly made out at Cambridge was that "America" would be given, as I have called it, to a tune altogether fresh, so that to hear this tune wholly played out might well become on the spot an inspiring privilege. If I indeed, I should add, said to myself "wholly," this was of course not a little straining a point; since, putting my initiation, my grasp of the exhibition, at its conceivable liveliest, far more of the supposed total was I inevitably to miss than to gather to my use. But I might gather what I could, and therein was exactly the adventure. To rinse my mouth of the European aftertaste *in order* to do justice to whatever of the native bitter-sweet might offer itself in congruous vessels— such a brave dash for discovery, and such only, would give a sense to my posture. With which it was unmistakable that I shouldn't in the least have painfully to strive; of such a force of impact was each impression clearly capable that I had much rather to steady myself, at any moment, where I stood, and quite to a sense of the luxury of the occasion, than to cultivate inquiry at the aggressive pitch. There was no need for curiosity —it was met by every object, I seemed to see, so much more than half way; unless indeed I put it better by saying that as *all* my vision partook of that principle the impulse and the object perpetually melted together. It wasn't for instance by the faintest process of inquiry that the *maison* Upham, where I three times daily sat at meat, had scarce to wait an hour to become as vivid a translation into American terms of Balzac's Maison Vauquer, in Le Pére Goriot, as I could have desired to deal with.

It would have been at once uplifting to see in the American terms a vast improvement on the prime version, had I not been here a bit baffled by the sense that the correspondence was not quite, after all, of like with like, and that the main scene of Balzac's action was confessedly and curiously sordid and even sinister, whereas its equivalent under the Harvard elms would rank decidedly as what we had *de mieux*, or in other words of most refined, in the "boarding" line, to show. I must have been further conscious that what we had de mieux in the social line appeared quite liable, on occasion, to board wherever it might—the situation in Balzac's world being on this head as different as possible. No one not deeply distressed or dismally involved or all but fatally compromised could have taken the chances of such an establishment at all; so that any comparison to our own particular advantage had to be, on reflection, nipped in the bud. There was a generic sameness, none the less, I might still reason; enough of that at least to show the two pictures as each in its way interesting—which was all that was required. The Maison Vauquer, its musty air thick with heavier social elements, might have been more so, for the Harvard elms overhung no strange Vautrin, no old Goriot, no young Rastignac; yet the interest of the Kirkland Street company couldn't, so to speak, help itself either, any more than I could help taking advantage of it. In one respect certainly, in the matter of talk as talk, we shone incomparably brighter; and if it took what we had de mieux to make our so regular resort a scene essentially of conversation, the point was none the less that our materials were there. I found the effect of this, very easily, as American as I liked—liked, that is, to think of it and to make all I might of it for being; about which in truth all difficulty vanished from the moment the local colour of the War broke in. So of course this element did at that season come back to us through every outward opening, and mean enough by contrast had been the questions amid which the Vauquer boarders grubbed. Anything even indirectly touched by our public story, stretching now into volume after volume of the very biggest print, took on that reflected light of dignity, of importance, or of mere gross salience, which passion charged with criticism, and criticism charged with the thousand menaced affections and connections, the whole of the reaction—charged in short with immediate intimate life—have a power, in such conditions, to fling as from a waving torch. The torch flared sufficiently about Miss Upham's board—save that she herself, ancient spinster, pushed it in dismay from her top of the table, blew upon it with vain scared sighs, and would have nothing to do with a matter so disturbing to the right temperature of her *plats*. We others passed it from hand to hand, so that it couldn't go quite out—since I must in fairness add that the element of the casual and the more *generally* ironic, the play of the studious or the irrepressibly social intelligence at large, couldn't fail to insist pretty constantly on its rights. There were quarters as well, I should note, in which the sense of local colour proceeding at all straight from the source I have named—reflected, that is, from camp and field—could but very soon run short; sharply enough do I recall for instance the felt, even if all so privately felt, limits of *my* poor stream of contributive remark (despite my habit, so fondly practised in the connection, of expatiating *in petto*). My poor stream would have trickled, truly, had it been able to trickle at all, from the most effective of my few occasions of "realising," up to that time, as to field and camp; literally as to camp in fact, since the occasion had consisted of a visit paid, or a pilgrimage, rather, ever so piously, so tenderly made, one August afternoon of the summer just ended, to a vast gathering of invalid and convalescent troops, under canvas and in roughly improvised shanties, at some point of the Rhode Island shore that figures to my memory, though with a certain vagueness, as Portsmouth Grove. (American local names lend themselves strangely little to retention, I find, if one has happened to deal for long years with almost any group of European designations — these latter springing, as it has almost always come to seem, straight from the soil where natural causes were anciently to root them, each with its rare identity. The bite into interest of the borrowed, the imposed, the "faked" label, growing but as by a dab of glue on an article of trade, is inevitably much less sharp.) Vagueness at best attends, however, the queer experience I glance at; what lives of it, in the ineffaceable way, being again, by my incurable perversity, my ambiguous economy, much less a matter of the "facts of the case," as they should, even though so dead and buried now, revive to help me through an anecdote, than the prodigiously subjective side of the experience, thanks to which it still presumes to flush with the grand air of an adventure. If I had not already so often brazened out my confession of the far from "showy" in the terms on which impressions could become indelibly momentous to me I might blush indeed for the thin tatter dragged in thus as an affair of record. It consisted at the time simply of an emotion — though the emotion, I should add, appeared to consist of everything in the whole world that my consciousness could hold. By *that* intensity did it hang as bravely as possible together, and by the title so made good has it handed itself endlessly down.

Owing to which it is that I don't at all know what troops were in question, a "mere" couple of Rhode Island regiments (nothing in those days could be too big to escape the application of the "mere,") or a congeries of the temporarily incapacitated, the more or less broken, picked from the veterans — so far as there already were such — of the East at large and directed upon the Grove as upon a place of stowage and sanitation. Discriminations of the prosaic order had little to do with my first and all but sole vision of the American soldier in his multitude, and above all — for that was markedly the colour of the whole thing — in his depression, his wasted melancholy almost; an effect that somehow corresponds for memory, I bethink myself, with the tender elegiac tone in which Walt Whitman was later on so admirably to commemorate him. The restrictions I confess to are abject, but both my sense and my aftersense of the exhibition I here allude to had, thanks to my situation, to do all the work they could in the way of representation to me of what was most publicly, most heroically, most wastefully, tragically, terribly going on. It had so to serve

for my particular nearest approach to a "contact" with the active drama—
I mean of course the collectively and scenically active, since the brush
of interest against the soldier single and salient was an affair of every
day—that were it not for just one other strange spasm of awareness, scarce
relaxed to this hour, I should have been left all but pitifully void of any
scrap of a substitute for the concrete experience. The long hot July 1st of
'63, on which the huge battle of Gettysburg had begun, could really
be—or rather couldn't possibly not be—a scrap of concrete experience
for any group of united persons, New York cousins and all, who, in a
Newport garden, restlessly strolling, sitting, neither daring quite to move
nor quite to rest, quite to go in nor quite to stay out, actually *listened* together, in their almost ignobly safe stillness, as to the boom of far-away
guns. This *was*, as it were, the War—the War palpably in Pennsylvania;
not less than my hour of a felt rage of repining at my doomed absence
from the sight of that march of the 54th Massachusetts out of Boston,
"Bob" Shaw at its head and our exalted Wilky among its officers, of which
a great sculptor was, on the spot of their vividest passing, to set the image
aloft forever. Poor other visitations, comparatively, had had to suffice for
me; I could take in fact for amusing, most of all (since that, thank goodness, was high gaiety), a couple of impressions of the brief preliminary
camp life at Readville during which we admired the charming composition of the 44th of the same State, under Colonel Frank Lee, and which
fairly made romantic for me Wilky's quick spring out of mere juvenility
and into such brightly-bristling ranks. He had begun by volunteering in
a company that gave him half the ingenuous youth of the circle within
our social ken for brothers-in-arms, and it was to that pair of Readville afternoons I must have owed my all so emphasised vision of handsome
young Cabot Russell, who, again to be his closest brother-in-arms in the
54th, irrecoverably lost himself, as we have seen, at Fort Wagner. A dry
desert, one must suppose, the life in which, for memory and appreciation
made one, certain single hours or compressed groups of hours have
found their reason for standing out through everything, for insistently living on, in the cabinet of intimate reference, the museum, as it were, of
the soul's curiosities—where doubtless at the same time an exhibition of
them to mere other eyes or ears or questioning logical minds may effect
itself in no plain terms. We recognise such occasions more and more as
we go on, and are surely, as a general thing, glad when, for the interest
of memory—which it's such a business to *keep* interesting—they constitute something of a cluster. In my queer cluster, at any rate, that flower
of the connection which answers to the name of Portsmouth Grove still
overtops other members of its class, so that to finger it again for a moment
is to make it perceptibly exhale its very principle of life. This was, for me,
at the time, neither more nor less than that the American soldier in his

multitude was the most attaching and affecting and withal the most amusing figure of romance conceivable; the great sense of my vision being thus that, as the afternoon light of the place and time lingered upon him, both to the seeming enhancement of his quality and of its own, romance of a more confused kind than I shall now attempt words for attended his every movement. It was the charmingest, touchingest, dreadfullest thing in the world that my impression of him should have to be somehow of his abandonment to a rueful humour, to a stoic reserve which could yet melt, a relation with him once established, into a rich communicative confidence; and, in particular, all over the place, of his own scanted and more or less baffled, though constantly and, as I couldn't not have it, pathetically, "knowing" devices.

The great point remained for me at all events that I could afterwards appear to myself to have done nothing but establish with him a relation, that I established it, to my imagination, in several cases—and all in the three or four hours—even to the pitch of the last tenderness of friendship. I recover that, strolling about with honest and so superior fellow-citizens, or sitting with them by the improvised couches of their languid rest, I drew from each his troubled tale, listened to his plaint on his special hard case—taking form, this, in what seemed to me the very poetry of the esoteric vernacular—and sealed the beautiful tie, the responsive sympathy, by an earnest offer, in no instance waved away, of such pecuniary solace as I might at brief notice draw on my poor pocket for. Yet again, as I indulge this memory, do I feel that I might if pushed a little rejoice in having to such an extent coincided with, not to say perhaps positively anticipated, dear old Walt—even if I hadn't come armed like him with oranges and peppermints. I ministered much more summarily, though possibly in proportion to the time and thanks to my better luck more pecuniarily; but I like to treat myself to making out that I can scarce have brought to the occasion (in proportion to the time again and to other elements of the case) less of the consecrating sentiment than he. I like further to put it in a light that, ever so curiously, if the good Walt was most inwardly stirred to his later commemorative accents by his participating in the common Americanism of his hospital friends, the familiar note and shared sound of which formed its ground of appeal, I found myself victim to a like moving force through quite another logic. It was literally, I fear, because our common Americanism carried with it, to my imagination, such a disclosed freshness and strangeness, working, as I might say, over such gulfs of dissociation, that I reached across to *their*, these hospital friends', side of the matter, even at the risk of an imperilled consistency. It had for me, the state in question, colour and form, accent and quality, with scarce less "authority" than if instead of the rough tracks or worn paths of my casual labyrinth I had trod the glazed halls of some school of natural history. What holds me now indeed is that such an institution might have exemplified then almost nothing but the aspects strictly native to our social and seasonal air; so simply and easily conceivable to the kindly mind were at that time these reciprocities, so great the freedom and pleasure of them compared with the restrictions imposed on directness of sympathy by the awful admixtures of to-day, those which offer to the would-be participant among us, on returns from sojourns wherever homogeneity and its entailed fraternity, its easy contacts, still may be seen to work, the strange shock of such amenities declined on any terms. Really not possible then, I think, the perception now accompanying, on American ground, this shock—the recognition, by any sensibility at all reflective, of the point where our national theory of absorption, assimilation and conversion appallingly breaks down; appallingly, that is, for those to whom the *consecrated* association, of the sort still at play where community has not been blighted, strongly speaks. Which remarks may reinforce the note of my unconsciousness of any difficulty for knowing in the old, the comparatively brothering, conditions what an American at least *was*. Absurd thus, no doubt, that the scant experience over which I perversely linger insists on figuring to me as quite a revel of the right confidence.

The revel, though I didn't for the moment yet know it, was to be renewed for me at Cambridge with less of a romantic intensity perhaps, but more usefully, so to put it, and more informingly; surrounded as I presently found myself at the Law School with young types, or rather with young members of a single type, not one of whom but would have enriched my imagined hall of congruous specimens. *That*, with the many months of it, was to be the real disclosure, the larger revelation; that was to be the fresh picture for a young person reaching the age of twenty in wellnigh grotesque unawareness of the properties of the atmosphere in which he but wanted to claim that he had been nourished. Of what I mean by this I shall in a moment have more to say—after pointing a trifle more, for our patience, the sense of my dilatation upon Portsmouth Grove. Perfectly distinct has remained the sail back to Newport by that evening's steamboat; the mere memory of which indeed—and I recall that I felt it inordinately long—must have been for me, just above, the spring of the whole reference. The sail was long, measured by my acute consciousness of paying physically for my excursion—which hadn't answered the least little bit for my impaired state. This last disobliging fact became one, at the same time, with an intensity, indeed a strange rapture, of reflection, which I may not in the least pretend to offer as a clear or coherent or logical thing, and of which I can only say, leaving myself there through the summer twilight, in too scant rest on a deck stool and against the bulwark, that it somehow crowned my little adventure of sympathy and wonder with a shining round of resignation—a realisation, as we nowadays put it, that, measuring wounds against wounds, or the compromised, the particular taxed condition, at the least, against all the rest of the debt then so generally and enormously due, one was no less exaltedly than wastefully engaged in the common fact of endurance. There are memories in truth too fine or too peculiar for notation, too intensely individual and supersubtle—call them what one will; yet which one may thus no more give up confusedly than one may insist on them vainly. Their kind is nothing ever to a present purpose unless they are in a manner statable, but is at the same time ruefully aware of threatened ridicule if they are overstated. Not that I in the least mind such a menace, however, in just adding that, soothed as I have called the admirable ache of my afternoon with that inward interpretation of it, I felt the latter—or rather doubtless simply the entire affair—absolutely overarched by the majestic manner in which the distress of our return drew out into the lucid charm of the night. To which I must further add that the hour seemed, by some wondrous secret, to know itself marked and charged and unforgettable—hinting so in its very own terms of cool beauty at something portentous in it, an exquisite claim then and there for lasting value and high authority.

# BOOKER T. WASHINGTON
## (1856–1915)

Though controversial in his stance regarding the social equality of blacks and whites, Washington was a key figure in the process of providing education to disadvantaged black students of the South. He often emphasized the need for gaining a secure economic position before social equality—a position that sparked much controversy among members of the struggle for civil liberty. His achievements included guiding the Tuskegee Institute through its transition from a one-teacher, fifty-student institute to a world-renowned center for the education of blacks. His papers span thirteen volumes and include correspondence with some of the other leading figures of the time. *Up from Slavery* (1901) was perhaps his most well-known work, and it brought his story to a wide, international audience.

Born in Virginia of a white father and black mother, Washington prided himself on having created personal greatness from nothing; in his two autobiographical books, he traced a Horatio Alger–like success story, putting himself forward as proof of the claim that the American dream was not bankrupt, and was still accessible to anyone with the desire to succeed. Like many autobiographers from Roman times to the present, Washington chose to focus on events, clinging to the surface of his life. His work is rarely personal; indeed, like that of U. S. Grant and many public figures, it often shades over into history and journalism. But the voice of Washington is distinct, and his work has inspired many African American writers and thinkers.

## FROM *Up from Slavery*

### ANXIOUS DAYS AND SLEEPLESS NIGHTS

The coming of Christmas, that first year of our residence in Alabama, gave us an opportunity to get a farther insight into the real life of the people. The first thing that reminded us that Christmas had arrived was the "foreday" visits of scores of children rapping at our doors, asking for "Chris'mus gifts! Chris'mus gifts!" Between the hours of two o'clock and five o'clock in the morning I presume that we must have had a half-hundred such calls. This custom prevails throughout this portion of the South to-day.

During the days of slavery it was a custom quite generally observed throughout all the Southern states to give the coloured people a week of holiday at Christmas, or to allow the holiday to continue as long as the "yule log" lasted. The male members of the race, and often the female members, were expected to get drunk. We found that for a whole week the coloured people in and around Tuskegee dropped work the day before Christmas, and that it was difficult to get any one to perform any service from the time they stopped work until after the New Year. Persons who at other times did not use strong drink thought it quite the proper thing to indulge in it rather freely during the Christmas week. There was a widespread hilarity, and a free use of guns, pistols, and gunpowder generally. The sacredness of the season seemed to have been almost wholly lost sight of.

During this first Christmas vacation I went some distance from the town to visit the people on one of the large plantations. In their poverty and ignorance it was pathetic to see their attempts to get joy out of the season that in most parts of the country is so sacred and so dear to the heart. In one cabin I noticed that all that the five children had to remind them of the coming of Christ was a single bunch of firecrackers, which they had divided among them. In another cabin, where there were at least a half-dozen persons, they had only ten cents' worth of ginger-cakes, which had been bought in the store the day before. In another family they had only a few pieces of sugarcane. In still another cabin I found nothing but a new jug of cheap, mean whiskey, which the husband and wife were making free use of, notwithstanding the fact that the husband was one of the local ministers. In a few instances I found that the people had gotten hold of some bright-coloured cards that had been designed for advertising purposes, and were making the most of those. In other homes some member of the family had bought a new pistol. In the majority of cases there was nothing to be seen in the cabin to remind one of the coming of the Saviour, except that the people had ceased work in the fields and were lounging about their homes. At night, during Christmas week, they usually had what they called a "frolic," in some cabin on the plantation. This meant a kind of rough dance, where there was likely to be a good deal of whiskey used, and where there might be some shooting or cutting with razors.

While I was making this Christmas visit I met an old coloured man who was one of the numerous local preachers, who tried to convince me, from the experience Adam had in the Garden of Eden, that God had cursed all labour, and that, therefore, it was a sin for any man to work. For that reason this man sought to do as little work as possible. He seemed at that time to be supremely happy, because he was living, as he expressed it, through one week that was free from sin.

In the school we made a special effort to teach our students the meaning of Christmas, and to give them lessons in its proper observance. In this we have been successful to a degree that makes me feel safe in saying that the season now has a new meaning, not only through all that immediate region, but, in a measure, wherever our graduates have gone.

At the present time one of the most satisfactory features of the Christmas and Thanksgiving seasons at Tuskegee is the unselfish and beautiful way in which our graduates and students spend their time in administering to the comfort and happiness of others, especially the unfortunate. Not long ago some of our young men spent a holiday in rebuilding a cabin for a helpless coloured woman who is about seventy-five years old. At another time I remember that I made it known in chapel, one night, that a very poor student was suffering from cold, because he needed a coat. The next morning two coats were sent to my office for him.

I have referred to the disposition on the part of the white people in the town of Tuskegee and vicinity to help the school. From the first, I resolved to make the school a real part of the community in which it was located. I was determined that no one should have the feeling that it was a foreign institution, dropped down in the midst of the people, for which they had no responsibility and in which they had no interest. I noticed that the very fact that they had been asked to contribute toward the purchase of the land made them begin to feel as if it was going to be their school, to a large degree. I noted that just in proportion as we made the white people feel that the institution was a part of the life of the community, and that, while we wanted to make friends in Boston, for example, we also wanted to make white friends in Tuskegee, and that we wanted to make the school of real service to all the people, their attitude toward the school became favourable.

Perhaps I might add right here, what I hope to demonstrate later, that, so far as I know, the Tuskegee school at the present time has no warmer and more enthusiastic friends anywhere than it has among the white citizens of Tuskegee and throughout the state of Alabama and the entire South. From the first, I have advised our people in the South to make friends in every straightforward, manly way with their next-door neighbour, whether he be a black man or a white man. I have also advised them, where no principle is at stake, to consult the interests of their local communities, and to advise with their friends in regard to their voting.

For several months the work of securing the money with which to pay for the farm went on without ceasing. At the end of three months enough was secured to repay the loan of two hundred and fifty dollars to General Marshall, and within two months more we had secured the entire five hundred dollars and had received a deed of the one hundred acres of land. This gave us a great deal of satisfaction. It was not only a source of satisfaction to secure a permanent location for the school, but it was equally satisfactory to know that the greater part of the money with which it was paid for had been gotten from the white and coloured people in the town of Tuskegee. The most of this money was obtained by holding festivals and concerts, and from small individual donations.

Our next effort was in the direction of increasing the cultivation of the land, so as to secure some return from it, and at the same time give the students training in agriculture. All the industries at Tuskegee have been started in natural and logical order, growing out of the needs of a community settlement. We began with farming, because we wanted something to eat.

Many of the students, also, were able to remain in school but a few weeks at a time, because they had so little money with which to pay their board. Thus another object which made it desirable to get an industrial system started was in order to make it available as a means of helping the students to earn money enough so that they might be able to remain in school during the nine months' session of the school year.

The first animal that the school came into possession of was an old blind horse given us by one of the white citizens of Tuskegee. Perhaps I may add here that at the present time the school owns over two hundred horses, colts, mules, cows, calves, and oxen, and about seven hundred hogs and pigs, as well as a large number of sheep and goats.

The school was constantly growing in numbers, so much so that, after we had got the farm paid for, the cultivation of the land begun, and the old cabins which we had found on the place somewhat repaired, we turned our attention toward providing a large, substantial building. After having given a good deal of thought to the subject, we finally had the plans drawn for a building that was estimated to cost about six thousand dollars. This seemed to us a tremendous sum, but we knew that the school must go backward or forward, and that our work would mean little unless we could get hold of the students in their home life.

One incident which occurred about this time gave me a great deal of satisfaction as well as surprise. When it became known in the town that we were discussing the plans for a new, large building, a Southern white man who was operating a sawmill not far from Tuskegee came to me and said that he would gladly put all the lumber necessary to erect the building on the grounds, with no other guarantee for payment than my word that it would be paid for when we secured some money. I told the man frankly that at the time we did not have in our hands one dollar of the money needed. Notwithstanding this, he insisted on being allowed to put the lumber on the grounds. After we had secured some portion of the money we permitted him to do this.

Miss Davidson again began the work of securing in various ways small contributions for the new building from the white and coloured people in and near Tuskegee. I think I never saw a community of people so happy over anything as were the coloured people over the prospect of this new building. One day, when we were holding a meeting to secure funds for its erection, an old, ante-bellum coloured man came a distance of twelve miles and brought in his ox-cart a large hog. When the meeting was in progress, he rose in the midst of the company and said that he had no money which he could give, but that he had raised two fine hogs, and that he had brought one of them as a contribution toward the expenses of the building. He closed his announcement by saying: "Any nigger that's got any love for his race, or any respect for himself, will bring a hog to the next meeting." Quite a number of men in the community also volunteered to give several days' work, each, toward the erection of the building.

After we had secured all the help that we could in Tuskegee, Miss Davidson decided to go North for the purpose of securing additional funds. For weeks she visited individuals and spoke in churches and before Sunday schools and other organizations. She found this work quite trying, and often embarrassing. The school was not known, but she was not long in winning her way into the confidence of the best people in the North.

The first gift from any Northern person was received from a New York lady whom Miss Davidson met on the boat that was bringing her North. They fell into a conversation, and the Northern lady became so much interested in the effort being made at Tuskegee that before they parted Miss Davidson was handed a check for fifty dollars. For some time before our marriage, and also after it, Miss Davidson kept up the work of securing money in the North and in the South by interesting people by personal visits and through correspondence. At the same time she kept in close touch with the work at Tuskegee, as lady principal and classroom teacher. In addition to this, she worked among the older people in and near Tuskegee, and taught a Sunday school class in the town. She was never very strong, but never seemed happy unless she was giving all of her strength to the cause which she loved. Often, at night, after spending the day in going from door to door trying to interest persons in the work at Tuskegee, she would be so exhausted that she could not undress herself. A lady upon whom she called, in Boston, afterward told me that at one time when Miss Davidson called to see her and sent up her card the lady was detained a little before she could see Miss Davidson, and when she entered the parlour she found Miss Davidson so exhausted that she had fallen asleep.

While putting up our first building, which was named Porter Hall, after Mr. A. H. Porter, of Brooklyn, N.Y., who gave a generous sum toward its erection, the need for money became acute. I had given one of our creditors a promise that upon a certain day he should be paid four hundred dollars. On the morning of that day we did not have a dollar. The mail arrived at the school at ten o'clock, and in this mail there was a check sent by Miss Davidson for exactly four hundred dollars. I could relate many instances of almost the same character. This four hundred dollars was given by two ladies in Boston. Two years later, when the work at Tuskegee had grown considerably, and when we were in the midst of a season when we were so much in need of money that the future looked doubtful and gloomy, the same two Boston ladies sent us six thousand dollars. Words cannot describe our surprise, or the encouragement that the gift brought to us. Perhaps I might add here that for fourteen years these same friends have sent us six thousand dollars each year.

As soon as the plans were drawn for the new building, the students began digging out the earth where the foundations were to be laid, working after the regular classes were over. They had not fully outgrown the idea that it was hardly the proper thing for them to use their hands, since they had come there, as one of them expressed it, "to be educated, and not to work." Gradually, though, I noted with satisfaction that a sentiment in favour of work was gaining ground. After a few weeks of hard work the foundations were ready, and a day was appointed for the laying of the corner-stone.

When it is considered that the laying of this corner-stone took place in the heart of the South, in the "Black Belt," in the centre of that part of our country that was most devoted to slavery; that at that time slavery had been abolished only about sixteen years; that only sixteen years before that no Negro could be taught from books without the teacher receiving the condemnation of the law or of public sentiment—when all this is considered, the scene that was witnessed on that spring day at Tuskegee was a remarkable one. I believe there are few places in the world where it could have taken place.

The principal address was delivered by the Hon. Waddy Thompson, the Superintendent of Education for the county. About the corner-stone were gathered the teachers, the students, their parents and friends, the county officials—who were white—and all the leading white men in that vicinity, together with many of the black men and women whom these same white people but a few years before had held a title to as property. The members of both races were anxious to exercise the privilege of placing under the corner-stone some memento.

Before the building was completed we passed through some very trying seasons. More than once our hearts were made to bleed, as it were, because bills were falling due that we did not have the money to meet. Perhaps no one who has not gone through the experience, month after month, of trying to erect buildings and provide equipment for a school when no one knew where the money was to come from, can properly appreciate the difficulties under which we laboured. During the first years at Tuskegee I recall that night after night I would roll and toss on my bed, without sleep, because of the anxiety and uncertainty which we were in regarding money. I knew that, in a large degree, we were trying an experiment—that of testing whether or not it was possible for Negroes to build up and control the affairs of a large educational institution. I knew that if we failed it would injure the whole race. I knew that the presumption was against us. I knew that in the case of white people beginning such an enterprise it would be taken for granted that they were going to succeed, but in our case I felt that people would be surprised if we succeeded. All this made a burden which pressed down on us, sometimes, it seemed, at the rate of a thousand pounds to the square inch.

In all our difficulties and anxieties, however, I never went to a white or a black person in the town of Tuskegee for any assistance that was in their power to render, without being helped according to their means. More than a dozen times, when bills figuring up into the hundreds of dollars were falling due, I applied to the white men of Tuskegee for small loans, often borrowing small amounts from as many as a half-dozen persons, to meet our obligations. One thing I was determined to do from the first, and that was to keep the credit of the school high; and this, I think I can say without boasting, we have done all through these years.

I shall always remember a bit of advice given me by Mr. George W. Campbell, the white man to whom I have referred as the one who induced General Armstrong to send me to Tuskegee. Soon after I entered upon the work Mr. Campbell said to me, in his fatherly way: "Washington, always remember that credit is capital."

At one time when we were in the greatest distress for money that we ever experienced, I placed the situation frankly before General Armstrong. Without hesitation he gave me his personal check for all the money which he had saved for his own use. This was not the only time that General Armstrong helped Tuskegee in this way. I do not think I have ever made this fact public before.

During the summer of 1882, at the end of the first year's work of the school, I was married to Miss Fannie N. Smith, of Malden, W.Va. We began keeping house in Tuskegee early in the fall. This made a home for our teachers, who now had been increased to four in number. My wife was also a graduate of the Hampton Institute. After earnest and constant

work in the interests of the school, together with her housekeeping duties, my wife passed away in May, 1884. One child, Portia M. Washington, was born during our marriage.

From the first, my wife most earnestly devoted her thoughts and time to the work of the school, and was completely one with me in every interest and ambition. She passed away, however, before she had an opportunity of seeing what the school was designed to be.

## A HARDER TASK THAN MAKING BRICKS WITHOUT STRAW

From the very beginning, at Tuskegee, I was determined to have the students do not only the agricultural and domestic work, but to have them erect their own buildings. My plan was to have them, while performing this service, taught the latest and best methods of labour, so that the school would not only get the benefit of their efforts, but the students themselves would be taught to see not only utility in labour, but beauty and dignity; would be taught, in fact, how to lift labour up from mere drudgery and toil, and would learn to love work for its own sake. My plan was not to teach them to work in the old way, but to show them how to make the forces of nature—air, water, steam, electricity, horse-power—assist them in their labour.

At first many advised against the experiment of having the buildings erected by the labour of the students, but I was determined to stick to it. I told those who doubted the wisdom of the plan that I knew that our first buildings would not be so comfortable or so complete in their finish as buildings erected by the experienced hands of outside workmen, but that in the teaching of civilization, self-help, and self-reliance, the erection of the buildings by the students themselves would more than compensate for any lack of comfort or fine finish.

I further told those who doubted the wisdom of this plan, that the majority of our students came to us in poverty, from the cabins of the cotton, sugar, and rice plantations of the South, and that while I knew it would please the students very much to place them at once in finely constructed buildings, I felt that it would be following out a more natural process of development to teach them how to construct their own buildings. Mistakes I knew would be made, but these mistakes would teach us valuable lessons for the future.

During the now nineteen years' existence of the Tuskegee school, the plan of having the buildings erected by student labour has been adhered to. In this time forty buildings, counting small and large, have been built, and all except four are almost wholly the product of student labour. As

an additional result, hundreds of men are now scattered throughout the South who received their knowledge of mechanics while being taught how to erect these buildings. Skill and knowledge are now handed down from one set of students to another in this way, until at the present time a building of any description or size can be constructed wholly by our instructors and students, from the drawing of the plans to the putting in of the electric fixtures, without going off the grounds for a single workman.

Not a few times, when a new student has been led into the temptation of marring the looks of some building by leadpencil marks or by the cuts of a jack-knife, I have heard an old student remind him: "Don't do that. That is our building. I helped put it up."

In the early days of the school I think my most trying experience was in the matter of brickmaking. As soon as we got the farm work reasonably well started, we directed our next efforts toward the industry of making bricks. We needed these for use in connection with the erection of our own buildings; but there was also another reason for establishing this industry. There was no brickyard in the town, and in addition to our own needs there was a demand for bricks in the general market.

I had always sympathized with the "Children of Israel," in their task of "making bricks without straw," but ours was the task of making bricks with no money and no experience.

In the first place, the work was hard and dirty, and it was difficult to get the students to help. When it came to brickmaking, their distaste for manual labour in connection with book education became especially manifest. It was not a pleasant task for one to stand in the mud-pit for hours, with the mud up to his knees. More than one man became disgusted and left the school.

We tried several locations before we opened up a pit that furnished brick clay. I had always supposed that brickmaking was very simple, but I soon found out by bitter experience that it required special skill and knowledge, particularly in the burning of the bricks. After a good deal of effort we moulded about twenty-five thousand bricks, and put them into a kiln to be burned. This kiln turned out to be a failure, because it was not properly constructed or properly burned. We began at once, however, on a second kiln. This, for some reason, also proved a failure. The failure of this kiln made it still more difficult to get the students to take any part in the work. Several of the teachers, however, who had been trained in the industries at Hampton, volunteered their services, and in some way we succeeded in getting a third kiln ready for burning. The burning of a kiln required about a week. Toward the latter part of the week, when it seemed as if we were going to have a good many thousand bricks in a few hours, in the middle of the night the kiln fell. For the third time we had failed.

The failure of this last kiln left me without a single dollar with which to make another experiment. Most of the teachers advised the abandoning of the effort to make bricks. In the midst of my troubles I thought of a watch which had come into my possession years before. I took this watch to the city of Montgomery, which was not far distant, and placed it in a pawn-shop. I secured cash upon it to the amount of fifteen dollars, with which to renew the brickmaking experiment. I returned to Tuskegee, and, with the help of the fifteen dollars, rallied our rather demoralized and discouraged forces and began a fourth attempt to make bricks. This time, I am glad to say, we were successful. Before I got hold of any money, the time-limit on my watch had expired, and I have never seen it since; but I have never regretted the loss of it.

Brickmaking has now become such an important industry at the school that last season our students manufactured twelve hundred thousand of first-class bricks, of a quality suitable to be sold in any market. Aside from this, scores of young men have mastered the brickmaking trade—both the making of bricks by hand and by machinery—and are now engaged in this industry in many parts of the South.

The making of these bricks taught me an important lesson in regard to the relations of the two races in the South. Many white people who had had no contact with the school, and perhaps no sympathy with it, came to us to buy bricks because they found out that ours were good bricks. They discovered that we were supplying a real want in the community. The making of these bricks caused many of the white residents of the neighbourhood to begin to feel that the education of the Negro was not making him worthless, but that in educating our students we were adding something to the wealth and comfort of the community. As the people of the neighbourhood came to us to buy bricks, we got acquainted with them; they traded with us and we with them. Our business interests became intermingled. We had something which they wanted; they had something which we wanted. This, in a large measure, helped to lay the foundation for the pleasant relations that have continued to exist between us and the white people in that section, and which now extend throughout the South.

Wherever one of our brickmakers has gone in the South, we find that he has something to contribute to the well-being of the community into which he has gone; something that has made the community feel that, in a degree, it is indebted to him, and perhaps, to a certain extent, dependent upon him. In this way pleasant relations between the races have been stimulated.

My experience is that there is something in human nature which always makes an individual recognize and reward merit, no matter under what colour of skin merit is found. I have found, too, that it is the visible, the tangible, that goes a long way in softening prejudices. The actual sight of a first-class house that a Negro has built is ten times more potent than pages of discussion about a house that he ought to build, or perhaps could build.

The same principle of industrial education has been carried out in the building of our own wagons, carts, and buggies, from the first. We now own and use on our farm and about the school dozens of these vehicles, and every one of them has been built by the hands of the students. Aside from this, we help supply the local market with these vehicles. The supplying of them to the people in the community has had the same effect as the supplying of bricks, and the man who learns at Tuskegee to build and repair wagons and carts is regarded as a benefactor by both races in the community where he goes. The people with whom he lives and works are going to think twice before they part with such a man.

The individual who can do something that the world wants done will, in the end, make his way regardless of his race. One man may go into a community prepared to supply the people there with an analysis of Greek sentences. The community may not at that time be prepared for, or feel the need of, Greek analysis, but it may feel its need of bricks and houses and wagons. If the man can supply the need for those, then, it will lead eventually to a demand for the first product, and with the demand will come the ability to appreciate it and to profit by it.

# W. E. B. DU BOIS

## (1868–1963)

By the end of his life, Du Bois would disown many of the things that had shaped his identity in his youth, including the whole of America itself. As he aged, he became an increasingly vocal spokesman for socialism, a move that ultimately led to his estrangement from the United States and his emigration to Ghana in 1961. Before he left the country, however, Du Bois actively supported the rights of America's black population and worked with the National Association for the Advancement of Colored People in its infancy.

"I have not always been right," he once said, "but I have always been sincere." His writings were often autobiographical, as in *The Souls of Black Folk* (1903), a series of essays on a variety of social issues. Through this volume, Du Bois expressed his alienation from the standard of American life, illustrating in great detail the sense of "double-consciousness" that he felt. Because of the color of his skin, he was prevented from seeing and feeling the nature of America in a manner similar to that of his white counterparts.

Editor of the NAACP's periodical, *Crisis*, Du Bois published over twenty-three books. He held a close working relationship of ideas with many of the major political figures of the era, including Booker T. Washington, with whom he sometimes disagreed on how to improve the lot of African Americans.

Some parts of *The Souls of Black Folk* (such as the chapter excerpted below) are written with intense lyricism and personal grace as well as well-modulated irony, revealing Du Bois as a writer of extraordinary power.

## FROM *The Souls of Black Folk*

### OF THE MEANING OF PROGRESS

Once upon a time I taught school in the hills of Tennessee, where the broad dark vale of the Mississippi begins to roll and crumple to greet the Alleghanies. I was a Fisk student then, and all Fisk men thought that Tennessee—beyond the Veil—was theirs alone, and in vacation time they sallied forth in lusty bands to meet the county school-commissioners. Young and happy, I too went, and I shall not soon forget that summer, seventeen years ago.

First, there was a Teachers' Institute at the county-seat; and there distinguished guests of the superintendent taught the teachers fractions and spelling and other mysteries,—white teachers in the morning, Negroes at night. A picnic now and then, and a supper, and the rough world was softened by laughter and song. I remember how—But I wander.

There came a day when all the teachers left the Institute and began the hunt for schools. I learn from hearsay (for my mother was mortally afraid of firearms) that the hunting of ducks and bears and men is wonderfully interesting, but I am sure that the man who has never hunted a country school has something to learn of the pleasures of the chase. I see now the white, hot roads lazily rise and fall and wind before me under the burning July sun; I feel the deep weariness of heart and limb as ten, eight, six miles stretch relentlessly ahead; I feel my heart sink heavily as I hear again and again, "Got a teacher? Yes." So I walked on and on—horses were too expensive—until I had wandered beyond railways, beyond stage lines, to a land of "varmints" and rattlesnakes, where the coming of a stranger was an event, and men lived and died in the shadow of one blue hill.

Sprinkled over hill and dale lay cabins and farmhouses, shut out from the world by the forests and the rolling hills toward the east. There I found at last a little school. Josie told me of it; she was a thin, homely girl of twenty, with a dark-brown face and thick, hard hair. I had crossed the stream at Watertown, and rested under the great willows; then I had gone to the little cabin in the lot where Josie was resting on her way to town. The gaunt farmer made me welcome, and Josie, hearing my errand, told me anxiously that they wanted a school over the hill; that but once since the war had a teacher been there; that she herself longed to learn,—and thus she ran on, talking fast and loud, with much earnestness and energy.

Next morning I crossed the tall round hill, lingered to look at the blue and yellow mountains stretching toward the Carolinas, then plunged into the wood, and came out at Josie's home. It was a dull frame cottage with four rooms, perched just below the brow of the hill, amid peach-trees. The father was a quiet, simple soul, calmly ignorant, with no touch of vulgarity. The mother was different,—strong, bustling, and energetic, with a quick, restless tongue, and an ambition to live "like folks." There was a crowd of children. Two boys had gone away. There remained two growing girls; a shy midget of eight; John, tall, awkward, and eighteen; Jim, younger, quicker, and better looking; and two babies of indefinite age. Then there was Josie herself. She seemed to be the centre of the family: always busy at service, or at home, or berry-picking; a little nervous and inclined to scold, like her mother, yet faithful, too, like her father. She had about her a certain fineness, the shadow of an unconscious moral heroism that would willingly give all of life to make life broader, deeper, and fuller for her and hers. I saw much of this family afterwards, and grew to love them for their honest efforts to be decent and comfortable, and for their knowledge of their own ignorance. There was with them no affectation. The mother would scold the father for being so "easy"; Josie would roundly berate the boys for carelessness; and all knew that it was a hard thing to dig a living out of a rocky side-hill.

I secured the school. I remember the day I rode horseback out to the commissioner's house with a pleasant young white fellow who wanted the white school. The road ran down the bed of a stream; the sun laughed and the water jingled, and we rode on. "Come in," said the commissioner,—"come in. Have a seat. Yes, that certificate will do. Stay to dinner. What do you want a month?" "Oh," thought I, "this is lucky"; but even then fell the awful shadow of the Veil, for they ate first, then I— alone.

The schoolhouse was a log hut, where Colonel Wheeler used to shelter his corn. It sat in a lot behind a rail fence and thorn bushes, near the sweetest of springs. There was an entrance where a door once was, and within, a massive rickety fireplace; great chinks between the logs served as windows. Furniture was scarce. A pale blackboard crouched in the corner. My desk was made of three boards, reinforced at critical points, and my chair, borrowed from the landlady, had to be returned every night. Seats for the children—these puzzled me much. I was haunted by a New England vision of neat little desks and chairs, but, alas! the reality was rough plank benches without backs, and at times without legs. They had the one virtue of making naps dangerous—possibly fatal, for the floor was not to be trusted.

It was a hot morning late in July when the school opened. I trembled when I heard the patter of little feet down the dusty road, and saw the growing row of dark solemn faces and bright eager eyes facing me. First came Josie and her brothers and sisters. The longing to know, to be a student in the great school at Nashville, hovered like a star above this child-woman amid her work and worry, and she studied doggedly. There were the Dowells from their farm over toward Alexandria,—Fanny, with her smooth black face and wondering eyes; Martha, brown and dull; the pretty girl-wife of a brother, and the younger brood.

There were the Burkes,—two brown and yellow lads, and a tiny haughty-eyed girl. Fat Reuben's little chubby girl came, with golden face and old-gold hair, faithful and solemn. 'Thenie was on hand early,—a jolly, ugly, good-hearted girl, who slyly dipped snuff and looked after her little bow-legged brother. When her mother could spare her, 'Tildy came,—a midnight beauty, with starry eyes and tapering limbs; and her brother, correspondingly homely. And then the big boys,—the hulking Lawrences; the lazy Neills, unfathered sons of mother and daughter; Hickman, with a stoop in his shoulders; and the rest.

There they sat, nearly thirty of them, on the rough benches, their faces shading from a pale cream to a deep brown, the little feet bare and swinging, the eyes full of expectation, with here and there a twinkle of mischief, and the hands grasping Webster's blue-black spelling-book. I loved my school, and the fine faith the children had in the wisdom of their teacher was truly marvellous. We read and spelled together, wrote a little, picked flowers, sang, and listened to stories of the world beyond the hill. At times the school would dwindle away, and I would start out. I would visit Mum Eddings, who lived in two very dirty rooms, and ask why little Lugene, whose flaming face seemed ever ablaze with the dark-red hair uncombed, was absent all last week, or why I missed so often the inimitable rags of Mack and Ed. Then the father, who worked Colonel Wheeler's farm on shares, would tell me how the crops needed the boys; and the thin, slovenly mother, whose face was pretty when washed, assured me that Lugene must mind the baby. "But we'll start them again next week." When the Lawrences stopped, I knew that the doubts of the old folks about book-learning had conquered again, and so, toiling up the hill, and getting as far into the cabin as possible, I put Cicero "pro Archia Poeta" into the simplest English with local applications, and usually convinced them—for a week or so.

On Friday nights I often went home with some of the children,— sometimes to Doc Burke's farm. He was a great, loud, thin Black, ever working, and trying to buy the seventy-five acres of hill and dale where he lived; but people said that he would surely fail, and the "white folks would get it all." His wife was a magnificent Amazon, with saffron face and shining hair, uncorseted and barefooted, and the children were strong and beautiful. They lived in a one-and-a-half-room cabin in the hollow of the farm, near the spring. The front room was full of great fat white beds, scrupulously neat; and there were bad chromos on the walls, and a tired centre-table. In the tiny back kitchen I was often invited to "take out and help" myself to fried chicken and wheat biscuit, "meat" and corn pone, string-beans and berries. At first I used to be a little alarmed at the approach of bedtime in the one lone bedroom, but embarrassment was very deftly avoided. First, all the children nodded and slept, and were stowed away in one great pile of goose feathers; next, the mother and the father discreetly slipped away to the kitchen while I went to bed; then, blowing out the dim light, they retired in the dark. In the morning all were up and away before I thought of awaking. Across the road, where fat Reuben lived, they all went outdoors while the teacher retired, because they did not boast the luxury of a kitchen.

I liked to stay with the Dowells, for they had four rooms and plenty of good country fare. Uncle Bird had a small, rough farm, all woods and hills, miles from the big road; but he was full of tales,—he preached now and then,—and with his children, berries, horses, and wheat he was happy and prosperous. Often, to keep the peace, I must go where life was less lovely; for instance, 'Tildy's mother was incorrigibly dirty, Reuben's larder was limited seriously, and herds of untamed insects wandered over the Eddingses' beds. Best of all I loved to go to Josie's, and sit on the porch, eating peaches, while the mother bustled and talked: how Josie had bought the sewing-machine; how Josie worked at service in winter, but that four dollars a month was "mighty little" wages; how Josie longed to go away to school, but that it "looked like" they never could get far enough ahead to let her; how the crops failed and the well was yet unfinished; and, finally, how "mean" some of the white folks were.

For two summers I lived in this little world; it was dull and humdrum. The girls looked at the hill in wistful longing, and the boys fretted and haunted Alexandria. Alexandria was "town,"—a straggling, lazy village of houses, churches, and shops, and an aristocracy of Toms, Dicks, and Captains. Cuddled on the hill to the north was the village of the colored folks, who lived in three- or four-room unpainted cottages, some neat and homelike, and some dirty. The dwellings were scattered rather aimlessly, but they centered about the twin temples of the hamlet, the Methodist, and the Hard-Shell Baptist churches. These, in turn, leaned gingerly on a sad-colored schoolhouse. Hither my little world wended its crooked way on Sunday to meet other worlds, and gossip, and wonder, and make the weekly sacrifice with frenzied priest at the altar of the "old-time religion." Then the soft melody and mighty cadences of Negro song fluttered and thundered.

I have called my tiny community a world, and so its isolation made it; and yet there was among us but a half-awakened common consciousness, sprung from common joy and grief, at burial, birth, or wedding; from a common hardship in poverty, poor land, and low wages; and, above all, from the sight of the Veil that hung between us and Opportunity. All this caused us to think some thoughts together; but these, when ripe for speech, were spoken in various languages. Those whose eyes twenty-five and more years before had seen "the glory of the coming of the Lord," saw in every present hindrance or help a dark fatalism bound to bring all things right in His own good time. The mass of those to whom slavery was a dim recollection of childhood found the world a puzzling thing: it asked little of them, and they answered with little, and yet it ridiculed their offering. Such a paradox they could not understand, and therefore sank into listless indifference, or shiftlessness, or reckless bravado. There were, however, some—such as Josie, Jim, and Ben—to whom War, Hell, and Slavery were but childhood tales, whose young appetites had been whetted to an edge by school and story and half-awakened thought. Ill could they be content, born without and beyond the World. And their weak wings beat against their barriers,—barriers of caste, of youth, of life; at last, in dangerous moments, against everything that opposed even a whim.

The ten years that follow youth, the years when first the realization comes that life is leading somewhere,—these were the years that passed after I left my little school. When they were past, I came by chance once more to the walls of Fisk University, to the halls of the chapel of melody. As I lingered there in the joy and pain of meeting old school-friends, there swept over me a sudden longing to pass again beyond the blue hill, and to see the homes and the school of other days, and to learn how life had gone with my school-children; and I went.

Josie was dead, and the gray-haired mother said simply, "We've had a heap of trouble since you've been away." I had feared for Jim. With a cultured parentage and a social caste to uphold him, he might have made a venturesome merchant or a West Point cadet. But here he was, angry with life and reckless; and when Farmer Durham charged him with stealing wheat, the old man had to ride fast to escape the stones which the furious fool hurled after him. They told Jim to run away; but he would not run, and the constable came that afternoon. It grieved Josie, and great awkward John walked nine miles every day to see his little brother through the bars of Lebanon jail. At last the two came back together in the dark night. The mother cooked supper, and Josie emptied her purse, and the boys stole away. Josie grew thin and silent, yet worked the more. The hill became steep for the quiet old father, and with the boys away there was little to do in the valley. Josie helped them to sell the old farm, and they moved nearer town. Brother Dennis, the carpenter, built a new house with six rooms; Josie toiled a year in Nashville, and brought back ninety dollars to furnish the house and change it to a home.

When the spring came, and the birds twittered, and the stream ran proud and full, little sister Lizzie, bold and thoughtless, flushed with the passion of youth, bestowed herself on the tempter, and brought home a nameless child. Josie shivered and worked on, with the vision of school-days all fled, with a face wan and tired,—worked until, on a summer's day, some one married another; then Josie crept to her mother like a hurt child, and slept—and sleeps.

I paused to scent the breeze as I entered the valley. The Lawrences have gone,—father and son forever,—and the other son lazily digs in the earth to live. A new young widow rents out their cabin to fat Reuben. Reuben is a Baptist preacher now, but I fear as lazy as ever, though his cabin has three rooms; and little Ella has grown into a bouncing woman, and is ploughing corn on the hot hillside. There are babies a-plenty, and one half-witted girl. Across the valley is a house I did not know before, and there I found, rocking one baby and expecting another, one of my schoolgirls, a daughter of Uncle Bird Dowell. She looked somewhat worried with her new duties, but soon bristled into pride over her neat cabin and the tale of her thrifty husband, and the horse and cow, and the farm they were planning to buy.

My log schoolhouse was gone. In its place stood Progress; and Progress, I understand, is necessarily ugly. The crazy foundation stones still marked the former site of my poor little cabin, and not far away, on six weary boulders, perched a jaunty board house, perhaps twenty by thirty feet, with three windows and a door that locked. Some of the window-glass was broken, and part of an old iron stove lay mournfully under the house. I peeped through the window half reverently, and found things that were more familiar. The blackboard had grown by about two feet, and the seats were still without backs. The county owns the lot now, I hear, and every year there is a session of school. As I sat by the spring and looked on the Old and the New I felt glad, very glad, and yet—

After two long drinks I started on. There was the great double log-house on the corner. I remembered the broken, blighted family that used to live there. The strong, hard face of the mother, with its wilderness of hair, rose before me. She had driven her husband away, and while I taught school a strange man lived there, big and jovial, and people talked. I felt sure that Ben and 'Tildy would come to naught from such a home. But this is an odd world; for Ben is a busy farmer in Smith County, "doing well, too," they say, and he had cared for little 'Tildy until last spring, when a lover married her. A hard life the lad had led, toiling for meat, and laughed at because he was homely and crooked. There was Sam Carlon, an impudent old skinflint, who had definite notions about "niggers," and hired Ben a summer and would not pay him. Then the hungry boy gathered his sacks together, and in broad daylight went into Carlon's corn; and when the hard-fisted farmer set upon him, the angry boy flew at him like a beast. Doc Burke saved a murder and a lynching that day.

The story reminded me again of the Burkes, and an impatience seized me to know who won in the battle, Doc or the seventy-five acres. For it is a hard thing to make a farm out of nothing, even in fifteen years. So I hurried on, thinking of the Burkes. They used to have a certain magnificent barbarism about them that I liked. They were never vulgar, never immoral, but rather rough and primitive, with an unconventionality that spent itself in loud guffaws, slaps on the back, and naps in the corner. I hurried by the cottage of the misborn Neill boys. It was empty, and they were grown into fat, lazy farm-hands. I saw the home of the Hickmans, but Albert, with his stooping shoulders, had passed from the world. Then I came to the Burkes' gate and peered through; the inclosure looked rough and untrimmed, and yet there were the same fences around the old farm save to the left, where lay twenty-five other acres. And lo! the cabin in the hollow had climbed the hill and swollen to a half-finished six-room cottage.

The Burkes held a hundred acres, but they were still in debt. Indeed, the gaunt father who toiled night and day would scarcely be happy out of debt, being so used to it. Some day he must stop, for his massive frame is showing decline. The mother wore shoes, but the lion-like physique of other days was broken. The children had grown up. Rob, the image of his father, was loud and rough with laughter. Birdie, my school baby of six, had grown to a picture of maiden beauty, tall and tawny. "Edgar is gone," said the mother, with head half bowed, — "gone to work in Nashville; he and his father couldn't agree."

Little Doc, the boy born since the time of my school, took me horse-back down the creek next morning toward Farmer Dowell's. The road and the stream were battling for mastery, and the stream had the better of it. We splashed and waded, and the merry boy, perched behind me, chattered and laughed. He showed me where Simon Thompson had bought a bit of ground and a home; but his daughter Lana, a plump, brown, slow girl, was not there. She had married a man and a farm twenty miles away. We wound on down the stream till we came to a gate that I did not recognize, but the boy insisted that it was "Uncle Bird's." The farm was fat with the growing crop. In that little valley was a strange still-ness as I rode up; for death and marriage had stolen youth and left age and childhood there. We sat and talked that night after the chores were done. Uncle Bird was grayer, and his eyes did not see so well, but he was still jovial. We talked of the acres bought, — one hundred and twenty-five, — of the new guest-chamber added, of Martha's marrying. Then we talked of death: Fanny and Fred were gone; a shadow hung over the other daughter, and when it lifted she was to go to Nashville to school. At last we spoke of the neighbors, and as night fell, Uncle Bird told me how, on a night like that, 'Thenie came wandering back to her home over yonder, to escape the blows of her husband. And next morning she died in the home that her little bow-legged brother, working and saving, had bought for their widowed mother.

My journey was done, and behind me lay hill and dale, and Life and

Death. How shall man measure Progress there where the dark-faced Josie lies? How many heartfuls of sorrow shall balance a bushel of wheat? How hard a thing is life to the lowly, and yet how human and real! And all this life and love and strife and failure,—is it the twilight of nightfall or the flush of some faint-dawning day?

Thus sadly musing, I rode to Nashville in the Jim Crow car.

# EMMA GOLDMAN
## (1869–1940)

Born into a Jewish family in Lithuania, Goldman emigrated to the United States in 1885. She became a leading anarchist and worked closely with Alexander Berkman, whom she affectionately dubbed Sasha. Referred to scathingly by J. Edgar Hoover as "Red Emma," she campaigned for the rights of workers and for personal freedom, traveling across the United States to lecture and organize resistance. She also traveled abroad to meet with like-minded people. In one memorable trip, she visited Russia and had a personal meeting with Lenin, whom she admired.

Goldman met Berkman in New York in 1889. She also met Johann Most, a violent revolutionary whose ideas inspired her. With Berkman, she conspired to murder Henry Clay Frick—an industrialist—for his suppression of the Homestead steel mill strike. Berkman was sentenced to prison for twenty-two years, but Goldman went free. She was imprisoned, however, in 1893, for inciting a riot. During her time in Blackwell's Island Penitentiary, she studied English carefully for the first time and became fluent. After getting out of prison, she ventured back to Europe, where she studied midwifery in Vienna—her new "profession," as she called it.

Goldman returned to America, where she lectured frequently on revolutionary politics, free love, birth control, and atheism. This activity led to further jail terms, and in 1919 she and Berkman were deported to the Soviet Union. But disillusionment with the Bolsheviks soon followed, and Goldman migrated to western Europe in 1921. She often lectured in Britain and the United States in her later years, and was finally buried in Chicago.

In *Living My Life* (1931), she wrote of her life, "I had lived its heights and its depths, in bitter sorrow and ecstatic joy, in black despair and fervent hope. I had drunk the cup to the last drop. I had lived my life. Would I had the gift to paint the life I had lived."

## FROM *Living My Life*

A renaissance was now taking place in anarchist ranks; greater activity was being manifested than at any time since 1887, especially among American adherents. *Solidarity*, an English publication started in 1892 by

S. Merlino and suspended later on, reappeared in '94, gathering about itself a number of very able Americans. Among them were John Edelman, William C. Owen, Charles B. Cooper, Miss Van Etton, an energetic trade-unionist, and a number of others. A social science club was organized, with weekly lectures. The work attracted considerable attention among the intelligent native element, not failing, of course, also to call forth virulent attacks in the press. New York was not the only city where anarchism was being expounded. In Portland, Oregon, the *Firebrand*, another English weekly, was being published by a group of gifted men and women, including Henry Addis and the Isaak family. In Boston Harry M. Kelly, a young and ardent comrade, had organized a co-operative printing shop which was publishing the *Rebel*. In Philadelphia activities were carried on by Voltairine de Cleyre, H. Brown, Perle McLeod, and other courageous advocates of our ideas. In fact, all over the United States the spirit of the Chicago martyrs had been resurrected. The voice of Spies and his comrades was finding expression in the native tongue as well as in every foreign language of the peoples in America.

Our work had received considerable incentive through the arrival of two British anarchists, Charles W. Mowbray and John Turner. The former had come in 1894, shortly after my release from prison, and was now active in Boston. John Turner, who was the more cultivated and better informed of the two, had been invited to the States by Harry Kelly. For some reason his lectures were at first poorly attended and it became necessary for us in New York to look after the arrangements. I had met John and his sister Lizzie during my stay in London. Both of them had strongly appealed to me by reason of their warmth, geniality, and friendliness. I loved especially to talk to John; he was familiar with the social movements in England and was himself closely allied with the trade-union and co-operative elements, as well as with the *Commonweal*, founded by William Morris. But his best efforts were devoted to the propaganda of anarchism. John Turner's coming to America gave me an opportunity to test my ability to speak in English, as I often had to preside at his meetings.

The free-silver campaign was at its height. The proposition for the free coinage of silver at the ratio with gold of sixteen to one had become a national issue almost overnight. It gained in strength by the sudden ascendancy of William Jennings Bryan who had stampeded the Democratic Convention by an eloquent speech and the catch phrase: "You shall not press down upon the brow of labour the crown of thorns, you shall not crucify mankind upon the cross of gold." Bryan was running for the presidency: the "silver-tongued" orator had caught the fancy of the man in the street. The American liberals, who so easily fall for every new political scheme, went over to Bryan on free silver almost to a man. Even some anarchists were carried away by his slogans. One day a well-known Chicago comrade, George Schilling, arrived in New York to enlist the co-operation of the Eastern radicals. George was an ardent follower of Benjamin Tucker, the leader of the individualist school of anarchism, and a contributor to his paper, *Liberty*. But, unlike Tucker, he was closer to the labour movement and also more revolutionary than his teacher. The wish for a popular awakening in the United States was father to George's belief that the free-silver issue would become a force to undermine both monopoly and the State. The vicious attacks on Bryan in the press helped his cause by leading George and many others to regard him as a martyr. The papers spoke of Bryan as a "tool in the blood-stained hands of Altgeld, the anarchist, and Eugene Debs, the revolutionist."

I could not share the enthusiasm for Bryan, partly because I did not believe in the political machine as a means of bringing about fundamental changes, and also because there was something weak and superficial about Bryan. I had a feeling that his main aim was to get into the White House rather than "strike off the chains" from the people. I resolved to steer clear of him. I sensed his lack of sincerity and I did not trust him. For this attitude I was assailed from two different sides on the same day. First it was Schilling who urged me to join the free-silver campaign. "What are you Easterners going to do," he asked when I met him, "when the West marches in revolutionary ranks towards the East? Are you going to continue talking, or will you join forces with us?" He assured me that my name had travelled to the West and that I could be a valuable factor in the popular movement to free the masses from their despoilers. George was very optimistic in his ardour, but he failed to convince me. We parted as friends, George shaking his head over my lack of judgment about the impending revolution.

In the evening we had a visitor, the former Burgess of Homestead, a man named John McLuckie. I remembered his determined stand during the steel strike against the importation of blacklegs and I appreciated his solidarity with the workers. I was glad to meet the large, jovial fellow, a true type of the old Jeffersonian democrat. He told me that he had been asked by Voltairine to see me about Sasha. He had gone to her to inform her that Berkman was no longer in the Western Penitentiary. He, as well as many other people in Homestead, believed that Berkman had never intended to kill Frick; he had committed the act only to arouse sympathy for the latter. The excessive sentence he had been given was merely a ruse on the part of the Pennsylvania courts to deceive the public. The Homestead workers felt sure that Alexander Berkman had been let out of prison long ago. Voltairine had given McLuckie material which proved how ridiculous his story was and had sent him to me for more proofs.

I listened to the man, unable to conceive that anyone in his senses could believe such a thing about Sasha. He had sacrificed his youth, he had already spent five years in the penitentiary, had suffered the dungeon, solitary confinement, and brutal physical attacks. Persecution by the prison authorities had even driven him to attempt suicide. Yet he was being suspected by the very people for whom he was willing to lay down his life. It was preposterous, cruel. I stepped into my room, took Sasha's letters, and handed them to McLuckie. "Read," I said, "and then tell me if you still believe the impossible stories you have just told me."

He took up one of the letters from the pile, read it carefully, then scanned several others. Presently he held out his hand. "My dear, brave girl," he said, "I am sorry, I am awfully sorry, to have doubted your friend." He assured me that he now realized how wrong he and his people had been. "You can count on me to help," he added, feelingly, "in any effort you may make to get Berkman out of prison." Then he referred to Bryan, dwelling on the exceptional opportunity to assist Sasha if I would join the free-silver campaign. My activities would bring me in close contact with the prominent politicians of the Democratic Party, and they could afterwards be approached to secure a pardon. He himself would undertake to see the leaders and he was certain of success if he could assure them of my services. He pointed out that I would have no responsibilities about the business end. He would travel with me and arrange everything. Of course, I would be paid a generous salary.

McLuckie was frank and decent, though evidently childishly ignorant of my ideas. Perhaps it was also his suggestion that I might help Sasha that made him sympathetic to me. Still, I could have nothing to do with Bryan, feeling he would use the workers merely as a stepping-stone to power.

My visitor took no offence. He left with regrets that I was so lacking in practical sense, but he promised faithfully to enlighten his people in Homestead in regard to Berkman.

Together with Ed and several other close friends I discussed the possible origin of the dreadful rumours about Sasha. I was sure that they had been created by the attitude of Most. I remembered that the press had widely commented on Most's statement that Sasha had used a "toy pistol to shoot Frick up a bit." Johann Most—my life was so full I had nearly forgotten him. The bitterness his betrayal of Sasha had aroused had given way to a dull feeling of disappointment in the man who had once meant so much to me. The wound he had struck had partly healed, yet leaving behind a sensitive scar. McLuckie's visit had torn the wound open again.

My encounters with Schilling and McLuckie made me aware of a large new field for activity. What I had done so far was only the first step of usefulness in our movement. I would go on a tour now, study the country and its people, come close to the pulse of American life. I would bring to the masses the message of a new social ideal. I was eager to start at once, but I determined first to become more proficient in English and to earn some money. I did not want to be dependent on the comrades or take pay for my lectures. Meanwhile I could continue my work in New York.

I was full of enthusiasm for the future, but in proportion as my spirits rose, Ed's interest in my aims waned. I had known for a long time that he begrudged every moment which took me away from him. I was also aware of our decided differences as far as the woman question was concerned. But outside of that, Ed had moved along with me, had always been helpful and ready to aid in my efforts. Now he became disgruntled, critical of everything I was doing. As the days passed, he grew more morose. Often on my return from a late meeting I would find him with a set face, frigidly silent, nervously swinging his leg. I yearned to come close to him, to share my thoughts and plans with him; but his reproachful look would numb me. In my room I would wait expectantly, but he would remain away and then I would hear him wearily drag himself to bed. It hurt me to the quick, for I loved him deeply. Outside of my interest in the movement and Sasha, my great passion for Ed had displaced everything else.

I still had a very tender feeling for my erstwhile artist lover, the more so because I thought he needed me. On my return from Europe I had found him very much changed. He had risen in his profession and was earning considerable money. He remained as generous to me as in our days of poverty, having aided me financially all through my stay in Vienna and later furnishing my new apartment. Indeed, there was no change in his attitude towards me. But it did not take me long to discover that the movement had lost its former meaning for Fedya. He now lived in a different circle, and his interests were different. Art auctions absorbed him, and all his leisure he spent at sales. He had craved beauty so long that, now that he had some means, he wanted to gorge himself with it. Studios became his great passion. Every few months he would furnish one with the most exquisite things, only to discard it shortly for another, which he would decorate with new hangings, vases, canvases, carpets, and what not. All the beautiful things in our flat had come from his *ateliers*. I could not bear the thought of Fedya's wandering so far away from our past interests that he would not offer any more financial help to the movement. But as he had never had much sense of material values, I was not surprised to find him so extravagant. I was even concerned more about his choice of new friends, nearly all of them men who worked on newspapers. A dissipated, cynical lot they were, their main objects in life being drink and women. Unhappily they had succeeded in imbuing

Fedya with the same spirit; I was grieved to see my idealistic friend going the way of so many empty in head and heart. Sasha had always felt that the social struggle would prove a mere passing phase in Fedya's life, but I had hoped that when Fedya should be drawn into other channels, they would be those of art. His drift towards meaningless and trivial pleasures, for which he was entirely too fine, was most painful. Fortunately he still felt close to us. He had great regard for Ed, and his affection for me, while no longer the same as in the past, was yet warm enough to counteract, at least partly, the disintegrating influence of his new surroundings.

He came often to our house. On one occasion he asked me to pose, this time for a pen-and-ink sketch he had promised Ed. During the sittings I thought of our common past, of our affection that had been so tender, perhaps too tender to survive the sway Ed's personality exercised over me; probably also because Fedya's love was too yielding for my turbulent nature, which could find expression only in the clashing of wills, in resistance and the surmounting of obstacles. Fedya still attracted me, but it was Ed who consumed me with intense longing, Ed who turned my blood to fire, Ed whose touch intoxicated and exalted me. The sudden change from his usual self to a discontented and hypercritical attitude was too galling to endure. But my pride would not let me make the first step to break his silence. Fedya told me that Ed had greatly admired his sketch of me and had praised it as a splendid piece of work, expressive of much of my being. In my presence, however, Ed would not say a word about it.

But one evening Ed's reserve broke down. "You are drifting away from me!" he cried excitedly. "I can see that my hopes of a beautiful life with you must be given up. You have wasted a year in Vienna, you have acquired a profession only to throw it over for those stupid meetings. You have no concern about anything else; your love has no thought of me or my needs. Your interest in the movement, for which you are willing to break up our life, is nothing but vanity, nothing but your craving for applause and glory and the limelight. You are simply incapable of a deep feeling. You have never understood or appreciated the love I have given you. I have waited and waited for a change, but I see it is useless. I will not share you with anybody or anything. You will have to choose!" He paced the room like a caged lion, turning from time to time to fasten his eyes on me. All that had been accumulating in him for weeks now streamed out in accusation and reproaches.

I sat in consternation. The familiar old demand that I "choose" kept droning in my ears. Ed, who had been my ideal, was like the others. He would have me forswear my interests and the movement, sacrifice everything for love of him. Most had repeatedly given me the same ultimatum. I stared at him unable to speak or move, while he continued stalking about the room in uncontrolled anger. Finally he picked up his coat and hat and left.

For hours I sat as if paralysed; then a violent ring brought me to my feet. It was a call to a confinement case. I took the bag which I had been keeping ready for weeks and walked out with the man who had come for me.

In a two-room flat on Houston Street, on the sixth floor of a tenement-house, I found three children asleep and the woman writhing in labour pains. There was no gas-jet, only a kerosene lamp, over which I had to heat the water. The man looked blank when I asked him for a sheet. It was Friday. His wife had washed Monday, he told me, and all the bed-linen had got dirty since. But I might use the table-cloth; it had been put on that very evening for the Sabbath. "Diapers or anything else ready for the baby?" I asked. The man did not know. The woman pointed to a bundle which consisted of a few torn shirts, a bandage, and some rags. Incredible poverty oozed from every corner.

With the use of the table-cloth and an extra apron I had brought I prepared to receive the expected comer. It was my first private case, and the shock over Ed's outburst helped to increase my nervousness. But I steeled myself and worked on desperately. Late in the morning I helped to bring the new life into the world. A part of my own life had died the evening before.

For a week my grief over Ed's absence was dulled by work. The care of several patients and Dr. White's operations, at which I assisted, left me little time for repining. The evenings were occupied with meetings in Newark, Paterson, and other near-by towns. But at night, alone in the flat, the scene with Ed haunted and tortured me. I knew he cared for me, but that he could leave as he did, stay away so long, and give no sign of his whereabouts made me resentful. It was impossible to reconcile myself to a love that denied the beloved the right to herself, a love that throve only at the expense of the loved one. I felt I could not submit to such a sapping emotion, but the next moment I would find myself in Ed's room, my burning face on his pillow, my heart contracting with yearning for him. At the end of two weeks my longing mastered all my resolutions; I wrote him at his place of work and begged him to return.

He came at once. Folding me to his heart, between tears and laughter, he cried: "You are stronger than I; I have wanted you every moment, ever since I closed that door. Every day I meant to come back, but I was too cowardly. Nights I have been walking round the house like a shadow. I wanted to come in and beg you to forgive and forget. I even went to the station when I knew you had to go to Newark and Paterson. I could not bear to think of your going home alone late at night. But I was afraid of your scorn, afraid you would send me away. Yes, you are braver and stronger than I. You are more natural. Women always are. Man is such a silly, civilized creature! Woman has retained her primitive impulses and she is more real."

We took up our common life again, but I spent less time on my public interests. Partly it was due to the numerous calls on my professional services, but more to my determination to devote myself to Ed. As the weeks passed, however, the still small voice kept on whispering that the final rupture would only temporarily be deferred. I clung desperately to Ed and his love to ward off the impending end.

My profession of midwife was not very lucrative, only the poorest of the foreign element resorting to such services. Those who had risen in the scale of material Americanism lost their native diffidence together with many other original traits. Like the American women they, too, would be confined only by doctors. Midwifery offered a very limited scope; in emergencies one was compelled to call for the aid of a physician. Ten dollars was the highest fee; the majority of the women could not pay even that. But while my work held out no hope of worldly riches, it furnished an excellent field for experience. It put me into intimate contact with the very people my ideal strove to help and emancipate. It brought me face to face with the living conditions of the workers, about which, until then, I had talked and written mostly from theory. Their squalid surroundings, the dull and inert submission to their lot, made me realize the colossal work yet to be done to bring about the change our movement was struggling to achieve.

Still more impressed was I by the fierce, blind struggle of the women of the poor against frequent pregnancies. Most of them lived in continual dread of conception; the great mass of the married women submitted helplessly, and when they found themselves pregnant, their alarm and worry would result in the determination to get rid of their expected offspring. It was incredible what fantastic methods despair could invent: jumping off tables, rolling on the floor, massaging the stomach, drinking nauseating concoctions, and using blunt instruments. These and similar methods were being tried, generally with great injury. It was harrowing, but it was understandable. Having a large brood of children, often many more than the weekly wage of the father could provide for, each additional child was a curse, "a curse of God," as orthodox Jewish women and Irish Catholics repeatedly told me. The men were generally more resigned, but the women cried out against Heaven for inflicting such cruelty upon them. During their labour pains some women would hurl anathema on God and man, especially on their husbands. "Take him away," one of my patients cried, "don't let the brute come near me—I'll kill him!" The tortured creature already had had eight children, four of whom had died in infancy. The remaining were sickly and undernourished, like most of the ill-born, ill-kept, and unwanted children who trailed at my feet when I was helping another poor creature into the world.

After such confinements I would return home sick and distressed, hating the men responsible for the frightful condition of their wives and children, hating myself most of all because I did not know how to help them. I could, of course, induce an abortion. Many women called me for that purpose, even going down on their knees and begging me to help them, "for the sake of the poor little ones already here." They knew that some doctors and midwives did such things, but the price was beyond their means. I was so sympathetic; wouldn't I do something for them? They would pay in weekly instalments. I tried to explain to them that it was not monetary considerations that held me back; it was concern for their life and health. I would relate the case of a woman killed by such an operation, and her children left motherless. But they preferred to die, they avowed; the city was then sure to take care of their orphans, and they would be better off.

I could not prevail upon myself to perform the much-coveted operation. I lacked faith in my skill and I remembered my Vienna professor who had often demonstrated to us the terrible results of abortion. He held that even when such practices prove successful, they undermine the health of the patient. I would not undertake the task. It was not any moral consideration for the sanctity of life; a life unwanted and forced into abject poverty did not seem sacred to me. But my interests embraced the entire social problem, not merely a single aspect of it, and I would not jeopardize my freedom for that one part of the human struggle. I refused to perform abortions and I knew no methods to prevent conception.

I spoke to some physicians about the matter. Dr. White, a conservative, said: "The poor have only themselves to blame; they indulge their appetites too much." Dr. Julius Hoffmann thought that children were the only joy the poor had. Dr. Solotaroff held out the hope of great changes in the near future when woman would become more intelligent and independent. "When she uses her brains more," he would tell me, "her procreative organs will function less." It seemed more convincing than the arguments of the other medicos, though no more comforting; nor was it of any practical help. Now that I had learned that women and children carried the heaviest burden of our ruthless economic system, I saw that it was mockery to expect them to wait until the social revolution arrives in order to right injustice. I sought some immediate solution for their purgatory, but I could find nothing of any use.

My home life was anything but harmonious, though externally all seemed smooth. Ed was apparently calm and contented again, but I felt cramped and nervous. If I attended a meeting and was detained later than expected, it would make me uneasy and I would hasten home in perturbation. Often I refused invitations to lecture because I sensed Ed's disapproval. Where I could not decline, I worked for weeks over my subject, my thoughts dwelling on Ed rather than on the matter in hand. I would wonder how this point or that argument might appeal to him and whether he would approve. Yet I never could get myself to read him my notes, and if he attended my meetings, his presence made me self-conscious, for I knew that he had no faith in my work. It served to weaken my faith in myself. I developed strange nervous attacks. Without preliminary warning I would fall to the ground as if knocked down by a heavy blow. I did not lose consciousness, being able to see and understand what was going on around me, but I was not able to utter a word. My chest felt convulsed, my throat compressed; I had an agonizing pain in my legs as if the muscles were being pulled asunder. This condition would last from ten minutes to an hour and leave me utterly exhausted. Solotaroff, failing to diagnose the trouble, took me to a specialist, who proved no wiser. Dr. White's examination also gave no results. Some physicians said it was hysteria, others an inverted womb. I knew the latter was the real cause, but I would not consent to an operation. More and more I had become convinced that my life would never know harmony in love for very long, that strife and not peace would be my lot. In such a life there was no room for a child.

From various parts of the country came requests for a series of lectures. I was very eager to go, but I lacked the courage to broach the matter to Ed. I knew he would not consent, and his refusal would most likely bring us nearer to a violent separation. My physicians had strongly advised a rest and change of scene, and now Ed surprised me by insisting that I ought to go away. "Your health is more important than any other consideration," he said, "but first you must drop the silly notion that you have to earn your own living." He was making enough for both now, and it would make him happy if I would give up my nursing and stop making myself ill by helping hapless brats into the world. He welcomed the opportunity to take care of me, to afford me leisure and recuperation. Later on, he said, I should be in condition to go on a tour. He realized how much I wanted it and he knew what an effort it was to me to play the devoted wife. He enjoyed the home I had made so beautiful for him, he went on, but he could see that I was not contented. He was sure a change would do me good, give me back my old spirit, and bring me back to him.

The weeks that followed were happy and peaceful. We were much together, making frequent trips to the country, attending concerts and operas. We took up reading together again, and Ed helped me to understand Racine, Corneille, Molière. He cared only for the classics; Zola and his contemporaries were repellent to him. But when alone during the day I indulged in the more modern literature, besides planning a number of lectures for my forthcoming tour.

In the midst of my preparations came the news of tortures in the Spanish prison of Montjuich. Three hundred men and women, mostly trade-unionists, with a sprinkling of anarchists, had been arrested in 1896 as a result of a bomb explosion in Barcelona during a religious procession. The entire world was appalled by the resurrection of the Inquisition, by prisoners being kept for days without food or water, flogged, and burned with hot irons. One even had had his tongue cut out. The fiendish methods were used to extort confessions from the unfortunates. Several went mad and in their delirium implicated their innocent comrades, who were immediately condemned to death. The person responsible for these horrors was the Prime Minister of Spain, Canovas del Castillo. Liberal-minded papers in Europe, like the *Frankfurter Zeitung* and the Paris *Intransigeant*, were arousing public sentiment against the nineteenth-century Inquisition. Advanced members of the House of Commons, the Reichstag, and the Chamber of Deputies were calling for action to stay the hand of Canovas. Only America remained dumb. Excepting the radical publications, the press maintained a conspiracy of silence. Together with my friends I strongly felt the necessity of breaking through that wall. In conference with Ed, Justus, John Edelman, and Harry Kelly, who had come from Boston, and with the co-operation of Italian and Spanish anarchists, we decided to start our campaign with a large mass meeting. A demonstration in front of the Spanish Consulate in New York was to follow. As soon as our efforts became public, the reactionary papers began to urge the authorities to stop "Red Emma," that term having stuck to me since the Union Square meeting. On the night of our gathering the police appeared in full force, crowding even the platform so that the speakers could hardly make a gesture without touching an officer. When my turn came to speak, I gave a detailed account of the methods that were being used in Montjuich, and called for a protest against the Spanish horrors.

The pent-up emotions of the audience, aroused to a high pitch, broke into thunderous applause. Before it fully subsided, a voice from the gallery called out: "Miss Goldman, don't you think someone of the Spanish Embassy in Washington or the Legation in New York ought to be killed in revenge for the conditions you have just described?" I felt intuitively that my questioner must be a detective, attempting to trap me. There was a movement among the police near me as if preparing to lay hands on me. The audience was hushed in tense expectation. For a moment I paused; then I replied calmly and deliberately: "No, I do not think any one of the Spanish representatives in America is important enough to be killed, but if I were in Spain now, I should kill Canovas del Castillo."

Several weeks later came the news that Canovas del Castillo had been shot dead by an anarchist whose name was Angiolillo. At once the New York papers started a veritable hunt for the leading anarchists to secure their opinions of the man and his deed. Reporters pestered me day and night for interviews. Did I know the man? Had I been in correspondence with him? Had I suggested to him that Canovas be killed? I had to disappoint them. I did not know Angiolillo and had never corresponded with him. All I knew was that he had acted while the rest of us had only talked about the fearful outrages.

We learned that Angiolillo had lived in London and that he was known among our friends as a sensitive young man, an ardent student, a lover of music and books, poetry being his passion. The Montjuich tortures had haunted him and he decided to kill Canovas. He went to Spain, expecting to find the Prime Minister in Parliament, but he learned that Canovas was recuperating from his "labours of State" at Santa Agueda, a fashionable summer resort. Angiolillo journeyed there. He met Canovas almost immediately, but the man was accompanied by his wife and two children. "I could have killed him then," Angiolillo said in court, "but I would not risk the lives of the innocent woman and children. It was Canovas I wanted; he alone was responsible for the crimes of Montjuich." He then visited the Castillo villa, introducing himself as the representative of a conservative Italian paper. When he was face to face with the Prime Minister, he shot him dead. Mme Canovas ran in at that moment and hit Angiolillo full in the face. "I did not mean to kill your husband," Angiolillo apologized to her, "I aimed only at the official responsible for the Montjuich tortures."

The *Attentat* of Angiolillo and his frightful death vividly recalled to me the period of July 1892. Sasha's Calvary had now lasted five years. How close I had come to sharing a similar fate!—the lack of a paltry fifty dollars had prevented my accompanying Sasha to Pittsburgh—but can one estimate the spiritual travail and suffering the experience involved? Yet the price was worth the lesson I had gained from Sasha's deed. Since then I had ceased to regard political acts, as some other revolutionists did, from a merely utilitarian standpoint or from the view of their propagandistic value. The inner forces that compel an idealist to acts of violence, often involving the destruction of his own life, had come to mean much more to me. I felt certain now that behind every political deed of that nature was an impressionable, highly sensitized personality and a gentle spirit. Such beings cannot go on living complacently in the sight of great human misery and wrong. Their reactions to the cruelty and injustice of the world must inevitably express themselves in some violent act, in supreme rending of their tortured soul.

I had spoken in Providence a number of times without the least trouble. Rhode Island was still one of the few States to maintain the old tradition of unabridged freedom of speech. Two of our open-air gatherings, attended by thousands, went off well. But the police had evidently decided to suppress our last meeting. Arriving with several friends at the square where the assembly was to take place, we found a member of the Socialist Labor Party talking, and, not wishing to interfere with him, we set up our box farther away. My good comrade John H. Cook, a very active worker, opened the meeting, and I began to speak. Just then a policeman came running towards us, shouting: "Stop your jabbering! Stop it this minute or I'll pull you off the box!" I went on talking. Someone called out: "Don't mind the bully—go right on!" The policeman came up, puffing heavily. When he got his breath he snarled, "Say, you, are you deaf? Didn't I tell you to stop? What d'you mean not obeying the law?" "Are you the law?" I retorted; "I thought it is your duty to maintain the law, not to break it. Don't you know the law in this State gives me the right of free speech?" "The hell it does," he replied, "I'm the law." The audience began hooting and jeering. The officer started to pull me off the improvised platform. The crowd looked threatening and began closing in on him. He blew his whistle. A patrol wagon dashed up to the square, and several policemen broke through the crowd with their clubs swinging. The officer, still holding on to me, shouted: "Drive those damn anarchists back so I can get this woman. She's under arrest." I was led to the patrol wagon and literally thrown into it.

At the police station I demanded to know by what right I had been interfered with. "Because you're Emma Goldman," the sergeant at the desk replied. "Anarchists have no rights in this community, see?" He ordered me locked up for the night.

It was the first time since 1893 that I had been arrested, but, constantly expecting to fall into the clutches of the law, I had made it a practice to carry a book with me when going to meetings. I wrapped my skirts around me, climbed up on the board placed for a bed in my cell, pressed close to the barred door, through which shimmered a light, and started to read. Presently I became aware of someone moaning in the adjoining cell. "What is it?" I called in a whisper; "are you ill?" A woman's voice replied between sobs: "My children, my motherless children! Who is going to take care of them now? My sick husband, what'll become of him?" Her weeping became louder. "Say, you drunken lout, stop that squealing!" a matron shouted from somewhere. The crying was checked, and I heard the woman walking up and down her cell like a caged animal. When she quieted down a little I asked her to tell me her troubles; perhaps I could be of help. I learned that she was the mother of six children, the eldest fourteen, the baby only a year old. Her husband had been ill for ten months, unable to work, and in her despair she had helped herself to a loaf of bread and a can of milk from the grocery store in which she had once worked. She was caught in the act and turned over to the police. She begged to be let off for the night in order not to frighten her family, but the officer insisted on her going with him, not even giving her a chance to send a message to her home. She was brought to the station-house after the evening meal. The matron told her she could order some food if she had the price. The woman had not eaten all day; she was faint with hunger and ill with anxiety; but she had no money.

I rapped for the matron and asked her to send out for supper for me. In less than fifteen minutes she returned with a tray of ham and eggs, hot potatoes, bread, butter, and a large pot of coffee. I had given her a two-dollar bill, and she handed back fifteen cents. "You have fancy prices here," I said. "Sure thing, kid, did you think this was a charity joint?" Seeing that she was in a good humour, I requested her to pass part of the meal to my neighbour. She did, but not without commenting: "You're a regular fool to waste such a feed on a common sneak-thief."

The next morning I was taken, together with my neighbour and other unfortunates, before a magistrate. I was held over under bond, and as the amount could not be raised immediately I was returned to the station-house. At one o'clock in the afternoon I was again called for, this time to see the Mayor. That individual, no less bulky and bloated than the policeman, informed me that if I would promise under oath never to return to Providence he would let me go. "That's nice of you, Mayor," I replied; "but inasmuch as you have no case against me, your offer isn't quite so generous as it appears, is it?" I told him that I would make no promises whatever, but that if it would relieve his mind, I could tell him that I was about to start on a lecture tour to California. "It may take three months or more, I don't know. But I do know that you and your city cannot do without me much longer than that, so I am determined to come back." The Mayor and his flunkies roared, and I was released.

On my arrival in Boston I was shocked by a report in the local papers of the shooting at Hazleton, Pennsylvania, of twenty-one strikers. The men were miners on their way to Latimer, in the same State, to induce the workers there to join the strike. The Sheriff had met them on the public road and would not allow them to go on. He commanded them to return to Hazleton, and when they refused, he and his posse opened fire.

The papers stated that the Sheriff had acted in self-defense; the mob had been threatening. Yet there was not one casualty among the posse, while twenty-one working-men had been mowed down and a number of others wounded. It was evident from the report that the men had gone out with empty hands, without any intention of offering resistance. Everywhere workers were slain, everywhere the same butchery! Montjuich, Chicago, Pittsburgh, Hazleton—the few for ever outraging and crushing the many. The masses were the millions, yet how weak! To awaken them from their stupor, to make them conscious of their power—that is the great need. Soon, I told myself, I should be able to reach them throughout America. With a tongue of fire I would rouse them to a realization of their dependence and indignity! Glowingly I visioned my first great tour and the opportunities it would offer me to plead our Cause. But presently my reverie was disturbed by the thought of Ed. Our common life—what would become of it? Why could it not go hand in hand with my work? My giving to humanity would only increase my own need, would make me love and want Ed more. He would, he must, understand; he had himself suggested my going away for a time. The image of Ed filled me with warmth, but my heart fluttered with apprehension.

I had been away from Ed only two weeks, but my longing for him was more intense than it had been on my return from Europe. I could hardly contain myself until the train came to a stop in the Grand Central Station, where he met me. At home everything seemed new, more beautiful and enticing. Ed's endearing words sounded like music in my ears. Sheltered and protected from the strife and conflict outside, I clung to him and basked in the sunshine of our home. My eagerness to go on a long tour paled under the fascination of my lover. A month of joy and abandon followed, but my dream was soon to suffer a painful awakening.

It was caused by Nietzsche. Ever since my return from Vienna I had been hoping that Ed would read my books. I had asked him to do so and he promised he would when he had more time. It made me very sad to find Ed so indifferent to the new literary forces in the world. One evening we were gathered at Justus's place at a farewell party. James Huneker was present and a young friend of ours, P. Yelineck, a talented painter. They began discussing Nietzsche. I took part, expressing my enthusiasm over the great poet-philosopher and dwelling on the impression of his works on me. Huneker was surprised. "I did not know you were interested in anything outside of propaganda," he remarked. "That is because you don't know anything about anarchism," I replied, "else you would understand that it embraces every phase of life and effort and that it undermines the old, outlived values." Yelineck asserted that he was an anarchist because he was an artist; all creative people must be anarchists, he held, because they need scope and freedom for their expression. Huneker insisted that art has nothing to do with any ism. "Nietzsche himself is the proof of it," he argued; "he is an aristocrat, his ideal is the superman because he has no sympathy with or faith in the common herd." I pointed out that Nietzsche was not a social theorist but a poet, a rebel and innovator. His aristocracy was neither of birth nor of purse; it was of the spirit. In that respect Nietzsche was an anarchist, and all true anarchists were aristocrats, I said.

Then Ed spoke. His voice sounded cold and constrained, and I sensed the tempest behind it. "Nietzsche is a fool," he said, "a man with a diseased mind. He was doomed from birth to the idiocy which finally overtook him. He will be forgotten in less than a decade, and so will all those other pseudo-moderns. They are contortionists in comparison with the truly great of the past."

"But you haven't read Nietzsche!" I objected heatedly; "how can you talk about him?" "Oh, yes, I have," he retorted, "I read long ago all the silly books you brought from abroad." I was dumbfounded. Huneker and Yelineck turned on Ed, but my hurt was too great to continue the discussion.

He had known how I had wanted him to share my books, how I had hoped and waited for him to recognize their value and significance. How could he have kept me in suspense, how could he have remained silent after he had read them? Of course, he had a right to his opinion: that I believed implicitly. It was not his differing from me that had stabbed me to the quick; it was his scorn and ridicule of what had come to mean so much to me. Huneker, Yelineck, strangers in a measure, welcomed my appreciation of the new spirit, while my own lover made me appear silly, childish, incapable of judgment. I wanted to run away from Justus's place, to be alone; but I checked myself. I could not bear an open conflict with Ed.

Late at night, when we returned home, he said to me: "Let's not spoil our beautiful three months; Nietzsche is not worth it." I felt wounded to the heart. "It isn't Nietzsche, it is you—you," I cried excitedly. "Under the pretext of a great love you have done your utmost to chain me to you, to rob me of all that is more precious to me than life. You are not content with binding my body, you want also to bind my spirit! First the movement and my friends—now it's the books I love. You want to tear me away from them. You're rooted in the old. Very well, remain there! But don't imagine you will hold me to it. You are not going to clip my wings, you shan't stop my flight. I'll free myself even if it means tearing you out of my heart."

He stood leaning against the door of his room, his eyes closed, giving no sign of having heard a word I said. But I no longer cared. I stepped into my own room, my heart cold and empty.

The last few days were outwardly calm, even friendly, Ed helping me to prepare for my departure. At the station he embraced me. I knew he wanted to say something, but he remained silent. I, too, could not speak.

When the train pulled out and Ed's form receded, I realized that our life would never be the same any more. My love had received too violent a shock. It was now like a cracked bell; never again would it ring the same clear, joyous song.

# ALEXANDER BERKMAN
## (1870–1936)

> While the four of us were having our dinner, and Solotaroff was pointing out to me the different people in the café, I suddenly heard a powerful voice call: "Extra-large steak! Extra cup of coffee!" My own capital was so small and the need for economy so great that I was startled by such apparent extravagance . . . I wondered who that reckless person could be and how he could afford such food. "Who is that glutton?" I asked. Solotaroff laughed aloud. "That is Alexander Berkman. He can eat for three. But he rarely has enough money for much food. When he has, he eats Sachs out of his supplies. I'll introduce him to you."
>
> —Emma Goldman, *Living My Life*

Goldman's description of Alexander Berkman quickly defines the man who eventually became her lover. Indeed, Berkman's desire to lead the life of a revolutionary would draw many others besides Goldman helplessly toward him. He was a man whose dedication to his cause led him to attempt the murder of one of the most prominent industrialists of the 1890s, Henry Clay Frick. *Prison Memoirs of an Anarchist* (1912) is a stirring description of political life on the left in the late nineteenth and early twentieth centuries. It also functions as an exposé of the conditions in prisons at the time of Berkman's crime and subsequent fifteen-year internment.

Berkman's ideas on workers' rights, prison reform, and homosexuality were ahead of their time. Though his autobiography does not delve into the specifics of Berkman's childhood—and is even incomplete as a testament to the development of his anarchist views—it manifests an overwhelming honesty.

## FROM *Prison Memoirs of an Anarchist*

### THE SPIRIT OF PITTSBURGH

### I

Like a gigantic hive the twin cities jut out on the banks of the Ohio, heavily breathing the spirit of feverish activity, and permeating the atmosphere with the rage of life. Ceaselessly flow the streams of human ants, meeting and diverging, their paths crossing and recrossing, leaving in their trail a thousand winding passages, mounds of structure, peaked and domed. Their huge shadows overcast the yellow thread of gleaming river that curves and twists its painful way, now hugging the shore, now hiding in affright, and again timidly stretching its arms toward the wrathful monsters that belch fire and smoke into the midst of the giant hive. And over the whole is spread the gloom of thick fog, oppressive and dispiriting—the symbol of our existence, with all its darkness and cold.

This is Pittsburgh, the heart of American industrialism, whose spirit moulds the life of the great Nation. The spirit of Pittsburgh, the Iron City! Cold as steel, hard as iron, its products. These are the keynote of the great Republic, dominating all other chords, sacrificing harmony to noise, beauty to bulk. Its torch of liberty is a furnace fire, consuming, destroying, devastating: a country-wide furnace, in which the bones and marrow of the producers, their limbs and bodies, their health and blood, are cast into Bessemer steel, rolled into armor plate, and converted into engines of murder to be consecrated to Mammon by his high priests, the Carnegies, the Fricks.

The spirit of the Iron City characterizes the negotiations carried on between the Carnegie Company and the Homestead men. Henry Clay Frick, in absolute control of the firm, incarnates the spirit of the furnace, is the living emblem of his trade. The olive branch held out by the workers after their victory over the Pinkertons has been refused. The ultimatum issued by Frick is the last word of Caesar: the union of the steelworkers is to be crushed, completely and absolutely, even at the cost of shedding the blood of the last man in Homestead; the Company will deal only with individual workers, who must accept the terms offered, without question or discussion; he, Frick, will operate the mills with non-union labor, even if it should require the combined military power of the State and the Union to carry the plan into execution. Millmen disobeying the order to return to work under the new schedule of reduced wages are to be discharged forthwith, and evicted from the Company houses.

## II

In an obscure alley, in the town of Homestead, there stands a one-story frame house, looking old and forlorn. It is occupied by the widow Johnson and her four small children. Six months ago, the breaking of a crane buried her husband under two hundred tons of metal. When the body was carried into the house, the distracted woman refused to recognize in the mangled remains her big, strong "Jack." For weeks the neighborhood resounded with her frenzied cry, "My husband! Where's my husband?" But the loving care of kind-hearted neighbors has now somewhat restored the poor woman's reason. Accompanied by her four little orphans, she recently gained admittance to Mr. Frick. On her knees she implored him not to drive her out of her home. Her poor husband was dead, she pleaded; she could not pay off the mortgage; the children were too young to work; she herself was hardly able to walk. Frick was very kind, she thought; he had promised to see what could be done. She would not listen to the neighbors urging her to sue the Company for damages. "The crane was rotten," her husband's friends informed her; "the government inspector had condemned it." But Mr. Frick was kind, and surely he knew best about the crane. Did he not say it was her poor husband's own carelessness?

She feels very thankful to good Mr. Frick for extending the mortgage. She had lived in such mortal dread lest her own little home, where dear John had been such a kind husband to her, be taken away, and her children driven into the street. She must never forget to ask the Lord's blessing upon the good Mr. Frick. Every day she repeats to her neighbors the story of her visit to the great man; how kindly he received her, how simply he talked with her. "Just like us folks," the widow says.

She is now telling the wonderful story to neighbor Mary, the hunchback, who, with undiminished interest, hears the recital for the twentieth time. It reflects such importance to know some one that had come in intimate contact with the Iron King; why, into his very presence! and even talked to the great magnate!

" 'Dear Mr. Frick,' says I," the widow is narrating, " 'dear Mr. Frick,' I says, 'look at my poor little angels—' "

A knock on the door interrupts her. "Must be one-eyed Kate," the widow observes. "Come in! Come in!" she calls out, cheerfully. "Poor Kate!" she remarks with a sigh. "Her man's got the consumption. Won't last long, I fear."

A tall, rough-looking man stands in the doorway. Behind him appear two others. Frightened, the widow rises from the chair. One of the children begins to cry, and runs to hide behind his mother.

"Beg pard'n, ma'am," the tall man says. "Have no fear. We are Deputy Sheriffs. Read this." He produces an official-looking paper. "Ordered to dispossess you. Very sorry, ma'am, but get ready. Quick, got a dozen more of—"

There is a piercing scream. The Deputy Sheriff catches the limp body of the widow in his arms.

## III

East End, the fashionable residence quarter of Pittsburgh, lies basking in the afternoon sun. The broad avenue looks cool and inviting: the stately trees touch their shadows across the carriage road, gently nodding their heads in mutual approval. A steady procession of equipages fills the avenue, the richly caparisoned horses and uniformed flunkies lending color and life to the scene. A cavalcade is passing me. The laughter of the ladies sounds joyous and care-free. Their happiness irritates me. I am thinking of Homestead. In mind I see the sombre fence, the fortifications and cannon; the piteous figure of the widow rises before me, the little children weeping, and again I hear the anguished cry of a broken heart, a shattered brain. . . .

And here all is joy and laughter. The gentlemen seem pleased; the ladies are happy. Why should they concern themselves with misery and want? The common folk are fit only to be their slaves, to feed and clothe them, build these beautiful palaces, and be content with the charitable crust. "Take what I give you," Frick commands. Why, here is his house! A luxurious place, with large garden, barns, and stable. That stable there, — it is more cheerful and habitable than the widow's home. Ah, life could be made livable, beautiful! Why should it not be? Why so much misery and strife? Sunshine, flowers, beautiful things are all around me. That is life! Joy and peace. . . . No! There can be no peace with such as Frick and these parasites in carriages riding on our backs, and sucking the blood of the workers. Fricks, vampires, all of them — I almost shout aloud — they are all one class. All in a cabal against *my* class, the toilers, the producers. An impersonal conspiracy, perhaps; but a conspiracy nevertheless. And the fine ladies on horseback smile and laugh. What is the misery of the People to *them*? Probably they are laughing at me. Laugh! Laugh! You despise me. I am of the People, but you belong to the Fricks. Well, it may soon be our turn to laugh. . . .

Returning to Pittsburgh in the evening, I learn that the conferences between the Carnegie Company and the Advisory Committee of the strikers have terminated in the final refusal of Frick to consider the demands of the millmen. The last hope is gone! The master is determined to crush his rebellious slaves.

## THE ATTENDANT

The door of Frick's private office, to the left of the reception-room, swings open as the colored attendant emerges, and I catch a flitting glimpse of a black-bearded, well-knit figure at a table in the back of the room.

"Mistah Frick is engaged. He can't see you now, sah," the negro says, handing back my card.

I take the pasteboard, return it to my case, and walk slowly out of the reception-room. But quickly retracing my steps, I pass through the gate separating the clerks from the visitors, and, brushing the astounded attendant aside, I step into the office on the left, and find myself facing Frick.

For an instant the sunlight, streaming through the windows, dazzles me. I discern two men at the further end of the long table.

"Fr——," I begin. The look of terror on his face strikes me speechless. It is the dread of the conscious presence of death. "He understands," it flashes through my mind. With a quick motion I draw the revolver. As I raise the weapon, I see Frick clutch with both hands the arm of the chair, and attempt to rise. I aim at his head. "Perhaps he wears armor," I reflect. With a look of horror he quickly averts his face, as I pull the trigger. There is a flash, and the high-ceilinged room reverberates as with the booming of cannon. I hear a sharp, piercing cry, and see Frick on his knees, his head against the arm of the chair. I feel calm and possessed, intent upon every movement of the man. He is lying head and shoulders under the large armchair, without sound or motion. "Dead?" I wonder. I must make sure. About twenty-five feet separate us. I take a few steps toward him, when suddenly the other man, whose presence I had quite forgotten, leaps upon me. I struggle to loosen his hold. He looks slender and small. I would not hurt him: I have no business with him. Suddenly I hear the cry, "Murder! Help!" My heart stands still as I realize that it is Frick shouting. "Alive?" I wonder. I hurl the stranger aside and fire at the crawling figure of Frick. The man struck my hand,—I have missed! He grapples with me, and we wrestle across the room. I try to throw him, but spying an opening between his arm and body, I thrust the revolver against his side and aim at Frick, cowering behind the chair. I pull the trigger. There is a click—but no explosion! By the throat I catch the stranger, still clinging to me, when suddenly something heavy strikes me on the back of the head. Sharp pains shoot through my eyes. I sink to the floor, vaguely conscious of the weapon slipping from my hands.

"Where is the hammer? Hit him, carpenter!" Confused voices ring in my ears. Painfully I strive to rise. The weight of many bodies is pressing on me. Now—it's Frick's voice! Not dead? . . . I crawl in the direction of the sound, dragging the struggling men with me. I must get the dagger from my pocket—I have it! Repeatedly I strike with it at the legs of the man near the window. I hear Frick cry out in pain—there is much shouting and stamping—my arms are pulled and twisted, and I am lifted bodily from the floor.

Police, clerks, workmen in overalls, surround me. An officer pulls my head back by the hair, and my eyes meet Frick's. He stands in front of me, supported by several men. His face is ashen gray; the black beard is streaked with red, and blood is oozing from his neck. For an instant a strange feeling, as of shame, comes over me; but the next moment I am filled with anger at the sentiment, so unworthy of a revolutionist. With defiant hatred I look him full in the face.

"Mr. Frick, do you identify this man as your assailant?"

Frick nods weakly.

The street is lined with a dense, excited crowd. A young man in civilian dress, who is accompanying the police, inquires, not unkindly:

"Are you hurt? You're bleeding."

I pass my hand over my face. I feel no pain, but there is a peculiar sensation about my eyes.

"I've lost my glasses," I remark, involuntarily.

"You'll be damn lucky if you don't lose your head," an officer retorts. . . .

## THE SHOP

### I

I stand in line with a dozen prisoners, in the anteroom of the Deputy's office. Humiliation overcomes me as my eye falls, for the first time in the full light of day, upon my striped clothes. I am degraded to a beast! My first impression of a prisoner in stripes is painfully vivid: he resembled a dangerous brute. Somehow the idea is associated in my mind with a wild tigress,—and I, too, must now look like that.

The door of the rotunda swings open, admitting the tall, lank figure of the Deputy Warden.

"Hands up!"

The Deputy slowly passes along the line, examining a hand here and there. He separates the men into groups; then, pointing to the one in which I am included, he says in his feminine accents:

"None crippled. Officers, take them, hm, hm, to Number Seven. Turn them over to Mr. Hoods."

"Fall in! Forward, march!"

My resentment at the cattle-like treatment is merged into eager expectation. At last I am assigned to work! I speculate on the character of "Number Seven," and on the possibilities of escape from there. Flanked by guards, we cross the prison yard in close lockstep. The sentinels on the wall, their rifles resting loosely on crooked arm, face the striped line winding snakelike through the open space. The yard is spacious and clean, the lawn well kept and inviting. The first breath of fresh air in two weeks violently stimulates my longing for liberty. Perhaps the shop will offer an opportunity to escape. The thought quickens my observation. Bounded north, east, and south by the stone wall, the two blocks of the cell-house form a parallelogram, enclosing the shops, kitchen, hospital, and, on the extreme south, the women's quarters.

"Break ranks!"

We enter Number Seven, a mat shop. With difficulty I distinguish the objects in the dark, low-ceilinged room, with its small, barred windows. The air is heavy with dust; the rattling of the looms is deafening. An atmosphere of noisy gloom pervades the place.

The officer in charge assigns me to a machine occupied by a lanky prisoner in stripes. "Jim, show him what to do."

Considerable time passes, without Jim taking the least notice of me. Bent low over the machine, he seems absorbed in the work, his hands deftly manipulating the shuttle, his foot on the treadle. Presently he whispers, hoarsely:

"Fresh fish?"

"What did you say?"

"You bloke, long here?"

"Two weeks."

"Wotcher doin'?"

"Twenty-one years."

"Quitcher kiddin'."

"It's true."

"Honest? Holy gee!"

The shuttle flies to and fro. Jim is silent for a while, then he demands, abruptly:

"Wat dey put you here for?"

"I don't know."

"Been kickin'?"

"No."

"Den you'se bugs."

"Why so?"

"Dis 'ere is crank shop. Dey never put a mug 'ere 'cept he's bugs, or else dey got it in for you."

"How do *you* happen to be here?"

"Me? De God damn —— got it in for me. See dis?" He points to a deep gash over his temple. "Had a scrap wid de screws. Almost knocked me glimmer out. It was dat big bull* dere, Pete Hoods. I'll get even wid *him*, all right, damn his rotten soul. I'll kill him. By God, I will. I'll croak 'ere, anyhow."

"Perhaps it isn't so bad," I try to encourage him.

"It ain't, eh? Wat d'*you* know 'bout it? I've got the con bad, spittin' blood every night. Dis dust's killin' me. Kill you, too, damn quick."

As if to emphasize his words, he is seized with a fit of coughing, prolonged and hollow.

The shuttle has in the meantime become entangled in the fringes of the matting. Recovering his breath, Jim snatches the knife at his side, and with a few deft strokes releases the metal. To and fro flies the gleaming thing, and Jim is again absorbed in his task.

"Don't bother me no more," he warns me, "I'm behind wid me work."

Every muscle tense, his long body almost stretched across the loom, in turn pulling and pushing, Jim bends every effort to hasten the completion of the day's task.

The guard approaches. "How's he doing?" he inquires, indicating me with a nod of the head.

"He's all right. But say, Hoods, dis 'ere is no place for de kid. He's got a twenty-one spot."†

"Shut your damned trap!" the officer retorts, angrily. The consumptive bends over his work, fearfully eyeing the keeper's measuring stick.

As the officer turns away, Jim pleads:

"Mr. Hoods, I lose time teachin'. Won't you please take off a bit? De task is more'n I can do, an' I'm sick."

"Nonsense. There's nothing the matter with you, Jim. You're just lazy, that's what you are. Don't be shamming, now. It don't go with *me*."

At noon the overseer calls me aside. "You are green here," he warns me, "pay no attention to Jim. He wanted to be bad, but we showed him different. He's all right *now*. You have a long time; see that you behave yourself. This is no playhouse, you understand?"

As I am about to resume my place in the line forming to march back to the cells for dinner, he recalls me:

*Guard.
†Sentence.

"Say, Aleck, you'd better keep an eye on that fellow Jim. He is a little off, you know."

He points toward my head, with a significant rotary motion.

## II

The mat shop is beginning to affect my health: the dust has inflamed my throat, and my eyesight is weakening in the constant dusk. The officer in charge has repeatedly expressed dissatisfaction with my slow progress in the work. "I'll give you another chance," he cautioned me yesterday, "and if you don't make a good mat by next week, down in the hole you go." He severely upbraided Jim for his inefficiency as instructor. As the consumptive was about to reply, he suffered an attack of coughing. The emaciated face turned greenish-yellow, but in a moment he seemed to recover, and continued working. Suddenly I saw him clutch at the frame, a look of terror spread over his face, he began panting for breath, and then a stream of dark blood gushed from his mouth, and Jim fell to the floor.

The steady whir of the looms continued. The prisoner at the neighboring machine cast a furtive look at the prostrate form, and bent lower over his work. Jim lay motionless, the blood dyeing the floor purple. I rushed to the officer.

"Mr. Hoods, Jim has—"

"Back to your place, damn you!" he shouted at me. "How dare you leave it without permission?"

"I just—"

"Get back, I tell you!" he roared, raising the heavy stick.

I returned to my place. Jim lay very still, his lips parted, his face ashen. Slowly, with measured step, the officer approached.

"What's the matter here?"

I pointed at Jim. The guard glanced at the unconscious man, then lightly touched the bleeding face with his foot.

"Get up, Jim, get up!"

The nerveless head rolled to the side, striking the leg of the loom.

"Guess he isn't shamming," the officer muttered. Then he shook his finger at me, menacingly: "Don't you ever leave your place without orders. Remember, *you!*"

After a long delay, causing me to fear that Jim had been forgotten, the doctor arrived. It was Mr. Rankin, the senior prison physician, a short, stocky man of advanced middle age, with a humorous twinkle in his eye. He ordered the sick prisoner taken to the hospital. "Did any one see the man fall?" he inquired.

"This man did," the keeper replied, indicating me.

While I was explaining, the doctor eyed me curiously. Presently he asked my name. "Oh, the celebrated case," he smiled. "I know Mr. Frick quite well. Not such a bad man, at all. But you'll be treated well here, Mr. Berkman. This is a democratic institution, you know. By the way, what is the matter with your eyes? They are inflamed. Always that way?"

"Only since I am working in this shop."

"Oh, he is all right, Doctor," the officer interposed. "He's only been here a week."

Mr. Rankin cast a quizzical look at the guard.

"You want him here?"

"Y-e-s: we're short of men."

"Well, *I* am the doctor, Mr. Hoods." Then, turning to me, he added: "Report in the morning on sick list."

III

The doctor's examination has resulted in my removal to the hosiery department. The change has filled me with renewed hope. A disciplinary shop, to which are generally assigned the "hard cases"—inmates in the first stages of mental derangement, or exceptionally unruly prisoners— the mat shop is the point of special supervision and severest discipline. It is the best-guarded shop, from which escape is impossible. But in the hosiery department, a recent addition to the local industries, I may find the right opportunity. It will require time, of course; but my patience shall be equal to the great object. The working conditions, also, are more favorable: the room is light and airy, the discipline not so stringent. My near-sightedness has secured for me immunity from machine work. The Deputy at first insisted that my eyes were "good enough" to see the numerous needles of the hosiery machine. It is true, I could see them; but not with sufficient distinctness to insure the proper insertion of the initial threads. To admit partial ability would result, I knew, in being ordered to produce the task; and failure, or faulty work, would be severely punished. Necessity drove me to subterfuge: I pretended total inability to distinguish the needles. Repeated threats of punishment failing to change my determination, I have been assigned the comparatively easy work of "turning" the stockings. The occupation, though tedious, is not exacting. It consists in gathering the hosiery manufactured by the knitting machines, whence the product issues without soles. I carry the pile to the table provided with an iron post, about eighteen inches high, topped with a small inverted disk. On this instrument the stockings are turned "inside out" by slipping the article over the post, then quickly "undressing" it. The hosiery thus "turned" is forwarded to the looping machines, by which the product is finished and sent back to me, once more to be "turned," preparatory to sorting and shipment.

Monotonously the days and weeks pass by. Practice lends me great dexterity in the work, but the hours of drudgery drag with heavy heel. I seek to hasten time by forcing myself to take an interest in the task. I count the stockings I turn, the motions required by each operation, and the amount accomplished within a given time. But in spite of these efforts, my mind persistently reverts to unprofitable subjects: my friends and the propaganda; the terrible injustice of my excessive sentence; suicide and escape.

My nights are restless. Oppressed with a nameless weight, or tormented by dread, I awake with a start, breathless and affrighted, to experience the momentary relief of danger past. But the next instant I am overwhelmed by the consciousness of my surroundings, and plunged into rage and despair, powerless, hopeless.

Thus day succeeds night, and night succeeds day, in the ceaseless struggle of hope and discouragement, of life and death, amid the externally placid tenor of my Pennsylvania nightmare.

# THEODORE DREISER
## (1871–1945)

Dreiser was among the dominant voices in American fiction in the early part of the twentieth century, writing evocative novels such as *Sister Carrie* (1900) and *An American Tragedy* (1925), which was based on a well-known murder case. The author's rough-hewn style and harsh realism were crucial elements in his work, and he remains a figure to reckon with.

The son of an intensely religious father and protective mother, he grew up in relative poverty. After a year at the University of Indiana, he turned to journalism and publishing. Although he worked elements of his own life into his novels and stories (in particular, his novel *The Genius* [1915] was based on incidents in his life), his most autobiographical writing is found in three books: *A Traveler at Forty* (1913), *A Hoosier Holiday* (1916), and *A Book about Myself* (1922). Each of these marks an interesting turn in the stream of American autobiographical writing. The zest of *A Hoosier Holiday* lifts it above the others; it is a wonderful "road book," the story of a trip by car taken with his friend Speed. In a way, this volume represents an early paean to the automobile, then a newfangled thing destined to alter forever the landscape of America.

## FROM *A Hoosier Holiday*

### RAILROADS AND A NEW WONDER OF THE WORLD

It wouldn't surprise me in the least if the automobile, as it is being perfected now, would make over the whole world's railway systems into something very different from what they are today. Already the railways are complaining that the automobile is seriously injuring business, and this is not difficult to understand. It ought to be so. At best the railways have become huge, clumsy, unwieldy affairs little suited to the temperamental needs and moods of the average human being. They are mass carriers, freight handlers, great hurry conveniences for overburdened commercial minds, but little more. After all, travel, however much it may be a matter of necessity, is in most instances, or should be, a matter of pleasure. If not, why go forth to roam the world so wide? Are not trees, flowers, attractive scenes, great mountains, interesting cities, and streets and terminals the objective? If not, why not? Should the discomforts become too great, as in the case of the majority of railroads, and any reasonable substitute offer itself, as the automobile, the old form of conveyance will assuredly have to give way.

Think what you have to endure on the ordinary railroad—and what other kind is there—smoke, dust, cinders, noise, the hurrying of masses of people, the ringing of bells, the tooting of whistles, the brashness and discourtesy of employees, cattle trains, coal trains, fruit trains, milk trains in endless procession—and then they tell you that these are necessary in order to give you the service you get. Actually our huge railways are becoming so freight logged and trainyard and train terminal infested, and four tracked and cinder blown, that they are a nuisance.

Contrast travel by railroad with the charm of such a trip as we were now making. Before the automobile, this trip, if it had been made at all, would have had to be made by train—in part at least. I would not have ridden a horse or in any carriage to Indiana—whatever I might have done after I reached there. Instead of green fields and pleasant ways, with the pleasure of stopping anywhere and proceeding at our leisure, substitute the necessity of riding over a fixed route, which once or twice seen, or ten times, as in my case, had already become an old story. For this is one of the drawbacks to modern railroading, in addition to all its other defects—it is so fixed; it has no latitude, no elasticity. Who wants to see the same old scenes over and over and over? One can go up the Hudson or over the Alleghanies or through the Grand Canyon of the Arizona once or twice, but if you have to go that way always, if you go at all—— But the prospect of new and varied roads, and of that intimate contact with woodland silences, grassy slopes, sudden and sheer vistas at sharp turns, streams not followed by endless lines of cars—of being able to change your mind and go by this route or that according to your mood—what a difference! These constitute a measureless superiority. And the cost per mile is not so vastly much more by automobile. Today it is actually making travel cheaper and quicker. Whether for a long tour or a short one, it appears to make man independent and give him a choice of life, which he must naturally prefer. Only the dull can love sameness.

North of Factoryville a little way—perhaps a score of miles—we encountered one of these amazing works of man which, if they become numerous enough, eventually make a country a great memory. They are the bones or articulatory ligaments of the body politic which, like the roads and viaducts and baths of ancient Rome, testify to the prime of its physical strength and after its death lie like whitening bones about the fields of the world which once it occupied.

We were coming around a curve near Nicholsen, Pennsylvania, approaching a stream which traversed this great valley, when across it from ridge's edge to ridge's edge suddenly appeared a great white stone or concrete viaduct or bridge—we could not tell at once which—a thing so colossal and impressive that we instantly had Speed stop the car so that we might remain and gaze at it. Ten huge arches—each say two hundred feet wide and two hundred feet high—were topped by eleven other arches say fifteen feet wide and forty feet high, and this whole surmounted by a great roadbed carrying several railway tracks, we assumed. The builders were still at work on it. As before the great Cathedral at Rouen or Amiens or Canterbury, or those giant baths in Rome which so gratify the imagination, so here, at Nicholsen, in a valley celebrated for nothing in particular and at the edge of a town of no size, we stood before this vast structure, gazing in a kind of awe. These arches! How really beautiful they were, how wide, how high, how noble, how symmetrically planned! And the smaller arches above, for all the actually huge size, how delicate and lightsomely graceful! How could they carry a heavy train so high in the air? But there they were, nearly two hundred and forty feet above us from the stream's surface, as we discovered afterwards, and the whole structure nearly twentyfour hundred feet long. We learned that it was the work of a great railroad corporation—a part of a scheme for straightening and shortening its line about three miles!— which incidentally was leaving a monument to the American of this day which would be stared at in centuries to come as evidencing the courage, the resourcefulness, the taste, the wealth, the commerce and the force of the time in which we are living—now.

It is rather odd to stand in the presence of so great a thing in the making and realize that you are looking at one of the true wonders of the world. As I did so I could not help thinking of all the great wonders America has already produced—capitals, halls, universities, bridges, monuments, water flumes, sea walls, dams, towering structures—yet the thought came to me how little of all that will yet *be* accomplished have *we* seen. What towers, what bridges, what palaces, what roads will not yet come! Numerous as these great things already are—a statue of Lincoln in Chicago, a building by Woolworth in New York, a sea wall at Galveston, an Ashokan dam in the Catskills, this bridge at Nicholsen—yet in times to come there will be thousands of these wonders—possibly hundreds of thousands where now there are hundreds. A great free people is hard at work day after day building, building, building—and for what?

Sometimes I think, like the forces and processes which produce embry-
onic life here or the coral islands in the Pacific, vast intelligences and personalities are at work, producing worlds and nations. As a child is builded
in the womb, so is a star. We socalled individuals are probably no more
than mere cell forms constructing something in whose subsequent movements, passions, powers we shall have no share whatsoever. Does the
momentary cell life in the womb show in the subsequent powers of the
man? Will we show in the subsequent life of the nation that we have
helped build? When one thinks of how little of all that is or will be one
has any part in—are we not such stuff as dreams are made of, and can we
feel anything but a slave's resignation?

While we were sightseeing, Speed was conducting a social conference of his own in the shade of some trees in one of the quiet streets of
Nicholsen. I think I have never seen anyone with a greater innate attraction for boys. Speed was only twentyfive himself. Boys seemed to understand Speed and to be hail-fellow-well-met with him, wherever he
was. In Dover, at the Water Gap, in Wilkes-Barré, Scranton—wherever
we chanced to stop, there was a boy or boys. He or they drew near and a
general conversation ensued. In so far as I could see, the mystery consisted of nothing more than a natural ability on Speed's part to take them
at their own value and on their own terms. He was just like any other boy
among them, questioning and answering quite as if he and they were all
grownups and very serious. Here in Nicholsen, as we came back, no less
than five youngsters were explaining to him all the facts and wonders of
the great bridge.

"Yes, and one man fell from the top of them there little arches way up
there last winter down to the back of the big arch and he almost died."

"Those little arches are forty feet above the big ones," another went on.

"Yes, but he didn't die," put in another informatively. "He just, now,
broke his back. But he almost died, though. He can't do any more work."

"That's too bad," I said, "and how does he manage to live now?"

"Well, his wife supports him, I believe," put in one quietly.

"He's goin' to get a pension, though," said another.

"There's a law now or something," volunteered a fourth. "They have
to give him money."

"Oh, I see," I said. "That's fine. Can any of you tell me how wide
those arches are—those big arches?"

"One hundred and eighty feet wide and two hundred feet high," volunteered one boy.

"And the little arches are sixteen feet and three inches wide and forty
feet high," put in another.

"And how long is it?"

"Two thousand, three hundred and ninetyfive feet from ridge to ridge," came with schoolboy promptness from three at once.

I was flabbergasted.

"How do you know all this?" I inquired.

"We learned it at school," said two. "Our teacher knows."

I was so entertained by the general spirit of this group that I wanted to stay awhile and listen to them. American boys—I know nothing of foreign ones—are so frank, free and generally intelligent. There was not the slightest air of sycophancy about this group. They were not seeking anything save temporary entertainment. Some of them wanted to ride a little way,—perhaps to the nearest store—but only a little way and then only when invited. They all looked so bright, and yet in this group you could easily detect the varying characteristics which, other things being equal, would make some successes materially and others failures, possibly. Here was the comparatively dull boy, the bashful boy, the shrewd boy, the easy going, pleasure loving boy. You could see it in their eyes. One of them, a tallish, leanish youth, had instantly on the appearance of Franklin and myself crowded the others back and stood closest, his shrewd, examining eyes taking in all our characteristics. By looking into his eyes I could see how shrewd, independent, and selfprotective he was. He was not in the least overawed like some of the others, but rather superior, like one who would have driven a clever bargain with us, if he might have, and worsted us at it.

Except for this bridge and these children, Nicholsen held nothing, at least nothing obvious. It was just a small town with retail stores, at one of which, a druggist's, we stopped for picture cards. One would have supposed, with so vast a thing as this bridge, there would have been excellent photographs of it; but no, there was none that was really good. The main street, some country roads, a wheat field which some rural poet had snapped—that was all. This country druggist's store was very flyspecked. I wished for Nicholsen's sake, as well as for my own, that something worthy had been prepared, which the sightseeing public might take away as a memento.

## A COUNTRY HOTEL

Beyond Nicholsen, somewhere in this same wondrous valley and in a winelike atmosphere, came New Milford and with it our noonday meal. We were rolling along aimlessly, uncertain where next we would pause. The sight of an old fashioned white hotel at a street corner with several rurals standing about and a row of beautiful elms over the way gave us our cue. "This looks rather inviting," said Franklin; and then, to the figure of a heavy nondescript in brown jeans who was sitting on a chair outside in the shade:

"Can't we get something to eat here?"

"You can," replied the countryman succinctly; "they'll be putting dinner on the table in a few minutes."

We went into the bar, Franklin's invariable opening for these meals being a cocktail, when he could get one. It was a cleanly room, but with such a field hand atmosphere about those present that I was a little disappointed, and yet interested. I always feel about most American country saloons that they are patronized by ditchers and men who do the rough underpaid work of villages, while in England and France I had a very different feeling.

I was much interested here by the proprietor, or, as he turned out afterward, one of two brothers who owned the hotel. He was an elderly man, stout and serious, who in another place perhaps and with a slightly different start in life might, I am sure, have been banker, railroad officer, or director. He was so circumspect, polite, regardful. He came to inquire in a serious way if we were going to take dinner? We were.

"You can come right in whenever you are ready," he commented.

Something in his tone and presence touched me pleasantly.

Because of the great heat—it was blazing outside—I had left my coat in the car and was arrayed in a brown khaki shirt and grey woolen trousers, with a belt. Because of the heat it did not occur to me that my appearance would not pass muster. But, no. Life's little rules of conduct are not so easily set aside, even in a country hotel. As I neared the diningroom door and was passing the coatrack, mine host appeared and, with a grace and tact which I have nowhere seen surpassed, and in a voice which instantly obviated all possibility of a disagreeable retort, he presented me a coat which he had taken from a hook and, holding it ready, said: "Would you mind slipping into this?"

"Pardon me," I said, "I have a coat in the car; I will get that."

"Don't trouble," he said gently; "you can wear this if you like. It will do."

I had to smile, but in an entirely friendly way. Something about the man's manner made me ashamed of myself—not that it would have been such a dreadful thing to have gone into the diningroom looking as I was, for I was entirely presentable, but that I had not taken greater thought to respect his conventions more. He was a gentleman running a country hotel—a real gentleman. I was the brash, smart asininity from the city seeking to have my own way in the country because the city looks down on the country. It hurt me a little and yet I felt repaid by having encountered a man who could fence so skilfully with the little and yet irritable and no doubt difficult problems of his daily life. I wanted to make friends with him, for I could see so plainly that he was really above the thing he was doing and yet content in some philosophical way to make the best of it. How this man came to be running a country hotel, with a bar attached, I should like to know.

After luncheon, I fell into a conversation with him, brief but interesting. He had lived here many years. The place over the way with the beautiful trees belonged to a former congressman. (I could see the forgotten dignitary making the best of his former laurels in this out-of-the-way place.) New Milford, a very old place, had been hurt by the growth of other towns. But now the automobile was beginning to do something for it. Last Sunday six hundred machines had passed through here. Only last week the town had voted to pave the principal street, in order to attract further travel. One could see by mine host's manner that his hotel business was picking up. I venture to say he offered to contribute liberally to the expense, so far as his ability would permit.

I could not help thinking of this man as we rode away, and I have been thinking of him from time to time ever since. He was so simple, so sincere, so honorably dull or conventional. I wish that I could believe there are thousands of such men in the world. His hotel was tasteless; so are the vast majority of other hotels, and homes too, in America. The dining room was execrable from one point of view; naïve, and pleasingly so, from another. One could feel the desire to "set a good table" and give a decent meal. The general ingredients were good as far as they went, but, alas! the average American does not make a good servant—for the public. The girl who waited on us was a poor slip, well intentioned enough, I am sure, but without the first idea of what to do. I could see her being selected by mine host because she was a good girl, or because her mother was poor and needed the money—never because she had been trained to do the things she was expected to do. Americans live in a world of sentiment in spite of all their business acumen, and somehow expect God to reward good intentions with perfect results. I adore the spirit, but I grieve for its inutility. No doubt this girl was dreaming (all the time she was waiting on us) of some four-corners merry-go-round where her beau would be waiting. Dear, naïve America! When will it be different from a dreaming child, and, if ever that time arrives, shall we ever like it as much again?

And then came Halstead and Binghamton, for we were getting on. I never saw a finer day nor ever enjoyed one more. Imagine smooth roads, a blue sky, white and black cattle on the hills, lovely farms, the rich green woods and yellow grainfields of a fecund August. Life was going by in a Monticelli-esque mood. Dooryards and houses seemed to be a compound of blowing curtains, cool deep shadows, women in summery dresses reading, and then an arabesque of bright flowers, goldenglow, canna, flowering sage, sweet elyssum, geraniums and sunflowers. At Halstead we passed an hotel facing the Susquehanna River, which seemed to me the ideal of what a summer hotel should be—gay with yellow and white awnings and airy balconies and painted with flowers. Before it was this blue river, a lovely thing, with canoes and trees and a sense of summer life.

Beyond, on a smooth white road, we met a man who was selling some kind of soap—a soap especially good for motorists. He came to us out of Binghamton, driving an old ramshackle vehicle, and hailed us as we were pausing to examine something. He was a tall, lean, shabby American, clothed in an ancient frock coat and soft rumpled felt hat, and looked like some small-town carpenter or bricklayer or maker of cement walks. By his side sat a youngish man, who looked nothing and said nothing, taking no part in what followed. He had a dreamy, speculative and yet harassed look, made all the more emphatic by a long pointed nose and narrow pointed chin.

"I've got something here I'd like to show you, gentlemen," he called, drawing rein and looking hopefully at Franklin and Speed.

"Well, we're always willing to look at something once," replied Franklin cheerfully and in a bantering tone.

"Very well, gentlemen," said the stranger, "you're just the people I'm looking for, and you'll be glad you've met me." Even as he spoke he had been reaching under the seat and produced a small can of something which he now held dramatically aloft. "It's the finest thing in the way of a hand or machine soap that has ever been invented, no akali (he did not seem to know there were two ls in the word), good for man or woman. Won't soil the most delicate fabric or injure the daintiest hands. I know, now, for I've been working on this for the last three years. It's my personal, private invention. The basis of it is cornmeal and healing, soothing oils. You rub it on your hands before you put them in water and it takes off all these spots and stains that come from machine oil and that ordinary turpentine won't take out. It softens them right up. Have you got any oil stains?" he continued, seizing one of Speed's genial hands. "Very good. This will take it right out. You haven't any water in there, have you, or a pan? Never mind. I'm sure this lady up here in this house will let me have some," and off he hustled with the air of a proselytizing religionist.

I was interested. So much enthusiasm for so humble a thing as a soap aroused me. Besides he was curious to look at—a long, lean, shambling zealot. He was so zealous, so earnest, so amusing, if you please, or hopeless. "Here really," I said, "is the basis of all zealotry, of all hopeless invention, of struggle and dreams never to be fulfilled." He looked exactly like the average inventor who is destined to invent and invent and invent and never succeed in anything.

"Well, there is character there, anyhow," said Franklin. "That long nose, that thin dusty coat, that watery blue, inventive eye—all mountebanks and charlatans and street corner fakers have something of this man in them—and yet——"

He came hustling back.

"Here you are now!" he exclaimed, as he put down a small washpan full of water. "Now you just take this and rub it in good. Don't be afraid; it won't hurt the finest fabric or skin. I know what all the ingredients are. I worked on it three years before I discovered it. Everybody in Binghamton knows me. If it don't work, just write me at any time and you can get your money back."

In his eager routine presentation of his material he seemed to forget that we were present, here and now, and could demand our money back before he left. In a fitting spirit of camaraderie Speed rubbed the soap on his hands and spots which had for several days defied ordinary soap-cleansing processes immediately disappeared. Similarly, Franklin, who had acquired a few stains, salved his hands. He washed them in the pan of water standing on the engine box, and declared the soap a success. From my lofty perch in the car I now said to Mr. Vallaurs (the name on the label of the bottle), "Well, now you've made fifteen cents."

"Not quite," he corrected, with the eye of a holy disputant. "There are eight ingredients in that besides the cornmeal and the bottle alone costs me four and one-half cents."

"Is that so?" I continued—unable to take him seriously and yet sympathizing with him, he seemed so futile and so prodigal of his energy. "Then I really suppose you don't make much of anything?"

"Oh, yes, I do," he replied, seemingly unconscious of my jesting mood, and trying to be exact in the interpretation of his profit. "I make a little, of course. I'm only introducing it now, and it takes about all I make to get it around. I've got it in all the stores of Binghamton. I've been in the chemical business for years now. I got up some perfumes here a few years ago, but some fellows in the wholesale business did me out of them."

"I see," I said, trying to tease him and so bring forth any latent animosity which he might be concealing against fate or life. He looked to me to be a man who had been kicked about from pillar to post. "Well, when you get this well started and it looks as though it would be a real success, some big soap or chemical manufacturer will come along and take it away from you. You won't make anything out of it."

"Won't I?" he rejoined defiantly, taking me with entire seriousness and developing a flash of opposition in his eyes. "No, he won't, either.

I've had that done to me before, but it won't happen this time. I know the tricks of them sharps. I've got all this patented. The last time I only had my application in. That's why I'm out here on this road today interducin' this myself. I lost the other company I was interested in. But I'm going to take better care of this one. I want to see that it gets a good start."

He seemed a little like an animated scarecrow in his mood.

"Oh, I know," I continued dolefully, but purely in a jesting way, "but they'll get you, anyhow. They'll swallow you whole. You're only a beginner; you're all right now, so long as your business is small, but just wait until it looks good enough to fight for and they'll come and take it away from you. They'll steal or imitate it, and if you say anything they'll look up your past and have you arrested for something you did twenty or thirty years ago in Oshkosh or Oskaloosa. Then they'll have your first wife show up and charge you with bigamy or they'll prove that you stole a horse or something. Sure—they'll get it away from you," I concluded.

"No, they won't either," he insisted, a faint suspicion that I was joking with him beginning to dawn on him. "I ain't never had but one wife and I never stole any horses. I've got this patented now and I'll make some money out of it, I think. It's the best soap"—(and here as he thought of his invention once more his brow cleared and his enthusiasm rose)— "the most all-round useful article that has ever been put on the market. You gentlemen ought really to take a thirty-cent bottle"—he went back and produced a large one—"it will last you a lifetime. I guarantee it not to soil, mar or injure the finest fabric or skin. Cornmeal is the chief ingredient and eight other chemicals, no akali. I wish you'd take a few of my cards"—he produced a handful of these—"and if you find anyone along the road who stands in need of a thing of this kind I wish you'd just be good enough to give 'em one so's they'll know where to write. I'm right here in Binghamton. I've been here now for twenty years or more. Every druggist knows me."

He looked at us with an unconsciously speculative eye—as though he were wondering what service we would be to him.

Franklin took the cards and gave him fifteen cents. Speed was still washing his hands, some new recalcitrant spots having been discovered. I watched the man as he proceeded to his rattletrap vehicle.

"Well, gentlemen, I'll be saying good day to you. Will you be so kind as to return that pan to that lady up there, when you're through with it? She was very accommodating about it."

"Certainly, certainly," replied Franklin, "we'll attend to it."

Once he had gone there ensued a long discussion of inventors and their fates. Here was this one, fifty years of age, if he was a day, and out on the public road, advertising a small soap which could not possibly bring him the reward he desired soon.

"You see, he's going the wrong way about it," Franklin said. "He's putting the emphasis on what he can do personally, when he ought to be seeing about what others can do for him; he should be directing as a manager, instead of working as a salesman. And another thing, he places too much emphasis upon local standards ever to become broadly successful. He said over and over that all the druggists and automobile supply houses in Binghamton handle his soap. That's nothing to us. We are, as it were, overland citizens and the judgments of Binghamton do not convince us of anything any more than the judgments of other towns and crossroad communities along our route. Every little community has its standards and its locally successful ones. The thing that will determine actual success is a man's ability or inability to see outside and put upon himself the test of a standard peculiar to no one community but common to all. This man was not only apparently somewhat mystified when we asked him what scheme he had to reach the broader market with his soap; he appeared never to have approached in his own mind that possibility at all. So he could never become more than partially successful or rich."

"Very true," I assented, "but a really capable man wouldn't work for him. He'd consider him too futile and try to take his treasure away from him and then the poor creature would be just where he was before, compelled to invent something else. Any man who would work for him wouldn't actually be worth having. It would be a case of the blind leading the blind."

There was much more of this—a long discussion. We agreed that any man who does anything must have so much more than the mere idea—must have vision, the ability to control and to organize men, a magnetism for those who are successful—in short, that mysterious something which we call personality. This man did not have it. He was a poor scrub, blown hither and yon by all the winds of circumstance, dreaming of some far-off supremacy which he never could enjoy or understand, once he had it.

# GERTRUDE STEIN
## (1874–1946)

Born into a well-off family, Stein studied psychology under William James at Radcliffe. "William James delighted her," we learn in the following excerpt from *The Autobiography of Alice B. Toklas*, which was written by Stein in the persona of her secretary and lifelong companion. She later studied medicine at the Johns Hopkins University, focusing on brain anatomy, but she soon opted for a life of writing. Her numerous books include novels, essays, and criticism, and she is widely considered an important experimental writer.

In 1903, she and Alice settled elegantly in Paris, where they held court and played host to countless important writers and artists, including Hemingway, Pound, Fitzgerald, Joyce, and Picasso. One remark that Stein made to Hemingway—"You are a lost generation"—has echoed down the corridors of literary history.

*The Autobiography of Alice B. Toklas* (1933) is a unique text: odd, amusing, often brilliant, as often annoying. Stein offers readers an intimate glimpse of expatriate life in Paris in the early decades of this century, and a remarkable self-portrait.

## FROM *The Autobiography of Alice B. Toklas*

### GERTRUDE STEIN BEFORE SHE CAME TO PARIS

Once more I have come to Paris and now I am one of the habitués of the rue de Fleurus. Gertrude Stein was writing The Making of Americans and she had just commenced correcting the proofs of Three Lives. I helped her correct them.

Gertrude Stein was born in Allegheny, Pennsylvania. As I am an ardent californian and as she spent her youth there I have often begged her to be born in California but she has always remained firmly born in Allegheny, Pennsylvania. She left it when she was six months old and has never seen it again and now it no longer exists being all of it Pittsburgh. She used however to delight in being born in Allegheny, Pennsylvania when during the war, in connection with war work, we used to have papers made out and they always immediately wanted to know one's birthplace. She used to say if she had been really born in California as I wanted her to have been she would never have had the pleasure of seeing the various french officials try to write, Allegheny, Pennsylvania.

When I first knew Gertrude Stein in Paris I was surprised never to see a french book on her table, although there were always plenty of english ones, there were even no french newspapers. But do you never read french, I as well as many other people asked her. No, she replied, you see I feel with my eyes and it does not make any difference to me what language I hear, I don't hear a language, I hear tones of voice and rhythms, but with my eyes I see words and sentences and there is for me only one language and that is english. One of the things that I have liked all these years is to be surrounded by people who know no english. It has left me more intensely alone with my eyes and my english. I do not know if it would have been possible to have english be so all in all to me otherwise. And they none of them could read a word I wrote, most of them did not even know that I did write. No, I like living with so very many people and being all alone with english and myself.

One of her chapters in The Making of Americans begins: I write for myself and strangers.

She was born in Allegheny, Pennsylvania, of a very respectable middle class family. She always says that she is very grateful not to have been born of an intellectual family, she has a horror of what she calls intellectual people. It has always been rather ridiculous that she who is good friends with all the world and can know them and they can know her, has always been the admired of the precious. But she always says some day they, anybody, will find out that she is of interest to them, she and her writing. And she always consoles herself that the newspapers are always interested. They always say, she says, that my writing is appalling but they always quote it and what is more, they quote it correctly, and those they say they admire they do not quote. This at some of her most bitter moments has been a consolation. My sentences do get under their skin, only they do not know that they do, she has often said.

She was born in Allegheny, Pennsylvania, in a house, a twin house. Her family lived in one and her father's brother's lived in the other one. These two families are the families described in The Making of Americans. They had lived in these houses for about eight years when Gertrude Stein was born. A year before her birth, the two sisters-in-law who had never gotten along any too well were no longer on speaking terms.

Gertrude Stein's mother as she describes her in The Making of Americans, a gentle pleasant little woman with a quick temper, flatly refused to see her sister-in-law again. I don't know quite what had happened but something. At any rate the two brothers who had been very successful business partners broke up their partnership, the one brother went to New York where he and all his family after him became very rich and the other brother, Gertrude Stein's family, went to Europe. They first went to Vienna and stayed there until Gertrude Stein was about three years old. All she remembers of this is that her brother's tutor once, when she was allowed to sit with her brothers at their lessons, described a tiger's snarl and that that pleased and terrified her. Also that in a picture-book that one of her brothers used to show her there was a story of the wanderings of Ulysses who when sitting sat on bent-wood dining room chairs. Also she remembers that they used to play in the public gardens and that often the old Kaiser Francis Joseph used to stroll through the gardens and sometimes a band played the austrian national hymn which she liked. She believed for many years that Kaiser was the real name of Francis Joseph and she never could come to accept the name as belonging to anybody else.

They lived in Vienna for three years, the father having in the meanwhile gone back to America on business and then they moved to Paris. Here Gertrude Stein has more lively memories. She remembers a little school where she and her elder sister stayed and where there was a little girl in the corner of the school yard and the other little girls told her not to go near her, she scratched. She also remembers the bowl of soup with french bread for breakfast and she also remembers that they had mutton and spinach for lunch and as she was very fond of spinach and not fond of mutton she used to trade mutton for spinach with the little girl opposite. She also remembers all of her three older brothers coming to see them at the school and coming on horse-back. She also remembers a black cat jumping from the ceiling of their house at Passy and scaring her mother and some unknown person rescuing her.

The family remained in Paris a year and then they came back to America. Gertrude Stein's elder brother charmingly describes the last days when he and his mother went shopping and bought everything that pleased their fancy, seal skin coats and caps and muffs for the whole family from the mother to the small sister Gertrude Stein, gloves dozens of gloves, wonderful hats, riding costumes, and finally ending up with a microscope and a whole set of the famous french history of zoology. Then they sailed for America.

This visit to Paris made a very great impression upon Gertrude Stein. When in the beginning of the war, she and I having been in England and there having been caught by the outbreak of the war and so not returning until October, were back in Paris, the first day we went out Gertrude Stein said, it is strange, Paris is so different but so familiar. And then reflectively, I see what it is, there is nobody here but the french (there were no soldiers or allies there yet), you can see the little children in their black aprons, you can see the streets because there is nobody on them, it is just like my memory of Paris when I was three years old. The pavements smell like they used (horses had come back into use), the smell of french streets and french public gardens that I remember so well.

They went back to America and in New York, the New York family tried to reconcile Gertrude Stein's mother to her sister-in-law but she was obdurate.

This story reminds me of Miss Etta Cone, a distant connection of Gertrude Stein, who typed Three Lives. When I first met her in Florence she confided to me that she could forgive but never forget. I added that as for myself I could forget but not forgive. Gertrude Stein's mother in this case was evidently unable to do either.

The family went west to California after a short stay in Baltimore at the home of her grandfather, the religious old man she describes in The Making of Americans, who lived in an old house in Baltimore with a large number of those cheerful pleasant little people, her uncles and her aunts.

Gertrude Stein has never ceased to be thankful to her mother for neither forgetting or forgiving. Imagine, she had said to me, if my mother had forgiven her sister-in-law and my father had gone into business with my uncle and we had lived and been brought up in New York, imagine, she says, how horrible. We would have been rich instead of being reasonably poor but imagine how horrible to have been brought up in New York.

I as a californian can very thoroughly sympathise.

And so they took the train to California. The only thing Gertrude Stein remembers of this trip was that she and her sister had beautiful big austrian red felt hats trimmed each with a beautiful ostrich feather and at some stage of the trip her sister leaning out of the window had her hat blown off. Her father rang the emergency bell, stopped the train, got the hat to the awe and astonishment of the passengers and the conductor. The only other thing she remembers is that they had a wonderful hamper of food given them by the aunts in Baltimore and that in it was a marvelous turkey. And that later as the food in it diminished it was renewed all along the road whenever they stopped and that that was always exciting. And also that somewhere in the desert they saw some red indians and that somewhere else in the desert they were given some very funny tasting peaches to eat.

When they arrived in California they went to an orange grove but she does not remember any oranges but remembers filling up her father's cigar boxes with little limes which were very wonderful.

They came by slow stages to San Francisco and settled down in Oak-

land. She remembers there the eucalyptus trees seeming to her so tall
and thin and savage and the animal life very wild. But all this and much
more, all the physical life of these days, she has described in the life of
the Hersland family in her Making of Americans. The important thing
to tell about now is her education.

Her father having taken his children to Europe so that they might
have the benefit of a european education now insisted that they should
forget their french and german so that their american english would be
pure. Gertrude Stein had prattled in german and then in french but she
had never read until she read english. As she says eyes to her were more
important than ears and it happened then as always that english was her
only language.

Her bookish life commenced at this time. She read anything that was
printed that came her way and a great deal came her way. In the house
were a few stray novels, a few travel books, her mother's well bound gift
books Wordsworth Scott and other poets, Bunyan's Pilgrim's Progress a
set of Shakespeare with notes, Burns, Congressional Records encyclo-
pedias etcetera. She read them all and many times. She and her brothers began to acquire other books. There was also the local free library and
later in San Francisco there were the mercantile and mechanics libraries
with their excellent sets of eighteenth century and nineteenth century authors. From her eighth year when she absorbed Shakespeare to her fifteenth year when she read Clarissa Harlowe, Fielding, Smollett etcetera
and used to worry lest in a few years more she would have read everything
and there would be nothing unread to read, she lived continuously with
the english language. She read a tremendous amount of history, she
often laughs and says she is one of the few people of her generation that
has read every line of Carlyle's Frederick the Great and Lecky's Constitutional History of England besides Charles Grandison and Wordsworth's
longer poems. In fact she was as she still is always reading. She reads anything and everything and even now hates to be disturbed and above all
however often she has read a book and however foolish the book may be
no one must make fun of it or tell her how it goes on. It is still as it always
was real to her.

The theatre she has always cared for less. She says it goes too fast, the
mixture of eye and ear bothers her and her emotion never keeps pace.
Music she only cared for during her adolescence. She finds it difficult to
listen to it, it does not hold her attention. All of which of course may
seem strange because it has been so often said that the appeal of her
work is to the ear and to the subconscious. Actually it is her eyes and
mind that are active and important and concerned in choosing.

Life in California came to its end when Gertrude Stein was about seventeen years old. The last few years had been lonesome ones and had

been passed in an agony of adolescence. After the death of first her mother and then her father she and her sister and one brother left California for the East. They came to Baltimore and stayed with her mother's people. There she began to lose her lonesomeness. She has often described to me how strange it was to her coming from the rather desperate inner life that she had been living for the last few years to the cheerful life of all her aunts and uncles. When later she went to Radcliffe she described this experience in the first thing she ever wrote. Not quite the first thing she ever wrote. She remembers having written twice before. Once when she was about eight and she tried to write a Shakespearean drama in which she got as far as a stage direction, the courtiers making witty remarks. And then as she could not think of any witty remarks gave it up.

The only other effort she can remember must have been at about the same age. They asked the children in the public schools to write a description. Her recollection is that she described a sunset with the sun going into a cave of clouds. Anyway it was one of the half dozen in the school chosen to be copied out on beautiful parchment paper. After she had tried to copy it twice and the writing became worse and worse she was reduced to letting some one else copy it for her. This, her teacher considered a disgrace. She does not remember that she herself did.

As a matter of fact her handwriting has always been illegible and I am very often able to read it when she is not.

She has never been able or had any desire to indulge in any of the arts. She never knows how a thing is going to look until it is done, in arranging a room, a garden, clothes or anything else. She cannot draw anything. She feels no relation between the object and the piece of paper. When at the medical school, she was supposed to draw anatomical things she never found out in sketching how a thing was made concave or convex. She remembers when she was very small she was to learn to draw and was sent to a class. The children were told to take a cup and saucer at home and draw them and the best drawing would have as its reward a stamped leather medal and the next week the same medal would again be given for the best drawing. Gertrude Stein went home, told her brothers and they put a pretty cup and saucer before her and each one explained to her how to draw it. Nothing happened. Finally one of them drew it for her. She took it to the class and won the leather medal. And on the way home in playing some game she lost the leather medal. That was the end of the drawing class.

She says it is a good thing to have no sense of how it is done in the things that amuse you. You should have one absorbing occupation and as for the other things in life for full enjoyment you should only contemplate results. In this way you are bound to feel more about it than those who know a little of how it is done.

She is passionately addicted to what the french call métier and she contends that one can only have one métier as one can only have one language. Her métier is writing and her language is english.

Observation and construction make imagination, that is granting the possession of imagination, is what she has taught many young writers. Once when Hemingway wrote in one of his stories that Gertrude Stein always knew what was good in a Cézanne, she looked at him and said, Hemingway, remarks are not literature.

The young often when they have learnt all they can learn accuse her of an inordinate pride. She says yes of course. She realizes that in english literature in her time she is the only one. She has always known it and now she says it.

She understands very well the basis of creation and therefore her advice and criticism is invaluable to all her friends. How often have I heard Picasso say to her when she has said something about a picture of his and then illustrated by something she was trying to do, racontez-moi cela. In other words tell me about it. These two even to-day have long solitary conversations. They sit in two little low chairs up in his apartment studio, knee to knee and Picasso says, expliquez-moi cela. And they explain to each other. They talk about everything, about pictures, about dogs, about death, about unhappiness. Because Picasso is a spaniard and life is tragic and bitter and unhappy. Gertrude Stein often comes down to me and says, Pablo has been persuading me that I am as unhappy as he is. He insists that I am and with as much cause. But are you, I ask. Well I don't think I look it, do I, and she laughs. He says, she says, that I don't look it because I have more courage, but I don't think I am, she says, no I don't think I am.

And so Gertrude Stein having been in Baltimore for a winter and having become more humanised and less adolescent and less lonesome went to Radcliffe. There she had a very good time.

She was one of a group of Harvard men and Radcliffe women and they all lived very closely and very interestingly together. One of them, a young philosopher and mathematician who was doing research work in psychology left a definite mark on her life. She and he together worked out a series of experiments in automatic writing under the direction of Münsterberg. The result of her own experiments, which Gertrude Stein wrote down and which was printed in the Harvard Psychological Review was the first writing of hers ever to be printed. It is very interesting to read because the method of writing to be afterwards developed in Three Lives and Making of Americans already shows itself.

The important person in Gertrude Stein's Radcliffe life was William James. She enjoyed her life and herself. She was the secretary of the philosophical club and amused herself with all sorts of people. She liked making sport of question asking and she liked equally answering them. She liked it all. But the really lasting impression of her Radcliffe life came through William James.

It is rather strange that she was not then at all interested in the work of Henry James for whom she now has a very great admiration and whom she considers quite definitely as her forerunner, he being the only nineteenth century writer who being an american felt the method of the twentieth century. Gertrude Stein always speaks of America as being now the oldest country in the world because by the methods of the civil war and the commercial conceptions that followed it America created the twentieth century, and since all the other countries are now either living or commencing to be living a twentieth century of life, America having begun the creation of the twentieth century in the sixties of the nineteenth century is now the oldest country in the world.

In the same way she contends that Henry James was the first person in literature to find the way to the literary methods of the twentieth century. But oddly enough in all of her formative period she did not read him and was not interested in him. But as she often says one is always naturally antagonistic to one's parents and sympathetic to one's grandparents. The parents are too close, they hamper you, one must be alone. So perhaps that is the reason why only very lately Gertrude Stein reads Henry James.

William James delighted her. His personality and his teaching and his way of amusing himself with himself and his students all pleased her. Keep your mind open, he used to say, and when some one objected, but Professor James, this that I say, is true. Yes, said James, it is abjectly true.

Gertrude Stein never had subconscious reactions, nor was she a successful subject for automatic writing. One of the students in the psychological seminar of which Gertrude Stein, although an undergraduate was at William James' particular request a member, was carrying on a series of experiments on suggestions to the subconscious. When he read his paper upon the result of his experiments, he began by explaining that one of the subjects gave absolutely no results and as this much lowered the average and made the conclusion of his experiments false he wished to be allowed to cut this record out. Whose record is it, said James. Miss Stein's, said the student. Ah, said James, if Miss Stein gave no response I should say that it was as normal not to give a response as to give one and decidedly the result must not be cut out.

It was a very lovely spring day, Gertrude Stein had been going to the opera every night and going also to the opera in the afternoon and had been otherwise engrossed and it was the period of the final examinations, and there was the examination in William James' course. She sat down with the examination paper before her and she just could not. Dear Professor James, she wrote at the top of her paper. I am so sorry but really I do not feel a bit like an examination paper in philosophy to-day, and left.

The next day she had a postal card from William James saying, Dear Miss Stein, I understand perfectly how you feel I often feel like that myself. And underneath it he gave her work the highest mark in his course.

When Gertrude Stein was finishing her last year at Radcliffe, William James one day asked her what she was going to do. She said she had no idea. Well, he said, it should be either philosophy or psychology. Now for philosophy you have to have higher mathematics and I don't gather that that has ever interested you. Now for psychology you must have a medical education, a medical education opens all doors, as Oliver Wendell Holmes told me and as I tell you. Gertrude Stein had been interested in both biology and chemistry and so medical school presented no difficulties.

There were no difficulties except that Gertrude Stein had never passed more than half of her entrance examinations for Radcliffe, having never intended to take a degree. However with considerable struggle and enough tutoring that was accomplished and Gertrude Stein entered Johns Hopkins Medical School.

Some years after when Gertrude Stein and her brother were just beginning knowing Matisse and Picasso, William James came to Paris and they met. She went to see him at his hotel. He was enormously interested in what she was doing, interested in her writing and in the pictures she told him about. He went with her to her house to see them. He looked and gasped, I told you, he said, I always told you that you should keep your mind open.

Only about two years ago a very strange thing happened. Gertrude Stein received a letter from a man in Boston. It was evident from the letter head that he was one of a firm of lawyers. He said in his letter that he had not long ago in reading in the Harvard library found that the library of William James had been given as a gift to the Harvard library. Among these books was the copy of Three Lives that Gertrude Stein had dedicated and sent to James. Also on the margins of the book were notes that William James had evidently made when reading the book. The man then went on to say that very likely Gertrude Stein would be very interested in these notes and he proposed, if she wished, to copy them out for her as he had appropriated the book, in other words taken it and considered it as his. We were very puzzled what to do about it. Finally a note was written saying that Gertrude Stein would like to have a copy of William James' notes. In answer came a manuscript the man himself had written and of which he wished Gertrude Stein to give him an opinion. Not knowing what to do about it all, Gertrude Stein did nothing.

After having passed her entrance examinations she settled down in

Baltimore and went to the medical school. She had a servant named Lena and it is her story that Gertrude Stein afterwards wrote as the first story of the Three Lives.

The first two years of the medical school were alright. They were purely laboratory work and Gertrude Stein under Llewelys Barker immediately betook herself to research work. She began a study of all the brain tracts, the beginning of a comparative study. All this was later embodied in Llewelys Barker's book. She delighted in Doctor Mall, professor of anatomy, who directed her work. She always quotes his answer to any student excusing him or herself for anything. He would look reflective and say, yes that is just like our cook. There is always a reason. She never brings the food to the table hot. In summer of course she can't because it is too hot, in winter of course she can't because it is too cold, yes there is always a reason. Doctor Mall believed in everybody developing their own technique. He also remarked, nobody teaches anybody anything, at first every student's scalpel is dull and then later every student's scalpel is sharp, and nobody has taught anybody anything.

These first two years at the medical school Gertrude Stein liked well enough. She always liked knowing a lot of people and being mixed up in a lot of stories and she was not awfully interested but she was not too bored with what she was doing and besides she had quantities of pleasant relatives in Baltimore and she liked it. The last two years at the medical school she was bored, frankly openly bored. There was a good deal of intrigue and struggle among the students, that she liked, but the practice and theory of medicine did not interest her at all. It was fairly well known among all her teachers that she was bored, but as her first two years of scientific work had given her a reputation, everybody gave her the necessary credits and the end of her last year was approaching. It was then that she had to take her turn in the delivering of babies and it was at that time that she noticed the negroes and the places that she afterwards used in the second of the Three Lives stories, Melanctha Herbert, the story that was the beginning of her revolutionary work.

As she always says of herself, she has a great deal of inertia and once started keeps going until she starts somewhere else.

As the graduation examinations drew near some of her professors were getting angry. The big men like Halstead, Osler etcetera knowing her reputation for original scientific work made the medical examinations merely a matter of form and passed her. But there were others who were not so amiable. Gertrude Stein always laughed, and this was difficult. They would ask her questions although as she said to her friends, it was foolish of them to ask her, when there were so many eager and anxious to answer. However they did question her from time to time and as she said, what could she do, she did not know the answers and they did not believe that she did not know them, they thought that she did not answer because she did not consider the professors worth answering. It was a difficult situation, as she said, it was impossible to apologise and explain to them that she was so bored she could not remember the things that of course the dullest medical student could not forget. One of the professors said that although all the big men were ready to pass her he intended that she should be given a lesson and he refused to give her a pass mark and so she was not able to take her degree. There was great excitement in the medical school. Her very close friend Marion Walker pleaded with her, she said, but Gertrude Gertrude remember the cause of women, and Gertrude Stein said, you don't know what it is to be bored.

The professor who had flunked her asked her to come to see him. She did. He said, of course Miss Stein all you have to do is to take a summer course here and in the fall naturally you will take your degree. But not at all, said Gertrude Stein, you have no idea how grateful I am to you. I have so much inertia and so little initiative that very possibly if you had not kept me from taking my degree I would have, well, not taken to the practice of medicine, but at any rate to pathological psychology and you don't know how little I like pathological psychology, and how all medicine bores me. The professor was completely taken aback and that was the end of the medical education of Gertrude Stein.

She always says she dislikes the abnormal, it is so obvious. She says the normal is so much more simply complicated and interesting.

It was only a few years ago that Marion Walker, Gertrude Stein's old friend, came to see her at Bilignin where we spend the summer. She and Gertrude Stein had not met since those old days nor had they corresponded but they were as fond of each other and disagreed as violently about the cause of women as they did then. Not, as Gertrude Stein explained to Marion Walker, that she at all minds the cause of women or any other cause but it does not happen to be her business.

During these years at Radcliffe and Johns Hopkins she often spent the summers in Europe. The last couple of years her brother had been settled in Florence and now that everything medical was over she joined him there and later they settled down in London for the winter.

They settled in lodgings in London and were not uncomfortable. They knew a number of people through the Berensons, Bertrand Russell, the Zangwills, then there was Willard (Josiah Flynt) who wrote Tramping With Tramps, and who knew all about London pubs, but Gertrude Stein was not very much amused. She began spending all her days in the British Museum reading the Elizabethans. She returned to her early love of Shakespeare and the Elizabethans, and became absorbed in Elizabethan prose and particularly in the prose of Greene. She had little notebooks full of phrases that pleased her as they had pleased her when she was a child. The rest of the time she wandered about the London streets and found them infinitely depressing and dismal. She never really got over this memory of London and never wanted to go back there, but in nineteen hundred and twelve she went over to see John Lane, the publisher and then living a very pleasant life and visiting very gay and pleasant people she forgot the old memory and became very fond of London.

She always said that that first visit had made London just like Dickens and Dickens had always frightened her. As she says anything can frighten her and London when it was like Dickens certainly did.

There were some compensations, there was the prose of Greene and it was at this time that she discovered the novels of Anthony Trollope, for her the greatest of the Victorians. She then got together the complete collection of his work some of it difficult to get and only obtainable in Tauchnitz and it is of this collection that Robert Coates speaks when he tells about Gertrude Stein lending books to young writers. She also bought a quantity of eighteenth century memoirs among them the Creevy papers and Walpole and it is these that she loaned to Bravig Imbs when he wrote what she believes to be an admirable life of Chatterton. She reads books but she is not fussy about them, she cares about neither editions nor make-up as long as the print is not too bad and she is not even very much bothered about that. It was at this time too that, as she says, she ceased to be worried about there being in the future nothing to read, she said she felt that she would always somehow be able to find something.

But the dismalness of London and the drunken women and children and the gloom and the lonesomeness brought back all the melancholy of her adolescence and one day she said she was leaving for America and she left. She stayed in America the rest of the winter. In the meantime her brother also had left London and gone to Paris and there later she joined him. She immediately began to write. She wrote a short novel.

The funny thing about this short novel is that she completely forgot about it for many years. She remembered herself beginning a little later writing the Three Lives but this first piece of writing was completely forgotten, she had never mentioned it to me, even when I first knew her. She must have forgotten about it almost immediately. This spring just two days before our leaving for the country she was looking for some manuscript of The Making of Americans that she wanted to show Bernard Faÿ and she came across these two carefully written volumes of this completely forgotten first novel. She was very bashful and hesitant about it, did not really want to read it. Louis Bromfield was at the house that evening and she handed him the manuscript and said to him, you read it.

# HELEN KELLER
## (1880–1968)

Even before Keller, who lost her sight and hearing at the age of nineteen months, learned to communicate through the use of her typewriter and signs, she maintained a strong curiosity about the world. She would follow the scent of violets and lilies into the garden, where she would feel her way along the boxwood hedges. She would take great comfort in these flowers; after a fit of anger at her inability to speak, see, or hear, she would come and bury her face in the flowers, soothed by their tangible presence.

Keller's education into the ways of language came at a late age, seven. Her first and only teacher, Anne Sullivan, gradually awakened in her the perception that every tactile thing had a name, and it was through the names of these things that people communicated. Because of the late age at which Keller learned to name things, she possessed, clearly in her memory, an awareness of the moment when she first began to understand.

In her later life, Keller accomplished many other things, including the earning of a diploma from Radcliffe College. The traumas and pain of everyday life were not lost on her either; she felt the sorrow of losing her loved ones, the pain of failure. But Keller's life was filled with an extraordinary beauty, and her fine perceptions—as recorded in her numerous volumes of autobiography, including *The Story of My Life* (1902)—endure as a testament to human valor.

## FROM *The Story of My Life*

The most important day I remember in all my life is the one on which my teacher, Anne Mansfield Sullivan, came to me. I am filled with wonder when I consider the immeasurable contrasts between the two lives which it connects. It was the third of March, 1887, three months before I was seven years old.

On the afternoon of that eventful day, I stood on the porch, dumb, expectant. I guessed vaguely from my mother's signs and from the hurrying to and fro in the house that something unusual was about to happen, so I went to the door and waited on the steps. The afternoon sun penetrated the mass of honeysuckle that covered the porch, and fell on my upturned face. My fingers lingered almost unconsciously on the familiar leaves and blossoms which had just come forth to greet the sweet southern spring. I did not know what the future held of marvel or surprise for me. Anger and bitterness had preyed upon me continually for weeks and a deep languor had succeeded this passionate struggle.

Have you ever been at sea in a dense fog, when it seemed as if a tangible white darkness shut you in, and the great ship, tense and anxious, groped her way toward the shore with plummet and sounding-line, and you waited with beating heart for something to happen? I was like that ship before my education began, only I was without compass or sounding-line, and had no way of knowing how near the harbour was. "Light! give me light!" was the wordless cry of my soul, and the light of love shone on me in that very hour.

I felt approaching footsteps. I stretched out my hand as I supposed to my mother. Some one took it, and I was caught up and held close in the arms of her who had come to reveal all things to me, and, more than all things else, to love me.

The morning after my teacher came she led me into her room and gave me a doll. The little blind children at the Perkins Institution had sent it and Laura Bridgman had dressed it; but I did not know this until afterward. When I had played with it a little while, Miss Sullivan slowly spelled into my hand the word "d-o-l-l." I was at once interested in this finger play and tried to imitate it. When I finally succeeded in making the letters correctly I was flushed with childish pleasure and pride. Running downstairs to my mother I held up my hand and made the letters for doll. I did not know that I was spelling a word or even that words existed; I was simply making my fingers go in monkey-like imitation. In the days that followed I learned to spell in this uncomprehending way a great many words, among them *pin, hat, cup* and a few verbs like *sit, stand* and *walk.* But my teacher had been with me several weeks before I understood that everything has a name.

One day, while I was playing with my new doll, Miss Sullivan put my big rag doll into my lap also, spelled "d-o-l-l" and tried to make me understand that "d-o-l-l" applied to both. Earlier in the day we had had a tussle over the words "m-u-g" and "w-a-t-e-r." Miss Sullivan had tried to impress it upon me that "m-u-g" is *mug* and that "w-a-t-e-r" is *water,* but I persisted in confounding the two. In despair she had dropped the subject for the time, only to renew it at the first opportunity. I became impatient at her repeated attempts and, seizing the new doll, I dashed it upon the floor. I was keenly delighted when I felt the fragments of the broken doll at my feet. Neither sorrow nor regret followed my passionate outburst. I had not loved the doll. In the still, dark world in which I lived there was no strong sentiment or tenderness. I felt my teacher sweep the fragments to one side of the hearth, and I had a sense of satisfaction that the cause of my discomfort was removed. She brought me my hat, and I knew I was going out into the warm sunshine. This thought, if a word-less sensation may be called a thought, made me hop and skip with plea-sure.

We walked down the path to the well-house, attracted by the fragrance of the honeysuckle with which it was covered. Some one was drawing water and my teacher placed my hand under the spout. As the cool stream gushed over one hand she spelled into the other the word *water*, first slowly, then rapidly. I stood still, my whole attention fixed upon the motions of her fingers. Suddenly I felt a misty consciousness as of some-thing forgotten—a thrill of returning thought; and somehow the mystery of language was revealed to me. I knew then that "w-a-t-e-r" meant the wonderful cool something that was flowing over my hand. That living word awakened my soul, gave it light, hope, joy, set it free! There were barriers still, it is true, but barriers that could in time be swept away.

I left the well-house eager to learn. Everything had a name, and each name gave birth to a new thought. As we returned to the house every ob-ject which I touched seemed to quiver with life. That was because I saw everything with the strange, new sight that had come to me. On enter-ing the door I remembered the doll I had broken. I felt my way to the hearth and picked up the pieces. I tried vainly to put them together. Then my eyes filled with tears; for I realized what I had done, and for the first time I felt repentance and sorrow.

I learned a great many new words that day. I do not remember what they all were; but I do know that *mother, father, sister, teacher* were among them—words that were to make the world blossom for me, "like Aaron's rod, with flowers." It would have been difficult to find a happier child than I was as I lay in my crib at the close of that eventful day and lived over the joys it had brought me, and for the first time longed for a new day to come.

*          *          *

I recall many incidents of the summer of 1887 that followed my soul's sudden awakening. I did nothing but explore with my hands and learn the name of every object that I touched; and the more I handled things and learned their names and uses, the more joyous and confident grew my sense of kinship with the rest of the world.

When the time of daisies and buttercups came Miss Sullivan took me by the hand across the fields, where men were preparing the earth for the seed, to the banks of the Tennessee River, and there, sitting on the warm grass, I had my first lessons in the beneficence of nature. I learned how the sun and the rain make to grow out of the ground every tree that is pleasant to the sight and good for food, how birds build their nests and live and thrive from land to land, how the squirrel, the deer, the lion and every other creature finds food and shelter. As my knowledge of things grew I felt more and more the delight of the world I was in. Long before I learned to do a sum in arithmetic or describe the shape of the earth, Miss Sullivan had taught me to find beauty in the fragrant woods, in every blade of grass, and in the curves and dimples of my baby sister's hand. She linked my earliest thoughts with nature, and made me feel that "birds and flowers and I were happy peers."

But about this time I had an experience which taught me that nature is not always kind. One day my teacher and I were returning from a long ramble. The morning had been fine, but it was growing warm and sultry when at last we turned our faces homeward. Two or three times we stopped to rest under a tree by the wayside. Our last halt was under a wild cherry tree a short distance from the house. The shade was grateful, and the tree was so easy to climb that with my teacher's assistance I was able to scramble to a seat in the branches. It was so cool up in the tree that Miss Sullivan proposed that we have our luncheon there. I promised to keep still while she went to the house to fetch it.

Suddenly a change passed over the tree. All the sun's warmth left the air. I knew the sky was black, because all the heat, which meant light to me, had died out of the atmosphere. A strange odour came from the earth. I knew it, it was the odour that always precedes a thunderstorm, and a nameless fear clutched at my heart. I felt absolutely alone, cut off from my friends and the firm earth. The immense, the unknown, enfolded me. I remained still and expectant; a chilling terror crept over me. I longed for my teacher's return; but above all things I wanted to get down from that tree.

There was a moment of sinister silence, then a multitudinous stirring of the leaves. A shiver ran through the tree, and the wind sent forth a blast that would have knocked me off had I not clung to the branch with might and main. The tree swayed and strained. The small twigs snapped and fell about me in showers. A wild impulse to jump seized me, but terror held me fast. I crouched down in the fork of the tree. The branches lashed about me. I felt the intermittent jarring that came now and then, as if something heavy had fallen and the shock had traveled up till it reached the limb I sat on. It worked my suspense up to the highest point, and just as I was thinking the tree and I should fall together, my teacher seized my hand and helped me down. I clung to her, trembling with joy to feel the earth under my feet once more. I had learned a new lesson — that nature "wages open war against her children, and under softest touch hides treacherous claws."

After this experience it was a long time before I climbed another tree. The mere thought filled me with terror. It was the sweet allurement of the mimosa tree in full bloom that finally overcame my fears. One beautiful spring morning when I was alone in the summer-house, reading, I became aware of a wonderful subtle fragrance in the air. I started up and instinctively stretched out my hands. It seemed as if the spirit of spring had passed through the summer-house. "What is it?" I asked, and the next minute I recognized the odour of the mimosa blossoms. I felt my way to the end of the garden, knowing that the mimosa tree was near the fence, at the turn of the path. Yes, there it was, all quivering in the warm sunshine, its blossom-laden branches almost touching the long grass. Was there ever anything so exquisitely beautiful in the world before! Its delicate blossoms shrank from the slightest earthly touch; it seemed as if a tree of paradise had been transplanted to earth. I made my way through a shower of petals to the great trunk and for one minute stood irresolute; then, putting my foot in the broad space between the forked branches, I pulled myself up into the tree. I had some difficulty in holding on, for the branches were very large and the bark hurt my hands. But I had a delicious sense that I was doing something unusual and wonderful, so I kept on climbing higher and higher, until I reached a little seat which somebody had built there so long ago that it had grown part of the tree itself. I sat there for a long, long time, feeling like a fairy on a rosy cloud. After that I spent many happy hours in my tree of paradise, thinking fair thoughts and dreaming bright dreams.

*     *     *

I had now the key to all language, and I was eager to learn to use it. Children who hear acquire language without any particular effort; the words that fall from others' lips they catch on the wing, as it were, delightedly, while the little deaf child must trap them by a slow and often painful process. But whatever the process, the result is wonderful. Gradually from naming an object we advance step by step until we have traversed the vast distance between our first stammered syllable and the sweep of thought in a line of Shakespeare.

At first, when my teacher told me about a new thing I asked very few questions. My ideas were vague, and my vocabulary was inadequate; but as my knowledge of things grew, and I learned more and more words, my field of inquiry broadened, and I would return again and again to the same subject, eager for further information. Sometimes a new word revived an image that some earlier experience had engraved on my brain.

I remember the morning that I first asked the meaning of the word, "love." This was before I knew many words. I had found a few early violets in the garden and brought them to my teacher. She tried to kiss me; but at that time I did not like to have any one kiss me except my mother. Miss Sullivan put her arm gently round me and spelled into my hand, "I love Helen."

"What is love?" I asked.

She drew me closer to her and said, "It is here," pointing to my heart, whose beats I was conscious of for the first time. Her words puzzled me very much because I did not then understand anything unless I touched it.

I smelt the violets in her hand and asked, half in words, half in signs, a question which meant, "Is love the sweetness of flowers?"

"No," said my teacher.

Again I thought. The warm sun was shining on us.

"Is this not love?" I asked, pointing in the direction from which the heat came, "Is this not love?"

It seemed to me that there could be nothing more beautiful than the sun, whose warmth makes all things grow. But Miss Sullivan shook her head, and I was greatly puzzled and disappointed. I thought it strange that my teacher could not show me love.

A day or two afterward I was stringing beads of different sizes in symmetrical groups—two large beads, three small ones, and so on. I had made many mistakes, and Miss Sullivan had pointed them out again and again with gentle patience. Finally I noticed a very obvious error in the sequence and for an instant I concentrated my attention on the lesson and tried to think how I should have arranged the beads. Miss Sullivan touched my forehead and spelled with decided emphasis, "Think."

In a flash I knew that the word was the name of the process that was going on in my head. This was my first conscious perception of an abstract idea.

For a long time I was still—I was not thinking of the beads in my lap, but trying to find a meaning for "love" in the light of this new idea. The sun had been under a cloud all day, and there had been brief showers; but suddenly the sun broke forth in all its southern splendour.

Again I asked my teacher, "Is this not love?"

"Love is something like the clouds that were in the sky before the sun came out," she replied. Then in simpler words than these, which at that time I could not have understood, she explained: "You cannot touch the clouds, you know; but you feel the rain and know how glad the flowers and the thirsty earth are to have it after a hot day. You cannot touch love either; but you feel the sweetness that it pours into everything. Without love you would not be happy or want to play."

The beautiful truth burst upon my mind—I felt that there were invisible lines stretched between my spirit and the spirits of others.

From the beginning of my education Miss Sullivan made it a practice to speak to me as she would speak to any hearing child; the only difference was that she spelled the sentences into my hand instead of speaking them. If I did not know the words and idioms necessary to express my thoughts she supplied them, even suggesting conversation when I was unable to keep up my end of the dialogue.

This process was continued for several years; for the deaf child does not learn in a month, or even in two or three years, the numberless idioms and expressions used in the simplest daily intercourse. The little hearing child learns these from constant repetition and imitation. The conversation he hears in his home stimulates his mind and suggests topics and calls forth the spontaneous expression of his own thoughts. This natural exchange of ideas is denied to the deaf child. My teacher, realizing this, determined to supply the kinds of stimulus I lacked. This she did by repeating to me as far as possible, verbatim, what she heard, and by showing me how I could take part in the conversation. But it was a long time before I ventured to take the initiative, and still longer before I could find something appropriate to say at the right time.

The deaf and the blind find it very difficult to acquire the amenities of conversation. How much more this difficulty must be augmented in the case of those who are both deaf and blind! They cannot distinguish the tone of the voice or, without assistance, go up and down the gamut of tones that give significance to words; nor can they watch the expression of the speaker's face, and a look is often the very soul of what one says.

*       *       *

The next important step in my education was learning to read.

As soon as I could spell a few words my teacher gave me slips of cardboard on which were printed words in raised letters. I quickly learned that each printed word stood for an object, an act, or a quality. I had a frame in which I could arrange the words in little sentences; but before I ever put sentences in the frame I used to make them in objects. I found the slips of paper which represented, for example, "doll," "is," "on," "bed" and placed each name on its object; then I put my doll on the bed with the words *is, on, bed* arranged beside the doll, thus making a sentence of the words, and at the same time carrying out the idea of the sentence with the things themselves.

One day, Miss Sullivan tells me, I pinned the word *girl* on my pinafore and stood in the wardrobe. On the shelf I arranged the words, *is, in, wardrobe*. Nothing delighted me so much as this game. My teacher and I played it for hours at a time. Often everything in the room was arranged in object sentences.

From the printed slip it was but a step to the printed book. I took my "Reader for Beginners" and hunted for the words I knew; when I found them my joy was like that of a game of hide-and-seek. Thus I began to read. Of the time when I began to read connected stories I shall speak later.

For a long time I had no regular lessons. Even when I studied most earnestly it seemed more like play than work. Everything Miss Sullivan taught me she illustrated by a beautiful story or a poem. Whenever anything delighted or interested me she talked it over with me just as if she were a little girl herself. What many children think of with dread, as a painful plodding through grammar, hard sums and harder definitions, is to-day one of my most precious memories.

I cannot explain the peculiar sympathy Miss Sullivan had with my pleasures and desires. Perhaps it was the result of long association with the blind. Added to this she had a wonderful faculty for description. She went quickly over uninteresting details, and never nagged me with questions to see if I remembered the day-before-yesterday's lesson. She introduced dry technicalities of science little by little, making every subject so real that I could not help remembering what she taught.

We read and studied out of doors, preferring the sunlit woods to the house. All my early lessons have in them the breath of the woods—the fine, resinous odour of pine needles, blended with the perfume of wild grapes. Seated in the gracious shade of a wild tulip tree, I learned to think that everything has a lesson and a suggestion. "The loveliness of things taught me all their use." Indeed, everything that could hum, or buzz, or sing, or bloom, had a part in my education—noisy-throated frogs, katydids and crickets held in my hand until, forgetting their embarrassment, they trilled their reedy note, little downy chickens and wildflowers, the dogwood blossoms, meadow-violets and budding fruit trees. I felt the bursting cotton-bolls and fingered their soft fiber and fuzzy seeds; I felt the low soughing of the wind through the cornstalks, the silky rustling of the long leaves, and the indignant snort of my pony, as we caught him in the pasture and put the bit in his mouth—ah me! how well I remember the spicy, clovery smell of his breath!

Sometimes I rose at dawn and stole into the garden while the heavy dew lay on the grass and flowers. Few know what joy it is to feel the roses pressing softly into the hand, or the beautiful motion of the lilies as they sway in the morning breeze. Sometimes I caught an insect in the flower I was plucking, and I felt the faint noise of a pair of wings rubbed together in a sudden terror, as the little creature became aware of a pressure from without.

Another favourite haunt of mine was the orchard, where the fruit ripened early in July. The large, downy peaches would reach themselves into my hand, and as the joyous breezes flew about the trees the apples tumbled at my feet. Oh, the delight with which I gathered up the fruit in my pinafore, pressed my face against the smooth cheeks of the apples, still warm from the sun, and skipped back to the house!

Our favourite walk was to Keller's Landing, an old tumble-down lumber-wharf on the Tennessee River, used during the Civil War to land soldiers. There we spent many happy hours and played at learning geography. I built dams of pebbles, made islands and lakes, and dug river-beds, all for fun, and never dreamed that I was learning a lesson. I listened with increasing wonder to Miss Sullivan's descriptions of the great round world with its burning mountains, buried cities, moving rivers of ice, and many other things as strange. She made raised maps in clay, so that I could feel the mountain ridges and valleys, and follow with my fingers the devious course of rivers. I liked this, too; but the division of the earth into zones and poles confused and teased my mind. The illustrative strings and the orange stick representing the poles seemed so real that even to this day the mere mention of temperate zone suggests a series of twine circles; and I believe that if any one should set about it he could convince me that white bears actually climb the North Pole.

Arithmetic seems to have been the only study I did not like. From the first I was not interested in the science of numbers. Miss Sullivan tried to teach me to count by stringing beads in groups, and by arranging kindergarten straws I learned to add and subtract. I never had patience to arrange more than five or six groups at a time. When I had accomplished this my conscience was at rest for the day, and I went out quickly to find my playmates.

In this same leisurely manner I studied zoölogy and botany.

Once a gentleman, whose name I have forgotten, sent me a collection of fossils — tiny mollusk shells beautifully marked, and bits of sandstone with the print of birds' claws, and a lovely fern in bas-relief. These were the keys which unlocked the treasures of the antediluvian world for me. With trembling fingers I listened to Miss Sullivan's descriptions of the terrible beasts, with uncouth, unpronounceable names, which once went tramping through the primeval forests, tearing down the branches of gigantic trees for food, and died in the dismal swamps of an unknown age. For a long time these strange creatures haunted my dreams, and this gloomy period formed a somber background to the joyous Now, filled with sunshine and roses and echoing with the gentle beat of my pony's hoof.

Another time a beautiful shell was given me, and with a child's surprise and delight I learned how a tiny mollusk had built the lustrous coil for his dwelling place, and how on still nights, when there is no breeze stirring the waves, the Nautilus sails on the blue waters of the Indian Ocean in his "ship of pearl." After I had learned a great many interesting things about the life and habits of the children of the sea—how in the midst of dashing waves the little polyps build the beautiful coral isles of the Pacific, and the foraminifera have made the chalk-hills of many a land— my teacher read me "The Chambered Nautilus," and showed me that the shell-building process of the mollusks is symbolical of the development of the mind. Just as the wonder-working mantle of the Nautilus changes the material it absorbs from the water and makes it a part of itself, so the bits of knowledge one gathers undergo a similar change and become pearls of thought.

Again, it was the growth of a plant that furnished the text for a lesson. We bought a lily and set it in a sunny window. Very soon the green, pointed buds showed signs of opening. The slender, fingerlike leaves on the outside opened slowly, reluctant, I thought, to reveal the loveliness they hid; once having made a start, however, the opening process went on rapidly, but in order and systematically. There was always one bud larger and more beautiful than the rest, which pushed her outer covering back with more pomp, as if the beauty in soft, silky robes knew that she was the lily-queen by right divine, while her more timid sisters doffed their green hoods shyly, until the whole plant was one nodding bough of loveliness and fragrance.

Once there were eleven tadpoles in a glass globe set in a window full of plants. I remember the eagerness with which I made discoveries about them. It was great fun to plunge my hand into the bowl and feel the tadpoles frisk about, and to let them slip and slide between my fingers. One day a more ambitious fellow leaped beyond the edge of the bowl and fell on the floor, where I found him to all appearance more dead than alive. The only sign of life was a slight wriggling of his tail. But no sooner had he returned to his element than he darted to the bottom, swimming round and round in joyous activity. He had made his leap, he had seen the great world, and was content to stay in his pretty glass house under the big fuchsia tree until he attained the dignity of froghood. Then he went to live in the leafy pool at the end of the garden, where he made the summer nights musical with his quaint love-song.

Thus I learned from life itself. At the beginning I was only a little mass of possibilities. It was my teacher who unfolded and developed them. When she came, everything about me breathed of love and joy and was full of meaning. She has never since let pass an opportunity to point out the beauty that is in everything, nor has she ceased trying in thought and action and example to make my life sweet and useful.

It was my teacher's genius, her quick sympathy, her loving tact which made the first years of my education so beautiful. It was because she seized the right moment to impart knowledge that made it so pleasant and acceptable to me. She realized that a child's mind is like a shallow brook which ripples and dances merrily over the stony course of its education and reflects here a flower, there a bush, yonder a fleecy cloud; and she attempted to guide my mind on its way, knowing that like a brook it should be fed by mountain streams and hidden springs, until it broadened out into a deep river, capable of reflecting in its placid surface, billowy hills, the luminous shadows of trees and the blue heavens, as well as the sweet face of a little flower.

Any teacher can take a child to the classroom, but not every teacher can make him learn. He will not work joyously unless he feels that liberty is his, whether he is busy or at rest; he must feel the flush of victory and the heart-sinking of disappointment before he takes with a will the tasks distasteful to him and resolves to dance his way bravely through a dull routine of textbooks.

My teacher is so near to me that I scarcely think of myself apart from her. How much of my delight in all beautiful things is innate, and how much is due to her influence, I can never tell. I feel that her being is inseparable from my own, and that the footsteps of my life are in hers. All the best of me belongs to her—there is not a talent, or an aspiration or a joy in me that has not been awakened by her loving touch.

# MARY ANTIN
## (1881–1949)

*The Promised Land* (1912) is the story of Mary Antin's flight from pogroms and ghettos in Russia to another kind of marginalization—economic destitution—in Boston's South End. Though her family did not do particularly well in the Promised Land, she herself was well educated in the public schools of Boston, and eventually got a job writing for newspapers.

Antin was only thirty at the time she wrote her autobiography, but she does not apologize for the premature nature of her story; instead, she defends her choice to write with a vitriolic voice. "I was born, I have lived, and I have been made over. Is it not time to write my life's story? I am just as much out of the way as if I were dead, for I am absolutely other than the person whose story I have to tell." Her transition from traditional Jewish culture to modernized American life is beautifully detailed, and her book is an important instance of the immigrant's tale: one of the major strains of American autobiography in the twentieth century. Like Benjamin Franklin, Antin is bent on self-invention; like Maxine Hong Kingston and others, she offers an immigration story of unusual vividness.

## FROM *The Promised Land*

### DOVER STREET

What happened next was Dover Street.

And what was Dover Street?

Ask rather, What was it not? Dover Street was my fairest garden of girlhood, a gate of paradise, a window facing on a broad avenue of life. Dover Street was a prison, a school of discipline, a battlefield of sordid strife. The air in Dover Street was heavy with evil odors of degradation, but a breath from the uppermost heavens rippled through, whispering of infinite things. In Dover Street the dragon poverty gripped me for a last fight, but I overthrew the hideous creature, and sat on his neck as on a throne. In Dover Street I was shackled with a hundred chains of disadvantage, but with one free hand I planted little seeds, right there in the mud of shame, that blossomed into the honeyed rose of widest freedom. In Dover Street there was often no loaf on the table, but the hand of some noble friend was ever in mine. The night in Dover Street was rent with the cries of wrong, but the thunders of truth crashed through the pitiful clamor and died out in prophetic silences.

Outwardly, Dover Street is a noisy thoroughfare cut through a South End slum, in every essential the same as Wheeler Street. Turn down any street in the slums, at random, and call it by whatever name you please, you will observe there the same fashions of life, death, and endurance. Every one of those streets is a rubbish heap of damaged humanity, and it will take a powerful broom and an ocean of soapsuds to clean it out.

Dover Street is intersected, near its eastern end, where we lived, by Harrison Avenue. That street is to the South End what Salem Street is to the North End. It is the heart of the South End ghetto, for the greater part of its length; although its northern end belongs to the realm of Chinatown. Its multifarious business bursts through the narrow shop doors, and overruns the basements, the sidewalk, the street itself, in pushcarts and open-air stands. Its multitudinous population bursts through the greasy tenement doors, and floods the corridors, the doorsteps, the gutters, the side streets, pushing in and out among the pushcarts, all day long and half the night besides.

Rarely as Harrison Avenue is caught asleep, even more rarely is it found clean. Nothing less than a fire or flood would cleanse this street. Even Passover cannot quite accomplish this feat. For although the tenements may be scrubbed to their remotest corners, on this one occasion, the cleansing stops at the curbstone. A great deal of the filthy rubbish accumulated in a year is pitched into the street, often through the windows; and what the ashman on his daily round does not remove is left to be trampled to powder, in which form it steals back into the houses from which it was so lately removed.

The City Fathers provide soap and water for the slums, in the form of excellent schools, kindergartens, and branch libraries. And there they stop: at the curbstone of the people's life. They cleanse and discipline the children's minds, but their bodies they pitch into the gutter. For there are no parks and almost no playgrounds in the Harrison Avenue district,— in my day there were none,—and such as there are have been wrenched from the city by public-spirited citizens who have no offices in City Hall. No wonder the ashman is not more thorough: he learns from his masters.

It is a pity to have it so, in a queen of enlightened cities like Boston. If we of the twentieth century do not believe in baseball as much as in philosophy, we have not learned the lesson of modern science, which teaches, among other things, that the body is the nursery of the soul; the instrument of our moral development; the secret chart of our devious progress from worm to man. The great achievement of recent science, of which we are so proud, has been the deciphering of the hieroglyphic of organic nature. To worship the facts and neglect the implications of the message of science is to applaud the drama without taking the moral to heart. And we certainly are not taking the moral to heart when we try to make a hero out of the boy by such foreign appliances as grammar and algebra, while utterly despising the fittest instrument for his uplifting— the boy's own body.

We had no particular reason for coming to Dover Street. It might just as well have been Applepie Alley. For my father had sold, with the goods, fixtures, and good-will of the Wheeler Street store, all his hopes of ever making a living in the grocery trade; and I doubt if he got a silver dollar the more for them. We had to live somewhere, even if we were not making a living, so we came to Dover Street, where tenements were cheap; by which I mean that rent was low. The ultimate cost of life in those tenements, in terms of human happiness, is high enough.

Our new home consisted of five small rooms up two flights of stairs, with the right of way through the dark corridors. In the "parlor" the dingy paper hung in rags and the plaster fell in chunks. One of the bedrooms was absolutely dark and air-tight. The kitchen windows looked out on a dirty court, at the back of which was the rear tenement of the estate. To us belonged, along with the five rooms and the right of way aforesaid, a block of upper space the length of a pulley line across this court, and the width of an arc described by a windy Monday's wash in its remotest wanderings.

The little front bedroom was assigned to me, with only one partner, my sister Dora. A mouse could not have led a cat much of a chase across this room; still we found space for a narrow bed, a crazy bureau, and a small table. From the window there was an unobstructed view of a lumberyard, beyond which frowned the blackened walls of a factory. The fence of the lumberyard was gay with theatre posters and illustrated advertisements of tobacco, whiskey, and patent baby foods. When the window was open, there was a constant clang and whirr of electric cars, varied by the screech of machinery, the clatter of empty wagons, or the rumble of heavy trucks.

There was nothing worse in all this than we had had before since our exile from Crescent Beach; but I did not take the same delight in the propinquity of electric cars and arc lights that I had till now. I suppose the tenement began to pall on me.

It must not be supposed that I enjoyed any degree of privacy, because I had half a room to myself. We were six in the five rooms; we were

bound to be always in each other's way. And as it was within our flat, so
it was in the house as a whole. All doors, beginning with the street door,
stood open most of the time; or if they were closed, the tenants did not
wear out their knuckles knocking for admittance. I could stand at any
time in the unswept entrance hall and tell, from an analysis of the med-
ley of sounds and smells that issued from doors ajar, what was going on
in the several flats from below up. That guttural, scolding voice, un-
remittent as the hissing of a steam pipe, is Mrs. Rasnosky. I make a guess
that she is chastising the infant Isaac for taking a second lump of sugar
in his tea. *Spam! Bam!* Yes, and she is rubbing in her objections with the
flat of her hand. That blubbering and moaning, accompanying an ele-
phantine tread, is fat Mrs. Casey, second floor, home drunk from an afternoon out, in fear of the vengeance of Mr. Casey; to propitiate whom
she is burning a pan of bacon, as the choking fumes and outrageous siz-
zling testify. I hear a feeble whining, interrupted by long silences. It is that
scabby baby on the third floor, fallen out of bed again, with nobody
home to pick him up.

To escape from these various horrors I ascend to the roof, where bacon
and babies and child-beating are not. But there I find two figures in calico wrappers, with bare red arms akimbo, a basket of wet clothes in front
of each, and only one empty clothes-line between them. I do not want
to be dragged in as a witness in a case of assault and battery, so I descend
to the street again, grateful to note, as I pass, that the third-floor baby is
still.

In front of the door I squeeze through a group of children. They are
going to play tag, and are counting to see who should be "it": —

> "My-mother-and-your-mother-went-out-to-hang-clothes;
> My-mother-gave-your-mother-a-punch-in-the-nose."

If the children's couplet does not give a vivid picture of the life, manners,
and customs of Dover Street, no description of mine can ever do so.

Frieda was married before we came to Dover Street, and went to live
in East Boston. This left me the eldest of the children at home. Whether
on this account, or because I was outgrowing my childish carelessness,
or because I began to believe, on the cumulative evidence of the Crescent Beach, Chelsea, and Wheeler Street adventures, that America, after
all, was not going to provide for my father's family, — whether for any or
all of these reasons, I began at this time to take bread-and-butter matters
more to heart, and to ponder ways and means of getting rich. My father
sought employment wherever work was going on. His health was poor;
he aged very fast. Nevertheless he offered himself for every kind of labor;
he offered himself for a boy's wages. Here he was found too weak, here

too old; here his imperfect English was in the way, here his Jewish appearance. He had a few short terms of work at this or that; I do not know the name of the form of drudgery that my father did not practise. But all told, he did not earn enough to pay the rent in full and buy a bone for the soup. The only steady source of income, for I do not know what years, was my brother's earnings from his newspapers.

Surely this was the time for me to take my sister's place in the workshop. I had had every fair chance until now: school, my time to myself, liberty to run and play and make friends. I had graduated from grammar school; I was of legal age to go to work. What was I doing, sitting at home and dreaming?

I was minding my business, of course; with all my might I was minding my business. As I understood it, my business was to go to school, to learn everything there was to know, to write poetry, become famous, and make the family rich. Surely it was not shirking to lay out such a programme for myself. I had boundless faith in my future. I was certainly going to be a great poet; I was certainly going to take care of the family.

Thus mused I, in my arrogance. And my family? They were as bad as I. My father had not lost a whit of his ambition for me. Since Graduation Day, and the school-committeeman's speech, and half a column about me in the paper, his ambition had soared even higher. He was going to keep me at school till I was prepared for college. By that time, he was sure, I would more than take care of myself. It never for a moment entered his head to doubt the wisdom or justice of this course. And my mother was just as loyal to my cause, and my brother, and my sister.

It is no wonder if I got along rapidly: I was helped, encouraged, and upheld by every one. Even the baby cheered me on. When I asked her whether she believed in higher education, she answered, without a moment's hesitation, "Ducka-ducka-da!" Against her I remember only that one day, when I read her a verse out of a most pathetic piece I was composing, she laughed right out, a most disrespectful laugh; for which I revenged myself by washing her face at the faucet, and rubbing it red on the roller towel.

It was just like me, when it was debated whether I would be best fitted for college at the High or the Latin School, to go in person to Mr. Tetlow, who was principal of both schools, and so get the most expert opinion on the subject. I never send a messenger, you may remember, where I can go myself. It was vacation time, and I had to find Mr. Tetlow at his home. Away out to the wilds of Roxbury I found my way—perhaps half an hour's ride on the electric car from Dover Street. I grew an inch taller and broader between the corner of Cedar Street and Mr. Tetlow's house, such was the charm of the clean, green suburb on a cramped waif from the slums. My faded calico dress, my rusty straw sailor hat, the color of my skin and all bespoke the waif. But never a bit daunted was I. I went up the steps to the porch, rang the bell, and asked for the great man with as much assurance as if I were a daily visitor on Cedar Street. I calmly awaited the appearance of Mr. Tetlow in the reception room, and stated my errand without trepidation.

And why not? I was a solemn little person for the moment, earnestly seeking advice on a matter of great importance. That is what Mr. Tetlow saw, to judge by the gravity with which he discussed my business with me, and the courtesy with which he showed me to the door. He saw, too, I fancy, that I was not the least bit conscious of my shabby dress; and I am sure he did not smile at my appearance, even when my back was turned.

A new life began for me when I entered the Latin School in September. Until then I had gone to school with my equals, and as a matter of course. Now it was distinctly a feat for me to keep in school, and my schoolmates were socially so far superior to me that my poverty became conspicuous. The pupils of the Latin School, from the nature of the institution, are an aristocratic set. They come from refined homes, dress well, and spend the recess hour talking about parties, beaux, and the matinée. As students they are either very quick or very hard-working; for the course of study, in the lingo of the school world, is considered "stiff." The girl with half her brain asleep, or with too many beaux, drops out by the end of the first year; or a one and only beau may be the fatal element. At the end of the course the weeding process has reduced the once numerous tribe of academic candidates to a cosey little family.

By all these tokens I should have had serious business on my hands as a pupil in the Latin School, but I did not find it hard. To make myself letter-perfect in my lessons required long hours of study, but that was my delight. To make myself at home in an alien world was also within my talents; I had been practising it day and night for the past four years. To remain unconscious of my shabby and ill-fitting clothes when the rustle of silk petticoats in the schoolroom protested against them was a matter still within my moral reach. Half a dress a year had been my allowance for many seasons; even less, for as I did not grow much I could wear my dresses as long as they lasted. And I had stood before editors, and exchanged polite calls with school-teachers, untroubled by the detestable colors and archaic design of my garments. To stand up and recite Latin declensions without trembling from hunger was something more of a feat, because I sometimes went to school with little or no breakfast; but even that required no special heroism, — at most it was a matter of self-control. I had the advantage of a poor appetite, too; I really did not need much breakfast. Or if I was hungry it would hardly show; I coughed so much that my unsteadiness was self-explained.

Everything helped, you see. My schoolmates helped. Aristocrats though they were, they did not hold themselves aloof from me. Some of the girls who came to school in carriages were especially cordial. They rated me by my scholarship, and not by my father's occupation. They teased and admired me by turns for learning the footnotes in the Latin grammar by heart; they never reproached me for my ignorance of the latest comic opera. And it was more than good breeding that made them seem unaware of the incongruity of my presence. It was a generous appreciation of what it meant for a girl from the slums to be in the Latin School, on the way to college. If our intimacy ended on the steps of the school-house, it was more my fault than theirs. Most of the girls were democratic enough to have invited me to their homes, although to some, of course, I was "impossible." But I had no time for visiting; school work and reading and family affairs occupied all the daytime, and much of the night time. I did not "go with" any of the girls, in the school-girl sense of the phrase. I admired some of them, either for good looks, or beautiful manners, or more subtle attributes; but always at a distance. I discovered something inimitable in the way the Back Bay girls carried themselves; and I should have been the first to perceive the incongruity of Commonwealth Avenue entwining arms with Dover Street. Some day, perhaps, when I should be famous and rich; but not just then. So my companions and I parted on the steps of the school-house, in mutual respect; they guiltless of snobbishness, I innocent of envy. It was a graciously American relation, and I am happy to this day to recall it.

The one exception to this rule of friendly distance was my chum, Florence Connolly. But I should hardly have said "chum." Florence and I occupied adjacent seats for three years, but we did not walk arm in arm, nor call each other nicknames, nor share our lunch, nor correspond in vacation time. Florence was quiet as a mouse, and I was reserved as an oyster; and perhaps we two had no more in common fundamentally than those two creatures in their natural state. Still, as we were both very studious, and never strayed far from our desks at recess, we practised a sort of intimacy of propinquity. Although Florence was of my social order, her father presiding over a cheap lunch room, I did not on that account feel especially drawn to her. I spent more time studying Florence than loving her, I suppose. And yet I ought to have loved her; she was such a good girl. Always perfect in her lessons, she was so modest that she recited in a noticeable tremor, and had to be told frequently to raise her voice. Florence wore her light brown hair brushed flatly back and braided in a single plait, at a time when pompadours were six inches high and braids hung in pairs. Florence had a pocket in her dress for her handkerchief, in a day when pockets were repugnant to fashion. All these things ought to have made me feel the kinship of humble circumstances, the comradeship of intellectual earnestness; but they did not.

The truth is that my relation to persons and things depended neither on social distinctions nor on intellectual or moral affinities. My attitude, at this time, was determined by my consciousness of the unique elements in my character and history. It seemed to me that I had been pursuing a single adventure since the beginning of the world. Through highways and byways, underground, overground, by land, by sea, ever the same star had guided me, I thought, ever the same purpose had divided my affairs from other men's. What that purpose was, where was the fixed horizon beyond which my star would not recede, was an absorbing mystery to me. But the current moment never puzzled me. What I chose instinctively to do I knew to be right and in accordance with my destiny. I never hesitated over great things, but answered promptly to the call of my genius. So what was it to me whether my neighbors spurned or embraced me, if my way was no man's way? Nor should any one ever reject me whom I chose to be my friend, because I would make sure of a kindred spirit by the coincidence of our guiding stars.

When, where in the harum-scarum life of Dover Street was there time or place for such self-communing? In the night, when everybody slept; on a solitary walk, as far from home as I dared to go.

I was not unhappy on Dover Street; quite the contrary. Everything of consequence was well with me. Poverty was a superficial, temporary matter; it vanished at the touch of money. Money in America was plentiful; it was only a matter of getting some of it, and I was on my way to the mint. If Dover Street was not a pleasant place to abide in, it was only a wayside house. And I was really happy, actively happy, in the exercise of my mind in Latin, mathematics, history, and the rest; the things that suffice a studious girl in the middle teens.

Still I had moments of depression, when my whole being protested against the life of the slum. I resented the familiarity of my vulgar neighbors. I felt myself defiled by the indecencies I was compelled to witness. Then it was I took to running away from home. I went out in the twilight and walked for hours, my blind feet leading me. I did not care where I went. If I lost my way, so much the better; I never wanted to see Dover Street again.

But behold, as I left the crowds behind, and the broader avenues were spanned by the open sky, my grievances melted away, and I fell to dreaming of things that neither hurt nor pleased. A fringe of trees against the sunset became suddenly the symbol of the whole world, and I stood and gazed and asked questions of it. The sunset faded; the trees withdrew. The wind went by, but dropped no hint in my ear. The evening star leaped out between the clouds, and sealed the secret with a seal of splendor.

A favorite resort of mine, after dark, was the South Boston Bridge, across South Bay and the Old Colony Railroad. This was so near home that I could go there at any time when the confusion in the house drove me out, or I felt the need of fresh air. I liked to stand leaning on the bridge railing, and look down on the dim tangle of railroad tracks below. I could barely see them branching out, elbowing, winding, and sliding out into the night in pairs. I was fascinated by the dotted lights, the significant red and green of signal lamps. These simple things stood for a complexity that it made me dizzy to think of. Then the blackness below me was split by the fiery eye of a monster engine, his breath enveloped me in blinding clouds, his long body shot by, rattling a hundred claws of steel; and he was gone, with an imperative shriek that shook me where I stood.

So would I be, swift on my rightful business, picking out my proper track from the million that cross it, pausing for no obstacles, sure of my goal.

After my watches on the bridge I often stayed up to write or study. It is late before Dover Street begins to go to bed. It is past midnight before I feel that I am alone. Seated in my stiff little chair before my narrow table, I gather in the night sounds through the open window, curious to assort and define them. As, little by little, the city settles down to sleep, the volume of sound diminishes, and the qualities of particular sounds stand out. The electric car lurches by with silent gong, taking the empty track by leaps, humming to itself in the invisible distance. A benighted team swings recklessly around the corner, sharp under my rattling window panes, the staccato pelting of hoofs on the cobblestones changed suddenly to an even pounding on the bridge. A few pedestrians hurry by, their heavy boots all out of step. The distant thoroughfares have long ago ceased their murmur, and I know that a million lamps shine idly in the idle streets.

My sister sleeps quietly in the little bed. The rhythmic dripping of a faucet is audible through the flat. It is so still that I can hear the paper crackling on the wall. Silence upon silence is added to the night; only the kitchen clock is the voice of my brooding thoughts, — ticking, ticking, ticking.

Suddenly the distant whistle of a locomotive breaks the stillness with a long-drawn wail. Like a threatened trouble, the sound comes nearer, piercingly near; then it dies out in a mangled silence, complaining to the last.

The sleepers stir in their beds. Somebody sighs, and the burden of all his trouble falls upon my heart. A homeless cat cries in the alley, in the voice of a human child. And the ticking of the kitchen clock is the voice of my troubled thoughts.

Many things are revealed to me as I sit and watch the world asleep. But the silence asks me many questions that I cannot answer; and I am glad when the tide of sound begins to return, by little and little, and I welcome the clatter of tin cans that announces the milkman. I cannot see him in the dusk, but I know his wholesome face has no problem in it.

It is one flight up to the roof; it is a leap of the soul to the sunrise. The morning mist rests lightly on chimneys and roofs and walls, wreathes the lamp-posts, and floats in gauzy streamers down the streets. Distant buildings are massed like palace walls, with turrets and spires lost in the rosy clouds. I love my beautiful city spreading all about me. I love the world. I love my place in the world.

# ZORA NEALE HURSTON
## (1891–1960)

Hurston struggled within the African American community and without, battling poverty and indifference to her great talent. She had a strong interest in black folklore and was an early expert on the culture of African Americans from Haiti, Bermuda, and Jamaica, as well as the rural and urban parts of the United States.

She was born in Eatonville, Florida, the first black township incorporated within the United States. This town often figures in her novels and autobiographical writings. She trained as an anthropologist at Barnard College and Columbia University, and became an important voice in the revival of interest in African American culture in the early part of this century. While publishing widely in the field of anthropology, she also wrote four novels between 1934 and 1938, as well as many stories and magazines articles.

Hurston is most widely known for *Their Eyes Were Watching God* (1937), an affecting novel that has acquired canonical status as an American masterpiece. But her autobiography, *Dust Tracks on a Road* (1942), is a work of similar quality, although its initial reception was controversial, with many black critics suggesting that she portrayed her life in terms far too sunny and uncomplicated by the reality of racism in America. In fact, Hurston's publisher had initially forced her to cut many passages that would have seriously complicated her portrayal of race relations in America.

## FROM *Dust Tracks on a Road*

### LOVE

What do I really know about love? I have had some experiences and feel fluent enough for my own satisfaction. Love, I find is like singing. Everybody can do enough to satisfy themselves, though it may not impress the neighbors as being very much. That is the way it is with me, but whether I know anything unusual, I couldn't say. Don't look for me to call a string of names and point out chapter and verse. Ladies do not kiss and tell any more than gentlemen do.

I have read many books where the heroine was in love for a long time without knowing it. I have talked with people and they have told me the same thing. So maybe that is the way it ought to be. That is not the way it is with me at all. I have been *out* of love with people for a long time, perhaps without finding it out. But when I fall *in*, I can feel the bump. That is a fact and I would not try to fool you. Love may be a sleepy, creeping thing with some others, but it is a mighty wakening thing with me. I feel the jar, and I know it from my head on down.

Though I started falling in love before I was seven years old, I never had a fellow until I was nearly grown. I was such a poor picker. I would have had better luck if I had stuck to boys around my own age, but that wouldn't do me. I wanted somebody with long pants on, and they acted as if they didn't know I was even born. The heartless wretches would walk right past my gate with grown women and pay me no attention at all, other than to say hello or something like that. Then I would have to look around for another future husband, only to have the same thing happen all over again.

Of course, in high school I received mushy notes and wrote them. A day or two, a week or month at most would see the end of the affair. Gone without a trace. I was in my Freshman year in college when I first got excited, really.

He could stomp a piano out of this world, sing a fair baritone and dance beautifully. He noticed me, too, and I was carried away. For the first time since my mother's death, there was someone who felt really close and warm to me.

This affair went on all through my college life, with the exception of two fallings-out. We got married immediately after I finished my work at Barnard College, which should have been the happiest day of my life. St. Augustine, Florida, is a beautiful setting for such a thing.

But, it was not my happiest day. I was assailed by doubts. For the first time since I met him, I asked myself if I really were in love, or if this had been a habit. I had an uncomfortable feeling of unreality. The day and the occasion did not underscore any features of nature or circumstance, and I wondered why. Who had canceled the well-advertised tour of the moon? Somebody had turned a hose on the sun. What I had taken for eternity turned out to be a moment walking in its sleep.

After our last falling-out, he asked me please to forgive him, and I said that I did. But now, had I really? A wind full of memories blew out of the past and brought a chilling fog. This was not the expected bright dawn. Rather, some vagrant ray had played a trick on the night. I could not bring myself to tell him my thoughts. I just couldn't, no matter how hard I tried, but there they were crowding me from pillar to post.

Back in New York, I met Mrs. Mason and she offered me a chance to return to my research work, and I accepted it. It seemed a way out without saying anything very much. Let nature take its course. I did not tell him about the arrangement. Rather, I urged him to return to Chicago to continue his medical work. Then I stretched my shivering insides out and went back to work. I have seen him only once since then. He has married again, and I hope that he is happy.

Having made such a mess, I did not rush at any serious affair right away. I set to work and really worked in earnest. Work was to be all of me, so I said. Three years went by. I had finished that phase of research and was considering writing my first book, when I met the man who was really to lay me by the heels. I met A.W.P.

He was tall, dark brown, magnificently built, with a beautifully modeled back head. His profile was strong and good. The nose and lips were especially good front and side. But his looks only drew my eyes in the beginning. I did not fall in love with him just for that. He had a fine mind and that intrigued me. When a man keeps beating me to the draw mentally, he begins to get glamorous.

I did not just fall in love. I made a parachute jump. No matter which way I probed him, I found something more to admire. We fitted each other like a glove. His intellect got me first for I am the kind of a woman that likes to move on mentally from point to point, and I like for my man to be there way ahead of me. Then if he is strong and honest, it goes on from there. Good looks are not essential, just extra added attraction. He had all of those things and more. It seems to me that God must have put in extra time making him up. He stood on his own feet so firmly that he reared back.

To illustrate the point, I got into trouble with him for trying to loan him a quarter. It came about this way.

I lived in the Graham Court at 116th Street and Seventh Avenue. He lived down in 64th Street, Columbus Hill. He came to call one night and everything went off sweetly until he got ready to leave. At the door he told me to let him go because he was going to walk home. He had spent the only nickel he had that night to come to see me. That upset me, and I ran to get a quarter to loan him until his pay day. What did I do that for? He flew hot. In fact he was the hottest man in the five boroughs. Why did I insult him like that? The responsibility was all his. He had known that he did not have his return fare when he left home, but he had wanted to come, and so he had come. Let him take the consequences for his own acts. What kind of coward did I take him for? How could he deserve my respect if he behaved like a cream puff? He was a *man*! No woman on earth could either lend him or give him a cent. If a man could not do for a woman, what good was he on earth? His great desire was to do for me. *Please* let him be a *man*!

For a minute I was hurt and then I saw his point. He had done a beautiful thing and I was killing it off in my blindness. If it pleased him to walk all of that distance for my sake, it pleased him as evidence of his devotion. Then too, he wanted to do all the doing, and keep me on the receiving end. He soared in my respect from that moment on. Nor did he ever change. He meant to be the head, *so help him over the fence!*

That very manliness, sweet as it was, made us both suffer. My career balked the completeness of his ideal. I really wanted to conform, but it was impossible. To me there was no conflict. My work was one thing, and he was all of the rest. But, I could not make him see that. Nothing must be in my life but himself.

But, I am ahead of my story. I was interested in him for nearly two years before he knew it. A great deal happened between the time we met and the time we had any serious talk.

As I said, I loved, but I did not say so, because nobody asked me. I made up my mind to keep my feelings to myself since they did not seem to matter to anyone else but me.

I went South, did some more concert work and wrote "Jonah's Gourd Vine" and "Mules and Men," then came back to New York.

He began to make shy overtures to me. I pretended not to notice for a while so that I could be sure and not be hurt. Then he gave me the extreme pleasure of telling me right out loud about it. It seems that he had been in love with me just as long as I had been with him, but he was afraid that I didn't mean him any good, as the saying goes. He had been trying to make me tell him something. He began by complimenting me on my clothes. Then one night we had attended the Alpha Phi Alpha fraternity dance—yes, he is an Alpha man—he told me that the white dress I was wearing was beautiful, but I did not have on an evening wrap rich enough to suit him. He had in mind just the kind he wanted to see me in, and when he made the kind of money he expected to, the first thing he meant to do was to buy me a gorgeous evening wrap and everything to go with it. He wanted *his* wife to look swell. He looked at me from under his eyelashes to see how I was taking it. I smiled and so he went on.

"You know, Zora, you've got a real man on your hands. You've got somebody to do for you. I'm tired of seeing you work so hard. I wouldn't want *my* wife to do anything but look after me. Be home looking like Skookums when I got there."

He always said I reminded him of the Indian on the Skookum Apples, so I knew he meant me to understand that he wanted to be coming home to me, and with those words he endowed me with Radio City, the General Motors Corporation, the United States, Europe, Asia and some outlying continents. I had everything!

So actively began the real love affair of my life. He was then a graduate of City College, and was working for his Master's degree at Columbia. He had no money. He was born of West Indian parents in the Columbus Hill district of New York City, and had nothing to offer but what it takes—a bright soul, a fine mind in a fine body, and courage. He is so modest that I do not think that he yet knows his assets. That was to make trouble for us later on.

It was a curious situation. He was so extraordinary that I lived in terrible fear lest women camp on his doorstep in droves and take him away from me. I found out later on that he could not believe that I wanted just him. So there began an agonizing tug of war. Looking at a very serious photograph of me that Carl Van Vechten had made, he told me one night in a voice full of feeling that that was the way he wanted me to look all the time unless I was with him. I almost laughed out loud. That was just the way I felt. I hated to think of him smiling unless he was smiling at me. His grins were too precious to be wasted on ordinary mortals, especially women.

If he could only have realized what a lot he had to offer, he need not have suffered so much through doubting that he could hold me. I was hog-tied and branded, but he didn't realize it. He could make me fetch and carry, but he wouldn't believe it. So when I had to meet people on business, or went to literary parties and things like that, it would drive him into a sulk, and then he would make me unhappy. I, too, failed to see how deeply he felt. I would interpret his moods as indifference and die, and die, and die.

He begged me to give up my career, marry him and live outside of New York City. I really wanted to do anything he wanted me to do, but that one thing I could not do. It was not just my contract with my publishers, it was that I had things clawing inside of me that must be said. I could not see that my work should make any difference in marriage. He was all and everything else to me but that. One did not conflict with the other in my mind. But it was different with him. He felt that he did not matter to me enough. He was the master kind. All, or nothing, for him.

The terrible thing was that we could neither leave each other alone, nor compromise. Let me seem too cordial with any male and something was going to happen. Just let him smile too broad at any woman, and no sooner did we get inside my door than the war was on! One night (I didn't decide this) something primitive inside me tore past the barriers and before I realized it I had slapped his face. That was a mistake. He was still smoldering from an incident a week old. A fellow had met us on Seventh Avenue and kissed me on my cheek. Just one of those casual things, but it had burned up A.W.P. So I had unknowingly given him an opening he had been praying for. He paid me off then and there with interest. No broken bones, you understand, and no black eyes. I realized afterwards that my hot head could tell me to beat him, but it would cost me something. I would have to bring head to get head. I couldn't get his and leave mine locked up in the dresser-drawer.

Then I knew I was too deeply in love to be my old self. For always a blow to my body had infuriated me beyond measure. Even with my parents, that was true. But somehow, I didn't hate him at all. We sat down on the floor and each one of us tried to take all the blame. He went out and bought some pie and I made a pot of hot chocolate and we were more affectionate than ever. The next day he made me a bookcase that I needed and you couldn't get a pin between us.

But fate was watching us and laughing. About a month later when he was with me, the telephone rang. Would I please come down to an apartment in the Fifties and meet an out-of-town celebrity? He was in town for only two days and he wanted to meet me before he left. When I turned from the phone, A.W.P. was changed. He begged me not to go. I reminded him that I had promised, and begged him to come along. He refused and walked out. I went, but I was most unhappy.

This sort of thing kept up time after time. He would not be reconciled to the thing. We were alternately the happiest people in the world, and the most miserable. I suddenly decided to go away to see if I could live without him. I did not even tell him that I was going. But I wired him from some town in Virginia.

Miss Barnicle of New York University asked me to join her and Alan Lomax on a short bit of research. I was to select the area and contact the subjects. Alan Lomax was joining us with a recording machine. So because I was delirious with joy and pain, I suddenly decided to leave New York and see if I could come to some decision. I knew no more at the end than I did when I went South. Six weeks later I was back in New York and just as much his slave as ever.

Really, I never had occasion to doubt his sincerity, but I used to drag my heart over hot coals by supposing. I did not know that I could suffer so. Then all of my careless words came to haunt me. For theatrical effect, I had uttered sacred words and oaths to others before him. How I hated myself for the sacrilege now! It would have seemed so wonderful never to have uttered them before.

But no matter how soaked we were in ecstasy, the telephone or the doorbell would ring, and there would be my career again. A charge had been laid upon me and I must follow the call. He said once with pathos in his voice, that at times he could not feel my presence. My real self had escaped him. I could tell from both his face and his voice that it hurt him terribly. It hurt me just as much to see him hurt. He really had nothing to worry about, but I could not make him see it. So there we were. Caught in a fiendish trap. We could not leave each other alone, and we could not shield each other from hurt. Our bitterest enemies could not have contrived more exquisite torture for us.

Another phase troubled me. As soon as he took his second degree, he was in line for bigger and better jobs. I began to feel that our love was slowing down his efforts. He had brains and character. He ought to go a long way. I grew terribly afraid that later on he would feel that I had thwarted him in a way and come to resent me. That was a scorching thought. Even if I married him, what about five years from now, the way we were going?

In the midst of this, I received my Guggenheim Fellowship. This was my chance to release him, and fight myself free from my obsession. He would get over me in a few months and go on to be a very big man. So I sailed off to Jamaica. But I freely admit that everywhere I set my feet down, there were tracks of blood. Blood from the very middle of my heart. I did not write because if I had written and he answered my letter, everything would have broken down.

So I pitched in to work hard on my research to smother my feelings. But the thing would not down. The plot was far from the circumstances, but I tried to embalm all the tenderness of my passion for him in "Their Eyes Were Watching God."

When I returned to America after nearly two years in the Caribbean, I found that he had left his telephone number with my publishers. For some time, I did not use it. Not because I did not want to, but because the moment when I should hear his voice something would be in wait for me. It might be warm and eager. It might be cool and impersonal, just with overtones from the grave of things. So I went South and stayed several months before I ventured to use it. Even when I returned to New York it took me nearly two months to get up my courage. When I did make the call, I cursed myself for the delay. Here was the shy, warm man I had left.

Then we met and talked. We both were stunned by the revelation that all along we had both thought and acted desperately in exile, and all to no purpose. We were still in the toils and after all my agony, I found out that he was a sucker for me, and he found out that I was in his bag. And I had a triumph that only a woman could understand. He had not turned into a tramp in my absence, but neither had he flamed like a newborn star in his profession. He confessed that he needed my aggravating presence to push him. He had settled down to a plodding desk job and reconciled himself. He had let his waistline go a bit and that bespoke his inside feeling. That made me happy no end. No woman wants a man all finished and perfect. You have to have something to work on and prod. That waistline went down in a jiffy and he began to discuss work-plans with enthusiasm. He could see something ahead of him besides time. I was happy. If he had been crippled in both legs, it would have suited me even better.

What will be the end? That is not for me to know. Life poses questions and that two-headed spirit that rules the beginning and the end of things called Death, has all the answers. And even if I did know all, I am supposed to have some private business to myself. Whatever I do know, I have no intention of putting but so much in the public ears.

Perhaps the oath of Hercules shall always defeat me in love. Once when I was small and first coming upon the story of The Choice of Hercules, I was so impressed that I swore an oath to leave all pleasure and take the hard road of labor. Perhaps God heard me and wrote down my words in His book. I have thought so at times. Be that as it may, I have the satisfaction of knowing that I have loved and been loved by the perfect man. If I never hear of love again, I have known the real thing.

So much for what I know about the major courses in love. However, there are some minor courses which I have not grasped so well, and would be thankful for some coaching and advice.

First is the number of men who pant in my ear on short acquaintance, "You passionate thing! I can see you are just *burning* up! Most men would be disappointing to you. It takes a man like me for you. Ahhh! I know that you will just wreck me! Your eyes and your lips tell me a lot. You are a walking furnace!" This amazes me sometimes. Often when this is whispered gustily into my ear, I am feeling no more amorous than a charter member of the Union League Club. I may be thinking of turnip greens with dumplings, or more royalty checks, and here is a man who visualizes me on a divan sending the world up in smoke. It has happened so often that I have come to expect it. There must be something about me that looks sort of couchy. Maybe it is a birthmark. My mother could have been frightened by a bed. There is nothing to be done about it, I suppose. But, I must say about these mirages that seem to rise around me, that the timing is way off on occasion.

Number two is, a man may lose interest in me and go where his fancy leads him, and we can still meet as friends. But if I get tired and let on about it, he is certain to become an enemy of mine. That forces me to lie like the cross-ties from New York to Key West. I have learned to frame it so that I can claim to be deserted and devastated by him. Then he goes off with a sort of twilight tenderness for me, wondering what it is that he's got that brings so many women down! I do not even have to show real tears. All I need to do is show my stricken face and dash away from him to hide my supposed heartbreak and renunciation. He understands that I am fleeing before his allure so that I can be firm in my resolution to save the pieces. He knew all along that he was a hard man to resist, so he visualized my dampened pillow. It is a good thing that some of them have sent roses as a poultice and stayed away. Otherwise, they might have found the poor, heartbroken wreck of a thing all dressed to kill and gone out for a high-heel time with the new interest, who has the new interesting things to say and do. Now, how to break off without acting deceitful and still keep a friend?

Number three is kin to Number two, in a way. Under the spell of moonlight, music, flowers, or the cut and smell of good tweeds, I sometimes feel the divine urge for an hour, a day or maybe a week. Then it is gone and my interest returns to corn pone and mustard greens, or rubbing a paragraph with a soft cloth. Then my ex-sharer of a mood calls up in a fevered voice and reminds me of every silly thing I said, and eggs me on to say them all over again. It is the third presentation of turkey hash after Christmas. It is asking me to be a seven-sided liar. Accuses me of being faithless and inconsistent if I don't. There is no inconsistency there. I was sincere for the moment in which I said the things. It is strictly a matter of time. It was true for the moment, but the next day or the next week, is not that moment. No two moments are any more alike than two snowflakes. Like snowflakes, they get that same look from being so plentiful and falling so close together. But examine them closely and see the multiple differences between them. Each moment has its own task and capacity; doesn't melt down like snow and form again. It keeps its character forever. So the great difficulty lies in trying to transpose last night's moment to a day which has no knowledge of it. That look, that tender touch, was issued by the mint of the richest of all kingdoms. That same expression of today is utter counterfeit, or at best the wildest of inflation. What could be more zestful than passing out canceled checks? It is wrong to be called faithless under circumstances like that. What to do?

I have a strong suspicion, but I can't be sure, that much that passes for constant love is a golded-up moment walking in its sleep. Some people know that it is the walk of the dead, but in desperation and desolation, they have staked everything on life after death and the resurrection, so they haunt the graveyard. They build an altar on the tomb and wait there like faithful Mary for the stone to roll away. So the moment has authority over all of their lives. They pray constantly for the miracle of the moment to burst its bonds and spread out over time.

But pay no attention to what I say about love, for as I said before, it may not mean a thing. It is my own bathtub singing. Just because my mouth opens up like a prayer book, it does not have to flap like a Bible. And then again, anybody whose mouth is cut cross-ways is given to lying, unconsciously as well as knowingly. So pay my few scattering remarks no mind as to love in general. I know only my part.

Anyway, it seems to be the unknown country from which no traveler ever returns. What seems to be a returning pilgrim is another person born in the strange country with the same-looking ears and hands. He is a stranger to the person who fared forth, and a stranger to family and old friends. He is clothed in mystery henceforth and forever. So, perhaps nobody knows, or can tell, any more than I. Maybe the old Negro folk rhyme tells all there is to know:

> Love is a funny thing; Love is a blossom;
> If you want your finger bit, poke it at a possum.

# PASCAL D'ANGELO
## (1894– )

Born in a peasant hamlet "comprised of a small group of stone houses near Introdacqua and not very far from the old walled city of Sulmona" in rural southern Italy, Pascal D'Angelo emigrated to the United States with his father in 1910 and worked with many of his countrymen as a "pick and shovel man." Carl van Doren, the editor of *The Nation*, discovered D'Angelo as a poet. He told the story in an introduction to D'Angelo's memoir, *A Son of Italy*, published in 1924: "I was wondering whether it was really worth any editor's trouble to offer an annual prize for poetry, and was, as usual, growing skeptical and more skeptical over the vales of rhymed and unrhymed mediocrity which I had to handle. So many poems and so few poets! Then, without warning or premonition, I came upon the letter to *The Nation* which Mr. D'Angelo now includes in his autobiography.

" 'This letter,' he said, 'is the cry of a soul stranded on the shores of darkness looking for light. . . . I am a worker, a pick and shovel man—what I want is an outlet to express what I can say besides work. . . . There are no words that can fitly express my living sufferings. . . . Let me free! Let me free! Free like the thought of love which haunts millions of minds. . . .'

"If this was not an authentic cry, I had never heard one. It drowned the loud noises of Vesey Street; it seemed to me to widen the walls of my cramped office. . . . Some incalculable chance had put the soul of a poet in the body of an Italian boy whose parents could not read or write and who came into no heritage but the family tradition of hopeless labor. . . . No American hereafter, watching a gang of brown Italians busy in a ditch, can help asking himself whether there is not some Pascal D'Angelo among them."

## FROM *Son of Italy*

In those days when work was rapidly picking up after a long slump, it was a matter of each man finding the very best he could. My case was typical: a long lay-off the previous year had left me in debt. And now there was a chance of making money. I was lured by the $2.25 per day promised on the state roads in Northern New Jersey, and went there alone. I spent all the money I had for the fare.

There were many various gangs working in the place: stone-breakers, stone-drillers, excavators, concrete workers and others, each with its own foreman. There were men loading stones of various sizes newly broken, on wagons; steam-rollers puffing along; gangs laying out first large stones, then smaller, and then sand. Over everything they put on tar and a covering of powder which we called "fine stuff."

I succeeded in getting work with the concrete gang. The road was progressing rapidly. There were rivulets over which little concrete bridges were required. Having no mixer for the concrete we had to mix the sand, stones and cement with our shovels right on the spot. And here came some of our hardest work, especially hard, as it was summer. On some of those cloudless days when the sun blazed down on us we would be carrying dusty bags full of heavy cement on our shoulders continuously. The dust mixed with the sweat beneath, burning the shoulders and itching. Very often after I had wiped my cheeks and around my neck with a dirty handkerchief I had to spread it out on the grass to dry while I staggered along through the flaming sunlight with my load. When dry the cement made the handkerchief appear petrified.

And the mixing. The foreman was getting angry that I wiped my face while the others worked bowed with the sweat pouring down over them. He snarled that it was just an excuse for raising my bowed body from the continual toil. This foreman's name was Domenick. He spoke in a weird Calabrese dialect and cursed always. He was a big broad-shouldered man, but his dry features were irregular and looked dissipated and his eyes were bloodshot. There was no appeal for one of us from his autocracy and he knew it. He had his spies in the gang and tyrannized over us—this foreman of the concrete workers. His threat of firing always awoke in us visions of aimless wanderings and dark months without jobs. And deep in his heart a man hates to go around begging for a job to be greeted with a sneer or a turned shoulder. Well, this foreman made us understand that in order to straighten our backs even a little, we needed a better excuse than that of wiping the sweat from our faces even though burning with cement dust. We said nothing, but bowed lower, while he stood straight watching us all the time. That was his job.

We had to dig foundations for these small bridges or "culverts." And always we found water; my feet were wet practically all the time. One day the foreman ordered us to go down into a short trench or foundation and make it deeper. The bottom was a deep pool of brown water. Most of the men had rubber boots; I had none. I hesitated.

The "boss" who was beginning to dislike me shouted harshly, "If you want your ten hours put down in the time book you'd better go down and dig; and hurry up about it." And down I went.

Often I'd try to put a piece of wood or flat stone under my feet; but usually the stone sank in the mire or my feet slipped away while working. So I invariably got wet. Rain or sunshine we had to work ahead; for our tyrant was that sort of man whom the contractors call "an excellent and efficient foreman."

One day while we were finishing one of those small bridges, it began to rain. The planks leading to the top of the foundation on which we had to climb were more vertical than horizontal. It was a steep climb up any time. And the rain rendered it more difficult by making the planks slippery. My job was to push wheelbarrows full of concrete up to the top of the foundation and dump the mixture down into the wooden forms. This was continuous and very hard work, for as soon as I returned an empty wheelbarrow, another full one greeted me. It was almost impossible to push a high-heaped wheelbarrow on the inclined slippery planks. I was going up with one not quite so full when the foreman shouted something to the men below.

Coming back I found the second wheelbarrow filled up to the brim. I paused. The foreman came running up, hot-faced. I said the load was too heavy to safely handle on the wet planks.

Grasping the handles he raised them and looking fiercely back, shouted, "Heavy, is it?"

"Well," I remarked, "anybody can do that. But look where I must go with it."

"I'll show you!" and he cursed. He started pushing the heavy wheelbarrow up toward the woodwork. But his feet began to slip a little and he saw that there might be danger for him. So he stopped and said, "But why should I go there? I'm the foreman. What do you think I have you here for?"

Meanwhile some of the bolder laborers, recognizing my right, began hurriedly to take off a few shovelfuls from the top of the overladen wheelbarrow. But the boss, cursing and threatening to fire the whole lot of them, made them put it back. And he ordered me to go ahead with the load. Without another word I bowed myself—a weakling under the force of necessity. The injustice of it split my thoughts like lightning, and I realized that a fire was smoldering in me. But what could I do? Rain was falling heavily. Not much time was given to decide. Almost without knowing it I found myself pushing upward a top-heavy wheelbarrow. While reaching near the top my feet slipped and I lost my balance. The wheelbarrow dropped down into the foundation. Wildly I threw out my hands and propped myself against the woodwork in order to avoid an inevitable fall. A rusty nail pierced my right hand. And I shrieked. Blood began to come out from both sides of my hand.

The foreman came running up. "Get out, you fool!" he shouted, "you can't work here any more!" And I couldn't.

All wet, tired, with bleeding, aching hand, I went back to the "shanty." My hand began to swell. I didn't know what to do. There was a small village further down the road but no drug store. There was only a grocery store that had peroxide. So I went down there through the rain, purchased a bottle and hurried back to medicate my hand. In the dark shanty there was an old stove but not lit. I could not dry my wet clothes. There was not even a good place where I could hang them out for the night. Outside it was still raining. I hung my dripping jacket near my wooden bed—a bed made of two boards nailed together. Some hours passed without my eating anything because I didn't feel much like eating. But even if I had been hungry, there was nothing more in the place except a loaf of stale bread and a piece of the cheapest and almost uneatable "Italian" salami made in America. In that condition, and feeling a repulsion toward an undesired food, I went to bed with an empty stomach. Now I began to be restless and felt the full pain of my wounded hand. My mind was dark. I felt like a hurt dog who slinks off to some corner where it can lick its wounds in silence.

Then the rest of the gang came straggling home through the downpour. They all made noise, and the chilly air of the shanty became foul with the sweat that steamed from them. One began to start a fire in the stove. A couple were arguing. There were shouts; and smoke filled the shanty. Some went to get food. There was frying in fat. After eating, one of them came over to ask me how I felt.

It was past midnight, but my eyes had not yet been closed. Everything was silent now save the beating of the rain outside and a sharp measured drip on the floor near the foot of my bed. The fever that was beating my wounded hand seemed little better, and sleep began to intensify. By about two o'clock in the morning I must have fallen asleep.

By five o'clock some of the men began to stir. They rose, yawned and spoke, and set about preparing their breakfast and some lunch to be taken on the job. Some whistled. An old fellow sang. Somebody was cursing outside that the wood was too wet and he couldn't get the fire going.

From a corner came a shout, "How is the weather? Is it worth while getting up?"

Someone shouted back, "It doesn't look so bad to-day. You'd better get your lunch ready."

About ten minutes to six a few started for the job. It was still quite dark, the sky showing through the open door in a gray turmoil of clouds and mists. Others began to leave, and by a quarter after six there was nobody around me. For a while I remained alone in that dim barnlike place. Then instinctively, in spite of my wounded hand, I felt the need of going to work and I too got up. Hurriedly I dressed and ran just as fast as I could in order to get to the job on time. I was hoping that foreman might have got over his anger and would give me some other work that I could do. It was just about one minute after seven when I came running up breathlessly. The last man had not yet picked his tools.

The foreman eyed me steadily and then said, "You are too late. If you want to work come at noon."

"But listen," I said quietly, "why must I lose five hours? If I am too late for seven o'clock can't I start at eight?"

He insisted, "No! I said noon." And he turned his broad back to me. From the tone of his voice and his demeanor I could see that, king-like, he had placed himself up in a tower of caprice—this ignorant man who had power over men. So, without adding any more futile words I did the only thing possible; slowly I walked back to the shanty and waited for noon.

Noon came. A distant whistle blew beyond some trees and then died out as if it were the last breath of silence. The sky had cleared and only a vague mist was blazing around the sun. Again I started out for the job, walking quickly through the throbbing brightness of the day. My wounded hand was very much swollen; I had tightened a handkerchief soaked in peroxide around it.

I was badly in need of money and realized that I had to submit under any circumstances. As soon as it was time to resume work I planted my-self meekly before Domenick.

But he, without any human consideration, said, "Take your shovel, go there with the others and mix the concrete!"

"But no," I interrupted gently, "I came here to see if you have any job that I can do." And I held out my swollen, bandaged hand. "Will you give me a job as water-boy? I can do that easily."

Apathetically he answered, "No. If you can't use a shovel then go home and stay there until your hand is healed. That's all." And with that, he went back to his work of watching the gang of workers. For an instant my thoughts were in a whirl. That is why many foremen carry re-volvers on the job. Then slowly I left the spot and began to plod my way home, if I could call that hovel "home."

I still remembered vividly—everybody remembered it—the heart-breaking times of the previous year, the long days out of a job when in-defatigable search was only rewarded by the repeated "No, no." I was without money and in debt; otherwise I wouldn't have cared so much.

Night and inevitable darkness came, and the tired workers returned home sullenly, like wild beasts toward their den. They divided them-selves into many groups, and each group began its own fire on the bare field in front of the shanty. I sat on a boulder quietly watching them, my wounded hand on my knee. Every now and then I would look at it tenderly like some mongrel who gently licks its wounded paw.

Now all the various fires began to glimmer and crackle, and the tongues of bright flames licked the velvet night. Some men were coming duskily with wood; some went for water; there was the welcome sound of pots; one man in each group chopped wood in the glow of the hungry fire. There were also a few among us who had no group to co-operate with and would hardly be getting our half-cooked supper before half past ten. And by then we would be so tired that with the pot still boiling on the two stones and the steam pouring up we would probably be half asleep. And many a man has lost his supper because the fire galloped along freely while he nodded. And finally when the smoke and bad odor awoke him the supper is hopelessly burned in the dirty pot. And many a time, tired and mad, a man has gone to sleep without eating.

The night was beautiful. The stars were like exquisite, happy, living spirits giving their bright laughter to the silent night. A few were beginning to munch their food. The rest were moving about or waiting. In spite of the soft weather they all seemed to be in ill humor. The night before, when coming into the shanty all wet, shouting and stamping about, they had been much more lively. And though not one of them said a word, it seemed that the balmy summer night had awakened deep in their hearts the vision of another land, lovely and balmy and calm. A land that doesn't know any such things as foremen, in small towns where one is never among strangers and people help one another.

While I was sitting there, along came a young fellow called Tony. He was the one who had asked me how I felt the night before, in the shanty. He was short and slender and had bright black eyes and wrinkled face when he smiled. Said he, "Why don't you go and see some other foreman for a job?" There were several scattered here and there each of them taking care of a different phase in the construction. These foremen boarded at various farms conveniently near the work. They got good wages and bonuses for watching us. They also put in time for us all and short-paid the men. Their food was ready for them at night and their beds were soft and clean. And we who did the work slept uncleanly in human sites.

I decided to follow Tony's advice, and started out immediately.

As I went down the road the moon arose and shone on the exquisite summer night. The warm wind came soft and steadily, the road gleamed delicately, and on the embankments to one side the cascades of dried loam appeared of fragile gold. There were not many trees around, but long stretches of indistinct fields lifting into nowhere.

Just then I noticed, stumbling a short distance ahead of me the big foreman Domenick who had caused me so much trouble. He was probably drunk. He had struck up a friendship with a woman in another farmhouse and was probably returning from her place. Immediately a fury such as I had never known before flared up in me. I hurried. Then I paused. But I have always abhorred violence. And a sudden pain from my swollen hand streaked through my being.

Just then, as I hesitated I felt a hand on my shoulder, not heavy, and gently laid. With a start I turned. It was old Michele who worked with some other foreman. He was also an Abbruzzese, but he came from the bright Adriatic coasts where groves of lemons and oranges grow right to the edge of the cliffs that overhang the sea. He had not spent his young manhood in this wretched endless labor and degradation among strangers. And his eyes were bright as if in them were still gleaming the hopes of youth. But now he was old and he liked drink.

He called me by name, "And where are you going, boy?" He was an intelligent man and spoke in excellent Italian. He had worked on our gang for a week and often mentioned Dante whom I thought was an ancient king. But now, old, the foreman took him on more in pity than anything and because he could talk so nicely to them.

I showed Michele my wounded hand and told him my predicament. He now spoke in his soft Abbruzzese dialect that is so much like ours of the uplands, "Boy," he said, "a stupid world drove nails through other hands—other hands."

I didn't know what he was talking about. But at times afterwards the image of that aimless old man has come before me like a frightful specter and at times like an alluring hope.

He laughed and took a hearty leave of me. I hurried along. Domenick had long since disappeared. Some lights of the houses gleamed around a turn of the road. There was a living haze around. And suddenly I felt the voluptuous summer night embracing me mother-like, and amazing with love. And my heart ached for home. And I dreamed of the moonrise over the rugged peaks of the eastern mountains when in among the black pinnacles are cups of molten silver overflowing and everybody looks up without knowing why.

But I was out to get a job. I shook my head at all these useless thoughts, and continued my way. Finally I reached the first farmhouse. The foreman came out. He told me his gang already had a water-boy, and shut the door. The second one, on a more distant farm, said that his gang was too small to have one. This was a lie. Completely discouraged, I decided that it was useless to go and see the third foreman who lived further down the long endless road. So I returned to the sty. I felt lost.

When I crossed the well-worn threshold one of the men put down his pipe and asked, "Hello! did you get any place?" He was a loud-mouthed, but good-natured Neapolitan whom I hardly knew.

I shook my head.

There was another older man sitting on a box near the door, and he asked, also in Neapolitan, "What has he been looking for?" This man was a stranger to me.

The first fellow, who must have been quite familiar with him, turned and said loudly, "Why I'll tell you. First of all you foremen and bosses seem to think that you are gods and kings around here. Why, look at this lad; yesterday he got hurt on the job; and his hand is still bleeding and swollen. He wants a light job that he can do; and nobody wants to give him any. That dog Domenick over there told him that he must wait until his hand is healed so he can use a shovel. But if he came out here without money—what the devil is he going to eat in the meanwhile? You know yourself how a man can be in a hole at times."

So I discovered that this stranger was a foreman in the excavation gang. He seemed not so bad as the others. He had just dropped around to have a chat with his fellow-townsman, luckily for me.

"Well, boy," he began half sympathetically, "come over to my gang tomorrow morning, south of here."

The next morning I arose feeling a little more certain and encouraged. I removed the handkerchief from my hand and put on a cleaner one, I tried to fry a couple of eggs in an old greasy pan. Then I took a half loaf of stale bread, split it, weakly, and put the half-fried eggs in between the pieces. I searched around for a piece of paper but could find none. I was in a hurry, the men were leaving, and I had to go further than they. Quickly I drew my other handkerchief from my pocket. It was still dirty with the blood that had oozed from my hand the day before. I wrapped the pieces of stale bread and the two fried eggs in it. And I took it with me as my lunch for noon.

So I worked every day with this new gang, carrying pail after pail of water to the men, who drank like mules. I had to go far off for the water and was unable to shift the heavy pail from one hand to the other. At times I had to pause on my way back; but this foreman seemed to be a little more considerate than the other, though he had his defects.

I worked there for about two weeks. My hand was not yet well healed. Then came the fortnightly pay-day. We were all waiting eagerly and thinking of the hour when the automobile with meats and vegetables would pass and we could buy something good. But when the usual hour for our money approached the pay-master failed to appear. An hour later one of the foremen who looked anxious, announced that the contractor had sent a telegram saying that he could not come that day but would be around to pay us about a day or two later. The approval was unanimous. We all went back to work happily, and eager to finish out that day like excited children waiting for a holiday.

About three o'clock in the afternoon the next day we saw a crowd getting together down the road. Someone came running up saying that another telegram had come. We all hurried over, the foreman first. The superintendent was there, white-faced. He read the telegram to us; then he explained that the contractor had gone bankrupt and that we didn't need to work out the day. The foremen crowded around him and started a hot argument.

Then, we all struck in despair. Like a flock of betrayed sheep we returned to the huge, barnlike shanty foolishly questioning one another. What could we do?

Some who had money or could get a loan returned to New York. Others went around begging the farmers nearby to give them work for the necessary fare. And I was there without money, and with a wounded hand, feeling full remorse for having made this newest change from my previous place.

But first, while most of the men were cursing eloquently a few of us had to sit down and laugh at one another.

### CHAPTER XII

That night I lingered a long time outside the shanty, thinking. And darkness made the vast solitudes of heaven populous with stars.

At first my mind was turbulent.

And I thought to myself, "Why, I am nothing more than a dog. A dog. But a dog is silent and slinks away when whipped, while I am filled with the urge to cry out, to cry out disconnected words, expressions of pain—anything—to cry out!"

I looked around. I felt a kinship with the beautiful earth. She was like some lovely hard-hearted lady in velvets and gaudy silks—one whom we could gaze at in admiration, but never dare approach. I felt a power that was forcing me to cry out to this world that was so fair, so soft and oblivious of our pains and petty sorrows. Then I had to laugh to myself. "After all," I thought, "what are my tiny woes to the eternal beauty of those stars, of these trees and even this short-lived grass?"

For a long time I paced the soft green in front of our shanty. Then I entered. The men inside were grumbling mournfully to one another, barely visible in the gloom. I had resigned myself to my fate. I was a poor laborer—a dago, a wop or some such creature—in the eyes of America. Well, what could I do?

Nothing.

Thereafter, for a long while until my numbed soul was again awakened, my prime interests were food and jobs. First of all I had to escape back to headquarters in New York. My credit was very bad.

I left the shanty with a couple of others; and we began to trudge aimlessly down the long road. At several farmhouses we paused to ask for work. None of the farmers seemed to care to give us any.

"What are you going to do?" asked a young bright-faced lad.

"Walk," grumbled my other companion, a Sicilian.

And walk we did. That night we slept in a most beautiful country side. But the mosquitoes and the gathering damp prevented our admiring the splendor of the broad starlit night.

Rising a little stiff-jointed the next morning we walked on. We were hungry; for a drink of water at a clear spring had not done much to soothe us. We had a little money between us, and on reaching a placid hamlet nestled amid soft green hills we made a quick run on the general store.

And who should be conducting the store but a paisano of mine! We shook hands long and vigorously and in a few minutes I was giving him a detailed account of everything that had passed in our village from the time he had come to America to the day, years later, when I left.

This good fellow-townsman of mine made the three of us sleep in his house that night. In real beds, too. And the next day he even loaned us the fare for New York, which I dutifully returned in time, as I hope my two companions did.

Back again to the railroad yard in Shady Side I went, humbly begging for a job. Fortunately for me, they needed men. And so it was that after my disastrous trip, I was again an inhabitant of our old box car.

Little by little a few other fellow-townsmen drifted back from unsuccessful jobs, and our original gang was in a way re-established.

Strange to say, I had become light-hearted after my troubles. Foremen would shout at me, and I laughed as soon as their backs were turned. I didn't care. I had resigned myself to the gradual eking out of my life. Work and food.

Up on Hudson Heights, on top of the Palisades, was a boarding house kept by a "paisana." And there I would spend the evenings, joking and fooling. I walked up and down with a broad smile on my face. And it was just by accident, and from this same sense of joking that my life took an upward turn.

First of all, a crowd of Mexican laborers were brought up from the south to work with us in the yard. At first they were kept separated from us, living in long shanties. But gradually a general mingling of laborers took place and we fraternized wonderfully with them. And I found some of them real gentlemen. There was one, a wiry young man, who had been with Villa and had been taken prisoner by the Americans. Besides

Spanish he could speak a strange Indian language that sounded very queer to me. That winter he and another older man came to live in our box car and our quarters, already crowded, became packed. They were lively fellows and would sing and play on a discordant guitar. Then at times the older one, Don Tomas, would start off reminiscing and put us all to sleep with his monotonous semi-comprehensible stories.

I began to learn some Spanish from these two Mexicans. The younger one received a Spanish weekly from some town in Texas. To my amusement he would sit hours at a time reading it. Little by little I became interested in the paper, and tried to pick out words that were like Italian. I had gotten to think of a newspaper as something to start a fire with or to wrap objects in. But now I began to read again—very little at first, I must confess. Somehow, I found English more to my liking than Spanish. And about once a week I even bought an English newspaper to look at. There was very little in them that I could understand, even though I spent many a puzzled hour trying to decipher the strange words. When I did learn a word and had discovered its meaning I would write it in big letters on the mouldy walls of the box car. And soon I had my first lesson in English all around me continually before my eyes.

One day a friend of mine who was a bartender in one of the many saloons that lined River Road took me to an Italian vaudeville show in a theater on the Bowery, New York. Included in the program was a short farce. I heard it and decided to myself that I could do better.

I went home and tried to write something after work. I began it in Italian, but unable to manage the language, on a sudden thought I decided to attempt it in English. After a few Sundays of hard work I had about three closely written pages of the most impossible English one could imagine. In triumph, I showed it to a couple of brakemen. They laughed long and loud. There was some doubt whether it was the jokes or the manhandled English which caused their hilarity. However, I gave myself the benefit of the doubt, and agreed with myself that I could write English.

Though I have long since burned most of these "prehistoric" attempts at English, I still have a few among my papers of which the following is an example:

> A farmer had not bean in this city very long beefore he falled in love with sumthing. And this sumthing happen to be a wooman whoo disliked him just as passionately he liked her. Now, please do not think that this tuirns out to be a joke. Farther from it. This is a seerious story in witch throbs the most violent of human passions. The life of an unfortunate farm swolled up by the whirlpulls of evil. Revealing the futile struggles of a mother who fites to save her son drunkard by liquor which he had not yet drunk. He was like

a drunken staggering alung the city streets and falls in some undignfied gutter out of which he emerges with his face embellished by mud and clothes smelling with heretofour unknown perfumes, made out of the too old manure and many other effective ingredients pertaining thereto.

He knelt beefore the wooman he lovd. Being largely dispose to obesity (fatness) whenver she moved away—which she did it on purpose—he would go after her (walking) on his knees. Most people become eloquent when drunken or in love and this farmer was not therefour exseption, "I love you" be begined, "I love you so much. I love you! Please come near! come nearer. You are my hope, my quween, my all! You are like a goddes beefore witch I am never tired of kneeling. You are the most beautful wooman in the world you are moor beautful then beauty. More beautful then one of our newly washed pig!" she went way and he called her back "At least help me to git up if you don want marry me." she went and he had a hard difficult job to get up.

So I began to write jokes in "English," most of them of my own invention or paraphrased from some paper. My jokes became known around the yard as great curiosities and things to laugh at. Several good-natured lads who worked there even brought me writing paper so that I could put down a few jokes for them. The things I wrote were not refined at all, but only of the type for my class of people.

Later, when I had learned to manage the English language a little better and could write with some degree of clarity, I put a prize of five cents on some good jokes. That is, if they could keep a straight face while reading a little collection of jokes that I presented them I would give them a nickel. But of course they always refused the nickel. Thus was my first climax in the rôle of English author.

One day I bought a small Webster's dictionary for a quarter (second-hand, if not third), half torn. But I thought I had gotten a treasure for the price. And I proceeded to memorize it. Thereafter I was continually going around the yard using the most unheard-of English words. But, insistently, I made them understand what I meant by spelling each word or writing them on a railroad tie.

From that time on I was continually asking questions and writing jokes and riddles—which were for me the heights of intellectual attainment.

One glorious winter night I was coming back toward the box car from a trip to Hudson Heights. With me were a couple of brakemen who were on a night shift and were going to work. They were young light-hearted American lads, always ready to joke with me.

I looked up. The sky was thick with stars. I remarked, "The stars are marching over the deep night. With whom are they going to war?"

"Eh? With whom . . . ?" they asked.

"With the emperor of Eternity."

"And who is he?"

"Death," I said.

They both laughed and took pains to make me understand that I was crazy. I walked ahead to my box car.

Shortly after this I began to project—ambitiously—a heart stirring tragedy. There was a small hall in back of one saloon on River Road owned by a Hungarian whose daughter I often spoke with. They were not bad people either, and she had beautiful blue eyes. Vaguely I made plans for producing a soul-rending show there, and charging admission, and making a good deal of money. Of course, I was to be the author of the sad play.

Now, just because I knew so little about the city, I determined to put my scene in the great metropolis. And the play was to start with a poor outcast who had to sleep in the subway. But when I sat down to write the speech of this poor being whose rest is disturbed by the rumbling trains, I didn't know what to say. Accordingly, I decided to investigate and spend a night in the subway, which I did very successfully in the matter of sleep. And I never wrote the sad tragedy, either.

But work, continual, hard, fatiguing work, made my attempts at writing few and short lived. I always was and am a pick and shovel man. That's all I am able to do, and that is what I am forced to do, even now. Work with my arms.

Wrecks in the yard were a daily occurrence. I could hardly concentrate my mind, when a man would come shouting, "All out! A wreck!" in the tunnel or away down the tracks toward the sugar refineries. Out I would have to go. And in a few minutes I would be starting long spells of intense, hurried labor to clear away the wreckage or repair the damaged tracks, in the red glow of flickering lanterns.

The superiority of my English was first recognized by the Italian laborers of my gang. Then brakemen and conductors who were practically all Americans began to notice me. And finally rumors of my accomplishments reached even the yard officials. I became quite celebrated in the Shady Side yard of the Erie Railroad as "that queer Italian laborer."

Then a group of young brakemen began a campaign to put down my little local fame. What they did was to bring new and difficult words every morning for me to define. Usually they would come about half an hour before working time, and cornering me would ask the meaning of some difficult word. If I could answer, all was well and they kept judiciously quiet for the rest of the day. But if I failed, then they would make it hot for me.

When noon came they would call me over to the space in front of the office where clerks, yard officials and girls were. And there they would, with plenty of noise, try to show me up to those who liked me.

But their efforts and mental ambushes were all useless—as useless as I could make them. One day they brought me before the whole crowd just to have me ridiculed, perhaps because they were high school lads. They gave me five words to define and I only knew the meaning of three. Throwing up their hands they began to proclaim themselves victorious.

But I calmly gave them two words that they had never heard of. Then I bet them that I could give them ten words and two more for good measure none of which they could understand.

I began, "Troglodyte," "sebaceous," "wen," "helot," "indeciduity," "murine," "bantling," "ubiquity," "clithrophobia," "nadir," and instead of adding two for good measure I added seven to make their debacle more horrible. And with a pencil against the office facade I wrote the seven words so that everyone might see their eternal defeat, "abettor," "caballine," "phlebotomy," "coeval," "octroon," "risible," "anorexia," "arable," then to complete, I added, "asininity." The defeat of these educated youths was, is and will be an eternal one, because there is no other pick and shovel man that can face them like that.

From the day of that triumph they nicknamed me "solution," and we all became good friends.

And so the months passed, with plenty of joking and foolishness and no end of work.

But at times I would stand in front of the box car on a clear night. Around would be the confusion, whistles, flashes and grinding sounds of the never-ending movement in the yard. I would steal a glance up at the stars. The stars have always been the wonder of my life. I had but lately learned, to my utter surprise, that there were other worlds besides this earth. And I had also discovered in a newspaper article that the stars were other suns with unseen worlds around them. And as I gazed upward I thought that perhaps there were other eyes in those viewless worlds that were gazing wondering in my direction. And how our glances must have met in the black mid-darkness of the infinite.

Such reveries were always broken by a rough shout from some of my fellow laborers to "come in and go to sleep!"

# F. SCOTT FITZGERALD
## (1896–1940)

A novelist and short story writer, Fitzgerald was known for his delicate evocations of the Jazz Age, which he once described as "a new generation grown up to find all Gods dead, all wars fought, all faiths in man shaken." His first novel, *This Side of Paradise* (1920), brought him instant fame and lots of money. Both were, eventually, a source of anguish. Fitzgerald went to Europe, where he joined Hemingway and Pound in Paris; with his beautiful wife, Zelda, he lived a life of lavish excess, which he chronicled in his stories and novels.

In 1925, he published *The Great Gatsby*, one of the unmistakable masterpieces of American fiction. But the novel was not economically successful, and Fitzgerald was forced increasingly to sell himself short by writing slick stories for popular magazines. He eventually wound up in Hollywood—a broken man, addicted to alcohol, possessed of a fading reputation. This was the period when he wrote his painful, exquisite essay "The Crack-Up" (1931). It remains a centerpiece of American autobiographical writing, a work of fierce honesty and remarkable self-interrogation in which he concludes, ruefully, that "the natural state of the sentient adult is a qualified unhappiness."

## "The Crack-Up"

*February, 1936*

Of course all life is a process of breaking down, but the blows that do the dramatic side of the work—the big sudden blows that come, or seem to come, from outside—the ones you remember and blame things on and, in moments of weakness, tell your friends about, don't show their effect all at once. There is another sort of blow that comes from within—that you don't feel until it's too late to do anything about it, until you realize with finality that in some regard you will never be as good a man again. The first sort of breakage seems to happen quick—the second kind happens almost without your knowing it but is realized suddenly indeed.

Before I go on with this short history, let me make a general observation—the test of a first-rate intelligence is the ability to hold two opposed ideas in the mind at the same time, and still retain the ability to function. One should, for example, be able to see that things are hopeless and yet be determined to make them otherwise. This philosophy fitted on to my early adult life, when I saw the improbable, the implausible, often the "impossible," come true. Life was something you dominated if you were any good. Life yielded easily to intelligence and effort, or to what proportion could be mustered of both. It seemed a romantic business to be a successful literary man—you were not ever going to be as famous as a movie star but what note you had was probably longer-lived—you were never going to have the power of a man of strong political or religious convictions but you were certainly more independent. Of course within the practice of your trade you were forever unsatisfied—but I, for one, would not have chosen any other.

As the twenties passed, with my own twenties marching a little ahead of them, my two juvenile regrets—at not being big enough (or good enough) to play football in college, and at not getting overseas during the war—resolved themselves into childish waking dreams of imaginary heroism that were good enough to go to sleep on in restless nights. The big problems of life seemed to solve themselves, and if the business of fixing them was difficult, it made one too tired to think of more general problems.

Life, ten years ago, was largely a personal matter. I must hold in balance the sense of the futility of effort and the sense of the necessity to struggle; the conviction of the inevitability of failure and still the determination to "succeed"—and, more than these, the contradiction between the dead hand of the past and the high intentions of the future. If I could do this through the common ills—domestic, professional and personal—then the ego would continue as an arrow shot from nothingness to nothingness with such force that only gravity would bring it to earth at last.

For seventeen years, with a year of deliberate loafing and resting out in the center—things went on like that, with a new chore only a nice prospect for the next day. I was living hard, too, but: "Up to forty-nine it'll be all right," I said. "I can count on that. For a man who's lived as I have, that's all you could ask."

—And then, ten years this side of forty-nine, I suddenly realized that I had prematurely cracked.

Now a man can crack in many ways—can crack in the head—in which case the power of decision is taken from you by others! or in the body, when one can but submit to the white hospital world; or in the nerves. William Seabrook in an unsympathetic book tells, with some pride and a movie ending, of how he became a public charge. What led to his alcoholism or was bound up with it, was a collapse of his nervous system. Though the present writer was not so entangled—having at the time not tasted so much as a glass of beer for six months—it was his nervous reflexes that were giving way—too much anger and too many tears.

Moreover, to go back to my thesis that life has a varying offensive, the realization of having cracked was not simultaneous with a blow, but with a reprieve.

Not long before, I had sat in the office of a great doctor and listened to a grave sentence. With what, in retrospect, seems some equanimity, I had gone on about my affairs in the city where I was then living, not caring much, not thinking how much had been left undone, or what would become of this and that responsibility, like people do in books; I was well insured and anyhow I had been only a mediocre caretaker of most of the things left in my hands, even of my talent.

But I had a strong sudden instinct that I must be alone. I didn't want to see any people at all. I had seen so many people all my life—I was an average mixer, but more than average in a tendency to identify myself, my ideas, my destiny, with those of all classes that I came in contact with. I was always saving or being saved—in a single morning I would go through the emotions ascribable to Wellington at Waterloo. I lived in a world of inscrutable hostiles and inalienable friends and supporters.

But now I wanted to be absolutely alone and so arranged a certain insulation from ordinary cares.

It was not an unhappy time. I went away and there were fewer people. I found I was good-and-tired. I could lie around and was glad to, sleeping or dozing sometimes twenty hours a day and in the intervals trying resolutely not to think—instead I made lists—made lists and tore them up, hundreds of lists: of cavalry leaders and football players and cities, and popular tunes and pitchers, and happy times, and hobbies and houses lived in and how many suits since I left the army and how many pairs of shoes (I didn't count the suit I bought in Sorrento that shrunk, nor the pumps and dress shirt and collar that I carried around for years and never wore, because the pumps got damp and grainy and the shirt and collar got yellow and starch-rotted). And lists of women I'd liked, and of the times I had let myself be snubbed by people who had not been my betters in character or ability.

—And then suddenly, surprisingly, I got better.

—And cracked like an old plate as soon as I heard the news.

That is the real end of this story. What was to be done about it will have to rest in what used to be called the "womb of time." Suffice it to say that after about an hour of solitary pillow-hugging, I began to realize that for two years my life had been a drawing on resources that I did not possess, that I had been mortgaging myself physically and spiritually up to the hilt. What was the small gift of life given back in comparison to that?—when there had once been a pride of direction and a confidence in enduring independence.

I realized that in those two years, in order to preserve something—an inner hush maybe, maybe not—I had weaned myself from all the things I used to love—that every act of life from the morning tooth-brush to the friend at dinner had become an effort. I saw that for a long time I had not liked people and things, but only followed the rickety old pretense of liking. I saw that even my love for those closest to me was become only an attempt to love, that my casual relations—with an editor, a tobacco seller, the child of a friend, were only what I remembered I *should* do, from other days. All in the same month I became bitter about such things as the sound of the radio, the advertisements in the magazines, the screech of tracks, the dead silence of the country—contemptuous at human softness, immediately (if secretively) quarrelsome toward hardness—hating the night when I couldn't sleep and hating the day because it went toward night. I slept on the heart side now because I knew that the sooner I could tire that out, even a little, the sooner would come that blessed hour of nightmare which, like a catharsis, would enable me to better meet the new day.

There were certain spots, certain faces I could look at. Like most Middle Westerners, I have never had any but the vaguest race prejudices—I always had a secret yen for the lovely Scandinavian blondes who sat on porches in St. Paul but hadn't emerged enough economically to be part of what was then society. They were too nice to be "chickens" and too quickly off the farmlands to seize a place in the sun, but I remember going round blocks to catch a single glimpse of shining hair—the bright shock of a girl I'd never know. This is urban, unpopular talk. It strays afield from the fact that in these latter days I couldn't stand the sight of Celts, English, Politicians, Strangers, Virginians, Negroes (light or dark), Hunting People, or retail clerks, and middlemen in general, all writers (I avoided writers very carefully because they can perpetuate trouble as no one else can)—and all the classes as classes and most of them as members of their class . . .

Trying to cling to something, I liked doctors and girl children up to the age of about thirteen and well-brought-up boy children from about eight years old on. I could have peace and happiness with these few categories of people. I forgot to add that I liked old men—men over seventy, sometimes over sixty if their faces looked seasoned. I liked Katharine Hepburn's face on the screen, no matter what was said about her pretentiousness, and Miriam Hopkins' face, and old friends if I only saw them once a year and could remember their ghosts.

All rather inhuman and undernourished, isn't it? Well, that, children, is the true sign of cracking up.

It is not a pretty picture. Inevitably it was carted here and there within its frame and exposed to various critics. One of them can only be described as a person whose life makes other people's lives seem like death—even this time when she was cast in the usually unappealing role of Job's comforter. In spite of the fact that this story is over, let me append our conversation as a sort of postscript:

"Instead of being so sorry for yourself, listen—" she said. (She always says "Listen," because she thinks while she talks—*really* thinks.) So she said: "Listen. Suppose this wasn't a crack in you—suppose it was a crack in the Grand Canyon."

"The crack's in me," I said heroically.

"Listen! The world only exists in your eyes—your conception of it. You can make it as big or as small as you want to. And you're trying to be a little puny individual. By God, if I ever cracked, I'd try to make the world crack with me. Listen! The world only exists through your apprehension of it, and so it's much better to say that it's not you that's cracked—it's the Grand Canyon."

"Baby et up all her Spinoza?"

"I don't know anything about Spinoza. I know—" She spoke, then, of old woes of her own, that seemed, in the telling, to have been more dolorous than mine, and how she had met them, over-ridden them, beaten them.

I felt a certain reaction to what she said, but I am a slow-thinking man, and it occurred to me simultaneously that of all natural forces, vitality is the incommunicable one. In days when juice came into one as an article without duty, one tried to distribute it—but always without success; to further mix metaphors, vitality never "takes." You have it or you haven't it, like health or brown eyes or honor or a baritone voice. I might have asked some of it from her, neatly wrapped and ready for home cooking and digestion, but I could never have got it—not if I'd waited around for a thousand hours with the tin cup of self-pity. I could walk from her door, holding myself very carefully like cracked crockery, and go away into the world of bitterness, where I was making a home with such materials as are found there—and quote to myself after I left her door:

*"Ye are the salt of the earth. But if the salt hath lost its savour, wherewith shall it be salted?"*

*Matthew* 5-13.

PASTING IT TOGETHER

*March, 1936*

In a previous article this writer told about his realization that what he had before him was not the dish that he had ordered for his forties. In fact—since he and the dish were one, he described himself as a cracked plate, the kind that one wonders whether it is worth preserving. Your editor thought that the article suggested too many aspects without regarding them closely, and probably many readers felt the same way—and there are always those to whom all self-revelation is contemptible, unless it ends with a noble thanks to the gods for the Unconquerable Soul.

But I had been thanking the gods too long, and thanking them for nothing. I wanted to put a lament into my record, without even the background of the Euganean Hills to give it color. There weren't any Euganean hills that I could see.

Sometimes, though, the cracked plate has to be retained in the pantry, has to be kept in service as a household necessity. It can never again be warmed on the stove nor shuffled with the other plates in the dishpan; it will not be brought out for company, but it will do to hold crackers late at night or to go into the ice box under left-overs . . .

Hence this sequel—a cracked plate's further history.

Now the standard cure for one who is sunk is to consider those in actual destitution or physical suffering—this is an all-weather beatitude for gloom in general and fairly salutory day-time advice for everyone. But at three o'clock in the morning, a forgotten package has the same tragic importance as a death sentence, and the cure doesn't work—and in a real dark night of the soul it is always three o'clock in the morning, day after day. At that hour the tendency is to refuse to face things as long as possible by retiring into an infantile dream—but one is continually startled out of this by various contacts with the world. One meets these occasions as quickly and carelessly as possible and retires once more back into the dream, hoping that things will adjust themselves by some great material or spiritual bonanza. But as the withdrawal persists there is less and less chance of the bonanza—one is not waiting for the fade-out of a single sorrow, but rather being an unwilling witness of an execution, the disintegration of one's own personality . . .

Unless madness or drugs or drink come into it, this phase comes to a dead-end, eventually, and is succeeded by a vacuous quiet. In this you can try to estimate what has been sheared away and what is left. Only when this quiet came to me, did I realize that I had gone through two parallel experiences.

The first time was twenty years ago, when I left Princeton in junior year with a complaint diagnosed as malaria. It transpired, through an X-ray taken a dozen years later, that it had been tuberculosis—a mild case, and after a few months of rest I went back to college. But I had lost certain offices, the chief one was the presidency of the Triangle Club, a musical comedy idea, and also I dropped back a class. To me college would never be the same. There were to be no badges of pride, no medals, after all. It seemed on one March afternoon that I had lost every single thing I wanted—and that night was the first time that I hunted down the spectre of womanhood that, for a little while, makes everything else seem unimportant.

Years later I realized that my failure as a big shot in college was all right—instead of serving on committees, I took a beating on English poetry; when I got the idea of what it was all about, I set about learning how to write. On Shaw's principle that "If you don't get what you like, you better like what you get," it was a lucky break—at the moment it was a harsh and bitter business to know that my career as a leader of men was over.

Since that day I have not been able to fire a bad servant, and I am astonished and impressed by people who can. Some old desire for personal dominance was broken and gone. Life around me was a solemn dream, and I lived on the letters I wrote to a girl in another city. A man does not recover from such jolts—he becomes a different person and, eventually, the new person finds new things to care about.

The other episode parallel to my current situation took place after the war, when I had again over-extended my flank. It was one of those tragic loves doomed for lack of money, and one day the girl closed it out on the basis of common sense. During a long summer of despair I wrote a novel instead of letters, so it came out all right, but it came out all right for a different person. The man with the jingle of money in his pocket who married the girl a year later would always cherish an abiding distrust, an animosity, toward the leisure class—not the conviction of a revolutionist but the smouldering hatred of a peasant. In the years since then I have never been able to stop wondering where my friends' money came from, nor to stop thinking that at one time a sort of *droit de seigneur* might have been exercised to give one of them my girl.

For sixteen years I lived pretty much as this latter person, distrusting the rich, yet working for money with which to share their mobility and the grace that some of them brought into their lives. During this time I had plenty of the usual horses shot from under me—I remember some of their names—*Punctured Pride, Thwarted Expectation, Faithless, Show-off, Hard Hit, Never Again.* And after awhile I wasn't twenty-five, then not even thirty-five, and nothing was quite as good. But in all these years I don't remember a moment of discouragement. I saw honest men through moods of suicidal gloom—some of them gave up and died; others adjusted themselves and went on to a larger success than mine; but my morale never sank below the level of self-disgust when I had put on some unsightly personal show. Trouble has no necessary connection with discouragement—discouragement has a germ of its own, as different from trouble as arthritis is different from a stiff joint.

When a new sky cut off the sun last spring, I didn't at first relate it to what had happened fifteen or twenty years ago. Only gradually did a certain family resemblance come through—an over-extension of the flank, a burning of the candle at both ends; a call upon physical resources that I did not command, like a man over-drawing at his bank. In its impact this blow was more violent than the other two but it was the same in kind—a feeling that I was standing at twilight on a deserted range, with an empty rifle in my hands and the targets down. No problem set—simply a silence with only the sound of my own breathing.

In this silence there was a vast irresponsibility toward every obligation, a deflation of all my values. A passionate belief in order, a disregard of motives or consequences in favor of guess work and prophecy, a feeling that craft and industry would have a place in any world—one by one, these and other convictions were swept away. I saw that the novel, which at my maturity was the strongest and supplest medium for conveying thought and emotion from one human being to another, was becoming subordinated to a mechanical and communal art that, whether in the hands of Hollywood merchants or Russian idealists, was capable of reflecting only the tritest thought, the most obvious emotion. It was an art in which words were subordinate to images, where personality was worn down to the inevitable low gear of collaboration. As long past as 1930, I had a hunch that the talkies would make even the best selling novelist as archaic as silent pictures. People still read, if only Professor Canby's book of the month—curious children nosed at the slime of Mr. Tiffany Thayer in the drug-store libraries—but there was a rankling indignity, that to me had become almost an obsession, in seeing the power of the written word subordinated to another power, a more glittering, a grosser power . . .

I set that down as an example of what haunted me during the long night—this was something I could neither accept nor struggle against, something which tended to make my efforts obsolescent, as the chain stores have crippled the small merchant, an exterior force, unbeatable—

(I have the sense of lecturing now, looking at a watch on the desk before me and seeing how many more minutes—).

Well, when I had reached this period of silence, I was forced into a measure that no one ever adopts voluntarily: I was impelled to think. God, was it difficult! The moving about of great secret trunks. In the first exhausted halt, I wondered whether I had ever thought. After a long time I came to these conclusions, just as I write them here:

(1) That I had done very little thinking, save within the problems of my craft. For twenty years a certain man had been my intellectual conscience. That was Edmund Wilson.

(2) That another man represented my sense of the "good life," though I saw him once in a decade, and since then he might have been hung. He is in the fur business in the Northwest and wouldn't like his name set down here. But in difficult situations I had tried to think what *he* would have thought, how *he* would have acted.

(3) That a third contemporary had been an artistic conscience to me— I had not imitated his infectious style, because my own style, such as it is, was formed before he published anything, but there was an awful pull toward him when I was on a spot.

(4) That a fourth man had come to dictate my relations with other people when these relations were successful: how to do, what to say. How to make people at least momentarily happy (in opposition to Mrs. Post's theories of how to make everyone thoroughly uncomfortable with a sort of systematized vulgarity). This always confused me and made me want to go out and get drunk, but this man had seen the game, analyzed it and beaten it, and his word was good enough for me.

(5) That my political conscience had scarcely existed for ten years save as an element of irony in my stuff. When I became again concerned with the system I should function under, it was a man much younger than myself who brought it to me, with a mixture of passion and fresh air.

So there was not an "I" any more—not a basis on which I could organize my self-respect—save my limitless capacity for toil that it seemed I possessed no more. It was strange to have no self—to be like a little boy left alone in a big house, who knew that now he could do anything he wanted to do, but found that there was nothing that he wanted to do—

(The watch is past the hour and I have barely reached my thesis. I have some doubts as to whether this is of general interest, but if anyone wants more, there is plenty left, and your editor will tell me. If you've had enough, say so—but not too loud, because I have the feeling that someone, I'm not sure who, is sound asleep—someone who could have helped me to keep my shop open. It wasn't Lenin, and it wasn't God.)

HANDLE WITH CARE

*April, 1936*

I have spoken in these pages of how an exceptionally optimistic young man experienced a crack-up of all values, a crack-up that he scarcely knew of until long after it occurred. I told of the succeeding period of desolation and of the necessity of going on, but without benefit of Henley's familiar heroics, "my head is bloody but unbowed." For a check-up of my spiritual liabilities indicated that I had no particular head to be bowed or unbowed. Once I had had a heart but that was about all I was sure of.

This was at least a starting place out of the morass in which I floundered: "I felt—therefore I was." At one time or another there had been many people who had leaned on me, come to me in difficulties or written me from afar, believed implicitly in my advice and my attitude toward life. The dullest platitude monger or the most unscrupulous Rasputin who can influence the destinies of many people must have some individuality, so the question became one of finding why and where I had changed, where was the leak through which, unknown to myself, my enthusiasm and my vitality had been steadily and prematurely trickling away.

One harassed and despairing night I packed a brief case and went off a thousand miles to think it over. I took a dollar room in a drab little town where I knew no one and sunk all the money I had with me in a stock of potted meat, crackers and apples. But don't let me suggest that the change from a rather overstuffed world to a comparative asceticism was any Research Magnificent—I only wanted absolute quiet to think out why I had developed a sad attitude toward sadness, a melancholy attitude toward melancholy and a tragic attitude toward tragedy—*why I had become identified with the objects of my horror or compassion.*

Does this seem a fine distinction? It isn't: identification such as this spells the death of accomplishment. It is something like this that keeps insane people from working. Lenin did not willingly endure the sufferings of his proletariat, nor Washington of his troops, nor Dickens of his London poor. And when Tolstoy tried some such merging of himself with the objects of his attention, it was a fake and a failure. I mention these because they are the men best known to us all.

It was dangerous mist. When Wordsworth decided that "there had passed away a glory from the earth," he felt no compulsion to pass away with it, and the Fiery Particle Keats never ceased his struggle against t. b.

nor in his last moments relinquished his hope of being among the English poets.

My self-immolation was something sodden-dark. It was very distinctly not modern—yet I saw it in others, saw it in a dozen men of honor and industry since the war. (I heard you, but that's too easy—there were Marxians among these men.) I had stood by while one famous contemporary of mine played with the idea of the Big Out for half a year; I had watched when another, equally eminent, spent months in an asylum unable to endure any contact with his fellow men. And of those who had given up and passed on I could list a score.

This led me to the idea that the ones who had survived had made some sort of clean break. This is a big word and is no parallel to a jail-break when one is probably headed for a new jail or will be forced back to the old one. The famous "Escape" or "run away from it all" is an excursion in a trap even if the trap includes the south seas, which are only for those who want to paint them or sail them. A clean break is something you cannot come back from; that is irretrievable because it makes the past cease to exist. So, since I could no longer fulfill the obligations that life had set for me or that I had set for myself, why not slay the empty shell who had been posturing at it for four years? I must continue to be a writer because that was my only way of life, but I would cease any attempts to be a person—to be kind, just or generous. There were plenty of counterfeit coins around that would pass instead of these and I knew where I could get them at a nickel on the dollar. In thirty-nine years an observant eye has learned to detect where the milk is watered and the sugar is sanded, the rhinestone passed for diamond and the stucco for stone. There was to be no more giving of myself—all giving was to be outlawed henceforth under a new name, and that name was Waste.

The decision made me rather exuberant, like anything that is both real and new. As a sort of beginning there was a whole shaft of letters to be tipped into the waste basket when I went home, letters that wanted something for nothing—to read this man's manuscript, market this man's poem, speak free on the radio, indite notes of introduction, give this interview, help with the plot of this play, with this domestic situation, perform this act of thoughtfulness or charity.

The conjuror's hat was empty. To draw things out of it had long been a sort of sleight of hand, and now, to change the metaphor, I was off the dispensing end of the relief roll forever.

The heady villainous feeling continued.

I felt like the beady-eyed men I used to see on the commuting train from Great Neck fifteen years back—men who didn't care whether the world tumbled into chaos tomorrow if it spared their houses. I was one with them now, one with the smooth articles who said:

"I'm sorry but business is business." Or:

"You ought to have thought of that before you got into this trouble." Or:

"I'm not the person to see about that."

And a smile—ah, I would get me a smile. I'm still working on that smile. It is to combine the best qualities of a hotel manager, an experienced old social weasel, a headmaster on visitors' day, a colored elevator man, a pansy pulling a profile, a producer getting stuff at half its market value, a trained nurse coming on a new job, a body-vender in her first rotogravure, a hopeful extra swept near the camera, a ballet dancer with an infected toe, and of course the great beam of loving kindness common to all those from Washington to Beverly Hills who must exist by virtue of the contorted pan.

The voice too—I am working with a teacher on the voice. When I have perfected it the larynx will show no ring of conviction except the conviction of the person I am talking to. Since it will be largely called upon for the elicitation of the word "Yes," my teacher (a lawyer) and I are concentrating on that, but in extra hours. I am learning to bring into it that polite acerbity that makes people feel that far from being welcome they are not even tolerated and are under continual and scathing analysis at every moment. These times will of course not coincide with the smile. This will be reserved exclusively for those from whom I have nothing to gain, old worn-out people or young struggling people. They won't mind—what the hell, they get it most of the time anyhow.

But enough. It is not a matter of levity. If you are young and you should write asking to see me and learn how to be a sombre literary man writing pieces upon the state of emotional exhaustion that often overtakes writers in their prime—if you should be so young and so fatuous as to do this, I would not do so much as acknowledge your letter, unless you were related to someone very rich and important indeed. And if you were dying of starvation outside my window, I would go out quickly and give you the smile and the voice (if no longer the hand) and stick around till somebody raised a nickel to phone for the ambulance, that is if I thought there would be any copy in it for me.

I have now at last become a writer only. The man I had persistently tried to be became such a burden that I have "cut him loose" with as little compunction as a Negro lady cuts loose a rival on Saturday night. Let the good people function as such—let the overworked doctors die in harness, with one week's "vacation" a year that they can devote to straightening out their family affairs, and let the underworked doctors scramble for cases at one dollar a throw; let the soldiers be killed and enter immediately into the Valhalla of their profession. That is their contract with the gods. A writer need have no such ideals unless he makes them for himself, and this one has quit. The old dream of being an entire man in the Goethe-Byron-Shaw tradition, with an opulent American touch, a sort of combination of J. P. Morgan, Topham Beauclerk and St. Francis of Assisi, has been relegated to the junk heap of the shoulder pads worn for one day on the Princeton freshman football field and the overseas cap never worn overseas.

So what? This is what I think now: that the natural state of the sentient adult is a qualified unhappiness. I think also that in an adult the desire to be finer in grain than you are, "a constant striving" (as those people say who gain their bread by saying it) only adds to this unhappiness in the end—that end that comes to our youth and hope. My own happiness in the past often approached such an ecstasy that I could not share it even with the person dearest to me but had to walk it away in quiet streets and lanes with only fragments of it to distil into little lines in books—and I think that my happiness, or talent for self-delusion or what you will, was an exception. It was not the natural thing but the unnatural—unnatural as the Boom; and my recent experience parallels the wave of despair that swept the nation when the Boom was over.

I shall manage to live with the new dispensation, though it has taken some months to be certain of the fact. And just as the laughing stoicism which has enabled the American Negro to endure the intolerable conditions of his existence has cost him his sense of the truth—so in my case there is a price to pay. I do not any longer like the postman, nor the grocer, nor the editor, nor the cousin's husband, and he in turn will come to dislike me, so that life will never be very pleasant again, and the sign *Cave Canem* is hung permanently just above my door. I will try to be a correct animal though, and if you throw me a bone with enough meat on it I may even lick your hand.

# MARY PAIK LEE
## (1900–    )

Of the accounts authored by Asian American women, Lee's comes from the rare perspective of a Korean immigrant at the turn of the century. Korean immigration to the United States began in 1900, and numbered less than ten thousand workers, most of whom relocated to Hawaii; immigration was halted in 1905 by the Korean government.

The Lee family entered America during this brief window. They traveled to Oahu in May of 1905, and, after one year there, resettled to Riverside, California. Lee's accounts of her childhood in California are sharp and very much those of a child; the colors are bright, and she focuses her attention on many sensation-oriented stories. Her account is less a literary venture than a slice of life, a clear-eyed account of experience in difficult circumstances. The autobiography does not stop with the end of Lee's childhood; she continues on into her married life, motherhood, and old age.

## FROM *Quiet Odyssey*

Mother told me there had been a lot of discussion for several days before the final decision was made for my parents, my brother, and me to leave Korea to find a better life elsewhere. Father was reluctant to leave, but his parents insisted, saying that his presence would not help them. They knew what would happen to them in the near future. They were prepared to face great hardship or worse, but they wanted at least one member of their family to survive and live a better life somewhere else. Such strong, quiet courage in ordinary people in the face of danger is really something to admire and remember always.

My second brother, Paik Daw Sun, was born on October 6, 1905, in Hawaii. Father was desperate, always writing to friends in other places, trying to find a better place to live. Finally, he heard from friends in Riverside, California, who urged him to join them: they said the prospects for the future were better in America; that a man's wages were ten to fifteen cents an hour for ten hours of work a day. After his year in

Hawaii was up, Father borrowed enough money from friends to pay for our passage to America on board the S. S. *China*.

We landed in San Francisco on December 3, 1906. As we walked down the gangplank, a group of young white men were standing around, waiting to see what kind of creatures were disembarking. We must have been a very queer-looking group. They laughed at us and spit in our faces; one man kicked up Mother's skirt and called us names we couldn't understand. Of course, their actions and attitudes left no doubt about their feelings toward us. I was so upset. I asked Father why we had come to a place where we were not wanted. He replied that we deserved what we got because that was the same kind of treatment that Koreans had given to the first American missionaries in Korea: the children had thrown rocks at them, calling them "white devils" because of their blue eyes and yellow or red hair. He explained that anything new and strange causes some fear at first, so ridicule and violence often result. He said the missionaries just lowered their heads and paid no attention to their tormentors. They showed by their action and good works that they were just as good as or even better than those who laughed at them. He said that is exactly what we must try to do here in America—study hard and learn to show Americans that we are just as good as they are. That was my first lesson in living, and I have never forgotten it.

Many old friends came with us from Hawaii. Some stayed in San Francisco, others went to Dinuba, near Fresno, but most headed for Los Angeles. We ourselves went straight to the railroad depot nearby and boarded a train for Riverside, where friends would be waiting for us. It was our first experience on a train. We were excited, but we felt lost in such a huge country. When we reached Riverside, we found friends from our village in Korea waiting to greet us.

In those days, Orientals and others were not allowed to live in town with the white people. The Japanese, Chinese, and Mexicans each had their own little settlement outside of town. My first glimpse of what was to be our camp was rows of one-room shacks, with a few water pumps here and there and little sheds for outhouses. We learned later that the shacks had been constructed for the Chinese men who had built the Southern Pacific Railroad in the 1880s.

We had reached Riverside without any plans and with very little money, not knowing what we could do for a living. After much discussion with friends, it was decided that Mother should cook for about thirty single men who worked in the citrus groves. Father did not like her to work, but it seemed to be the only way we could make a living for ourselves. She would make their breakfast at 5 A.M., pack their lunches, and cook them supper at 7 P.M. But my parents did not have the cooking utensils we needed, so Father went to the Chinese settlement and told them of our situation. He could not speak Chinese but he wrote *hanmun,* the character writing that is the same in Korean and Chinese. He asked for credit, promising to make regular payments from time to time. They trusted him and agreed to give us everything we needed to get started: big iron pots and pans, dishes, tin lunch pails, chopsticks, and so forth. They also gave us rice and groceries.

The Korean men went to the dumpyard nearby and found the materials to build a shack large enough for our dining area. They made one long table and two long benches to seat thirty men. Father made a large stove and oven with mud and straw, and he found several large wine barrels to hold the water for drinking and cooking. That was the start of our business. Mother had long, thick black hair that touched the ground. It became a nuisance in her work, so Father cut it short, leaving just enough to coil in a bun on the back of her head. It must have caused her much grief to lose her beautiful hair, but she never complained. We had already lost everything else that meant anything to us.

We lived in a small one-room shack built in the 1880s. The passing of time had made the lumber shrink, so the wind blew through the cracks in the walls. There was no pretense of making it livable — just four walls, one window, and one door — nothing else. We put mud in the cracks to keep the wind out. The water pump served several shacks. We had to heat our bath water in a bucket over an open fire outside, then pour it into a tin tub inside. There was no gas or electricity. We used kerosene lamps, and one of my chores was to trim the wicks, clean the glass tops, and keep the bowls filled with kerosene.

The Chinese men who had lived there in the 1880s must have slept on the floor. Father solved the problem of where we were going to sleep by building shelves along the four walls of our shack. Then he found some hay to put on each shelf. He put a blanket over the hay, rolled up some old clothes for a pillow — and that was a bed for a child. I used a block of wood for my pillow. It became such a habit with me that even to this day I do not like a soft pillow. My parents themselves slept on the floor.

After our shelter was taken care of, I looked around and found that all our immediate neighbors were old friends from Korea. Philip Ahn, who became a movie actor many years later, lived across from us. His father was Mr. Ahn Chang-ho. Mr. Ahn and my father, who had been boy-hood friends in Korea, felt like brothers to each other and kept in touch through the years. It was good to see so many familiar faces again, and we felt happy to be there together.

Every day after school and on weekends, my older brother and I had to pile enough firewood up against the kitchen shack to last until the next day. Father found some wheels and boards at the dumpyard to make a long flatbed for carrying the wood, but we had to make several trips each day. An acre of trees grew some distance from us, where we found plenty of broken branches to gather up.

Meung's job was to keep the wine barrels filled with water so Mother could do her work. I cleaned the oil lamps, kept our shack in order, looked after my baby brother, and heated the bath water for the men at 6 P.M. so they could bathe before supper. The workers' bathhouse had just one large tub inside; I heated the water by building a fire under the floor. The men washed themselves with a hose before entering the tub.

Every Saturday Meung and I went to a slaughterhouse some distance away to get the animal organs that the butchers threw out—pork and beef livers, hearts, kidneys, entrails, tripe—all the things they considered unfit for human consumption. We were not alone—Mexican children came there also. They needed those things to survive just as we did. The butchers stood around laughing at us as we scrambled for the choice pieces. When I told Father I didn't want to go there anymore because they were making fun of us, he said we should thank God that they did not know the value of what they threw out; otherwise, we would go hungry.

Meung started school at the Washington Irving School, not far from our settlement. When I was ready to go, Father asked a friend who spoke a little English—a Mr. Song—to take me. My first day at school was a very frightening experience. As we entered the schoolyard, several girls formed a ring around us, singing a song and dancing in a circle. When they stopped, each one came over to me and hit me in the neck, hurting and frightening me. They ran away when a tall woman came towards us. Her bright yellow hair and big blue eyes looking down at me were a fearful sight; it was my first close look at such a person. She was welcoming me to her school, but I was frightened. When she addressed me, I answered in Korean, "I don't understand you." I turned around, ran all the way home, and hid in our shack. Father laughed when he heard about my behavior. He told me there was nothing to be afraid of; now that we were living here in America, where everything is different from Korea, we would have to learn to get along with everyone.

The next day when I went to school with my brother, the girls did not dance around us; I guess the teacher must have told them not to do it. I learned later that the song they sang was:

> Ching Chong, Chinaman,
> Sitting on a wall.
> Along came a white man,
> And chopped his head off.

The last line was the signal for each girl to "chop my head off" by giving me a blow on the neck. That must have been the greeting they gave to all the Oriental kids who came to school the first day.

Because our Korean names were too difficult for them to remember, the children at school always said "Hey you!" when they wanted our attention. I told Meung that it was too late to change our names, but we should give American names to our siblings. So we started with Paik Daw Sun, who had been born in Hawaii, by calling him Ernest. When another brother was born in Riverside on August 8, 1908, we named him Stanford.

Meung was only three years older than I, but he was extremely observant and considerate for his age. He told me to stop playing around and to notice how much work our mother had to do. He said that to help her, every day before school he would wash the baby's diapers, and I was to hang them on the line. After school, before going for firewood, I was to take them in, fold them, and put them away. Meanwhile he would fill the wine barrels with water from the pump. We followed this routine from then on. I was always taking care of the babies, bathing them every night, changing their diapers, and feeding them midnight bottles. He heated their bath water in a bucket outside so I could give them baths in the tin tub inside our shack.

There was one large building for community meetings in Riverside, where religious services were held on Sundays. We didn't have a minister, but several persons read the Bible and discussed it. Father preached there whenever he had time. An American lady named Mrs. Stewart, who lived in Upland, used to come to our church on Sundays. She was interested in the Korean people and brought presents for everyone at Christmastime. She gave me the first and only doll I ever had.

Meung and I had a special "gang" consisting of six members about the same age. We ran to school together, ran home for lunch, back to school, and home again. On the way to school there was a large mulberry bush growing in the front lawn of one house. Whenever we passed, we noticed the big black berries that had fallen on the lawn. They looked so tempting that we just had to stop and see what they tasted like. They were so delicious we couldn't stop eating them. After that, every time we passed that house we helped ourselves, but we had an uneasy feeling about whether it was right or wrong to take the fruit. We childishly decided that it was all right because the berries were on the ground and weren't picked off the bush. We had a big argument about it one day. When Meung said it was wrong to take something that belonged to someone else, my girlfriend got so angry she picked up a piece of firewood and hit him on the head. When we told Father about it, he said that the berries belonged to the owner of the bush, whether they were on the bush or on the ground. That settled our arguments. From then on we looked the other way every time we passed that house.

An old Chinese peddler used to come to our place once a week with fruits and vegetables on his wagon. I told Philip Ahn to climb up the front of his wagon and talk to him while I climbed up the back and filled my apron with small potatoes, lima beans, and corn, which we roasted in hot ashes. It was our first taste of such vegetables, and they were so good. But the old man got wise to us after a while, so whenever we approached his wagon, he used the horsewhip on us.

One evening, as I was helping Mother wash the lunch pails the men brought back, I asked her what kind of work the men were doing. She told me they were picking oranges, which gave me an idea, but I didn't dare to tell her about it. After breakfast the next day, as I passed out the lunch pails, I asked some of the men why they never brought me an orange. I said I had never seen or tasted one. That evening as I took in the lunch pails, they felt a bit heavy; when I opened one I saw a beautiful orange for the first time. I was so excited I told Father about it. He must have talked to the men, because there were only a few oranges after that. It helped make the work of washing the lunch pails seem less tiring to find a few. One night some time later, when I took in the lunch pails every single one felt heavy. I got really excited, but to my surprise, each pail had a rock in it. When I asked why, the men said they were afraid I would scold them if they didn't bring something, but there were no more oranges to be picked. Everybody had a good laugh about it.

After the orange season was over, the men picked lemons and grapefruit. In the fall there was work in the walnut groves. The men would shake the walnuts from the trees with long poles, then the women and children would gather them up in sacks, take them to a clearing, and peel off the outer shells [hulls]. They got paid by the sack for their labor. Between the walnut harvest and the time to prune the orange trees, the men got a short rest. When there was no work in the citrus groves, Father worked at the Riverside Cement Company on the edge of town.

Two incidents happened in Riverside that will always remain in my memory. The first was when I told Father I needed a coat to wear to school. He said that he would see what he could do about it. He rode to town on his bicycle to buy some material, and he made a coat for me. Since we did not have a sewing machine, he had to sew it by hand one evening. It was a beautiful red coat; I was so happy to wear it. All the girls at school wanted to know where I had purchased it. They couldn't believe my father had made it himself. When I asked Mother how Father could do such a wonderful thing, she smiled and said that, among other things, Father had been an expert tailor in Korea. He had studied to be a minister and had taught the Korean language to missionaries, but tailoring was how he made a living.

My second memory is equally wondrous. One evening Father woke us up in the middle of the night and said a wonderful thing was happening in the sky. Looking out the window, we saw a big star with a very long sparkling tail that seemed to stretch across the whole sky. The tail was full of small sparkling stars. It was a spectacular, awesome sight, a bit frightening to us children. We didn't understand what was going on and couldn't sleep the rest of the night, wondering what it meant and if everything would be all right the next day.

* * *

We lived in Riverside for four or five years, but Father became concerned about Mother's health—the work of cooking for thirty men was too much for her. She was a small woman, only four feet eleven inches tall, and she was expecting another baby. So we paid off the Chinese merchants who had helped us get started, paid all our debts to friends, and moved to Claremont, not too far away. It was a quiet college town with many school buildings. We moved into a duplex building, where an old friend, Martha Kim, was living with her parents. It was across the street from the railroad station and a huge citrus-packing house. Those were the days before frozen fruit juices, so after the choice fruit was packed, the culls were piled up in boxes back of the buildings to be taken to the dump once a week. Because of this, we were fortunate that we could enjoy all the discarded fruit.

Our move to Claremont turned out to be our first experience with the American way of living. The new house seemed huge after our little shack. It had several rooms with beds, chairs, and other furniture. The kitchen had a gas stove, electric lights, and a sink with faucets for cold and hot water. But all that was as nothing compared with what we found in the bathroom. There was a big white tub with faucets at one end—I couldn't believe it was the place for taking our baths. And the biggest surprise of all was the toilet. Father flushed it to show us how it operated. He must have seen these wonders before somewhere, because he wasn't surprised at anything. For the first time, I felt glad that we had come to America.

Father found a job as a janitor in the nearby apartment buildings. He told Meung and me to ask the tenants if we could do their laundry, and also to ask our schoolteachers the same thing. On foot, Meung had to pick up the dirty laundry in a big basket and return it later. I helped with the laundry before and after school and with the ironing at night. In Claremont we had our first experience with an electric iron. Before this we had heated the old "sad irons," as they were called in those days, on the wood stove. It was such a relief to use the electric iron. No more going back and forth to the wood stove for a hot iron. No more kerosene lamps, hunting for firewood, and outhouses. Life was getting better.

Every Saturday Father bought a beef roast, and every Sunday we had pot roast with mashed potatoes and bread. This was our introduction to American food, and it tasted wonderful. A small group of Koreans lived in Claremont. They came together to worship on Sundays in an old building. There was no minister, so Father preached there several times. Arthur was born in Claremont on December 2, 1910. The memory of our short stay there is a pleasant one.

Unfortunately Father's wages were so low in Claremont that it was difficult to make a living. So, a year later, we moved to Colusa in northern California, hoping to find work there. It turned out we had made a disastrous move. Father could not find any kind of work. There was a depression in 1911, and the situation was so bad the Salvation Army offered a bowl of soup and a piece of bread to each hungry person in town. But when I asked if we could go and get some, Father said no. He didn't want us to be humiliated by asking for help.

The feeling towards Orientals in southern California had not been friendly, but we had been tolerated. In the northern part of the state, we found the situation to be much worse. Although we found a house on the outskirts of town, the townspeople's attitude towards us was chilling. Father told Meung and me to ask our schoolteachers for their laundry. Once again, Meung had to fetch and deliver, carrying a basket on foot. Since we lived on the outskirts of town, it was a hard job for him, but he never complained. But because of the negative feeling towards Orientals in Colusa, we never got enough clothes to launder, and we could not earn enough money to meet our needs.

After paying the rent, light, water, and other bills, we had very little left over for food. Mother would tell me to buy a five-pound sack of flour, a small can of baking powder, salt, and two cans of Carnation milk for the baby. The two cans of milk had to last for one week: it was diluted with so much water, it didn't look like anything nourishing. Mother made tiny biscuits each morning and served one biscuit and a tin cup of water to each of us three times a day. During the time we lived in Colusa, we had no rice, meat, or anything besides biscuits to eat. Nonetheless, when we sat down to eat, Father would pray, thanking God for all our blessings. This used to irritate me. At the age of eleven years, I couldn't think of anything to be thankful for. Once he was sitting out on the porch smoking after dinner, and I asked him what we had to be so thankful for. He said, "Don't you remember why we came here?" I had forgotten that the fate of our family in Korea was much worse than ours. Nevertheless, my stomach ached for lack of food, and I had severe cramps. One evening the pain was so bad I got up to fill myself with water, which helped somewhat. As I neared the kitchen, I saw Father and Mother sitting across from each other at the table holding hands, with tears flowing down their

faces. I realized then how much agony they were suffering, and that my
own feelings were as nothing compared with theirs. I had been so absorbed in myself that the thought of my parents' suffering had never entered my mind. Seeing them that way made me realize how ignorant I
was. It awakened me to the realities of life.

I thought maybe I could get work cleaning someone's home to help
out. Since my schoolteacher was the only one I could talk to, I asked her
if she knew where I could get housework. She said that the principal lived
in a big house, that his wife might need someone to help her. So I went
to the principal and asked if his wife needed someone to do the cleaning
in his home. He said that he would find out and let me know.

The next day I went to his office and found out that his wife was willing to try me. She said I should work before and after school, and all day
Saturdays and Sundays. The wages were to be one dollar a week. In my
ignorance, that sounded good to me. I asked where he lived and walked
past it on my way home. It was a big, beautiful house, quite far from ours,
with a large lawn in front and colorful flowers all around. When I told Father about it, he shook his head and didn't say a word. As if he didn't
know it, I said that one dollar would buy twenty loaves of bread, and that
it would help feed the younger children who were hungry. Bread cost five
cents a loaf then. He said it was too much work for me, but I could try it.
Father left the room and went outside to smoke his pipe. Many years
later, he told me he had felt humiliated to hear his eleven-year-old
daughter tell him that her one-dollar-a-week wages were needed to feed
the family. I was too young and ignorant to know how my words had hurt
him.

I was totally ignorant of what my employers expected of me, but I was
stubborn enough to make the attempt. My secret reason for wanting this
job was that I was hoping to get something more than a tiny biscuit and
water to eat, but my punishment came in an unexpected way. Before I
left home in the morning, Father gave me advice about how I was to behave in my first American home. He showed me how to set a table with
napkins, and so forth. He said I should eat in the kitchen, never with the
family. I left home at 6 A.M., reached the principal's house before 7 A.M.,
and was surprised to see his wife. She looked like the pictures of the fat
lady in the circus—a huge woman. I also met her son, who was about
twenty years old. I helped the woman prepare breakfast and I set the
table. Before they sat down to eat, she gave me a cup of black coffee with
no sugar, milk, or cream, and she took the trouble to slice a piece of
bread so thin that, when I held it up to the light of the window, I could
see the outline of the tree outside. That was about the same amount of
food I would have had at home. I had to laugh at myself.

After the family finished eating, I cleared the table, washed the dishes, and cleaned up in the kitchen. Then I had to walk to school while the principal drove in his car. His son had a car also. Very few people in town owned cars, so two cars in one home was certainly unusual. When I told Father about it, he said that it *was* surprising, considering the low salaries of teachers. About fifteen years later, as I was passing a newsstand, I saw the principal's name in the headline of a paper. I stopped to read it. The article stated that Mr. So-and-So had been arrested for embezzling school funds. This had apparently been going on for years. No wonder he had a big, beautiful home and two cars in the family.

After school I went back to the principal's house, helped his wife prepare dinner, and set the table. Then I cleaned the other rooms while dinner was being prepared. She gave me a piece of bread and a few spoons of this and that for my meal. When I cleared the table, she put all the leftovers in dishes, covered them tightly, and put them in the ice box. I guess she was afraid I would eat their food. After washing the dishes and cleaning up the kitchen, I was told I could leave.

On Saturdays, I had to wash all the sheets, pillowcases, towels, and clothes in a big washtub, scrubbing them on a washboard in the backyard, rinsing them, hanging them on a line to dry, and taking them into the house after they were dry. There were no washing machines in those days. Everything had to be done by hand. On Sunday mornings, I sprinkled all the clothes that needed ironing and ironed all day. By nightfall, I was so tired I could hardly walk home. I had to admit to myself that the work was too much for me. Finally, summer vacation came. Father said that he was going to Dinuba, near Fresno, to work in the fruit orchards there to try to make some money. Thus, I should stay home and help Mother while he was away. I was really glad to have an excuse to quit my job. After that, I learned to listen to my elders and not to be such a stubborn fool over things I knew nothing about.

One day we heard music outside the house. Looking out the window, we saw a small truck painted in bright colors with a big picture of an ice cream cone filled with white ice cream. All my younger brothers had their faces pressed against the window, wondering what the truck was. We had never tasted ice cream. Seeing so many children, the man thought that surely someone would come out to buy from him. After waiting several minutes, he gave up and left. The children looked around at Father with questions in their eyes, not daring to say a word. That must have been an agonizing moment for my parents. I looked at their sad, desperate faces and felt sorry for them. Father asked all of us to come into the kitchen and sit down at the table. He took out all the money he had and said that we were not earning enough money to buy everything we wanted, and that we had to pay for several things before we could even buy food to eat. Picking up a few coins, he said, "We have to save this much every week in order to pay the rent for this house, otherwise the owner will not let us live here. Then we have to pay so much for the electric lights, gas for the stove, water, and laundering supplies. That is why we cannot buy enough food to eat three times a day. There is nothing left for such things as ice cream cones." It was a lesson in economics that even a five-year-old child could understand. There were five children in the family then, and ice cream cones cost five cents apiece. Twenty-five cents was a lot of money when one did not have it. From then on, the children never looked out the window when the music sounded, and the ice cream man never stopped at our house. The children never asked for anything after that.

# RICHARD WRIGHT
## (1908–1960)

An extremely versatile writer, Wright was born on a plantation in Mississippi, near Natchez, where his erratic, troubled father was a mill worker and school-teacher. After his father's desertion, Wright shuffled among orphanages or accompanied his weary mother as she moved from city to city, living an itinerant, impoverished life on the hoof. In 1927, at nineteen, he joined the Communist Party in Chicago and began writing, which for him was a form of social action as well as a means of achieving identity.

Writing novels, stories, and essays in defense of his ideals, Wright produced an important body of work that includes *Uncle Tom's Children* (1938), a miscellaneous first collection; *Native Son* (1940), a wrenching novel about a young black man who is thrust into a life of crime; *The Outsider* (1953), a polemical novel on the theme of alienation among black people in America; and *Black Power* (1954), a remarkable piece of reportage focused on West Africa. *Black Boy: A Record of Childhood and Youth,* his deeply felt memoir, which counts among the handful of canonical works in this genre, was published in 1945 and is excerpted here.


## FROM *Black Boy*

Summer again. The old problem of hunting for a job. I told the woman for whom I was working, a Mrs. Bibbs, that I needed an all-day job that would pay me enough money to buy clothes and books for the next school term. She took the matter up with her husband, who was a foreman in a sawmill.

"So you want to work in the mill, hunh?" he asked.

"Yes, sir."

He came to me and put his hands under my arms and lifted me from the floor, as though I were a bundle of feathers.

"You're too light for our work," he said.

"But maybe I could do *something* there," I said.

"That's the problem," he said soberly. "The work's heavy and dangerous." He was silent and I knew that he considered the matter closed. That was the way things were between whites and blacks in the South;

many of the most important things were never openly said; they were understated and left to seep through to one. I, in turn, said nothing; but I did not leave the room; my standing silent was a way of asking him to reconsider, telling him that I wanted ever so much to try for a job in his mill. "All right," he said finally. "Come to the mill in the morning. I'll see what I can do. But I don't think that you'll like it."

I was at the mill at dawn the next morning and saw men lifting huge logs with tackle blocks. There were scores of buzzing steel saws biting into green wood with loud whines.

"Watch out!" somebody yelled.

I looked around and saw a black man pointing above my head; I glanced up. A log was swinging toward me. I scrambled out of its path. The black man came to my side.

"What do you want here, boy?"

"Mr. Bibbs, the foreman, told me to look around. I'm looking for a job," I said.

The man gazed at me intently.

"I wouldn't try for this if I was you," he said. "If you know this game, all right. But this is dangerous stuff for a guy that's green." He held up his right hand from which three fingers were missing. "See?"

I nodded and left.

Empty days. Long days. Bright hot days. The sun heated the pavements until they felt like the top of an oven. I spent the mornings hunting for jobs and I read during the afternoons. One morning I was walking toward the center of town and passed the home of a classmate, Ned Greenley. He was sitting on his porch, looking glum.

"Hello, Ned. What's new?" I asked.

"You've heard, haven't you?" he asked.

"About what?"

"My brother, Bob?"

"No, what happened?"

Ned began to weep softly.

"They killed him," he managed to say.

"The white folks?" I asked in a whisper, guessing.

He sobbed his answer. Bob was dead; I had met him only a few times, but I felt that I had known him through his brother.

"What happened?"

"Th-they t-took him in a c-car . . . Out on a c-country road . . . Th-they shot h-him," Ned whimpered.

I had heard that Bob was working at one of the hotels in town.

"Why?"

"Th-they said he was fooling with a white prostitute there in the hotel," Ned said.

Inside of me my world crashed and my body felt heavy. I stood looking down the quiet, sun-filled street. Bob had been caught by the white death, the threat of which hung over every male black in the South. I had heard whispered tales of black boys having sex relations with white prostitutes in the hotels in town, but I had never paid any close attention to them; now those tales came home to me in the form of the death of a man I knew.

I did not search for a job that day; I returned home and sat on my porch too, and stared. What I had heard altered the look of the world, induced in me a temporary paralysis of will and impulse. The penalty of death awaited me if I made a false move and I wondered if it was worthwhile to make any move at all. The things that influenced my conduct as a Negro did not have to happen to me directly; I needed but to hear of them to feel their full effects in the deepest layers of my consciousness. Indeed, the white brutality that I had not seen was a more effective control of my behavior than that which I knew. The actual experience would have let me see the realistic outlines of what was really happening, but as long as it remained something terrible and yet remote, something whose horror and blood might descend upon me at any moment, I was compelled to give my entire imagination over to it, an act which blocked the springs of thought and feeling in me, creating a sense of distance between me and the world in which I lived.

A few days later I sought out the editor of the local Negro newspaper and found that he could not hire me. I had doubts now about my being able to enter school that fall. The empty days of summer rolled on. Whenever I met my classmates they would tell me about the jobs they had found, how some of them had left town to work in summer resorts in the North. Why did they not tell me of these jobs? I demanded of them. They said that they simply had not thought of it, and as I heard the words fall from their lips my sense of isolation became doubly acute. But, after all, what would make them think of me in connection with jobs when for years I had encountered them only casually in the classroom? I had had no association with them; the religious home in which I lived, my mush-and-lard-gravy poverty had cut me off from the normal processes of the lives of black boys my own age.

One afternoon I made a discovery in the home that stunned me. I was talking to my cousin, Maggie, who was a few months younger than I, when Uncle Tom entered the room. He paused, stared at me with silent hostility, then called his daughter. I gave the matter no thought. A few moments later I rose from my chair, where I had been reading, and was on my way down the hall when I heard Uncle Tom scolding his daughter. I caught a few phrases:

"Do you want me to break your neck? Didn't I tell you to stay away from him? That boy's a dangerous fool, I tell you! Then why don't you keep away from him? And make the other children keep away from him! Ask me no questions, but do as I tell you! Keep away from him, or I'll skin you!"

And I could hear my cousin's whimpering replies. My throat grew tight with anger. I wanted to rush into the room and demand an explanation, but I held still. How long had this been going on? I thought back over the time since Uncle Tom and his family had moved into the house, and I was filled with dismay as I recalled that on scarcely any occasion had any of his children ever been alone with me. Be careful now, I told myself; don't see what isn't there . . . But no matter how carefully I weighed my memories, I could recall no innocent intimacy, no games, no playing, none of the association that usually exists between young people living in the same house. Then suddenly I was reliving that early morning when I had held Uncle Tom at bay with my razors. Though I must have seemed brutal and desperate to him, I had never thought of myself as being so, and now I was appalled at how I was regarded. It was a flash of insight which revealed to me the true nature of my relations with my family, an insight which altered the entire course of my life. I was now definitely decided upon leaving home. But I would remain until the ninth grade term had ended. There were many days when I spoke to no one in the home except my mother. My life was falling to pieces and I was acutely aware of it. I was poised for flight, but I was waiting for some event, some word, some act, some circumstance to furnish the impetus.

I returned to my job at Mrs. Bibb's and bought my schoolbooks; my clothing remained little better than rags. Luckily the studies in the ninth—my last year at school—were light; and, during a part of the term the teacher turned over the class to my supervision, an honor that helped me emotionally and made me hope faintly. It was even hinted that, if I kept my grades high, it would be possible for me to teach in the city school system.

During that winter my brother came home from Chicago; I was glad to see him, though we were strangers. But it was not long before I felt that the affection shown him by the family was far greater than that which I had ever had from them. Slowly my brother grew openly critical of me, taking his cue from those about him, and it hurt. My loneliness became organic. I felt walled in and I grew irritable. I associated less and less with my classmates, for their talk was now full of the schools they planned to attend when the term was over. The cold days dragged mechanically: up early and to my job, splitting wood, carrying coal, sweeping floors, then off to school and boredom.

The school term ended. I was selected as valedictorian of my class and assigned to write a paper to be delivered at one of the public auditoriums. One morning the principal summoned me to his office.

"Well, Richard Wright, here's your speech," he said with smooth bluntness and shoved a stack of stapled sheets across his desk.

"What speech?" I asked as I picked up the papers.

"The speech you're to say the night of graduation," he said.

"But, professor, I've written my speech already," I said.

He laughed confidently, indulgently.

"Listen, boy, you're going to speak to both *white* and colored people that night. What can you alone think of saying to them? You have no experience . . ."

I burned.

"I know that I'm not educated, professor," I said. "But the people are coming to hear the students, and I won't make a speech that you've written."

He leaned back in his chair and looked at me in surprise.

"You know, we've never had a boy in this school like you before," he said. "You've had your way around here. Just how you managed to do it, I don't know. But, listen, take this speech and say it. I know what's best for you. You can't afford to just say *anything* before those white people that night." He paused and added meaningfully: "The superintendent of schools will be there; you're in a position to make a good impression on him. I've been a principal for more years than you are old, boy. I've seen many a boy and girl graduate from this school, and none of them was too proud to recite a speech I wrote for them."

I had to make up my mind quickly; I was faced with a matter of principle. I wanted to graduate, but I did not want to make a public speech that was not my own.

"Professor, I'm going to say my own speech that night," I said.

He grew angry.

"You're just a young, hotheaded fool," he said. He toyed with a pencil and looked up at me. "Suppose you don't graduate?"

"But I passed my examinations," I said.

"Look, mister," he shot at me, "I'm the man who says who passes at this school."

I was so astonished that my body jerked. I had gone to this school for two years and I had never suspected what kind of man the principal was; it simply had never occurred to me to wonder about him.

"Then I don't graduate," I said flatly.

I turned to leave.

"Say, you. Come here," he called.

I turned and faced him; he was smiling at me in a remote, superior sort of way.

"You know, I'm glad I talked to you," he said. "I was seriously thinking of placing you in the school system, teaching. But, now, I don't think that you'll fit."

He was tempting me, baiting me; this was the technique that snared black young minds into supporting the southern way of life.

"Look, professor, I may never get a chance to go to school again," I said. "But I like to do things right."

"What do you mean?"

"I've no money. I'm going to work. Now, this ninth-grade diploma isn't going to help me much in life. I'm not bitter about it; it's not your fault. But I'm just not going to do things this way."

"Have you talked to anybody about this?" he asked me.

"No, why?"

"Are you sure?"

"This is the first I've heard of it, professor," I said, amazed again.

"You haven't talked to any white people about this?"

"No, sir!"

"I just wanted to know," he said.

My amazement increased; the man was afraid now for his job!

"Professor, you don't understand me." I smiled.

"You're just a young, hot fool," he said, confident again. "Wake up, boy. Learn the world you're living in. You're smart and I know what you're after. I've kept closer track of you than you think. I know your relatives. Now, if you play safe," he smiled and winked, "I'll help you to go to school, to college."

"I want to learn, professor," I told him. "But there are some things I don't want to know."

"Good-bye," he said.

I went home, hurt but determined. I had been talking to a "bought" man and he had tried to "buy" me. I felt that I had been dealing with something unclean. That night Griggs, a boy who had gone through many classes with me, came to the house.

"Look, Dick, you're throwing away your future here in Jackson," he said. "Go to the principal, talk to him, take his speech and say it. I'm saying the one he wrote. So why can't you? What the hell? What can you lose?"

"No," I said.

"Why?"

"I know only a hell of a little, but my speech is going to reflect that," I said.

"Then you're going to be blacklisted for teaching jobs," he said.

"Who the hell said I was going to teach?" I asked.

"God, but you've got a will," he said.

"It's not will. I just don't want to do things that way," I said.

He left. Two days later Uncle Tom came to me. I knew that the principal had called him in.

"I hear that the principal wants you to say a speech which you've rejected," he said.

"Yes, sir. That's right," I said.

"May I read the speech you've written?" he asked.

"Certainly," I said, giving him my manuscript.

"And may I see the one that the principal wrote?"

I gave him the principal's speech too. He went to his room and read them. I sat quiet, waiting. He returned.

"The principal's speech is the better speech," he said.

"I don't doubt it," I replied. "But why did they ask me to write a speech if I can't deliver it?"

"Would you let me work on your speech?" he asked.

"No, sir."

"Now, look, Richard, this is your future . . ."

"Uncle Tom, I don't care to discuss this with you," I said.

He stared at me, then left. The principal's speech was simpler and clearer than mine, but it did not say anything; mine was cloudy, but it said what I wanted to say. What could I do? I had half a mind not to show up at the graduation exercises. I was hating my environment more each day. As soon as school was over, I would get a job, save money, and leave.

Griggs, who had accepted a speech written by the principal, came to my house each day and we went off into the woods to practice orating; day in and day out we spoke to the trees, to the creeks, frightening the birds, making the cows in the pastures stare at us in fear. I memorized my speech so thoroughly that I could have recited it in my sleep.

The news of my clash with the principal had spread through the class and the students became openly critical of me.

"Richard, you're a fool. You're throwing away every chance you've got. If they had known the kind of fool boy you are, they would never have made you valedictorian," they said.

I gritted my teeth and kept my mouth shut, but my rage was mounting by the hour. My classmates, motivated by a desire to "save" me, pestered me until I all but reached the breaking point. In the end the principal had to caution them to let me alone, for fear I would throw up the sponge and walk out.

I had one more problem to settle before I could make my speech. I was the only boy in my class wearing short pants and I was grimly determined to leave school in long pants. Was I not going to work? Would I not be on my own? When my desire for long pants became known at home, yet another storm shook the house.

"You're trying to go too fast," my mother said.

"You're nothing but a child," Uncle Tom pronounced.

"He's beside himself," Granny said.

I served notice that I was making my own decisions from then on. I borrowed money from Mrs. Bibbs, my employer, made a down payment on a pearl-gray suit. If I could not pay for it, I would take the damn thing back after graduation.

On the night of graduation I was nervous and tense; I rose and faced the audience and my speech rolled out. When my voice stopped there was some applause. I did not care if they liked it or not; I was through. Immediately, even before I left the platform, I tried to shunt all memory of the event from me. A few of my classmates managed to shake my hand as I pushed toward the door, seeking the street. Somebody invited me to a party and I did not accept. I did not want to see any of them again. I walked home, saying to myself: The hell with it! With almost seventeen years of baffled living behind me, I faced the world in 1925.

# EUDORA WELTY
## (1909– )

"As you have seen," Welty concludes in *One Writer's Beginnings* (1984), "I am a writer who came of a sheltered life. A sheltered life can be a daring life as well. For all serious daring starts from within." That Welty has led a daring life of the mind is clear from her autobiography, which tells the story of her entrance into the world of thought and feeling. Like Hemingway and Annie Dillard, she writes beautifully about her sense of vocation as a writer. In the vein of Helen Keller and Mary Antin, she describes her awakening to the world in memorable language.

Welty's short fiction—gathered in her *Collected Stories* (1980)—has won a great deal of well-deserved praise. (Her wildly funny tale "Why I Live at the P.O." has earned the status of a modern classic.) Her novels, too, reveal a writer of uncanny originality, as in *The Optimist's Daughter*, awarded a Pulitzer Prize in 1973.

## FROM *One Writer's Beginnings*

I had the window seat. Beside me, my father checked the progress of our train by moving his finger down the timetable and springing open his pocket watch. He explained to me what the position of the arms of the semaphore meant; before we were to pass through a switch we would watch the signal lights change. Along our track, the mileposts could be read; he read them. Right on time by Daddy's watch, the next town sprang into view, and just as quickly was gone.

Side by side and separately, we each lost ourselves in the experience of not missing anything, of seeing everything, of knowing each time what the blows of the whistle meant. But of course it was not the same experience: what was new to me, not older than ten, was a landmark to him. My father knew our way mile by mile; by day or by night, he knew where we were. Everything that changed under our eyes, in the flying countryside, was the known world to him, the imagination to me. Each in our own way, we hungered for all of this: my father and I were in no other respect or situation so congenial.

In Daddy's leather grip was his traveler's drinking cup, collapsible; a lid to fit over it had a ring to carry it by; it traveled in a round leather box. This treasure would be brought out at my request, for me to bear to the water cooler at the end of the Pullman car, fill to the brim, and bear back to my seat, to drink water over its smooth lip. The taste of silver could almost be relied on to shock your teeth.

After dinner in the sparkling dining car, my father and I walked back to the open-air observation platform at the end of the train and sat on the folding chairs placed at the railing. We watched the sparks we made fly behind us into the night. Fast as our speed was, it gave us time enough to see the rose-red cinders turn to ash, each one, and disappear from sight. Sometimes a house far back in the empty hills showed a light no bigger than a star. The sleeping countryside seemed itself to open a way through for our passage, then close again behind us.

The swaying porter would be making ready our berths for the night, pulling the shade down just so, drawing the green fishnet hammock across the window so the clothes you took off could ride along beside you, turning down the tight-made bed, standing up the two snowy pillows as high as they were wide, switching on the eye of the reading lamp, starting the tiny electric fan—you suddenly saw its blades turn into gauze and heard its insect murmur; and drawing across it all the pair of thick green theaterlike curtains—billowing, smelling of cigar smoke—between which you would crawl or dive headfirst to button them together with yourself inside, to be seen no more that night.

When you lay enclosed and enwrapped, your head on a pillow parallel to the track, the rhythm of the rail clicks pressed closer to your body as if it might be your heart beating, but the sound of the engine seemed to come from farther away than when it carried you in daylight. The whistle was almost too far away to be heard, its sound wavering back from the engine over the roofs of the cars. What you listened for was the different sound that ran under you when your own car crossed on a trestle, then another sound on an iron bridge; a low or a high bridge—each had its pitch, or drumbeat, for your car.

Riding in the sleeper rhythmically lulled me and waked me. From time to time, waked suddenly, I raised my window shade and looked out at my own strip of the night. Sometimes there was unexpected moonlight out there. Sometimes the perfect shadow of our train, with our car, with me invisibly included, ran deep below, crossing a river with us by the light of the moon. Sometimes the encroaching walls of mountains woke me by clapping at my ears. The tunnels made the train's passage resound like the "loud" pedal of a piano, a roar that seemed to last as long as a giant's temper tantrum.

But my father put it all into the frame of regularity, predictability, that was his fatherly gift in the course of our journey. I saw it going by, the outside world, in a flash. I dreamed over what I could see as it passed, as well as over what I couldn't. Part of the dream was what lay beyond, where the path wandered off through the pasture, the red clay road climbed and went over the hill or made a turn and was hidden in trees, or toward a river whose bridge I could see but whose name I'd never know. A house back at its distance at night showing a light from an open doorway, the morning faces of the children who stopped still in what they were doing, perhaps picking blackberries or wild plums, and watched us go by—I never saw with the thought of their continuing to be there just the same after we were out of sight. For now, and for a long while to come, I was proceeding in fantasy.

I learned much later—after he was dead, in fact, the time when we so often learn fundamental things about our parents—how well indeed he knew the journey, and how he happened to do so. He fell in love with my mother, and she with him, in West Virginia when she was a teacher in the mountain schools near her home and he was a young man from Ohio who'd gone over to West Virginia to work in the office of a lumber construction company. When they decided to marry, they saw it as part of the adventure of starting a new life to go to a place far away and new to both of them, and that turned out to be Jackson, Mississippi. From rural Ohio and rural West Virginia, that must have seemed, in 1904, as far away as Bangkok might possibly seem to young people today. My father went down and got a job in a new insurance company being formed in Jackson. This was the Lamar Life. He was promoted almost at once, made secretary and one of the directors, and he was to stay with the company for the rest of his life. He set about first thing finding a house in Jackson, then a town of six or eight thousand people, for them to live in until they could build a house of their own. So during the engagement, he went the thousand miles to see her when he could afford it. The rest of the time—every day, sometimes twice a day—the two of them sent letters back and forth by this same train.

Their letters had all been kept by that great keeper, my mother; they were in one of the trunks in the attic—the trunk that used to go on the train with us to West Virginia and Ohio on summer trips. I didn't in the end feel like a trespasser when I came to open the letters: they brought my parents before me for the first time as young, as inexperienced, consumed with the strength of their hopes and desires, as *living* on these letters. I would have known my mother's voice in her letters anywhere. But I wouldn't have so quickly known my father's. Annihilating those miles between them—the miles I came along to travel with him, that first time on the train—those miles he knew nearly altogether by heart, he wrote more often than any once a day, and mailed his letters directly onto the mail car—letters that are so ardent, so direct and tender in expression, so urgent, that they seemed to bare, along with his love, the rest of his whole life to me.

On the train I saw that world passing my window. It was when I came to see it was *I* who was passing that my self-centered childhood was over. But it was not until I began to write, as I seriously did only when I reached my twenties, that I found the world out there revealing, because (as with my father now) *memory* had become attached to seeing, love had added itself to discovery, and because I recognized in my own continuing longing to keep going, the need I carried inside myself to know—the apprehension, first, and then the passion, to connect myself to it. Through travel I first became aware of the outside world; it was through travel that I found my own introspective way into becoming a part of it.

This is, of course, simply saying that the outside world is the vital component of my inner life. My work, in the terms in which I see it, is as dearly matched to the world as its secret sharer. My imagination takes its strength and guides its direction from what I see and hear and learn and feel and remember of my living world. But I was to learn slowly that both these worlds, outer and inner, were different from what they seemed to me in the beginning.

The best college in the state was very possibly the private liberal-arts one right here in Jackson, but I was filled with desire to go somewhere away and enter a school I'd never passed on the street. My parents thought that I was too young at sixteen to live for my first year too far from home. Mississippi State College for Women was well enough accredited and two hundred miles to the north.

There I landed in a world to itself, and indeed it was all new to me. It was surging with twelve hundred girls. They came from every nook and corner of the state, from the Delta, the piney woods, the Gulf Coast, the black prairie, the red clay hills, and Jackson—as the capital city and the only sizeable town, a region to itself. All were clearly differentiated sections, at that time, and though we were all put into uniforms of navy blue so as to unify us, it could have been told by the girls' accents, by their bearings, the way they came into the classroom and the way they ate, where they'd grown up. This was my first chance to learn what the body of us were like and what differences in background, persuasion of mind, and resources of character there were among Mississippians—at that, among only half of us, for we were all white. I missed the significance of both what was in, and what was out of, our well-enclosed but vibrantly alive society. What was never there was money enough provided by our

Legislature for education, and what was always there was a faculty accomplishing that education as a *feat*. Mississippi State College for Women, the oldest institution of its kind in America, poverty-stricken, enormously overcrowded, keeping within the tradition we were all used to in Mississippi, was conscientiously and, on the average, well taught by a dedicated faculty remaining and growing old there.

It was life in a crowd. We'd fight to get our mail in the basement post office, on rainy mornings, surrounded by other girls doing the Three Graces, where the gym teacher would have had to bring her first-period class indoors to practice. Even a gym piano, in competition with girls screaming over their letters and opening the food packages from home, was almost defeated. When we all had to crowd into compulsory chapel, one or two little frail undernourished students would faint sometimes — we had a fifteen-minute long Alma Mater to sing.

Old Main, the dormitory where I lived, had been built in 1860. It was packed to the roof with freshmen, three, four, or a half-dozen sometimes to the room, rising up four steep flights of wooden stairs. The chapel clock striking the hour very close by would shake our beds under us. It was the practice to use the fire escape to go to class, and at night to slip outside for a few minutes before going to bed.

It was the iron standpipe kind of fire escape, with a tin chute running down through it — all corkscrew turns from top to bottom, with holes along its passage where girls at fire drill could pour out of the different floors, and a hole at the bottom to pitch you out onto the ground, head still whirling.

It seemed impossible to be alone. Only music students had a good way. On a spring night you might hear one of them alone in a practice room of the Music Building, playing her heart out at an open window. It would be something like "Pale Hands I Loved Beside the Shalimar (Where Are You Now?)" — she'd be imagining of course that what she sent floating in the air was from someone else singing this song to *her*. At other times, when some strange song with low gutteral notes and dragging movement, dramatically working up to a crescendo, was heard later still through that same open window, we freshmen told one another that was Miss Pohl, the spectacular gym teacher with the flying gray hair, who was, we had heard and believed, a Russian by birth, who'd been crossed, long years ago, in love. She may have indeed been crossed in love, but she was a Mississippian, just like us.

A time could be seized, close to bedtime, when it was possible to slip down the fire escape and, before the doors were all locked against my getting back, walk to an iron fountain on the campus and around it, with poetry running through my head. I'd bought the first book for my shelf from the college bookstore, *In April Once,* by William Alexander Percy, our chief Mississippi poet. Its first poem was one written from New York City, entitled "Home."

> *I have a need of silence and of stars.*
> *Too much is said too loudly. I am dazed.*
> *The silken sound of whirled infinity*
> *Is lost in voices shouting to be heard . . .*

Where I walked at that moment, within the little town of Columbus, and further within the iron gates of the campus of a girls' college at night, now everywhere going to bed, and while I said the poem to myself, around me was nothing *but* silence and stars. This did not impinge upon my longing. In the beautiful spring night, I was dedicated to *wanting* a beautiful spring night. To be *transported* to it was what I wanted. Whatever a poem was about—that it could be called "Home" didn't matter—it was about somewhere else, somewhere distant and far.

I was lucky enough to have found for myself, at the very beginning, an outside shell, that of freshman reporter on our college newspaper, *The Spectator.* I became a wit and humorist of the parochial kind, and the amount I was able to show off in print must have been a great comfort to me. (I saw *The Bat* and wrote "The Gnat," laid in MSCW. The Gnat assumes the disguise of our gym uniform—navy blue serge one-piece with pleated bloomers reaching below the knee, and white tennis shoes—and enters through the College Library, after hours; our librarian starts screaming at his opening line, "Beulah Culbertson, I have come for those fines.") I'd been a devoted reader of S. J. Perelman, Corey Ford, and other humorists who appeared in *Judge* magazine, and I'd imagined that with these as a springboard, I could swim.

After great floods struck the state and Columbus had been overflowed by the Tombigbee River, I contributed an editorial to *The Spectator* for its April Fool issue. This lamented that five of our freshman class got drowned when the waters rose, but by this Act of God, it went on, there was that much more room now for the rest of us. Years later, a Columbus newspaperman, on whose press our paper was printed, told me that H. L. Mencken had picked up this chirp out of me for *The American Mercury* as sample thinking from the Bible Belt. But by chance, in the home of a town student, I had just met my first intellectual. Within a few moments he had lent me *Candide!* It was just published, the first Modern Library book (I believe the very first)—that thin little book with leatherlike covers that heated up, while you read, warmer than your hand. Voltaire, too, I could call on.

But I learned my vital lesson in the classroom.

Mr. Lawrence Painter, the only man teacher in the college, spent his life conducting the MSCW girls in their sophomore year through English Survey, from "Summer is y-comen in" to "I have a rendezvous with Death." In my time a handsome, learned, sandy-haired man—wildly popular, of course, on campus—he got instant silence when he would throw open the book and begin to read aloud to us.

In high-school freshman English, we had committed to memory "Whan that Aprille with his shoures soote . . ." which as poetry was not less remote to our ears than "Arma virumque cano . . ." I had come unprepared for the immediacy of poetry.

I felt the shock closest to this a year later at the University of Wisconsin when I walked into my art class and saw, in place of the bowl of fruit and the glass bottle and ginger jar of the still life I used to draw at MSCW, a live human being. As we sat at our easels, a model, a young woman, lightly dropped her robe and stood, before us and a little above us, holding herself perfectly contained, in her full self and naked. Often that year in Survey Course, as Mr. Painter read, poetry came into the room where we could see it and all around it, free-standing poetry. As we listened, Mr. Painter's, too, was a life class.

After I transferred, in my junior year, to the University of Wisconsin, I made in this far, new place a discovery for myself that has fed my life ever since. I express a little of my experience in a story, one fairly recent and not yet completed. It's the story of a middle-aged man who'd come from a farm in the Middle West, who's taciturn and unhappy as a teacher of linguistics and now has reached a critical point in his life. The scene is New Orleans; he and a woman are walking at night (they are really saying goodbye) and he speaks of himself without reserve to her for the first time.

He'd put himself through the University of Wisconsin, he tells her:

> "And I happened to discover Yeats, reading through some of the stacks in the library. I read the early and then the later poems all in the same one afternoon, standing up, by the window . . . I read 'Sailing to Byzantium,' standing up in the stacks, read it by the light of falling snow. It seemed to me that if I could stir, if I could move to take the next step, I could go out into the poem the way I could go out into that snow. That it would be falling on my shoulders. That it would pelt me on its way down—that I could move in it, live in it—that I could die in it, maybe. So after that I had to *learn* it," he said. "And I told myself that I would. That I accepted the invitation."

The experience I describe in the story had indeed been my own, snow and all; the poem that smote me first was "The Song of Wandering Aengus"; it was the poem that turned up, fifteen years or so later, in my stories of *The Golden Apples* and runs all through that book.

At length too, at Wisconsin, I learned the word for the nature of what I had come upon in reading Yeats. Mr. Ricardo Quintana lecturing to his class on Swift and Donne used it in its true meaning and import. The word is *passion*.

It was my mother who emotionally and imaginatively supported me in my wish to become a writer. It was my father who gave me the first dictionary of my own, a Webster's Collegiate, inscribed on the flyleaf with my full name (he always included Alice, my middle name, after his mother) and the date, 1925. I still consult it. It was also he who expressed his reservations that I wouldn't achieve financial success by becoming a writer, a sensible fear; nevertheless he fitted me out with my first typewriter, my little red Royal Portable, which I carried off to the University of Wisconsin. It was also he who advised me, after I'd told him I still meant to try writing, even though I didn't expect to sell my stories to *The Saturday Evening Post* which paid well, to go ahead and try myself—but to prepare to earn my living some other way. My supportive parents had already very willingly agreed that I go farther from home for my last two years of college and sent me to Wisconsin—my father's choice for its high liberal-arts reputation. Now that I'd been graduated from there, they sent me to my first choice of a place to prepare for a job: New York City, at Columbia University Graduate School of Business. (As certain as I was of wanting to be a writer, I was certain of *not* wanting to be a teacher. I lacked the instructing turn of mind, the selflessness, the patience for teaching, and I had the unreasoning feeling that I'd be trapped. The odd thing is that when I did come to write my stories, the longest list of my characters turns out to be schoolteachers. They are to a great extent my heroines.)

My father did not bring it up, but of course I knew that he had another reason to worry about my decision to write. Though he was a reader, he was not a lover of fiction, because fiction is not true, and for that flaw it was forever inferior to fact. If reading fiction was a waste of time, so was the writing of it. (Why is it, I wonder, that humor didn't count? Wodehouse, for one, whom both of us loved, was a flawless fiction writer.)

But I was not to be in time to show him what I could do, to hear what he thought, on the evidence, of where I was headed.

My father had given immense study to the erection of the new Lamar Life home office building on Capitol Street, which was completed in 1925—"Jackson's first skyscraper." It is a delicately imposing Gothic building of white marble, thirteen stories high with a clock tower at the top.

It had been designed, as my father had asked of the Fort Worth architect, to be congenial with the Episcopal parish church that stood next door to it and with the fine Governor's Mansion that faced it from across the street. The architect pleased him with his gargoyles: the stone decorations of the main entrance took the form of alligators, which related it as well to Mississippi.

At every stage of the building, Daddy took his family to see as much as we could climb over, usually on Sunday mornings. At last we could climb by the fire escape to reach the top. We stood on the roof, with the not-yet-working clock towering at our backs, and viewed all Jackson below, spread to its seeable limits, its green rim, where the still river-like Pearl River and the still-unpaved-over Town Creek meandered and joined together in their unmolested swamp, with "the country" beyond. We were located where we stood there—part of our own map.

At the grand opening, the whole of the new building was lighted from a top to bottom and the Company—its business now expanded into other Southern states—had a public reception. My father made a statement at the time: "Not a dollar was borrowed nor a security sold for the erection of this new building, and it is all paid for. The building will stand, now and always, free from all debt, as a most valuable asset to policy-holders."

It was a crowning year of his life. At the same time that the new building was going up, so was our new house, designed by the same architect. The house was on a slight hill (my mother never could see the hill) covered with its original forest pines, on a gravel road then a little out from town, and was built in a style very much of its day, of stucco and brick and beams in the Tudor style. We had moved in, and Mother was laying out the garden.

Six years later, my father was dead.

The Lamar Life tower is overshadowed now, and you can no longer read the time on its clocktower from all over town, as he'd wanted to be possible always, but the building's grace and good proportion contrast tellingly with the overpowering, sometimes brutal, character of some of the structures that rise above it. Renovators have sandblasted away the alligators that graced the entrance. But the Company still has its home there, and my father is remembered.

My father's enthusiasm for business was not the part of him that he passed on to his children. But his imaginative conception of the building, and his pride in seeing it go up and his love of working in his tenth-floor office with the windows open to the view on three sides, may well have entered into his son Edward. He went on to become an architect, especially gifted in design, who had a hand in a number of public buildings and private houses to be seen today in Jackson. Walter was a more literal kind of inheritor; after taking his master's degree in mathematics he went into the office of an insurance company—not the Lamar Life, but another.

Plans for the Company had included the launching of a radio station, and its office was a cubbyhole installed in the base of the tower. After my father was dead and the Great Depression remained with us, I got a part-time job there. My first paid work was in communications: Mississippi's first radio station, operating there under the big clock, to which he would have given his nod of approval.

My first full-time job was rewarding to me in a way I could never have foreseen in those early days of my writing. I went to work for the state office of the Works Progress Administration as junior publicity agent. (This was of course one of President Roosevelt's national measures to combat the Great Depression.) Traveling over the whole of Mississippi, writing news stories for county papers, taking pictures, I saw my home state at close hand, really for the first time.

With the accretion of years, the hundreds of photographs—life as I found it, all unposed—constitute a record of that desolate period; but most of what I learned for myself came right at the time and directly out of the *taking* of the pictures. The camera was a hand-held auxiliary of wanting-to-know.

It had more than information and accuracy to teach me. I learned in the doing how *ready* I had to be. Life doesn't hold still. A good snapshot stopped a moment from running away. Photography taught me that to be able to capture transience, by being ready to click the shutter at the crucial moment, was the greatest need I had. Making pictures of people in all sorts of situations, I learned that every feeling waits upon its gesture; and I had to be prepared to recognize this moment when I saw it. These were things a story writer needed to know. And I felt the need to hold transient life in *words*—there's so much more of life that only words can convey—strongly enough to last me as long as I lived. The direction my mind took was a writer's direction from the start, not a photographer's, or a recorder's.

Along Mississippi roads you'd now and then see bottle trees; you'd see them alone or in crowds in the front yard of remote farmhouses. I photographed one—a bare crape myrtle tree with every branch of it ending in the mouth of a colored glass bottle—a blue Milk of Magnesia or an orange or green pop bottle; reflecting the light, flashing its colors in the sun, it stood as the centerpiece in a little thicket of peach trees in bloom. Later, I wrote a story called "Livvie" about youth and old age: the death of an old, proud, possessive man and the coming into flower, after dormant years, of his young wife—a spring story. Numbered among old Solomon's proud possessions is this bottle tree.

I know that the actual bottle tree, from the time of my actual sight of it, was the origin of my story. I know equally well that the bottle tree appearing in the story is a projection from my imagination; it isn't the real one except in that it is corrected by reality. The fictional eye sees in, through, and around what is really there. In "Livvie," old Solomon's bottle tree stands bright with dramatic significance, it stands vulnerable, ready for invading youth to sail a stone into the bottles and shatter them, as Livvie is claimed by love in the bursting light of spring. This I saw could be brought into being in the form of a story.

I was always my own teacher. The earliest story I kept a copy of was, I had thought, sophisticated, for I'd had the inspiration to lay it in Paris. I wrote it on my new typewriter, and its opening sentence was, "Monsieur Boule inserted a delicate dagger into Mademoiselle's left side and departed with a poised immediacy." I'm afraid it was a perfect example of what my father thought "fiction" mostly was. I was ten years older before I redeemed that in my first published story, "Death of a Traveling Salesman." I back-slid, for I found it hard to save myself from starting stories to show off what I could write.

In "Acrobats in a Park," though I laid the story in my home town, I was writing about Europeans, acrobats, adultery, and the Roman Catholic Church (seen from across the street), in all of which I was equally ignorant. In real life I fell easily under the spell of all traveling artists. En route to New Orleans, entertainments of many kinds would stop over in those days for a single performance in Jackson's Century Theatre. Galli-Curci came, so did Blackstone the Magician, so did Paderewski, so did *The Cat and the Canary* and the extravaganza *Chu Chin Chow*. Our family attended them all. My stories from the first drew visiting performers in, beginning modestly with a ladies' trio of the Redpath Chatauqua in "The Winds" and going so far as Segovia in "Music from Spain." Then, as now, my imagination was magnetized toward transient artists—toward the transience as much as the artists.

I must have seen "Acrobats in a Park" at the time I wrote the story as exotic, free of any experience as I knew it. And yet in the simplest way it isn't unrelated. The acrobats I led in procession into Smith Park in Jackson, Mississippi, were a *family*. They sat down in our family park, eating their lunch under a pin-oak tree I knew intimately. A father, a mother, and their children made up the troupe. At the center of the little story is the Zorros' act: the feat of erecting a structure of their bodies that holds together, interlocked, and stands like a wall, the Zorro Wall. Writing about the family act, I was writing about the family itself, its strength as a unit, testing its frailty under stress. I treated it in an artificial and oddly formal way; the stronghold of the family is put on public view as a structure built each night; on the night before the story opens, the Wall has come down when the most vulnerable member slips, and the act is done for. But from various points within it and from outside it, I've been writing about the structure of the family in stories and novels ever since. In spite of my unpromising approach to it, my fundamental story form might have been trying to announce itself to me.

My first good story began spontaneously, in a remark repeated to me by a traveling man—our neighbor—to whom it had been spoken while he was on a trip into North Mississippi: "He's gone to borry some fire." The words, which carried such lyrical and mythological and dramatic overtones, were real and actual—their hearer repeated them to me.

As usual, I began writing from a distance, but "Death of a Traveling Salesman" led me closer. It drew me toward what was at the center of it, to a cabin back in the red clay hills—perhaps just such a house as I used to see from far off on a train at night, with the firelight or lamplight showing yellow from its open doorway. In writing the story I approached and went inside with my traveling salesman, and had him, pressed by imminent death, figure out what was there:

> Bowman could not speak. He was shocked with knowing what was really in this house. A marriage, a fruitful marriage. That simple thing. Anyone could have had that.

Writing "Death of a Traveling Salesman" opened my eyes. And I had received the shock of having touched, for the first time, on my real subject: human relationships. Daydreaming had started me on the way; but story writing, once I was truly in its grip, took me and shook me awake.

# WALLACE STEGNER
## (1909–1993)

Wallace Stegner was one of the most vivid and versatile writers of the American West in the twentieth century. In nearly sixty years of writing, he published short stories and novels, essays and works of travel, biography, autobiography, and history. His last book was an elegiac hymn to the West: *Where the Bluebird Sings to the Lemonade Springs* (1992).

Stegner is perhaps best known for his fiction, which includes the Pulitzer Prize–winning novel *Angle of Repose* (1971) and *The Spectator Bird* (1976), which won a National Book Award. Central to Stegner's fiction is a sense of place and a keen interest in human values.

Although he wrote and published a great deal, Stegner had a long career in the academy. He taught at Harvard from 1939 until 1945, then moved to Stanford, where he directed the program in writing from 1946 until 1971.

In 1962, Stegner published *Wolf Willow*, a memoir that is subtitled *A History, a Story, and a Memory of the Last Plains Frontier*. Drawing on his various forms of writing, he is by turns historian, autobiographer, nature writer, and fiction maker. This remarkable work is commonly regarded as a classic of American autobiography, a book of deep wisdom and nostalgia, brilliantly evoked.

## FROM *Wolf Willow*

A muddy little stream, a village grown unfamiliar with time and trees. I turn around and retrace my way up Main Street and park and have a Coke in the confectionery store. It is run by a Greek, as it used to be, but whether the same Greek or another I would not know. He does not recognize me, nor I him. Only the smell of his place is familiar, syrupy with old delights, as if the ghost of my first banana split had come close to breathe on me. Still in search of something or someone to make the town fully real to me, I get the telephone book off its nail by the wall telephone and run through it, sitting at the counter. There are no more than seventy or eighty names in the Whitemud section. I look for Huffman—none. Bickerton—none. Fetter—none. Orullian—none. Stenhouse—none. Young—one, but not by a first name I remember. There are a few names I do remember—Harold Jones and William Christenson and Nels Sieverud and Jules LaPlante. (That last one startles me. I always thought his name was Jewell.) But all of the names I recognize are those of old-timers, pioneers of the town. Not a name that I went to school with, not a single person who would have shared as a contemporary my own experience of this town in its earliest years, when the river still ran clear and beaver swam in it in the evenings. Who in town remembers Phil Lott, who used to run coyotes with wolfhounds out on the South Bench? Who remembers in the way I do the day he drove up before Leaf's store in his democrat wagon and unloaded from it two dead hounds and the lynx that had killed them when they caught him unwarily exposed out on the flats? Who remembers in *my* way that angry and disgusted scene, and shares my recollection of the stiff, half-disemboweled bodies of the hounds and the bloody grin of the lynx? Who feels it or felt it, as I did and do, as a parable, a moral lesson for the pursuer to respect the pursued?

Because it is not shared, the memory seems fictitious, and so do other memories: the blizzard of 1916 that marooned us in the schoolhouse for a night and a day, the time the ice went out and brought both Martin's dam and the CPR bridge in kindling to our doors, the games of fox-and-geese in the untracked snow of a field that is now a grove, the nights of skating with a great fire leaping from the river ice and reflecting red from the cutbanks. I have used those memories for years as if they really happened, have made stories and novels of them. Now they seem uncorroborated and delusive. Some of the pioneers still in the telephone book would remember, but pioneers' memories are no good to me. Pioneers would remember the making of the town; to me, it was made, complete, timeless. A pioneer's child is what I need now, and in this town the pioneers' children did not stay, but went on, generally to bigger places farther west, where there was more opportunity.

Sitting in the sticky-smelling, nostalgic air of the Greek's confectionery store, I am afflicted with the sense of how many whom I have known are dead, and how little evidence I have that I myself have lived what I remember. It is not quite the same feeling I imagined when I contemplated driving out to the homestead. That would have been absolute denial. This, with its tantalizing glimpses, its hints and survivals, is not denial but only doubt. There is enough left to disturb me, but not to satisfy me. So I will go a little closer. I will walk on down into the west bend and take a look at our house.

In the strange forest of the school yard the boys are friendly, and their universal air of health, openness, and curiosity reassures me. This is still a good town to be a boy in. To see a couple of them on the prowl with air rifles (in my time we would have been carrying .22's or shotguns, but we would have been of the same tribe) forces me to readjust my disappointed estimate of the scrub growth. When one is four feet high, ten-foot willows are a sufficient cover, and ten acres are a wilderness.

By now, circling and more than half unwilling, I have come into the west end of town, have passed Corky Jones's house (put off till later that meeting) and the open field beside Downs's where we used to play run-sheep-run in the evenings, and I stand facing the four-gabled white frame house that my father built. It ought to be explosive with nostalgias and bright with recollections, for this is where we lived for five or six of my most impressionable years, where we all nearly died with the flu in 1918, where my grandmother "went crazy" and had to be taken away by a Mountie to the Provincial asylum because she took to standing silently in the door of the room where my brother and I slept—just hovered there for heaven knows how long before someone discovered her watching and listening in the dark. I try to remember my grandmother's face and cannot; only her stale old-woman's smell after she became incontinent. I can summon up other smells, too—it is the smells that seem to have stayed with me: baking paint and hot tin and lignite smoke behind the parlor heater; frying scrapple, which we called headcheese, on chilly fall mornings after the slaughtering was done; the rich thick odor of doughnuts frying in a kettle of boiling lard (I always got to eat the "holes"). With effort, I can bring back Christmases, birthdays, Sunday School parties in that house, and I have not forgotten the licking I got when, aged about six, I was caught playing with my father's loaded .30-.30 that hung above the mantel just under the Rosa Bonheur painting of three white horses in a storm. After that licking I lay out behind the chopping block all one afternoon watching my big dark heavy father as he worked at one thing and another, and all the time I lay there I kept aiming an empty cartridge case at him and dreaming murder.

Even the dreams of murder, which were bright enough at the time, have faded; he is long dead, and if not forgiven, at least propitiated. My mother too, who saved me from him so many times, and once missed saving me when he clouted me with a chunk of stove wood and knocked me over the woodbox and broke my collarbone: she too has faded. Standing there looking at the house where our lives entangled themselves in one another, I am infuriated that of that episode I remember less her love and protection and anger than my father's inept contrition. And walking all around the house trying to pump up recollection, I notice principally that the old barn is gone. What I see, though less changed than the town in general, still has power to disturb me; it is all dreamlike, less real than memory, less convincing than the recollected odors.

Whoever lives in the house now is a tidy housekeeper; the yard is neat, the porch swept. The corner where I used to pasture my broken-legged colt is a bed of flowers, the yard where we hopefully watered our baby spruces is a lawn enclosed by a green hedge. The old well with the hand pump is still in the side yard. For an instant my teeth are on edge with the memory of the dry screech of that pump before a dipperful of priming water took hold, and an instant later I feel the old stitch in my side from an even earlier time, the time when we still carried water from the river, and I dipped a bucket down into the hole in the ice and toted it, staggering and with the other arm stuck stiffly out, up the dugway to the kitchen door.

Those instants of memory are persuasive. I wonder if I should knock on the door and ask the housewife to let me look around, go upstairs to our old room in the west gable, examine the ceiling to see if the stains from the fire department's chemicals are still there. My brother and I used to lie in bed and imagine scenes and faces among the blotches, giving ourselves inadvertent Rorschach tests. I have a vivid memory, too, of the night the stains were made, when we came out into the hard cold from the Pastime Theater and heard the firehouse bell going and saw the volunteer fire department already on the run, and followed them up the ditch toward the glow of the fire, wondering whose house, until we got close and it was ours.

It is there, and yet it does not flow as it should, it is all a pumping operation. I half suspect that I am remembering not what happened but something I have written. I find that I am as unwilling to go inside that house as I was to try to find the old homestead in its ocean of grass. All the people who once shared the house with me are dead; strangers would have effaced or made doubtful the things that might restore them in my mind.

Behind our house there used to be a footbridge across the river, used by the Carpenters and others who lived in the bottoms, and by summer swimmers from town. I pass by the opaque and troubling house to the cutbank. The twin shanties that through all the town's life have served as men's and women's bath houses are still there. In winter we used to hang our frozen beef in one of them. I remember iron evenings when I went out with a lantern and sawed and haggled steaks from a rocklike hind quarter. But it is still an academic exercise; I only remember it, I do not feel the numb fingers and the fear that used to move just beyond the lantern's glow.

Then I walk to the cutbank edge and look down, and in one step the past comes closer than it has yet been. There is the gray curving cutbank, not much lower than I remember it when we dug cave holes in it or tunneled down its drifted cliff on our sleds. The bar is there at the inner curve of the bend, and kids are wallowing in a quicksandy mudhole and shrieking on an otter slide. They chase each other into the river and change magically from black to white. The water has its old quiet, its whirlpools spin lazily into deep water. On the footbridge, nearly exactly where it used to be, two little girls lie staring down into the water a foot below their noses. Probably they are watching suckers that lie just as quietly against the bottom. In my time we used to snare them from the bridge with nooses of copper wire.

It is with me all at once, what I came hoping to re-establish, an ancient, unbearable recognition, and it comes partly from the children and the footbridge and the river's quiet curve, but much more from the smell. For here, pungent and pervasive, is the smell that has always meant my childhood. I have never smelled it anywhere else, and it is as evocative as Proust's madeleine and tea.

But what is it? Somehow I have always associated it with the bath house, with wet bathing suits and damp board benches, heaps of clothing, perhaps even the seldom rinsed corners where desperate boys had made water. I go into the men's bath house, and the smell is there, but it does not seem to come from any single thing. The whole air smells of it, outside as well as in. Perhaps it is the river water, or the mud, or something about the float and footbridge. It is the way the old burlap-tipped diving board used to smell; it used to remain in the head after a sinus-flooding dive.

I pick up a handful of mud and sniff it. I step over the little girls and bend my nose to the wet rail of the bridge. I stand above the water and sniff. On the other side I strip leaves off wild rose and dogwood. Nothing doing. And yet all around me is that odor that I have not smelled since I was eleven, but have never forgotten—have *dreamed*, more than once. Then I pull myself up the bank by a gray-leafed bush, and I have it. The tantalizing and ambiguous and wholly native smell is no more than the shrub we called wolf willow, now blooming with small yellow flowers.

It is wolf willow, and not the town or anyone in it, that brings me home. For a few minutes, with a handful of leaves to my nose, I look across at the clay bank and the hills beyond where the river loops back on itself, enclosing the old sports and picnic ground, and the present and all the years between are shed like a boy's clothes dumped on the bathhouse bench. The perspective is what it used to be, the dimensions are restored, the senses are as clear as if they had not been battered with sensation for forty alien years. And the queer adult compulsion to return to one's beginnings is assuaged. A contact has been made, a mystery touched. For the moment, reality is made exactly equivalent with memory, and a hunger is satisfied. The sensuous little savage that I once was is still intact inside me.

Later, looking from the North Bench hills across my restored town, I can see the river where it shallows and crawls southeastward across the prairie toward the Milk, the Missouri, and the Gulf, and I toy with the notion that a man is like the river or the clouds, that he can be constantly moving and yet steadily renewed. The sensuous little savage, at any rate, has not been rubbed away or dissolved; he is as solid a part of me as my skeleton.

And he has a fixed and suitably arrogant relationship with his universe, a relationship geometrical and symbolic. From his center of sensation and question and memory and challenge, the circle of the world is measured, and in that respect the years of experience I have loaded upon my savage have not altered him. Lying on a hillside where I once sprawled among the crocuses, watching the town herd and snaring May's emerging gophers, I feel how the world still reduces me to a point and then measures itself from me. Perhaps the meadowlark singing from a fence post—a meadowlark whose dialect I recognize—feels the same way. All points on the circumference are equidistant from him; in him all radii begin; all diameters run through him; if he moves, a new geometry creates itself around him.

No wonder he sings. It is a good country that can make anyone feel so.

And it is a fact that once I have, so to speak, recovered myself as I used to be, I can look at the town, whose childhood was exactly contemporary with my own, with more understanding. It turns out to have been a special sort of town—special not only to me, in that it provided the indispensable sanctuary to match the prairie's exposure, but special in its belated concentration of Plains history. The successive stages of the Plains frontier flowed like a pageant through these Hills, and there are men still alive who remember almost the whole of it. My own recollections cover only a fragment; and yet it strikes me that this is *my* history. My disjunct, uprooted, cellular family was more typical than otherwise on the frontier. But more than we knew, we had our place in a human movement. What this town and its surrounding prairie grew from, and what they grew into, is the record of my tribe. If I am native to anything, I am native to this.

# MARY McCARTHY
## (1912–1989)

"Many a time, in the course of doing these memoirs, I have wished that I were writing fiction," McCarthy wrote in her *Memories of a Catholic Girlhood* (1957), a document full of pain, beginning with the death of her parents from the great influenza of 1918. At six, she moved with her brothers to the home of her abusive great-uncle, who insisted that the children work far beyond their capacities.

By contrast, the Catholic convent in Seattle where she eventually moved was idyllic. She remained there until her graduation from high school, never returning to see her cruel guardians. Her intellectual life was awakened at Vassar College, in Poughkeepsie, New York, where she suddenly found her voice as a writer. While her novels are delicious to read, especially *The Groves of Academe* (1952) and *The Group* (1963), her memoir of childhood is easily among her best books—an affecting and self-revelatory document by one of the sharpest literary minds of her generation.

## FROM *Memories of a Catholic Girlhood*

### A TIN BUTTERFLY

The man we had to call Uncle Myers was no relation to us. This was a point on which we four orphan children were very firm. He had married our great-aunt Margaret shortly before the death of our parents and so became our guardian while still a benedict—not perhaps a very nice eventuality for a fat man of forty-two who has just married an old maid with a little income to find himself summoned overnight from his home in Indiana to be the hired parent of four children, all under seven years old.

When Myers and Margaret got us, my three brothers and me, we were a handful; on this there were no two opinions in the McCarthy branch of the family. The famous flu epidemic of 1918, which had stricken our little household en route from Seattle to Minneapolis and carried off our parents within a day of each other, had, like all God's devices, a meritorious aspect, soon discovered by my grandmother McCarthy: a merciful end had been put to a regimen of spoiling and coddling, to Japanese houseboys, iced cakes, picnics, upset stomachs, diamond rings (imagine!), an ermine muff and neckpiece, furred hats and coats. My grandmother thanked her stars that Myers and her sister Margaret were available to step into the breach. Otherwise, we might have had to be separated, an idea that moistened her hooded grey eyes, or been taken over by "the Protestants"—thus she grimly designated my grandfather Preston, a respectable Seattle lawyer of New England antecedents who, she many times declared with awful emphasis, had refused to receive a Catholic priest in his house! But our Seattle grandparents, coming on to Minneapolis for the funeral, were too broken up, she perceived, by our young mother's death to protest the McCarthy arrangements. Weeping, my Jewish grandmother (Preston, born Morganstern), still a beauty, like her lost daughter, acquiesced in the wisdom of keeping us together in the religion my mother had espoused. In my sickbed, recovering from the flu in my grandmother McCarthy's Minneapolis house, I, the eldest and the only girl, sat up and watched the other grandmother cry, dampening her exquisite black veil. I did not know that our parents were dead or that my sobbing grandmother—whose green Seattle terraces I remembered as delightful to roll down on Sundays—had just now, downstairs in my grandmother McCarthy's well-heated sun parlor, met the middle-aged pair who had come on from Indiana to undo her daughter's mistakes. I was only six years old and had just started school in a Sacred Heart convent on a leafy boulevard in Seattle before the fatal November trek back east, but I was sharp enough to see that Grandmother Preston did not belong here, in this dour sickroom, and vain enough to pride myself on drawing the inference that something had gone awry.

We four children and our keepers were soon installed in the yellow house at 2427 Blaisdell Avenue that had been bought for us by my grandfather McCarthy. It was situated two blocks away from his own prosperous dwelling, with its grandfather clock, tapestries, and Italian paintings, in a block that some time before had begun to "run down." Flanked by two-family houses, it was simply a crude box in which to stow furniture, and lives, like a warehouse; the rooms were small and brownish and for some reason dark, though I cannot think why, since the house was graced by no ornamental planting; a straight cement driveway ran up one side; in the back, there was an alley. Downstairs, there were a living room, a "den," a dining room, a kitchen, and a lavatory; upstairs, there were four bedrooms and a bathroom. The dingy wallpaper of the rooms in which we children slept was promptly defaced by us; bored without our usual toys, we amused ourselves by making figures on the walls with our wet tongues. This was our first crime, and I remember it because the violence of the whipping we got surprised us; we had not known we were doing wrong. The splotches on the walls remained through the years to fix this first whipping and the idea of badness in our minds; they stared at us in the evenings when, still bored but mute and tamed, we learned to make shadow figures on the wall—the swan, the rabbit with its ears wiggling—to while away the time.

It was this first crime, perhaps, that set Myers in his punitive mold. He saw that it was no sinecure he had slipped into. Childless, middle-aged, he may have felt in his slow-turning mind that his inexperience had been taken advantage of by his wife's grandiloquent sister, that the vexations outweighed the perquisites; in short, that he had been sold. This, no doubt, was how it must have really looked from where he sat—in a brown leather armchair in the den, wearing a blue work shirt, stained with sweat, open at the neck to show an undershirt and lion-blond, glinting hair on his chest. Below this were workmen's trousers of a brownish-gray material, straining at the buttons and always gaping slightly, just below the belt, to show another glimpse of underwear, of a yellowish white. On his fat head, frequently, with its crest of bronze curly hair, were the earphones of a crystal radio set, which he sometimes, briefly, in a generous mood, fitted over the grateful ears of one of my little brothers.

A second excuse for Myers' behavior is manifest in this description. He had to contend with Irish social snobbery, which looked upon him dispassionately from four sets of green eyes and set him down as "not a gentleman." "My father was a gentleman and you're not"—what I meant by these categorical words I no longer know precisely, except that my father had had a romantic temperament and was a spendthrift; but I suppose there was also included some notion of courtesy. Our family, like many Irish Catholic new-rich families, was filled with aristocratic delusions; we children were always being told that we were descended from the kings of Ireland and that we were related to General "Phil" Sheridan, a dream of my great-aunt's. More precisely, my great-grandfather on this side had been a streetcar conductor in Chicago.

But at any rate Myers (or Meyers) Shriver (or Schreiber—the name had apparently been Americanized) was felt to be beneath us socially. Another count against him in our childish score was that he was a German, or, rather, of German descent, which made us glance at him fearfully in 1918, just after the armistice. In Minneapolis at that time, there was great prejudice among the Irish Catholics, not only against the Protestant Germans, but against all the northern bloods and their hateful Lutheran heresy. Lutheranism to us children was, first of all, a religion for servant girls and, secondly, a sort of yellow corruption associ-

ated with original sin and with Martin Luther's tongue rotting in his
mouth as God's punishment. Bavarian Catholics, on the other hand,
were singled out for a special regard; we saw them in an Early Christian
light, brunette and ringleted, like the Apostles. This was due in part to the
fame of Oberammergau and the Passion Play, and in part to the fact that
many of the clergy in our diocese were Bavarians; all through this period
I confided my sins of disobedience to a handsome, dark, young Father El-
derbush. Uncle Myers, however, was a Protestant, although, being too indolent, he did not go to church; he was not one of us. And the discovery
that we could take refuge from him at school, with the nuns, at church,
in the sacraments, seemed to verify the ban that was on him; he was
truly outside grace. Having been impressed with the idea that our religion was a sort of logical contagion, spread by holy books and good example, I could never understand why Uncle Myers, bad as he was, had
not caught it; and his obduracy in remaining at home in his den on Sundays, like a somnolent brute in its lair, seemed to me to go against nature.

Indeed, in the whole situation there was something unnatural and inexplicable. His marriage to Margaret, in the first place: he was younger
than his wife by three years, and much was made of this difference by my
grandmother McCarthy, his wealthy sister-in-law, as though it explained
everything in a slightly obscene way. Aunt Margaret, née Sheridan, was
a well-aged quince of forty-five, with iron-gray hair shading into black, a
stiff carriage, high-necked dresses, unfashionable hats, a copy of *Our
Sunday Visitor* always under her arm—folded, like a flail—a tough dry
skin with soft colorless hairs on it, like dust, and furrowed and corrugated,
like the prunes we ate every day for breakfast. It could be said of her that
she meant well, and she meant especially well by Myers, all two hundred
and five pounds, dimpled double chin, and small, glinting, gross blue
eyes of him. She called him "Honeybunch," pursued him with attentions, special foods, kisses, to which he responded with tolerance, as
though his swollen passivity had the character of a male thrust or assertion. It was clear that he did not dislike her, and that poor Margaret, as
her sister said, was head over heels in love with him. To us children, this
honeymoon rankness was incomprehensible; we could not see it on either side for, quite apart from everything else, both parties seemed to us
very old, as indeed they were, compared to our parents, who had been
young and handsome. That he had married her for her money occurred
to us inevitably, though it may not have been so; very likely it was his
power over her that he loved, and the power he had to make her punish
us was perhaps her strongest appeal to him. They slept in a bare, ugly
bedroom with a tall, cheap pine chiffonier on which Myers' black wallet and his nickels and dimes lay spread out when he was at home—did
he think to arouse our cupidity or did he suppose that this stronghold of

his virility was impregnable to our weak desires? Yet, as it happened, we did steal from him, my brother Kevin and I—rightfully, as we felt, for we were allowed no pocket money (two pennies were given us on Sunday morning to put into the collection plate) and we guessed that the money paid by our grandfather for the household found its way into Myers' wallet.

And here was another strange thing about Myers. He not only did nothing for a living but he appeared to have no history. He came from Elkhart, Indiana, but beyond this fact nobody seemed to know anything about him—not even how he had met my aunt Margaret. Reconstructed from his conversation, a picture of Elkhart emerged for us that showed it as a flat place consisting chiefly of ball parks, poolrooms, and hardware stores. Aunt Margaret came from Chicago, which consisted of the Loop, Marshall Field's, assorted priests and monsignors, and the black-and-white problem. How had these two worlds impinged? Where our family spoke freely of its relations, real and imaginary, Myers spoke of no one, not even a parent. At the very beginning, when my father's old touring car, which had been shipped on, still remained in our garage, Myers had certain seedy cronies whom he took riding in it or who simply sat in it in our driveway, as if anchored in a houseboat; but when the car went, they went or were banished. Uncle Myers and Aunt Margaret had no friends, no couples with whom they exchanged visits—only a middle-aged, black-haired, small, emaciated woman with a German name and a yellow skin whom we were taken to see one afternoon because she was dying of cancer. This protracted death had the aspect of a public execution, which was doubtless why Myers took us to it; that is, it was a spectacle and it was free, and it inspired restlessness and depression. Myers was the perfect type of rootless municipalized man who finds his pleasures in the handouts or overflow of an industrial civilization. He enjoyed standing on a curbstone, watching parades, the more nondescript the better, the Labor Day parade being his favorite, and next to that a military parade, followed by the commercial parades with floats and girls dressed in costumes; he would even go to Lake Calhoun or Lake Harriet for doll-carriage parades and competitions of children dressed as Indians. He liked bandstands, band concerts, public parks devoid of grass; skywriting attracted him; he was quick to hear of a department-store demonstration where colored bubbles were blown, advertising a soap, to the tune of "I'm Forever Blowing Bubbles," sung by a mellifluous soprano. He collected coupons and tinfoil, bundles of newspaper for the old rag-and-bone man (thus interfering seriously with our school paper drives), free samples of cheese at Donaldson's, free tickets given out by a neighborhood movie house to the first installment of a serial—in all the years we lived with him, we never saw a full-length movie but only those truncated beginnings. He was also fond of streetcar rides (could the system have been municipally owned?), soldiers' monuments, cemeteries, big, coarse flowers like cannas and cockscombs set in beds by city gardeners. Museums did not appeal to him, though we did go one night with a large crowd to see Marshal Foch on the steps of the Art Institute. He was always weighing himself on penny weighing machines. He seldom left the house except on one of these purposeless errands, or else to go to a ball game, by himself. In the winter, he spent the days at home in the den, or in the kitchen, making candy. He often had enormous tin trays of decorated fondants cooling in the cellar, which leads my brother Kevin to think today that at one time in Myers' life he must have been a pastry cook or a confectioner. He also liked to fashion those little figures made of pipe cleaners that were just then coming in as favors in the better candy shops, but Myers used *old* pipe cleaners, stained yellow and brown. The bonbons, with their pecan or almond topping, that he laid out in such perfect rows were for his own use; we were permitted to watch him set them out, but never—and my brother Kevin confirms this—did we taste a single one.

In the five years we spent with Myers, the only candy I ever had was bought with stolen money and then hidden in the bottom layer of my paper-doll set; the idea of stealing to buy candy and the hiding place were both lifted from Kevin. Opening my paper-doll box one day, I found it full of pink and white soft-sugar candies, which it seemed to me God or the fairies had sent me in response to my wishes and prayers, until I realized that Kevin was stealing, and using my paper-doll box for a cache; we had so few possessions that he had no place of his own to hide things in. Underneath the mattress was too chancy, as I myself found when I tried to secrete magazines of Catholic fiction there; my aunt, I learned, was always tearing up the bed and turning the mattress to find out whether you had wet it and attempted to hide your crime by turning it over. Reading was forbidden us, except for schoolbooks and, for some reason, the funny papers and magazine section of the Sunday Hearst papers, where one read about leprosy, the affairs of Count Boni de Castellane, and a strange disease that turned people to stone creepingly from the feet up.

This prohibition against reading was a source of scandal to the nuns who taught me in the parochial school, and I think it was due to their intervention with my grandmother that finally, toward the end, I was allowed to read openly the Camp Fire Girls series, *Fabiola,* and other books I have forgotten. Myers did not read; before the days of the crystal set, he passed his evenings listening to the phonograph in the living room: Caruso, Harry Lauder, "Keep the Home Fires Burning," "There's a Sweet Little Nest," and "Listen to the Mocking Bird." It was his pleasure to make the four of us stand up in a line and sing to him the same tunes he had just heard on the phonograph, while he laughed at my performance, for I tried to reproduce the staccato phrasing of the sopranos, very loudly and off key. Also, he hated long words, or, rather, words that he regarded as long. One summer day, in the kitchen, when I had been ordered to swat flies, I said, "They disappear so strangely," a remark that he mimicked for years whenever he wished to humiliate me, and the worst of this torture was that I could not understand what was peculiar about the sentence, which seemed to me plain ordinary English, and, not understanding, I knew that I was in perpetual danger of exposing myself to him again.

So far as we knew, he had never been in any army, but he liked to keep smart military discipline. We had frequently to stand in line, facing him, and shout answers to his questions in chorus. "Forward *march!*" he barked after every order he gave us. The Fourth of July was the only holiday he threw himself into with geniality. Anything that smacked to him of affectation or being "stuck-up" was subject to the harshest reprisals from him, and I, being the oldest, and the one who remembered my parents and the old life best, was the chief sinner, sometimes on purpose, sometimes unintentionally.

When I was eight, I began writing poetry in school: "Father Gaughan is our dear parish priest / And he is loved from west to east." And "Alas, Pope Benedict is dead, / The sorrowing people said." Pope Benedict at that time was living, and, as far as I know, in good health; I had written this opening couplet for the rhyme and the sad idea; but then, very conveniently for me, about a year later he died, which gave me a feeling of fearsome power, stronger than a priest's power of loosing and binding. I came forward with my poem and it was beautifully copied out by our teacher and served as the school's elegy at a memorial service for the Pontiff. I dared not tell that I had had it ready in my desk. Not long afterward, when I was ten, I wrote an essay for a children's contest on "The Irish in American History," which won first the city and then the state prize. Most of my facts I had cribbed from a series on Catholics in American history that was running in *Our Sunday Visitor.* I worked on the assumption that anybody who was Catholic must be Irish, and then, for good measure, I went over the singers of the Declaration of Independence and added any name that sounded Irish to my ears. All this was clothed in rhetoric invoking "the lilies of France"—God knows why, except that I was in love with France and somehow, through Marshal MacMahon, had made Lafayette out an Irishman. I believe that even Kosciusko figured as an Irishman *de coeur.* At any rate, there was a school ceremony, at which I was presented with the city prize (twenty-five dollars, I think, or perhaps that was the state prize); my aunt was in the audience in her best mallard-feathered hat, looking, for once, proud and happy. She spoke kindly to me as we walked home, but when we came to our ugly house, my uncle silently rose from his chair, led me into the dark downstairs lavatory, which always smelled of shaving cream, and furiously beat me with the razor strop—to teach me a lesson, he said, lest I become stuck-up. Aunt Margaret did not intervene. After her first look of discomfiture, her face settled into folds of approval; she had been too soft. This was the usual tribute she paid Myers' greater discernment—she was afraid of losing his love by weakness. The money was taken, "to keep for me," and that, of course, was the end of it. Such was the fate of anything considered "much too good for her," a category that was rivaled only by its pendant, "plenty good enough."

We were beaten all the time, as a matter of course, with the hairbrush across the bare legs for ordinary occasions, and with the razor strop across the bare bottom for special occasions, like the prize-winning. It was as though these ignorant people, at sea with four frightened children, had taken a Dickens novel—*Oliver Twist*, perhaps, or *Nicholas Nickleby*—for a navigation chart. Sometimes our punishments were earned, sometimes not; they were administered gratuitously, often, as preventive medicine. I was whipped more frequently than my brothers, simply by virtue of seniority; that is, every time one of them was whipped, I was whipped also, for not having set a better example, and this was true for all four of us in a descending line. Kevin was whipped for Preston's misdeeds and for Sheridan's, and Preston was whipped for Sheridan's, while Sheridan, the baby and the favorite, was whipped only for his own. This naturally made us fear and distrust each other, and only between Kevin and myself was there a kind of uneasy alliance. When Kevin ran away, as he did on one famous occasion, I had a feeling of joy and defiance, mixed with the fear of punishment for myself, mixed with something worse, a vengeful anticipation of the whipping *he* would surely get. I suppose that the two times I ran away, his feelings were much the same—envy, awe, fear, admiration, and a certain evil thrill, collusive with my uncle, at the thought of the strop ahead. Yet, strange to say, nobody was beaten on these historic days. The culprit, when found, took refuge at my grandmother's, and a fearful hush lay over the house on Blaisdell Avenue at the thought of the monstrous daring and deceitfulness of the run-away; Uncle Myers, doubtless, was shaking in his boots at the prospect of explanations to the McCarthy family council. The three who remained at home were sentenced to spend the day upstairs, in strict silence. But if my uncle's impartial application of punishment served to make us each other's enemies very often, it did nothing to establish discipline, since we had no incentive to behave well, not knowing when we might be punished for something we had not done or even for something that by ordinary standards would be considered good. We knew not when we would offend, and what I learned from this, in the main, was a policy of lying and concealment; for several years after we were finally liberated, I was a problem liar.

Despite Myers' quite justified hatred of the intellect, of reading and education (for he was right—it *was* an escape from him), my uncle, like all dictators, had one book that he enjoyed. It was *Uncle Remus*, in a red cover—a book I detested—which he read aloud to us in his den over and over again in the evenings. It seemed to me that this reduction of human life to the level of talking animals and this corruption of language to dialect gave my uncle some very personal relish. He knew I hated it and he rubbed it in, trotting my brother Sheridan on his knee as he dwelt on some exploit of Br'er Fox's with many chuckles and repetitions. In *Uncle Remus*, he had his hour, and to this day I cannot read anything in dialect or any fable without some degree of repugnance.

A distinction must be made between my uncle's capricious brutality and my aunt's punishments and repressions, which seem to have been dictated to her by her conscience. My aunt was not a bad woman; she was only a believer in method. Since it was the family theory that we had been spoiled, she undertook energetically to remedy this by quasi-scientific means. Everything we did proceeded according to schedule and in line with an over-all plan. She was very strong, naturally, on toilet-training, and everything in our life was directed toward the after-breakfast session on "the throne." Our whole diet—not to speak of the morning orange juice with castor oil in it that was brought to us on the slightest pretext of "paleness"—was centered around this levee. We had prunes every day for breakfast, and corn-meal mush, Wheatena, or farina, which I had to eat plain, since by some medical whim it had been decided that milk was bad for me. The rest of our day's menu consisted of parsnips, turnips, rutabagas, carrots, boiled potatoes, boiled cabbage, onions, Swiss chard, kale, and so on; most green vegetables, apparently, were too dear to be appropriate for us, though I think that, beyond this, the family had a sort of moral affinity for the root vegetable, stemming, perhaps, from everything fibrous, tenacious, watery, and knobby in the Irish peasant stock. Our desserts were rice pudding, farina pudding, overcooked custard with little air holes in it, prunes, stewed red plums, rhubarb, stewed pears, stewed dried peaches. We must have had meat, but I have only the most indistinct recollection of pale lamb stews in which the carrots outnumbered the pieces of white, fatty meat and bone and gristle; certainly we did not have steak or roasts or turkey or fried chicken, but perhaps an occasional boiled fowl was served to us with its vegetables (for I do remember the neck, shrunken in its collar of puckered skin, coming to me as my portion, and the fact that if you sucked on it, you could draw out an edible white cord), and doubtless there was meat loaf and beef stew. There was no ice cream, cake, pie, or butter, but on rare mornings we had johnnycake or large woolly pancakes with Karo syrup.

We were not allowed to leave the table until every morsel was finished, and I used to sit through half a dark winter afternoon staring at the cold carrots on my plate, until, during one short snowy period, I found that I could throw them out the back window if I raised it very quietly. (Unfortunately, they landed on the tar roofing of a sort of shed next to the back porch, and when the snow finally melted, I met a terrible punishment.) From time to time, we had a maid, but the food was so wretched that we could not keep "girls," and my aunt took over the cooking, with sour enthusiasm, assisted by her sister, Aunt Mary, an arthritic, white-haired, wan, devout old lady who had silently joined our household and earned her keep by helping with the sewing and dusting and who tried to stay out of Myers' way. With her gentle help, Aunt Margaret managed to approximate, on a small scale, the conditions prevailing in the orphan asylums we four children were always dreaming of being let into.

Myers did not share our diet. He sat at the head of the table, with a napkin around his neck, eating the special dishes that Aunt Margaret prepared for him and sometimes putting a spoonful on the plate of my youngest brother, who sat next to him in a high chair. At breakfast, he had corn flakes or shredded wheat with bananas or fresh sliced peaches, thought by us to be a Lucullan treat. At dinner, he had pigs' feet and other delicacies I cannot remember. I only know that he shared them with Sheridan, who was called Herdie, as my middle brother was called Pomps, or Pompsie—childish affectionate nicknames inherited from our dead parents that sounded damp as gravemold in my aunt Margaret's flannelly voice, which reminded one of a chest rag dipped in asafetida to ward off winter throat ailments.

In addition to such poultices, and mustard plasters, and iron pills to fortify our already redoubtable diet, we were subject to other health fads of the period and of my great-aunt's youth. I have told elsewhere of how we were put to bed at night with our mouths sealed with adhesive tape to prevent mouth-breathing; ether, which made me sick, was used to help pull the tape off in the morning, but a grimy, gray, rubbery remainder was usually left on our upper lips and in the indentations of our pointed chins when we set off for school in our heavy outer clothes, long underwear, black stockings, and high shoes. Our pillows were taken away from us; we were given a sulphur-and-molasses spring tonic, and in the winter, on Saturdays and Sundays, we were made to stay out three hours in the morning and three in the afternoon, regardless of the temperature. We had come from a mild climate, in Seattle, and at fifteen, twenty, or twenty-four below zero we could not play, even if we had had something to play with, and used simply to stand in the snow, crying, and beating sometimes on the window with our frozen mittens, till my aunt's angry face would appear there and drive us away.

No attempt was made to teach us a sport, winter or summer; we were forbidden to slide in Fairoaks Park nearby, where in winter the poorer children made a track of ice down a hill, which they flashed down sitting or standing, but I loved this daring sport and did it anyway, on the way home from school, until one day I tore my shabby coat on the ice and was afraid to go home. A kind woman named Mrs. Corkerey, who kept a neighborhood candy store across from our school, mended it for me, very skillfully, so that my aunt never knew; nevertheless, sliding lost its lure for me, for I could not risk a second rip.

The neighbors were often kind, surreptitiously, and sometimes they "spoke" to the sisters at the parochial school, but everyone, I think, was afraid of offending my grandparents, who diffused an air of wealth and pomp when they entered their pew at St. Stephen's Church on Sunday. Mrs. Corkerey, in fact, got herself and me in trouble by feeding me in the mornings in her kitchen above the candy store when I stopped to pick up her daughter, Clarazita, who was in my class. I used to lie to Mrs. Corkerey and say that I had had no breakfast (when the truth was that I was merely hungry), and she went to the nuns finally in a state of indignation. The story was checked with my aunt, and I was obliged to admit that I had lied and that they did feed me, which must have disillusioned Mrs. Corkerey forever with the pathos of orphaned childhood. It was impossible for me to explain to her then that what I needed was her pity and her fierce choleric heart. Another neighbor, Mr. Harrison, a well-to-do old bachelor or widower who lived in the corner house, used sometimes to take us bathing, and it was thanks to his lessons that I learned to swim—a strange antiquated breast stroke—copied from an old man with a high-necked bathing suit and a beard. In general, we were not supposed to have anything to do with the neighbors or with other children. It was a rule that other children were not allowed to come into our yard or we to go into theirs, nor were we permitted to walk to school with another boy or girl. But since we were in school most of the day, five days a week, our guardians could not prevent us from making friends despite them; other children were, in fact, very much attracted to us, pitying us for our woebegone condition and respecting us because we were thought to be rich. Our grandmother's chauffeur, Frank, in her winter Pierce-Arrow and summer Locomobile, was well known in the neighborhood, waiting outside church on Sunday to take her home from Mass. Sometimes we were taken, too, and thus our miserable clothes and underfed bodies were associated with high financial status and became a sort of dubious privilege in the eyes of our classmates.

We both had enviable possessions and did not have them. In the closet in my bedroom, high on the top shelf, beyond my reach even standing on a chair, was a stack of cardboard doll boxes, containing wonderful French dolls, dressed by my Seattle grandmother in silks, laces, and satins, with crepe-de-Chine underwear and shoes with high heels. These and other things were sent us every year at Christmastime, but my aunt had decreed that they were all too good for us, so they remained in their boxes and wrappings, *verboten*, except on the rare afternoon, perhaps once in a twelvemonth or so, when a relation or a friend of the family would come through from the West, and then down would come the dolls, out would come the baseball gloves and catchers' masks and the watches and the shiny cars and the doll houses, and we would be set to playing with these things on the floor of the living room while the visitor tenderly looked on. As soon as the visitor left, bearing a good report of our household, the dolls and watches and cars would be whisked away, to come out again for the next emergency. If we had been clever, we would have refused this bait and paraded our misery, but we were too simple to do anything but seize the moment and play out a whole year's playtime in this gala hour and a half. Such techniques, of course, are common in concentration camps and penal institutions, where the same sound calculation of human nature is made. The prisoners snatch at their holiday; they trust their guards and the motto *"Carpe diem"* more than they do the strangers who have come to make the inspection. Like all people who have been mistreated, we were wary of being taken in; we felt uneasy about these visitors—Protestants from Seattle—who might be much worse than our uncle and aunt. The latter's faults, at any rate, we knew. Moreover, we had been subjected to propaganda: we had been threatened with the Seattle faction, time and again, by our uncle, who used to jeer and say to us, *"They'd* make you toe the chalk line."

The basis, I think, of my aunt's program for us was in truth totalitarian: she was idealistically bent on destroying our privacy. She imagined herself as enlightened in comparison with our parents, and a super-ideal of health, cleanliness, and discipline softened in her own eyes the measures she applied to attain it. A nature not unkindly was warped by bureaucratic zeal and by her subservience to her husband, whose masterful autocratic hand cut through our nonsense like a cleaver. The fact that our way of life resembled that of an orphan asylum was not a mere coincidence; Aunt Margaret strove purposefully toward a corporate goal. Like most heads of institutions, she longed for the eyes of Argus. To the best of her ability, she saw to it that nothing was hidden from her. Even her health measures had this purpose. The aperients we were continually dosed with guaranteed that our daily processes were open to her inspection, and the monthly medical check-up assured her, by means of stethoscope and searchlight and tongue depressor, that nothing was happening inside us to which she was not privy. Our letters to Seattle were written under her eye, and she scrutinized our homework sharply, though her arithmetic, spelling, and grammar were all very imperfect. We prayed, under supervision, for a prescribed list of people. And if we were forbidden companions, candy, most toys, pocket money, sports, reading, entertainment, the aim was not to make us suffer but to achieve efficiency. It was simpler to interdict other children than to inspect all the children with whom we might want to play. From the standpoint of efficiency, our lives, in order to be open, had to be empty; the books we might perhaps read, the toys we might play with figured in my aunt's mind, no doubt, as what the housewife calls "dust catchers"—around these distractions, dirt might accumulate. The inmost folds of consciousness, like the belly button, were regarded by her as unsanitary. Thus, in her spiritual outlook, my aunt was an early functionalist.

Like all systems, my aunt's was, of course, imperfect. Forbidden to read, we told stories, and if we were kept apart, we told them to ourselves in bed. We made romances out of our schoolbooks, even out of the dictionary, and read digests of novels in the *Book of Knowledge* at school. My uncle's partiality for my youngest brother was a weakness in him, as was my aunt Mary's partiality for me. She was supposed to keep me in her room, sewing on squares of cheap cotton, making handkerchiefs with big, crude, ugly hems, and ripping them out and making them over again, but though she had no feeling for art or visual beauty (she would not even teach me to darn, which is an art, or to do embroidery, as the nuns did later on, in the convent), she liked to talk of the old days in Chicago and to read sensational religious fiction in a magazine called the *Extension*, which sometimes she let me take to my room, with a caution against being caught. And on the Sunday walks that my uncle headed, at the end of an interminable streetcar ride, during which my bigger brothers had to scrunch down to pass for under six, there were occasions on which he took us (in military order) along a wooded path, high above the Mississippi River, and we saw late-spring harebells and, once, a coral-pink snake. In Minnehaha Park, a favorite resort, we were allowed to play on the swings and to examine the other children riding on the ponies or on a little scenic railway. Uncle Myers always bought himself a box of Cracker Jack, which we watched him eat and delve into, to find the little favor at the bottom—a ritual we deeply envied, for, though we sometimes had popcorn at home (Myers enjoyed popping it) and even, once or twice, homemade popcorn balls with molasses, we had never had more than a taste of this commercial Cracker Jack, with peanuts in it, which seemed to us the more valuable because *he* valued it and would often come home eating a box he had bought at a ball game. But one Sunday, Uncle Myers, in full, midsummer mood, wearing his new pedometer, bought my brother Sheridan a whole box for himself.

Naturally, we envied Sheridan—the only blond among us, with fair red-gold curls, while the rest of us were all pronounced brunets, with thick black brows and lashes—as we watched him, the lucky one, munch the sticky stuff and fish out a painted tin butterfly with a little pin on it at the bottom. My brothers clamored around him, but I was too proud to show my feelings. Sheridan was then about six years old, and this butterfly immediately became his most cherished possession—indeed, one of the few he had. He carried it about the house with him all the next week, clutched in his hand or pinned to his shirt, and my two other brothers followed him, begging him to be allowed to play with it, which slightly disgusted me, at the age of ten, for I knew that I was too sophisticated to care for tin butterflies and I felt in this whole affair the instigation of my uncle. He was relishing my brothers' performance and saw to it, strictly, that Sheridan clung to his rights in the butterfly and did not permit anybody to touch it. The point about this painted tin butterfly was not its intrinsic value; it was the fact that it was virtually the only toy in the house that had not been, so to speak, socialized, but belonged privately to one individual. Our other playthings—a broken-down wooden swing, an old wagon, a dirty sandbox, and perhaps a fire engine or so and some defaced blocks and twisted second-hand train tracks in the attic— were held by us all in common, the velocipedes we had brought with us from Seattle having long ago foundered, and the skipping rope, the jacks, the few marbles, and the pair of rusty roller skates that were given us being decreed to be the property of all. Hence, for a full week this butterfly excited passionate emotions, from which I held myself stubbornly apart, refusing even to notice it, until one afternoon, at about four o'clock, while I was doing my weekly chore of dusting the woodwork, my white-haired aunt Mary hurried softly into my room and, closing the door behind her, asked whether I had seen Sheridan's butterfly.

The topic wearied me so much that I scarcely lifted my head, answering no, shortly, and going on with my dusting. But Aunt Mary was gently persistent: Did I know that he had lost it? Would I help her look for it? This project did not appeal to me, but in response to some faint agitation in her manner, something almost pleading, I put down my dustcloth and helped her. We went all over the house, raising carpets, looking behind curtains, in the kitchen cupboards, in the Victrola, everywhere but in the den, which was closed, and in my aunt's and uncle's bedroom. Somehow—I do not know why—I did not expect to find the butterfly, partly, I imagine, because I was indifferent to it and partly out of the fatalism that all children have toward lost objects, regarding them as irretrievable, vanished into the flux of things. At any rate I was right: we did not find it and I went back to my dusting, vindicated. Why should *I* have to look for Sheridan's stupid butterfly, which he ought to have taken better care of? "Myers is upset," said Aunt Mary, still hovering, uneasy and diffident, in the doorway. I made a slight face, and she went out, plaintive, remonstrant, and sighing, in her pale, high necked, tight-buttoned dress.

It did not occur to me that I was suspected of stealing this toy, even when Aunt Margaret, five minutes later, burst into my room and ordered me to come and look for Sheridan's butterfly. I protested that I had already done so, but she paid my objections no heed and seized me roughly by the arm. "Then do it again, Miss, and mind that you find it." Her voice was rather hoarse and her whole furrowed iron-gray aspect somewhat tense and disarrayed, yet I had the impression that she was not angry with me but with something in outer reality—what one would now call fate or contingency. When I had searched again, lackadaisically, and again found nothing, she joined in with vigor, turning everything upside down. We even went into the den, where Myers was sitting, and searched all around him, while he watched us with an ironical expression, filling his pipe from a Bull Durham sack. We found nothing, and Aunt Margaret led me upstairs to my room, which I ransacked while she stood and watched me. All at once, when we had finished with my bureau drawers and my closet, she appeared to give up. She sighed and bit her lips. The door cautiously opened and Aunt Mary came in. The two sisters looked at each other and at me. Margaret shrugged her shoulders. "She hasn't got it, I do believe," she said.

She regarded me then with a certain relaxing of her thick wrinkles, and her heavy-skinned hand, with its wedding ring, came down on my shoulder. "Uncle Myers thinks you took it," she said in a rusty whisper, like a spy or a scout. The consciousness of my own innocence, combined with a sense of being let into the confederacy of the two sisters, filled me with excitement and self-importance. "But I didn't, Aunt Margaret," I began proclaiming, making the most of my moment. "What would I want with his silly old butterfly?" The two sisters exchanged a look. "That's what I said, Margaret!" exclaimed old Aunt Mary sententiously. Aunt Margaret frowned; she adjusted a bone hairpin in the coiled rings of her unbecoming coiffure. "Mary Therese," she said to me, solemnly, "if you know anything about the butterfly, if one of your brothers took it, tell me now. If we don't find it, I'm afraid Uncle Myers will have to punish you." "He *can't* punish me, Aunt Margaret," I insisted, full of righteousness. "Not if I didn't do it and *you* don't think I did it." I looked up at her, stagily trustful, resting gingerly on this solidarity that had suddenly appeared between us. Aunt Mary's pale old eyes watered. "You mustn't let Myers punish her, Margaret, if you don't think she's done wrong." They both glanced up at the Murillo Madonna that was hanging on my stained wall. Intelligence passed between them and I was sure that, thanks to our Holy Mother, Aunt Margaret would save me. "Go along, Mary Therese," she said hoarsely. "Get yourself ready for dinner. And don't you say a word of this to your uncle when you come downstairs."

When I went down to dinner, I was exultant, but I tried to hide it. Throughout the meal, everyone was restrained; Herdie was in the dumps about his butterfly, and Preston and Kevin were silent, casting covert looks at me. My brothers, apparently, were wondering how I had avoided punishment, as the eldest, if for no other reason. Aunt Margaret was rather flushed, which improved her appearance slightly. Uncle Myers had a cunning look, as though events would prove him right. He patted Sheridan's golden head from time to time and urged him to eat. After dinner, the boys filed into the den behind Uncle Myers, and I helped Aunt Margaret clear the table. We did not have to do the dishes, for at this time there was a "girl" in the kitchen. As we were lifting the white table-cloth and the silence pad, we found the butterfly—pinned to the silence pad, right by my place.

My hash was settled then, though I did not know it. I did not catch the significance of its being found at *my* place. To Margaret, however, this was grimly conclusive. She had been too "easy," said her expression; once again Myers had been right. Myers went through the formality of interrogating each of the boys in turn ("No, sir," "No, sir," "No, sir") and even, at my insistence, of calling in the Swedish girl from the kitchen. Nobody knew how the butterfly had got there. It had not been there before dinner, when the girl set the table. My judges therefore concluded that I had had it hidden on my person and had slipped it under the table-cloth at dinner, when nobody was looking. This unanimous verdict maddened me, at first simply as an indication of stupidity—how could they be so dense as to imagine that I would hide it by my own place, where it was sure to be discovered? I did not really believe that I was going to be punished on such ridiculous evidence, yet even I could form no theory of how the butterfly had come there. My first base impulse to accuse the maid was scoffed out of my head by reason. What would a grownup want with a silly six-year-old's toy? And the very unfairness of the condemnation that rested on me made me reluctant to transfer it to one of my brothers. I kept supposing that the truth somehow would out, but the interrogation suddenly ended and every eye avoided mine.

Aunt Mary's dragging step went up the stairs, the boys were ordered to bed, and then, in the lavatory, the whipping began. Myers beat me with the strop, until his lazy arm tired; whipping is hard work for a fat man, out of condition, with a screaming, kicking, wriggling ten-year-old in his grasp. He went out and heaved himself, panting, into his favorite chair and I presumed that the whipping was over. But Aunt Margaret took his place, striking harder than he, with a hairbrush, in a businesslike, joyless way, repeating, "Say you did it, Mary Therese, say you did it." As the blows fell and I did not give in, this formula took on an intercessory note, like a prayer. It was clear to me that she was begging me to surrender and give Myers his satisfaction, for my own sake, so that the whipping could stop. When I finally cried out "All right!" she dropped the hairbrush with a sigh of relief; a new doubt of my guilt must have been visiting her, and my confession set everything square. She led me in to my uncle, and we both stood facing him, as Aunt Margaret, with a firm but not ungentle hand on my shoulder, whispered, "Just tell him, 'Uncle Myers, I did it,' and you can go to bed." But the sight of him, sprawling in his leather chair, complacently waiting for this, was too much for me. The words froze on my tongue. I could not utter them to *him*. Aunt Margaret urged me on, reproachfully, as though I were breaking our compact, but as I looked straight at him and assessed his ugly nature, I burst into yells. "I didn't! I didn't!" I gasped, between screams. Uncle Myers shot a vindictive look at his wife, as though he well understood that there had been collusion between us. He ordered me back to the dark lavatory and symbolically rolled up his sleeve. He laid on the strop decisively, but this time I was beside myself, and when Aunt Margaret hurried in and tried to reason with me, I could only answer with wild cries as Uncle Myers, gasping also, put the strop back on its hook. "You take her," he articulated, but Aunt Margaret's hairbrush this time was perfunctory, after the first few angry blows that punished me for having disobeyed her. Myers did not take up the strop again; the whipping ended, whether from fear of the neighbors or of Aunt Mary's frail presence upstairs or sudden guilty terror, I do not know; perhaps simply because it was past my bedtime.

I finally limped up to bed, with a crazy sense of inner victory, like a saint's, for I had not recanted, despite all they had done or could do to me. It did not occur to me that I had been unchristian in refusing to answer a plea from Aunt Margaret's heart and conscience. Indeed, I rejoiced in the knowledge that I had *made* her continue to beat me long after she must have known that I was innocent; this was her punishment for her condonation of Myers. The next morning, when I opened my eyes on the Murillo Madonna and the Baby Stuart, my feeling of triumph abated; I was afraid of what I had done. But throughout that day and the next, they did not touch me. I walked on air, incredulously and, no doubt, somewhat pompously, seeing myself as a figure from legend: my strength was *as* the strength of ten because my *heart* was pure! Afterward, I was beaten, in the normal routine way, but the question of the butterfly was closed forever in that house.

In my mind, there was, and still is, a connection between the butterfly and our rescue, by our Protestant grandfather, which took place the following year, in the fall or early winter. Already defeated, in their own view, or having ceased to care what became of us, our guardians, for the first time, permitted two of us, my brother Kevin and me, to be alone with this strict, kindly lawyer, as we walked the two blocks between our house and our grandfather McCarthy's. In the course of our walk, between the walls of an early snow, we told Grandpa Preston everything, overcoming our fears and fixing our minds on the dolls, the baseball gloves, and the watches. Yet, as it happened, curiously enough, albeit with a certain aptness, it was not the tale of the butterfly or the other atrocities that chiefly impressed him as he followed our narration with precise legal eyes but the fact that I was not wearing my glasses. I was being punished for breaking them in a fall on the school playground by having to go without; and I could not see why my account of this should make him flush up with anger—to me it was a great relief to be free of those disfiguring things. But he shifted his long, lantern jaw and, settling our hands in his, went straight as a writ up my grandfather McCarthy's front walk. Hence it was on a question of health that this good American's alarms finally alighted; the rest of what we poured out to him he either did not believe or feared to think of, lest he have to deal with the problem of evil.

On health grounds, then, we were separated from Uncle Myers, who disappeared back into Elkhart with his wife and Aunt Mary. My brothers were sent off to the sisters in a Catholic boarding school, with the exception of Sheridan, whom Myers was permitted to bear away with him, like a golden trophy. Sheridan's stay, however, was of short duration. Very soon, Aunt Mary died, followed by Aunt Margaret, followed by Uncle Myers; within five years, still in the prime of life, they were all gone, one, two, three, like ninepins. For me, a new life began, under a happier star. Within a few weeks after my Protestant grandfather's visit, I was sitting in a compartment with him on the train, watching the Missouri River go westward to its source, wearing my white-gold wrist watch and a garish new red hat, a highly nervous child, fanatical against Protestants, who, I explained to Grandpa Preston, all deserved to be burned at the stake. In the dining car, I ordered greedily, lamb chops, pancakes, sausages, and then sat, unable to eat them. "Her eyes," observed the waiter, "are bigger than her stomach."

Six or seven years later, on one of my trips east to college, I stopped in Minneapolis to see my brothers, who were all together now, under the roof of a new and more indulgent guardian, my uncle Louis, the hand-somest and youngest of the McCarthy uncles. All the old people were dead; my grandmother McCarthy, but recently passed away, had left a fund to erect a chapel in her name in Texas, a state with which she had no known connection. Sitting in the twilight of my uncle Louis' screened porch, we sought a common ground for our reunion and found it in Uncle Myers. It was then that my brother Preston told me that on the fa-mous night of the butterfly, he had seen Uncle Myers steal into the din-ing room from the den and lift the tablecloth, with the tin butterfly in his hand.

# THOMAS MERTON
## (1915–1968)

In *The Seven Storey Mountain* (1948), the poet Thomas Merton writes about his conversion to Roman Catholicism and his decision to become a priest. "I had not shaped my life to this situation," he says, "I had not been building up to this." But a sense of spiritual crisis led him in this direction, a crisis elaborated at considerable length in his affecting autobiography.

Merton, who became a monk, was a prolific author, writing poems and essays, books of religious meditation and theological speculation during the fifties and sixties. Among his books are *The Living Bread* (1956), *Disputed Questions* (1960), and *Faith and Violence: Christian Teaching and Christian Practice* (1968). *The Asian Journal* (1973) and his *Collected Poems* (1977) were published after his untimely death on a visit to the Far East. Merton's work has strong affinities with the tradition of spiritual autobiography that begins with Saint Augustine's *Confessions* and continues on through Jonathan Edwards, Elizabeth Ashbridge, and—in recent years—writers such as Kathleen Norris.

## FROM *The Seven Storey Mountain*

When we went back to New York, in the middle of August, the world that I had helped to make was finally preparing to break the shell and put forth its evil head and devour another generation of men.

At Olean we never read any newspapers, and we kept away from radios on principle, and for my own part the one thing that occupied my mind was the publication of the new novel. Having found an old copy of *Fortune* lying around Benjie's premises, I had read an article in it on the publishing business: and on the basis of that article I had made what was perhaps the worst possible choice of a publisher—the kind of people who would readily reprint everything in the *Saturday Evening Post* in diamond letters on sheets of gold. They were certainly not disposed to be sympathetic to the wild and rambling thing I had composed on the mountain.

And it was going to take them a good long time to get around to telling me about it.

For my own part, I was walking around New York in the incomparable agony of a new author waiting to hear the fate of his first book—an agony which is second to nothing except the torments of adolescent love. And because of my anguish I was driven, naturally enough, to fervent though interested prayer. But after all God does not care if our prayers are interested. He wants them to be. Ask and you shall receive. It is a kind of pride to insist that none of our prayers should ever be petitions for our own needs: for this is only another subtle way of trying to put ourselves on the same plane as God—acting as if we had no needs, as if we were not creatures, not dependent on Him and dependent, by His will, on material things too.

So I knelt at the altar rail in the little Mexican church of Our Lady of Guadalupe on Fourteenth Street, where I sometimes went to Communion, and asked with great intensity of desire for the publication of the book, if it should be for God's glory.

The fact that I could even calmly assume that there was some possibility of the book giving glory to God shows the profound depths of my ignorance and spiritual blindness: but anyway, that was what I asked. But now I realize that it was a very good thing that I made that prayer.

It is a matter of common belief among Catholics that when God promises to answer our prayers, He does not promise to give us exactly what we ask for. But we can always be certain that if he does not give us that, it is because He has something much better to give us instead. That is what is meant by Christ's promise that we will receive all that we ask in His Name. *Quodcumque petimus adversus utilitatem salutis, non petimus in nomine Salvatoris.*

I think I prayed as well as I could, considering what I was, and with considerable confidence in God and in Our Lady, and I knew I would be answered. I am only just beginning to realize how well I was answered. In the first place the book was never published, and that was a good thing. But in the second place God answered me by a favor which I had already refused and had practically ceased to desire. He gave me back the vocation that I had half-consciously given up, and He opened to me again the doors that had fallen shut when I had not known what to make of my Baptism and the grace of that First Communion.

But before He did this I had to go through some little darkness and suffering.

I think those days at the end of August 1939 were terrible for everyone. They were grey days of great heat and sultriness and the weight of physical oppression by the weather added immeasurably to the burden of the news from Europe that got more ominous day by day.

Now it seemed that at last there really would be war in earnest. Some sense of the craven and perverted esthetic excitement with which the

Nazis were waiting for the thrill of this awful spectacle made itself felt negatively, and with hundredfold force, in the disgust and nausea with which the rest of the world expected the embrace of this colossal instrument of death. It was a danger that had, added to it, an almost incalculable element of dishonor and insult and degradation and shame. And the world faced not only destruction, but destruction with the greatest possible defilement: defilement of that which is most perfect in man, his reason and his will, his immortal soul.

All this was obscure to most people, and made itself felt only in a mixture of disgust and hopelessness and dread. They did not realize that the world had now become a picture of what the majority of its individuals had made of their own souls. We had given our minds and wills up to be raped and defiled by sin, by hell itself: and now, for our inexorable instruction and reward, the whole thing was to take place all over again before our eyes, physically and morally, in the social order, so that some of us at least might have some conception of what we had done.

In those days, I realized it myself. I remember one of the nights at the end of August when I was riding on the subway, and suddenly noticed that practically nobody in the car was reading the evening paper, although the wires were hot with news. The tension had become so great that even this toughest of cities had had to turn aside and defend itself against the needles of such an agonizing stimulation. For once everybody else was feeling what Lax and I and Gibney and Rice had been feeling for two years about newspapers and news.

There was something else in my own mind—the recognition: "I myself am responsible for this. My sins have done this. Hitler is not the only one who has started this war: I have my share in it too . . ." It was a very sobering thought, and yet its deep and probing light by its very truth eased my soul a little. I made up my mind to go to confession and Communion on the First Friday of September.

The nights dragged by. I remember one, when I was driving in from Long Island where I had been having dinner at Gibney's house at Port Washington. The man with whom I was riding had a radio in the car, and we were riding along the empty Parkway, listening to a quiet, tired voice from Berlin. These commentators' voices had lost all their pep. There was none of that lusty and doctrinaire elation with which the news broadcasters usually convey the idea that they know all about everything. This time you knew that nobody knew what was going to happen, and they all admitted it. True, they were all agreed that the war was now going to break out. But when? Where? They could not say.

All the trains to the German frontier had been stopped. All air service had been discontinued. The streets were empty. You got the feeling that things were being cleared for the first great air-raid, the one that everyone had been wondering about, that H. G. Wells and all the other people had written about, the one that would wipe out London in one night . . .

The Thursday night before the first Friday of September I went to confession at St. Patrick's Cathedral and then, with characteristic stupidity, stopped in at Dillon's, which was a bar where we went all the time, across the street from the stage-door of the Center Theater. Gibney and I used to sit there waiting for the show to end, and we would hang around until one or two in the morning with several girls we knew who had bits to play in it. This evening, before the show was out, I ran into Jinny Burton, who was not in the show, but could have been in many better shows than that, and she said she was going home to Richmond over Labor Day. She invited me to come with her. We arranged to meet in Pennsylvania Station the following morning.

When it was morning, I woke up early and heard the radios. I could not quite make out what they were saying, but the voices were not tired any more: there was much metallic shouting which meant something had really happened.

On my way to Mass, I found out what it was. They had bombed Warsaw, and the war had finally begun.

In the Church of St. Francis of Assisi, near the Pennsylvania Station, there was a High Mass. The priest stood at the altar under the domed mosaic of the apse and his voice rose in the solemn cadences of the Preface of the Mass—those ancient and splendid and holy words of the Immortal Church. *Vere dignum et justum est aequum et salutare nos tibi semper et ubique gratias agere, Domine sancte, Pater omnipotens, aeterne Deus . . .*

It was the voice of the Church, the Bride of Christ who is in the world yet not of it, whose life transcends and outlives wars and persecutions and revolutions and all the wickedness and cruelty and rapacity and injustice of men. It is truly meet and just always and in all things to give Thee thanks, Holy Lord, omnipotent Father, eternal God: a tremendous prayer that reduces all wars to their real smallness and insignificance in the face of eternity. It is a prayer that opens the door to eternity, that springs from eternity and goes again into eternity, taking our minds with it in its deep and peaceful wisdom. Always and in all things to give Thee thanks, omnipotent Father. Was it thus that she was singing, this Church, this one Body, who had already begun to suffer and to bleed again in another war?

She was thanking Him *in* the war, *in* her suffering: not for the war and for the suffering, but for His love which she knew was protecting her, and us, in this new crisis. And raising up her eyes to Him, she saw the eternal God alone through all these things, was interested in His action alone, not in the bungling cruelty of secondary causes, but only in His love, His wisdom. And to Him the Church, His Bride, gave praise through Christ, through Whom all the angelic hierarchies praise Him . . .

I knelt at the altar rail and on this the first day of the Second World War received from the hand of the priest, Christ in the Host, the same Christ Who was being nailed again to the cross by the effect of my sins, and the sin of the whole selfish, stupid, idiotic world of men.

There was no special joy in that week-end in Virginia. On the Saturday afternoon when we started out from Richmond to go to Urbanna, where Jinny's family had a boat they were going to sail in a regatta, we got the news about the sinking of the *Athenia*, and then, that evening, I suddenly developed a pain in an impacted wisdom tooth. It raged all night and the next day I staggered off to the regatta, worn out with sleeplessness and holding a jaw full of pain.

Down at the dock where there was a gas-pump for the motor boats and a red tank full of Coca-Cola on ice, we stood out of the sun in the doorway of a big shed smelling of ropes and pitch, and listened to a man talking on the radio from London.

His voice was reassuring. The city had not yet been bombed.

We started out of the cove, and passed through the mouth into the open estuary of the Rappahannock, blazing with sun, and everybody was joking about the *Bremen*. The big German liner had sailed out of New York without warning and had disappeared. Every once in a while some high drawling Southern female voice would cry:

"There's the *Bremen*."

I had a bottle of medicine in my pocket, and with a match and a bit of cotton I swabbed the furious impacted tooth.

Nevertheless, when I got back to New York, it turned out that the war was not going to be so ruthless after all—at least so it seemed. The fighting was fierce in Poland, but in the west there was nothing doing. And now that the awful tension was over, people were quieter and more confident than they had been before the fighting had started.

I went to a dentist who hammered and chipped at my jaw until he got the wisdom tooth out of my head, and then I went back to Perry Street and lay on my bed and played some ancient records of Bix Beiderbecke, Paul Whiteman's trumpet player, and swabbed my bleeding mouth with purple disinfectant until the whole place reeked of it.

I had five stitches in my jaw.

The days went by. The city was quiet and confident. It even began to get gay again. Whatever happened, it was evident that America was not going to get into the war right away, and a lot of people were saying that it would just go on like this for years, a sort of state of armed waiting and sniping, with the big armies lined up in their impregnable fortified areas. It was as if the world were entering upon a strange new era in which the pretence of peace had defined itself out into what it was, a state of permanent hostility that was nevertheless not quite ready to fight. And some people thought we were just going to stay that way for twenty years.

For my own part, I did not think anything about it, except that the grim humor of Russia's position in the war could not help but strike me: for now, after a loud outcry and a great storm of crocodile tears over Chamberlain's betrayal of Czechoslovakia the year before, the Reds were comfortably allied with Germany and blessing, with a benign smile, the annihilation of Poland, ready themselves to put into effect some small designs of their own regarding the Finns.

The party line had evolved indeed, and turned itself into many knots since the days of the 1935 Peace Strike and the Oxford Pledge. We had once been led to believe that all wars were wars of aggression and wars of aggression were the direct product of capitalism, masking behind Fascism and all the other movements with colored shirts, and therefore no one should fight at all. It now turned out that the thing to do was support the aggressive war of the Soviets against Finland and approve the Russian support of German aggression in Poland.

The September days went by, and the first signs of fall were beginning to be seen in the clearing of the bright air. The days of heat were done. It was getting on toward that season of new beginnings, when I would get back to work on my Ph.D., and when I hoped possibly to get some kind of job as an instructor at Columbia, in the College or in Extension.

These were the things I was thinking about when one night Rice and Bob Gerdy and I were in Nick's on Sheridan Square, sitting at the curved bar while the room rocked with jazz. Presently Gibney came in with Peggy Wells, who was one of the girls in that show at the Center Theater, the name of which I have forgotten. We all sat together at a table and talked and drank. It was just like all the other nights we spent in those places. It was more or less uninteresting but we couldn't think of anything else to do and there seemed to be no point in going to bed.

After Rice and Gerdy went home, Gibney and Peggy and I still sat there. Finally it got to be about four o'clock in the morning. Gibney did not want to go out on Long Island, and Peggy lived uptown in the Eighties.

They came to Perry Street, which was just around the corner.

It was nothing unusual for me to sleep on the floor, or in a chair, or on a couch too narrow and too short for comfort—that was the way we lived, and the way thousands of other people like us lived. One stayed up all night, and finally went to sleep wherever there happened to be room for one man to put his tired carcass.

It is a strange thing that we should have thought nothing of it, when if anyone had suggested sleeping on the floor as a penance, for the love of God, we would have felt that he was trying to insult our intelligence and dignity as men! What a barbarous notion! Making yourself uncomfortable as a penance! And yet we somehow seemed to think it quite logical to sleep that way as part of an evening dedicated to pleasure. It shows how far the wisdom of the world will go in contradicting itself. "From him that hath not, it shall be taken away even that which he hath."

I suppose I got some five or six hours of fitful sleep, and at about eleven we were all awake, sitting around dishevelled and half stupefied, talking and smoking and playing records. The thin, ancient, somewhat elegiac cadences of the long dead Beiderbecke sang in the room. From where I sat, on the floor, I could see beyond the roofs to a patch of clear fall sky.

At about one o'clock in the afternoon I went out to get some breakfast, returning with scrambled eggs and toast and coffee in an armful of cardboard containers, different shapes and sizes, and pockets full of new packs of cigarettes. But I did not feel like smoking. We ate and talked, and finally cleared up all the mess and someone had the idea of going for a walk to the Chicken Dock. So we got ready to go.

Somewhere in the midst of all this, an idea had come to me, an idea that was startling enough and momentous enough by itself, but much more astonishing in the context. Perhaps many people will not believe what I am saying.

While we were sitting there on the floor playing records and eating this breakfast the idea came to me: "I am going to be a priest."

I cannot say what caused it: it was not a reaction of especially strong disgust at being so tired and so uninterested in this life I was still leading, in spite of its futility. It was not the music, not the fall air, for this conviction that had suddenly been planted in me full grown was not the sick and haunting sort of a thing that an emotional urge always is. It was not a thing of passion or of fancy. It was a strong and sweet and deep and insistent attraction that suddenly made itself felt, but not as movement of appetite towards any sensible good. It was something in the order of conscience, a new and profound and clear sense that this was what I really ought to do.

How long the idea was in my mind before I mentioned it, I cannot say. But presently I said casually:

"You know, I think I ought to go and enter a monastery and become a priest."

Gibney had heard that before, and thought I was fooling. The statement aroused no argument or comment, and anyway, it was not one to which Gibney was essentially unsympathetic. As far as he was concerned, any life made sense except that of a business man.

As we went out the door of the house I was thinking:

"I am going to be a priest."

When we were on the Chicken Dock, my mind was full of the same idea. Around three or four in the afternoon Gibney left and went home to Port Washington. Peggy and I sat looking at the dirty river for a while longer. Then I walked with her to the subway. In the shadows under the elevated drive over Tenth Avenue I said:

"Peggy, I mean it, I am going to enter a monastery and be a priest."

She didn't know me very well and anyway, she had no special ideas about being a priest. There wasn't much she could say. Anyway, what did I expect her to say?

I was glad, at last, to be alone. On that big wide street that is a continuation of Eighth Avenue, where the trucks run down very fast and loud— I forget its name—there was a little Catholic library and a German bakery where I often ate my meals. Before going to the bakery to get dinner and supper in one, I went to the Catholic library, St. Veronica's. The only book about religious Orders they seemed to have was a little green book about the Jesuits but I took it and read it while I ate in the bakery.

Now that I was alone, the idea assumed a different and more cogent form. Very well: I had accepted the possibility of the priesthood as real and fitting for me. It remained for me to make it, in some sense, more decisive.

What did that mean? What was required? My mind groped for some sort of an answer. What was I supposed to do, here and now?

I must have been a long time over the little book and these thoughts. When I came out into the street again, it was dusk. The side streets, in fact, were already quite dark. I suppose it was around seven o'clock.

Some kind of an instinct prompted me to go to Sixteenth Street, to the Jesuit Church of St. Francis Xavier. I had never been there. I don't know what I was looking for: perhaps I was thinking primarily of talking to some one of the Fathers there—I don't know.

When I got to Sixteenth Street, the whole building seemed dark and empty, and as a matter of fact the doors of the church were locked. Even the street was empty. I was about to go away disappointed, when I noticed a door to some kind of a basement under the church.

Ordinarily I would never have noticed such a door. You went down a couple of steps, and there it was, half hidden under the stairs that led up to the main door of the church. There was no sign that the door was anything but locked and bolted fast.

But something prompted me: "Try that door."

I went down the two steps, put my hand on the heavy iron handle. The door yielded and I found myself in a lower church, and the church was full of lights and people and the Blessed Sacrament was exposed in a monstrance on the altar, and at last I realized what I was supposed to do, and why I had been brought here.

It was some kind of a novena service, maybe a Holy Hour, I don't know: but it was nearly ending. Just as I found a place and fell on my knees, they began singing the *Tantum Ergo*. . . . All these people, workmen, poor women, students, clerks, singing the Latin hymn to the Blessed Sacrament written by St. Thomas Aquinas.

I fixed my eyes on the monstrance, on the white Host.

And then it suddenly became clear to me that my whole life was at a crisis. Far more than I could imagine or understand or conceive was now hanging upon a word—a decision of mine.

I had not shaped my life to this situation: I had not been building up to this. Nothing had been further from my mind. There was, therefore, an added solemnity in the fact that I had been called in here abruptly to answer a question that had been preparing, not in my mind, but in the infinite depths of an eternal Providence.

I did not clearly see it then, but I think now that it might have been something in the nature of a last chance. If I had hesitated or refused at that moment—what would have become of me?

But the way into the new land, the promised land, the land that was not like the Egypt where I persisted in living, was now thrown open again: and I instinctively sensed that it was only for a moment.

It was a moment of crisis, yet of interrogation: a moment of searching, but it was a moment of joy. It took me about a minute to collect my thoughts about the grace that had been suddenly planted in my soul, and to adjust the weak eyes of my spirit to its unaccustomed light, and during that moment my whole life remained suspended on the edge of an abyss: but this time, the abyss was an abyss of love and peace, the abyss was God.

It would be in some sense a blind, irrevocable act to throw myself over. But if I failed to do that . . . I did not even have to turn and look behind me at what I would be leaving. Wasn't I tired enough of all that?

So now the question faced me:

"Do you really want to be a priest? If you do, say so . . ."

The hymn was ending. The priest collected the ends of the humeral veil over his hands that held the base of the monstrance, and slowly lifted it off the altar, and turned to bless the people.

I looked straight at the Host, and I knew, now, Who it was that I was looking at, and I said:

"Yes, I want to be a priest, with all my heart I want it. If it is Your will, make me a priest—make me a priest."

When I had said them, I realized in some measure what I had done with those last four words, what power I had put into motion on my behalf, and what a union had been sealed between me and that power by my decision.

# ALFRED KAZIN

## (1915–1998)

Alfred Kazin was the epitome of the urban Jewish intellectual. Indeed, he spent most of his life in New York City, where he educated himself in the New York Public Library. His first major publication was *On Native Grounds* (1942), a vastly erudite and original reading of modern American prose literature. Kazin made a lifelong study of American writers and published countless influential studies, including *Contemporaries* (1962), *Bright Book of Life* (1973), *American Procession* (1984), and *God and the American Writer* (1997).

A *Walker in the City* (1951) remains an important piece of urban autobiography, a book about being a Jew in America and about walking in a city that one has come to love. Kazin writes movingly about the immigrant's sense of being suspended between two worlds: the modern secular one, represented by the movies, and the ancient world of Jewish culture, which seemed to oppose all forms of modernity. Those conflicting worlds are symbolized in his memoir by the "old neighborhood" of Brownsville and the cosmopolitan world of Manhattan, separated only by a bridge.

## FROM *A Walker in the City*

Chester Street at last, and the way home.

On my right hand the "Stadium" movie house—the sanctuary every Saturday afternoon of my childhood, the great dark place of all my dream life. On my left the little wooden synagogue where I learned my duties as a Jew and at thirteen, having reached the moral estate of a man, stood up at the high desk before the Ark *(Blessed be He, Our Lord and Our Shield!)* and was confirmed in the faith of my fathers.

Right hand and left hand: two doorways to the East. But the first led to music I heard in the dark, to inwardness; the other to ambiguity. That poor worn synagogue could never in my affections compete with that movie house, whose very lounge looked and smelled to me like an Oriental temple. It had Persian rugs, and was marvelously half-lit at all hours of the day; there were great semi-arcs of colored glass above the entrance to the toilets, and out of the gents' came a vaguely foreign, deliciously stinging deodorant that prepared me, on the very threshold of the movie auditorium itself, for the magic within. There was never anything with such expectancy to it as that twilit lounge. I would even delay in it a little, to increase my pleasure in what lay ahead; and often shut my eyes just as I entered the auditorium, knowing that as soon as I opened them again a better world would take me in.

In the wonderful darkness of the movies there was nothing to remind me of Brownsville—nothing but the sudden alarm of a boy who, reminding himself at six o'clock that it was really time to get home, would in his haste let himself out by the great metal fire door in front. Then the gritty light on Bristol Street would break up the images on the screen with a meanness that made me shudder.

I always feared that light for the same reason: it seemed to mock imagination. I could never finally leave the movies, while the light of Saturday afternoon still filled the streets, without feeling the sadness that Spinoza describes as coming after lust, and would stare amazed, numb and depleted at the mica dots gleaming in the pavement and at the people still busily moving up and down Chester Street. There was something in the everyday look of the streets that reproached me; they seemed to know I had come back to them unwillingly. But deep inside the darkness of the movies everything that was good in life, everything that spoke straight to the imagination, began in some instant dark fusion between the organ music from the pit and the cycles of terror that started up again each Saturday afternoon in the "episodes." Walking home afterward, everything I felt came to me as the first ominously repeated notes of Schubert's *Unfinished* when the hero jumped from roof to roof just ahead of the crooks; the horn calls in Weber's overture to *Oberon* when Tarzan fell into the lion trap, his mouth opening in a silent scream I heard all along my spine; Sinding's *Rustle of Spring* when the sky darkened just before a storm—music that was as uncontainable as water or light or air, that shifted its course with each new breath it took, and showed me the rapids, the storms, the plunging mountain falls of consciousness itself. Where were those notes racing in me? Oh where were they racing? What had that music been preparing for me so deep in the bowels of the earth? Whenever that shadowy organist in the pit, whose face I could never see as he bent over the faintly lighted rows of keys, began one of those three pieces he played for "episodes," my throat would beat wildly in premonition, but I knew a secret happiness, as if my mind had at last been encouraged to seek its proper concerns.

Not so in the synagogue. It was dark enough, but without any illusion or indulgence for a boy; and it had a permanently stale smell of snuff, of vinegar, of beaten and scarred wood in the pews, of the *rebbitsin's* cooking from the kitchen next door, of the dusty velvet curtains over the Ark, of the gilt brocade in the prayer shawls, of ancient prayer books and commentaries which in their chipped black bindings and close black print on the yellowing paper looked as if they had come down to us from Moses and the Prophets, with the reverent kiss of each generation in the margins. The synagogue was old, very old; it must once have been a farmhouse; it was one of the oldest things in Brownsville and in the world; it was old in every inch of the rotting wooden porch, in the crevices deep in the doors over the Ark, in the little company of aged and bearded men smelling of snuff who were to be seen there every day at twilight, wrapped in their black-striped prayer shawls, their eyes turned to Jerusalem, mumbling and singing in their threadbare voices— "*Blessed, praised, glorified, extolled and exalted shall be the Holy Name of the Supreme King of Kings! Blessed is He, for He is the First and the Last, and besides Him there is no God!*"

*As it was for Abraham and Isaac, Jacob and Benjamin* . . . Old as the synagogue was, old as it looked and smelled in its every worn and wooden corner, it seemed to me even older through its ties to that ancestral world I had never seen. Its very name, Dugschitz, was taken from the little Polish village my mother came from; everyone in the congregation was either a relative or an old neighbor—a *lantsman*. I belonged to that synagogue as a matter of course; I was my mother's son. My father, as an honest Social Democrat and enlightened free thinker, was tolerant in these matters, and with good-humored indifference let my mother claim me among her "brethren." When he came around to the synagogue at all, it was to exchange greetings at the New Year, and to listen, as he said, to the cantor trying for the high notes; he liked singing.

There was another synagogue halfway down the block, much larger and no doubt more impressive in every way; I never set foot in it; it belonged to people from another province in Russia. The little wooden synagogue was "our" place. All good *Dugschitzer* were expected to show up in it at least once a year, had their sons confirmed in it as a matter of course, and would no doubt be buried from it when their time came. Members of the congregation referred to each other in a homely familiar way, using not the unreal second names so many Jews in Russia had been given for the Czar's census, but the first names in their familiar order—Dovid Yossel's or Khannah Sorke's; some were known simply by some distinguishing physical trait, the Rakhmiel lame in one foot. There were little twists and turns to the liturgy that were strictly "ours," a particularly nostalgic way of singing out the opening words of prayers that only *Dugschitzer* could possibly know. If the *blind* Rakhmiel—the Rakhmiel in the back bench who was so nearsighted that he might fairly be described as blind—skipped two lines in the prayer book, the sexton would clutch his hands in despair and call out mockingly, "*Bene-*

*shalélem; Bless the Lord!* Will you just listen to the way he *reads?"* There were scornful little references to the way *outsiders* did things—people from Warsaw, for example, who gave every sound a pedantic roll; or Galicians, who, as everyone knew, were coarse-grained, had no taste, took cream with herring, and pronounced certain words in so uncouth a manner that it made you ache with laughter just to hear them. What did it matter that our congregation was poor, our synagogue small and drab? It was sufficient to the handful of *us* in Brownsville, and from birth to death would regather us in our ties to God, to the tradition of Israel, and to each other. On a Saturday when a boy had been confirmed, and the last loving proud *Amen!* had been heard from the women where they sat at the back separated from us by a gauze curtain, and a table in an open space between the pews had been laden with nut-cake, fruit, herring, and wine, and the brethren had gathered to toast the boy and his parents and each other in their rejoicing for Israel, we were all—no matter what we knew of each other or had suffered from each other—one plighted family.

Though there was little in the ritual that was ever explained to me, and even less in the atmosphere of the synagogue that in my heart I really liked, I assumed that my feelings in the matter were of no importance; I belonged there before the Ark, with the men, sitting next to an uncle. I felt a loveless intimacy with the place. It was not exclusively a house of "worship," not frigid and formal as we knew all churches were. It had been prayed in and walked through and lived in with such easy familiarity that it never seemed strange to come on young boys droning their lessons under the long twisted yellow flytrap hung from the ceiling, the *shammes*, the sexton, waddling about in his carpet slippers carrying a fly swatter, mumbling old Hebrew tunes to himself—*Ái! Bái! Biddle Bái Dóm!*—as he dashed after a fly, while his wife, whom we mockingly called the *rebbitsin*, the rabbi's wife, red-faced over her pots in the kitchen next door, shrieked curses against the boys playing punchball in the street—*bandits* and *murderers*, she would call the police!—who were always just about to break her windows. The wood in the benches and in the high desk before the Ark had taken on with age and long use such a deep rosy mirror shine that on those afternoons when I strayed in on my way back from school, I would think that if only I bent over it long enough I might see my own face reflected in the wood. I never did. Secretly, I thought the synagogue a mean place, and went only because I was expected to. Whenever I crossed the splintered and creaking porch into that stale air of snuff, of old men and old books, and saw the dusty gilt brocade on the prayer shawls, I felt I was being pulled into some mysterious and ancient clan that claimed me as its own simply because I had been born a block away. Whether I agreed with its beliefs or not, I belonged; whether I assented to its rights over me or not, I belonged;

whatever I thought of them, no matter how far I might drift from that place, I belonged. This was understood in the very nature of things; I was a Jew. It did not matter how little I knew or understood of the faith, or that I was always reading alien books; I belonged, I had been expected, I was now to take my place in the great tradition.

For several months before my confirmation at thirteen, I appeared every Wednesday afternoon before a choleric old *melamed*, a Hebrew teacher, who would sit across the table eating peas, and with an incredulous scowl on his face listen to me go over and over the necessary prayers and invocations, slapping me sharply on the hands whenever I stammered on a syllable. I had to learn many passages by heart, but never understood most of them, nor was I particularly expected to understand them; it was as if some contract in secret cipher had been drawn up between the Lord of Hosts and Gita Fayge's son Alfred which that *Amerikaner idiót*, as the *melamed* called me, could sign with an x. In the "old country" the *melamed* might possibly have encouraged me to understand the text, might even have discussed it with me. Here it was understood that I would go through the lessons simply for form's sake, because my mother wished to see me confirmed; the *melamed* expected nothing more of me. In his presence I stammered more wildly than ever, and on each line. "*Idiót!*" he would scream. "They have produced an *idiót* in you, *idiót!*" Sitting back in his chair, he would hear me out with a look of contemptuous resignation as I groaned and panted my way to the end of each passage, heave sighs of disgust at the ceiling, and mechanically take up some peas to throw them into his mouth one by one, always ready to lean across the table with his bitter smile and slap my hands.

Still, I had to go through with it; I was a Jew. Yet it puzzled me that no one around me seemed to take God very seriously. We neither believed nor disbelieved. He was our oldest habit. For me, He was horribly the invisible head above the Board of Superintendents, the Almighty Judge Who watched you in every thought and deed, and to Whom I prayed for help in passing midterms and finals, His prophetess Deborah leading me safely through so long as I remembered to say under my breath as I walked in the street, *"Desolate were the open towns in Israel, they were desolate, until that I arose, Deborah."* He filled my world with unceasing dread; He had such power over me, watched me so unrelentingly, that it puzzled me to think He had to watch all the others with the same care; one night I dreamed of Him as a great engineer in some glasswalled control tower high in the sky glaring fixedly at a brake on which my name alone was written. In some ways He was simply a mad tyrant, someone I needed constantly to propitiate. Deborah alone would know how to intercede for me. Then He became a good-luck piece I carried around to get me the things I needed. I resented this God of Israel and of the Board of Superintendents; He would never let me rest.

I could not even speak of Him to others—not to the aged and bearded men in the synagogue always smelling of snuff, who spoke of the Talmud with a complacent little smile on their faces; not to the young Zionist pioneers in their clubhouses off Pitkin Avenue, who were busily learning to be farmers in the Land of Israel and chilled me with that same complacency whenever they formed their lips around the word *Jew*; certainly not to those strangers standing on the steps of the little Protestant church on Rockaway or to the Italians in the new red-brick Catholic church just off East New York Avenue, at the borders of Brownsville. He was my private burden, my peculiar misfortune.

Yet I never really wanted to give Him up. In some way it would have been hopeless to justify to myself—I had feared Him so long—He fascinated me, He seemed to hold the solitary place I most often went back to. There was a particular sensation connected with this—not of peace, not of certainty, not of goodness—but of depth; as if it were there I felt right to myself at last.

# JAMES BALDWIN
## (1924–1987)

"I had never thought of myself as an essayist: the idea had never entered my mind. Even—or, perhaps, especially now—I find it hard to re-create the journey," says Baldwin, whose collection of autobiographical essays, *Notes of a Native Son* (1955), has become a central text in American literature. Baldwin's modesty is remarkable when coupled with the quality of his essays, many of which have become classics of the form. His nervousness may have stemmed from the aspect of personal revelation that autobiographical writing inevitably requires.

*Notes of a Native Son* centers on Baldwin's early childhood in Harlem, the death of his father, an evangelical minister, and his adult life as a refuge seeker in Switzerland and Paris, where he eventually found his calling as a novelist and essayist. Baldwin, whose novels include *Go Tell It on the Mountain* (1953) and *Giovanni's Room* (1956), would live most of his adult life as an expatriate, returning only periodically to the country of his birth. Much of his writing is focused on race relations, and the feelings of estrangement and hopelessness often found in the black community in America. In this, he draws strength from earlier African American writers, from W. E. B. Du Bois and Booker T. Washington through Zora Neale Hurston, and anticipates (in his reformist political zeal) the writings of Malcom X, Eldridge Cleaver, and others.

## FROM *Notes of a Native Son*

On the 29th of July, in 1943, my father died. On the same day, a few hours later, his last child was born. Over a month before this, while all our energies were concentrated in waiting for these events, there had been, in Detroit, one of the bloodiest race riots of the century. A few hours after my father's funeral, while he lay in state in the undertaker's chapel, a race riot broke out in Harlem. On the morning of the 3rd of August, we drove my father to the graveyard through a wilderness of smashed plate glass.

The day of my father's funeral had also been my nineteenth birthday. As we drove him to the graveyard, the spoils of injustice, anarchy, discontent, and hatred were all around us. It seemed to me that God himself had devised, to mark my father's end, the most sustained and brutally dissonant of codas. And it seemed to me, too, that the violence which rose all about us as my father left the world had been devised as a corrective for the pride of his eldest son. I had declined to believe in that apocalypse which had been central to my father's vision; very well, life seemed to be saying, here is something that will certainly pass for an apocalypse until the real thing comes along. I had inclined to be contemptuous of my father for the conditions of his life, for the conditions of our lives. When his life had ended I began to wonder about that life and also, in a new way, to be apprehensive about my own.

I had not known my father very well. We had got on badly, partly because we shared, in our different fashions, the vice of stubborn pride. When he was dead I realized that I had hardly ever spoken to him. When he had been dead a long time I began to wish I had. It seems to be typical of life in America, where opportunities, real and fancied, are thicker than anywhere else on the globe, that the second generation has no time to talk to the first. No one, including my father, seems to have known exactly how old he was, but his mother had been born during slavery. He was of the first generation of free men. He, along with thousands of other Negroes, came North after 1919 and I was part of that generation which had never seen the landscape of what Negroes sometimes call the Old Country.

He had been born in New Orleans and had been a quite young man there during the time that Louis Armstrong, a boy, was running errands for the dives and honky-tonks of what was always presented to me as one of the most wicked of cities—to this day, whenever I think of New Orleans, I also helplessly think of Sodom and Gomorrah. My father never mentioned Louis Armstrong, except to forbid us to play his records; but there was a picture of him on our wall for a long time. One of my father's strong-willed female relatives had placed it there and forbade my father to take it down. He never did, but he eventually maneuvered her out of the house and when, some years later, she was in trouble and near death, he refused to do anything to help her.

He was, I think, very handsome. I gather this from photographs and from my own memories of him, dressed in his Sunday best and on his way to preach a sermon somewhere, when I was little. Handsome, proud, and ingrown, "like a toe-nail," somebody said. But he looked to me, as I grew older, like pictures I had seen of African tribal chieftains: he really should have been naked, with war-paint on and barbaric mementos, standing among spears. He could be chilling in the pulpit and indescribably cruel in his personal life and he was certainly the most bitter man I have ever met; yet it must be said that there was something else in him, buried in him, which lent him his tremendous power and, even, a rather crushing charm. It had something to do with his blackness, I think—he was very black—with his blackness and his beauty, and with the fact that he knew that he was black but did not know that he was beautiful. He claimed to be proud of his blackness but it had also been the cause of much humiliation and it had fixed bleak boundaries to his life. He was not a young man when we were growing up and he had already suffered many kinds of ruin; in his outrageously demanding and protective way he loved his children, who were black like him and menaced, like him; and all these things sometimes showed in his face when he tried, never to my knowledge with any success, to establish contact with any of us. When he took one of his children on his knee to play, the child always became fretful and began to cry; when he tried to help one of us with our homework the absolutely unabating tension which emanated from him caused our minds and our tongues to become paralyzed, so that he, scarcely knowing why, flew into a rage and the child, not knowing why, was punished. If it ever entered his head to bring a surprise home for his children, it was, almost unfailingly, the wrong surprise and even the big watermelons he often brought home on his back in the summertime led to the most appalling scenes. I do not remember, in all those years, that one of his children was ever glad to see him come home. From what I was able to gather of his early life, it seemed that this inability to establish contact with other people had always marked him and had been one of the things which had driven him out of New Orleans. There was something in him, therefore, groping and tentative, which was never expressed and which was buried with him. One saw it most clearly when he was facing new people and hoping to impress them. But he never did, not for long. We went from church to smaller and more improbable church, he found himself in less and less demand as a minister, and by the time he died none of his friends had come to see him for a long time. He had lived and died in an intolerable bitterness of spirit and it frightened me, as we drove him to the graveyard through those unquiet, ruined streets, to see how powerful and overflowing this bitterness could be and to realize that this bitterness now was mine.

When he died I had been away from home for a little over a year. In that year I had had time to become aware of the meaning of all my father's bitter warnings, had discovered the secret of his proudly pursed lips and rigid carriage: I had discovered the weight of white people in the world. I saw that this had been for my ancestors and now would be for me an awful thing to live with and that the bitterness which had helped to kill my father could also kill me.

He had been ill a long time—in the mind, as we now realized, reliving instances of his fantastic intransigence in the new light of his affliction and endeavoring to feel a sorrow for him which never, quite, came true. We had not known that he was being eaten up by paranoia, and the discovery that his cruelty, to our bodies and our minds, had been one of the symptoms of his illness was not, then, enough to enable us to forgive him. The younger children felt, quite simply, relief that he would not be coming home anymore. My mother's observation that it was he, after all, who had kept them alive all these years meant nothing because the problems of keeping children alive are not real for children. The older children felt, with my father gone, that they could invite their friends to the house without fear that their friends would be insulted or, as had sometimes happened with me, being told that their friends were in league with the devil and intended to rob our family of everything we owned. (I didn't fail to wonder, and it made me hate him, what on earth we owned that anybody else would want.)

His illness was beyond all hope of healing before anyone realized that he was ill. He had always been so strange and had lived, like a prophet, in such unimaginably close communion with the Lord that his long silences which were punctuated by moans and hallelujahs and snatches of old songs while he sat at the living-room window never seemed odd to us. It was not until he refused to eat because, he said, his family was trying to poison him that my mother was forced to accept as a fact what had, until then, been only an unwilling suspicion. When he was committed, it was discovered that he had tuberculosis and, as it turned out, the disease of his mind allowed the disease of his body to destroy him. For the doctors could not force him to eat, either, and, though he was fed intravenously, it was clear from the beginning that there was no hope for him.

In my mind's eye I could see him, sitting at the window, locked up in his terrors; hating and fearing every living soul including his children who had betrayed him, too, by reaching towards the world which had despised him. There were nine of us. I began to wonder what it could have felt like for such a man to have had nine children whom he could barely feed. He used to make little jokes about our poverty, which never, of course, seemed very funny to us; they could not have seemed very funny to him, either, or else our all too feeble response to them would never have caused such rages. He spent great energy and achieved, to our chagrin, no small amount of success in keeping us away from the people who surrounded us, people who had all-night rent parties to which we listened when we should have been sleeping, people who cursed and drank and flashed razor blades on Lenox Avenue. He could not understand why, if they had so much energy to spare, they could not use it to make their lives better. He treated almost everybody on our block with a most uncharitable asperity and neither they, nor, of course, their children were slow to reciprocate.

The only white people who came to our house were welfare workers and bill collectors. It was almost always my mother who dealt with them, for my father's temper, which was at the mercy of his pride, was never to be trusted. It was clear that he felt their very presence in his home to be a violation: this was conveyed by his carriage, almost ludicrously stiff, and by his voice, harsh and vindictively polite. When I was around nine or ten I wrote a play which was directed by a young, white schoolteacher, a woman, who then took an interest in me, and gave me books to read and, in order to corroborate my theatrical bent, decided to take me to see what she somewhat tactlessly referred to as "real" plays. Theater-going was forbidden in our house, but, with the really cruel intuitiveness of a child, I suspected that the color of this woman's skin would carry the day for me. When, at school, she suggested taking me to the theater, I did not, as I might have done if she had been a Negro, find a way of discouraging her, but agreed that she should pick me up at my house one evening. I then, very cleverly, left all the rest to my mother, who suggested to my father, as I knew she would, that it would not be very nice to let such a kind woman make the trip for nothing. Also, since it was a schoolteacher, I imagine that my mother countered the idea of sin with the idea of "education," which word, even with my father, carried a kind of bitter weight.

Before the teacher came my father took me aside to ask *why* she was coming, what *interest* she could possibly have in our house, in a boy like me. I said I didn't know but I, too, suggested that it had something to do with education. And I understood that my father was waiting for me to say something—I didn't quite know what; perhaps that I wanted his protection against this teacher and her "education." I said none of these things and the teacher came and we went out. It was clear, during the brief interview in our living room, that my father was agreeing very much against his will and that he would have refused permission if he had dared. The fact that he did not dare caused me to despise him: I had no way of knowing that he was facing in that living room a wholly unprecedented and frightening situation.

Later, when my father had been laid off from his job, this woman became very important to us. She was really a very sweet and generous woman and went to a great deal of trouble to be of help to us, particularly during one awful winter. My mother called her by the highest name she knew: she said she was a "christian." My father could scarcely disagree but during the four or five years of our relatively close association he never trusted her and was always trying to surprise in her open, Midwestern face the genuine, cunningly hidden, and hideous motivation. In later years, particularly when it began to be clear that this "education" of mine was going to lead me to perdition, he became more explicit and warned me that my white friends in high school were not really my friends and that I would see, when I was older, how white people would do anything to keep a Negro down. Some of them could be nice, he admitted, but none of them were to be trusted and most of them were not even nice. The best thing was to have as little to do with them as possible. I did not feel this way and I was certain, in my innocence, that I never would.

But the year which preceded my father's death had made a great change in my life. I had been living in New Jersey, working in defense plants, working and living among southerners, white and black. I knew about the south, of course, and about how southerners treated Negroes and how they expected them to behave, but it had never entered my mind that anyone would look at me and expect *me* to behave that way. I learned in New Jersey that to be a Negro meant, precisely, that one was never looked at but was simply at the mercy of the reflexes the color of one's skin caused in other people. I acted in New Jersey as I had always acted, that is as though I thought a great deal of myself—I had to *act* that way—with results that were, simply, unbelievable. I had scarcely arrived before I had earned the enmity, which was extraordinarily ingenious, of all my superiors and nearly all my co-workers. In the beginning, to make matters worse, I simply did not know what was happening. I did not know what I had done, and I shortly began to wonder what *anyone* could possibly do, to bring about such unanimous, active, and unbearably vocal hostility. I knew about jim-crow but I had never experienced it. I went to the same self-service restaurant three times and stood with all the Princeton boys before the counter, waiting for a hamburger and coffee; it was always an extraordinarily long time before anything was set before me; but it was not until the fourth visit that I learned that, in fact, nothing had ever been set before me: I had simply picked something up. Negroes were not served there, I was told, and they had been waiting for me to realize that I was always the only Negro present. Once I was told this, I determined to go there all the time. But now they were ready for me and, though some dreadful scenes were subsequently enacted in that restaurant, I never ate there again.

It was the same story all over New Jersey, in bars, bowling alleys, diners, places to live. I was always being forced to leave, silently, or with mutual imprecations. I very shortly became notorious and children giggled behind me when I passed and their elders whispered or shouted—they really believed that I was mad. And it did begin to work on my mind, of course; I began to be afraid to go anywhere and to compensate for this I went places to which I really should not have gone and where, God knows, I had no desire to be. My reputation in town naturally enhanced my reputation at work and my working day became one long series of acrobatics designed to keep me out of trouble. I cannot say that these acrobatics succeeded. It began to seem that the machinery of the organization I worked for was turning over, day and night, with but one aim: to eject me. I was fired once, and contrived, with the aid of a friend from New York, to get back on the payroll; was fired again, and bounced back again. It took a while to fire me for the third time, but the third time took. There were no loopholes anywhere. There was not even any way of getting back inside the gates.

That year in New Jersey lives in my mind as though it were the year during which, having an unsuspected predilection for it, I first contracted some dread, chronic disease, the unfailing symptom of which is a kind of blind fever, a pounding in the skull and fire in the bowels. Once this disease is contracted, one can never be really carefree again, for the fever, without an instant's warning, can recur at any moment. It can wreck more important things than race relations. There is not a Negro alive who does not have this rage in his blood—one has the choice, merely, of living with it consciously or surrendering to it. As for me, this fever has recurred in me, and does, and will until the day I die.

My last night in New Jersey, a white friend from New York took me to the nearest big town, Trenton, to go to the movies and have a few drinks. As it turned out, he also saved me from, at the very least, a violent whipping. Almost every detail of that night stands out very clearly in my memory. I even remember the name of the movie we saw because its title impressed me as being so patly ironical. It was a movie about the German occupation of France, starring Maureen O'Hara and Charles Laughton and called *This Land Is Mine*. I remember the name of the diner we walked into when the movie ended: it was the "American Diner." When we walked in the counterman asked what we wanted and I remember answering with the casual sharpness which had become my habit: "We want a hamburger and a cup of coffee, what do you think we want?" I do not know why, after a year of such rebuffs, I so completely failed to anticipate his answer, which was, of course, "We don't serve Negroes here." This reply failed to discompose me, at least for the moment. I made some sardonic comment about the name of the diner and we walked out into the streets.

This was the time of what was called the "brown-out," when the lights in all American cities were very dim. When we re-entered the streets something happened to me which had the force of an optical illusion, or a nightmare. The streets were very crowded and I was facing north. People were moving in every direction but it seemed to me, in that instant, that all of the people I could see, and many more than that, were moving toward me, against me, and that everyone was white. I remember how their faces gleamed. And I felt, like a physical sensation, a *click* at the nape of my neck as though some interior string connecting my head to my body had been cut. I began to walk. I heard my friend call after me, but I ignored him. Heaven only knows what was going on in his mind, but he had the good sense not to touch me—I don't know what would have happened if he had—and to keep me in sight. I don't know what was going on in my mind, either; I certainly had no conscious plan. I wanted to do something to crush these white faces, which were crushing me. I walked for perhaps a block or two until I came to an enormous, glittering, and fashionable restaurant in which I knew not even the intercession of the Virgin would cause me to be served. I pushed through the doors and took the first vacant seat I saw, at a table for two, and waited.

I do not know how long I waited and I rather wonder, until today, what I could possibly have looked like. Whatever I looked like, I frightened the waitress who shortly appeared, and the moment she appeared all of my fury flowed towards her. I hated her for her white face, and for her great, astounded, frightened eyes. I felt that if she found a black man so frightening I would make her fright worth-while.

She did not ask me what I wanted, but repeated, as though she had learned it somewhere, "We don't serve Negroes here." She did not say it with the blunt, derisive hostility to which I had grown so accustomed, but, rather, with a note of apology in her voice, and fear. This made me colder and more murderous than ever. I felt I had to do something with my hands. I wanted her to come close enough for me to get her neck between my hands.

So I pretended not to have understood her, hoping to draw her closer. And she did step a very short step closer, with her pencil poised incongruously over her pad, and repeated the formula: ". . . don't serve Negroes here."

Somehow, with the repetition of that phrase, which was already ringing in my head like a thousand bells of a nightmare, I realized that she would never come any closer and that I would have to strike from a distance. There was nothing on the table but an ordinary water-mug half full of water, and I picked this up and hurled it with all my strength at her. She ducked and it missed her and shattered against the mirror behind the bar. And, with that sound, my frozen blood abruptly thawed, I returned from wherever I had been, I *saw*, for the first time, the restaurant, the people with their mouths open, already, as it seemed to me, rising as one man, and I realized what I had done, and where I was, and I was frightened. I rose and began running for the door. A round, potbellied man grabbed me by the nape of the neck just as I reached the doors and began to beat me about the face. I kicked him and got loose and ran into the streets. My friend whispered, *"Run!"* and I ran.

My friend stayed outside the restaurant long enough to misdirect my pursuers and the police, who arrived, he told me, at once. I do not know what I said to him when he came to my room that night. I could not have said much. I felt, in the oddest, most awful way, that I had somehow betrayed him. I lived it over and over and over again, the way one relives an automobile accident after it has happened and one finds oneself alone and safe. I could not get over two facts, both equally difficult for the imagination to grasp, and one was that I could have been murdered. But the other was that I had been ready to commit murder. I saw nothing very clearly but I did see this: that my life, my *real* life, was in danger, and not from anything other people might do but from the hatred I carried in my own heart.

# GORE VIDAL
## (1925– )

After attending Exeter, Vidal served briefly in the armed forces during World War II; aboard ship in the Pacific, he began writing fiction, and his first novel was published when he was twenty. Novel followed novel, including *The City and the Pillar* (1948)—one of the first public treatments of the subject of homosexuality in American fiction. He wrote numerous scripts for television and Hollywood, as well as stage plays, in the fifties. Among Vidal's most well-known later novels are *Myra Breckinridge* (1968), *Burr* (1973), *Lincoln* (1984), and *The Smithsonian Institution* (1998).

His brilliant and witty essays, gathered in *United States: Essays. 1952–1992*, reveal a uniquely gifted and well-stocked mind, and a sensibility rare in our time: that of the genuine satirist. His memoir, *Palimpsest* (1995), reveals little about the interior man, but it does paint a vivid portrait of the author's times. Like the memoirs of U. S. Grant or Malcolm X, Vidal's book is more memoir than autobiography, describing the social milieu of the author, giving flesh to the ghosts who wandered through his life, like the playwright Tennessee Williams, whom Vidal nicknames the Glorious Bird.

## FROM *Palimpsest*

### ROME AND THE GLORIOUS BIRD

. . . The house is full of workmen. The electrician—rather sulky—has come and gone with the telephone, so I cannot ring out. The carpenter repairs furniture, carefully replacing eighteenth-century patina with a bright and shiny chocolate veneer whose formula will die with him. The cook has gone to the village to do the shopping. In this heat, tuna-fish salad. A characteristic of Italy is that no job is ever properly finished, thus maintaining an eternal and often highly irritable relationship between contractor and artisan. For the artisan, a finished job is like a finished tomb was for Pharaoh: a signal that he is now ready to die.

My own mood is irritable this morning. A kaleidoscope of impressions keeps thought at bay. My collected essays have just been published. The reviews are arriving. I look at them; Howard reads them. As the book represents forty years of essay writing, the reception is benign. I am plainly at the end of the road. So, I suspect, is literature, a serious matter that I cannot say I take very seriously. Each culture plays the games it needs to play. The novel has given way to the audio-visual just as interactive computers now replace conversation and sex for Americans, if that recent poll is to be believed.

Not to want, was the Buddha's recipe for the blessed absence of pain. As it has turned out, I have got so much more than I ever wanted—or needed—that I am close to serenity. Even so, when I wake up, I take my blood pressure—normal this morning; blood sugar, too. Were I to follow the Buddha's fivefold way, I should not bother about such things. But I am a child of the sick West and cannot be other.

I look about the room where I have been at work for almost a quarter century. Proofs of unread novels accumulate on the coffee table. I sit at a large table that was in the house when we bought it. Everything since *Burr* has been written at this table. Lately, we have acquired a television set to watch the news on CNN and old movies. Videocassettes are beginning to crowd out the books. To the left of the fireplace, a chiaroscuro Neapolitan painting by Viola. "Typical of early eighteenth-century South German painting," boomed the journalist Joe Alsop. As Joe was an expert on everything, he was generally wrong on almost everything, particularly his subject, politics. For thirty years we were losing to Communism, according to Joe; he was a romantic goose, but endearing.

To the right, a Eugene Berman painting, a ruin whose perspective is slightly off; next to Eugene, a Tuscan landscape by his brother, Leonid. Eugene lived in Rome, surrounded by a vast illegally acquired Etruscan collection that the director John Huston tried, illegally, to buy. Where is it now? Eugene was a friend of Carmen Angleton, sister of James Jesus Angleton, the madman of the CIA, and an associate of my sister's friend Cord Meyer, whose wife, a mistress of Jack Kennedy, was mysteriously murdered and her diary vanished, supposedly taken by Angleton. . . . Everything has so many chains of association in our unexpectedly Jacobean republic that nothing any longer surprises.

Ordinarily, I don't think much about the past. A friend was surprised to hear me say that there was not one moment of my past that I would like to relive. Apparently, I am unlike others in this. In fact, everyone I've put that question to has a list of times and places and people to be revisited. I am only at home in the present, and view with dislike the numerous letters from biographers. On my desk there are now two new requests for recollection—of Alec Guinness and Terry Southern. Who next? I like both, but what on earth has one got to say about either that will be interesting? Little anecdotes are not my style. Of course, I could review their life work, but I charge for writing reviews.

When I last saw Alec, he was about to move into the Connaught Hotel in London, where I was staying. "Good," he said. "We shall see each other. I shall be filming for a month in town. A TV thing." I said that, alas, I was leaving the next day for Pittsburgh. "Why Pittsburgh?"

"I, too, am filming, a movie. As an actor this time." Alec's pale brows knit. "A *television* film?" he asked. "No. A theatrical film." The eyes became, as Daphne du Maurier would say, *mere slits.* "How *long* will you be in Pittsburgh?" When I answered two days, he sighed with quiet pleasure, "Ah, a *small* part."

While filming *With Honors* in Chicago, I was told that since the star, Joe Pesci, had a degree of control over the cast, the producer proposed five names to him for the part of the villainous Harvard professor. Four English actors and me. Alec's name headed the list. Pesci is supposed to have said, "Why do we always have to go get an English asshole for this sort of part when we have one of our own?" Thus, I was hired.

The above is a demonstration of how memory works—or doesn't work. One thing recalls another, and then the mind starts to shape the material. As I am supposed to be remembering myself, I am central to these memories; I am, however, happier to be at the edge, as one is in an essay, studying someone else or what someone else has made art of, like Alec's splendid caricature of Kenneth Tynan in *The Lavender Hill Mob*, eerily precise even down to the way that Ken, who was to die of emphysema, stagily held a cigarette between ring and little fingers. Ken also, despite— no, I am sure, because of—his lifelong stammer, was the Player King in Alec's *Hamlet.* What was Ken's performance like? Alec sighed. "He elected to play the part as a Chinese, a curious choice. But then I was bad, too. The only original thing about the production was that I insisted that there be no staircases on the set. I have found in life—if not onstage—that I have *never* had an intelligent conversation with anyone—much less a monologue—on the stairs of my house."

I have always preferred the company of actors to writers. But given the choice, who does not? Of the two professions, actors are the most modest and the least secure; they also tell better stories. Writers tend to self-pity and crude envy. I suppose my own self-pity is adequate to the task of being, for half a century, a writer, but as I have never experienced sexual jealousy of anyone, I have also never been envious of another writer. If a reviewer prefers X to me, I will dislike the reviewer, not X. Also, the reverse of envy, I am drawn to those writers who do what I cannot do. In reading someone wonderful—full of wonders—like Calvino, empathy takes over and I start to feel that what he wrote I wrote. This can be exhilarating. Whenever Tennessee had a successful play, it was like my own. When I wrote a successful play, Tennessee would be distraught. The Glorious Bird, as I called him, would make hissing sounds through that sharp beak, feathers aflutter, beady eyes wide with alarm, nest invaded.

Now, after much circling, I am ready to take the plunge into the heart of 1948.

"I particularly like New York on hot summer nights when all the . . . uh, superfluous people are off the streets." Those were the first words Tennessee addressed to me; then the foggy blue eyes blinked, and a nervous chuckle filled the moment's silence before I said whatever I said.

As I later wrote: "Curtain rising. The place: an apartment at the American Academy in Rome. Occasion: a party for some newly arrived Americans, among them Frederic Prokosch, Samuel Barber. The month: February 1948. The day: glittering. What else could any day be in the golden age?"

I am pleased that I can remember so clearly my first meeting with the Glorious Bird. Usually, I forget first meetings, excepting always those solemn audiences granted by the old and famous when I was young and green.

I thought Tennessee ancient. After all, I was twenty-two. He was thirty-seven. A *Streetcar Named Desire* had been running in New York for more than a year when we met that evening in a flat on the Janiculum hill with a view of what was, in those days, a quiet city where hardly anyone was superfluous unless it was us, the first group of American writers and artists to arrive in Rome after the war.

In 1946 and 1947 Europe was still out-of-bounds for foreigners; hence, my Guatemalan phase. But by 1948 the Italians had begun to pull themselves together, demonstrating once more their astonishing ability to cope with disaster, so neatly balanced by their inability to deal with success.

Rome was strange to all of us. For one thing, Italy had been sealed off not only by war but by Fascism. Since the early thirties, few English or American artists knew Italy well. Those who did included mad Ezra Pound, gentle Max Beerbohm, spurious Bernard Berenson, and, of course, the wealthy Anglo-American historian Harold Acton, in stately residence at Florence. By 1948 Acton had written about both the Bourbons of Naples and the later Medici of Florence; he was also prone to the writing of memoirs. And so, wanting no doubt to flesh out yet another chapter in the ongoing story of a long and marvelously uninteresting life, Acton came down to Rome to look at the new invaders. What he believed he saw and heard, he subsequently published in a little volume called *More Memoirs of an Aesthete,* a work to be cherished for its remarkable number of unaesthetic misprints and misspellings.

"After the First World War American writers and artists had emigrated to Paris; now they pitched upon Rome." So Acton begins. "According to Stendhal, the climate was enough to gladden anybody, but this was not the reason; one of them explained to me that it was the facility of finding taxis, and very little of Rome can be seen from a taxi. Classical and Romantic Rome was no more to them than a picturesque background. Tennessee Williams, Victor [he means Frederic] Prokosch and Gore Vidal created a bohemian annexe to the American Embassy . . ." To like Rome for its available taxis is splendid stuff and I wish I had said it. (Did I?) Certainly whoever did was putting Acton on, since the charm of Rome, for us, if not the Italians, was the lack of automobiles of any kind. But Acton is only just easing into his formidable stride. More to come.

Toward the end of March, Tennessee gave a party to inaugurate his new flat on the Via Aurora (in the golden age even the street names were apt). Somehow or other, Acton got himself invited. I remember him floating like some large pale fish through the crowded room; from time to time, he would make a sudden lunge at this or that promising bit of bait while Tennessee, he tells us, "wandered as a lost soul among the guests he [had] assembled in an apartment which might have been in New York. . . . Neither he nor any of the group I met with him spoke Italian, yet he had a typically Neapolitan protégé who could speak no English."

At this time Tennessee and I had been in Rome for only a few weeks and French, not Italian, was the second language of the reasonably well educated American of that era. On the other hand, Prokosch knew Italian, German, and French; he also bore with becoming grace the heavy weight of a Yale doctorate in Middle English. But to Acton the author of *The Asiatics,* the translator of Hölderlin and Louise Labé was just another barbarian whose works "fell short of his perfervid imagination, [he] had the dark good looks of an advertiser of razor blades . . ." Happily, "Gore Vidal, the youngest in age, aggressively handsome in a clean-limbed sophomore style, had success written all over him. . . . His candour was engaging but he was slightly on the defensive, as if he anticipated an attack on his writings or his virtue." Well, the young GV wasn't so dumb: Seeing the old one-two plainly in the middle distance, he kept sensibly out of reach.

"A pudgy, taciturn, moustached little man without any obvious distinction." Thus Acton describes Tennessee. He then zeroes in on the "protégé" from Naples, a young man whom Acton calls "Pierino." Acton tells us that Pierino had many complaints about Tennessee and his friends, mostly due to the language barrier. The boy was also eager to go to America. Pierino was enthralled, Acton tells us, by Acton. "You are the first *galantuomo* who has spoken to me this evening." After making a date to see the *galantuomo* later on that evening, Pierino split. Acton then told Tennessee, "as tactfully as I could, that his young protégé felt neglected. [Tennessee] rubbed his chin thoughtfully and said nothing, a little perplexed. There was something innocently childish about his expression." It does not occur to the memoirist that Tennessee might have been alarmed at his strange guest's bad manners. "Evidently he was not aware that Pierino wanted to be taken to America and I have wondered since whether he took him there, for that was my last meeting with Tennessee Williams." It must be said that Acton managed to extract quite a lot of copy out of a single meeting. To put his mind at rest, Tennessee did take Pierino to America, and Pierino is now a married man and doing, as they say, well.

"This trifling episode illustrated the casual yet condescending attitude of certain foreigners towards the young Italians they cultivated on account of their Latin charm, without any interest in their character, aspirations or desires." This sentiment or sentimentality could be put just as well the other way around—and with far more accuracy. Italian "trade" has never had much interest in the character, aspirations, or desires of those to whom they rent their ass. When Acton meditates upon the Italian Boy, a sweet and sickly hypocrisy clouds his usually sharp prose and we are in E. M. Forsterland, where the lower orders (male) are worshiped and entirely misunderstood. But magnum of sour grapes to one side, Acton is by no means inaccurate. Certainly he got right Tennessee's indifference to place, art, history. The Bird seldom read a book, and the only history he knew was his own; he depended, finally, on a romantic genius to get him through life. Above all, he was a survivor.

From the Bird's memoirs: "Life that winter in Rome: a golden dream, and I don't just mean Raffaello [Acton's "Pierino"] and the mimosa and total freedom of life. Stop there: what I do mean is the total freedom of life and Raffaello and the mimosa . . ." That season we were, all of us, symbolically, out of jail. Free of poverty and hack work, Tennessee had metamorphosed into the Glorious Bird while I had left behind me, as I've already noted, a lifetime of servitude. So it was, at the beginning of that golden dream, we met.

Tennessee's version: "[Gore] had just published a best-seller, called *The City and the Pillar*, which was one of the first homosexual novels of consequence. I had not read it but I knew that it had made the best-seller lists and that it dealt with a 'forbidden subject.' " Later, Tennessee actu-

ally read the book—the only novel of mine that he was ever able to get
through. Tennessee was so taken in by the style that he thought that I was
writing, most artlessly, the story of my own life.

"My parents were just like yours," he said, "particularly my father." At
first, I didn't know what he was talking about. Then I recalled my description of Jim Willard's lower-middle-class family in Virginia, which I
had simply made up out of my head with some help, perhaps, from
James T. Farrell's *Studs Lonigan*. I told him that everything in the book
was made up except the passion of Jim Willard for Bob Ford.

Tennessee didn't care for the ending, "I don't think you realized what
a good book you had written." He found the fight at the end melodra-
matic—that from Tennessee, whose heroes, when not castrated, are eaten
alive by small boys in Amalfi, just below where I live. I should note that
whenever *Suddenly, Last Summer* appears on Italian television, the local
boys find it irresistibly funny.

I told Tennessee about Jimmie Trimble, and how I had no idea what
would have happened had we ever met again and so, aware of the American panic on the subject, I had visualized the worst possible ending,
rather, I added slyly, as Shakespeare had done for *Romeo and Juliet* and
as Tennessee himself would do over and over again. Love is Death is Romance.

"Gore was a handsome kid, about twenty-four, and I was quite taken
by his wit as well as his appearance." Incidentally, I am mesmerized by
the tributes to my beauty that keep cropping up in the memoirs of the period. At the time, nobody reliable thought to tell me. In fact, it was my
impression that I was not making out as well as most people because,
with characteristic malice, Nature had allowed the actor Guy Madison
to look like Guy Madison and not me.

"We found that we had interests in common and we spent a lot of time
together. Please don't imagine that I'm suggesting that there was a romance." I don't remember whether or not I ever told Tennessee that I
had actually seen but not met him the previous year. He was following
me up Fifth Avenue while I, in turn, was stalking yet another quarry. I
recognized him: He wore a blue bow tie with white polka dots. In no
mood for literary encounters, I gave him a scowl and he abandoned the
chase just north of Rockefeller Center. I don't recall how my own pursuit ended. We walked—cruised—a lot in the golden age.

"I believe we also went to Florence that season and were entertained
by that marvelous old aesthete Berenson." No, that was someone else.
"And then one afternoon Gore took me to the Convent of the Blue Nuns
to meet the great philosopher and essayist, by then an octogenarian and
semi-invalid, Santayana." I had to drag Tennessee to meet Santayana.
Neither had heard of the other.

In 1985, after the Bird's death, I wrote:

> *Thirty-seven years ago, in March 1948, Tennessee Williams and I celebrated his thirty-seventh birthday in Rome, except that he said that it was his thirty-fourth birthday. Years later, when confronted with the fact that he had been born in 1911 not 1914, he said, serenely, "I do not choose to count as part of my life the three years that I spent working for a shoe company." Actually, he had spent ten months, not three years, in the shoe company, and the reason that he had changed his birthdate was to qualify for a play contest open to those twenty-five or under. No matter. I thought him very old in 1948.*

I must say I was somewhat awed by Tennessee's success. In his *Memoirs*—and life—he went on and on about the years of poverty, yet, starting with *The Glass Menagerie* (1944), he had an astonishingly productive and successful fifteen years. But even at that high moment in Rome, the Bird's eye was coldly realistic. "Baby, the playwright's working career is a short one. There's always somebody new to take your place."

Tennessee worked every morning on whatever was at hand. If there was no play to be finished or new dialogue to be sent round to the theater, he would open a drawer and take out the draft of a story already written and begin to rewrite it. I once found him revising a short story that had just been published. "Why," I asked, "rewrite what's already in print?" He looked at me, vaguely; then he said, "Well, obviously it's not finished." And went back to his typing.

In Paris, he gave me the story "Rubio y Morena" to read. I didn't like it. So fix it, he said. He knew, of course, that there is no fixing someone else's story (or life), but he was curious to see what I would do. So I reversed backward-running sentences, removed repetitions, eliminated half those adjectives and adverbs that he always insisted do their work in pairs. I was proud of the result. He was deeply irritated. "What you have done is remove my *style*, which is all that I have."

Tennessee could not possess his own life until he had written about it. This is common. To start with, there would be, let us say, a sexual desire for someone. Consummated or not, the desire ("something that is made to occupy a larger space than that which is afforded by the individual being") would produce reveries. In turn, the reveries would be written down as a story. But should the desire still remain unfulfilled, he would make a play of the story and then—and this is why he was so compulsive a working playwright—he would have the play produced so that he could, at relative leisure, like God, rearrange his original experience into something that was no longer God's and unpossessable but *his*. The Bird's frantic lifelong pursuit of—and involvement in—play productions was not just ambition or a need to be busy; it was the only way that he ever had of being entirely alive. The sandy encounters with his first real love, a dancer, on the beach at Provincetown and the dancer's later death ("an awful flower grew in his brain"), instead of being forever lost, were forever his once they had been translated to the stage, where living men and women could act out his text and with their immediate flesh close at last the circle of desire. "For love I make characters in plays," he wrote; and did.

I had long since forgotten why I called him the Glorious Bird until I came to reread his stories for a preface that I would write. The image of the bird is everywhere in his work. The bird is flight, poetry, life. The bird is time, death: "Have you ever seen the skeleton of a bird? If you have you will know how completely they are still flying." In his last story, written at seventy-one, "The Negative," he wrote of a poet who can no longer assemble a poem. "Am I a wingless bird?" he writes; and soars no longer.

One of the bird's academic biographers wanted to know if he had ever said anything witty or wise. I suppose too much had been made of his later years, when he was often on pills or drunk and not always coherent. But, at his best, he was corrosively funny. After listening to a boorish youth in a bar repeat for the hundredth time, "Live and let live is my motto," the Bird finally said, with grave courtesy, "Surely, in your situation, there is no alternative philosophy."

The fiercely busy and tragical director Kazan was Stanislavsky to the Bird's Chekhov. Where Tennessee or Chekhov intended a comic effect, the two directors insisted on fierce passion and tears. Invariably, at the end of *A Streetcar Named Desire*, when the audience was barking like seals as the broken Blanche DuBois is led away, with the poignant cry, "I have always depended upon the kindness of strangers," the Bird's whoop of laughter would echo in the snuffling theater, and he would say, loudly, "Now she's off to the bughouse."

In London I acted as interpreter between the Bird and Claire Bloom when she was about to take on the role of Blanche. The Bird didn't think she was right for the part, but he had agreed to the production. Claire was jittery. He offered her a cigarette. "I don't smoke," she said, grabbing the cigarette and inhaling deeply as he lit it. "Except one, just before dinner, always in the evening," she babbled. The Bird looked at her suspiciously; then he said, "Do you have any questions about the play?"

"Yes." Claire pulled herself together. "What happens *after* the final curtain?"

The Bird sat back in his chair, narrowed his eyes. "No actress has ever asked me that question." He shut his eyes; thought. "She will enjoy her time in the bin. She will seduce one or two of the more comely young doctors. Then she will be let free to open an attractive boutique in the French Quarter . . ."

"She wins?"

"Oh, yes," said the Bird. "Blanche wins." The result was splendid. Claire gained greater and greater strength as the play proceeded and, at the end, she leaves for the bin as for a coronation. Audiences cheered, not knowing how one psychological adjustment, made in the smoke of one cigarette at dusk, had changed the nature of a famous play.

At eleven-thirty every morning, a tourist boat passes below the house, and from four hundred meters below, I hear a woman's voice describing, first in Italian, then in English, the villa of Gore Vidal. I hear my name clearly but cannot make out exactly what she is saying. Last year Nureyev said that she also discussed him as he lay in bed on his island off Positano. "She come to me first. *Nine* o'clock." He rather enjoyed her. I don't. I feel as if I were being forced to listen in on an extension telephone where I am being discussed. Doubtless, I am reacting against my mother who was a compulsive eavesdropper, as well as interceptor of the mail of others.

Nina's spying backfired during a September–July romance that she was having with an actor in Southampton. On an extension telephone, she heard him speak lovingly to a man in New York whom he was to see the following day. Furiously, Nina confronted him. Not only was he two-timing her, he was, as she had always feared—let's face it—a sexual degenerate. He admitted the first; denied the second because "That was not a man," he said. "That was the actress Edith Atwater. She has a very deep voice, and we are being married tomorrow." Later, Edith was in a road company of my play *The Best Man*. Once we made eye contact at a rehearsal and, without a word, both laughed at Nina.

## THE GUEST OF THE BLUE NUNS

Years after 1948, Frederic Prokosch was to write a book called *Voices* in which he described every famous person he had ever met. He had kept careful notes, he assured the reader. I gave him a wary review, and praised him for literary virtues that had been unfairly overlooked for more than a generation. But I was uneasy with his "voices" of the great, since it was plain to me that he had simply made up most of them. The few that he did catch from real life, like Auden, are sharp and one does hear a real voice; but with George Santayana, say, whom I took him to meet in Rome, he simply invents, rather lazily, what he thinks Santayana *ought* to have said as opposed to what he did say.

Santayana is largely forgotten now, but he was once a commanding philosopher known for his silver style and elusive persona. In 1935, he published his only novel, *The Last Puritan*, an attractive story that I read as a boy, half guessing at the emotional currents that he sets in motion when he describes how a New England Puritan youth, Oliver Alden (alpha omega, beginning and end) tries to find himself. Even I, a pubescent, could identify with his search. But then it is a book for the young. Later I read *The Idea of Christ in the Gospels*. I also made a number of partially successful attempts to grasp Santayana's formal philosophy. This was the background to our meeting, which took place simply enough.

I presented myself at the convent of the Blue Nuns on the Celian hill. A sister—the nuns are Irish—met me in the hall. What was my business? I would like to see Professor Santayana (Professor has more resonance in Italy than it has for us). I am a young American student, I added, as bait. Well, I was American and twenty-two.

The nun left me at the entrance to a long hallway with doors to left and right. She opened one of them, on the right. A small figure glided toward me, the light behind him. Santayana's routine with callers was simple. If he was interested, he would invite them back to his cell; if not, he would say a few polite words and withdraw.

We shook hands, he looked up at me with bright round black eyes that reminded me of someone I knew well. He wore a dressing gown, a Byronic shirt open at the neck, and a faded mauve-gray waistcoat from the 1890s. The voice—although I have an aural memory and can usually mimic almost anyone, I cannot recall his voice other than that it was agreeable, very much Harvard of the last century, where he had taught alongside William James . . . well, *counter* to William James. Santayana's father had been Spanish, as was his mother, who later married a Sturges of Boston. He looked Spanish but sounded Sturges; he had made himself the first—and perhaps last—Epicurean Puritan.

"Come in," he said after a few words of exchange. As the bright eyes stared at me, I realized that they were the eyes, and indeed the face, of my beloved grandmother Gore, gone mysteriously bald.

The cell had an iron bed, with a screen partly around it, a small bookcase with fewer than a dozen books; a writing table with chair; a second chair for visitors. He had lived at the Bristol Hotel during the war, but when the Nazis came, it had seemed politic to vanish into the convent-hospital. He was eighty-five when I met him.

"I shall talk and you shall listen," he said, with a smile. "You can ask questions, of course. But remember I am *very* deaf." I felt like Phaedo with Socrates. He held up a section of a book whose binding he had removed. As he finished reading each section, he would drop it into a wastebasket, "I am reading someone called Toynbee. Do you know him? No? I gather he is some sort of preacher who involves himself with history. The footnotes are not entirely worthless. Perhaps you know my *new* young friend, Robert Lowell?" I said that I had met him. "He writes to me regularly. He is gifted as a poet, isn't he? I no longer write poetry." This seemed to mean, Nor read it either. But he had read Lowell's *Lord Weary's Castle*. "What a difficult time he is going to have, though I don't dare tell him so. He is a Lowell. From Boston. He is also a poet and now . . . now . . . he is a Roman Catholic convert. Isn't that all perhaps too much for one young man?"

I did not know Lowell well enough in 1948 to be able to remark that Lowell was also, periodically, mad as a hatter and a great torment to the three talented women he married. I always liked to compete with the sane Lowell in conversation—and competition was what he most enjoyed. Once at my house on the Hudson, we talked of Caesar. I remarked on Cicero's report to Atticus on Caesar's visit to his house, and how delighted Cicero was when Caesar—the true politician—praised his consulship.

Lowell moved smoothly in to take the trick. "And remember," he said, "Cicero's remark on how unnerving it was to have Caesar for a houseguest?"

What is the point to any knowledge unless one can share it? Did we learn these things in school? No, we read them on our own in order to meet the personages of the past with whom Lowell was as eager to compete as with his contemporaries. He was forever making up lists of the best, second best, third best this or that (usually poets). I told Mary McCarthy that he was currently making more and more far-fetched comparisons, like, Is Mary McCarthy a better critic than Saint-Beuve? Mary's eyes become adamantine. I recovered quickly: "Well, that's too reasonable as you're both critics. It's as if he . . ." Mary finished for me: "As if he had said, Is Mary McCarthy a better general than Joan of Arc?"

"Tell me, do you know a Mr. Edmund Wilson? He came to see me. He led me to believe that he was a very famous man of letters, which no doubt he is. He said that I had sent him a book. I said that he was mistaken. He said that, no, I had signed it to Edmund Wilson. At first I was firm, but then I remembered that when the American army came—and, oh! how glad we were to see them in Rome!" The black eyes glittered with a fine obsidian malice. "And an army major came here with several of my books for me to sign and as I was so grateful, so *very* grateful for this liberation, I threw caution to the winds and signed copies to this one and to that one. Edmund Wilson was apparently that one."

Wilson had paid his call on Santayana three years before me, in April 1945. He wrote it up immediately, and so his detailed account is apt to be more precise than mine forty-five years later: "He received me with simplicity and courtesy and excused himself for reclining on a little chaise longue with a blanket over his legs." I don't remember a chaise longue. The comedy of the autographed copy of his memoirs, *Persons and Places*, was duly played. Santayana told me that although he sometimes signed books for people, he never wrote the person's name unless he knew him. Wilson had taken it for granted that Santayana had sent him a book as an *hommage* to the powerful critic of *The New Yorker* magazine. "Santayana seemed to want to slip away from the subject, but I was nonplused and embarrassed at coming to see him when he did not know who I was." Fame. "With a freedom that surprised me, however, he at once began talking about his recent books: *Persons and Places* and *The Middle Span*."

I didn't talk to him about these two memoirs because I'd not yet read them. I did ask about *The Idea of Christ in the Gospels*, written in the convent. I had had a long argument with a friend about Santayana's chapter on Christ's miracles. As Santayana gravely—even reverently—describes each miracle, the analyzed miracle becomes ever more absurd as, all the while, he maintains the usual priestly line that since all life is a miracle, then what we may not understand could be . . . and so on. I was blunt: Does *he* actually believe in them? The answer was quick. "Oh, no." He smiled what Wilson called his "mischievous smile" and paused: "On the ground, of course, that there is not enough evidence." Wilson remarks that someone said that Santayana was a Catholic in everything but faith. Santayana himself is supposed to have said, "There is no God and Mary is his mother."

I asked about Henry James. He gave a sort of imitation of Henry's paraphrastic style; then sighed. "Oh, the James brothers!" He sounded as if he were invoking the outlaws. Perhaps he was; Santayana was about twenty years old when Jesse James hit the dust. "One was a novelist who thought he was a philosopher," the old man said—for the hundredth time?—"and the other was a philosopher who thought he was a novelist." I cannot remember much else, though I did take notes in a diary that winter and spring in Rome. I must look them up.

I brought the composer Samuel Barber, Prokosch, and Tennessee to meet him. He was amused, I think, by the first two and mystified by the Bird. Although the Bird had never heard of him, the Bird's bright eye watched him carefully and the Bird's perfect ear picked up Santayana's reading of the line "That was in the days when I had young secretaries." Later, the Bird repeated the line with relish and rolled his eyes heavenward.

I saw Santayana two or three times alone. He never asked me a question about myself, and I never volunteered information. He had given

Wilson the same treatment: "One of the wonderful things about him was the readiness and grace with which he played a classical role: that of the sage who has made it his business to reflect on all kinds of men and who will talk about the purpose and practice of life with anyone who likes to discuss them—as with me, whom he didn't know from Adam . . ."

I recall two arias. One that began on the subject of the mystics, in which he tended to include the egotists, as he called them, of German philosophy. This ended on the pure Santayanan note, a plainspoken, even wide-eyed statement, swiftly canceled by an unexpected comment: "I am not a mystic." Full stop. Then the eyes—yes, widened, and the mischievous smile switched on: "But I can *imagine* what it must be like." This reopens the door to reveal . . . what? Another door, I should think. What is mysticism but imagination?

Finally, on the transience of reputation and of history itself. "In America literary reputations come and go so swiftly," I complained, fatuously. The answer was swift. "It would be insufferable if they did *not*."

I commented on how bloody the century that we had lived in was. He looked surprised. "Why, I have lived most of my life in one of the longest periods of peace ever known. I was born at the end of the American Civil War while those two German wars together lasted—how long? Nine years? Out of the eighty-five years that I've been alive, nine years of war is nothing." Plainly, he was suggesting that I must cultivate the long view. We spoke of the coming election in Italy. American propaganda daily told us that Italy was in danger of going Communist, and if that happened, Western civilization would be extinguished.

I have just shut my eyes. I used to be able to summon up scenes at will, but now aging memory is so busy weeding its own garden that, promiscuously, it pulls up roses as well as crabgrass. In any case, the room is too full of light for me to see clearly what is—much less what was. I ask him why he never wrote another novel.

A great smile: "How could I? You see, I've never really knocked about that much." I liked the "knocked about."

I open my eyes in present time but continue to hear, if not see, Santayana talking about a possible Communist takeover of Italy. He is disconcertingly blithe. "Why not? After all, they have tried everything else. This will be something new for them, something perhaps even useful, because who knows what life will be like in a . . . in a wolf pack? Who knows what sort of new energies, relationships, loyalties will emerge?" The irony shone along with the morning sun on the pale bald head.

Then he opened a picture book and showed me colored sketches of Guards officers in some nineteenth-century regiment. "The illustrations are nice."

I rose to go. This was my last visit. Alarmed by our imperial propaganda machine, I feared that Italy was about to undergo the standard "bloodbath" that our press is always eager to draw for other people. I said goodbye.

"I shall give you a book," he said. From the bookcase, he took a copy of the second volume of his memoirs, *The Middle Span*. "What is your name?" I told him. "You see," he said, as he carefully wrote at his table, "I shall write 'for' you. I rarely do this, except of course when liberated by the American army." I have the book on my desk: "For Gore Vidal, George Santayana, April 1, 1948."

"It is your April Fool's present." He led me to the door to the corridor. "How old are you?"

"Twenty-two."

"You have written a book?"

"Three, in fact."

"You look young for your age, but then your head is small in proportion to your body." In those days I wore a crew cut. "When I was your age I wanted to be an architect at Harvard. But there was an opening in philosophy . . ." He walked me slowly down the corridor to the entrance hall. "I've often wondered what life would have been like as an architect. I'm not sure that I could have handled the mathematical part very well, but I believe that I would have been good at decoration."

He gave me his cold old hand. I shook it. "I think you will have a happy life." He smiled and the black eyes glittered. "Because you lack superstition. If you come back to Rome, pay me a call, assuming that I'm still here." I did, but did not see him. He was to live four more years.

Prokosch's Santayana is entirely made up: "His head sags a little. His eyes begin to water. His voice rose imperceptibly, as though for a final effort. 'We are sailing ever deeper into the dark, uncharted waters. The lights in the lighthouses are beginning to go out. Is there anything to guide us? Is there anyone worth listening to? I wake up in the middle of the night and I'm cold with terror.' " I fear this is a libel, and I grow irritated with my dead friend Fritz.

Wilson gets the tone right: "This little husk of a man, at once so ascetic and so cheerful, sustaining at eighty-one so steady an intellectual energy, inhabiting a convent cell, among the layers of historical debris that composed the substance of Rome, intact and unmoved by the tides of invasions and revolution that have been brawling back and forth around him; and when he talked about these outside occurrences it was as if he attached them to history: the war was an event like any other which would presently belong to the past." A past that Santayana belongs to— as well as Wilson and Prokosch and nearly everyone else that I knew in 1948, all past and gone.

Years later I became a friend of Philip Rahv, a literary critic as well as editor of *Partisan Review*. The only row that I ever had with Philip was when he remarked, in passing, that Santayana had sent him an essay from Rome (probably a chapter of *Dominations and Powers*), which Philip had sent back, unread, because, "What's *he* got to say to us now?" I said, "Everything," and more.

There is a strain of flippant anti-Semitism in Santayana's letters and *obiter dicta* that makes uncomfortable reading, but it is all a part of a general dislike of both nationalism and tribalism. As he wrote to his Jewish assistant at Harvard: "[Nationalism] is at once interior and exterior, or political; how can Italian, Balkan, Irish or Zionist Americans combine in an entity between the two? . . . It is the difficulty of realizing either of these ideals that seems to me to make nationality a problem rather than a solution." The idea of any people as "chosen" he finds romantic in the worst sense; finally, it is not the Jews that disturb him but the Germans. As early as the First War, he found that in their tribes there was "something sinister at work, something at once hollow and aggressive." *Egotism in German Philosophy* describes how, after Napoleon's invasion, Fichte and Hegel cobbled together a worldview that Providence intended for the German people "to occupy the supreme place in the history of the universe." Of this "revealed philosophy" Santayana notes, "It is the heir of Judaism," and he finds it to be not so much religious as a mad idealism in service to the state: "In this philosophy imagination that is sustained is called knowledge, illusion that is coherent is called truth, and will that is systematic is called virtue." This was written in 1916.

The most famous of Santayana's aphorisms is: "Those who cannot remember the past are condemned to repeat it." A generation later the forgetful Germans made a second bid for supremacy, and again failed. Santayana despised fanaticism; after all, the title of his five-volume "philosophy" is *The Life of Reason*. He was a materialist of the Epicurean school of Democritus and Lucretius; and he suspected that despite all his notions of the tribe and self and will and God and "*Skepticism and Animal Faith*," "Chaos is perhaps at the bottom of everything."

# MALCOLM X

## (1925–1965)

The assassination of Malcolm X on February 21, 1965, several months before his fortieth birthday, remains one of the most shocking moments in a decade of assassinations and political unrest. At the time of his death, the famed Black Muslim leader was changing his thoughts and ideological positions regarding race in America. Dismayed by the "secular practices" he saw occurring among the followers of Elijah Muhammad's separatist movement, and deeply touched by several pilgrimages to Mecca, Malcolm X was modifying his stance, moving toward the center of a varied political landscape.

Always an electrifying speaker and personality, he is the subject of one of the most riveting of American autobiographies. As told to Alex Haley, who was admonished to be a "writer, not an interpreter," the *Autobiography of Malcolm X* (1964) spins along in a fury of ideology and voice. From his fiery, early speeches (in which he castigated the white race for stepping on the backs of black people) to his later, more conciliatory works, Malcolm X was always an eloquent and impassioned proponent of his cause. While he discloses little of himself in this book, he nevertheless communicates a fierce sensibility (rather like Emma Goldman and Alexander Berkman); his attention is always directed outward, toward the world, refusing the inward gaze one sees more often in autobiographical writing.

## FROM *The Autobiography of Malcom X*

The more places I represented Mr. Muhammad on television and radio, and at colleges and elsewhere, the more letters came from people who had heard me. I'd say that ninety-five percent of the letters were from white people.

Only a few of the letters fell into the "Dear Nigger X" category, or the death-threats. Most of my mail exposed to me the white man's two major dreads. The first one was his own private belief that God wrathfully is going to destroy this civilization. And the white man's second most pervading dread was his image of the black man entering the body of the white woman.

An amazing percentage of the white letter-writers agreed entirely with Mr. Muhammad's analysis of the problem—but not with his solution. One odd ambivalence was how some letters, otherwise all but championing Mr. Muhammad, would recoil at the expression "white devils." I tried to explain this in subsequent speeches:

"Unless we call one white man, by name, a 'devil,' we are not speaking of any *individual* white man. We are speaking of the *collective* white man's *historical* record. We are speaking of the collective white man's cruelties, and evils, and greeds, that have seen him *act* like a devil toward the non-white man. Any intelligent, honest, objective person cannot fail to realize that this white man's slave trade, and his subsequent devilish actions are directly *responsible* for not only the *presence* of this black man in America, but also for the *condition* in which we find this black man here. You cannot find *one* black man, I do not care who he is, who has not been personally damaged in some way by the devilish acts of the collective white man!"

Nearly every day, some attack on the "Black Muslims" would appear in some newspapers. Increasingly, a focal target was something that I had said, "Malcolm X" as a "demagogue." I would grow furious reading any harsh attack upon Mr. Muhammad. I didn't care what they said about me.

Those social workers and sociologists—they tried to take me apart. Especially the black ones, for some reason. Of course, I knew the reason; the white man signed their paychecks. If I wasn't "polarizing the community," according to this bunch, I had "erroneously appraised the racial picture." Or in some statement, I had "over-generalized." Or when I had made some absolutely true point, "Malcolm X conveniently manipulated. . . ."

Once, one of my Mosque Seven Muslim brothers who worked with teenagers in a well-known Harlem community center showed me a confidential report. Some black senior social worker had been given a month off to investigate the "Black Muslims" in the Harlem area. Every paragraph sent me back to the dictionary—I guess that's why I've never forgotten one line about me. Listen to this: "The dynamic interstices of the Harlem sub-culture have been oversimplified and distorted by Malcolm X to meet his own needs."

Which of us, I wonder, knew more about that Harlem ghetto "sub-culture"? I, who had hustled for years in those streets, or that black snob status-symbol-educated social worker?

But that's not important. What's important, to my way of thinking about it, is that among America's 22 million black people so relatively few have been lucky enough to attend a college—and here was one of those who had been lucky. Here was, to my way of thinking, one of those "educated" Negroes who never had understood the true intent, or purpose, or application of education. Here was one of those stagnant educations, never used except for parading a lot of big words.

Do you realize this is one of the major reasons why America's white man has so easily contained and oppressed America's black man? Because until just lately, among the few educated Negroes scarcely any applied their education, as I am forced to say the white man does—in searching and creative thinking, to further themselves and their own kind in this competitive, materialistic, dog-eat-dog white man's world. For generations, the so-called "educated" Negroes have "led" their black brothers by echoing the white man's thinking—which naturally has been to the exploitive white man's advantage.

The white man—give him his due—has an extraordinary intelligence, an extraordinary cleverness. His world is full of proof of it. You can't name a thing the white man can't make. You can hardly name a scientific problem he can't solve. Here he is now solving the problems of sending men exploring into outer space—and returning them safely to earth.

But in the arena of dealing with human beings, the white man's working intelligence is hobbled. His intelligence will fail him altogether if the humans happen to be non-white. The white man's emotions supersede his intelligence. He will commit against non-whites the most incredible spontaneous emotional acts, so psyche-deep is his "white superiority" complex.

Where was the A-bomb dropped . . . "to save American lives"? Can the white man be so naive as to think the clear import of this *ever* will be lost upon the non-white two-thirds of the earth's population?

Before that bomb was dropped—right over here in the United States, what about the one hundred thousand loyal naturalized and native-born Japanese American citizens who were herded into camps, behind barbed wire? But how many German-born naturalized Americans were herded behind barbed wire? They were *white!*

Historically, the non-white complexion has evoked and exposed the "devil" in the very nature of the white man.

What else but a controlling emotional "devil" so blinded American white intelligence that it couldn't foresee that millions of black slaves, "freed," then permitted even limited education, would one day rise up as a terrifying monster within white America's midst?

The white man's brains that today explore space should have told the slavemaster that any slave, if he is educated, will no longer fear his master. History shows that an educated slave always begins to ask, and next demand, equality with his master.

Today, in many ways the black man sees the collective white man in

America better than that white man can see himself. And the 22 million blacks realize increasingly that physically, politically, economically, and even to some degree socially, the aroused black man can create a turmoil in white America's vitals—not to mention America's international image.

I had not intended to stray off. I had been telling how in 1963 I was trying to cope with the white newspaper, radio, and television reporters who were determined to defeat Mr. Muhammad's teachings.

I developed a mental image of reporters as human ferrets—steadily sniffing, darting, probing for some way to trick me, somehow to corner me in our interview exchanges.

Let some civil rights "leader" make some statement, displeasing to the white public power structure, and the reporters, in an effort to whip him back into line, would try to use me. I'll give an example. I'd get a question like this: "Mr. Malcolm X, you've often gone on record as disapproving of the sit-ins and similar Negro protest actions—what is your opinion of the Montgomery boycott that Dr. King is leading?"

Now my feeling was that although the civil rights "leaders" kept attacking us Muslims, still they were black people, still they were our own kind, and I would be most foolish to let the white man maneuver me against the civil rights movement.

When I was asked about the Montgomery boycott, I'd carefully review what led up to it. Mrs. Rosa Parks was riding home on a bus and at some bus stop the white cracker bus driver ordered Mrs. Parks to get up and give her seat to some white passenger who had just got on the bus. I'd say, "Now, just *imagine* that! This good, hard-working, Christian-believing black woman, she's paid her money, she's in her seat. Just because she's *black*, she's asked to get up! I mean, sometimes even for *me* it's hard to believe the white man's arrogance!"

Or I might say, "No one will ever know exactly what emotional ingredient made this relatively trivial incident a fuse for those Montgomery Negroes. There had been *centuries* of the worst kind of outrages against Southern black people—lynchings, rapings, shootings, beatings! But you know history has been triggered by trivial-seeming incidents. Once a little nobody Indian lawyer was put off a train, and fed up with injustice, he twisted a knot in the British Lion's tail. *His* name was Mahatma Gandhi!"

Or I might copy a trick I had seen lawyers use, both in life and on television. It was a way that lawyers would slip in before a jury something otherwise inadmissible. (Sometimes I think I really might have made it as a lawyer, as I once told that eighth-grade teacher in Mason, Michigan, I wanted to be, when he advised me to become a carpenter.) I would slide right over the reporter's question to drop into his lap a logical-extension hot potato for him.

"Well, sir, I see the same boycott reasoning for Negroes asked to join the Army, Navy, and Air Force. Why should we go off to die somewhere to preserve a so-called 'democracy' that gives a white immigrant of one day more than it gives the black man with four hundred years of slaving and serving in this country?"

Whites would prefer fifty local boycotts to having 22 million Negroes start thinking about what I had just said. I don't have to tell you that it never got printed the way I said it. It would be turned inside out if it got printed at all. And I could detect when the white reporters had gotten their heads together; they quit asking me certain questions.

If I had developed a good point, though, I'd bait a hook to get it said when I went on radio or television. I'd seem to slip and mention some recent so-called civil rights "advance." You know, where some giant industry had hired ten showpiece Negroes; some restaurant chain had begun making more money by serving Negroes; some Southern university had enrolled a black freshman without bayonets—like that. When I "slipped," the program host would leap on that bait: "Ahhh! Indeed, Mr. Malcolm X—you can't deny *that's* an advance for your race!"

I'd jerk the pole then. "I can't turn around without hearing about some 'civil rights advance'! White people seem to think the black man ought to be shouting 'hallelujah'! Four hundred years the white man has had his foot-long knife in the black man's back—and now the white man starts to *wiggle* the knife out, maybe six inches! The black man's supposed to be *grateful*? Why, if the white man jerked the knife *out*, it's still going to leave a *scar*!"

Similarly, just let some mayor or some city council somewhere boast of having "no Negro problem." That would get off the newsroom teletypes and it would soon be jammed right in my face. I'd say they didn't need to tell me where this was, because I knew that all it meant was that relatively very few Negroes were living there. That's true the world over, you know. Take "democratic" England—when 100,000 black West Indians got there, England stopped the black migration. Finland welcomed a Negro U.S. Ambassador. Well, let enough Negroes follow him to Finland! Or in Russia, when Khrushchev was in power, he threatened to cancel the visas of black African students whose anti-discrimination demonstration said to the world, "Russia, too. . . ."

The Deep South white press generally blacked me out. But they front-paged what I felt about Northern white and black Freedom Riders going *South* to "demonstrate." I called it "ridiculous"; their own Northern ghettoes, right at home, had enough rats and roaches to kill to keep all of the Freedom Riders busy. I said that ultra-liberal New York had more integration problems than Mississippi. If the Northern Freedom Riders wanted more to do, they could work on the roots of such ghetto evils as the little children out in the streets at midnight, with apartment keys on strings around their necks to let themselves in, and their mothers and fathers drunk, drug addicts, thieves, prostitutes. Or the Northern Freedom Riders could light some fires under Northern city halls, unions, and major industries to give more jobs to Negroes to remove so many of them from the relief and welfare rolls, which created laziness, and which deteriorated the ghettoes into steadily worse places for humans to live. It was all—it *is* all—the absolute truth; but what did I want to *say* it for? Snakes couldn't have turned on me faster than the liberal.

Yes, I will pull off that liberal's halo that he spends such efforts cultivating! The North's liberals have been for so long pointing accusing fingers at the South and getting away with it that they have fits when they are exposed as the world's worst hypocrites.

I believe my own life *mirrors* this hypocrisy. I know nothing about the South. I am a creation of the Northern white man and of his hypocritical attitude toward the Negro.

The white Southerner was always given his due by Mr. Muhammad. The white Southerner, you can say one thing—he is honest. He bares his teeth to the black man; he tells the black man, to his face, that Southern whites never will accept phony "integration." The Southerner white goes further, to tell the black man that he means to fight him every inch of the way—against even the so-called "tokenism." The advantage of this is the Southern black man never has been under any illusions about the opposition he is dealing with.

You can say for many Southern white people that, individually, they have been paternalistically helpful to many individual Negroes. But the Northern white man, he grins with his teeth, and his mouth has always been full of tricks and lies of "equality" and "integration." When one day all over America, a black hand touched the white man's shoulder, and the white man turned, and there stood the Negro saying "Me, too . . . ," why, that Northern liberal shrank from that black man with as much guilt and dread as any Southern white man.

Actually, America's most dangerous and threatening black man is the one who has been kept sealed up by the Northerner in the black ghettoes—the Northern white power structure's system to keep talking democracy while keeping the black man out of sight somewhere, around the corner.

The word "integration" was invented by a Northern liberal. The word has no real meaning. I ask you: in the racial sense in which it's used so much today, whatever "integration" is supposed to mean, can it precisely be defined? The truth is that "integration" is an *image*, it's a foxy Northern liberal's smoke-screen that confuses the true wants of the American black man. Here in these fifty racist and neo-racist states of North America, this word "integration" has millions of white people confused, and angry, believing wrongly that the black masses want to live mixed up with the white man. That is the case only with the relative handful of these "integration"-mad Negroes.

I'm talking about these "token-integrated" Negroes who flee from their poor, downtrodden black brothers—from their own self-hate, which is what they're really trying to escape. I'm talking about these Negroes you will see who can't get enough of nuzzling up to the white man. These "chosen few" Negroes are more white-minded, more anti-black, than even the white man is.

Human rights! Respect as *human beings!* That's what America's black masses want. That's the true problem. The black masses want not to be shrunk from as though they are plague-ridden. They want not to be walled up in slums, in the ghettoes, like animals. They want to live in an open, free society where they can walk with their heads up, like men, and women!

Few white people realize that many black people today dislike and avoid spending any more time than they must around white people. This "integration" image, as it is popularly interpreted, has millions of vain, self-exalted white people convinced that black people want to sleep in bed with them—and that's a lie! Or you can't *tell* the average white man that the Negro man's prime desire isn't to have a white woman—another lie! Like a black brother recently observed to me, "Look, you ever smell one of them *wet?*"

The black masses prefer the company of their own kind. Why, even these fancy, bourgeois Negroes—when they get back home from the fancy "integrated" cocktail parties, what do they do but kick off their shoes and talk about those white liberals they just left as if the liberals were dogs. And the white liberals probably do the very same thing. I can't be sure about the whites, I am never around them in private—but the bourgeois Negroes know I'm not lying.

I'm telling it like it *is!* You *never* have to worry about me biting my tongue if something I know as truth is on my mind. Raw, naked truth exchanged between the black man and the white man is what a whole lot more of is needed in this country—to clear the air of the racial mirages, clichés, and lies that this country's very atmosphere has been filled with for four hundred years.

In many communities, especially small communities, white people have created a benevolent image of themselves as having had so much "good-will toward our Negroes," every time any "local Negro" begins suddenly letting the local whites know the truth—that the black people are sick of being hind-tit, second-class, disfranchised, that's when you hear, uttered so sadly, "Unfortunately now because of this, our whites of good-will are starting to turn against the Negroes. . . . It's so regrettable . . . progress *was* being made . . . but now our communications between the races have broken down!"

What are they talking about? There never was any *communication*. Until after World War II, there wasn't a single community in the entire United States where the white man heard from any local Negro "leaders" the truth of what Negroes felt about the conditions that the white community imposed upon Negroes.

You need some proof? Well, then, why was it that when Negroes did start revolting across America, virtually all of white America was caught up in surprise and even shock? I would hate to be general of an army as badly informed as the American white man has been about the Negro in this country.

This is the situation which permitted Negro combustion to slowly build up to the revolution-point, without the white man realizing it. All over America, the local Negro "leader," in order to survive as a "leader," kept reassuring the local white man, in effect, "Everything's all right, everything's right in hand, boss!" When the "leader" wanted a little something for his people: "Er, boss, some of the people talking about we sure need a better school, boss." And if the local Negroes hadn't been causing any "trouble," the "benevolent" white man might nod and give them a school, or some jobs.

The white men belonging to the power structures in thousands of communities across America know that I'm right! They know that I am describing what has been the true pattern of "communications" between the "local whites of good-will" and the local Negroes. It has been a pattern created by domineering, ego-ridden whites. Its characteristic design permitted the white man to feel "noble" about throwing crumbs to the black man, instead of feeling guilty about the local community's system of cruelly exploiting Negroes.

But I want to tell you something. This pattern, this "system" that the white man created, of teaching Negroes to hide the truth from him behind a façade of grinning, "yessir-bossing," foot shuffling and head-scratching—that system has done the American white man more harm than an invading army would do to him.

Why do I say this? Because all this has steadily helped this American white man to build up, deep in his psyche, absolute conviction that he *is* "superior." In how many, many communities have, thus, white men who didn't finish high school regarded condescendingly university-educated local Negro "leaders," principals of schools, teachers, doctors, other professionals?

The white man's system has been imposed upon non-white peoples all over the world. This is exactly the reason why wherever people who are anything but white live in this world today, the white man's governments are finding themselves in deeper and deeper trouble and peril.

Let's just face truth. Facts! Whether or not the white man of the world is able to face truth, and facts, about the true reasons for his troubles—that's what essentially will determine whether or not *he* will now survive.

Today we are seeing this revolution of the non-white peoples, who just a few years ago would have frozen in horror if the mighty white nations so much as lifted an eyebrow. What it is, simply, is that black and brown and red and yellow peoples have, after hundreds of years of exploitation and imposed "inferiority" and general misuse, become, finally, do-or-die sick and tired of the white man's heel on their necks.

How can the white American government figure on selling "democracy" and "brotherhood" to non-white peoples—if they read and hear every day what's going on right here in America, and see the better-than-a-thousand-word photographs of the American white man denying "democracy" and "brotherhood" even to America's native-born non-whites? The world's non-whites know how this Negro here has loved the American white man, and slaved for him, tended to him, nursed him. This Negro has jumped into uniform and gone off and died when this America was attacked by enemies both white and non-white. Such a faithful, loyal non-white as *this*—and *still* America bombs him, and sets dogs on him, and turns fire hoses on him, and jails him by the thousands, and beats him bloody, and inflicts upon him all manner of other crimes.

Of course these things, known and refreshed every day for the rest of the world's non-whites, are a vital factor in these burnings of ambassadors' limousines, these stonings, defilings, and wreckings of embassies and legations, these shouts of "White man, go home!," these attacks on white Christian missionaries, and these bombings and tearing down of flags.

Is it clear why I have said that the American white man's malignant superiority complex has done him more harm than an invading army?

The American black man should be focusing his every effort toward building his *own* businesses, and decent homes for himself. As other ethnic groups have done, let the black people, wherever possible, however possible, patronize their own kind, hire their own kind, and start in those ways to build up the black race's ability to do for itself. That's the only way the American black man is ever going to get respect. One thing the white man never can give the black man is self-respect! The black man never can become independent and recognized as a human being who is truly equal with other human beings until he has what they have, and until he is doing for himself what others are doing for themselves.

The black man in the ghettoes, for instance, has to start self-correcting his own material, moral, and spiritual defects and evils. The black man needs to start his own program to get rid of drunkenness, drug addiction, prostitution. The black man in America has to lift up his own sense of values.

Only a few thousands of Negroes, relatively a very tiny number, are taking any part in "integration." Here, again, it is those few bourgeois Negroes, rushing to throw away their little money in the white man's luxury hotels, his swanky nightclubs, and big, fine, exclusive restaurants. The white people patronizing those places can afford it. But these Negroes you see in those places can't afford it, certainly most of them can't. Why, what does some Negro one installment payment away from disaster look like somewhere downtown out to dine, grinning at some headwaiter who has more money than the Negro? Those bourgeois Negroes out draping big tablecloth-sized napkins over their knees and ordering quail under glass and stewed snails—why, Negroes don't even *like* snails! What they're doing is proving they're integrated.

If you want to get right down to the real outcome of this so-called "integration," what you've got to arrive at is intermarriage.

I'm right *with* the Southern white man who believes that you can't have so-called "integration," at least not for long, without intermarriage increasing. And what good is this for anyone? Let's again face reality. In a world as color-hostile as this, man or woman, black or white, what do they want with a mate of the other race?

Certainly white people have served enough notice of their hostility to any blacks in their families and neighborhoods. And the way most Negroes feel today, a mixed couple probably finds that black families, black communities, are even more hostile than the white ones. So what's bound to face "integrated" marriages, except being unwelcomed, unwanted, "misfits" in whichever world they try to live in? What we arrive at is that "integration," socially, is no good for either side. "Integration," ultimately, would destroy the white race . . . and destroy the black race.

The white man's "integrating" with black women has already changed the complexion and characteristics of the black race in America. What's been proved by the "blacks" whose complexions are "whiter" than many "white" people? I'm told that there are in America today between two and five million "white Negroes," who are "passing" in white society. Imagine their torture! Living in constant fear that some black person they've known might meet and expose them. Imagine every day living a lie. *Imagine* hearing their own white husbands, their own white wives, even their own white children, talking about "those Negroes."

I would doubt if anyone in America has heard Negroes more bitter against the white man than some of those I have heard. But I will tell you that, without any question, the *most* bitter anti-white diatribes that I have ever heard have come from "passing" Negroes, living as whites, among whites, exposed every day to what white people say among themselves regarding Negroes—things that a recognized Negro never would hear. Why, if there was a racial showdown, these Negroes "passing" within white circles would become the black side's most valuable "spy" and ally.

Europe's "brown babies," now young men and women who are starting to marry, and produce families of their own . . . have their experiences throughout their lives, scarred as racial freaks, proved anything positive for "integration"?

"Integration" is called "assimilation" if white ethnic groups alone are involved: it's fought against tooth and nail by those who want their heritage preserved. Look at how the Irish threw the English out of Ireland. The Irish knew the English would engulf them. Look at the French-Canadians, fanatically fighting to keep their identity.

In fact, history's most tragic result of a mixed, therefore diluted and weakened, ethnic identity has been experienced by a white ethnic group—the Jew in Germany.

He had made greater contributions to Germany than Germans themselves had. Jews had won over half of Germany's Nobel Prizes. Every culture in Germany was led by the Jew; he published the greatest newspaper. Jews were the greatest artists, the greatest poets, composers, stage directors. But those Jews made a fatal mistake—assimilating.

From World War I to Hitler's rise, the Jews in Germany had been increasingly intermarrying. Many changed their names and many took other religions. Their own Jewish religion, their own rich Jewish ethnic and cultural roots, they anesthetized, and cut off . . . until they began thinking of themselves as "Germans."

And the next thing they knew, there was Hitler, rising to power from the beer halls—with his emotional "Aryan master race" theory. And right at hand for a scapegoat was the self-weakened, self-deluded "German" Jew.

Most mysterious is how did those Jews—with all of their brilliant minds, with all of their power in every aspect of Germany's affairs—how did those Jews stand almost as if mesmerized, watching something which did not spring upon them overnight, but which was gradually developed—a monstrous plan for their own *murder*.

Their self-brainwashing had been so complete that not long after, in the gas chambers, a lot of them were still gasping, "It *can't* be true!"

If Hitler *had* conquered the world, as he meant to—that is a shuddery thought for every Jew alive today.

The Jew never will forget that lesson. Jewish intelligence eyes watch every neo-Nazi organization. Right after the war, the Jews' Haganah mediating body stepped up the longtime negotiations with the British. But this time, the Stern gang was shooting the British. And this time the British acquiesced and helped them to wrest Palestine away from the Arabs, the rightful owners, and then the Jews set up Israel, their own country—the one thing that every race of man in the world respects, and understands.

Not long ago, the black man in America was fed a dose of another form of the weakening, lulling and deluding effects of so-called "integration." It was that "Farce on Washington," I call it.

The idea of a mass of blacks marching on Washington was originally the brainchild of the Brotherhood of Sleeping Car Porters' A. Philip Randolph. For twenty or more years the March on Washington idea had floated around among Negroes. And, spontaneously, suddenly now, that idea caught on.

Overalled rural Southern Negroes, small town Negroes, Northern ghetto Negroes, even thousands of previously Uncle Tom Negroes began talking "March!"

Nothing since Joe Louis had so coalesced the masses of Negroes. Groups of Negroes were talking of getting to Washington any way they could—in rickety old cars, on buses, hitch-hiking—walking even, if they had to. They envisioned thousands of black brothers converging together upon Washington—to lie down in the streets, on airport runways, on government lawns—demanding of the Congress and the White House some concrete civil rights action.

This was a national bitterness; militant, unorganized, and leaderless. Predominantly, it was young Negroes, defiant of whatever might be the consequences, sick and tried of the black man's neck under the white man's heel.

The white man had plenty of good reasons for nervous worry. The right spark—some unpredictable emotional chemistry—could set off a black uprising. The government knew that thousands of milling, angry blacks not only could completely disrupt Washington—but they could erupt in Washington.

The White House speedily invited in the major civil rights Negro "leaders." They were asked to stop the planned March. They truthfully said they hadn't begun it, they had no control over it—the idea was national, spontaneous, unorganized, and leaderless. In other words, it was a black powder keg.

Any student of how "integration" can weaken the black man's movement was about to observe a master lesson.

The White House, with a fanfare of international publicity, "approved," "endorsed," and "welcomed" a March on Washington. The big civil rights organization right at this time had been publicly squabbling about donations. The *New York Times* had broken the story. The N.A.A.C.P. had charged that other agencies' demonstrations, highly publicized, had attracted a major part of the civil rights donations—while the N.A.A.C.P. got left holding the bag, supplying costly bail and legal talent for the other organizations' jailed demonstrators.

It was like a movie. The next scene was the "big six" civil rights Negro "leaders" meeting in New York City with the white head of a big philanthropic agency. They were told that their money-wrangling in public was damaging their image. And a reported $800,000 was donated to a United Civil Rights Leadership council that was quickly organized by the "big six."

Now, what had instantly achieved black unity? The white man's money. What string was attached to the money? Advice. Not only was there this donation, but another comparable sum was promised, for sometime later on, after the March . . . obviously if all went well.

That original "angry" March on Washington was now about to be entirely changed.

Massive international publicity projected the "big six" as March on Washington leaders. It was news to those angry grass-roots Negroes steadily adding steam to their March plans. They probably assumed that now those famous "leaders" were endorsing and joining them.

Invited next to join the March were four famous white public figures: one Catholic, one Jew, one Protestant, and one labor boss.

The massive publicity now gently hinted that the "big ten" would "supervise" the March on Washington's "mood," and its "direction."

The four white figures began nodding. The word spread fast among so-called "liberal" Catholics, Jews, Protestants, and laborites: it was "democratic" to join this black March. And suddenly, the previously March-nervous whites began announcing *they* were going.

It was as if electrical current shot through the ranks of bourgeois Negroes—the very so-called "middle-class" and "upper-class" who had earlier been deploring the March on Washington talk by grass-roots Negroes.

But white people, now, were going to march.

Why, some downtrodden, jobless, hungry Negro might have gotten trampled. Those "integration"-mad Negroes practically ran over each other trying to find out where to sign up. The "angry blacks" March suddenly had been made chic. Suddenly it had a Kentucky Derby image. For the status-seeker, it was a status symbol. "Were you *there?*" You can hear that right today.

It had become an outing, a picnic.

The morning of the March, any rickety carloads of angry, dusty, sweating small-town Negroes would have gotten lost among the chartered jet planes, railroad cars, and air-conditioned buses. What originally was planned to be an angry riptide, one English newspaper aptly described now as "the gentle flood."

Talk about "integrated"! It was like salt and pepper. And, by now, there wasn't a single logistics aspect uncontrolled.

The marchers had been instructed to bring no signs—signs were provided. They had been told to sing one song: "We Shall Overcome." They had been told *how* to arrive, *when*, *where* to arrive, *where* to assemble, when to *start* marching, the *route* to march. First-aid stations were strategically located—even where to *faint!*

Yes, I was there. I observed that circus. Who ever heard of angry revolutionists all harmonizing "We Shall Overcome . . . Su-um Day . . ." while tripping and swaying along arm-in-arm with the very people they were supposed to be angrily revolting against? Who ever heard of angry revolutionists swinging their bare feet together with their oppressor in lily-pad park pools, with gospels and guitars and "I Have A Dream" speeches?

And the black masses in America were—and still are—having a nightmare.

These "angry revolutionists" even followed their final instructions: to leave early. With all of those thousands upon thousands of "angry revolutionists," so few stayed over that the next morning the Washington hotel association reported a costly loss in empty rooms.

Hollywood couldn't have topped it.

In a subsequent press poll, not one Congressman or Senator with a previous record of opposition to civil rights said he had changed his views. What did anyone expect? How was a one-day "integrated" picnic going to counter-influence these representatives of prejudice rooted deep in the psyche of the American white man for four hundred years?

The very fact that millions, black and white, believed in this monumental farce is another example of how much this country goes in for the surface glossing over, the escape ruse, surfaces, instead of truly dealing with its deep-rooted problems.

What that March on Washington did do was lull Negroes for a while. But inevitably, the black masses started realizing they had been smoothly hoaxed again by the white man. And, inevitably, the black man's anger rekindled, deeper than ever, and there began bursting out in different cities, in the "long, hot summer" of 1964, unprecedented racial crises.

# GAY TALESE
## (1932– )

Raised in Ocean City, New Jersey, Talese was the son of immigrants from the patriarchal world of southern Italy. His abiding interest in his cultural heritage would lead him to write *Unto the Sons* (1992), an epic memoir of his family's migration to the New World. Mixing social history with family stories, interviews, letters, and diaries, Talese fashioned a tale of displacement, confusion, lost tradition, and heroic will.

He began his writing career as a journalist, joining the reportorial staff of the *New York Times* in 1955. He remained there for a decade. During the sixties and seventies, he contributed many essays on a variety of cultural topics to *Esquire*, and is often considered (with Tom Wolfe) one of the founding fathers of the New Journalism. His immensely popular, highly crafted nonfiction works include *The Kingdom and the Power* (1969), *Honor Thy Father* (1971), and *Thy Neighbor's Wife* (1980).

## FROM *Unto the Sons*

The beach in winter was dank and desolate, and the island dampened by the frigid spray of the ocean waves pounding relentlessly against the beachfront bulkheads, and the seaweed-covered beams beneath the white houses on the dunes creaked as quietly as the crabs crawling nearby.

The boardwalk that in summer was a festive promenade of suntanned couples and children's balloons, of carousel tunes and colored lights spinning at night from the Ferris wheel, was occupied in winter by hundreds of sea gulls perched on the iron railings facing into the wind. When not resting they strutted outside the locked doors of vacated shops, or circled high in the sky, holding clams in their beaks that they soon dropped upon the boardwalk with a splattering *cluck*. Then they zoomed down and pounced on the exposed meat, pecking and pulling until there was nothing left but the jagged, salty white chips of empty shells.

By midwinter the shell-strewn promenade was a vast cemetery of clams, and from a distance the long elevated flat deck of the boardwalk resembled a stranded aircraft carrier being attacked by dive-bombers—and oddly juxtaposed in the fog behind the dunes loomed the rusting remains of a once sleek four-masted vessel that during a gale in the winter of 1901 had run aground on this small island in southern New Jersey called Ocean City.

The steel-hulled ship, flying a British flag and flaunting hundred-fifty-foot masts, had been sailing north along the New Jersey coast toward New York City, where it was scheduled to deliver one million dollars' worth of Christmas cargo it had picked up five months before in Kobe, Japan. But during the middle of the night, while a number of crewmen drank rum and beer in a premature toast to the long journey's end, a fierce storm rose and destroyed the ship's sails, snapped its masts, and drove it into a sandbar within one hundred yards of the Ocean City boardwalk.

Awakened by the distress signals that flared in the night, the alarmed residents of Ocean City—a conservative community founded in 1879 by Methodist ministers and other Prohibitionists who wished to establish an island of abstinence and propriety—hastened to help the sailors, who were soon discovered to be battered but unharmed and smelling of sweat, salt water, and liquor.

After the entire thirty-three-man crew had been escorted to shore, they were sheltered and fed for days under the auspices of the town's teetotaling elders and ministers' wives; and while the sailors expressed gratitude for such hospitality they privately cursed their fate in being shipwrecked on an island so sedate and sober. But soon they were relocated by British nautical authorities, and the salvageable cargo was barged to New York to be sold at reduced prices. And the town returned to the tedium of winter.

The big ship, however, remained forever lodged in the soft white sand—unmovable, slowly sinking, a sight that served Ocean City's pious guardians as a daily reminder of the grim consequences of intemperate guidance. But as I grew up in the late 1930s, more than three decades after the shipwreck—when the visible remnants at low tide consisted only of the barnacle-bitten ridge of the upper deck, the corroded brown rudder post and tiller, and a single lopsided mast—I viewed the vessel as a symbol of adventure and risk; and during my boyhood wanderings along the beach I became enchanted with exotic fantasies of nights in foreign ports, of braving the waves and wind with wayward men, and of escaping the rigid confines of this island on which I was born but never believed I belonged.

I saw myself always as an alien, an outsider, a drifter who, like the shipwrecked sailors, had arrived by accident. I felt different from my young friends in almost every way, different in the cut of my clothes, the food in my lunch box, the music I heard at home on the record player, the ideas and inner thoughts I revealed on those rare occasions when I was open and honest.

I was olive-skinned in a freckle-faced town, and I felt unrelated even to my parents, especially my father, who was indeed a foreigner—an unusual man in dress and manner, to whom I bore no physical resemblance and with whom I could never identify. Trim and elegant, with wavy dark hair and a small rust-colored moustache, he spoke English with an accent and received letters bearing strange-looking stamps.

These letters sometimes contained snapshots of soldiers wearing uniforms with insignia and epaulets unlike any I had seen on the recruitment posters displayed throughout the island. They were my uncles and cousins, my father explained to me quietly one day early in World War II, when I was ten; they were fighting in the Italian army, and—it was unnecessary for him to add—their enemy included the government of the United States.

I became increasingly sensitive to this fact when I sat through the newsreels each week at the local cinema; next to my unknowing classmates, I watched with private horror the destruction by Allied bombers of mountain villages and towns in southern Italy to which I was ancestrally linked through a historically ill-timed relationship with my Italian father. At any moment I half expected to see up on the screen, gazing down at me from a dust-covered United States Army truck filled with disheveled Italian prisoners being guarded at gunpoint, a sad face that I could identify from one of my father's snapshots.

My father, on the other hand, seemed to share none of my confused sense of patriotism during the war years. He joined a citizens' committee of shore patrolmen who kept watch along the waterfront at night, standing with binoculars on the boardwalk under the stanchioned lights that on the ocean side were painted black as a precaution against discovery by enemy submarines.

He made headlines in the local newspaper after a popular speech to the Rotary Club in which he reaffirmed his loyalty to the Allied cause, declaring that were he not too old for the draft (he was thirty-nine) he would proudly join the American troops at the front, in a uniform devotedly cut and stitched with his own hands.

Trained as an apprentice tailor in his native village, and later an assistant cutter in a prominent shop in Paris that employed an older Italian cousin, my father arrived in Ocean City circuitously and impulsively at the age of eighteen in 1922 with very little money, an extensive wardrobe, and the outward appearance of a man who knew exactly where he was going, when in fact nothing was further from the truth. He knew no one in town, barely knew the language, and yet, with a self-assurance that has always mystified me, he adjusted to this unusual island as readily as he could cut cloth to fit any size and shape.

Having noticed a "For Sale" sign in the window of a tailor shop in the center of town, my father approached the asthmatic owner, who was desperate to leave the island for the drier climate of Arizona. After a brief negotiation, my father acquired the business and thus began a lengthy, spirited campaign to bring the rakish fashion of the Continental boulevardier to the comparatively continent men of the south Jersey shore.

But after decorating his windows with lantern-jawed mannequins holding cigarettes and wearing Borsalino hats, and draping his counters with bolts of fine imported fabrics—and displaying on his walls such presumably persuasive regalia as his French master tailor's diploma bordered by cherubim and a Greek goddess—my father made so few sales during his first year that he was finally forced to introduce into his shop a somewhat undignified gimmick called the Suit Club.

At the cost of one dollar per week, Suit Club members would print their names and addresses on small white cards and, after placing the cards in unmarked envelopes, would deposit them into a large opaque vase placed prominently atop a velvet-covered table next to a fashion photograph of a dapper man and woman posing with a greyhound on the greensward of an ornate country manor.

Each Friday evening just prior to closing time, my father would invite one of the assembled Suit Club members to close his eyes and pick from the vase a single envelope, which would reveal the name of the fortunate winner of a free suit, to be made from fabric selected by that individual; after two fittings, it would be ready for wearing within a week.

Since as many as three or four hundred people were soon paying a dollar each week to partake in this raffle, my father was earning on each free suit a profit perhaps three times the average cost of a custom-made suit in those days—to say nothing of the additional money he earned when he enticed a male winner into purchasing an extra pair of matching trousers.

But my father's bonanza was abruptly terminated one day in 1928, when an anonymous complaint sent to City Hall, possibly by a rival tailor, charged that the Suit Club was a form of gambling clearly outlawed under the town charter; thus ended for all time my father's full-time commitment to the reputable but precarious life of an artist with a needle and thread. My father did *not* climb down from an impoverished mountain in southern Italy and forsake the glorious lights of Paris and sail thousands of miles to the more opportunistic shores of America to end up as a poor tailor in Ocean City, New Jersey.

So he diversified. Advertising himself as a ladies' furrier who could alter or remodel old coats as well as provide resplendent new ones (which he obtained on consignment from a Russian Jewish immigrant who resided in nearby Atlantic City), my father expanded his store to accommodate a refrigerated fur storage vault and extended the rear of the building to include a dry-cleaning plant overseen by a black Baptist deacon who during Prohibition operated a small side business in bootlegging. Later, in the 1930s, my father added a ladies' dress boutique, having as partner and wife a well-tailored woman who once worked as a buyer in a large department store in Brooklyn.

He met her while attending an Italian wedding in that borough in December 1927. She was a bridesmaid, a graceful and slender woman of twenty with dark eyes and fair complexion and a style my father immediately recognized as both feminine and prepossessing. After a few dances at the reception under the scrutiny of her parents, and the frowns of the saxophone player in the band with whom she had recently gone out on a discreet double date, my father decided to delay his departure from Brooklyn for a day or two so that he might ingratiate himself with her. This he did with such panache that they were engaged within a year, and married six months later, after buying a small white house near the Ocean City beach, where, in the winter of 1932, I was born and awoke each morning to the smell of espresso and the roaring sound of the waves.

My first recollection of my mother was of a fashionable, solitary figure on the breezy boardwalk pushing a baby carriage with one hand while with the other stabilizing on her head a modish feathered hat at an unwavering angle against the will of the wind.

As I grew older I learned that she cared greatly about exactness in appearance, preciseness in fit, straightness in seams; and, except when positioned on a pedestal in the store as my father measured her for a new suit, she seemed to prefer standing at a distance from other people, conversing with customers over a counter, communicating with her friends via telephone rather than in person. On those infrequent occasions when her relatives from Brooklyn would visit us in Ocean City, I noticed how quickly she backed away from their touch after offering her cheek for a kiss of greeting. Once, during my preschool days as I accompanied her on an errand, I tried to hold on to her, to put my hand inside the pocket of her coat not only for the warmth but for a closer feeling with her presence. But when I tried this I felt her hand, gently but firmly, remove my own.

It was as if she were incapable of intimate contact with anyone but my father, whom she plainly adored to the exclusion of everyone else; and the impression persisted throughout my youth that I was a kind of orphan in the custody of a compatible couple whose way of life was strange and baffling.

One night at the dinner table when I casually picked up a loaf of Italian bread and placed it upside down in the basket, my father became furious and, without further explanation, turned the loaf right side up and demanded that I never repeat what I had done. Whenever we attended the cinema as a family we left before the end, possibly because of my parents' inability or unwillingness to relate to the film's content, be it drama or comedy. And although my parents spent their entire married life living along the sea, I never saw them go sailing, fishing, or swimming, and rarely did they even venture onto the beach itself.

In my mother's case I suspect her avoidance of the beach was due to her desire to prevent the sun from scorching and darkening her fair skin. But I believe my father's aversion to the sea was based on something deeper, more complex, somehow related to his boyhood in southern Italy. I suggest this because I often heard him refer to his region's coastline as foreboding and malarial, a place of piracy and invasion; and as an avid reader of Greek mythology—his birthplace is not far from the renowned rock of Scylla, where the Homeric sea monster devoured sailors who had escaped the whirlpool of Charybdis—my father was prone to attaching chimerical significance to certain bizarre or inexplicable events that occurred during his youth along the streams and lakes below his village.

I remember overhearing, when I was eleven or twelve, my father complaining to my mother that he had just experienced a sleepless night during which he had been disturbed by beachfront sounds resembling howling wolves, distant but distinct, and reminiscent of a frightful night back in 1914 when his entire village had been stirred by such sounds; when the villagers awoke they discovered that the azure water of their lake had turned a murky red.

It was a mournful precursor of things to come, my father explained to my mother: his own father would soon die unexpectedly of an undiagnosed ailment, and a bloody world war would destroy the lives of so many of his young countrymen, including his older brother.

I, too, had sometimes heard in Ocean City at night what sounded like wolves echoing above the sand dunes; but I knew they were really stray dogs, part of the large population of underfed pets and watchdogs abandoned each fall by summer merchants and vacationers during the peak years of the Depression, when the local animal shelter was inadequately staffed or closed entirely.

Even in summertime the dogs roamed freely on the boardwalk during the Depression, mingling with the reduced number of tourists who strolled casually up and down the promenade, passing the restaurants of mostly unoccupied tables, the soundless bandstand outside the music pavilion, and the carousel's riderless wooden horses.

My mother loathed the sight and smell of these dogs; and as if her disapproval provoked their spiteful nature, they followed her everywhere. Moments after she had emerged from the house to escort me to school before her mile walk along deserted streets to join my father at the store, the dogs would appear from behind fences and high-weeded yards and trail her by several paces in a quiet trot, softly whimpering and whining, or growling or panting with their tongues extended.

While there were a few pointers and terriers, spaniels and beagles, they were mostly mongrels of every breed and color, and *all* of them seemed unintimidated by my mother, even after she abruptly turned and glared at them and tried to drive them away with a sweeping gesture of her right arm in the air. They never attacked her or advanced close enough to nip at her high heels; it was mainly a game of territorial imperative that they played each morning with her. By the winter of 1940, the dogs had definitely won.

At this time my mother was caring for her second and final child, a daughter four years my junior; and I think that the daily responsibility of rearing two children, assisting in the store, and being followed, even when we children accompanied her, by the ragged retinue of dogs—a few of which often paused to copulate in the street as my sister and I watched in startled wonderment—drove my mother to ask my father to sell our house on the isolated north end of the island and move us into the more populated center of town.

This he unhesitatingly did, although in the depressed real estate market of that time he was forced to sell at an unfavorable price. But he also benefitted from these conditions by obtaining at a bargain on the main street of Ocean City a large brick building that had been the offices of a weekly newspaper lately absorbed in a merger. The spacious first floor of the building, with its high ceiling and balcony, its thick walls and deep interior, its annex and parking lot, provided more than enough room for my father's various enterprises—his dress shop and dry-cleaning service, his fur storage vaults and tailoring trade.

More important to my mother, however, was the empty floor of the building, an open area as large as a dance hall that would be converted into an apartment offering her both a convenient closeness to my father and the option of distance from everyone else when she so desired. Since she also decorated this space in accord with her dictum that living quarters should be designed less to be lived in than to be looked at and admired, my sister and I soon found ourselves residing in an abode that was essentially an extended showroom. It was aglow with crystal chandeliers and sculpted candles in silver holders, and it had several bronze claw-footed marble-topped coffee tables surrounded by velvet sofas and chairs that bespoke comfort and taste but nonetheless conveyed the message that should we children ever take the liberty of reclining on their cushions and pillows, we should, upon rising, be certain we did not leave them rumpled or scattered or even at angles asymmetrical to the armrests.

Not only did my father not object to this fastidiously decorative ambience, he accentuated it by installing in the apartment several large mirrors that doubled the impression of almost everything in view, and also concealed in the rear of the apartment the existence of three ersatz bedrooms that for some reason my parents preferred not to acknowledge.

Each bed was separately enclosed within an L-shaped ten-foot-high partition that on the inside was backed by shelves and closets and on the outside was covered entirely with mirror. Whatever was gained by this arrangement was lost whenever a visitor bumped into a mirror. And while I never remember at night being an unwitting monitor of my parents' intimacy, I do know that otherwise in this domestic hall of mirrors we as a family hardly ever lost sight of one another.

Most embarrassing to me were those moments when, on entering the apartment unannounced after school, I saw reflected in a mirror, opposite a small alcove, the bowed head of my father as he knelt on the red velvet of a prie-dieu in front of a wall portrait of a bearded, brown-robed medieval monk. The monk's face was emaciated, his lips seemed dry, and as he stood on a rock in sandals balancing a crosier in his right arm, his dark, somber eyes looked skyward as if seeking heavenly relief from the sins that surrounded him.

Ever since my earliest youth I had heard again and again my father's astonishing tales about this fifteenth-century southern Italian miracle worker, Saint Francis of Paola. He had cured the crippled and revived the dead, he had multiplied food and levitated and with his hands stopped mountain boulders from rolling down upon villages; and one day in his hermitage, after an alluring young woman had tempted his celibacy, he had hastily retreated and leaped into an icy river to extinguish his passion.

The denial of pleasure, the rejection of worldly beauty and values, dominated the entire life of Saint Francis, my father had emphasized, adding that Francis as a boy had slept on stones in a cave near my father's own village, had fasted and prayed and flagellated himself, and had finally established a credo of punishing piety and devotion that endures in southern Italy to this day, almost six hundred years after the birth of the saint.

I myself had seen other portraits of Saint Francis in the Philadelphia homes of some of my father's Italian friends whom we occasionally visited on Sunday afternoons; and while I never openly doubted the veracity of Francis's achievements, I never felt comfortable after I had climbed the many steps of the private staircase leading to the apartment and opened the living room door to see my father kneeling in prayer before this almost grotesque oil painting of a holy figure whose aura suggested agony and despair.

Prayer for me was either a private act witnessed exclusively by God or a public act carried out by the congregation or by me and my classmates in parochial school. It was not an act to be on exhibition in a family parlor in which I, as a nonparticipating observer, felt suddenly like an interloper, a trapped intruder in spiritual space, an awkward youth who dared not disturb my father's meditation by announcing my presence. And yet I could not unobtrusively retreat from the room, or remain unaffected or even unafraid as I stood there, stifled against the wall, overhearing during these war years of the 1940s my father's whispered words as he sought from Saint Francis nothing less than a miracle.

# HARRY CREWS
## (1935– )

Born in Bacon County, Georgia, Crews was the son of a farmer, a country boy whose infectious love of the natural world is communicated in all of his numerous books of fiction and nonfiction.

Since 1974, Crews has been teaching in the English department at the University of Florida in Gainesville, which he also attended as a student.

The author of more than a dozen novels, he drew wide admiration for his memoir, A Childhood: The Biography of a Place (1978). In that brilliant and funny book, he recalls his first six years as the family moved from farm to farm in Bacon County, an impoverished place that was nevertheless rich in anecdote.

## FROM A Childhood: The Biography of a Place

In early December 1935 daddy loaded us up in the wagon with Daisy between the shaves. He put the mattress and bedsteads and table and benches and the Home Comfort, Number 8, stove—put it all in the wagon with me, six months old at the time, and my brother, who was four years old, up on the mattress bundled in quilts, and mamma beside him on the crossboard and started down the six miles of washboard road to the Cash Carter place.

Cash Carter didn't own it; it just went by his name. If the house were still standing today, it would still go by his name. A farm in Bacon County took a man's name, not always the first man who owned it, but some man's name, and once the name was taken, it held the name as long as it stood, no matter who lived there. It was a tradition that gave direction to the county. Farmers as a rule didn't move around much, but subsistence farmers—tenants out on the fringe of things—moved a lot, much more than most people would imagine, moved from one patch of farmed-out land to another, from one failed crop to a place where they thought there was hope of making a good one. Because they moved, it helped for the farms to hold the same name forever. It gave people's lives points of reference.

When we got there, daddy had to start building all over again. He worked from very early in the morning until very late at night, usually for as long as he and Daisy could see. During that first year he built a log tobacco barn and a lot for Daisy, and in the fall of the following year he managed to put up a little tenant house himself and move widow Ella Thomas into it with her three boys, ages ten, fourteen, and sixteen. They worked with daddy and mama, hoeing and weeding the forty acres in cultivation, helping with the turpentine timber, and taking in new ground. He paid the family fifty cents a day in wages.

It pleases me that right after daddy moved to the Cash Carter place he became good friends with the sorriest man in the county, Pete Fretch. Pete's affectionate name for his wife was "nigger." She was a thin, starved gray thing who moved about quiet as a shadow on her bare feet. Her mouth, nearly toothless, was always stained by the cud of snuff caught between lip and gum. Pete, when he wasn't busy telling lies or stealing, used to spend his time whipping his wife with a four-plait cowhip.

Anybody in that part of the county who had something stolen would just go on over to Pete's little tar-paper shack and say: "All right, Pete, where's my wheelbarrow?" or "Where's my singletrees?" or "Where's my shoat hog?" And Pete, if he had whatever was missing, and he usually did, would give it up, always with a marvelous and convoluted excuse about how the hog had just wandered up to his place, or how he'd been walking down by the Harrikin four days ago to go catfishing and happened to find the singletrees in a ditch. He'd say he wondered at the time who them singletrees belonged to and how come they were in the ditch.

But if the notion struck him, and it almost never did, Pete could do just about anything there was to do. He could build a good drawing chimney, a chimney that would never back up and smoke the house, or he could butcher a hog quicker than a blink (no doubt from long practice of butchering other people's hogs in the woods and making off with the meat before he was caught) or make the best sausage meat in South Georgia or build anything: houses or barns or lots, the boards of which were true as a plumb line and tight as if they'd been made of brick.

In 1936, he built a wash trough for mama. She washed clothes in that trough for as long as we farmed. It was made out of a tree three feet thick and twenty feet long. He dug out one end of it for a place where mama could wash her clothes and dug out the other end for a place to rinse. He made it using a chisel and an ax and a drawing knife and fire. He chopped and hewed and chipped and burned it deeper, smoothed it out with litered knots. Finally, he flattened off the bottom so it would stand steady. When he finished, it was so symmetrical it might have been calibrated on a machine.

Daddy tried to give him a quarter for his work. Pete refused it. This strange, sorry, violent man would not spend one minute of his life doing anything for anybody for cash money. But he would do anything for a friend and *always* refuse money for it. Since there was hardly anybody who could stand him as a friend, the question of whether or not to work rarely came up.

Daddy had worked progressively harder since the day he got married. He was having a lot of trouble with his heart, and it wasn't unusual for him to fall in the field. He might fall anywhere, doing anything, and sometimes it was as much as an hour before he could move about freely again. But as soon as he could, he went directly back to the task at hand. He had also lost the two front teeth out of his top gum from pyorrhea, and his weight was down to 155 pounds. He had, as they said, gone to nothing but breath and britches. But he insisted on working as hard as ever. It was his custom to get up in the morning and build a fire in the stove, leaving mama and my brother and me in the bed asleep and get out to the lot, bridle and harness Daisy, and get to the field and work there until mama took a hammer and beat on an old plow point hanging up on the front porch.

When he heard the ringing plow point, he would come to the house, eat his breakfast, and go directly back to the field. The same thing was repeated at dinnertime in the middle of the day and again at night. It was an unusual day when he didn't go back to the field if it was light enough to see after he had eaten supper. If it was too dark to go back to the field, he worked on the mule lot or on the tenant house or on Daisy's harness; which he managed to hold together with bailing wire.

His color had gone bad. There was a wildness in his eyes, but he resisted going to the doctor. Doctors meant money, and the little he had he desperately needed to keep everything together: the farm, his wife and babies.

It was during this time when daddy was working himself to death, practically living in the field, that something happened that will forever epitomize the experience of my people. It was a bright, hot summer day. It had not rained in nearly a month. The crop was doing well that year. Mama had been cleaning house since daylight and was scrubbing the floor of the last room, using homemade lye and a scrub brush made out of cornshucks.

It was midafternoon, and as she worked, she could see daddy through the open, screenless window out in the field. He was spraying the tobacco for cutworms. While she scrubbed, I was in the doorway leading into the room in a little playpen daddy had built for me.

They had done better than usual the first year there on the Cash Carter place and had managed to buy two yearling cows, the first they had ever owned. She looked up from her work and saw the two yearlings walking along the fence row toward the barrel of lead poisoning daddy had in a turpentine barrel on a sled. Mama knew they were going to drink out of the barrel, and if they did, they would die right where they were standing because the poison daddy was putting on the tobacco was deadly.

She leaned out of the window and hollered for him, but he was down between the tobacco rows with the sprayer, a long metal cylinder that was filled with air pressure using a hand pump. The sprayer was strapped to his back, and the hissing air and blowing spray made it impossible for him to hear her. So she threw down her shuck scrub brush and ran out of the house toward the field.

Halfway there, she heard me scream and knew immediately what had happened. When she got back to the house, I had turned over my playpen and crawled into the room where she had been working. Some of the pieces of lye had not melted, and I was sitting on the floor screaming, holding a lump of raw lye in each hand, and worse, I had put some of it in my mouth. Blood was running from my lips and tongue. She snatched me up and ran for daddy, who put Daisy to the wagon, and they galloped the eight miles to town to Dr. Sharp's office.

It turned out not to be as bad as it looked. I had not swallowed any of the lye, and the burns in my mouth and on my hands were not serious.

When they got back home, the yearling cows were dead, lying already stiff by the barrel of lead poisoning.

Daddy strapped the sprayer on and went back to work in the tobacco. He worked until it was so dark he couldn't see, and then he hitched Daisy to the only two cows he'd ever owned and dragged them off behind the field for the buzzards to eat. He was afraid to butcher them because of the poison.

Ever since mama first told me that story of the day they lost the cows I have thought a great deal about my daddy in that time, of how tragic it was and how typical. The world that circumscribed the people I come from had so little margin for error, for bad luck, that when something went wrong, it almost always brought something else down with it. It was a world in which survival depended on raw courage, a courage born out of desperation and sustained by a lack of alternatives.

When the crop was finally gathered and sold, daddy took most of the money he had made that year, sold the turpentine rights to his timber, and paid off the mortgage that the bank held on the place. In spite of all that had happened, things were looking pretty good for him. He owned a little over 200 acres free and clear, and he had enough money to start his next crop.

But that same year on April 17, 1937, it all caught up with him, and he went down. They had a particularly bad winter, and even in mid-April it was still cold. All of us were sleeping in the same bed that night. Mama woke up shortly after dawn and was surprised to see him still in the bed beside her. No fire in the stove, none in the fireplace. And daddy still in bed where the light of day never found him. But he had butchered hogs not long before that and prepared the smokehouse to cure the meat, all of which is exhausting work, and she thought he was just tired out from it all and had overslept. She got quietly out of bed, got a fire going in the stove, and made breakfast.

About the time she got the grits bubbling and the biscuits in the oven and the water heated in the reservoir and the kitchen warm from the stove, my brother, who was then five years old, came walking in, yawning, wearing his cotton gown. Mama told him to go in and wake up his daddy. He went back into the bedroom and stood beside the bed watching his daddy and watching me, then twenty-one months old, sleeping at his side. Hoyet thought to play a trick on his daddy, an affectionate little-boy trick, and he reached over and twisted his daddy's nose to wake him up, twisted it gently, and then harder, and finally harder still. But daddy didn't move.

He went back into the kitchen and said: "Daddy won't wake up and his nose is cold."

He was dead, had died sometime in the night in his sleep of a massive heart attack, so massive and so sudden that he didn't move enough to wake his wife, who was sleeping with her head on his arm.

She screamed and ran into the yard. She stood there for a long time mindlessly screaming in a terror for her husband's death. Her screaming brought widow Ella Thomas out of her little tenant house, and then her three children, and finally the house that day was filled with her people and daddy's.

The door was taken down, as it usually was in those days, for a cooling board, and the body placed upon it. Ordinarily the women of the family would have gathered and washed the corpse and dressed it and closed its eyes and combed its hair and shaved it for burial. But mama, for reasons she cannot now name, but which I have always thought of as a statement of her love and respect for her husband, had an embalmer come from Waycross, thirty miles away.

When daddy was drained of blood, the blood was buried out behind the house in a deep hole but not deep enough to keep a dog we had then, a hound dog whose name was Sam, from knowing what was buried there. Sam lay on the buried blood and howled all night and continued to howl for three days and nights running until he was almost dead himself from exhaustion because he would take no food or water.

Even the coffin was not built by the men of the family, as it customarily would have been. Rather, it was brought from the Mincy Funeral Home, the same place the embalmer came from in Waycross. Daddy was dressed in the only suit of clothes he had and placed in his box. The entire expense for the coffin, having it brought from Waycross, and the job of work done by the embalmer was just under $60.

Two days later, on April 19, 1937, the coffin was loaded onto the wagon he bought with the money from the sale of the Model T Ford that he'd put up on blocks all those years ago. Daisy was hitched to the wagon, and other wagons drawn by mules carrying members of the family set off for Corinth Freewill Baptist Church ten miles away. One of the men riding the second wagon with his wife, Dinah, was daddy's older brother Pascal. Eight months later, in December, Pascal would be divorced from Dinah and mama would marry him.

They went the long slow way to the graveyard there behind a tiny white clapboard church and put daddy in the ground with a wooden marker at his head. Later mama would find the money, $150, for a slab and headstone of Georgia marble. The same man who had baptized her when she was fourteen and later joined her and daddy in marriage, Preacher Will Davis, said the last words over the open grave on that day unlike April at all, but rainy and blustery and still cold.

The two closest graves to the one daddy lies in today are the graves of babies. One died in 1927 and the other in 1928. They were both Smith babies. The first one had lived to be ten months old, the other eight months old. For reasons I cannot name, it has always seemed profoundly right to me that two babies lie there so close to him who cared so much for babies and who had been told so early that he would never have any and who, once having them, lost them not because they died, but because he himself went down so early.

The night after the day daddy was buried, somebody went in the smokehouse and stole all the meat that had been cured and hung there before he died. There were nine middlings of meat hanging, and sausage in boxes, and headcheese in muslin cloth, and somebody took it all, everything but one little piece about as big as a man's hand hanging in the back of the smokehouse.

Mama knows who got the meat, not because she has any hard proof, but because in her heart she knows, and I know, too, but the one who got it is himself lying in the same graveyard daddy's in and I see no reason to name him.

He was one of my daddy's friends. I do not say he was *supposedly* or *apparently* a friend. He *was* a friend, and a close one, but he stole the meat anyway. Not many people may be able to understand that or sympathize with it, but I think I do. It was a hard time in that land, and a lot of men did things for which they were ashamed and suffered for the rest of their lives. But they did them because of hunger and sickness and because they could not bear the sorry spectacle of their children dying from lack of a doctor and their wives growing old before they were thirty.

# VIVIAN GORNICK

## (1935– )

The quintessential urban dweller, Vivian Gornick was born in New York City, graduated from City College, and received her master's degree from New York University. She made her living for nearly a decade as a writer for the *Village Voice*. Her wide-ranging interests are suggested simply by the titles of her books, which include *In Search of Ali Mahmoud: An American Woman in Egypt* (1973), *The Romance of American Communism* (1977), *Essays in Feminism* (1978), *Women in Science: Portraits from a World in Transition* (1983), and *The End of the Novel of Love* (1997).

Her memoir, *Fierce Attachments*, which appeared in 1987, is focused on her complex, often trying relationship with her mother. In some of the most memorable passages, she recalls her childhood in the forties. She also writes movingly about trying to define herself as an intellectual in the fifties—a role that seemed, at least to her, to remove her from the world of her mother. Indeed, it became necessary for her (as for Mary McCarthy, Joyce Carol Oates, Maxine Hong Kingston, and many others) to redefine appropriate behavior for a woman. Part of the work of autobiography, for Gornick, involves this redefinition.

## FROM *Fierce Attachments*

A glorious day, today: New York hard-edged in the clear autumn sun, buildings sharply outlined against the open sky, streets crowded with pyramids of fruits and vegetables, flowers in papier-mâché vases cutting circles on the sidewalk, newspaper stands vivid in black and white. On Lexington Avenue, in particular, an outpouring of lovely human bustle at noon, a density of urban appetites and absorptions.

I have agreed to walk with my mother late in the day but I've come uptown early to wander by myself, feel the sun, take in the streets, be in the world without the interceding interpretations of a companion as voluble as she. At Seventy-third Street I turn off Lexington and head for the Whitney, wanting a last look at a visiting collection. As I approach the museum some German Expressionist drawings in a gallery window catch my eye. I walk through the door, turn to the wall nearest me, and come face to face with two large Nolde watercolors, the famous flowers. I've looked often at Nolde's flowers, but now it's as though I am seeing them for the first time: that hot lush diffusion of his outlined, I suddenly realize, in intent. I see the burning quality of Nolde's intention, the serious patience with which the flowers absorb him, the clear, stubborn concentration of the artist on his subject. I *see* it. And I think, It's the concentration that gives the work its power. The space inside me enlarges. That rectangle of light and air inside, where thought clarifies and language grows and response is made intelligent, that famous space surrounded by loneliness, anxiety, self-pity, it opens wide as I look at Nolde's flowers.

In the museum lobby I stop at the permanent exhibit of Alexander Calder's circus. As usual, a crowd is gathered, laughing and gaping at the wonderfulness of Calder's sighing, weeping, triumphing bits of cloth and wire. Beside me stand two women. I look at their faces and I dismiss them: middle-aged Midwestern blondes, blue-eyed and moony. Then one of them says, "It's like second childhood," and the other one replies tartly, "Better than anyone's first." I'm startled, pleasured, embarrassed. I think, What a damn fool you are to cut yourself off with your stupid amazement that *she* could have said *that*. Again, I feel the space inside widen unexpectedly.

That space. It begins in the middle of my forehead and ends in the middle of my groin. It is, variously, as wide as my body, as narrow as a slit in a fortress wall. On days when thought flows freely or better yet clarifies with effort, it expands gloriously. On days when anxiety and self-pity crowd in, it shrinks, how fast it shrinks! When the space is wide and I occupy it fully, I taste the air, feel the light. I breathe evenly and slowly. I am peaceful and excited, beyond influence or threat. Nothing can touch me. I'm safe. I'm free. I'm thinking. When I lose the battle to think, the boundaries narrow, the air is polluted, the light clouds over. All is vapor and fog, and I have trouble breathing.

Today is promising, tremendously promising. Wherever I go, whatever I see, whatever my eye or ear touches, the space radiates expansion. I want to think. No, I mean today I *really* want to think. The desire announced itself with the word "concentration."

I go to meet my mother. I'm flying. Flying! I want to give her some of this shiningness bursting in me, siphon into her my immense happiness at being alive. Just because she is my oldest intimate and at this moment I love everybody, even her.

"Oh, Ma! What a day I've had," I say.

"Tell me," she says. "Do you have the rent this month?"

"Ma, listen . . ." I say.

"That review you wrote for the *Times*," she says. "It's for sure they'll pay you?"

"Ma, stop it. Let me tell you what I've been feeling," I say.

"Why aren't you wearing something warmer?" she cries. "It's nearly winter."

The space inside begins to shimmer. The walls collapse inward. I feel breathless. Swallow slowly, I say to myself, slowly. To my mother I say, "You *do* know how to say the right thing at the right time. It's remarkable, this gift of yours. It quite takes my breath away."

But she doesn't get it. She doesn't know I'm being ironic. Nor does she know she's wiping me out. She doesn't know I take her anxiety personally, feel annihilated by her depression. How can she know this? She doesn't even know I'm there. Were I to tell her that it's death to me, her not knowing I'm there, she would stare at me out of her eyes crowding up with puzzled desolation, this young girl of seventy-seven, and she would cry angrily, "You don't understand! You have never understood!"

Mama and Nettie quarreled, and I entered City College. In feeling memory these events carry equal weight. Both inaugurated open conflict, both drove a wedge between me and the unknowing self, both were experienced as subversive and warlike in character. Certainly the conflict between Nettie and my mother seemed a strategic plan to surround and conquer. Incoherent as the war was, shot through with rage and deceit, its aims apparently confused and always denied, it never lost sight of the enemy: the intelligent heart of the girl who if not bonded to one would be lost to both. City College, as well, seemed no less concerned with laying siege, to the ignorant mind if not the intelligent heart. Benign in intent, only a passport to the promised land, City of course was the real invader. It did more violence to the emotions than either Mama or Nettie could have dreamed possible, divided me from them both, provoked and nourished an unshared life inside the head that became a piece of treason. I lived among my people, but I was no longer one of them.

I think this was true for most of us at City College. We still used the subways, still walked the familiar streets between classes, still returned to the neighborhood each night, talked to our high-school friends, and went to sleep in our own beds. But secretly we had begun to live in a world inside our heads where we read talked thought in a way that separated us from our parents, the life of the house and that of the street. We had been initiated, had learned the difference between hidden and expressed thought. This made us subversives in our own homes.

As thousands before me have said, "For us it was City College or nothing." I enjoyed the solidarity those words invoked but rejected the implied deprivation. At City College I sat talking in a basement cafeteria until ten or eleven at night with a half dozen others who also never wanted to go home to Brooklyn or the Bronx, and here in the cafeteria my education took root. Here I learned that Faulkner was America, Dickens was politics, Marx was sex, Jane Austen the idea of culture, that I came from a ghetto and D. H. Lawrence was a visionary. Here my love of literature named itself, and amazement over the life of the mind blossomed. I discovered that people were transformed by ideas, and that intellectual conversation was immensely erotic.

We never stopped talking. Perhaps because we did very little else (restricted by sexual fear and working-class economics, we didn't go to the theater and we didn't make love), but certainly we talked so much because most of us had been reading in bottled-up silence from the age of six on and City College was our great release. It was not from the faculty that City drew its reputation for intellectual goodness, it was from its students, it was from us. Not that we were intellectually distinguished, we weren't; but our hungry energy vitalized the place. The idea of intellectual life burned in us. While we pursued ideas we felt known, to ourselves and to one another. The world made sense, there was ground beneath our feet, a place in the universe to stand. City College made conscious in me inner cohesion as a first value.

I think my mother was very quickly of two minds about me and City, although she had wanted me to go to school, no question about that, had been energized by the determination that I do so (instructed me in the middle of her first year of widowhood to enter the academic not the commercial course of high-school study), and was even embattled when it became something of an issue in the family.

"Where is it written that a working-class widow's daughter should go to college?" one of my uncles said to her, drinking coffee at our kitchen table on a Saturday morning in my senior year in high school.

"Here it is written," she had replied, tapping the table hard with her middle finger. "Right here it is written. The girl goes to college."

"Why?" he had pursued.

"Because I say so."

"But why? What do you think will come of it?"

"I don't know. I only know she's clever, she deserves an education, and she's going to get one. This is America. The girls are not cows in the field only waiting for a bull to mate with." I stared at her. Where had *that* come from? My father had been dead only five years, she was in full widowhood swing.

The moment was filled with conflict and bravado. She felt the words she spoke but she did not mean them. She didn't even know what she meant by an education. When she discovered at my graduation that I wasn't a teacher she acted as though she'd been swindled. In her mind a girl child went in one door marked college and came out another marked teacher.

"You mean you're not a teacher?" she said to me, eyes widening as her two strong hands held my diploma down on the kitchen table.

"No," I said.

"What have you been doing there all these years?" she asked quietly.

"Reading novels," I replied.

She marveled silently at my chutzpah.

But it wasn't really a matter of what I could or could not do with the degree. We were people who knew how to stay alive, she never doubted I would find a way. No, what drove her, and divided us, was me thinking. She hadn't understood that going to school meant I would start thinking: coherently and out loud. She was taken by violent surprise. My sentences got longer within a month of those first classes. Longer, more complicated, formed by words whose meaning she did not always know. I had never before spoken a word she didn't know. Or made a sentence whose logic she couldn't follow. Or attempted an opinion that grew out of an abstraction. It made her crazy. Her face began to take on a look of animal cunning when I started a sentence that could not possibly be concluded before three clauses had hit the air. Cunning sparked anger, anger flamed into rage. "What are you talking about?" she would shout at me. "What *are* you talking about? Speak English, please! We all understand English in this house. Speak it!"

Her response stunned me. I didn't get it. Wasn't she pleased that I could say something she didn't understand? Wasn't that what it was all about? I was the advance guard. I was going to take her into the new world. All she had to do was adore what I was becoming, and here she was refusing. I'd speak my new sentences, and she would turn on me as though I'd performed a vile act right there at the kitchen table.

She, of course, was as confused as I. She didn't know why she was angry, and if she'd been told she was angry she would have denied it, would have found a way to persuade both herself and any interested listener that she was proud I was in school, only why did I have to be such a showoff? Was that what going to college was all about? Now, take Mr. Lewis, the insurance agent, an educated man if ever there was one, got a degree from City College in 1929, 1929 mind you, and never made you feel stupid, always spoke in simple sentences, but later you thought about what he had said. That's the way an educated person should talk. Here's this snotnose kid coming into the kitchen with all these big words, sentences you can't make head or tail of . . .

I was seventeen, she was fifty. I had not yet come into my own as a qualifying belligerent but I was a respectable contender and she, naturally, was at the top of her game. The lines were drawn, and we did not fail one another. Each of us rose repeatedly to the bait the other one tossed out. Our storms shook the apartment: paint blistered on the wall, linoleum cracked on the floor, glass shivered in the window frame. We barely kept our hands off one another, and more than once we approached disaster.

One Saturday afternoon she was lying on the couch. I was reading in a nearby chair. Idly she asked, "What are you reading?" Idly I replied, "A comparative history of the idea of love over the last three hundred years." She looked at me for a moment. "That's ridiculous," she said slowly. "Love is love. It's the same everywhere, all the time. What's to compare?" "That's absolutely not true," I shot back. "You don't know what you're talking about. It's only an idea, Ma. That's all love is. Just an idea. You think it's a function of the mysterious immutable being, but it's not! There is, in fact, no such thing as the mysterious immutable being . . ." Her legs were off the couch so fast I didn't see them go down. She made fists of her hands, closed her eyes tight, and howled, "I'll kill you-u-u! Snake in my bosom, I'll kill you. How dare you talk to me that way?" And then she was coming at me. She was small and chunky. So was I. But I had thirty years on her. I was out of the chair faster than her arm could make contact, and running, running through the apartment, racing for the bathroom, the only room with a lock on it. The top half of the bathroom door was a panel of frosted glass. She arrived just as I turned the lock, and couldn't put the brakes on. She drove her fist through the glass, reaching for me. Blood, screams, shattered glass on both sides of the door. I thought that afternoon, One of us is going to die of this attachment.

# FRANK CONROY

## (1936– )

Conroy has written one of the most striking and well-known of contemporary memoirs, *Stop-Time* (1967), an account of his coming-of-age in the late forties and fifties. This intricately shaped and delicate work has something of the same tone one heard in J. D. Salinger's *Catcher in the Rye*, as when Conroy writes, "It came to me that the world was insane. Not just people. The world."

Conroy's memoir has everything a good novel has: suspense, vivid characters (his family, in particular), and a strongly realized sense of the physical world. The child of an alcoholic father who dies when he is twelve, Conroy writes about his childhood, adolescence, and young manhood with unusual frankness and grace, his prose often moving beautifully into poetry and aphorism. In "Losing My Cherry," the particularly engaging chapter that follows, he writes about his sexual initiation—a rite of passage common to all but paradoxically always unique as well.

## FROM *Stop-Time*

### LOSING MY CHERRY

Alison and I were fond of each other, but we lived in different worlds. To defend ourselves we had been forced to extremes—Alison's of disengagement and calmness, mine of rebellion and anger. We sent heartfelt but necessarily simple messages to each other, like mountaineers from peak to peak. "How are you over there? I love you, but I can hardly hear you. I don't pretend to understand you, but I wish you well." By a monumental effort Alison had created a life for herself quite separate from the chaos of the family. As a child she'd shown remarkable self-sufficiency, reliability, and good sense, and had therefore won the right to be left alone. Or so she thought. Actually it was not so much a right she had won as it was Jean's and Dagmar's lack of interest. They were preoccupied with their own problems. As a teen-ager she did nothing to endanger that privilege. She was a model student and eventually became president of the student government at Washington Irving High School. She never argued with her mother, or allowed herself to be sucked into Jean's harangues. In many ways it was as if she were a guest in the house, or a boarder who had her own family somewhere else. When she won a scholarship to Barnard College no one was surprised. She'd been a good, industrious girl for so long everyone took it for granted. "I never have to worry about Alison," my mother would say. "Alison is a sensible girl." What we didn't know was the terrible price she was paying to keep up the front.

In her senior year at college Alison acquired a steady boy friend, Jack, a tall, good-looking fellow she'd met in the dramatic group. Because of an anomaly in his earlier education he was a freshman, although only a year younger than herself. I liked him immediately. In classic little-brother style I made something of a pest of myself, but he never seemed to mind. Coming home, I often went straight up to Alison's room, eager to talk and enjoy some reflected warmth. Her room, separated from the others by a long hall, was always tidy and managed, in a cold house, to convey a bit of cosiness. There was a fake leopard-skin bedspread, brown corduroy drapes, books, a throw rug, and a few tasteful knickknacks. It was like the rooms one sees in magazines. I'd knock on the door, give them a couple of seconds, and walk in. They were usually on the couch on the far side of the room, in mild disarray, but fully clothed. Unlike young people these days, it took Jack and Alison quite a while to achieve the ultimate union. She had, I later learned, a hymen as tough as the plastic window on a convertible.

"Hi. Can I come in?"

"You are in," Alison said, taking her arms from his shoulders.

"Well, I can come back later if . . ."

"You're here now. It wears off after a while."

"What wears off?"

"Never mind." She laughed, sitting up.

"How's the boy?" Jack asked.

"Pretty good. There's a great movie on the late show tonight. Mickey Rooney."

"Oh yeah?"

"We have to go over your history paper," Alison reminded him.

"Oh, it's okay," he said. "It's good enough the way it is."

"No. We'll rewrite it together." She reached forward and smoothed down the hair on the back of his neck. "We'll make something of you yet, young man."

"Anybody want a glass of milk?" I asked.

When I came back they were kissing. I sat down and drank my milk, watching abstractedly.

"Hmm," she said. "Delicious."

"You sound like you want to eat him."

"Maybe I do."

"Disgusting," I said. "Cannibalism. That's very unhealthy sexually."

She laughed, and sticking her finger in his ear, said coyly, "I'm a very sexually unhealthy person, in a certain healthy kind of way." She jumped up from the couch. "Oh, isn't he beautiful?" she cried. "Isn't he the most beautiful thing you've ever *seen?*"

"All right," I said. "Cut it out."

"My sexy freshman. My wild black Irishman."

"Alison, for Christ sake."

"Well, let me preen a little!" she said, suddenly annoyed. "Let me enjoy it."

"I don't know how you put up with all that goo," I said to Jack.

He winked. "It's not so bad when you get used to it."

"He loves it," Alison said. "He loves every minute of it."

"Yeah," I said. "Okay."

"You'll find out about it," she said. "It'll happen to you."

"In a pig's ass."

"Don't be vulgar."

"How about Mickey Rooney?" I asked Jack. "I'll go down and get some oatmeal cookies."

"Is it a western?"

"Jack, you *can't,*" Alison said quickly. "You got a C minus on the last quiz." She came down on his lap and put her arms around him. "How am I going to make you into a beautiful silver-haired professor with a beautiful pipe in a beautiful book-lined library if you don't cooperate?" She kissed him on the ear. "I'm your mentor, remember. You've put yourself in my capable hands."

They started kissing some more, their jaws working, and after a while I got up and left, closing the door behind me.

It was the winter of my seventeenth birthday, presumably my last year of high school. I made a half-hearted attempt to pass my courses, knowing that in any event I'd have to go to summer school to make up for previous failures. I wanted the diploma that year. I wanted to get it over with so I could leave the country, go to Denmark and meet my grandparents, see Paris, but mostly just get away from home. I withdrew into myself and let the long months go by, spending my time reading, playing the piano, and watching television. Jean too had retreated into himself. He'd watch the screen silently for hours on end, wrapped up in a blanket Indian fashion, never moving his head. Night after night I'd lie in bed, with a glass of milk and a package of oatmeal cookies beside me, and read one paperback after another until two or three in the morning. I read everything, without selection, buying all the fiction on the racks of the local drugstore—D. H. Lawrence, Moravia, Stuart Engstrand, Aldous Huxley, Frank Yerby, Mailer, Twain, Gide, Dickens, Philip Wylie, Tolstoi, Hemingway, Zola, Dreiser, Vardis Fisher, Dostoievsky, G. B. Shaw, Thomas Wolfe, Theodore Pratt, Scott Fitzgerald, Joyce, Frederick Wakeman, Orwell, McCullers, Remarque, James T. Farrell, Steinbeck, de Maupassant, James Jones, John O'Hara, Kipling, Mann, Saki, Sinclair Lewis, Maugham, Dumas, and dozens more. I borrowed from the public library ten blocks away and from the rental library at Womrath's on Madison Avenue. I read very fast, uncritically, and without retention, seeking only to escape from my own life through the imaginative plunge into another. Safe in my room with milk and cookies I disappeared into inner space. The real world dissolved and I was free to drift in fantasy, living a thousand lives, each one more powerful, more accessible, and more real than my own. It was around this time that I first thought of becoming a writer. In a cheap novel the hero was asked his profession at a cocktail party. "I'm a novelist," he said, and I remember putting the book down and thinking, my God what a beautiful thing to be able to say.

The piano kept me occupied when I didn't feel like books. Music had always affected me strongly. As a small boy I'd stand on the coffee table in the living room and conduct scratchy records of Grieg, Rachmaninoff, and Tchaikovsky with a pencil, watching myself in the mirror all the while. I memorized pieces well enough to anticipate tempo changes with exactitude. My baton technique was flamboyant and I moved around as much as the limited area of the coffee table allowed. More than once, carried away by the sweep and grandeur of it all, I fell off. But I always climbed back up.

There were violent scenes with my mother. I was beginning to realize I could outsmart her in arguments, and equally important, that I was too big for her to attempt the use of force. I adopted an attitude of haughty independence, as if I didn't care what she said or how she felt, and loosed a storm of sarcasm and invective whenever she threatened to overpower me emotionally and destroy my pose. I remember actually laughing once when, speechless and spluttering, she threw a shoe at me. "You missed," I said with tremendous outward calm, "why don't you try again?" We groped through life in mutual misunderstanding, unable to help each other, unable to think of anything more intelligent to do than endure the war, hoping that somehow, mysteriously, it would end.

Summer school was ridiculously easy. I cut classes with impunity and showed up for the tests with no more preparation than a vague memory of what I'd learned at Stuyvesant. It was enough to get me through.

The school library had twenty or thirty back issues of the London *Illustrated News* as well as a few copies of *Punch*. I spent hours looking through them, soaking up their strangeness, projecting myself across the sea. I wasn't going to England, but it didn't matter. The magazines were proof that another world existed, that many other worlds existed into which I might escape. I counted the days until my departure, frustrated by the slowness of time. Life around me was meaningless—my grades, the struggle at home, the fact that I probably wasn't going to college, everything was eclipsed by the fact that soon, soon, in a matter of weeks, I would leave it behind. Finally, at last, I was going to *get out*.

A few students crossed the hall in the distance but no one was coming my way. I pulled open the door and entered the stairwell. A wire-mesh door closed off the up staircase. There was a foot and a half of space at the top. I climbed the door carefully, shoving the pointed toes of my shoes into the wire and pulling myself up with hooked fingers. On top, I slipped through sideways and fell to the steps on the other side. Instantly lightheaded and alert, as if waking from sleep, I climbed the stairs.

Three stories above the floors in which school was in session I wandered through deserted corridors, whistling, peering into empty classrooms, stopping every now and then to throw a few blackboard erasers into the ventilation cowls up near the ceiling. In the music room sunlight streamed through the huge windows. I sat on the sill and smoked a cigarette, watching the tenement rooftops far below. Flocks of pigeons circled in the air over the Lower East Side. Striding down the aisle to the grand piano I clapped my hands in imitation of an audience applauding the featured soloist. I opened the piano, took a short bow, and sat down at the keyboard. I played the blues in the key of C.

I paused in the aisle, unsure which of my two favorite techniques to use. I could sit in the row in front of her, drape my arm over the back of the seat next to me and attempt to contact her knee with my hand, or I could sit next to her, with one empty seat between us, and play footsie. The small balcony was almost empty. I entered her row and sat down. From the corner of my eye I could see her white raincoat going on and off in the reflected light from the screen below. I watched the movie for half an hour before making my move. Shifting around in my seat, I extended my legs in the darkness until my foot almost touched hers. After a while I raised my toe and applied a gentle pressure to the side of her foot. To my astonishment she answered immediately, giving me three firm, unmistakable taps. I moved into the seat next to her and she turned her head for the first time.

"It's you!" I said. I'd picked her up in another theater a few weeks before.

"Didn't you know?" Her accent was heavy. She was Belgian, nineteen, and she had a job looking after two children.

"No. Of course not."

"I hoped I should see you again."

I put my arm around her. "Me too." Congratulating myself on my luck, I kissed her cheek. She turned and I kissed her mouth. She wasn't very pretty, and there was an odd bloodless quality to her, almost as if she was undernourished, but she was a girl, the most cooperative girl I'd ever met. I slipped my free hand over her breast.

"The movie is bad," she said.

Fifteen minutes later, my leg up on the seat in front to screen us off, I had my hand between her legs, slipping my finger in and out of her wet sex.

"There," she whispered. "No, there. Yes. That's right."

She reached out and grabbed me through my trousers. Her fingers touched and pressed. She unzipped my fly. She pulled me out into the cool air and squeezed. I couldn't believe what was happening. She struggled to get her hand all the way inside. "That's what I want," she said as her hand closed over me.

"Let's go somewhere," I said after a while.

"Where?"

"We'll find someplace." My mind was racing. If I could get her alone she would let me fuck her. Under the stairs in the service entrance to my house. In the alley. In the park. Anyplace dark. "Let's go."

"We better not."

"Why?"

"You know why."

"No, I don't. It isn't wrong." I stared at her profile. Her mouth was set in a faint smile, barely perceptible. I pulled her shoulder gently. "Come on. It's all right."

She leaned forward, sitting on the edge of her seat, and stared out over my shoulder into the darkness. For a moment I thought she was going to leave me—simply walk out on her own and go home—but then she looked at me, nodded, and stood up. I followed her down the aisle, my eyes locked on her back.

As we emerged from the theater I turned toward the park. "This way." The marquee lights threw our shadows on the sidewalk in front of us, long, thin shadows stretching away up the block, growing longer and fainter as we walked.

"You're going too fast," she said.

"I'm sorry." As we passed my house I gave up the idea of the alley or the service stairs. We continued toward the park in silence. I was conscious only of movement, of the girl beside me, and of the blood roaring in my head.

At the corner of Madison Avenue she said, "I'm scared."

"Why?"

She didn't answer.

"What is there to be scared of?" I helped her over the curb. She shook her head, watching the sidewalk moving under us. Suddenly I understood. "You mean you're scared of having a baby."

"Yes."

"Don't worry. We'll take care of that." It flashed through my mind that I could buy a prophylactic at the drugstore on the corner. Then I remembered I'd spent the last of my money for the theater ticket.

We went into the park through the same entrance I had used as a child. After a few steps I led her off the path into the darkness. There was a place I remembered from years ago—a little hollow between the footpath and the sunken roadway to the West Side. Leading her by the hand, I found it quickly.

"Let's put your coat on the ground," I said.

She took it off slowly and gave it to me. I spread it over the rough grass and went down on my knees. We remained motionless as someone walked along the path on the other side of the bushes. Light from a distant lamp post filtered through the trees and played over her shoulders and neck. When the footsteps died away she came down into the darkness and lay beside me.

She lifted her hips as I raised her skirt, and again as I pulled her panties to her ankles. Opening my clothes I looked down at her white belly glowing in the shadows.

"Do it," she said. "Before someone comes."

I got on top of her and, after a moment of blind fumbling, drove myself into her. She cried out in pain and threw her head to one side.

"What's the matter?" I asked, pausing, but she didn't answer and I began to move again. I found myself thrusting hard once more, and when she didn't flinch I got up on my elbows and quickened the pace. She lay motionless, her head averted.

As I fucked her, a certain moment arrived when I realized her body had changed. Her sex was no longer simply the entrance way one penetrated in search of deeper, more intangible mysteries. It had become, all at once, *slippery*—a lush blossom beyond which there was no need to go.

Afterward, I lay still, dazzled. Coming out of her was a shock. I seemed to be floating weightless in space. On my hands and knees I paused to feel the earth and orient myself. A noisy bus went past in the sunken roadway. I looked up and she was on her feet, waiting.

"Hurry," she said. "I am so late."

We walked to the subway without talking. At the top of the stairs she turned to me. "Goodbye."

"I'll look for you," I said, aware of how feeble it sounded, knowing we would never meet again. "We'll see each other."

She started down.

"Goodbye," I said.

She turned, holding the rail. "What is your name?"

"Frank." I said quickly. "Frank Conroy."

She turned again and went down the stairs into the roar of an arriving train.

# JOYCE CAROL OATES
## (1938– )

Oates was born and raised in Lockport, New York, a region that has often figured in her stories and novels. A poet, critic, and playwright as well as writer of fiction, she has been extremely prolific in a career that has brought her a wide and admiring readership for work marked by acute psychological insights, emotional intensity, and expressive language. Her novels include *A Garden of Earthly Delights* (1967), *Expensive People* (1968), *them* (1969), *Bellefleur* (1980), *You Must Remember This* (1987), and *What I Lived For* (1994).

Like Vivian Gornick, Oates is driven (in the excerpt that follows, taken from a 1997 anthology titled *I've Always Meant to Tell You*) to define herself against her mother. In doing so, she is reaching for self-definition, attempting to come to terms with the role of daughter in an age when the traditional roles have been called into question.

## "A Letter to My Mother Carolina Oates on Her 78th Birthday November 8, 1995"

*Dear Mom,*
    I've always meant to tell you . . .
    I've long rehearsed telling you . . .
    I've meant so many times to tell you, and Daddy . . .
    How the human world divides into two: those who speak unhesitantly, smoothly saying *I love you*—and possibly not mean it; and those too shy or constrained by family custom or temperament to utter the words *I love you*—though they mean it. To the depths of what's called the soul.

How deep inside me, imprinted in infant memory, the sight of my young parents leaning over me, gazing at me smiling, lifting me in their arms. The wonder, the unspeakable mystery. Radiant unnamed faces of first love.

For this I've long believed: we carry our young parents within us, so much more vivid and alive, pulsing-alive, than any memory of ourselves as infants, children. We carry our young parents within us everywhere, through life. No wonder is ever quite equivalent to that first wonder. Blinking up from a crib, gaping in absolute trust and amazement lacking words to stammer, even to *think Who are you? Why do you care for me? What does it mean, we are here together? Only hold me, hold me. Only feed me, love me, forever.*

An inventory of our lives. The back fields shimmering in sunshine, humming with summer insects, iridescent dragonflies' wings. The countryside, farm region of western New York State, northern Erie County near the Niagara County border, near the Tonawanda Creek and the Erie Barge canal. Waking to such days, a succession of days—what happiness! To a child, eternity is this morning, this hour. Forever is now. Permanent.

Into the pear orchard: a harvest of greeny-yellow Bartlett pears. How hard they've seemed, like stone, green stone, for weeks. And now ripe, ready to be picked. That ripe sun-warmed smell. Picking pears, a single pear, a single gesture. Placing, not dropping, the pear into the bushel basket. You taught me patience: Like this! Daddy was the one who used the ladder. A harvest of pears—so many. At least it seemed like so many. Some of the pears were for us to eat then, some were for canning; most were sold by the roadside, in quart baskets, pecks, bushels. We sold apples, too—not so many, since we had only a few apple trees. And black cherries (sweet) and red cherries (sour). And tomatoes—those juicy plump red First Lady tomatoes, pole climbers, with their strong tart smell. And sweet corn, peppers, onions.

But it's the pear orchard I remember most vividly. Beyond the swing that seated four people, an old-fashioned metal-and-wood swing Daddy painted blue, the orchard, to the very rear of our property, the fragrance of pears, the perfect shapes of pears, smooth skins sometimes touched with a russet-red blush as with a delicate watercolor brush like the petals of your favorite rose, Double Delight.

Those long summer days. Cicadas screaming out of the trees. *Listen to those crazy things!* you'd say, laughing. The very music of the country, of deep intransigent summer; like crickets at dusk, the cries of owls in the near distance, a faint dry rustling of leaves. Flashes of lightning—"heat lightning"—silent nervous ripping-veins of flame renting the sky and disappearing in seemingly the same instant. *You look, it's already gone.* How nature, how the world surrounding us, *is* us; yet shrouded in mystery. You and I are in the back field picking corn, tomatoes. We're in the barn, we're feeding chickens in the mottled pecked-at dirt surrounding the chicken coop, tossing grain, what childish pleasure in tossing grain, and the chickens come clucking, fretting, plumping their wings, and the big rooster, his lurid-red comb, his mad yellow eye, that look of male impatience to all roosters, and I'm squealing, shrinking back to avoid the rooster who pecks at feet when he's in a bad mood, and where is my chicken?—my pet chicken—Happy Chicken, so-called? A reddish-brown bird, with a bad limp. *If you pet a chicken the right way, if you show you're not going to hurt it, it will go very still and crouch down.* We're in the kitchen, upstairs in the farmhouse, you're cooking tomatoes, simmering them slowly into a thick ripe sauce in a large pan on the stove beneath the bright yellow plastic General Electric clock (bought with stamps from Loblaw's, pasted assiduously into a little booklet, the accumulation of months) with its shiny black numerals and red hands moving slowly, imperially, unswerving through the days. Those long summer days I believed, as a child, would never end.

I've always meant to tell you how in awe I am of . . .
How hypnotized, entranced I've been by . . .
Since I became mature enough, in high school perhaps . . .
Most powerfully, painfully since I've become of the adults of the world, like you . . . though so much older now than you were through my childhood, girlhood, my luminous and fascinating memories . . .
Dedicating how many of my books to you. How many times *Again, for my parents Carolina and Frederic Oates, and in memory of that world, now vanishing, that continues to nourish.*

That vanishing world. Before I was born. So vast, so mysterious falling away like a seeming edge to the horizon that shifts into shadows even as we push eagerly forward, hoping to illuminate, to see.
I've always meant to tell you though it would have been impossible to tell you, impossible to choose the words, for such words embarrass, such words make self-conscious what must remain unconscious or at any rate unspoken, always I've meant to tell you how in awe I am of the lives you and Daddy lived; your strength, your resilience, your good humor; your utter lack of self-pity; never complaining, except perhaps jokingly as if to indicate *That's the way the world is, you might as well laugh.*
The yearning, the wonder. I've always believed that some secret must reside in you, and your world, before I came into being, let alone into consciousness. My birth, June 16, 1938. When you were twenty years old. And Daddy was twenty-four. In our old precious snapshots, some of them a bit mangled, what an attractive young couple you are: you, with your bushy-springy hair and sweet smile, a look of girlish hope, openness,

Daddy with his swarthy features, stiff-crested dark hair and heavy eye-brows, easy smile. Radiant faces of first love, romance.

What a precious hoard of twenty or so snapshots, old family snapshots, scattered across my desk.

The earliest is of Blanche Oates, later Blanche Woodside, Daddy's mother, an attractive dark-haired young woman in her early or mid-twenties. When was this picture taken, and by whom? I can only guess, about 1914. (The year of Daddy's birth.) No one living could even haz-ard a guess who might have taken it.

Most of these precious pictures are of you, Daddy, my brother Fred, and me, taken in the 1940s and 1950s. All have a much-thumbed, much-contemplated look.

How unknowing we are, taking pictures! The very concept—"taking a picture." Unable to guess what significance this fleeting moment among a vertiginous ceaseless cascade of similar moments will acquire in later years; how *representative*. For such images give distinct, visible, daylight shapes to our every-shifting and ever-precarious memories.

These snapshots are of the early 1940s. My favorites. There's quite a dramatic shot of Daddy kneeling, very handsome with sleek thick dark hair and a look of some solemnity for the camera, with me, a child of per-haps four? five? on his knee. We're in the leafy backyard near one of the pear orchards. I'm in a pretty floral dress, my curly, inclined-to-snarl hair beribboned, wearing white anklet socks, no doubt new white shoes. Daddy's and Mommy's little girl, dressed for some special occasion.

Can it be—over fifty years have passed?

*Fifty years.*

Well, here we are, in that long-ago lost time, as in a region of Time it-self, oblivious of our circumstances. You are a pretty, young mother in your midtwenties, with springy-curly hair, a white flower in your hair, slender, smiling, in an elaborately buttoned dress, very likely a new spring dress, and white spring shoes. In one of the snapshots we're standing in the very spot Daddy had posed with me, I seem to be clowning for the camera, what a show-off spoiled child I must have been, firstborn, en-joying sovereignty as a child in the farmhouse in Millersport among adults for five years before my brother Robin was born. (In fact I was clowning for Daddy wielding the blue box Kodak camera I wasn't al-lowed to play with, that in later years would be a household relic whose interior workings, subtly distorting magnifying lenses, and very smell, impossible to describe, would fascinate me. How moon-faced I am, at the age of four or five; how rather plumpish, like one of those luxury dolls with "real"-seeming skin. I don't recognize myself at all, feel no kinship with that child at all, the kinship I feel is with you, my mother gazing down at me so sweetly with what motherly indulgence and patience. *Who has been secure in his mother's love,* Freud has speculated, from his narrowly masculine perspective, *will be secure through life.*

In other pictures taken that day or at that general time you and I are similarly posed in that leafy space, a world of trees it seems, childhood's green world. In one of my favorite pictures, you and I are sitting together in the grass, you're holding a tiny black kitten in your hands and I'm in the crook of your arm, this is in fact May 14, 1941, as you've noted on the back of the snapshot. Is this kitten my first? (We had so many kittens, so many cats on the farm! I think I must have loved them all!) Behind us is what appears to be a cherry tree, long vanished from my memory as from that landscape. (Where, decades later, miraculously it seems to one who has moved so often, of a generation of Americans who have moved yet more often, you still live. Almost seventy-eight years on the same land.) And beyond the cherry tree is the farmhouse owned by my (adoptive) grandfather John Bush and my (adoptive) grandmother Lena Bush with whom we lived, one not-large, fairly typical farm family, for all the years of my childhood and adolescence. The farmhouse is always old in my memory, built in 1888, in any case its foundations laid in 1888, but it doesn't look particularly old in these snapshots, a durable woodframe two-story steep-roofed house like many others in rural western New York, then and now. In the snapshots, the house appears about to dissolve in light; in my memory, and in other, subsequent snapshots, the house is sided with a gritty practicable gray, "simulated brick" made of asphalt. Did Daddy put the siding on the house? I suspect he did. And there's the outside cellar door, at an angle against the rear of the house. Gone forever, these cellar doors! A commonplace of a vanished America, like the hefty rain barrel at the corner or the house. Virtually every house, of a certain economic level at least, had rain barrels in those days, strategically positioned to collect rain running down roofs. Unfathomable to the inhabitants of that world, still recovering from the Depression, our contemporary indifference to "usable" water allowed to fall and drain away into mere earth.

If I could slip back into that instant, as the shutter clicks!

But I can't, of course. This species of time travel is wholly imaginary. Our lives are time travel, moving in one direction only. We accompany one another as long as we can; as long as time grants us.

*My father was killed and I never knew why. No one would say. Now there's no one I can ask. My mother didn't want me, there were too many children I guess, nine children counting me, I was a baby when my father died, not a year old. My mother gave me to her sister Lena who didn't have any children. I felt so bad, I used to cry all the time . . . my mother didn't*

*want me. It was so strange! I went to visit them, they had a farm in Pendle-*
*ton, only about three miles away on the other side of the creek. They weren't*
*really very nice to me. I don't know why, I guess they thought I was better*
*off here with Aunt Lena and Uncle John, not so many children to feed I*
*guess. My father's name was Steve and my mother's name was Elizabeth.*
*I never knew my father of course. He was Hungarian, my mother was Hun-*
*garian, she and her sister Lena married two brothers in Budapest, Steve*
*and John, and they all came over together. This must have been 1900 or so.*
*My mother never learned English, always spoke Hungarian. She was a*
*short, plump woman, a pleasant woman, with curly hair like mine. She*
*didn't want me, it was so strange . . . she had so many children she had to*
*give me away. There was Leslie, he was the oldest; then Mary, I didn't get*
*to know too well; then Steve, who was kicked by a horse, wasn't ever quite*
*right in the head and always lived at home with Ma; then Elsie, I came to*
*be so close with Elsie; then Johnny; then Edith; then George, I wasn't too*
*close with George. It's a long time ago but I remember crying a lot, when*
*I was a little girl and my mother didn't want me.*

It *is* a mystery how my (biological) grandfather Bush died, in or near
a tavern, in or near Lockport, who killed him, murdered him, with what
sort of weapon, and was the assailant arrested, tried, sent to prison?—a
family legend, yet blurred, dreamlike. *Now there's no one I can ask.*

An eerie symmetry: my father's grandfather, too, died violently, in
Hartland, New York, north of Lockport, a suicide.

Of these old tragedies, if tragedy is the right term and not rather misadventures, sheer bad luck, no one ever spoke during my childhood,
girlhood, young adulthood. Now, old family secrets seem to matter less,
even as their details have faded, their very contours blurred as bad dreams
recounted by others.

How ironic, as a writer I've been constantly queried why do you write
about violent acts? What do you know of violence? And my replies are polite, thoughtful, abstract and even idealistic. I might say that my entire
life, indeed the lives of both my parents, have been shaped by "violent
acts"—yet that would not be entirely accurate, since I knew very little of
these old, near-forgotten family tales, tales of the Bushes and the Mor-
gensterns, through most of my life. Only the past decade or so has been
illuminating in this regard—like a door opening to a shadowy passage-
way, but only just opening a few inches, never to be budged any farther.

Yet: what romance, in that world. Because you inhabited it, you and
Daddy, it's transformed.

You came, in 1918, an infant, to live with your uncle John and aunt
Lena on their farm in Millersport, never formally adopted, that was how

things were done in those days, no need for lawyers, government intervention, blood relatives in any case. Your uncle John, my "grandfather"
Bush. He was a farmer, a blacksmith, later a factory worker in
Tonawanda. *So tough and strong, a hard-drinking man, a true Hungarian,
what a character! A jug of hard cider on the kitchen floor beside his chair
even at breakfast. Chewed tobacco, rolled his own cigarettes. His long underwear, his bristly chin, whiskers. Everyone had horses then, blacksmiths
were in demand. John Bush was tough and strong, could practically lift a
horse. If a horse acted up while he was shoeing it, tried to get away, he'd
wrestle it down, sometimes he'd hit it with his hammer. Yes he was tough!
And Lena, your grandmother Bush we called her—a plump, pretty woman
when she was young, like her sister Elizabeth. She never learned to read
English but she could speak it, in her way. She never learned to drive a car,
and Ma didn't either, so the sisters didn't see much of each other. They only
lived a few miles apart, and were sisters, from the old country, but didn't
see each other much. That was how women were in the old days.*

And how you were, when you married.
Hardly more than a girl, when you and Daddy met. You'd gone to the
one-room schoolhouse, Lockport District #7, to which I and my brother
Robin would later go, and you'd gone to a Catholic school in Swormville,
about four miles away, dropping out after eighth grade to work at home
and on the farm. Meeting Fred Oates, a brash young man, a boy really,
hardly nineteen, one day in Lockport when you were with a friend of his,
driving in the friend's car. *He stopped for a light, and somebody yanked
open the car door and surprised us both—it was Fred! That was how we
met, that day. He always did surprising things, things you couldn't predict,
you know what Dad is like.* You fell in love, and swiftly I gather. Fred
Oates was such a handsome boy, quick-tempered, volatile, possibly a little wild but good-hearted, kind and intelligent. He had an Irish father
named Carlton Oates, a drinker, "no good"—a man who'd walked out on
his young wife and child, years before, refusing to support them—but a
beautiful, well-spoken mother. Blanche Oates *so dignified, so well-dressed
and chic, I was afraid of her at first.* (In fact, no one knew at the time, in
1936, that Blanche Oates, formerly Blanche Morningstar, had been born
Morgenstern, the daughter of German Jews who had immigrated to rural
western New York in the 1890s, changed their name in 1894, seemed to
have hidden their Jewishness from their neighbors and even from their
several daughters.) Fred Oates too had dropped out of school, worked for
a Lockport sign painter and would shortly go to work at Harrison Radia-
tor, the Lockport division of General Motors, where he would be a loyal
and inventive employee, in the tool and dye design shop, for the next

forty years. You were married in 1937, and your first baby was born in 1938, named Joyce Carol; your second, in 1943, Fred Jr., nickname "Robin"; your third, Lynn Ann, in 1956.

An inventory of our lives. The lost world of laundry; clotheslines, clothespins, sheets, towels, trousers, dresses, and underwear, socks flapping in the wind, a ceaseless wind it seemed, how crude by present-day standards, how primitive; yet there was pleasure in it, in even the repetition, the familiarity. Each item of laundry lifted by hand, smoothed and affixed to the line with wooden pins, in later years plastic pins. From my small room on the second floor rear of the house I could glance out at any time when the laundry was hanging on the line and see a reflection of our household, our family, like ghost-figures glimpsed in water.

Who taught me patience, if not you? The sometimes-consoling rituals of housekeeping, small simple finite tasks executed with love or at any rate bemused affection, cheerful resignation. You tried to teach me to knit, and to sew, for which feminine activities I demonstrated little talent if, at the outset, energy and hope. You had more success teaching me to iron, a dreamy mesmerizing task I seem to have liked, as girls will, in small intermittent doses. Though not so much as I came to like vacuuming, a more robust, even acrobatic activity: the very opposite, I've often thought, of the obsessive activity of "creating art." And I enjoyed cooking with you, cooking under your easygoing tutelage. Just the two of us, you and me, preparing supper together in the kitchen. *This is how you set the timer for the oven. This is how you use the Mixmaster—see the speeds? This is how you whip egg whites. This is how you stir the macaroni to keep it from sticking in the pan. This is how you make a Jell-O mold. This is how you set the table, paper napkin neatly folded in two at the left side of the plates. This is how you smile when you don't especially feel like smiling, this is how you laugh when you don't especially feel like laughing, this is how you prepare a life.*

Item: a large fringed knitted afghan of orange, brown, white wool
Item: a knitted quilt, of many brightly colored wool squares, predominately red, yellow, green
Item: a pale peach-colored sweater coat with a matching belt
Item: a crimson sweater coat with matching belt
Item: a turquoise jacket, matching skirt (light fabric)
Item: a dove-gray jacket, matching skirt (wool)
Item: a dark red jacket, matching skirt (wool)
Item: a fine-knit pale pink jacket-sweater with matching belt
Item: a jacket of soft autumnal brown-floral check with a russet-red skirt (wool)

Item:   a camel's-hair skirt
Item:   a lilac silk dress, long-sleeved, with lace trim
Item:   a dark blue velour dress
Item:   a crimson velour dress
Item:   a long dark red cocktail skirt (light wool)
Item:   a long purple velvet skirt
Item:   a dark blue and black floral checked cocktail dress (silk)
Items: a white silk long-sleeved blouse (raw silk); a pumpkin-colored
        silk blouse; a pink blouse, ruffled; a raw silk deep-pink blouse with
        pleated bodice; a dark blue silk blouse, with tie; a maroon silk
        blouse, with tie; a dove-gray silk blouse with a fine-stitched collar;
        a dark gold blouse; plus shirts in cotton, rayon, flannel, some long-
        sleeved, some short.
Items: a black vest (rayon, wool), a beige vest (velour)
Items: summer dresses, summer skirts of various colors, fabrics

All of these, and more, you've made for me. How many hours of effort,
concentration, skill in these things so delicately fashioned, so exquisitely
sewed or knitted. What infinite patience in such creation. What love.
An inventory of our lives.

The old farmhouse was razed years ago, the very site of its foundation
filled with earth, all trace of its existence obliterated. Yet I see it clearly,
and the lilac tree that grew close beside the back door, a child-sized tree
into which I climbed in a crook of whose twisty sinewy limbs I sat, a
dreamy child given to solitude in places near the house, near you. Within
the range of your raised voice. *Joyce, Joy-ce!* Why is it always a misty-hazy
summer day, that peculiar translucence to the light that means the air is
heavy with moisture though the sky is cloudless, the sun prominent overhead? The house of my childhood is the house of recurring dreams yet
subtly altered, the rooms mysterious, their dimensions uncertain, always
there is a promise, alarming yet tantalizing, of rooms yet undiscovered,
through a back wall, in the attic perhaps, or the cellar, rooms yet to be
explored, beckoning. Your presence permeates the house, you are the
house, its mysterious infinite rooms. You are the hazy light, the rich
smell of damp earth, sunshine and grass, ripening pears. You are the
humming buzzing not-quite-audible sound of fields, of distance. I see
you pushing me on the swing, your hair reddish brown, you're wearing
a shirt and pale blue "pedal pushers," I'm a lanky child of nine or ten on
the swing Daddy made for me, the swing I loved, tough hemp rope hanging from a metal pipe secured between the branches of two tall trees in
the backyard. I see you pushing me, I see myself stretching my legs upward, straining higher, higher, squealing with childish excitement, fear-

less, reckless, flying into the sky. So often I have wanted to tell you how in patches of abrupt sunshine hundred of miles and thousands of days from home I am pulled back into that world as into the most seductive and most nourishing of dreams, I'm filled with a sense of wonder, and awe, and fear, regret for all that has passed, and for what must be surrendered, what we can imagine as life but cannot ever explain, cannot possibly put into words for all our effort, cannot utter aloud, dare not utter aloud, this succession of small particular moments like the movement of the red second hand on the General Electric clock, moments linked together as pearls are linked together to constitute a necklace, linked by tough, invisible string, the interior mystery. We were lucky, and we were happy, and I think we've always known.

# MAXINE HONG KINGSTON

## (1940– )

Born in Stockton, California, the eldest of six children, Kingston was raised by a powerful mother who had been a doctor and midwife in China, but who in the New World was relegated to the role of laundry worker and field hand. Similarly, her father had been a scholar in China; in California, he was also forced to survive by taking menial jobs. Kingston graduated from the University of California at Berkeley in 1962 and later taught there.

The struggle to escape an intricately threaded past and rigid social order, to balance the world of her Chinese home life with the demands of modern American existence, forms the center of *The Woman Warrior* (1976), a celebrated memoir by Kingston that crosses the normal boundaries of the genre as it blends fact and fiction, often drawing on myths and legends (such as that of the female warrior whose savage presence makes her a kind of protective goddess and guardian angel to a young woman oppressed by a potentially submissive role she does not wish to inherit).

The appearance of ghosts is a common theme in *The Woman Warrior*, with its subtitle—*Memoirs of a Girlhood among Ghosts*—serving to inform the reader that Kingston's world is one where the supernatural and the ordinary coexist. Like many female autobiographers before her, Kingston used the genre itself to affirm her identity. This was especially difficult for a woman born into the fiercely patriarchal culture of Chinese Americans. Her tale has similarities to that told by many second-generation Americans, but it has a particular cultural flavor here, shot through with folklore carried over from China to North America.

## FROM *The Woman Warrior*

My American life has been such a disappointment.

"I got straight A's, Mama."

"Let me tell you a true story about a girl who saved her village."

I could not figure out what was my village. And it was important that I do something big and fine, or else my parents would sell me when we made our way back to China. In China there were solutions for what to do with little girls who ate up food and threw tantrums. You can't eat straight A's.

When one of my parents or the emigrant villagers said, "Feeding girls is feeding cowbirds," I would thrash on the floor and scream so hard I couldn't talk. I couldn't stop.

"What's the matter with her?"

"I don't know. Bad, I guess. You know how girls are. 'There's no profit in raising girls. Better to raise geese than girls.' "

"I would hit her if she were mine. But then there's no use wasting all that discipline on a girl. 'When you raise girls, you're raising children for strangers.' "

"Stop that crying!" my mother would yell. "I'm going to hit you if you don't stop. Bad girl! Stop!" I'm going to remember never to hit or to scold my children for crying, I thought, because then they will only cry more.

"I'm not a bad girl," I would scream. "I'm not a bad girl. I'm not a bad girl." I might as well have said, "I'm not a girl."

"When you were little, all you had to say was 'I'm not a bad girl,' and you could make yourself cry," my mother says, talking-story about my childhood.

I minded that the emigrant villagers shook their heads at my sister and me. "One girl—and another girl," they said, and made our parents ashamed to take us out together. The good part about my brothers being born was that people stopped saying, "All girls," but I learned new grievances. "Did you roll an egg on *my* face like that when *I* was born?" "Did you have a full-month party for *me*?" "Did you turn on all the lights?" "Did you send *my* picture to Grandmother?" "Why not? Because I'm a girl? Is that why not?" "Why didn't you teach me English?" "You like having me beaten up at school, don't you?"

"She is very mean, isn't she?" the emigrant villagers would say.

"Come children. Hurry. Hurry. Who wants to go out with Great-Uncle?" On Saturday mornings my great-uncle, the ex-river pirate, did the shopping. "Get your coats, whoever's coming."

"I'm coming. I'm coming. Wait for me."

When he heard girls' voices, he turned on us and roared, "No girls!" and left my sisters and me hanging our coats back up, not looking at one another. The boys came back with candy and new toys. When they walked through Chinatown, the people must have said, "A boy—and another boy—and another boy!" At my great-uncle's funeral I secretly tested out feeling glad that he was dead—the six-foot bearish masculinity of him.

I went away to college—Berkeley in the sixties—and I studied, and I marched to change the world, but I did not turn into a boy. I would have liked to bring myself back as a boy for my parents to welcome with chickens and pigs. That was for my brother, who returned alive from Vietnam.

If I went to Vietnam, I would not come back; females desert families. It was said, "There is an outward tendency in females," which meant that I was getting straight A's for the good of my future husband's family, not my own. I did not plan ever to have a husband. I would show my mother and father and the nosey emigrant villagers that girls have no outward tendency. I stopped getting straight A's.

And all the time I was having to turn myself American-feminine, or no dates.

There is a Chinese word for the female *I*—which is "slave." Break the women with their own tongues!

I refused to cook. When I had to wash dishes, I would crack one or two. "Bad girl," my mother yelled, and sometimes that made me gloat rather than cry. Isn't a bad girl almost a boy?

"What do you want to be when you grow up, little girl?"

"A lumberjack in Oregon."

Even now, unless I'm happy, I burn the food when I cook. I do not feed people. I let the dirty dishes rot. I eat at other people's tables but won't invite them to mine, where the dishes are rotting.

If I could not-eat, perhaps I could make myself a warrior like the swordswoman who drives me. I will—I must—rise and plow the fields as soon as the baby comes out.

Once I get outside the house, what bird might call me; on what horse could I ride away? Marriage and childbirth strengthen the swordswoman, who is not a maid like Joan of Arc. Do the women's work; then do more work, which will become ours too. No husband of mine will say, "I could have been a drummer, but I had to think about the wife and kids. You know how it is." Nobody supports me at the expense of his own adventure. Then I get bitter: no one supports me; I am not loved enough to be supported. That I am not a burden has to compensate for the sad envy when I look at women loved enough to be supported. Even now China wraps double binds around my feet.

When urban renewal tore down my parents' laundry and paved over our slum for a parking lot, I only made up gun and knife fantasies and did nothing useful.

From the fairy tales, I've learned exactly who the enemy are. I easily recognize them—business-suited in their modern American executive guise, each boss two feet taller than I am and impossible to meet eye to eye.

I once worked at an art supply house that sold paints to artists. "Order more of that nigger yellow, willya?" the boss told me. "Bright, isn't it? Nigger yellow."

"I don't like that word," I had to say in my bad, small-person's voice that makes no impact. The boss never deigned to answer.

I also worked at a land developers' association. The building industry was planning a banquet for contractors, real estate dealers, and real estate editors. "Did you know the restaurant you chose for the banquet is being picketed by CORE and the NAACP?" I squeaked.

"Of course I know." The boss laughed. "That's why I chose it."

"I refuse to type these invitations," I whispered, voice unreliable.

He leaned back in his leather chair, his bossy stomach opulent. He picked up his calendar and slowly circled a date. "You will be paid up to here," he said. "We'll mail you the check."

If I took the sword, which my hate must surely have forged out of the air, and gutted him, I would put color and wrinkles into his shirt.

It's not just the stupid racists that I have to do something about, but the tyrants who for whatever reason can deny my family food and work. My job is my own only land.

To avenge my family, I'd have to storm across China to take back our farm from the Communists; I'd have to rage across the United States to take back the laundry in New York and the one in California. Nobody in history has conquered and united both North America and Asia. A descendant of eighty pole fighters, I ought to be able to set out confidently, march straight down our street, get going right now. There's work to do, ground to cover. Surely, the eighty pole fighters, though unseen, would follow me and lead me and protect me, as is the wont of ancestors.

Or it may well be that they're resting happily in China, their spirits dispersed among the real Chinese, and not nudging me at all with their poles. I mustn't feel bad that I haven't done as well as the swordswoman did; after all, no bird called me, no wise old people tutored me. I have no magic beads, no water gourd sight, no rabbit that will jump in the fire when I'm hungry. I dislike armies.

I've looked for the bird. I've seen clouds make pointed angel wings that stream past the sunset, but they shred into clouds. Once at a beach after a long hike I saw a seagull, tiny as an insect. But when I jumped up to tell what miracle I saw, before I could get the words out I understood that the bird was insect-size because it was far away. My brain had momentarily lost its depth perception. I was that eager to find an unusual bird.

The news from China has been confusing. It also had something to do with birds. I was nine years old when the letters made my parents, who are rocks, cry. My father screamed in his sleep. My mother wept and crumpled up the letters. She set fire to them page by page in the ashtray, but new letters came almost every day. The only letters they opened without fear were the ones with red borders, the holiday letters that mustn't carry bad news. The other letters said that my uncles were made to kneel on broken glass during their trials and had confessed to being landowners. They were all executed, and the aunt whose thumbs were twisted off drowned herself. Other aunts, mothers-in-law, and cousins disappeared; some suddenly began writing to us again from communes or from Hong Kong. They kept asking for money. The ones in communes got four ounces of fat and one cup of oil a week, they said, and had to work from 4 A.M. to 9 P.M. They had to learn to do dances waving red kerchiefs; they had to sing nonsense syllables. The Communists gave axes to the old ladies and said, "Go and kill yourself. You're useless." If we overseas Chinese would just send money to the Communist bank, our relatives said, they might get a percentage of it for themselves. The aunts in Hong Kong said to send money quickly; their children were begging on the sidewalks and mean people put dirt in their bowls.

When I dream that I am wire without flesh, there is a letter on blue airmail paper that floats above the night ocean between here and China. It must arrive safely or else my grandmother and I will lose each other.

My parents felt bad whether or not they sent money. Sometimes they got angry at their brothers and sisters for asking. And they would not simply ask but have to talk-story too. The revolutionaries had taken Fourth Aunt and Uncle's store, house, and lands. They attacked the house and killed the grandfather and oldest daughter. The grandmother escaped with the loose cash and did not return to help. Fourth Aunt picked up her sons, one under each arm, and hid in the pig house, where they slept that night in cotton clothes. The next day she found her husband, who had also miraculously escaped. The two of them collected twigs and yams to sell while their children begged. Each morning they tied the faggots on each other's back. Nobody bought from them. They ate the yams and some of the children's rice. Finally Fourth Aunt saw what was wrong. "We have to shout 'Fuel for sale' and 'Yams for sale,' " she said. "We can't just walk unobtrusively up and down the street." "You're right," said my uncle, but he was shy and walked in back of her. "Shout," my aunt ordered, but he could not. "They think we're carrying these sticks home for our own fire," she said. "Shout." They walked about miserably, silently, until sundown, neither of them able to advertise themselves. Fourth Aunt, an orphan since the age of ten, mean as my mother, threw her bundle down at his feet and scolded Fourth Uncle, "Starving to death, his wife and children starving to death, and he's too damned shy to raise his voice." She left him standing by himself and afraid to return empty-handed to her. He sat under a tree to think, when he spotted a pair of nesting doves. Dumping his bag of yams, he climbed up and caught the birds. That was when the Communists trapped him, in the tree. They criticized him for selfishly taking food for his own family and killed him, leaving his body in the tree as an example. They took the birds to a commune kitchen to be shared.

It is confusing that my family was not the poor to be championed. They were executed like the barons in the stories, when they were not barons. It is confusing that birds tricked us.

What fighting and killing I have seen have not been glorious but slum grubby. I fought the most during junior high school and always cried. Fights are confusing as to who has won. The corpses I've seen had been rolled and dumped, sad little dirty bodies covered with a police khaki blanket. My mother locked her children in the house so we couldn't look at dead slum people. But at news of a body, I would find a way to get out; I had to learn about dying if I wanted to become a swordswoman. Once there was an Asian man stabbed next door, words on cloth pinned to his corpse. When the police came around asking questions, my father said, "No read Japanese. Japanese words. Me Chinese."

I've also looked for old people who could be my gurus. A medium with red hair told me that a girl who died in a far country follows me wherever I go. This spirit can help me if I acknowledge her, she said. Between the head line and heart line in my right palm, she said, I have the mystic cross. I could become a medium myself. I don't want to be a medium. I don't want to be a crank taking "offerings" in a wicker plate from the frightened audience, who, one after another, asked the spirits how to raise rent money, how to cure their coughs and skin diseases, how to find a job. And martial arts are for unsure little boys kicking away under fluorescent lights.

I live now where there are Chinese and Japanese, but no emigrants from my own village looking at me as if I had failed them. Living among one's own emigrant villagers can give a good Chinese far from China glory and a place. "That old busboy is really a swordsman," we whisper when he goes by, "He's a swordsman who's killed fifty. He has a tong ax in his closet." But I am useless, one more girl who couldn't be sold. When I visit the family now, I wrap my American successes around me like a private shawl; I *am* worthy of eating the food. From afar I can believe my family loves me fundamentally. They only say, "When fishing for treasures in the flood, be careful not to pull in girls," because that is what one says about daughters. But I watched such words come out of my own mother's and father's mouths; I looked at their ink drawing of poor people snagging their neighbors' flotage with long flood hooks and pushing the girl babies on down the river. And I had to get out of hating range. I read in an anthropology book that Chinese say, "Girls are necessary too"; I have never heard the Chinese I know make this concession. Perhaps it was a saying in another village. I refuse to shy my way anymore through our Chinatown, which tasks me with the old sayings and the stories.

The swordswoman and I are not so dissimilar. May my people understand the resemblance soon so that I can return to them. What we have in common are the words at our backs. The ideographs for *revenge* are "report a crime" and "report to five families." The reporting is the vengeance—not the beheading, not the gutting, but the words. And I have so many words—"chink" words and "gook" words too—that they do not fit on my skin.

# SAMUEL F. PICKERING, JR.

## (1941– )

A prolific essayist whose autobiographical rambles have been collected in a dozen volumes over the past two decades, Pickering often writes about family and place. Born and raised in Nashville, Tennessee, he was educated at Sewanee, Cambridge University, and Princeton, where he received a Ph.D. in English literature. After a period of teaching at Dartmouth and traveling in the Middle East, Pickering settled into a professorship at the University of Connecticut.

As a critic in the *Smithsonian* once wrote, "Reading Pickering . . . is like taking a walk with your oldest, wittiest friend." Among Pickering's volumes of essays are *The Blue Caterpillar* and *Living to Prowl*, both published in 1997. The essay included here, "Son and Father," appeared in *The Right Distance* (1987).

## "Son and Father"

"The more I see of old people," my father said in the last letter he wrote me, "the greater my feeling is that the bulk of them should be destroyed."

"Not you," I thought when I read the letter, "at least not yet."

For years I imagined that I was different from, even better than, my father. Then one evening I walked into his room to ask about a book and found him asleep on his bed. Although I had seen him sleeping countless times, I was startled. His pajamas were inside out, as mine invariably are, and I noticed that we slept in the same position, left arm bent under the pillow, hand resting on the headboard; right leg pulled high toward the chest, and left thrust back and behind with the toes pointed, seemingly pushing us up and through the bed. Suddenly I realized Father and I were remarkably alike, the greatest difference being only the years that lay between us. At first I was upset. I had never consciously rejected family, but like the bottom of the bed against which I appeared to be pushing at night, my father and his life provided a firmness against which I could press and thrust myself off into something better.

As I looked at the old man lying on the bed, his thin ankles and knobby feet sticking out of his pajamas like fallen branches, I felt warm and comfortable. Instead of being parted by time and youth's false sense of superiority, we were bound together by patterns of living. His life could teach me about my future and my past, but, I thought, how little I knew about him. How well, I wondered, did any son know a father—particularly an only son, the recipient of so much love and attention that he worried about having a self and turned inward, often ignoring the parents about him and responding aggressively to concern with a petulant "leave me alone."

In his letter Father said that he and Mother disagreed about the past. "I tell her," he wrote, "that her recollections are remarkable, albeit not necessarily accurate." My memories of Father are ordinary and consist of a few glimpses: such things, for example, as his running alongside and steadying me when I learned to ride a bicycle and his fondness for chocolate. Mother liked chocolate too, and whenever Father was given a box of candy, he hid it in his closet where Mother could not reach it. The closet was dark, and as he grew older and his sight failed, he kept a flashlight in a shoebox. In a way, I suppose, past events resemble leaves on a tree. A multitude of little things make up life in full bloom, but as time passes, they fall and disappear without a trace. A few seeds blow into the garage, or memory, and get wedged behind spades, axes, and bits of lumber. If found or remembered, they are usually swept aside. Does it matter that Father rolled and chewed his tongue while telling a story or that after having drinks before dinner he would talk with his mouth full and embarrass me? Particular place is often necessary if the seeds lodged in memory are to sprout and grow green. Sadly, places vanish almost as quickly as leaves in October.

The Sulgrave Apartments, where I lived for eight years, and the long alley behind stretching through neighborhoods and drawing gangs of children to its treasures have vanished. When I was five I entered Ransome School. For the first months, Father walked all the way to school with me: along West End; across Fairfax, where Mr. Underwood the policeman waved at us; under the railway trestle and up Iroquois; past three small streets, Howell, Harding, and Sutherland. Slowly, as I grew surer, Father walked less of the distance with me; one morning he did not cross Sutherland; sometime later, he stopped at Harding, then Howell. Eventually he left me at the corner of Fairfax and I made my own way to Ransome under the watchful eye of Mr. Underwood. What I did when I was five, I can do no longer. The trestle and tracks with their caches of spikes, Iroquois, Harding, Howell, Sutherland, and Ransome itself, a scrapbook of small faces, have disappeared. All the associations that would freshen memory have been torn down for an interstate, going to Memphis or Birmingham, I am not sure which. Great washes of cars and trucks pour down ramps and rush through my old neighborhood. Traffic is so heavy that I rarely drive on West End, and when I must, the congestion makes me so nervous and the driving takes such concentration that I never think of Ransome, Mr. Underwood, or a little boy and a tall, thin man holding hands as they walked to school.

Father grew up in Carthage, Tennessee, a town of some two thousand people set high above the Cumberland River on red clay bluffs fifty-five miles east of Nashville. Since Carthage was the seat of Smith County, sidewalks ran along Main Street, and Father and his brother Coleman used to roller skate from their house to Grandfather's insurance agency, downtown over the bank. Life in Carthage was slow and from my perspective appealingly unsophisticated. On the front page of the weekly newspaper alongside an ad for Tabler's Buckeye Pile Ointment were excerpts from the sermons of the Reverend Sam P. Jones, the local Methodist minister. "I wouldn't give whiskey to a man until he had been dead for three days," Jones said. "When an old red-nosed politician gets so he isn't fit for anything else," he declared, "the Democrat Party send him to the Legislature." When a resident went away, a notice duly appeared on the front page. "D. B. Kittrell," the paper informed readers, "went to Nashville last week with about 40 fat hogs and has not yet returned."

Not much money was to be made in Carthage, and people lived comfortably. Every morning Grandpa Pickering walked downtown and had coffee with friends, after which he came home for breakfast. Only then did he go to his office. Grandfather's house was a white, clapboard, two-story Victorian with a bright tin roof. A porch ran around two sides; at one corner of the porch was a cupola; on top was a weathervane. Huge sugar maples stood in the front yard, and about the house were bushes of white hydrangeas; in spring they seemed like mountains of snow to me. In back of the house was the well, sheds, fields, a tobacco barn, and then a long slope down to the river. Bessie the maid cooked Grandfather's breakfast. She made wonderful shortcake, and whenever I was in Carthage, she gave me sweet coffee to drink. Bessie's first marriage had not been a success; James, her husband, was unfaithful, and one night when he returned from gallivanting, she shot him. Although James lost a leg, he did not die, and Grandfather got Bessie off with a suspended sentence. Later, after Grandfather's death, Bessie married a preacher and moved to Nashville. On Thanksgiving and Christmas she often came to our house and cooked. The last time she came she asked me if I was still catching bugs and snakes.

I don't remember any snakes in Carthage, and the only bugs I recall catching are tobacco worms. I took a bucket from the back porch and after walking down to the tobacco patch filled it with worms. Then I drew a big circle in the dust on the road and in the middle dumped the worms. The first worm to detach itself from the squirming green pile and to crawl out of the circle I returned to the bucket and carried back to the field. The others I crushed. Tobacco worms are big and fat, and if I lined up worm and sole just right and put my foot down quickly heel to toe, I could occasionally squirt a worm's innards two feet.

Grandfather died when I was young, and I have few memories of him. During the last months of his life, he was bedridden. Beside his bed was always a stack of flower magazines. All seemed to have been filled with pictures of zinnias, bright red and orange and occasionally purple zinnias, the only flower Father ever grew. Grandma Pickering outlived her husband, and I have clearer memories of her. She was strong-willed and opinionated, once confessing to me that she voted for Roosevelt the first time. In some ways Carthage may have been too small for her; she was interested in literature, and after her death I found scrapbooks filled with newspaper clippings, poems, reviews, and articles. Most of the poems were conventionally inspirational or religious and were typically entitled "Symbols of Victory" and "Earth Is Not Man's Abiding Place." Occasionally, though, I found other kinds of poetry, poems for the dreamer, not the moralist, poems which did not teach but which sketched moods. Pasted on the bottom of a page containing an article on "Shakespeare's Ideals of Womanhood" and a review of *For Whom the Bell Tolls* were two lines:

> I've reached the land of Golden-rod,
> Afar I see it wave and nod.

Much as it is hard to think of Father skating along the sidewalks of Carthage, so it is difficult to think of Grandma Pickering as a dreamer. Instead of bright, beckoning goldenrod, I associate her with a rusting red Studebaker. Almost until the day she died, she drove, and whenever she left Carthage for Nashville, the sheriff radioed ahead to the highway patrol, warning, "Mrs. Pickering's on the road." Along the way, patrolmen watched out for her, and when she reached Lebanon, one telephoned Father and then he and Mother and I drove out to a Stuckey's near the city limits and waited. After what seemed forever, she eventually appeared, inevitably with cars backed up behind her by the score, something that embarrassed me terribly.

Father told me little about his childhood in Carthage. I know only that he had an Airedale named Jerry; that on Rattlesnake Mountain, the hill just outside town, he once saw a huge snake; that he almost died after eating homemade strawberry ice cream at a birthday party; and that Lucy, the talented little girl next door, died from trichinosis. Report cards pro-

vided most of what I know about Father's childhood, and in Grandmother's scrapbooks I found several. Father entered first grade in 1915;
Lena Douglas taught him reading, spelling, writing, arithmetic, and language; his average for the year in all subjects was ninety-nine and a half;
for his first two years he was remarkably healthy and only missed three
days of school. The Carthage schools proved too easy, and for a year in
high school Father attended KMI, Kentucky Military Institute, a place
about which he never spoke except to say, "Children should not be sent
to military schools." After KMI Father returned to Carthage, skipped two
grades, graduated from high school, and in 1925 entered Vanderbilt.

One of my undergraduate nicknames was "Machine," and once or
twice when I walked into class intent on an A, people made whirring or
clanking sounds. Father, it seems, rarely attended class; every semester at
Vanderbilt his quality credits were reduced because of absences. In 1927
he skipped so many classes that the dean called him in for a conference.
Story had it that if the dean got out of his chair and put his arm around
a student's shoulders, the student was certain to be dismissed from school.
Midway through the interview, the dean rose and approached Father.
Swiftly Father got up and walked around the desk, and thus conversation
proceeded in circular fashion, with the dean lecturing and pursuing and
Father explaining and running. The result was probation, not expulsion.
It was a wonder that Father had enough energy to elude the dean, because he never attended gym class, a required course. Before graduation
one of Father's physician friends wrote a letter, urging the suspension of
the requirement in Father's case, explaining, "Pickering has a lameness
in his back." After reading the letter, the dean said, "No more lies, Pickering; out of my office." Father left silently and graduated.

Although Father majored in English during the great years of Vanderbilt's English department—the years of the Fugitives and the Agrari-
ans—his college experiences were personal, not intellectual. From
Carthage he brought with him the small-town world of particulars and
familial relationships. For him, as for me, reality was apparent and truth
clear, and he had little interest in hidden structures or highly wrought
reasoning, making Ds in psychology and philosophy. In later years he
rarely talked about classroom matters unless there was a story attached.
When John Crowe Ransom assigned two poems to be written, Father exhausted his inspiration and interest on the first and got his roommate,
who had a certain lyrical ability, to write the other. The week following
the assignment, Professor Ransom read Father's two poems to the class,
remarking, "It is inconceivable to me that the same person could have
written these poems."

"A matter of mood, Mr. Ransom," Father explained, and he was right.
Whose mood seems beside the point, especially when the nonpoetic

have to write verse. I inherited Father's poetic skills, and in sixth grade when I was assigned a poem, I turned to him and he turned out "The Zoo," a very effective piece for twelve-year-olds, featuring, among other animals, a polar bear with white hair, a chimp with a limp, an antelope on the end of a rope, and a turtle named Myrtle. Despite his lack of poetic talent, Father read a fair amount of poetry and was fond of quoting verse, particularly poems like Tennyson's "The Splendour Falls," the sounds of which rang cool and clear like bells. Father's favorite poet was Byron; and the dying gladiator was a companion of my childhood, while the Coliseum seemed to stand not in faraway Rome but just around the corner of another day. College, however, probably had little to do with Father's enjoyment of Byron; the source was closer to home, Father's grandfather William Blackstone Pickering. On a shelf in our library I found *The Works of Lord Byron in Verse and Prose*, published in Hartford in 1840 by Silas Andrus and Son. The book was inscribed "Wm. B. Pickering from his father." Over the inscription a child wrote, "Sammie F. Pickering." Under that in a firm, youthful handwriting was written "Samuel Pickering, Beta House, Vanderbilt University, 1926."

Often holding three jobs at once, Father worked his way through Vanderbilt and simply did not have much time for classes. Yet he was always a reading man, and at times I suspected that there was nothing he had not read. Years later at his office, he kept books in the top drawer of his desk. When business was slow, he pulled the drawer out slightly, and after placing a pad and pencil in front of himself for appearances, he read. Despite the college jobs, such a reader should have done better than the Bs, Cs, and Ds Father made in English. In part the small-town world of Carthage may have been responsible for his performance. Carthage was a world of particulars, not abstractions, a place in which Tabler's Buckeye Pile Ointment "Cures Nothing but Piles," a town in which Mrs. Polk, a neighbor, could burst into Grandfather's kitchen crying that her daughter Mary, who had gone to Nashville, was "ruined."

"Oh, Lord," Grandfather exclaimed, "was she taken advantage of?"

"Yes," Mrs. Polk answered, "she had her hair bobbed."

At Vanderbilt during the 1920s literary criticism was shifting from the personal and anecdotal to the intellectual and the abstract. Instead of explaining ordinary life, it began to create an extraordinary world of thought far from piles and bobbed hair. For Father such a shift led to boredom and the conviction that although literary criticism might entertain some people, it was ultimately insignificant. In the sixty years that have passed since Father entered Vanderbilt, criticism has become more rarefied, and the result is, as a friend and critic wrote me, "we write books that even our mothers won't read."

Carthage influenced more than Father's school work; it determined the course of his career. Although Grandmother dreamed of the land of goldenrod, she stayed in Carthage and joined the Eastern Star. After graduating from Vanderbilt in 1929, Father went to work in the personnel department of the Travelers Insurance Company. Years later, he told me that he had made a mistake. "I did what my father did," he said; "I should have done something different, even run off to sea." An old man's thoughts often wander far from the path trod by the young man, and running away to sea is only accomplished in books and dreamed about when the house is quiet and the children asleep. For his insurance business, Grandfather traveled about Smith County in a buggy; occasionally he took the train to Nashville. Once when he was trying to settle a claim over a mule which had been struck by lightning (no mule ever died a natural death in Tennessee; mules were the lightning rods of the animal world), he stayed overnight at Chestnut Mound with Miss Fanny and Godkin Hayes. The next morning after breakfast, when he was climbing into his buggy, Miss Fanny asked Grandfather if he ever went to Difficult Creek, Tennessee, saying she had heard he was quite a traveler and had been to Nashville.

"Yes, ma'am," Grandfather answered. "I go there right much."

"Well, the next time you go," Miss Fanny said, "will you please say hello to Henry McCracken; he's my brother and I haven't seen him in over twenty years."

"What!" my grandfather exclaimed; "Difficult Creek is only twelve miles away, just on the other side of the Caney Fork River. Roane's Ferry will take you across in eight minutes."

"Oh, Mr. Sam," Miss Fanny answered wistfully, "I do want to see my brother, but I just can't bring myself to cross the great Caney Fork River."

Father crossed the Caney Fork, but he didn't travel far. After working in Washington and Richmond, he was sent to Nashville in the late thirties. From that time on he refused to be transferred. Beyond Difficult Creek lay the little town of Defeated Creek, and for most of his life Father was content to meander through a small circle of miles and visit with the Miss Fannys he met. Personnel, however, may have been too easy for him. Reading books in the office, he became a character, albeit a competent one. "He was a bumblebee," a man told me; "he shouldn't have been able to fly, but he did. What's more he did things that couldn't be done." By the 1960s, though, the topography of Father's world changed. The wild growth of wealth changed the course of Defeated Creek, making it swing closer to home. People suddenly became not who they knew or what they were but how much money they made. Strangers appeared, and instead of being identified by a rich string of anecdotes, they became bank accounts or corporations. It was almost impossible not to be swept up by the wash of money, and as Father's friends grew wealthy

and began to possess the glittering goods of the world and to take trips beyond simple goldenrod to lands where orchids hung heavy from trees and
butterflies bigger than fans waved in the sun, Father became envious. Although he occasionally criticized the affluence of certain groups—physicians, for example—he was not resentful. What troubled him most, I
think, was how wealth changed conversation. Despite his wide reading,
there was little room for him or Miss Fanny in talk about Bali or Borneo.

Disregard for possessions tempered Father's resentment of wealth. Although he liked shoes, both good and bad, and as a handsome man was
vain on occasions like Christmas, when he wore a red vest, clothes, for
example, mattered little to him. Outside the office he wore khaki trousers
and checkered shirts that he bought at Sears. So long as the interior of
the house was tasteful, something he knew Mother managed well, Father
paid no attention to it. If a visitor admired something, Father was likely
to offer it to him, especially, it seemed, if it was a family piece: an envelope of Confederate money or a Bible published in 1726 and listing forgotten generations of ancestors. As a child, I learned to hide things.
When I found a box of old letters in a storeroom at Aunt Lula's house, I
hid them in the attic. When the day came, as I knew it would, when Father asked for them, saying he had a friend who would like to have them,
I lied and said that I lost them. Of course saving everything was beyond
me, and I once resented his forays through my things. Even today when
I want a good tricycle for my children, I resent his giving away the English trike that Mother's father bought me in New York. Now, though, I
understand Father's desire to rid himself of possessions. I behave similarly. I wear Sears trousers and shirts from J. C. Penney's. I have turned
down positions that would greatly increase my salary because I like the
little out-of-the-way place where I live. I, too, alas, give away possessions.
"You are the only teacher I have ever met," a graduate student told me
recently, "who has two offices and not a single book." I don't have any
books because I have given them away, out of, I think, the same compulsion that led Father to give away things and that kept him from becoming wealthy: the desire to keep life as clean and as simple as possible.

Wealth clutters life, bringing not simply possessions but temptation.
Money lures one from the straight and clear into the darkly complex.
The sidewalks in Carthage ran in narrow lines to the courthouse. Skating along them, a boy was always aware of where he was: in front of the
Reeds' house, then the Ligons', the Fishers', the McGinnises', and then
by the drugstore, the five and ten, King's barbershop, and finally the
bank and post office. Wealth bends lines and makes it difficult for even
the most adept skater to roll through life without losing his way or falling
into the dirt. Instead of enriching, wealth often lessens life. At least that's
the way I think Father thought, for he spurned every chance to become

wealthy. For some twenty years he managed the affairs of his Aunt Lula, Grandmother's widowed sister. Father being her nearest relative, Aunt Lula called upon him whenever anything went wrong. For three summers in a row, Aunt Lula fell ill during Father's two-week summer vacation, and we hurried back to Nashville from the beach to put her in the hospital. Aunt Lula owned a farm, 750 acres of land just outside Nashville in Williamson County. The farm had been in the family for generations, and when I came home from college at Christmas, I spent mornings roaming over it rabbit hunting.

Aunt Lula did not have a will, and when Father's closest friend, a lawyer, learned this, he urged Father to let him draw one up for her. "For God's sakes, Sam," he said; "you have nursed her for years. She would want you to have the farm. I will make out the will tonight and you have her sign it tomorrow." Father demurred, and when Aunt Lula died, two relatives who had never met her shared the estate. Father put the land up for sale and received a bid of seventy-five thousand dollars.

"Borrow the money," Mother advised, "and buy the land yourself. Nashville is growing by leaps and bounds, and the farm is worth much more."

"That would not be right," Father answered, and the land was sold. Six years later it was resold for over a million dollars. Father kept the lines of his life straight and his temptations few, and I admire him for it; yes at night when I think about the three teaching jobs I have taken this summer so the house can be painted and dead oaks felled in the yard, I sometimes wish he had not sold the farm. This is not to say that Father did not understand the power of money. He thought it important for other people and urged me to make the most of my chances, citing his younger brother Coleman as a warning. According to Father, Coleman was the talented Pickering and could have done practically anything; yet, Father recounted, he refused to grasp opportunities. Satisfied to live simply, Coleman was in truth Father's brother, a man wary of complexity, determined to remain independent and free from entangling responsibilities.

After forty most people I know realize that their actions and thoughts are inconsistent. Worried about gypsy moths, a child's stuttering, or slow-running drains, they have little time for principle and not simply neglect but recognize and are comfortable with the discrepancy between words and deeds. To some extent Father's attitude toward wealth reflected this state of mind. Behind his behavior, however, also lay the perennial conflict between the particular and the abstract or the general. From infancy through school people are taught the value of general truths or principles, the sanctity, for example, of honor and truth itself. As one grows older and attempts to apply principles to real human beings, one learns that rules are cruelly narrow and, instead of bettering life, often lead to unhappiness. The sense of principle or belief in general truth is so deeply ingrained, however, that one rarely repudiates it. Instead, one continues to pay lip service to it and actually believe in its value while never applying it to particular individuals. Thus during the turmoil over integration in Nashville during the 1950s and early '60s, Father sounded harshly conservative. One day, though, while he and Mother and I were walking along Church Street, we came upon four toughs, or hoods as they were then called, harassing a black woman. "You there," Father bellowed, all 136 pounds of him swelling with his voice; "who do you think you are?" Then as mother and I wilted into a doorway, he grabbed the biggest tough and, shaking him, said, "Apologize to this lady. This is Tennessee, and people behave here."

"Yes, sir, yes, sir," the man responded meekly and apologized.

Father then turned to the woman, and while the toughs scurried away, took off his hat and said, "Ma'am, I am sorry for what happened. You are probably walking to the bus stop; if you don't mind, my wife and I and our son would like to walk with you."

Although Father expounded political and moral generalities during the isolation of dinner, he never applied them to the hurly-burly of his friends' lives. He delighted in people too much to categorize and thus limit his enjoyment of them. Not long after the incident on Church Street, Father was invited to join the Klan. Around ten or eleven each morning, a man appeared outside the Travelers building, selling doughnuts and sweet rolls. As could be expected from a man who did not have to work too hard and who loved candy, Father always bought a doughnut and a cup of coffee and then chatted a bit. On this occasion, the man said, "Mr. Pickering, I have known you for some time, and you seem a right thinking man. This Friday there is going to be a meeting of the Klan at Nolensville, and I'd like for you to attend and become a member."

"That's mighty nice of you to invite me," Father replied, "but I believe I will just continue to vote Republican."

As could be expected, Father was inconsistent toward me. Of things he thought comparatively unimportant—sports, for example—he rarely said much, except to moan about the Vanderbilt football team. When I was in high school, he picked me up after football practice, and unlike some boys' fathers, who filmed practices, had conferences with the coaches, and caused their sons untold misery, Father never got in the way. About social matters he behaved differently, urging me to do the things he never did—join service clubs, for example. "They will help your career," he explained. When he heard me taking a political stance that was not generally accepted and thereby safe, he intervened. Ten years ago I spent three months in the Soviet Union. On my return people often asked me questions; once during a discussion with businessmen Father overheard me say something "risky." "Pay no attention to my son," he interrupted; "he has been brainwashed." That ended the conversation.

Of Father's courtship of Mother, I know and want to know little. Toward the end of his life, he refused to tell me family stories, saying, "You will publish them." Quite right—I would publish almost anything except an account of his and Mother's love affair. Theirs was a good and typical marriage with much happiness and sadness during the early and middle years and with many operations at the end. They were very different, but they stumbled along in comparative harmony.

"When I first met him," Mother told me; "I thought him the damnedest little pissant."

"Your mother," Father often said, "does not appreciate my sense of humor." That was a loss, because laughing was important to Father, and for much of his life, he played practical jokes. Practical jokes are an almost implicit recognition of the foolishness of man's endeavors. Involving actual individuals rather than comparative abstractions like word play, for example, such humor flourishes in stable communities in which people's positions remain relatively constant and clearly defined. The popularity of practical jokes waned as the South grew wealthy. Money undermined community both by making people more mobile and by changing the terms by which position was defined. As people became financial accomplishments, not neighbors, cousins, sons, and daughters, they took themselves more seriously. When they, rather than a web of relationships over which they had comparatively little control, determined what they were, their actions grew increasingly significant. No more could the practical joker be seen as a friend; no more was his laughter benign, even fond. Instead, threatening the basis of identity by mocking, he undermined society. By the late 1960s Father had stopped playing practical jokes; before then, though, the going was good.

After selling some rocky, farmed-out land to a company that wanted to construct a shopping center, one of Father's acquaintances, Tuck Gobbett, built a twenty-room house outside Nashville. Known locally as the Taj Mahal, the house had everything: sauna bath, swimming pool, Japanese shoji screens around the garage, and even a pond with swans purchased from a New York dealer. In its garishness the house was marvelous, and Father enjoyed it, saying only, "The birds were a mistake. As soon as snapping turtles find the pond, it's good-bye swans." He was right; two years later the turtles came, and the swans disappeared. Father decided Gobbett went too far, however, when he got rid of the off-brand beagles he had always owned and bought an Afghan hound. The dog had a royal pedigree, and when Gobbett advertised in a kennel-club magazine that the dog was standing at stud, Father saw his chance. "Why is it," he asked me years later, "that mongrel people always want pure-bred dogs." Father then read about Afghans, learning quite a bit about blood lines. Able to disguise his voice, he telephoned Gobbett, explaining that he lived in Birmingham and was the owner of a champion bitch. He had, he said, seen the advertisement in the kennel-club magazine and wondered about the possibility of breeding the animals. Of course, he continued, he would first have to scrutinize the pedigree of Gobbett's dog. After Gobbett detailed his dog's ancestry, Father then supplied that of the bitch, which, not surprisingly, came from the best Afghan stock in the nation. Saying he would need time to investigate the Gobbetts' dog, Father hung up, promising to call within a week. During the week Father visited Gobbett. When asked about news, Gobbett excitedly described the telephone call, saying the bitch had "an absolutely first-class pedigree" and the puppies would be worth a thousand dollars apiece.

The next week Father telephoned, saying he looked into the dog and thought the pedigree would do. Although the owner of the bitch usually received all the puppies except for one from a breeding, Father said he did not want a single puppy. After this remark, he said he had pressing business and would call the following week to make arrangements for the mating. Gobbett was ebullient. "What fools there are in the world," he said; "there is money to be made in these dogs. The puppies will make me a man to be reckoned with in Afghan circles." As could be expected, completing the arrangements was not easy, but after a month and a half of conversations, the date and place were set. Then at the end of the final telephone call, almost as an afterthought, Father said, "There is just one thing though."

"What's that?" Gobbett asked.

"Oh, nothing important," Father said; "my dog has been spayed, but I don't suppose that will make a difference."

Father's humor was rarely bawdy, and the jokes he told were usually stories, gentle tales about foolishness. My favorite, one that I have often told, was called "Edgar the Cat." Two bachelor brothers, Herbert and James, lived with their mother and James's cat Edgar in a little town not unlike Carthage. James was particularly attached to Edgar, and when he had to spend several days in Nashville having work done on his teeth, he left Herbert meticulous instructions about Edgar. At the end of his first day away from home, James telephoned Herbert. "Herbert," he said, "how is Edgar?"

"Edgar is dead," Herbert answered immediately.

There was a pause; then James said, "Herbert, you are terribly insensitive. You know how close I was to Edgar and you should have broken the news to me slowly."

"How?" Herbert said.

"Well," James said, "when I asked about Edgar tonight, you should have said 'Edgar's on the roof, but I have called the fire department to get him down.'"

"Is that so?" said Herbert.

"Yes," James answered, "and tomorrow when I called you could have said the firemen were having trouble getting Edgar down but you were hopeful they would succeed. Then when I called the third time you could have told me that the firemen had done their best but unfortunately Edgar had fallen off the roof and was at the veterinarian's, where he was receiving fine treatment. Then when I called the last time you could have said that although everything humanly possible had been done for Edgar he had died. That's the way a sensitive man would have told me about Edgar. And, oh, before I forget," James added, "how is mother?"

"Uh," Herbert said, pausing for a moment, "she's on the roof."

There was an innocence in Father's humor, perhaps a sign of softness, something that contributed to his not grabbing Aunt Lula's farm. In the eighteenth and early nineteenth centuries, Pickerings were Quakers and, so far as I can tell, gentle people who did not struggle or rage against life but who took things as they came, people who copied poems into family Bibles while recording the deaths of children. When seven-year-old Marthelia died in 1823, her father wrote:

> When the Icy hand of death
> his sabre drew!
> To cut down the budding
> rose of morn!!
> He held his favorite motto
> full in view—
> The fairest Bud must the
> tomb adorn!!!

In general Pickerings lived quiet lives, cultivating their few acres and avoiding the larger world with its abstractions of honor, service, and patriotism. For them country meant the counties in which they lived, not the imperial nation. Years ago I knew John Kennedy had things backwards when he said, "Ask not what your country can do for you, but what you can do for your country." The great excuse for country, with its borders dividing brothers, was that it bettered the life of the individual.

With the exception of the Civil War, the struggles of the nation have not touched us. Coming of age between battles, few Pickerings have looked at the dark side of man's heart. Perhaps because of this, we are soft and, in our desires, subconscious or conscious, to remain free, have become evasive. Few things are simple, though, and this very evasiveness may be a sign of a shrewd or even tough vitality. Aware that those who respond to challenges and fight for a cause or success often are ground under, we have learned to live unobtrusively and blossom low to the ground and out of sight. Even when a Pickering does respond to a call, it's usually not for him. In 1942 the navy rejected Father's application for Officers' Training School because he was too thin. In 1944 Father was drafted; two days before he was slated to leave for training camp and after a series of farewell parties, he received a telegram instructing him not to report, explaining that he was too thin.

Not long ago my daughter Eliza McClarin Pickering was born. She was born, fittingly enough, in a hospital in a relatively small town. For four days she was the only baby in the maternity ward, and the nurses let me wander in and out at my convenience. With little to do, the nurses drank coffee, ate doughnuts, and talked. One night as I stood looking at Eliza in her crib, I overheard a conversation at the nurses' station around the corner. "I have worked at four hospitals," one nurse declared confidentially, "but this is the worst for poking I have ever seen. There's Shirley," she said, warming to the subject, "she runs out to the parking lot and gets poked every chance she gets. And Kate, there's not a bed on the third floor that she hasn't been poked in." Like Homer's account of those slain at the sack of Troy, the nurse's list of fallen was long and colorful. During the recital, the second nurse was silent. Finally, though, she spoke. "My word," she said in mild astonishment, "it's just a whirlwind of festivities."

Although few strong breezes blow through the lives of Pickerings, there are festivities, not shining affairs strung with bright lights but quiet events lit by words. After being married on my grandfather's farm in Hanover, Virginia, Father and Mother spent their first night together in the Jefferson Hotel in Richmond. Early the next morning they started for Nashville in Father's Ford coupe. On the outskirts of Richmond, they stopped for gas, and Mother bought a newspaper to look at the wedding pictures. She spread the paper out on the front seat and was looking at the pictures with Father when the man who was cleaning the windshield spoke up, saying, "It's a pity about that wedding. I feel so sorry for the girl."

"What do you mean," Father answered, jumping in before Mother could respond.

"Well," the man said, "she didn't marry the man she wanted to. She was in love with a poor insurance man but her father made her marry a rich fellow."

"Who told you that?" Father asked.

"Oh," the man answered, "a colored preacher that comes through here told me all about it. He preaches up in Hanover and some of the members of his congregation work at her father's farm."

"Hmmm," Father said, "I hate to ruin your story, but look at the picture of the groom, and then look at me. This," he said gesturing toward Mother after the man had a good look, "is that unfortunate girl, and I am the poor insurance man. The preacher was wrong; sometimes in life poor folks carry off the prizes." And that's what Father did in a quiet way all his days. No prize of his was mentioned in an obituary; his name was not associated with any accomplishment; yet in the few acres he tilled and even beyond, at least as far as Carthage, he was known.

While at Vanderbilt, Father bought an old car. On a trip to Carthage it broke down, and, having to hurry back to Nashville to take an examination, one of the few times he attended class, Father left the car in Carthage and took the train. For a modest fee George Jackson, a black man, agreed to drive the car to Nashville once it was repaired. Father wrote out careful instructions and drew a map. Alas, George lost both, but this did not deter him. On arriving in Nashville, he stopped in a residential area, went up to a house, and asked where "young Mr. Samuel Pickering" lived. Amazingly, the people in the house knew Father. They gave George clear directions, and he delivered the car. When Father learned that the map had gone astray and George had lost his way, he asked him how he knew whom to ask for instructions. "Mister Sam," George answered, "everybody knows you." The one time Father told this story, he laughed, then said, "What a world we have lost. Not a better world," he added, "but a different one. At times I miss it." Not, old man, so much as I miss you—not so much as I miss you.

# ERICA JONG
## (1942– )

"The older we get, the more Jewish we become in my family," writes Erica Jong in her vivid memoir, *Fear of Fifty* (1994). Jong's title, of course, echoes that of her most widely read novel, *Fear of Flying*, which was published in 1973 to worldwide acclaim. That novel was a bulletin from the front lines of the women's movement. Her later novels include *Fanny: Being the True History of the Adventures of Fanny Hackabout-Jones* (1980), *Any Woman's Blues* (1990), and *Inventing Memory: A Novel of Mothers and Daughters* (1997)—all of them featuring intelligent, high-energy, robustly sexual women.

Jong began her career as a poet, with *Fruits & Vegetables* (1971), and has continued to write and publish poetry, including a volume of selected poems in 1991 called *Becoming Light*.

## FROM *Fear of Fifty*

### HOW I GOT TO BE JEWISH

> To be a Jew in the twentieth century
> Is to be offered a gift.
>
> —Muriel Rukeyser, "Letter to the Front"

> News of America travelled quickly around the European shtetls. Word was that even if the streets of the "Golden Land" weren't paved with gold, at least a Jew had a chance.
>
> —Jeff Kisseloff, *You Must Remember This*

The older we get, the more Jewish we become in my family. My mother's father declared himself an atheist in his communist youth, so we never belonged to a synagogue or had bat mitzvahs. But we wind up in Hebrew homes for the aged and in cemeteries with Hebrew letters over the gates. Thus does our heritage claim us—even in America, our promised land. In my family, if you're still protesting that you're Unitarian, you're just not *old* enough. (I refer, of course, to one of my ex-husbands, who, having married a shiksa, worships at the local Unitarian church. That will change, I predict.)

My father, on the other hand, sends money to Israel and carries around a card that supposedly will expedite his admission to Mount Sinai Hospital and, after that, heaven, identifying him as a Big Donor. This is the sort of thing he would have done riffs on in his vaudeville days. Now Molly does those riffs. The young are cruel. They *have* to be to supplant the old. The old are such a burden, so territorial, so inclined to hold on to their money. The young have to be tough to grow up at all.

After all, what does the ritual of circumcision say to a Jewish son? *"Watch out. Next time I'll cut off the whole thing."* So Jewish boys are horny, but also full of fear about whether their cocks will survive their horniness. Alexander Portnoy is the archetypal good Jewish boy. The good Jewish boy and the bad Jewish boy inhabit the same skin—if not the same foreskin. Jewish girls are luckier. Their sexuality is less damaged—whatever those jokes about dropping emery boards may imply. Girls are allowed to be sexual as long as they keep it inside the family. Marriage is sacred as long as you marry an Oedipal stand-in. Jewish adultery is an oxymoron. We read Updike for that. Jewish men who cheat end up like Sol Wachtler or Woody Allen. In big trouble. Even Jewish lesbians are required to have silverware and bone china from Tiffany's. Jewish lesbians are required to fall in love with women who remind them of their mothers. And, in today's feminist times, are doctors or lawyers.

How did I get to be Jewish? I with no religious training? Jews are made by the existence of anti-Semitism—or so said Jean-Paul Sartre, who knew. And despite myths to the contrary, there is *plenty* of anti-Semitism in America (otherwise we'd be saying "Next year in Oyster Bay" or "Grosse Pointe" instead of "Next year in Jerusalem"). But American anti-Semitism takes the clever form of class snobbery. Let me show you what I mean.

We say that America is a classless society, but really it is not. It's just that our class distinctions are so much subtler than those of other countries that sometimes we don't even see them as class distinctions. They are uniquely American class distinctions and they follow us all our lives. We go happily into the Hebrew Home for the Aged, having learned that where aging and death are concerned, only our own kind *want* us. When we're young and cute, we can hang out with goyim—but as the sun goes down, we revert to knishes and *knaydlach*. We do mitzvahs—of the sort that I have done by getting my aunt into the Hebrew Home. We suddenly remember that—like "community service" in high school—we have to rack up 613 mitzvahs to be considered good Jews. At fifty, we take those mitzvahs seriously—unlike community service in high school. How much time, after all, do we have? Not much. Better get busy—women especially. We're not exactly shoo-ins. The Orthodox rabbis still won't let us pray at the Wailing Wall, so why do we assume they'll let us into that obscure heaven of the Jews? If men need 613 mitzvahs, I figure women need 1,839.

When I was growing up in a New York that seemed dominated by Jews whose parents or grandparents had fled from Europe, I never consciously thought about Jewishness. Or about class. And yet invisible barriers ruled my life—barriers that still stand.

Even in childhood I knew that my best friend, Glenda Glascock, who was Episcopalian and went to private school, was considered classier than me. We lived in the same gloomy Gothic apartment house near Central Park West. We both had parents who were artists. But Glenda's name ended with *cock* and mine did not. I knew that names ending in *cock* were intrinsically classier.

What was my name anyway?

My father was born Weisman and became Mann. My mother was called Yehuda by her Russian Jewish parents when she was born in England, but the intransigent Englishman in the registry office had changed it first to Judith and then to Edith ("good English names")—leaving the resultant impression that Jews were not even allowed to keep their own names. The dominant culture around our (mental) ghetto required names that did not *sound* Jewish or foreign. That left a strong impression too.

There were categories of Americans in our supposedly egalitarian country, and I did not belong to the better (as in "better dresses") category. Glenda did. Her last name bespoke this. Even her nickname— Jewish girls did not have nicknames like Glenni then—bespoke this. And yet we were close as twins, best buddies, in and out of each other's apartments—until we took a bath together one day and she accused me of making peepee in the bathwater because that was "what Jews did." I was outraged, having done no such thing. (Unless my memory censors.)

"Who says they do that?"

"My mother," said Glenni confidently.

So I reported this conversation to my parents and grandparents, and mysteriously my friendship with Glenni cooled.

She went off to private school. I did not. I was in some "Intellectually Gifted Program" at P.S. 87, at Seventy-seventh Street and Amsterdam Avenue—a great Victorian pile in those days, with girls' and boys' entrances. There I discovered other class stratifications. The closer you lived to Central Park West and the "better" your building, the more classy you were. Now I had status. Below me were poorer Jewish kids whose parents had fled the Holocaust and who lived in lesser buildings further west, Irish kids who lived in tenements on side streets, and the first sprinkling of Puerto Rican kids to arrive in New York. They lived in other tenements, on West Side Storyish side streets. In the forties, New York was far from being racially integrated. I did not meet black kids from Harlem until I went to the High School of Music and Art, where talent, not neighborhood, was the qualification. The only African-Americans we met—called Negroes then—were servants. In childhood, my world was Jewish, Irish, Hispanic—with Jews lording it over everyone else.

The WASP kids were, by this time, off in private school, meeting their own kind so they could go to Yale, run the CIA, and rule the world (like George and Barbara Bush). Jewish kids did not go to private school in *that* New York—unless they were superrich, had disciplinary problems, or were Orthodox.

I figured out pretty soon that in my school I was high class, but that in the world I was not. The kids on television shows and in reading primers did not have names like Weisman, Rabinowitz, Plotkin, Ratner, or Kisselgoff. Certainly not Gonzales or O'Shea. There was another America out there in televisionland and we were not part of it. In that other America, girls were named things like Gidget and boys were named things like Beaver Cleaver. Our world was not represented—except when the credits rolled by.

Kept out of this *proper* America, we learned to control it by reinventing it (or representing it—as in agent). Some of our parents already did this as actors, producers, or writers, so we knew this was a possible path for us. Others were businessmen, or artists turned businessmen—like my father. The point was we were outsiders longing to be insiders. In those days, we knew that Princeton and Yale might not want us—unless we were rich enough to buy the school. We knew our initials were MCA, not CIA. We knew we were not born into the ruling class, so we invented our own ruling class. Mike Ovitz, not George Bush. Swiftly Lazar, not Bill Clinton. Mort Janklow, not Al Gore.

How much the world has changed since the forties! And how *little!* Except for Henry Kissinger, who has changed these laws of class and caste? Not even Mike Ovitz. What you see your parents do is what you think *you* can do. So are we defined, designed. Since my father was a songwriter-musician turned importer, my grandfather a portrait painter, my mother a housewife and portrait painter, I just *assumed* that I would do something creative. I also just *assumed* that I would graduate from college, and live in a "good building" forever. I also assumed that I would never turn out to be anything like those American families I saw on TV.

My family was fiercely proud to be Jewish, but not religious—unless our religion was buying new English Mary Janes at Saks and English leather leggings and velvet-collared chesterfield coats at De Pinna. We were dressed like little English princesses, and I understood that this was the class to which we aspired.

Dress tells you everything about aspiration. I hated the damned leather leggings but had to wear them because Princesses Elizabeth and Margaret did. How did *they* get to be princesses of the Jews? Better not ask. It was tacitly understood, just as it was understood that Glascock was a better name than Weisman (or even Mann).

I smile writing all this. I am trying (clumsily, I fear) to reenter that world of 1940s New York with its "air-cooled" movie palaces (complete with towering matrons and wrapper-strewn children's sections), its striped awnings on apartment buildings in summer, its dime bus fares, its telephone exchanges (I was ENdicott 2), its candy stores and soda fountains, its marble lunch counters that sold the most delicious bacon, lettuce, and tomato sandwiches and fresh-dipped ice cream cones.

Gone, gone forever. But just as sunlight on a series of paving stones or the taste of tea-soaked cake returned Proust* to his halcyon childhood, I sometimes stop on a street corner in New York and am taken back to the forties. The smells do it. The mouths of the subway stations still, on occasion, blow a blast of cotton candy–bubble gum breath, mixed with sweat and popcorn, with piss and (its precursor) beer, and, inhaling deeply, I am taken back to being six years old, standing in the subway, staring at a forest of knees. In childhood, you feel you'll never grow up. And the world will always be incomprehensible. First you are all mouth, then you have a name, then you are a member of a family, then you begin to ask the hard questions about better/worse that are the beginning of class consciousness. Human beings are naturally hierarchical beasts. Democracy is not their native religion.

It was in junior high that my world opened up beyond Seventy-seventh Street and the West Side. Because my parents and I were both terrified of the violence of the local junior high, I went to private school—a deliciously comic place where the paying students were mostly Park Avenue Jews and the scholarship students mostly WASPs from Washington Heights whose parents were professors, clergy, missionaries.

The teachers were genteel and WASPy, like the scholarship students, and they had proper American-sounding names like the TV people. The school had been started by two redoubtable New England ladies named Miss Birch and Miss Wathen, who were probably lovers—but in those days we called them spinsters. One of them looked like Gertrude Stein, the other like Alice B. Toklas. They pronounced "shirt" as if it had three

*Note to reviewer: I'm not comparing myself to Proust, but am I allowed to have read him?

*i*'s in the middle, and they pronounced "poetry" as if it were poy-et-try (*poy* rhyming with *goy*). I knew this was classy. I knew this was WASP.

At Birch-Wathen, most of the Jewish kids were wealthier than I. They lived on the East Side in apartments hung with expensive art and some of them had German names. They went to Temple Emanu-El—my nephews now call it Temple Episco-Pal—and took dancing and deportment (what an old-fashioned word!) at Viola Wolf's. Again my sense of class was up for grabs. With my Russian grandparents and my West Side bohemian home, I didn't fit in with these kids either. And the scholarship kids all stuck together. I thought them snotty—though now I realize they must have been scared to death. The paying students got bigger allowances—and some of them came to school in chauffeured Cadillacs, Lincolns, or Rollses. That must have seemed daunting to kids who rode the subway. It seemed daunting to me.

Cliques splintered us. The Park Avenue kids stuck with their own kind. The scholarship kids did the same.

I floated between the two groups, never knowing where I belonged, now shoplifting at Saks with the rich kids (the richer the kids, I learned, the more they shoplifted), now wandering up to Columbia with the scholarship kids (whose parents were professors). I felt I belonged nowhere. Ashamed that my father was a businessman, I used to wish he were a professor. If you couldn't have a name that ended with *cock*, or an apartment on Fifth or Park, you ought to have a Ph.D. at least.

When high school began, I joined still another new world—a world that was racially mixed and full of kids from the ghetto. (We called it Harlem then.) Chosen for their talent to draw or sing or play an instrument, these kids were the most diverse group I'd ever met. Their class was talent. And like all insecure people, they shoved it in your face.

It was in high school that I began to find my true class. Here the competition was not about money or color or neighborhood but about how well you drew or played. At Music and Art, new hierarchies were created, hierarchies of virtuosity. Was your painting in the semiannual exhibition? Were you tapped to perform in the orchestra or on WQXR? By now, we all knew we did not belong in televisionland America—and we were *proud* of it. Being outsiders was a badge of merit. We had no teams, no cheerleaders, and the cool class uniform was early beatnik: black stockings, handmade sandals, and black lipstick for the girls; black turtlenecks, black jeans, black leather jackets for the boys. Stringy hair was requisite for both sexes. We experimented with dope. We cruised the Village hoping to be mistaken for hipsters. We carried books by Kafka, Genet, Sartre, Allen Ginsberg. We stared existentially into our cappuccino at Rienzi's or the Peacock. We wanted to seduce black jazz musicians, but were afraid to. We had found our class at last.

Many of us rose to the top of it. I count among my high school classmates pop singers, television producers, directors, actors, painters, novelists. Many are household names. A few earn tens of millions of dollars
a year. Most of us went to college—but it was not finally a B.A. or a
Ph.D. that defined our status. It was whether or not we stayed hot, were
racing up the charts with a bullet, were going into syndication, on the
bestseller list, into twenty-five foreign languages. Even the professors envied *this* status: Money and name recognition level all classes in America. Hence the obsession with celebrity. Even in Europe you can pass
into the "best" circles, though the rules of class are quite different there.

Having done my time with the Eurotrash set, I'm always amazed at
how an aristocratic name still covers a multitude of sins in Europe. In
England, in Germany, a lord or ladyship, a *Graf* or *Gräfin*, a *von* or *zu*,
still carries weight. Italians are more cynical about titles. The classiest
friends I have in Italy may be *contesse, marchesi,* or *principi,* but they're
too cool to advertise it. They'd rather be famous for a hit record, or a big
book. But go to the chic watering spots—St. Moritz, for example—and
membership in the best clubs still goes by family, not by individual
achievement. Walk into the Corviglia Club and say you're Ice-T or
Madonna. Honey—you won't get in, while any old Niarchos or von
Ribbentrop will.

Many of my European friends still inhabit a world where a name and
old money can become a positive *bar* to achievement. There is so much
*more* to do than merely work. If you have to be in Florence in June, in
Paris in July, in Tuscany in August, in Venice in September, in Sologne
in October, in New York in November, in St. Bart's in December and
January, in St. Moritz in February, in New York in March, in Greece in
April, in Prague in May—how on earth can you take (let alone hold) a
job? And the fittings. And the balls. And the spas. And the dryings out!
As a husband of Barbara Hutton's once asked: "When would I have *time*
to work?" True class means never even having to *talk* about it. (Work, I
mean.)

Americans are intrinsically unclassy—so the Jews *almost* fit in. All we
talk about is our work. All we want to do is make our first names so recognized we don't even *need* a last (Ms. Ciccione [Madonna] is the ultimate American here). We believe in change as fervently as Europeans
believe in the status quo. We believe that money will buy us into heaven
(with heaven defined as toned muscles, no flab at the chin, interest on
interest, and a name that cows maître d's). Once that's accomplished, we
can start to save the world: plow some money into AIDS research, the
rain forest, political candidates. Maybe we can even run for office ourselves! (Witness Mr. Perot.) In a society where pop name recognition
means everything, celebrities are more equal than everyone else. But

celebrity status is hell to keep in shape (just like an aging body). It needs a host of trainers, PR experts, publishers, media consultants. Plus you have to keep turning out new product—and possibly even new scandal. (Witness Woody Allen.) Maybe the reason celebrities marry so often is simply to keep their names in the news. And maybe—whether they intend it or not—they create scandal to hype their movies. (Again, witness Woody Allen, né Allen Konigsberg.)

Ah—we are back to the question of Jews and names. Can we keep our names? As long as we keep them *hot*. Otherwise, we also have to change them. We may have, as political theorist Benjamin Barber says, "an aristocracy of everyone," but not everyone can be hot at once. Thus, the drive for class becomes as relentless and chronic in America as the diet. No matter how hot you are, you're always in danger of growing cold.

It's a lot like mortality, isn't it? No wonder Carpe Diem is our motto. This is what makes America such a restless country and its top-class celebrities so insecure.

Ah, friends, I long to be born into a membership in the Corviglia Club. But I suspect I never would have written any books.

Did you ever wonder why Jews are such relentless scribes? You may have thought it was because we are people of the book. You may have thought it was because we come from homes where reading is stressed. You may have thought it was repressed sexuality. All that is true. But I submit the *real* reason is our need constantly to define our class. By writing, we reinvent ourselves. By writing, we create pedigrees.

# JAMES ALAN McPHERSON
## (1943– )

McPherson was raised in Savannah, Georgia, during a time when segregation was still a dominant cultural factor. His writing career began in the late sixties, when one of his stories was awarded a prize by the editors of the *Atlantic Monthly*. McPherson began serving as a contributing editor of that magazine in 1969; he also started to teach at various universities, including the University of Iowa.

His first book of stories, *Elbow Room* (1977), was awarded a Pulitzer Prize and catapulted him into the front rank of contemporary fiction writers. This remarkable collection was full of stories about black Americans—ministers, professors, convicts, business people—making huge efforts to forge a sense of identity. The stories were shot through with good humor and human warmth, characteristics that recurred in McPherson's later work, such as *Crabcakes* (1998), a book of lyrical evocations of the author's life. "Going Up to Atlanta" (found in the 1987 anthology *A World Unsuspected*) is an affecting meditation on a series of family photographs and on the admixture of shame and pride involved in being the son of a gifted father whose talents were thwarted.

## FROM "Going Up to Atlanta"

The only picture I have of my father was taken sometime in the 1930s, at his mother's family home in Hardeeville, South Carolina, when he was a young man. I have known all along that he liked comic books. Someone has pointed out to me that he is wearing a down jacket. The wearing of down jackets did not become fashionable until many years after this picture was taken. But a down jacket would be most comfortable during the cool, rainy winters that settle into the coastal areas of Georgia and South Carolina. My father's roots were in this region. Knowing its climate, he must have dressed with an eye toward comfort.

Someone else has noted that he seems arrogant. I cannot remember him this way, although some arrogance, for him, was possible. But most likely his arms are crossed and his eyes are closed and his head is tilted because he is asleep. I have learned that he suffered from narcolepsy, an inherited disorder that causes a person to fall asleep at absolutely any time. My brother, Richard, inherited this condition from my father. I note that my father has small hands. This is surprising, considering the fact that he labored all his life as an electrician. I want to believe that he was not fated to be a laborer.

When my father died, in late December 1961, I had just returned to Savannah from Morris Brown College in Atlanta. In my own mind, my father had died many years before. I attended the funeral, but grew angry when the Methodist minister who conducted the services said, "We all knew Mac, and we all know he's better off where he is now."

I did not attend the burial.

### Moving Pictures

In California, many years ago, I saw a Japanese film called *Sansho the Bailiff*. The film is about Japan during its Middle Ages, when slavery existed as an institution. It tells the story of a family.

The Governor of a certain province, who is an aristocrat, decides on his own that human slavery is wrong. He decrees its abolition. But the decree threatens the human property of Sansho the Bailiff, who is the most powerful slaveholder in the province. The Shogun immediately revokes the Governor's decree, because it threatens to undermine the social order, and transfers the offending Governor to a remote province, where his personal feelings about slavery will pose no threat. The departing Governor sends his family, a wife and two children, to live with her parents. While traveling, they are kidnapped by slave traders. The mother is sold into prostitution. The two children are sold to Sansho the Bailiff. They grow up as slaves. The son becomes dehumanized and loses his memory of his former life and therefore his identity. He becomes such a good slave that he is promoted to the rank of trustee. It becomes his job to mutilate, kill or bury any slave who tries to escape or who dies of work or of old age. During one trip outside the slave compound, a very beautiful thing happens. The young man and his sister are gathering branches in order to bury an old woman. They have to break some branches from trees. They both pull at a branch together. It breaks and they fall down. The fall is a repetition of a similar fall they had, as children, when they were gathering branches for a fire the night the family was captured by slave traders. This ritual gesture, recalling the last happy moment they shared before becoming slaves, revives the young man's former psychological habits. He begins, slowly, to reclaim himself. His sister, at the sacrifice of her own life, eventually helps him to escape. He eludes the slave catchers and, after great difficulty, petitions the Shogun to restore his family name. Recognizing the offspring of his former official, the Shogun makes the young man Governor of the province. He now occupies the same position as his father, who by now is dead. The son immediately issues a decree outlawing slavery. Whereas his father, an aristocrat, had outlawed slavery out of his own intuitive distaste for the institution, the son, having been a slave, has an *earned* contempt for the dehumanizing aspects of the institution. Even though his sister is dead and his mother is now an aged, mutilated prostitute, the son does achieve the father's original desire. But he achieves it for reasons that are personally and emotionally sound.

He *learns*.

I learned from this film that, among the Asians, the offspring can ennoble the ancestor.

### In Atlanta

My father's half brother, Thomas McPherson, Jr., is closer to my age than he is to my father's. He was born, during my grandfather's second marriage, after my father had achieved adulthood. James Allen McPherson, Sr., my father, was himself like a father to Thomas McPherson, Jr.

In the late 1960s, Thomas, a trained minister, became District Director of the Equal Employment Opportunity Commission. His office in Atlanta covered Georgia, South Carolina and Alabama. I visited him there once and met some of his employees. One especially cheerful older white man was very pleased to meet me. His name was Bill Harris. My uncle Thomas introduced us, and explained that Bill Harris, because he was once Sheriff of Chatham County, Georgia (which included Savannah), once knew my father very well. Bill Harris had arrested my father many times, not for any personal offense but for "cheating and swindling," for not completing work he had contracted to do. Bill Harris shook my hand and said, "Everybody liked Mac. It's just that he couldn't hold his liquor."

I remembered Bill Harris. I remembered one night he came to our house to arrest my father. I was about six. My father had come home to say good-bye to us. His ambition had always been to go up to Atlanta and start over. He had come to see us one last time before he left Savannah. We lived on the top floor of a duplex at 509 1/2 West Walburg Street. It was a cool winter night, in December, and we had no lights or heat except for the fireplace in the bedroom. For light we used candles and an oil lamp. I remember the four of us, and my mother, standing at the top of the stairs. Mary, my older sister, was holding the lamp. All of us were crying while my father said good-bye. Just as he turned to walk down the stairs, the front door opened and Bill Harris, the Sheriff of Chatham County, came in the door and said, "All right, Mac, get your hat."

I think now that if he had not loved us enough to come to the house to say good-bye, he would have gotten away.

## Augusta

Thomas McPherson, Sr., my grandfather, lived at 1635 15th Street in Augusta. I associate Augusta with Christmas.

Thomas McPherson, Sr., was for most of his life an insurance salesman for Guaranty Life Insurance Company. He married twice. His first marriage was to Alice Scarborough of Hardeeville, South Carolina. That marriage lasted until shortly after my father was born. His second marriage, when he was in middle age, was to Josephine Martin of Blackshare, Georgia. She was my mother's first cousin. By this marriage he had two children, Thomas and Eva, and moved from Savannah to Augusta. There he led a poor but respectable life. In Savannah, we lived almost always in poverty: public welfare, clothes from the Salvation Army, no lights or heat for years at a time, double sessions in the segregated public schools, work at every possible job that would pay the bills. Each year at Christmas, if my father was not with us, my grandfather would try to arrange to bring us to Augusta, so we could share the family Christmas at his home. Sometimes we would go by train. Other times he would try to arrange a ride for the four of us with the insurance men with whom he worked. I can't remember whether or not my grandfather owned a car.

When I think about Augusta, I remember ambrosia. It was made with coconuts, apples, pecans, oranges and lots of spices. It would be served with Christmas dinner, late at night, when people would not notice the small amounts of food. But in the mornings, there was the anticipation of toys. Sometimes we would get old toys that had been repaired by Thomas and Eva. Thomas had a chicken coop in their backyard, and he liked to show me how, with the sound of his voice, he had trained the chickens to cut off and on, off and on, the light in their coop. He had a bicycle, and would take time to ride me on the back seat of it before he went to work. Once, when I had a very bad cold, Thomas bought a lemon for me. I remember that lemon after all these years because the gesture was grounded in love.

I also remember my grandfather, who had a nervous condition, sitting at the head of the table and moving his hands up and down, up and down, to steady his nerves. After the meal, which was the high point of Christmas Day, he would say to his wife, "Joe, I enjoyed the meal." And she would answer, "I'm glad you did, Mr. Mac." Afterwards, before it was time to go to bed, I would sit alone in the living room and draw Christmas trees. I had, then, great talent as a drawer of Christmas trees. I still love trains because sometimes we would take the Nancy Hanks, run by the Georgia Central Line, from Savannah to Augusta.

Janie McPherson
*"Aunt China"*

Whenever I ran away, I would get as far as Aunt China's house. I would say, "Aunt China, I'm running away." She would look severely at me and say, "What's wrong with you, boy? Here, sit down and eat some of these greens and rice." I loved Aunt China. She was the wife of Robert McPherson, my grandfather's brother, and lived on West 32nd Street in Savannah. I think she was pure African.

My Uncle Bob, Robert McPherson, was only one of my grandfather's brothers. The others were Joe, B.J. and George. My Uncle George, whom I never met, was a Presiding Elder in the African Methodist Episcopal Church. The family agreed that he could preach the fuzz off a Georgia peach. Uncle Bob and Aunt China were like parents to my father. I think now that he must have run away to their house many times, even after he was a full-grown man. I know that, when I was a boy, I could always find out where he was if I went there.

Aunt China was a very strong woman. She never asked "real" questions, but seemed to know everything. She seemed never bothered by anything in life. All of us leaned on her, absorbed her strength. She seemed to assume that everything in life could be cured by a good meal and a good night's sleep. I liked to go there when I ran away.

Several days before my father died, he sent word that he wanted to see me. He had been living in a rented room in 33rd Lane, just a few blocks away from Aunt China's house. I did not go to see him. But when the news came that he was dead, I ran away to Aunt China's. This was one of the few days when she was not at home. I was making up my mind to go on to the rooming house where my father had just died, and I was walking down 32nd Lane, when I saw Aunt China coming up the lane toward me. Down the lane, in the distance behind her, I could see an ambulance loading my father's body. It was the only time I ever saw my Aunt China cry. She took me home with her and kept crying and saying, *"I told that fool. I told that boy."*

## Houses

The stable houses were Aunt China's on 32nd Street and wherever my Aunt Beulah Collins was, anyplace in Savannah. The others were places we lived.

We lived at 509 1/2 West Walburg Street, next door to a funeral parlor, from the time I was born until 1951. Then we moved to 2010 West Bulloch Street and lived there until 1953. Then we moved to Green Cove Springs, Florida, for a summer. Then we moved back to Savannah and lived there with our cousin, Cassie Harper, until 1955. Then we moved to the east side of town, into a small apartment at 508 East Henry Street. In 1957 we moved to 1006 1/2 Montgomery Street, into a duplex owned by an electrician named T. J. Hopkins. We lived there until 1960. Then we moved to 316 West Hall Street, about five blocks away. In 1963 my mother moved into a housing project named Catton Homes.

During all this time, I liked Aunt China's house the best. I could always go there from the other places. Of the other places, I liked the duplex on Montgomery Street the best. The adjoining apartment was vacant, and I could get into it through a hole in the closet of one of the bedrooms. I liked to crawl through that hole, sit on the floor in the empty, quiet apartment and be alone.

### Ebony, North Carolina
### *Eva McPherson (Clayton)*

In 1980, I went to North Carolina to see Eva, my father's half sister. She is a very successful woman and was, at that time, a County Commissioner. Except for brief exchanges at funerals, I had not seen her since I was a child.

I asked Eva about my father. She told me that he was considered a "brain." She said that, in his day, he was the only licensed black master electrician in the entire state of Georgia. I asked her what had happened to him. She said she did not know. I asked her whether he chased women. She said that he was a faithful husband, but liked to drink and gamble. She said his only real love was electricity. She said that he had invented a device once that, when placed over an outlet, would reduce the *cost*, but not the flow, of electricity. She said that the officials threatened to take away his license if he ever tried to market it. She said that I was not the first in my immediate family to attend college. She said that my father had attended the same college I finished, Morris Brown College in Atlanta, but had been expelled after the first semester for gambling. She said that, during World War II, he had been deferred from active service because he taught a course at Savannah State College, a course in engineering, that was considered essential. She said that he was a completely self-taught man, having never attended any grade beyond one college semester. I asked Eva how it was that such a gifted man could wind up dying of frost exposure in a rented room in a dirt lane in Savannah. Eva said she did not know.

I told Eva that I believed my father had been frustrated by having his license taken from him and by having to work for an older man, T. J. Hopkins, as a common electrician. I told her that I believed that my father had considered Hopkins a father-substitute, against whom he was always rebelling. Eva said this was inaccurate. She said that the older man, Hopkins, had been my father's student. She said that Mr. Hopkins had never been a master electrician, only a licensed one, and that my father had never wanted to work for him. She said that his ambition, always, had been to start his own company in Savannah or in Atlanta. I asked her why I had never been told these things.

Eva said she did not know.

### Samuel James Collins, Jr.
### "Bro"

Sam Collins is the oldest son of Beulah Collins, my mother's sister. It was Beulah Collins who drew my mother out of Green Cove Springs, Florida, and into Savannah. Beulah had left Green Cove Springs to marry a man named Samuel Collins who lived in Savannah. He was an ice-man by trade. He sent so many letters to Mary Smalls, my mother's mother, back in Green Cove Springs, letters that kept reciting the line "Beulah and me is having a wonderful time. We eat collard greens every day," that Mary Smalls became suspicious. She sent my mother, the oldest daughter, into Savannah to see about Beulah. While there she lived with her first cousin, Josephine Martin, who had just married a man named Thomas McPherson, Sr. James McPherson, the grown son of my mother's cousin's new husband, was sitting around the house reading comic books. My mother never went back to Green Cove Springs.

Samuel and Beulah Collins had four children: Barbara and Lucille, Sam and Harry. When we were growing up we were as close as brothers and sisters. I loved their mother with them. There was always laughter and life in their house. Sometimes, at Thanksgiving or at Christmas, when we had nothing to eat, Beulah would steal a can of mackerel for us from the family for whom she worked. My mother would make mackerel croquettes. But the best things about my Aunt Beulah's house were the magical things that happened on weekends. I would go there on Friday evenings and would not have to leave until Sunday night. Bro would tell me some of the things I could not have learned on my own.

We were not as close after we became adolescents. I had to work all the time, and go to school. My world was made up of school and jobs and reading. Bro moved into the street culture. In this way, through word of mouth, he came to know my father much better than I did. He joined the group of men who stood around the fire on the corner of Anderson and 31st streets. My father was also part of that group.

Years later, Samuel Collins told me that the men around the fire used to call my father "Papasqualli," their version of a Creek or Cherokee word meaning "Chief." He said that whenever the men had an argument, before they came to blows over the issue in dispute, one of them would say, "Well, let's go ask Mac." He said my father would delight the men around the fire with his command of language. He would say things like, "I think I shall repair to the bathroom." Samuel Collins said that, once, when one of the men said something negative about my mother, my father picked him up and threw him into the fire. He said that, usually, my father was a gentle man.

## T. J. HOPKINS

Called "Major" publicly by influential people in the white community, Mr. Hopkins was the only other licensed electrician in Savannah who was black. He had served in the U.S. Army, had attended school. He was always willing to employ my father, to give him a job as a common electrician. Once, after my father had gotten out of prison and had resumed working for him, Mr. Hopkins rented my father an apartment in his duplex just over the office of his company at 2010 Montgomery Street. My father had only to go downstairs to work and back upstairs to his family. Mr. Hopkins even allowed my brother and me to work for him, sorting electrical parts and cleaning out his office. In this way we could help our father pay off the rent. Nights, Mr. Hopkins sat at the main desk in his office talking on the telephone. Seated in the white glare of the neon lights, he looked, to anyone watching through the plate-glass window, like an actor on stage.

But my father was always losing his temper and quitting the job. His ambition was to regain his old license as a master electrician and start his own company. He had tried this many times and had always failed. Many of the men who worked for Hopkins were former members of my father's old crews. They were still loyal to him. Sometimes, a few of them would quit when he quit, and would not go back until *he* was forced, by family pressures, to go back. Mr. Hopkins was always willing to take him back.

But my father's ambition, always, was to regain his license and then go up to Atlanta, where he could start his own company.

### REIDSVILLE

The people at Reidsville would always welcome my father back. He was not a criminal, but many of the hardened criminals there loved him. My father was a great cook, and was always assigned to the kitchen. I think he was considered too valuable to waste on the road gang.

We used to go from Savannah to Reidsville to see my father. I was always very ashamed to see him come into the visiting room because there was a wire screen between him and us. But at the same time I was glad to see him. We always wore our best clothes when we went to Reidsville. My father, because he worked in the kitchen, gained weight there. He was always healthier after he had settled into the routine of prison life. But during one of his last stays, they gave him electric shock treatments. When he came back to Savannah, after that time, he went back to work for Hopkins without complaining. But he began to drink almost all the time. Sometime after that, when I was twelve or thirteen, I stopped trying to see him. If I saw him on Anderson Street after school, I would turn and walk the other way.

The last time I saw my father alive, I was seventeen. I had gotten a National Defense Student Loan and was about to go to college in Atlanta. I went looking for him one night and found him, standing by the fire, on the corner of Anderson and 31st streets. I had, by this time, been working every possible kind of job to help support the family I thought he had abandoned. During all my years in Savannah, I had never had peace or comfort or any chance to rely on anyone else. I blamed him for it. I was very bitter toward him. That night I lectured him, telling him to straighten himself out, as I had, and be a man. He said he was hungry and wanted something to eat. I bought a meal for him with money I had earned on my own. After he had eaten it he said to me, "And a little child shall lead them."

This was the last thing he ever said to me. . . .

### AFFLUENCE

Mary remembers that we were among the first black families in Savannah to have an electric stove. We also had a maid, a woman named

Delphene, who used to help our mother with us and who used to give us baths. Mary also remembers that, at one time, my father had his own company and his own truck. It had painted on it: "McPherson & Company: Electrical Contractor." Mary also remembers that our father always gave us money when he came home from work on Fridays. She said that all the kids in the neighborhood would be waiting with us for him to come home. He always gave everyone a share of his earnings. But he would do it by ages, giving the older children more money. Mary said it did not seem to matter to him that his own children expected the best treatment. I do not remember these things. I remember, though, that my father always wanted a street in Savannah named for him.

I also remember attending the best school for "colored" children in the city of Savannah. It was St. Mary's, a Catholic school, on West 36th Street. All the teachers were white nuns. All the students were black. If you talked at St. Mary's when the nuns were out of the room, one of their spies would report you when they came back. Then the talkers had to hold out their palms so the nuns could smack them with a ruler. I never talked. I learned to read very quietly. I was never smacked.

My father always did more than anyone else to support the shows and parties that were put on at St. Mary's. He had a friend named Mr. Simon, a white man who ran an ice-cream plant. My father would always take my brother and me there to pick up five- and ten-gallon cartons of ice cream for the shows at St. Mary's. I think that Mr. Simon had affection for my father. They would always embrace when he went in there. The nuns were very happy to have the free ice cream. My sister, Mary, was always a star in the show.

During my three years at St. Mary's, I was trained to be a Catholic. Mary and Richard and I learned the rosary, attended mass, lit candles. But toward the end of my third year, the priest in charge of St. Mary's called us out of class and into his office. He told us that our father had not paid our tuition for some time, but that since we were such good students he was going to pay it himself. He pulled a wad of money out of his pocket and showed it to us.

I never knew whether my father paid what was owed to St. Mary's. Toward the end of my third year, and my sister's fourth, we were transferred from St. Mary's to the Florence Street School. The black children there had to attend double sessions: half went from early in the morning until noon, and the others went from early afternoon until five or six o'clock. I was put into group five, among the retarded people, during the last part of third grade and through all of fourth. I sat at my desk and never said a word. I read my sister's fifth-grade books on the sly.

## PAULSON STREET SCHOOL

After we moved to East Henry Street, I had to attend Paulson Street School. This was where all the mean people went. They would throw rocks at you, push you in the halls, trying to make you fight. I did not want to fight anyone. During the years at Paulson we were eligible for the free lunch program. This was available, through the state, for anyone on public welfare. Every six weeks, when he was making out his report, the teacher would ask me before the entire class, "McPherson, is your father still in jail?"

During those years at Paulson I developed a reputation for remotion. I just did not want to talk. Once, a boy named Leon Chaplin, who shared a desk with me, asked if he could sharpen my pencil with his new knife. I refused to give it to him. Leon insisted that I hand it over. I refused. He said that if I did not give him my pencil he would stab me. I refused to give it to him. Leon stabbed me, under cover of the desk, in the left thigh. I grabbed him and took the knife away. The teacher saw us wrestling and thought that I had attacked him. I told her he had stabbed me. She demanded to see the evidence. Because I would have had to take down my pants, I refused to show her the mark. After that I was watched.

During the course in first aid, we were required to demonstrate artificial respiration techniques. Our grades depended on our learned skills in this exercise. But during this time our mother was buying all our clothes from the Salvation Army, and there were holes in my shoes. For this reason, I refused to kneel down and demonstrate how much I knew about artificial respiration. I knew that the other kids would laugh at the holes in my shoes. I did not want them to laugh. The teacher kept demanding that I kneel down. I kept refusing. I finally flunked the course.

But during this same time, I discovered the Colored Branch of the Carnegie Public Library less than a block away from where we lived on East Henry Street. I liked going there to read all day.

## BOOKS

At first the words, without pictures, were a mystery. But then, suddenly, they all began to march across the page. They gave up their secret meanings, spoke of other worlds, made me know that pain was a part of other peoples' lives. After a while, I could read faster and faster and faster

and faster. After a while, I no longer believed in the world in which I
lived.

I loved the Colored Branch of the Carnegie Public Library.

## "Daddy Slick" and "Mama Della"

These were people who had no respectability. They were my father's
friends. They owned and ran a place on 32nd and Burroughs streets
where men gambled and where moonshine whiskey was sold. I loved to
go in there and look for my father. He loved to gamble and be in there
with the other men.

To get into Daddy Slick's place, you had to walk through the dry black
dirt on Burroughs Street until you came to a big yard enclosed by a high
wooden fence. You could not look over the fence, but you could ring a
buzzer on a wooden door in the gate. A peephole would open, and you
had to say to someone, "Is my daddy here?" Once you were recognized,
the wooden door would open and you would be allowed into a courtyard
where ducks and geese and flamingos and chickens were strutting and
scratching in the black dirt. Directly across the courtyard was the house
in which Daddy Slick and Mama Della lived. To the right of the house,
at a distance, was another house, a much smaller house also made of
wood. It looked almost like a toyhouse and was painted bright colors.
This was where people drank and gambled. To get in, you had to knock
on another wood door and be inspected through another peephole. Inside that place, it was always dark. But there would be music from a
bright jukebox, and light from the pinball machines, and people would
be drinking. Daddy Slick or Mama Della always sat behind the counter
facing the door. They always saw you before you saw them. Daddy Slick
was very fat and Mama Della was very thin. Daddy Slick always wore a
round, flat touring hat. People said he had a photographic memory and
never forgot anything, especially the amount of money people owed him.

He sat with his legs apart so his belly would have room to spread. He
or Mama Della always gave you a Coke or an orange soda or a nickel or
a dime. In the wall near the counter was another door. In that room people gambled. My father was almost always in there. I always wanted to go
in there, but was never allowed to. I would have to sit at the counter and
wait for him to come out. Sometimes I would play one of the pinball machines. When my father came out, he would always buy something for
me, no matter whether he had won or lost in the gambling room. Once,
because he had promised to buy me a television for my birthday, I played
hooky from school and waited all day at Daddy Slick's for him to finish
gambling. He had just won a lot of money playing bolita. But when he

came out, in the late afternoon, he had lost everything. He could no longer afford the down payment on the used television set we had already chosen. He tried to give me his wristwatch instead. I refused to take it.

Daddy Slick also sold bolita. Someone told me once that my father won at bolita so often that after a while no dealer in town would sell him a ticket. But he was liked by all the men who spent time at Daddy Slick's. Whenever he was in jail at Christmas or at Thanksgiving, Daddy Slick or Mama Della, or one of the men, would bring a box of groceries to our house. These people had their own code.

## ELECTRICITY
### 1957

I think that a certain kind of creative man finds one thing he likes to do and then does it for the rest of his life. I think that if he is really *good* at what he does, if he is really creative, he masters the basics and then begins to *play* with the conventions of the thing. My father was a master electrician.

During one of the times he came back from Reidsville, we lived on East Henry Street. He was working again for T. J. Hopkins, and was trying to be a man in all the conventional ways. He liked to cook for us, liked to drop by the house to see us whenever he passed it during work hours. He liked to fix things. One day he was repairing the light fixture above the face bowl in the bathroom. He asked me to hold one of his hands and to grip the faucet of the bathtub with my other hand. I did this. Then he licked the index finger of his free hand and stuck it up into the empty socket where the lightbulb had been. As the electricity passed through him and into me and through me and was grounded in the faucet of the bathtub, my father kept saying, "Pal, I won't hurt you. I won't hurt you." If I had let go of the faucet, both of us would have died. If I had let go of his hand, he would have died.

That day, I know now, my father was trying to regain my trust.

## BLACK AND WHITE

Once, when a story about me was in the Savannah papers, an old white man called up my mother. He introduced himself as a former Chatham County official who had known my father through his work as an electrician. My mother said he asked, "Is this Mac's son?" Then he said, "Mac was a brilliant man. That liquor just got to him." Then he said, "Mable, I never had anything against the colored. Now both of us are old. Can I come around sometime and sit with you?"

Richard, my brother, knows more about the public side of my father than I do. He and my father worked together on a number of jobs. He told me that when they were wiring a store for a Greek on East Broad Street, my father's and my brother's skills came under the watchful eye of a redneck. He and his son were pouring concrete for the Greek. The redneck watched my brother for a while, and then said to his son, "You see there? If *you* worked as hard as that little nigger over there you'd get someplace." Richard said he turned to my father and saw him laughing. The sight of this, considering the insult, made my brother cry. Then my father said to Richard, "Look, if you get hot over something like that, you'll stay hot all your life."

Richard also told me that part of his job with my father was to take certain papers to a state agency as soon as a job was completed. He said there was a receptionist's desk in the lobby of the building to which he was required to go. This was during the time of official segregation, and the white female receptionist would always stop him at her desk and try to prevent him from going upstairs. But then the official in charge of the agency would come to the head of the stairs and say, "Is that you, little Mac? Come on up." He would sign the papers without looking at them.

The Jewish community of Savannah, which was old Sephardic, knew and respected my father for his intelligence and skill. They knew who his children were. Sometimes on Christmas Eve, when our lights were off and we had no food or presents or Christmas tree, my father, if he was not at Reidsville, would appear well after dark with money he had either borrowed or won at gambling. He would break the law by turning on our electricity himself, and then he would take us downtown to shop. Certain merchants would keep their stores open for him far past closing time on Christmas Eve. I never believed in Santa Claus, but I believed that my father, sometimes, possessed a special magic.

Last Christmas my mother gave me the best Christmas present in the world, and all Christmas Day I felt as if my father were still keeping the stores open late on Christmas Eve. She said he loved to buy groceries after he had been paid for doing a job. She said that one night he came home with sacks and sacks of groceries, bought with money he had just collected from poor white people for work completed. He told her, "Mable, those people don't have anything. They paid me because they're proud. I'm going to take half of these groceries out to them." Since my mother valued security, she said, she got very mad.

## WENDELL PHILLIPS SIMMS

Mr. Simms ran a fish market on the corner of West Broad and Walburg streets. His father had been a slave who escaped to the North during the years just before the Civil War. He had joined the abolitionists, had taken the name Wendell Phillips, and had returned to Savannah during the Reconstruction. He brought the traditions of freemasonry into the black community of Savannah. His son, Wendell Phillips Simms, was a thirty-third degree Mason. I did not know this when I was growing up.

Mr. Simms had five children: Robert, Ruth, Merelus, Louis and Richard. Merelus and I were born on the same day, next door to each other. We were natural playmates. Mr. Simms and my father, in the early days, exchanged turns taking us to school. But after a while, they did not get along. The clash of personalities, I think, resulted from the differences in their perspectives. My father seemed to love everybody. Mr. Simms had deep suspicions of the world outside his fish market. My father drank and gambled. Mr. Simms did not. My father was always looking out for other people. Mr. Simms looked out for himself. My father took great chances. Mr. Simms always hedged his bets. My father improvised. Mr. Simms practiced great efficiency. Mr. Simms did not seem to respect my father. Whenever he spoke to me of him, I could hear condescension in his voice. Mr. Simms thought, long before I did, that my father was irresponsible.

When I went into their fish market, after school, I would talk with Merelus and Louis while they cleaned and weighed fish. Mr. Simms would recite poems like "Invictus" and "Keep A-goin" while he cleaned fish. He knew all the nineteenth-century declamatory gestures. He seemed to believe the words he recited. He practiced great self-reliance and had a quiet contempt for Christianity. He kept his contacts with white people to a minimum. He preferred to catch his own fish in the Savannah River rather than buy them from the local wholesalers. He once attacked a truckload of Klansmen with a crowbar.

When I was about six, Mr. Simms began making bricks. He designed a device in his backyard for pressing and baking cement blocks. Over the years, day after day, he and his family made thousands of bricks. They tore down parts of their house as more room for the bricks was required. I liked to watch them from our kitchen window. Merelus and Louis and Richard would climb up the pyramid of cement blocks and talk with us through our kitchen window. My father agreed to do the wiring for the new house, and I wanted very badly for him to have some part in the creation. But by the time the house was ready for wiring he had lost control of his own life. Mr. Simms finished the house, by himself, and moved his family into it. I was invited there to visit a number of times. Mr. Simms had broken his health completing the house, but he was very proud of what he had done. When he spoke of my father, there was that familiar contempt in his voice. He died, in the house, shortly after he had settled his family into it.

Several years later, the Urban Renewal leveled the entire west side of Savannah, including Mr. Simms's house, to make room for a massive housing project named Catton Homes.


## Mr. Hopkins under the Neon Light

We owed Mr. Hopkins many hundreds of dollars when we moved out of his duplex on Montgomery Street. He had offered to let us stay, and he offered to let my brother and me work for him, in the absence of our father, in order to pay off the debt. My brother, Richard, did work for him for a while, but then my mother found another apartment and insisted that we move. We moved into an apartment in a slum that had many rats. I could not understand why she had not accepted Mr. Hopkins's kindness.

Years later, when I understood, I thought that Richard should be the one to repay Mr. Hopkins the money we owed him. I wrote a check for a certain amount and gave it to Richard and asked him to go in and put the money on Mr. Hopkins's desk. I don't know whether Richard ever turned over the money. I don't know whether he ever understood.


## In the Fish Market

Louis Simms is the third son of Wendell Phillips Simms. Unlike Merelus, he left Savannah. Like his oldest brother, Robert, he joined the U.S. Army and became an officer. He served in Vietnam, then in Europe, then returned to Savannah to be close to his mother. When Mrs. Simms died, he moved to Michigan to be close to his older sister, Ruth. Both he and I wound up in the Middle West, and we have a bond based on common memories. Louis remembers all the details.

Since childhood, Louis has kept everybody honest. He tells the truth, even though it hurts. Sometimes I feel that his father and my own are still debating essential issues: the advantages of efficiency over improvisation, the self-negation that can come from Christian belief, whether it is better to laugh at or to attack intruding Klansmen, whether it is best, or extremely dangerous, to call attention to intelligence and ambition in black males. Louis is wise in a pragmatic sense. He spent most of his boyhood making cement bricks.

Once, years ago, I was invited back to Savannah by the Poetry Society of Georgia. They asked me to give the Gilmer Lecture. It was a ritual occasion. The obligation of the exile is that, when he returns home, he must take something beautiful with him. At the time of the speech I had nothing to take home except forgiveness for my father. But to forgive him, I had to forgive the entire community. I wanted, twenty years late, to give a funeral oration for an intelligent and creative man. I wanted to say to the people, "This is a small part of the good thing that was destroyed." In the speech I gave I tried my very best to do this. My uncle, Thomas McPherson, was in the audience. He told me later, "James, you sure were generous to Savannah." But Savannah was also part of my father. I was trying to take the best parts of him home for burial.

Sometime later, I let Louis Simms read the speech. He called to my attention some of the concrete details that I had left out. He said:

"Although I followed the themes of your Gilmer Lecture—the merging of white and black cultures, your personal growth, the myth of racial classification, and change—I found some elements of the Savannah experience (the Southern experience, really) missing, and others, incredulous. I found it incredulous, totally unbelievable, that you could remember *no* specific incidents of oppression, to yourself or others around you. It is *impossible* for you to have been born in the South of the forties and not have experienced specific incidents of racial oppression. You may have suppressed those experiences in your subconscious, but they happened.

"You sharply forgot to mention that time and time and time again, your father had been unjustly denied an electrician's license—and he was the best. Yes, Mr. Mac was the best, or so my father and mother told me. My father and mother also told me, and my brother and sister, that the lily-white test administrators would never release your father's test results. This refusal by *white folk* to grant your father an electrician's license and release his test scores, along with scores of other rejections and humiliations—the inheritance of all black people—caused your father irrevocable pain. The pain may have even caused him to masquerade—as many unpleasantries have undoubtedly caused you to masquerade—his hostilities toward whites. He turned to drink for relief, you turn to 'ideas.'

"Those black folk who did not have other escape mechanisms, had to masquerade, or face the sure prospect of being blown to pieces, physically and psychologically. Believe me, your father's alleged status as the first black master electrician in Georgia came at a terrible drain on his inner resources. His effort to become an electrician, much less a master electrician, was a great leap from the abyss of despair. I'm not talking abstractly now. Two years ago, I did a paper for an E.E.O. case in Labor Relations on 'Blacks and the Law in Skilled Trades.' The electrical trade was, and still is, more discriminatory towards blacks than any other skilled trade. The electrical trade, in fact, has almost totally excluded blacks. When writing this paper, so as not to become abstract, I thought of your father, Mr. Mac . . ."

## The Ancestral Home

There is not one house where I lived as a child still standing. My family is scattered. All of us have, in one way or another, gone up to Atlanta. But my mother still resides in Savannah. Her one ambition, for many years, was to have us all come home. We went, whenever she was sick, but we could not stay there with her.

My brother lingered in Atlanta, biding his time. He has my father's genius for things electrical and mechanical. He is a mechanic for a major airline. For years now, he has been the only black mechanic in his shop. He once expected promotion to foreman of his shop. He took the standardized tests and outscored his peers. The rule was changed to make the election of a foreman democratic. He played politics, made friends, did favors. Finally, a somewhat friendly white peer told him, "Mac, your only trouble is your father was the wrong color." After every new foreman is elected, my brother still receives calls at his home during his off hours. These calls are from his peers, and they explain technical problems that they cannot solve. They ask, "Mac, what should we do?"

My brother, Richard, is "Papasqualli" now, up in Atlanta.

Many years ago, I tried to go back as close to Savannah as I could. As usual, my mother was calling all of her children home. It was my fate, on the way back to Savannah, to enter a time-warp in Charlottesville, Virginia. I lived, as an intelligent black male, through the first fifty years of this century. And when, some years later, I emerged, I found that I had learned, emotionally, every previously hidden dimension of my father's life. I love him now for what he had to endure. I am determined now, for very personal reasons, to live well beyond the forty-eight years allotted to him, in any Atlanta I can find.

Like all permanent exiles, I have learned to be at home inside myself.

## A Positive-Negative

There is, I know now, in the hidden places of human nature, a lust for power over the souls and the talents and therefore the bodies of special people. I don't believe there was any of this craving in my father. He had a passion for something that transcended it. He loved electricity, loved to play with it, and must have found some connection with God within the mysteries of that invisible flow. His will to believe in this, I think, allowed him to maintain the illusion that people were better in fact than they are in life.

For forty-eight years, I want to believe, he practiced an enigmatic form of his own secular religion.

### Obligations

Honor thy father and thy mother:
that thy days may be long upon the land
which the Lord thy God giveth thee.
*The Book of Exodus*

# RICHARD RODRIGUEZ
## (1944– )

Born of Mexican parents, Rodriguez was raised in Sacramento, California. He graduated from Stanford and later took an M.A. at Columbia, then did further graduate work at the University of California at Berkeley. His first book, *Hunger of Memory* (1981), describes his journey through the American educational system and the loss of ethnicity that was the odd, unexpected result of that journey. His second major book, excerpted here, is *Days of Obligation* (1992), subtitled *An Argument with My Mexican Father.* This memoir deals with a major issue in the author's life: his ethnicity, or lack of it. Although his parents spoke Spanish to him, he felt increasingly cut off from Mexican culture and did not visit Mexico until he was an adult.

*Days of Obligation* is a complex, poetic work in which Rodriguez meditates, often elliptically, on his Mexican past, with its complex mixture of native (Indian) peoples and Europeans. "I take it as an Indian achievement that I am alive," he writes in "India," which follows. Exactly how this is the case is the subject of this remarkable piece, which combines autobiography and cultural analysis.

FROM *Days of Obligation*

### INDIA

At sunrise the next day, the time the Indians appointed, they came according to their promise, and brought us a large quantity of fish with certain roots. . . . They sent their women and children to look at us. . . .

*Álvar Núñez Cabeza de Vaca*

I used to stare at the Indian in the mirror. The wide nostrils, the thick lips. Starring Paul Muni as Benito Juárez. Such a long face—such a long nose—sculpted by indifferent, blunt thumbs, and of such common clay. No one in my family had a face as dark or as Indian as mine. My face could not portray the ambition I brought to it. What could the United

States of America say to me? I remember reading the ponderous conclusion of the Kerner Report in the sixties: two Americas, one white, one black—the prophecy of an eclipse too simple to account for the complexity of my face.

*Mestizo* in Mexican Spanish means mixed, confused. Clotted with Indian, thinned by Spanish spume.

What could Mexico say to me?

Mexican philosophers powwow in their tony journals about Indian "fatalism" and "Whither Mexico?" *El fatalismo del indio* is an important Mexican philosophical theme; the phrase is trusted to conjure the quality of Indian passivity as well as to initiate debate about Mexico's reluctant progress toward modernization. Mexicans imagine their Indian part as deadweight: the Indian stunned by modernity; so overwhelmed by the loss of what is genuine to him—his language, his religion—that he sits weeping like a medieval lady at the crossroads; or else he resorts to occult powers and superstitions, choosing to consort with death because the purpose of the world has passed him by.

One night in Mexico City I ventured from my hotel to a distant *colonia* to visit my aunt, my father's only sister. But she was not there. She had moved. For the past several years she has moved, this woman of eighty-odd years, from one of her children to another. She takes with her only her papers and books—she is a poetess—and an upright piano painted blue. My aunt writes love poems to her dead husband, Juan—keeping Juan up to date, while rewatering her loss. Last year she sent me her *obras completas*, an inch-thick block of bound onionskin. And with her poems she sent me a list of names, a genealogy braiding two centuries, two continents, to a common origin: eighteenth-century Salamanca. No explanation is attached to the list. Its implication is nonetheless clear. We are—my father's family is (despite the evidence of my face)—of Europe. We are not Indian.

On the other hand, a Berkeley undergraduate approached me one day, creeping up as if I were a stone totem to say, "God, it must be cool to be related to Aztecs."

\*     \*     \*

I sat down next to the journalist from Pakistan—the guest of honor. He had been making a tour of the United States under the auspices of the U.S. State Department. Nearing the end of his journey now, he was having dinner with several of us, American journalists, at a Chinese restaurant in San Francisco. He said he'd seen pretty much all he wanted to see in America. His wife, however, had asked him to bring back some American Indian handicrafts. Blankets. Beaded stuff. He'd looked everywhere.

The table was momentarily captured by the novelty of his dilemma.

You can't touch the stuff nowadays, somebody said. So rare, so expensive. Somebody else knew of a shop up on Sacramento Street that sells authentic Santa Fe. Several others remembered a store in Chinatown where moccasins, belts—"the works"—were to be found. All manufactured in Taiwan.

The Pakistani journalist looked incredulous. His dream of America had been shaped by American export-Westerns. Cowboys and Indians are yin and yang of America. He had seen men dressed like cowboys on this trip. But (turning to me): Where are the Indians?

(Two Indians staring at one another. One asks where are all the Indians, the other shrugs.)

\*       \*       \*

I grew up in Sacramento thinking of Indians as people who had disappeared. I was a Mexican in California; I would no more have thought of myself as an Aztec in California than you might imagine yourself a Viking or a Bantu. Mrs. Ferrucci up the block used to call my family "Spanish." We knew she intended to ennoble us by that designation. We also knew she was ignorant.

I was ignorant.

In America the Indian is relegated to the obligatory first chapter—the "Once Great Nation" chapter—after which the Indian is cleared away as easily as brush, using a very sharp rhetorical tool called an "alas." Thereafter, the Indian reappears only as a stunned remnant—Ishi, or the hundred-year-old hag blowing out her birthday candle at a rest home in Tucson; or the teenager drunk on his ass in Plaza Park.

Here they come down Broadway in the Fourth of July parades of my childhood—middle-aged men wearing glasses, beating their tom-toms; Hey-ya-ya-yah; Hey-ya-ya-yah. They wore Bermuda shorts under their loincloths. High-school kids could never refrain from the answering Woo-woo-woo, stopping their mouths with the palms of their hands.

In the 1960s, Indians began to name themselves Native Americans, recalling themselves to life. That self-designation underestimated the ruthless idea Puritans had superimposed upon the landscape. America is an idea to which native are inimical. The Indian represented permanence and continuity to Americans who were determined to call this country new. Indians must be ghosts.

I collected conflicting evidence concerning Mexico, it's true, but I never felt myself the remnant of anything. Mexican magazines arrived in our mailbox from Mexico City; showed pedestrians strolling wide ocher boulevards beneath trees with lime-green leaves. My past was at least this coherent: Mexico was a real place with plenty of people walking around in it. My parents had come from somewhere that went on without them.

When I was a graduate student at Berkeley, teaching remedial English, there were a few American Indians in my classroom. They were unlike any other "minority students" in the classes I taught. The Indians drifted in and out. When I summoned them to my office, they came and sat while I did all the talking.

I remember one tall man particularly, a near-somnambulist, beautiful in an off-putting way, but interesting, too, because I never saw him without the current issue of *The New York Review of Books* under his arm, which I took as an advertisement of ambition. He eschewed my class for weeks at a time. Then one morning I saw him in a café on Telegraph Avenue, across from Cody's. I did not fancy myself Sidney Poitier, but I was interested in this moody brave's lack of interest in me, for one, and then *The New York Review*.

Do you mind if I sit here?

Nothing.

Blah, Blah, Blah . . . N. Y. R. B. ?—entirely on my part—until, when I got up to leave:

"You're not Indian, you're Mexican," he said. "You wouldn't understand."

He meant I was cut. Diluted.

Understand what?

He meant I was not an Indian in America. He meant he was an enemy of the history that had otherwise created me. And he was right, I didn't understand. I took his diffidence for chauvinism. I read his chauvinism as arrogance. He didn't see the Indian in my face? I saw his face—his refusal to consort with the living—as the face of a dead man.

As the landscape goes, so goes the Indian? In the public-service TV commercial, the Indian sheds a tear at the sight of an America polluted beyond his recognition. Indian memory has become the measure against which America gauges corrupting history when it suits us. Gitchigoomeism—the habit of placing the Indian outside history—is a white sentimentality that relegates the Indian to death.

An obituary from *The New York Times* (September 1989—dateline Alaska): An oil freighter has spilled its load along the Alaskan coast. There is a billion-dollar cleanup, bringing jobs and dollars to Indian villages.

> The modern world has been closing in on English Bay . . . with glacial slowness. The oil spill and the resulting sea of money have accelerated the process, so that English Bay now seems caught on the cusp of history.

The omniscient reporter from *The New York Times* takes it upon himself to regret history on behalf of the Indians.

> Instead of hanging salmon to dry this month, as Aleut natives have done for centuries . . . John Kvasnikoff was putting up a three thousand dollar television satellite dish on the bluff next to his home above the sea.

The reporter from *The New York Times* knows the price modernity will exact from an Indian who wants to plug himself in. Mind you, the reporter is confident of his own role in history, his freedom to lug a word processor to some remote Alaskan village. About the reporter's journey, *The New York Times* is not censorious. But let the Indian drop one bead from custom, or let his son straddle a snowmobile—as he does in the photo accompanying the article—and *The New York Times* cries Boo-hoo-hoo yah-yah-yah.

Thus does the Indian become the mascot of an international ecology movement. The industrial countries of the world romanticize the Indian who no longer exists, ignoring the Indian who does—the Indian who is poised to chop down his rain forest, for example. Or the Indian who reads *The New York Times.*

Once more in San Francisco: I flattered myself that the woman staring at me all evening "knew my work." I considered myself an active agent, in other words. But, after several passes around the buffet, the woman cornered me to say she recognized me as an "ancient soul."

Do I lure or am I just minding my own business?

Is it the nature of Indians—not verifiable in nature, of course, but in the European description of Indians—that we wait around to be "discovered"?

Europe discovers. India beckons. Isn't that so? India sits atop her lily pad through centuries, lost in contemplation of the horizon. And, from time to time, India is discovered.

In the fifteenth century, sailing Spaniards were acting according to scientific conjecture as to the nature and as to the shape of the world. Most thinking men in Europe at the time of Columbus believed the world to be round. The voyage of Columbus was the test of a theory believed to be true. Brave, yes, but pedantic therefore.

The Indian is forever implicated in the roundness of the world. America was the false India, the mistaken India, and yet veritable India, for all that—India—the clasp, the coupling mystery at the end of quest.

This is as true today as of yore. Where do the Beatles go when the world is too much with them? Where does Jerry Brown seek the fat farm of his soul? India, man, India!

India waits.

India has all the answers beneath her passive face or behind her veil or between her legs. The European has only questions, questions that are assertions turned inside out, questions that can only be answered by sailing toward the abysmal horizon.

The lusty Europeans wanted the shortest answers. They knew what they wanted. They wanted spices, pagodas, gold.

Had the world been flat, had the European sought the unknown, then the European would have been as great a victor over history as he has portrayed himself to be. The European would have outdistanced history—even theology—if he could have arrived at the shore of some prelapsarian state. If the world had been flat, then the European could have traveled outward toward innocence.

But the world was round. The entrance into the Indies was a reunion of peoples. The Indian awaited the long-separated European, the inevitable European, as the approaching horizon.

Though perhaps, too, there was some demiurge felt by the human race of the fifteenth century to heal itself, to make itself whole? Certainly, in retrospect, there was some inevitability to the Catholic venture. If the world was round, continuous, then so, too, were peoples?

According to the European version—the stag version—of the pageant of the New World, the Indian must play a passive role. Europe has been accustomed to play the swaggart in history—Europe striding through the Americas, overturning temples, spilling language, spilling seed, spilling blood.

And wasn't the Indian the female, the passive, the waiting aspect to the theorem—lewd and promiscuous in her embrace as she is indolent betimes?

Charles Macomb Flandrau, a native of St. Paul, Minnesota, wrote a book called *Viva Mexico!* in 1908, wherein he described the Mexican Indian as "incorrigibly plump. One never ceases to marvel at the superhuman strength existing beneath the pretty and effeminate modeling of their arms and legs and backs. . . . The legs of an American 'strong man' look usually like an anatomical chart, but the legs of the most powerful Totonac Indian—and the power of many of them is beyond belief—would serve admirably as one of those idealized extremities on which women's hosiery is displayed in shop windows."

In Western Civilization histories, the little honeymoon joke Europe tells on itself is of mistaking America for the extremities of India. But India was perhaps not so much a misnomer as was "discoverer" or "conquistador."

Earliest snapshots of Indians brought back to Europe were of naked little woodcuts, arms akimbo, resembling Erasmus, or of grandees in capes and feathered tiaras, courtiers of an Egyptified palace of nature. In European museums, she is idle, recumbent at the base of a silver pineapple tree or the pedestal of the Dresden urn or the Sèvres tureen—the muse of European adventure, at once wanderlust and bounty.

Many tribes of Indians were prescient enough, preserved memory enough, or were lonesome enough to predict the coming of a pale stranger from across the sea, a messianic twin of completing memory or skill.

None of this could the watery Europeans have known as they marveled at the sight of approaching land. Filled with the arrogance of discovery, the Europeans were not predisposed to imagine that they were being watched, awaited.

*     *     *

That friend of mine at Oxford loses patience whenever I describe my face as mestizo. Look at my face. What do you see?

An Indian, he says.

Mestizo, I correct.

Mestizo, mestizo, he says.

Listen, he says. I went back to my mother's village in Mexico last summer and there was nothing mestizo about it. Dust, dogs, and Indians. People there don't even speak Spanish.

So I ask my friend at Oxford what it means to him to be an Indian.

He hesitates. My friend has recently been taken up as amusing by a bunch of rich Pakistanis in London. But, facing me, he is vexed and in earnest. He describes a lonely search among his family for evidence of Indian-ness. He thinks he has found it in his mother; watching his mother in her garden.

Does she plant corn by the light of the moon?

She seems to have some relationship with the earth, he says quietly.

So there it is. The mystical tie to nature. How else to think of the Indian except in terms of some druidical green thumb? No one says of an English matron in her rose garden that she is behaving like a Celt. Because the Indian has no history—that is, because history books are the province of the descendants of Europeans—the Indian seems only to belong to the party of the first part, the first chapter. So that is where the son expects to find his mother, Daughter of the Moon.

Let's talk about something else. Let's talk about London. The last time I was in London, I was walking toward an early evening at the Queen's Theatre when I passed that Christopher Wren church near Fortnum & Mason. The church was lit; I decided to stop, to savor the spectacle of what I expected would be a few Pymish men and women rolled into balls of fur at evensong. Imagine my surprise that the congregation was young—dressed in army fatigues and Laura Ashley. Within the chancel, cross-legged on a dais, was a South American shaman.

Now, who is the truer Indian in this picture? Me . . . me on my way to the Queen's Theatre? Or that guy on the altar with a Ph.D. in death?

*   *   *

We have hurled—like starlings, like Goths—through the castle of European memory. Our reflections have glanced upon the golden coach that carried the Emperor Maximilian through the streets of Mexico City, thence onward through the sludge of a hundred varnished paintings.

I have come at last to Mexico, the country of my parents' birth. I do not expect to find anything that pertains to me.

We have strained the rouge cordon at the thresholds of imperial apartments; seen chairs low enough for dwarfs, commodious enough for angels.

We have imagined the Empress Carlota standing in the shadows of an afternoon; we have followed her gaze down the Paseo de la Reforma toward the distant city. The Paseo was a nostalgic allusion to the Champs-Elysées, we learn, which Maximilian re-created for his tempestuous, crowlike bride.

Come this way, please. . . .

European memory is not to be the point of our excursion. Señor Fuentes, our tour director, is already beginning to descend the hill from Chapultepec Castle. What the American credit-card company calls our "orientation tour" of Mexico City had started late and so Señor Fuentes has been forced, regrettably,

". . . This way, please . . ."

to rush. Señor Fuentes is consumed with contrition for time wasted this morning. He intends to uphold his schedule, as a way of upholding Mexico, against our expectation.

We had gathered at the appointed time at the limousine entrance to our hotel, beneath the banner welcoming contestants to the Señorita Mexico pageant. We—Japanese, Germans, Americans—were waiting promptly at nine. There was no bus. And as we waited, the Señorita Mexico contestants arrived. Drivers leaned into their cabs to pull out long-legged señoritas. The drivers then balanced the señoritas onto stiletto heels (the driveway was cobbled) before they passed the señoritas, *en pointe*, to the waiting arms of officials.

Mexican men, meanwhile—doormen, bellhops, window washers, hotel guests—stopped dead in their tracks, wounded by the scent and spectacle of so many blond señoritas. The Mexican men assumed fierce expressions, nostrils flared, brows knit. Such expressions are masks—the men intend to convey their adoration of prey—as thoroughly ritualized as the smiles of beauty queens.

By now we can see the point of our excursion beyond the parched trees of Chapultepec Park—the Museo Nacional de Antropología—which is an air-conditioned repository for the artifacts of the Indian civilizations of Meso-America, the finest anthropological museum in the world.

"There will not be time to see everything," Señor Fuentes warns as he ushers us into the grand salon, our first experience of the suffocating debris of The Ancients. Señor Fuentes wants us in and out of here by noon.

Whereas the United States traditionally has rejoiced at the delivery of its landscape from "savagery," Mexico has taken its national identity only from the Indian, the mother. Mexico measures all cultural bastardy against the Indian; equates civilization with India—Indian kingdoms of a golden age; cities as fabulous as Alexandria or Benares or Constantinople; a court as hairless, as subtle as the Pekingese. Mexico equates barbarism with Europe—beardedness—with Spain.

It is curious, therefore, that both modern nations should similarly apostrophize the Indian, relegate the Indian to the past.

Come this way, please. Mrs. . . . Ah . . . this way, please.

Señor Fuentes wears an avocado-green sports coat with gold buttons. He is short. He is rather elegant, with a fine small head, small hands, small feet; with his two rows of fine small teeth like a nutcracker's teeth, with which he curtails consonants as cleanly as bitten thread. Señor Fuentes is brittle, he is watchful, he is ironic, he is metropolitan; his wit is quotational, literary, wasted on Mrs. Ah.

He is not our equal. His demeanor says he is not our equal. We mistake his condescension for humility. He will not eat when we eat. He will not spend when we shop. He will not have done with Mexico when we have done with Mexico.

Señor Fuentes is impatient with us, for we have paused momentarily outside the museum to consider the misfortune of an adolescent mother who holds her crying baby out to us. Several of us confer among ourselves in an attempt to place a peso value on the woman's situation. We do not ask for the advice of Señor Fuentes.

For we, in turn, are impatient with Señor Fuentes. We are in a bad mood. The air conditioning on our "fully air-conditioned coach" is nonexistent. We have a headache. Nor is the city air any relief, but it is brown, fungal, farted.

Señor Fuentes is a mystery to us, for there is no American equivalent to him; for there is no American equivalent to the subtleties he is paid to describe to us.

Mexico will not raise a public monument to Hernán Cortés, for example, the father of Mexico—the rapist. In the Diego Rivera murals in the presidential palace, the Aztec city of Tenochtitlán is rendered—its blood temples and blood canals—as haughty as Troy, as vulnerable as Pompeii. Any suggestion of the complicity of other tribes of Indians in overthrowing the Aztec empire is painted over. Spaniards appear on the horizons of Arcadia as syphilitic brigands and demon-eyed priests.

The Spaniard entered the Indian by entering her city—the floating city—first as a suitor, ceremoniously; later by force. How should Mexico honor the rape?

In New England the European and the Indian drew apart to regard each other with suspicion over centuries. Miscegenation was a sin against Protestant individualism. In Mexico the European and the Indian consorted. The ravishment of fabulous Tenochtitlán ended in a marriage of blood—a "cosmic race," the Mexican philosopher José Vasconcelos has called it.

Mexico's tragedy is that she has no political idea of herself as rich as her blood.

The rhetoric of Señor Fuentes, like the murals of Diego Rivera, resorts often to the dream of India—to Tenochtitlán, the capital of the world before conquest. "Preconquest" in the Mexican political lexicon is tantamount to "prelapsarian" in the Judeo-Christian scheme, and hearkens to a time Mexico feels herself to have been whole, a time before the Indian was separated from India by the serpent Spain.

Three centuries after Cortés, Mexico declared herself independent of Spain. If Mexico would have no yoke, then Mexico would have no crown, then Mexico would have no father. The denial of Spain has persisted into our century.

The priest and the landowner yet serve Señor Fuentes as symbols of the hated Spanish order. Though, in private, Mexico is Catholic; Mexican mothers may wish for light-skinned children. Touch blond hair and good luck will be yours.

In private, in Mexican Spanish, *indio* is a seller of Chiclets, a sidewalk squatter. *Indio* means backward or lazy or lower-class. In the eyes of the world, Mexico raises a magnificent museum of anthropology—the finest in the world—to honor the Indian mother.

In the nave of the National Cathedral, we notice the floor slopes dramatically. "The cathedral is sinking," Señor Fuentes explains as a hooded figure approaches our group from behind a column. She is an Indian woman; she wears a blue stole; her hands are cupped, beseeching; tear marks ream her cheeks. In Spanish, Señor Fuentes forbids this apparition: "Go ask *padrecito* to pry some gold off the altar for you."

"Mexico City is built upon swamp," Señor Fuentes resumes in English. "Therefore, the cathedral is sinking." But it is clear that Señor Fuentes believes the sinkage is due to the oppressive weight of Spanish Catholicism, its masses of gold, its volumes of deluded suspiration.

Mexican political life can only seem Panglossian when you consider an anti-Catholic government of an overwhelmingly Catholic population. Mexico is famous for politicians descended from Masonic fathers and Catholic mothers. Señor Fuentes himself is less a Spaniard, less an Indian, perhaps, than an embittered eighteenth-century man, clinging to the witty knees of Voltaire against the chaos of twentieth-century Mexico.

Mexico blamed the ruin of the nineteenth century on the foreigner, and with reason. Once emptied of Spain, the palace of Mexico became the dollhouse of France. Mexico was overrun by imperial armies. The greed of Europe met the Manifest Destiny of the United States in Mexico. Austria sent an archduke to marry Mexico with full panoply of candles and bishops. The U.S. reached under Mexico's skirt every chance he got.

"Poor Mexico, so far from God, so close to the United States."

Señor Fuentes dutifully attributes the mot to Porfirio Díaz, the Mexican president who sold more of Mexico to foreign interests than any other president. It was against the regime of Porfirio Díaz that Mexicans rebelled in the early decades of this century. Mexico prefers to call its civil war a "revolution."

Mexico for Mexicans!

The Revolution did not accomplish a union of Mexicans. The Revolution did not accomplish a restoration of Mexicans to their landscape. The dust of the Revolution parted to reveal—not India—but Marx *ex machina*, the Institutional Revolutionary Party, the PRI—a political machine appropriate to the age of steam. The Institutional Revolutionary Party, as its name implies, was designed to reconcile institutional pragmatism with revolutionary rhetoric. And the PRI worked for a time, because it gave Mexico what Mexico most needed, the stability of compromise.

The PRI appears everywhere in Mexico—a slogan on the wall, the politician impersonating a journalist on the evening news, the professor at his podium. The PRI is in its way as much a Mexican institution as the Virgin of Guadalupe.

Now Mexicans speak of the government as something imposed upon them, and they are the victims of it. But the political failure of Mexico must be counted a failure of Mexicans. Whom now shall Señor Fuentes blame for a twentieth century that has become synonymous with corruption?

Well, as long as you stay out of the way of the police no one will bother you, is conventional Mexican wisdom, and Mexico continues to live her daily life. In the capital, the air is the color of the buildings of Siena. Telephone connections are an aspect of the will of God. Mexicans drive on the sidewalks. A man on the street corner seizes the opportunity of stalled traffic to earn his living as a fire-eater. His ten children pass among the cars and among the honking horns to collect small coins.

Thank you. Thank you very much. A pleasure, Mrs. . . . Ah. Thank you very much.

Señor Fuentes bids each farewell. He accepts tips within a handshake. He bows slightly. We have no complaint with Señor Fuentes, after all. The bus was not his fault. Mexico City is not his fault. And Señor Fuentes will return to his unimaginable Mexico and we will return to our rooms to take aspirin and to initiate long-distance telephone calls. Señor Fuentes will remove his avocado-green coat and, having divested, Señor Fuentes will in some fashion partake of what he has successfully kept from us all day, which is the life and the drinking water of Mexico.

*   *   *

The Virgin of Guadalupe symbolizes the entire coherence of Mexico, body and soul. You will not find the story of the Virgin within hidebound secular histories of Mexico—nor indeed within the credulous repertoire of Señor Fuentes—and the omission renders the history of Mexico incomprehensible.

One recent afternoon, within the winy bell jar of a very late lunch, I told the story of the Virgin of Guadalupe to Lynn, a sophisticated twentieth-century woman. The history of Mexico, I promised her, is neither mundane nor masculine, but it is a miracle play with trapdoors and sequins and jokes on the living.

In the sixteenth century, when Indians were demoralized by the routing of their gods, when millions of Indians were dying from the plague of Europe, the Virgin Mary appeared pacing on a hillside to an Indian peasant named Juan Diego—his Christian name, for Juan was a convert. It was December 1531.

On his way to mass, Juan passed the hill called Tepayac . . .

> Just as the East was beginning to kindle
> To dawn. He heard there a cloud
> Of birdsong bursting overhead
> Of whistles and flutes and beating wings
> —Now here, now there—
> A mantle of chuckles and berries and rain
> That rocked through the sky like the great Spanish bell
> In Mexico City;
> At the top of the hill there shone a light

And the light called out a name to him
With a lady's voice.
Juan, Juan,
The Lady-light called.
Juan crossed himself, he fell to his knees,
He covered his eyes and prepared to be blinded.

He could see through his hands that covered his face
As the sun rose up from behind her cape,
That the poor light of day
Was no match for this Lady, but broke upon her
Like a waterfall,
A rain of rings.
She wore a gown the color of dawn.
Her hair was braided with ribbons and flowers
And tiny tinkling silver bells. Her mantle was sheer
And bright as rain and embroidered with thousands of twinkling
        stars.
A clap before curtains, like waking from sleep;
Then a human face,
A mother's smile;
Her complexion as red as cinnamon bark;
Cheeks as brown as pérsimmon.

Her eyes were her voice,
As modest and shy as a pair of doves
In the eaves of her brow. Her voice was
Like listening. This lady spoke
In soft Nahuatl, the Aztec tongue
(As different from Spanish
As some other season of weather,
As doves in the boughs of a summer tree
Are different from crows in a wheeling wind,
Who scatter destruction and
Caw caw caw caw) —
Nahuatl like rain, like water flowing, like drips in a cavern,
Or glistening thaw,
Like breath through a flute,
With many stops and plops and sighs . . .

Peering through the grille of her cigarette smoke, Lynn heard and she seemed to approve the story.

At the Virgin's behest, this Prufrock Indian must go several times to the bishop of Mexico City. He must ask that a chapel be built on Tepayac where his discovered Lady may share in the sorrows of her people. Juan

Diego's visits to the Spanish bishop parody the conversion of the Indians by the Spaniards. The bishop is skeptical.

The bishop wants proof.

The Virgin tells Juan Diego to climb the hill and gather a sheaf of roses as proof for the bishop—Castilian roses—impossible in Mexico in December of 1531. Juan carries the roses in the folds of his cloak, a pregnant messenger. Upon entering the bishop's presence, Juan parts his cloak, the roses tumble; the bishop falls to his knees.

In the end—with crumpled napkins, torn carbons, the bitter dregs of coffee—Lynn gave the story over to the Spaniards.

The legend concludes with a concession to humanity—proof more durable than roses—the imprint of the Virgin's image upon the cloak of Juan Diego . . .

A Spanish trick, Lynn said. A recruitment poster for the new religion, no more, she said (though sadly). An itinerant diva with a costume trunk. Birgit Nilsson as Aïda.

Why do we assume Spain made up the story?

The importance of the story is that Indians believed it. The jokes, the vaudeville, the relegation of the Spanish bishop to the role of comic adversary, the Virgin's chosen cavalier, and especially the brown-faced Mary—all elements spoke directly to Indians.

The result of the apparition and of the miraculous image of the Lady remaining upon the cloak of Juan Diego was a mass conversion of Indians to Catholicism.

The image of Our Lady of Guadalupe (privately, affectionately, Mexicans call her La Morenita—Little Darkling) has become the unofficial, the private flag of Mexicans. Unique possession of her image is a more wonderful election to Mexicans than any political call to nationhood. Perhaps Mexico's tragedy in our century, perhaps Mexico's abiding grace thus far, is that she has no political idea of herself as compelling as her icon.

The Virgin appears everywhere in Mexico. On dashboards and on calendars, on playing cards, on lampshades and cigar boxes; within the loneliness and tattooed upon the very skins of Mexicans.

Nor is the image of Guadalupe a diminishing mirage of the sixteenth century, but she has become more vivid with time, developing in her replication from earthy shades of melon and musk to bubble-gum pink, Windex blue, to achieve the hard, literal focus of holy cards or baseball cards; of Krishna or St. Jude or the Atlanta Braves.

Mexico City stands as the last living medieval capital of the world. Mexico is the creation of a Spanish Catholicism that attempted to draw continents together as one flesh. The success of Spanish Catholicism in

Mexico resulted in a kind of proof—a profound concession to humanity:
the *mestizaje*.

What joke on the living? Lynn said.

The joke is that Spain arrived with missionary zeal at the shores of contemplation. But Spain had no idea of the absorbent strength of Indian
spirituality.

By the waters of baptism, the active European was entirely absorbed
within the contemplation of the Indian. The faith that Europe imposed
in the sixteenth century was, by virtue of the Guadalupe, embraced by
the Indian. Catholicism has become an Indian religion. By the twenty-
first century, the locus of the Catholic Church, by virtue of numbers, will
be Latin America, by which time Catholicism itself will have assumed
the aspect of the Virgin of Guadalupe.

Brown skin.

\*       \*       \*

*Time* magazine dropped through the chute of my mailbox a few years
ago with a cover story on Mexico entitled "The Population Curse." From
the vantage point of Sixth Avenue, the editors of Time-Life peer down
into the basin of Mexico City—like peering down into the skull of a
pumpkin—to contemplate the nightmare of fecundity, the tangled mass
of slime and hair and seed.

America sees death in all that life; sees rot. Life—not illness and
poverty; not death—life becomes the curse of Mexico City in the opinion of *Time* magazine.

For a long time I had my own fear of Mexico, an American fear. Mexico's history was death. Her stature was tragedy. A race of people that
looked like me had disappeared.

I had a dream about Mexico City, a conquistador's dream. I was lost
and late and twisted in my sheet. I dreamed streets narrower than they actually are—narrow as old Jerusalem. I dreamed sheets, entanglements,
bunting, hanging larvaelike from open windows, distended from balconies and from lines thrown over the streets. These streets were not
empty streets. I was among a crowd. The crowd was not a carnival crowd.
This crowd was purposeful and ordinary, welling up from subways, ascending from stairwells. And then the dream followed the course of all
my dreams. I must find the airport—the American solution—I must
somehow escape, fly over.

Each face looked like mine. But no one looked at me.

I have come at last to Mexico, to the place of my parents' birth. I have
come under the protection of an American credit-card company. I have
canceled this trip three times.

As the plane descends into the basin of Mexico City, I brace myself for some confrontation with death, with India, with confusion of purpose that I do not know how to master.

Do you speak Spanish? the driver asks in English.

Andrés, the driver employed by my hotel, is in his forties. He lives in the Colonia Roma, near the airport. There is nothing about the city he does not know. This is his city and he is its memory.

Andrés's car is a dark-blue Buick—about 1975. Windows slide up and down at the touch of his finger. There is the smell of disinfectant in Andrés's car, as there is in every bus or limousine or taxi I've ridden in Mexico—the smell of the glycerine crystals in urinals. Dangling from Andrés's rearview mirror is the other appliance common to all public conveyance in Mexico—a rosary.

Andrés is a man of the world, a man, like other working-class Mexican men, eager for the world. He speaks two languages. He knows several cities. He has been to the United States. His brother lives there still.

In the annals of the famous European discoverers there is invariably an Indian guide, a translator—willing or not—to facilitate, to preserve Europe's stride. These seem to have become fluent in pallor before Europe learned anything of them. How is that possible?

The most famous guide in Mexican history is also the most reviled by Mexican histories—the villainess Marina—"La Malinche." Marina became the lover of Cortés. So, of course, Mexicans say she betrayed India for Europe. In the end, she was herself betrayed, left behind when Cortés repaired to his Spanish wife.

Nonetheless, Marina's treachery anticipates the epic marriage of Mexico. La Malinche prefigures, as well, the other, the beloved female aspect of Mexico, the Virgin of Guadalupe.

Because Marina was the seducer of Spain, she challenges the boast Europe has always told about India.

I assure you Mexico has an Indian point of view as well, a female point of view:

*I opened my little eye and the Spaniard disappeared.*

*Imagine a dark pool; the Spaniard dissolved; the surface triumphantly smooth.*

*My eye!*

*The spectacle of the Spaniard on the horizon, vainglorious—the shiny surfaces, clanks of metal; the horses, the muskets, the jingling bits.*

*Cannot you imagine me curious? Didn't I draw near?*

European vocabularies do not have a silence rich enough to describe the force within Indian contemplation. Only Shakespeare understood that Indians have eyes. Shakespeare saw Caliban eyeing his master's books—well, why not his master as well? The same dumb lust.

WHAT DAT? is a question philosophers ask. And Indians.

Shakespeare's comedy, of course, resolves itself to the European's applause. The play that Shakespeare did not write is Mexico City.

Now the great city swells under the moon; seems, now, to breathe of itself—the largest city in the world—a Globe, kind Will, not of your devising, not under your control.

The superstition persists in European travel literature that Indian Christianity is the thinnest veneer covering an ulterior altar. But there is a possibility still more frightening to the European imagination, so frightening that in five hundred years such a possibility has scarcely found utterance.

What if the Indian were converted?

The Indian eye becomes a portal through which the entire pageant of European civilization has already passed; turned inside out. Then the baroque is an Indian conceit. The colonial arcade is an Indian detail.

Look once more at the city from La Malinche's point of view. Mexico is littered with the shells and skulls of Spain, cathedrals, poems, and the limbs of orange trees. But everywhere you look in this great museum of Spain you see living Indians.

Where are the *conquistadores?*

Postcolonial Europe expresses pity or guilt behind its sleeve, pities the Indian the loss of her gods or her tongue. But let the Indian speak for herself. Spanish is now an Indian language. Mexico City has become the metropolitan see of the Spanish-speaking world. In something like the way New York won English from London after World War I, Mexico City has captured Spanish.

The Indian stands in the same relationship to modernity as she did to Spain—willing to marry, to breed, to disappear in order to ensure her inclusion in time; refusing to absent herself from the future. The Indian has chosen to survive, to consort with the living, to live in the city, to crawl on her hands and knees, if need be, to Mexico City or L.A.

I take it as an Indian achievement that I am alive, that I am Catholic, that I speak English, that I am an American. My life began, it did not end, in the sixteenth century.

The idea occurs to me on a weekday morning, at a crowded intersection in Mexico City: Europe's lie. Here I am in the capital of death. Life surges about me; wells up from subways, wave upon wave; descends from stairwells. Everywhere I look. Babies. Traffic. Food. Beggars. Life. Life coming upon me like sunstroke.

Each face looks like mine. No one looks at me.

Where, then, is the famous conquistador?

*We have eaten him,* the crowd tells me, *we have eaten him with our eyes.*

I run to the mirror to see if this is true.

It is true.

In the distance, at its depths, Mexico City stands as the prophetic example. Mexico City is modern in ways that "multiracial," ethnically "diverse" New York City is not yet. Mexico City is centuries more modern than racially "pure," provincial Tokyo. Nothing to do with computers or skyscrapers.

Mexico City is the capital of modernity, for in the sixteenth century, under the tutelage of a curious Indian whore, under the patronage of the Queen of Heaven, Mexico initiated the task of the twenty-first century—the renewal of the old, the known world, through miscegenation. Mexico carries the idea of a round world to its biological conclusion.

*       *       *

For a time when he was young, Andrés, my driver, worked in Alpine County in northern California.

And then he worked at a Lake Tahoe resort. He remembers the snow. He remembers the weekends when blond California girls would arrive in their ski suits and sunglasses. Andrés worked at the top of a ski lift. His job was to reach out over a little precipice to help the California girls out of their lift chairs. He would maintain his grasp until they were balanced upon the snow. And then he would release them, watch them descend the winter slope—how they laughed!—oblivious of his admiration, until they disappeared.

# PAUL MONETTE

## (1945–1995)

A poet, novelist, screenwriter, and memoirist who died of AIDS, Monette was a pioneer in writing about this horrific epidemic. *Borrowed Time: An AIDS Memoir* (1988) is among the finest examples of a genre that has sadly flourished as the disease itself has taken root, especially in gay communities. This award-winning memoir seems likely to outlive the disease that set this tragic story in motion. It is, at its most elemental level, a love story, conveyed so movingly that the book transcends the genre of "gay literature." It is also a universal story of human loss, written with the kind of lyric precision one might expect of a poet. Monette focuses on the final nineteen months in the life of Roger Horwitz, his companion, celebrating the bravery of a man wracked by pain. It is an urbane, intelligent, harrowing book.

## FROM *Borrowed Time: An AIDS Memoir*

I don't know if I will live to finish this. Doubtless there's a streak of self-importance in such an assertion, but who's counting? Maybe it's just that I've watched too many sicken in a month and die by Christmas, so that a fatal sort of realism comforts me more than magic. All I know is this: The virus ticks in me. And it doesn't care a whit about our categories—when is full-blown, what's AIDS-related, what is just sick and tired? No one has solved the puzzle of its timing. I take my drug from Tijuana twice a day. The very friends who tell me how vigorous I look, how well I seem, are the first to assure me of the imminent medical breakthrough. What they don't seem to understand is, I used up all my optimism keeping my friend alive. Now that he's gone, the cup of my own health is neither half full nor half empty. Just half.

Equally difficult, of course, is knowing where to start. The world around me is defined now by its endings and its closures—the date on the grave that follows the hyphen. Roger Horwitz, my beloved friend, died of complications of AIDS on October 22, 1986, nineteen months and ten days after his diagnosis. That is the only real date anymore, casting its ice shadow over all the secular holidays lovers mark their calendars by. Until that long night in October, it didn't seem possible that any day could supplant the brute equinox of March 12—the day of Roger's diagnosis in 1985, the day we began to live on the moon.

The fact is, no one knows where to start with AIDS. Now, in the seventh year of the calamity, my friends in L.A. can hardly recall what it felt like any longer, the time before the sickness. Yet we all watched the toll mount in New York, then in San Francisco, for years before it ever touched us here. It comes like a slowly dawning horror. At first you are equipped with a hundred different amulets to keep it far away. Then someone you know goes into the hospital, and suddenly you are at high noon in full battle gear. They have neglected to tell you that you will be issued no weapons of any sort. So you cobble together a weapon out of anything that lies at hand, like a prisoner honing a spoon handle into a stiletto. You fight tough, you fight dirty, but you cannot fight dirtier than it.

I remember a Saturday in February 1982, driving Route 10 to Palm Springs with Roger to visit his parents for the weekend. While Roger drove, I read aloud an article from *The Advocate:* "Is Sex Making Us Sick?" There was the slightest edge of irony in the query, an urban cool that seems almost bucolic now in its innocence. But the article didn't mince words. It was the first in-depth reporting I'd read that laid out the shadowy nonfacts of what till then had been the most fragmented of rumors. The first cases were reported to the Centers for Disease Control (CDC) only six months before, but they weren't in the newspapers, not in L.A. I note in my diary in December '81 ambiguous reports of a "gay cancer," but I know I didn't have the slightest picture of the thing. Cancer of the *what?* I would have asked, if anyone had known anything.

I remember exactly what was going through my mind while I was reading, though I can't now recall the details of the piece. I was thinking: How is this not me? Trying to find a pattern I was exempt from. It was a brand of denial I would watch grow exponentially during the next few years, but at the time I was simply relieved. Because the article appeared to be saying that there was a grim progression toward this undefined catastrophe, a set of preconditions—chronic hepatitis, repeated bouts of syphilis, exotic parasites. No wonder my first baseline response was to feel safe. It was *them*—by which I meant the fast-lane Fire Island crowd, the Sutro Baths, the world of High Eros.

Not us.

I grabbed for that relief because we'd been through a rough patch the previous autumn. Till then Roger had always enjoyed a sort of no-nonsense good health: not an abuser of anything, with a constitutional aversion to hypochondria, and not wed to his mirror save for a minor alarm as to the growing dimensions of his bald spot. In the seven years we'd been together I scarcely remember him having a cold or taking an aspirin. Yet in October '81 he had struggled with a peculiar bout of intestinal flu. Nothing special showed up in any of the blood tests, but over a period of weeks he experienced persistent symptoms that didn't neatly connect: pains in his legs, diarrhea, general malaise. I hadn't been feeling notably bad myself, but on the other hand I was a textbook hypochondriac, and I figured if Rog was harboring some kind of bug, so was I.

The two of us finally went to a gay doctor in the Valley for a further set of blood tests. It's a curious phenomenon among gay middle-class men that anything faintly venereal had better be taken to a doctor who's "on the bus." Is it a sense of fellow feeling perhaps, or a way of avoiding embarrassment? Do we really believe that only a doctor who's *our* kind can heal us of the afflictions that attach somehow to our secret hearts? There is so much magic to medicine. Of course we didn't know then that those few physicians with a large gay clientele were about to be swamped beyond all capacity to cope.

The tests came back positive for amoebiasis. Roger and I began the highly toxic treatment to kill the amoeba, involving two separate drugs and what seems in memory thirty pills a day for six weeks, till the middle of January. It was the first time I'd ever experienced the phenomenon of the cure making you sicker. By the end of treatment we were both weak and had lost weight, and for a couple of months afterward were susceptible to colds and minor infections.

It was only after the treatment was over that a friend of ours, diagnosed with amoebas by the same doctor, took his slide to the lab at UCLA for a second opinion. And that was my first encounter with lab error. The doctor at UCLA explained that the slide had been misread; the squiggles that looked like amoebas were in fact benign. The doctor shook his head and grumbled about "these guys who do their own lab work." Roger then retrieved his slide, took it over to UCLA and was told the same: no amoebas. We had just spent six weeks methodically ingesting poison for no reason at all.

So it wasn't the *Advocate* story that sent up the red flag for us. We'd been shaken by the amoeba business, and from that point on we operated at a new level of sexual caution. What is now called safe sex did not use to be so clearly defined. The concept didn't exist. But it was quickly becoming apparent, even then, that we couldn't wait for somebody else to define the parameters. Thus every gay man I know has had to come to a point of personal definition by way of avoiding the chaos of sexually transmitted diseases, or STD as we call them in the trade. There was obviously no one moment of conscious decision, a bolt of clarity on the shimmering freeway west of San Bernardino, but I think of that day when I think of the sea change. The party was going to have to stop. The evidence was too ominous: We *were making ourselves sick.*

Not that Roger and I were the life of the party. Roger especially didn't march to the different drum of *so many men, so little time,* the motto and anthem of the sunstruck summers of the mid-to-late seventies. He'd managed not to carry away from his adolescence the mark of too much repression, or indeed the yearning to make up for lost time. In ten years he had perhaps half a dozen contacts outside the main frame of our relationship, mostly when he was out of town on business. He was comfortable with relative monogamy, even at a time when certain quarters of the gay world found the whole idea trivial and bourgeois. I realize that in the world of the heterosexual there is a generalized lip service paid to exclusive monogamy, a notion most vividly honored in the breach. I leave the matter of morality to those with the gift of tongues; it was difficult enough for us to fashion a sexual ethics just for us. In any case, I was the one in the relationship who suffered from lost time. I was the one who would go after a sexual encounter as if it were an ice cream cone—casual, quick, good-bye.

But as I say, who's counting? I only want to make it plain to start with that we got very alert and very careful as far back as the winter of '82. That gut need for safety took hold and lingered, even as we got better again and strong. Thus I'm not entirely sure what I thought on another afternoon a year and a half later, when a friend of ours back from New York reported a conversation he'd had with a research man from Sloan-Kettering.

"He thinks all it takes is one exposure," Charlie said, this after months of articles about the significance of repeated exposure. More tenaciously than ever, we all wanted to believe the whole deepening tragedy was centered on those at the sexual frontiers who were fucking their brains out. The rest of us were fashioning our own little Puritan forts, as we struggled to convince ourselves that a clean slate would hold the nightmare at bay.

Yet with caution as our watchword starting in February of '82, Roger was diagnosed with AIDS three years later. So the turning over of new leaves was not to be on everybody's side. A lot of us were already ticking and didn't even know. The magic circle my generation is trying to stay within the borders of is only as real as the random past. Perhaps the young can live in the magic circle, but only if those of us who are ticking will tell our story. Otherwise it goes on being *us* and *them* forever, built like a wall higher and higher, till you no longer think to wonder if you are walling it out or in.

For us the knowing began in earnest on the first of September, 1983. I'd had a call a couple of days before from my closest friend, Cesar Albini, who'd just returned to San Francisco after a summer touring Europe with a group of students. He said he'd been having trouble walking because of a swollen gland in his groin, and he was going to the hospital to have it biopsied. He reassured me he was feeling fine and wasn't expecting anything ominous, but figured he'd check it out before school started again. AIDS didn't even cross my mind, though cancer did. Half joking, Cesar wondered aloud if he dared disturb our happy friendship with bad news.

"If it's bad," I said, "we'll handle it, okay?"

But I really didn't clutch with fear, or it was only a brief stab of the hypochondriacal sort. Roger and I were busy getting ready for a four-day trip to Big Sur, something we'd done almost yearly since moving to California in 1977. We were putting the blizzard of daily life on hold, looking forward to a dose of raw sublime that coincided with our anniversary—September 3, the day we met.

Cesar was forty-three, only ten months older than Roger. Born in Uruguay, possessed of a great heart and inexhaustible energy, he had studied in Europe and traveled all over, once spending four months going overland from Paris to China at a total cost of five hundred dollars. He was the first Uruguayan ever to enter Afghanistan through the mountains—on a camel, if I remember right. He spoke French, Italian, Spanish and English with equal fluency, and he tended to be the whole language department of a school. We'd both been teaching at secondary schools in Massachusetts when we met, and we goaded one another to make the move west that had always been our shared dream. Thus Cesar had relocated to San Francisco in July of '76, and Roger and I landed in L.A. four days after Thanksgiving the following year.

Cesar wasn't lucky in matters of the heart. He was still in the closet during his years back east, and the move to San Francisco was an extraordinary rite of passage for him. He always wanted a great love, but the couple of relationships he'd been involved in scarcely left the station. Still, he was very proud and indulged in no self-pity. He learned to accept the limited terms of the once-a-week relations he found in San Francisco, and broke through to the freedom of his own manhood without the mythic partner. The open sexual exultation that marked San Francisco in those days was something he rejoiced in.

Yet even though he went to the baths a couple of times a week, Cesar wasn't into anything *weird*—or that's how I might have put it at that stage of my own denial. No hepatitis, no history of VD, built tall and fierce—of course he was safe. The profile of AIDS continued to be mostly a matter of shadows. The L.A. *Times* wasn't covering it, though by then I had come to learn how embattled things had grown in New York. The Gay Men's Health Crisis was up to its ears in clients; Larry Kramer was screaming at the mayor; and the body count was appearing weekly in the *Native*. A writer I knew slightly was walking around with Kaposi's sarcoma. A young composer kept getting sicker and sicker, though he stubbornly didn't fit the CDC's hopelessly narrow categories, so that case was still officially a toss-up. And again, we're talking New York.

I came home at six on the evening of the first, and Roger met me gravely at the door. "There's a message from Cesar," he said. "It's not good."

Numbly I played back the answering machine, where so much appalling misery would be left on tape over the years to come, as if a record were crying out to be kept. "I have a little bit of bad news." Cesar's voice sounded strained, almost embarrassed. He left no details. I called and called him throughout the evening, convinced I was about to hear cancer news. The lymph nodes, of course—a hypochondriac knows all there is to know about the sites of malignancy. Already I was figuring what the treatments might be; no question in my mind but that it was treatable. I had Cesar practically cured by the time I reached Tom, a friend and former student of his. But as usual with me in crisis, I was jabbering and wouldn't let Tom get a word in. Finally he broke through: "He's got it."

"Got what?"

It's not till you first hear it attached to someone you love that you realize how little you know about it. My mind went utterly blank. The carefully constructed wall collapsed as if a 7.5 quake had rumbled under it. At that point I didn't even know the difference between KS and the opportunistic infections. I kept picturing that swollen gland in his groin, thinking: What's *that* got to do with AIDS? And a parallel track in my mind began careening with another thought: the swollen glands in my own groin, always dismissed by my straight doctor as herpes-related and "not a significant sign."

"We're not going to die young," Cesar used to say with a wag of his finger, his black Latin eyes dancing. "We won't get out of it *that* easily!" Then he would laugh and clap his hands, downing the coffee he always took with cream and four sugars. It looked like pudding.

I reached him very late that night and mouthed again the same words I'd said so bravely two days before: We'll deal with it. There is no end to the litany of reassurance that springs to your lips to ward away the specter. They've caught it early; you're fine; there's got to be some kind of treatment. That old chestnut, the imminent breakthrough. You fling these phrases instinctively, like pennies down a well. Cesar and I bent backward to calm each other. It was just a couple of lesions in the groin; you could hardly see them. And the reason everything was going to be all right was really very simple: We would fight this thing like demons.

But the hollowness and disbelief pursued Roger and me all the way up the gold coast. Big Sur was towering and bracing as ever—exalted as Homer's Ithaca, as Robinson Jeffers described it. We were staying at Ventana, the lavish inn high in the hills above the canyon of the Big Sur River. We used the inn as a base camp for our day-long hikes, returning in the evening to posh amenities worthy of an Edwardian big-game hunt. On the second morning we walked out to Andrew Molera Beach, where the Big Sur empties into the Pacific. Molera stretches unblemished for five miles down the coast, curving like a crescent moon, with weathered headlands clean as Scotland. It was a kind of holy place for Roger and me, like the yearly end of a quest.

"What if we got it?" I said, staring out at the otters belly up in the kelp beds, taking the sun.

I don't remember how we answered that, because of course there wasn't any answer. Merely to pose the question was by way of another shot at magic. Mention the unmentionable and it will go away, like shining a light around a child's bedroom to shoo the monster. The great ache we were feeling at that moment was for our stricken friend, and we were too ignorant still to envision the medieval tortures that might await him.

But I know that the roll of pictures I took that day was my first conscious memorializing of Roger and me, as if I could hold the present as security on the future.

# ANNIE DILLARD
## (1945– )

Born in Pittsburgh and educated at Hollins College, in Virginia, Dillard is best known for *Pilgrim at Tinker Creek,* which won a Pulitzer Prize in nonfiction in 1974. This beautifully written account of a year spent in the Roanoke Valley of the Blue Ridge Mountains offers a natural history of that region as well as a delicate evocation of consciousness. It has earned its status as a classic of contemporary nature writing.

Dillard's books are unusually varied, in both theme and genre. She has published a book of poetry, *Tickets for a Prayer Wheel* (1974), a novel, and various collections of essays, including *Teaching a Stone to Talk* (1982). Her lyrical memoir, *An American Childhood* (1987), traces the emergence of her intense relation to the physical world and her gift for detailed observation. Since 1979, she has been on the faculty of Wesleyan University.

## FROM *An American Childhood*

The interior life is often stupid. Its egoism blinds it and deafens it; its imagination spins out ignorant tales, fascinated. It fancies that the western wind blows on the Self, and leaves fall at the feet of the Self for a reason, and people are watching. A mind risks real ignorance for the sometimes paltry prize of an imagination enriched. The trick of reason is to get the imagination to seize the actual world—if only from time to time.

When I was five, growing up in Pittsburgh in 1950, I would not go to bed willingly because something came into my room. This was a private matter between me and it. If I spoke of it, it would kill me.

Who could breathe as this thing searched for me over the very corners of the room? Who could ever breathe freely again? I lay in the dark.

My sister Amy, two years old, was asleep in the other bed. What did she know? She was innocent of evil. Even at two she composed herself attractively for sleep. She folded the top sheet tidily under her prettily outstretched arm; she laid her perfect head lightly on an unwrinkled pillow, where her thick curls spread evenly in rays like petals. All night long she slept smoothly in a series of pleasant and serene, if artificial-looking, positions, a faint smile on her closed lips, as if she were posing for an ad for sheets. There was no messiness in her, no roughness for things to cling to, only a charming and charmed innocence that seemed then to protect her, an innocence I needed but couldn't muster. Since Amy was asleep, furthermore, and since when I needed someone most I was afraid to stir enough to wake her, she was useless.

I lay alone and was almost asleep when the damned thing entered the room by flattening itself against the open door and sliding in. It was a transparent, luminous oblong. I could see the door whiten at its touch; I could see the blue wall turn pale where it raced over it, and see the maple headboard of Amy's bed glow. It was a swift spirit; it was an awareness. It made noise. It had two joined parts, a head and a tail, like a Chinese dragon. It found the door, wall, and headboard; and it swiped them, charging them with its luminous glance. After its fleet, searching passage, things looked the same, but weren't.

I dared not blink or breathe; I tried to hush my whooping blood. If it found another awareness, it would destroy it.

Every night before it got to me it gave up. It hit my wall's corner and couldn't get past. It shrank completely into itself and vanished like a cobra down a hole. I heard the rising roar it made when it died or left. I still couldn't breathe. I knew—it was the worst fact I knew, a very hard fact—that it could return again alive that same night.

Sometimes it came back, sometimes it didn't. Most often, restless, it came back. The light stripe slipped in the door, ran searching over Amy's wall, stopped, stretched lunatic at the first corner, raced wailing toward my wall, and vanished into the second corner with a cry. So I wouldn't go to bed.

It was a passing car whose windshield reflected the corner streetlight outside. I figured it out one night.

Figuring it out was as memorable as the oblong itself. Figuring it out was a long and forced ascent to the very rim of being, to the membrane of skin that both separates and connects the inner life and the outer world. I climbed deliberately from the depths like a diver who releases the monster in his arms and hauls himself hand over hand up an anchor chain till he meets the ocean's sparkling membrane and bursts through it; he sights the sunlit, becalmed hull of his boat, which had bulked so ominously from below.

I recognized the noise it made when it left. That is, the noise it made called to mind, at last, my daytime sensations when a car passed—the sight and noise together. A car came roaring down hushed Edgerton

Avenue in front of our house, stopped at the corner stop sign, and passed on shrieking as its engine shifted up the gears. What, precisely, came into the bedroom? A reflection from the car's oblong windshield. Why did it travel in two parts? The window sash split the light and cast a shadow.

Night after night I labored up the same long chain of reasoning, as night after night the thing burst into the room where I lay awake and Amy slept prettily and my loud heart thrashed and I froze.

There was a world outside my window and contiguous to it. If I was so all-fired bright, as my parents, who had patently no basis for comparison, seemed to think, why did I have to keep learning this same thing over and over? For I had learned it a summer ago, when men with jackhammers broke up Edgerton Avenue. I had watched them from the yard; the street came up in jagged slabs like floes. When I lay to nap, I listened. One restless afternoon I connected the new noise in my bedroom with the jackhammer men I had been seeing outside. I understood abruptly that these worlds met, the outside and the inside. I traveled the route in my mind: You walked downstairs from here, and outside from downstairs. "Outside," then, was conceivably just beyond my windows. It was the same world I reached by going out the front or the back door. I forced my imagination yet again over this route.

The world did not have me in mind; it had no mind. It was a coincidental collection of things and people, of items, and I myself was one such item—a child walking up the sidewalk, whom anyone could see or ignore. The things in the world did not necessarily cause my overwhelming feelings; the feelings were inside me, beneath my skin, behind my ribs, within my skull. They were even, to some extent, under my control.

I could be connected to the outer world by reason, if I chose, or I could yield to what amounted to a narrative fiction, to a tale of terror whispered to me by the blood in my ears, a show in light projected on the room's blue walls. As time passed, I learned to amuse myself in bed in the darkened room by entering the fiction deliberately and replacing it by reason deliberately.

When the low roar drew nigh and the oblong slid in the door, I threw my own switches for pleasure. It's coming after me; it's a car outside. It's after me. It's a car. It raced over the wall, lighting it blue wherever it ran; it bumped over Amy's maple headboard in a rush, paused, slithered elongate over the corner, shrank, flew my way, and vanished into itself with a wail. It was a car.

Our parents and grandparents, and all their friends, seemed insensible to their own prominent defect, their limp, coarse skin.

We children had, for instance, proper hands; our fluid, pliant fingers joined their skin. Adults had misshapen, knuckly hands loose in their skin like bones in bags; it was a wonder they could open jars. They were loose in their skins all over, except at the wrists and ankles, like rabbits.

We were whole, we were pleasing to ourselves. Our crystalline eyes shone from firm, smooth sockets; we spoke in pure, piping voices through dark, tidy lips. Adults were coming apart, but they neither noticed nor minded. My revulsion was rude, so I hid it. Besides, we could never rise to the absolute figural splendor they alone could on occasion achieve. Our beauty was a mere absence of decrepitude; their beauty, when they had it, was not passive but earned; it was grandeur; it was a party to power, and to artifice, even, and to knowledge. Our beauty was, in the long run, merely elfin. We could not, finally, discount the fact that in some sense they owned us, and they owned the world.

Mother let me play with one of her hands. She laid it flat on a living-room end table beside her chair. I picked up a transverse pinch of skin over the knuckle of her index finger and let it drop. The pinch didn't snap back; it lay dead across her knuckle in a yellowish ridge. I poked it; it slid over intact. I left it there as an experiment and shifted to another finger. Mother was reading *Time* magazine.

Carefully, lifting it by the tip, I raised her middle finger an inch and released it. It snapped back to the tabletop. Her insides, at least, were alive. I tried all the fingers. They all worked. Some I could lift higher than others.

"That's getting boring."

"Sorry, Mama."

I refashioned the ridge on her index-finger knuckle; I made the ridge as long as I could, using both my hands. Moving quickly, I made parallel ridges on her other fingers—a real mountain chain, the Alleghenies; Indians crept along just below the ridgetops, eyeing the frozen lakes below them through the trees.

Skin was earth; it was soil. I could see, even on my own skin, the joined trapezoids of dust specks God had wetted and stuck with his spit the morning he made Adam from dirt. Now, all these generations later, we people could still see on our skin the inherited prints of the dust specks of Eden.

I loved this thought, and repeated it for myself often. I don't know where I got it; my parents cited Adam and Eve only in jokes. Someday I would count the trapezoids, with the aid of a mirror, and learn precisely how many dust specks Adam comprised—one single handful God wetted, shaped, blew into, and set firmly into motion and left to wander about in the fabulous garden bewildered.

The skin on my mother's face was smooth, fair, and tender; it took impressions readily. She napped on her side on the couch. Her face skin pooled on the low side; it piled up in the low corners of her deep-set eyes and drew down her lips and cheeks. How flexible was it? I pushed at a puddle of it by her nose.

She stirred and opened her eyes. I jumped back.

She reminded me not to touch her face while she was sleeping. Anybody's face.

When she sat up, her cheek and brow bone bore a deep red gash, the mark of a cushion's welting. It was textured inside precisely with the upholstery's weave and brocade.

Another day, after a similar nap, I spoke up about this gash. I told her she had a mark on her face where she'd been sleeping.

"Do I?" she said; she ran her fingers through her hair. Her hair was short, blond, and wavy. She wore it swept back from her high, curved forehead. The skin on her forehead was both tight and soft. It would only barely shift when I tried to move it. She went to the kitchen. She was not interested in the hideous mark on her face. "It'll go away," I said. "What?" she called.

I noticed the hair on my father's arms and legs; each hair sprang from a dark dot on his skin. I lifted a hair and studied the puckered tepee of skin it pulled with it. Those hairs were in there tight. The greater the strain I put on the hair, the more puckered the tepee became, and shrunken within, concave. I could point it every which way.

"Ouch! Enough of that."

"Sorry, Daddy."

At the beach I felt my parent's shinbones. The bones were flat and curved, like the slats in a Venetian blind. The long edges were sharp as swords. But they had unexplained and, I thought, possibly diseased irregularities: nicks, bumps, small hard balls, shallow ridges, and soft spots. I was lying between my parents on an enormous towel through which I could feel the hot sand.

Loose under their shinbones, as in a hammock, hung the relaxed flesh of their calves. You could push and swing this like a baby in a sling. Their heels were dry and hard, sharp at the curved edge. The bottoms of their toes had flattened, holding the imprint of life's smooth floors even when they were lying down. I would not let this happen to me. Under certain conditions, the long bones of their feet showed under their skin. The bones rose up long and miserably thin in skeletal rays on the slopes of their feet. This terrible sight they ignored also.

In fact, they were young. Mother was twenty-two when I was born, and Father twenty-nine; both appeared to other adults much younger than they were. They were a handsome couple. I felt it overwhelmingly when they dressed for occasions. I never lost a wondering awe at the transformation of an everyday, tender, nap-creased mother into an exalted and dazzling beauty who chatted with me as she dressed.

Her blue eyes shone and caught the light, and so did the platinum waves in her hair and the pearls at her ears and throat. She was wearing a black dress. The smooth skin on her breastbone rent my heart, it was so familiar and beloved; the black silk bodice and the simple necklace set off its human fineness. Mother was perhaps a bit vain of her long and perfect legs, but not too vain for me; despite her excited pleasure, she did not share my view of her beauty.

"Look at your father," she said. We were all in the dressing room. I found him in one of the long mirrors, where he waggled his outthrust chin over the last push of his tie knot. For me he made his big ears jiggle on his skull. It was a wonder he could ever hear anything; his head was loose inside him.

Father's enormousness was an everyday, stunning fact; he was taller than everyone else. He was neither thin nor stout; his torso was supple, his long legs nimble. Before the dressing-room mirror he produced an anticipatory soft-shoe, and checked to see that his cuffs stayed down.

Now they were off. I hoped they knocked them dead; I hoped their friends knew how witty they were, and how splendid. Their parties at home did not seem very entertaining, although they laughed loudly and often fetched the one-man percussion band from the basement, or an old trumpet, or a snare drum. We children could have shown them how to have a better time. Kick the Can, for instance, never palled. A private game called Spider Cow, played by the Spencer children, also had possibilities: The spider cow hid and flung a wet washcloth at whoever found it, and erupted from hiding and chased him running all over the house.

But implicitly and emphatically, my parents and their friends were not interested. They never ran. They did not choose to run. It went with being old, apparently, and having their skin half off.

# SCOTT RUSSELL SANDERS
## (1945– )

A professor of English at the University of Indiana, Sanders was raised in the Midwest and educated at Brown University. An important essayist and advocate for the environment, he has also written over half a dozen volumes of fiction and books for children. In *Writing from the Center* (1995), he addresses the central concerns of his work in a sequence of a dozen essays that take up the question of how one can live "a meaningful, gathered life in a world that seems broken and scattered." In considering this question, Sanders looks closely at the layers of human relations that create a sense of community, beginning with the family. In one of these essays, "Buckeye" (which follows), he explores the mysteries of familiar connections as well as those peculiar attachments to a particular landscape that matter. It is also a thoughtful meditation on death and, in the fullest sense, inheritance.

## "Buckeye"

Years after my father's heart quit, I keep in a wooden box on my desk the two buckeyes that were in his pocket when he died. Once the size of plums, the brown seeds are shriveled now, hollow, hard as pebbles, yet they still gleam from the polish of his hands. He used to reach for them in his overalls or suit pants and click them together, or he would draw them out, cupped in his palm, and twirl them with his blunt carpenter's fingers, all the while humming snatches of old tunes.

"Do you really believe buckeyes keep off arthritis?" I asked him more than once.

He would flex his hands and say, "I do so far."

My father never paid much heed to pain. Near the end, when his worn knee often slipped out of joint, he would pound it back in place with a rubber mallet. If a splinter worked into his flesh beyond the reach of tweezers, he would heat the blade of his knife over a cigarette lighter and slice through the skin. He sought to ward off arthritis not because he feared pain but because he lived through his hands, and he dreaded the swelling of knuckles, the stiffening of fingers. What use would he be if he could no longer hold a hammer or guide a plow? When he was a boy he had known farmers not yet forty years old whose hands had curled into claws, men so crippled up they could not tie their own shoes, could not sign their names.

"I mean to tickle my grandchildren when they come along," he told me, "and I mean to build doll houses and turn spindles for tiny chairs on my lathe."

So he fondled those buckeyes as if they were charms, carrying them with him when our family moved from Ohio at the end of my childhood, bearing them to new homes in Louisiana, then Oklahoma, Ontario, and Mississippi, carrying them still on his final day when pain a thousand times fiercer than arthritis gripped his heart.

The box where I keep the buckeyes also comes from Ohio, made by my father from a walnut plank he bought at a farm auction. I remember the auction, remember the sagging face of the widow whose home was being sold, remember my father telling her he would prize that walnut as if he had watched the tree grow from a sapling on his own land. He did not care for pewter or silver or gold, but he cherished wood. On the rare occasions when my mother coaxed him into a museum, he ignored the paintings or porcelain and studied the exhibit cases, the banisters, the moldings, the parquet floors.

I remember him planing that walnut board, sawing it, sanding it, joining piece to piece to make foot stools, picture frames, jewelry boxes. My own box, a bit larger than a soap dish, lined with red corduroy, was meant to hold earrings and pins, not buckeyes. The top is inlaid with pieces fitted so as to bring out the grain, four diagonal joints converging from the corners toward the center. If I stare long enough at those converging lines, they float free of the box and point to a center deeper than wood.

I learned to recognize buckeyes and beeches, sugar maples and shagbark hickories, wild cherries, walnuts, and dozens of other trees while tramping through the Ohio woods with my father. To his eyes, their shapes, their leaves, their bark, their winter buds were as distinctive as the set of a friend's shoulders. As with friends, he was partial to some, craving their company, so he would go out of his way to visit particular trees, walking in a circle around the splayed roots of a sycamore, laying his hand against the trunk of a white oak, ruffling the feathery green boughs of a cedar.

"Trees breathe," he told me. "Listen."

I listened, and heard the stir of breath.

He was no botanist; the names and uses he taught me were those he had learned from country folks, not from books. Latin never crossed his lips. Only much later would I discover that the tree he called ironwood, its branches like muscular arms, good for axe handles, is known in the books as hophornbeam; what he called tuliptree or canoewood, ideal for log cabins, is officially the yellow poplar; what he called hoop ash, good for barrels and fence posts, appears in books as hackberry.

When he introduced me to the buckeye, he broke off a chunk of the gray bark and held it to my nose. I gagged.

"That's why the old-timers called it stinking buckeye," he told me. "They used it for cradles and feed troughs and peg legs."

"Why for peg legs?" I asked.

"Because it's light and hard to split, so it won't shatter when you're clumping around."

He showed me this tree in late summer, when the fruits had fallen and the ground was littered with prickly brown pods. He picked up one, as fat as a lemon, and peeled away the husk to reveal the shiny seed. He laid it in my palm and closed my fist around it so the seed peeped out from the circle formed by my index finger and thumb. "You see where it got the name?" he asked.

I saw: what gleamed in my hand was the eye of a deer, bright with life. "It's beautiful," I said.

"It's beautiful," my father agreed, "but also poisonous. Nobody eats buckeyes, except maybe a fool squirrel."

I knew the gaze of deer from living in the Ravenna Arsenal, in Portage County, up in the northeastern corner of Ohio. After supper we often drove the Arsenal's gravel roads, past the munitions bunkers, past acres of rusting tanks and wrecked bombers, into the far fields where we counted deer. One June evening, while mist rose from the ponds, we counted three hundred and eleven, our family record. We found the deer in herds, in bunches, in amorous pairs. We came upon lone bucks, their antlers lifted against the sky like the bare branches of dogwood. If you were quiet, if your hands were empty, if you moved slowly, you could leave the car and steal to within a few paces of a grazing deer, close enough to see the delicate lips, the twitching nostrils, the glossy, fathomless eyes.

The wooden box on my desk holds these grazing deer, as it holds the buckeyes and the walnut plank and the farm auction and the munitions bunkers and the breathing forests and my father's hands. I could lose the box, I could lose the polished seeds, but if I were to lose the memories I would become a bush without roots, and every new breeze would toss me about. All those memories lead back to the northeastern corner of Ohio, the place where I came to consciousness, where I learned to connect feelings with words, where I fell in love with the earth.

It was a troubled love, for much of the land I knew as a child had been ravaged. The ponds in the Arsenal teemed with bluegill and beaver, but they were also laced with TNT from the making of bombs. Because the wolves and coyotes had long since been killed, some of the deer, so plump in the June grass, collapsed on the January snow, whittled by hunger to racks of bones. Outside the Arsenal's high barbed fences, many of the farms had failed, their barns caving in, their topsoil gone. Ravines were choked with swollen couches and junked washing machines and cars. Crossing fields, you had to be careful not to slice your feet on tin cans or shards of glass. Most of the rivers had been dammed, turning fertile valleys into scummy playgrounds for boats.

One free-flowing river, the Mahoning, ran past the small farm near the Arsenal where our family lived during my later years in Ohio. We owned just enough land to pasture three ponies and to grow vegetables for our table, but those few acres opened onto miles of woods and creeks and secret meadows. I walked that land in every season, every weather, following animal trails. But then the Mahoning, too, was doomed by a government decision; we were forced to sell our land, and a dam began to rise across the river.

If enough people had spoken for the river, we might have saved it. If enough people had believed that our scarred country was worth defending, we might have dug in our heels and fought. Our attachments to the land were all private. We had no shared lore, no literature, no art to root us there, to give us courage, to help us stand our ground. The only maps we had were those issued by the state, showing a maze of numbered lines stretched over emptiness. The Ohio landscape never showed up on postcards or posters, never unfurled like tapestry in films, rarely filled even a paragraph in books. There were no mountains in that place, no waterfalls, no rocky gorges, no vistas. It was a country of low hills, cut over woods, scoured fields, villages that had lost their purpose, roads that had lost their way.

"Let us love the country of here below," Simone Weil urged. "It is real; it offers resistance to love. It is this country that God has given us to love. He has willed that it should be difficult yet possible to love it." Which is the deeper truth about buckeyes, their poison or their beauty? I hold with the beauty; or rather, I am held by the beauty, without forgetting the poison. In my corner of Ohio the gullies were choked with trash, yet cedars flickered up like green flames from cracks in stone; in the evening bombs exploded at the ammunition dump, yet from the darkness came the mating cries of owls. I was saved from despair by knowing a few men and women who cared enough about the land to clean up trash, who planted walnuts and oaks that would long outlive them, who imagined a world that would have no call for bombs.

How could our hearts be large enough for heaven if they are not large enough for earth? The only country I am certain of is the one here below. The only paradise I know is the one lit by our everyday sun, this land of difficult love, shot through with shadow. The place where we learn this love, if we learn it at all, shimmers behind every new place we inhabit.

A family move carried me away from Ohio thirty years ago; my schooling and marriage and job have kept me away ever since, except for visits in memory and in flesh. I returned to the site of our farm one cold November day, when the trees were skeletons and the ground shone with the yellow of fallen leaves. From a previous trip I knew that our house had been bulldozed, our yard and pasture had grown up in thickets, and the reservoir had flooded the woods. On my earlier visit I had merely gazed from the car, too numb with loss to climb out. But on this November day, I parked the car, drew on my hat and gloves, opened the door, and walked.

I was looking for some sign that we had lived there, some token of our affection for the place. All that I recognized, aside from the contours of the land, were two weeping willows that my father and I had planted near the road. They had been slips the length of my forearm when we set them out, and now their crowns rose higher than the telephone poles. When I touched them last, their trunks had been smooth and supple, as thin as my wrist, and now they were furrowed and stout. I took off my gloves and laid my hands against the rough bark. Immediately I felt the wince of tears. Without knowing why, I said hello to my father, quietly at first, then louder and louder, as if only shouts could reach him through the bark and miles and years.

Surprised by sobs, I turned from the willows and stumbled away toward the drowned woods, calling to my father. I sensed that he was nearby. Even as I called, I was wary of grief's deceptions. I had never seen his body after he died. By the time I reached the place of his death, a furnace had reduced him to ashes. The need to see him, to let go of him, to let go of this land and time, was powerful enough to summon mirages; I knew that. But I also knew, stumbling toward the woods, that my father was here.

At the bottom of a slope where the creek used to run, I came to an expanse of gray stumps and withered grass. It was a bay of the reservoir from which the water had retreated, the level drawn down by engineers or drought. I stood at the edge of this desolate ground, willing it back to life, trying to recall the woods where my father had taught me the names of trees. No green shoots rose. I walked out among the stumps. The grass crackled under my boots, breath rasped in my throat, but otherwise the world was silent.

Then a cry broke overhead and I looked up to see a red-tailed hawk launching out from the top of an oak. I recognized the bird from its band of dark feathers across the creamy breast and the tail splayed like rosy fingers against the sun. It was a red-tailed hawk for sure; and it was also my father. Not a symbol of my father, not a reminder, not a ghost, but the man himself, right there, circling in the air above me. I knew this as clearly as I knew the sun burned in the sky. A calm poured through me. My chest quit heaving. My eyes dried.

Hawk and father wheeled above me, circle upon circle, wings barely moving, head still. My own head was still, looking up, knowing and being known. Time scattered like fog. At length, father and hawk stroked the air with those powerful wings, three beats, then vanished over a ridge.

The voice of my education told me then and tells me now that I did not meet my father, that I merely projected my longing onto a bird. My education may well be right; yet nothing I heard in school, nothing I've read, no lesson reached by logic has ever convinced me as utterly or stirred me as deeply as did that red-tailed hawk. Nothing in my education prepared me to love a piece of the earth, least of all a humble, battered country like northeastern Ohio; I learned from the land itself.

Before leaving the drowned woods, I looked around at the ashen stumps, the wilted grass, and for the first time since moving from this place I was able to let it go. This ground was lost; the flood would reclaim it. But other ground could be saved, must be saved, in every watershed, every neighborhood. For each home ground we need new maps, living maps, stories and poems, photographs and paintings, essays and songs. We need to know where we are, so that we may dwell in our place with a full heart.

# KATHLEEN NORRIS
## (1947– )

Writing in a tradition of American spiritual autobiography with deep roots in the seventeenth and eighteenth centuries, the poet Kathleen Norris has published a remarkable sequence of memoirs, beginning with *Dakota: A Spiritual Geography* (1993) and moving through *The Cloister Walk* (1996) and, most recently, *Amazing Grace: A Vocabulary of Faith* (1998). In these volumes, Norris describes her inner journey as a poet, wife, feminist, Benedictine oblate (she spent two extensive periods in residence at St. John's Abbey in Minnesota), and resettler in her home state of South Dakota. In *The Cloister Walk*, she meditates on her renewal of faith while adhering to the ancient practice of Benedictine monasticism. She writes in a lyrical voice with a fierce sense of urgency and deep, experiential knowledge.

## FROM *The Cloister Walk*

### ACEDIA

*From Late Latin, from Greek* akedia, *indifference.*
*a (absence) + kedos (care)*

—AMERICAN HERITAGE DICTIONARY

*The malice of sloth lies not merely in the neglect of duty (though that can be a symptom of it) but in the refusal of joy. It is allied to despair.*

—Evelyn Waugh, *Acedia*, in *The Seven Deadly Sins*

*Amma Syncletica said: There is a grief that is useful, and there is a grief that is destructive. The first sort consists in weeping over one's own faults and weeping over the weakness of one's neighbors, in order not to lose one's purpose, and attach oneself to the perfect good. But there is also a grief that comes from the enemy, full of mockery, which some call accidie. This spirit must be cast out, mainly by prayer and psalmody.*

—*The Sayings of the Desert Fathers*

Severe lethargy has set in, what the desert monks might have called "acedia" or "listlessness," and in the Middle Ages was considered sloth, but these days is most often termed "depression." I had thought that I was merely tired and in need of rest at year's end, but it drags on, becoming the death-in-life that I know all too well, when my capacity for joy shrivels up and, like drought-stricken grass, I die down to the roots to wait it out. The simplest acts demand a herculean effort, the pleasure I normally take in people and the world itself is lost to me. I can be with people I love, and know that I love them, but feel nothing at all. I am observing my life more than living it.

I recognize in all of this the siege of what the desert monks termed the "noonday demon." It suggests that whatever I'm doing, indeed my entire life of "doings," is not only meaningless but utterly useless. This plunge into the chill waters of pure realism is incapacitating, and the demon likes me this way. It suggests sleep when what I need most is to take a walk. It insists that I shut myself away when what I probably need is to be with other people. It mocks the rituals, routines, and work that normally fill my day; why do them, why do anything at all, it says, in the face of so vast an emptiness. Worst of all, even though I know that the ancient remedies—prayer, psalmody, scripture reading—would help to pull me out of the morass, I find myself incapable of acting on this knowledge. The exhaustion that I'm convinced lies behind most suicides finds its seed in acedia; the rhythms of daily life, and of the universe itself, the everyday glory of sunrise and sunset and all the "present moments" in between seem a disgusting repetition that stretches on forever. It would be all too easy to feel that one wants no part of it any more.

The first experience of acedia that I recall (although I did not know to name it as such) occurred when I was fifteen years old, a scholarship student at a prep school in Honolulu. The job I held in partial payment of my scholarship was a pleasant one; during the noon hour, I answered the phone and did secretarial work at the Music School. Not being in the school cafeteria gave me a chance to diet, and my normal fare, in what now strikes me as a comical parody of the monastic desert, was a model of severity: Metrecal wafers, a low-cal soda, and an apple or an orange. (For readers who have never tasted Metrecal, allow me to suggest fresh asphalt with a hint of chocolate and the bitter afterglow of saccharin.) One day as I was unpacking my lunch, a lunch that my mother had faithfully packed for me, I suddenly saw the future stretch out before me: days and days of lunches that one day my mother would not be packing for me, that I would be responsible for myself. Day upon day of eating and excreting, of working at this job or that, of monotony, the futile round.

When, in my thirties, I encountered the monk Evagrius's classic description of the "noonday demon," I recognized my experience of many years before. He speaks of the depressing thought that suddenly "depicts life stretching out for a long period of time, and brings before the mind's eye the toil of the ascetic struggle, and . . . leaves no leaf unturned to induce the monk to forsake his cell and drop out of the fight." At fifteen I had no "cell" but a small bedroom in Navy housing near Pearl Harbor (which was luxurious to me because until recently I had been sharing a room with my two younger sisters). I had no knowledge of monks, or of ascetic practice. But I had been visited by the noonday demon and, in ways I was not to become fully aware of for many years, my life was changed forever. The fear of the daily had intruded into my consciousness at a time when it could do real harm. A shy, pudgy teenager, suffering from the loneliness that so many teenagers feel, I had just become more lonely. My fearful thoughts of the future seemed so absurd I could not speak of them to anyone.

Some thirty years later, I am back in Honolulu, in fragrant Manoa Valley, not far from that school. A letter-press book has come for me in the mail, exquisitely made by a friend, full of poems I wrote during a year at St. John's. The book, and the poems themselves, are a great gift, I know, but I can't bring myself to open the box. After a few days, when I finally do unpack it, the book's beauty seems remote. My mother and sister-in-law admire it—yes, it's lovely, I say, agreeing with them. But I can't feel it. They know this, and it troubles them. But they're tolerant; we share the hope that I'll soon snap out of it. Drugs, therapy, someone might suggest. The last time it got this bad I did consult with a doctor. We discussed many options, and what she suggested to me I treasure still: exercise, she said, and spiritual direction.

I have promised to go to services this Sunday, at the modest but spirited Disciples of Christ church where my brother is a pastor. I still feel half-dead but do my best to sing with the congregation. One of the verses of "Spirit of God, Descend Upon My Heart"—"I ask no dreams, no prophet ecstasies, no sudden rending of the veil of clay, no angel visitant, no opening skies; but take the dimness of my soul away"—makes me realize that I'm praying for the first time in days, and that it's working. The rest of that service is a giddy blur; I felt alive again, appropriately enough, on a Sunday morning. In his sermon, my brother says, "God's language is silence; how do we translate it?" He speaks of gifts differing, gifts of the Spirit coming to each of us, for the common good. The title of the closing hymn, "There Is Sunshine in My Heart Today," seems like icing on the cake. The melody is appropriately zippy, upbeat, the lyrics as thoroughly Protestant as the title would suggest, and I enjoy every bit of it.

When last I was home and attending church, the children's choir sang "Jesus Wants Me for a Sunbeam," a song I remember singing as a child.

I suppose I loved it then. What made their song so marvelous in the context of our worship that day was that it was followed by a reading from Jeremiah 14 that made it clear that God did *not* want Jeremiah for a sunbeam. Gifts differing, I suppose. And I suppose that both of the hymns that have touched me today could be labeled "pietistic," not sufficiently concerned with the larger picture, the larger world. But it's acedia that made my world small, a self-centered hell—"Is there no way out of the mind?" Sylvia Plath once asked, anguished, in a poem—and these hymns that have released me to live in the real world again. In the context of this worship service, both hymns seem fine to me, not uncaring, not irresponsible, but merely a glad response to grace. I wonder if Christians might be permitted a certain gladness on Sunday morning. Even if the universe is mostly hydrogen atoms, and the few human beings who exist in it are continually at war with one another, even if time and space stretch out into the void. Here, in this ordinary church service, I have gained the strength to live this moment, the present moment, for the first time in days. I recall something that I read recently in a book on monastic practices: "A life of prayer," the monk Charles Cummings wrote, "is a life of beginning all over again." Ashamed of my own unsteadiness, my lack of courage and, in the words of another hymn, my heart so "prone to wander from the God I love," I have the strength to take it all up again. This is a day to begin.

## THE CLOISTER WALK

*Love is intensity, that second in which the doors of time and space open just a crack . . .*

—Octavio Paz

*How but in custom and in ceremony
Are innocence and beauty born?*

—William Butler Yeats, "A Prayer for My Daughter"

I know exactly what I was doing at 10:30 A.M. on Sunday, May 31, 1992, but have no idea where I was. The enormous church of St. John's Abbey in Collegeville, Minnesota, designed by Marcel Breuer, was familiar to me, as I'd gone there nearly every day for the previous nine months to join the monks in their Liturgy of the Hours. On that Sunday morning I learned how little I knew about the place.

I was walking down the center aisle, trying to keep to the slow, deliberate pace the liturgy director had established as we proceeded down the cloister walk into the church. But it was hard, because I was alone now, and had little to gauge myself by. As instructed, I was holding the scriptures, a big book of lectionary readings, out in front of me at a little more than shoulder height. Following me, walking two by two, were nearly two hundred monks in black habits, and bringing up the rear, two acolytes and a priest who would preside at this Mass on the Seventh Sunday of Easter. The congregation of several hundred had risen for the first hymn as I started slowly down the aisle.

An incongruous thought danced through my mind: even Mae West never entered a room followed by this many men. I seemed incongruous, too, someone with a checkered past, who until the last few years hadn't been to church much since high school. Breathing deeply, to get my bearings, I found that I was walking a path with a downward tilt much more steep than I had realized. By contrast, the altar loomed before me, brilliant white, a simple but powerful shape. The magnificent folds of concrete holding up the roof seemed weightless, and the expanse above me limitless, the ceiling lifted clean off by the sound of the pipe organ.

It was the reverse of an experience most adults have had, of returning to a place that had seemed vast in childhood, and finding it pathetically small. This church was a place I thought I knew, a big space I'd tamed by my daily presence there. Now I was discovering that it was wild after all, and could roar like the sea. Walking on the terrazzo floor, I was reminded of a recurring dream, in which I move through the galaxy, stepping delicately (and sometimes leaping) from star to star. This sunlit room now seemed such an expanse, my every step daring an enormous distance.

My mind chugged along: don't stumble on the steps, remember to bow at the altar and put the lectionary on the ambo. Take the first choir stall on the left but don't sit down, because the monks will enter there. They swept past me like small black clouds to take their places with me in the front row, and I found the voice to sing the last verse of the hymn as the liturgy began to flow in all directions around me. The quantum effect.

I did my reading, a text from the Book of Acts about the stoning of Stephen. "I see an opening in the sky," Stephen said, and I thought, "Amen." Good liturgy can act like an icon, a window into a world in which our concepts of space, time, and even stone are pleasurably bent out of shape. Good liturgy is a living poem, and ceremony is the key.

Any outsider writing about monastic life runs the risk of romanticizing it. I've simply described what I experienced one Sunday morning at St. John's. I'm assuming, hoping even, that some of the monks were wondering what was for dinner, or thinking dark thoughts about a confrere who had annoyed them at breakfast, or regretting a sharp remark they'd made over the pool table the night before. Good ceremony makes room for all the dimensions of human experience in the hope that, together, we will discover something that transforms us. This is why I suspect that individuals can't create true ceremony for themselves alone. Ceremony requires that we work with others in the humbling give-and-take of communal existence.

Monastic people seek to weave ceremony through every mundane part of life: how one eats, how one dresses, how one treats tools, or enters a church are not left to whim. Ceremony is so large a part of what Benedictines do that it becomes second nature to many of them. The monastic life has this in common with the artistic one: both are attempts to pay close attention to objects, events, and natural phenomena that otherwise would get chewed up in the daily grind. One of the things I like most about monastic people is the respect they show for the holy hours of sunrise and sunset, and in these days when the horrors of sexual warfare fill the news, I find it nothing short of miraculous to be with a group of grown men who will sing at close of day: "Day is done, but love unfailing / dwells ever here." The fact that Christian monastics, men and women both, have been singing such gentle hymns at dusk for seventeen hundred years makes me realize that ceremony and tradition, things I've been raised to distrust as largely irrelevant, can be food for the soul.

Ceremony forces a person to slow down, and as many of us live at a frenzied pace, encountering monastic prayer, or a traditional monastic meal—eaten in silence while a passage from scripture or a religious book is read aloud—can feel like skidding to a halt. My nine months' immersion in the slow, steady rhythms of monastic life was a kind of gestation. But now that I'm back "in the world," now that my husband and I have come home from Minnesota, I'm not sure what I'm giving birth to. At times I'm homesick for a place that isn't mine, homesick for two hundred monks and their liturgy. Most people have the sense not to get themselves into such a predicament. What do I do now for ceremony, and community?

My instinct is to keep as much of the monastery in me as possible. Now I honor the coming of dawn with a long walk instead of going to church, but small difference, if I can turn it toward prayer. I keep some Benedictine practices, as best as I can: reading psalms daily, singing hymns, and also doing *lectio*, a meditative reading of scripture. Otherwise I suspect my world would go flat. And sometimes it does: sometimes I'm closed off from both beauty and pain, suffering from what the world calls "depression" but the ancient monks would call listlessness or *acedia*. Drought times, when I have to hunker down and wait for rain, for hope.

I keep in touch with my monastic friends at St. John's, and at other, smaller communities in the Dakotas that I visit frequently. Above all, I try to remember where I am: a small town on the Great Plains that may not be here in fifty years. But even in this hamlet of 1600 souls, considered insignificant by the rest of the world, there is much that people need to tell. I became more reclusive over the last year, but when I'm with people I try to listen to them. Alice, for one. When the Presbyterian church recently held its Sunday service in the park, the minister sharing a flatbed truck with a local country-western band, Alice and I were standing over to the side. A country woman, the wife of a retired rancher in poor health, she was someone I'd missed when I was away. Her only child, a young man of thirty-five, had died unexpectedly the year before. She stood there, swaying to the music, the steel guitar whining through "What a Friend We Have in Jesus," and said, "I haven't danced in three years." "Well, it's time, then, Alice," I said. And so we danced.

# JOHN ELDER
## (1947– )

A nature writer, literary critic, and environmental activist, Elder is also co-editor of *The Norton Book of Nature Writing* (1990). The son of a Baptist minister, he was born and raised in California, where he attended Pomona College. After graduate school at Yale, he moved to Vermont, where he has taught literature and environmental studies for over twenty years at Middlebury College. His books include *Imagining the Earth: Poetry and the Vision of Nature* (1985)—an important study of American nature poetry—and *Following the Brush* (1993), a lyrical reflection on the author's confrontation with Japanese culture.

His recent memoir, *Reading the Mountains of Home* (1998), combines literary criticism (in particular, a critical reading of Robert Frost's seminal poem "Directive") and environmental history within the context of a personal narrative—a highly original format. Elder's voice, at once sinuous and deeply reflective, owes something to Thoreau, one of his great predecessors in the tradition of meditative autobiography.

## FROM *Reading the Mountains of Home*

I visited my father in Hillhaven Convalescent Home shortly before he died. His gaunt head was propped up on a lofty white pillow, and his arms looked thin and frail lying on top of the sheets. Looking at his arms, though, I thought of a day when I was a boy of six and he and I rowed a borrowed skiff way out into the Gulf of Mexico. The boat had been in storage for years, so that the bottom was dried out and leaky. Water began to well up, then suddenly rushed through the separating planks. Our boat sank with us too far from shore even to make out the white porch railings of our little vacation house. But my father calmly said to put my arms around his neck so that he could swim us in. I remember the total security I felt, resting on the smooth, powerful muscles of his back, watching the sweep of his arms through the brown water. I drowsed along, safe with my father above the invisible currents of the deep. I remembered that strength in Hillhaven, looking down at his thin arms and bony, age-spotted hands. I remember it now, in the life-and-death of this Vermont wilderness.

Death and life are both embodied in a nurse log. Nature is always unified for one who can let go and identify with a life that transcends individuality. But certain propositions are much easier to affirm in the abstract, and such letting go sometimes requires first being overturned and uprooted. Frost's first volume of poetry, *A Boy's Will*, was published in 1913. One stanza of "In Hardwood Groves" from that volume connects the need to fall back into the fund of life not only with blow-down but also with the annual descent of leaves.

> Before the leaves can mount again
> To fill the trees with another shade,
> They must go down past things coming up,
> They must go down into the dark decayed.

I feel Frost's struggle in the reiterated "must," as in the phrase "dark decayed." Decomposition at the bacterial level may be easier to contemplate if one leaves one's own body out of the picture. But only with an inclusive perspective on the universal breakdown of organisms can one look past it to new life. Only by adopting a time-line that comprehends the visitations of glaciers and the rise and fall of whole forests may one draw the lesson home. This is the tough but liberating view of life taught by the memory-tangled, ever-new New England woods.

Without Frost, it would have been much harder for me to appreciate the human meaning of these woods. Growing up in northern California, I was within a bike ride of Muir Woods. That grove of redwoods was my criterion for natural integrity as I began to enjoy nature on my own. When I eventually moved east to attend graduate school, the woods of Connecticut left me feeling disappointed and disoriented. They seemed to lack the sublime beauty of the redwoods with their grand columns rising through the filtered light, their forest floor almost devoid of underbrush. Walking in a little patch of forest near Guilford, Connecticut, I felt how small the trees were, how little they conformed to the monolithic simplicity of the redwoods, and how littered the forest floor felt with its broken branches and leaf-duff everywhere. I felt closed into a messy room rather than released into natural grandeur. Another grad student from the West repeated to me the libel, based on the relative smallness and proximity of landforms in this part of the country, that being in New England was like living in a teacup. Right, I thought, and in the tattered leaves that slid around my boots I'd found the dregs.

But Frost offers a vision of sublimity based not on spaciousness and noble clarity but rather on endurance in the face of loss, unity in fragmentation, and the warmth of decay. These are primarily physical truths for him, not metaphysical ones. Snow covers and temporarily arrests the decomposition of this forest floor, but beneath it lie the vestiges of several successive growing seasons. The top layer—"fit[ting] the earth like a leather glove," as Frost has it at the beginning of "In Hardwood Groves"—is composed of the brown but intact leaves of the previous fall. Beneath them is a layer of fragments and skeletons, sometimes just the spines of leaves, or the tips, or the outlines of maple or red oak leaves defining a webwork of holes. Just below those shards, and yet another year earlier, are found the crumbly little indistinguishable scraps, the chaff of three seasons' winnowing. And then comes the sweet black dirt. This soil is the "dark decayed," a layer of renewal from which sweet nutrients seep down into the mineral mix, food for the trees that hang overhead in familial continuity.

A forester named George Kessler introduced me to the concept of soil horizons. The decaying leaves and fragments mark the O, or organic, horizon, while the topsoil, lying beneath that fertile litter, is the A horizon. Below that comes the B horizon, or subsoil, which contains relatively little organic material. Slicing down into the forest floor, he showed me the lines of demarcation from the light brown of duff to the black of topsoil to the mineral-rich red-brown of the subsoil. New England, like the West, has its own big sky, but its horizons stretch beneath our boots. The circulation of water is like wind for this saturated soil. It bears leaves and ashes down through three horizons, then lifts them into trees that, even in early January, have their buds fully formed and ready to receive the spring.

As I began this year's long hike northward toward Bristol and home, a notable essay on Frost came out in the *New Yorker* of September 26, 1994. Joseph Brodsky's "On Grief and Reason" was impressive, as one strong poet's serious reading of another always is. But it also helped me understand my own reading of Frost more clearly, through certain reservations I felt about his. Brodsky says of the earlier poet that "on the surface, he looks very positively predisposed toward his surroundings—particularly toward nature. His fluency, his 'being versed in country things' alone can produce this impression." But unlike the inescapably *historical* reference that European poets bring to a foray out of doors, Brodsky writes,

> when an American walks out of his house and encounters a tree it is a meeting of equals. Man and tree face each other in their respective primal power, free of references: neither has a past, and as to whose future is greater, it is a toss-up. Basically, it's epidermis meeting bark. Our man returns to his cabin in a state of bewilderment, to say the least, if not in actual shock or terror.

In fact, though, nature *always* has a past, and an awareness of natural history includes and lifts up into coherence the history both of individuals and of humanity as a whole. Many writers have experienced America as an Eden, or a hell, of unnamed forms, just as Brodsky describes. But Frost is absolutely not one of them. He constantly reads the past within the present, and earns this large vision in part by encountering and admitting the disintegration of his own individuality. "Nature for this poet is neither friend nor foe, nor is it the backdrop for human drama; it is this poet's terrifying self-portrait," Brodsky writes. But his proposition, like Thompson's opposition between the spiritual and the secular, is built upon a false dichotomy. For Frost, at least, true self-portraiture must also depict one's place on earth. He would refute both the self-creating impulses of high Romanticism and the environmentalism of "vast, pristine, and untrammeled" lands removed from all human endeavors. Frost in this way anticipates our contemporary, Gary Snyder. For both writers, sublimity finally depends less upon spatial extent than upon temporal expansiveness.

As Brodsky says, Frost is often unsettled by nature, discovering within it the darkness of his own shadow. But Frost also looks intently at each of the dynamic forms in which he glimpses aspects of himself. He rarely just encounters a "tree," with "bark." More often, the tree is named: beech or maple, hemlock, pine, or larch, with its size, its profile against the sky, its moment in the cycles of foliage and succession specified within the poem. Frost seems at times almost overwhelmed by the concreteness and multiplicity of nature. As "In Hardwood Groves" shows, the ceaseless transformations of nature, like the human condition itself, can be "too much for us." But the tug of a diverse, living world always renews his poetry.

D. H. Lawrence expressed his admiration for Thomas Hardy in a way that also bears on Frost's poetry.

> This is the wonder of Hardy's novels, and gives them their beauty. The vast, unexplored morality of life itself, what we call the immorality of nature, surrounds us in its eternal incomprehensibility, and in its midst goes on the little human morality play, with its queer frame of morality and its mechanized movement; seriously, portentously, till some one of the protagonists chances to look out of the charmed circle, weary of the stage, to look into the wilderness raging round.

"Incomprehensibility" affirms the vastness and complexity of nature. Frost's woods, like Hardy's heath, offer the possibility for getting seriously lost when the merely human realm has become too much for us. "Directive," even in a moment when it mocks the "excitement" of Vermont's "upstart" trees, always acknowledges that incomparably larger natural processes are at work. Frost pays such close attention to the particular forms and lives amid the Green Mountains because they both disorient and reorient him, because they insist upon an enlarged frame of reference. He reads the story of a glacier in the erratics dotting Vermont's long central ridge. And he helps me, as I lift my boot across the hummock of a moldering root-circle, to bear in mind the cycles of a forest's buried life.

Hiking out to Briggs Hill Road, I compounded my boot prints from the way in, making them spread out like snowshoes as I slid back down to the present. I was also walking once more through my memories, occasioned by this road, of Rachel as a toddler, "not twenty years ago." The path bore me back down to the present world, in which she is a stylish, black-clad college student. Rachel slyly tests me when we ride together in the car by playing alternative and hard-core rock, as far from the Dylan and Beatles of my own college years as the littered forests of New England are remote from the redwood groves. Despite all the years since Rachel's childhood, though, I can always picture with perfect clarity how she was *then*—just as in looking at the deep blue clintonia berries of late summer I always have a superimposed image of their yellow lilybells swaying beside the trail in June. In opening the car door now and sliding behind the wheel of a world in which my father is no longer alive, I can also still picture how he used to push Rachel on her Big Wheel when she was three or so. It was a comical scene, since his technique was to position an old golf club against the back of her vehicle so that he wouldn't have to bend over as he propelled her around the sidewalks for hour after patient, cheerful hour.

And here I am back in Bristol, working in our barn as the afternoon of this long day draws to a close. A couple of shop-lights shine down, plugged into an outlet on the deck with a long orange extension cord. A kerosene heater roars at my back and almost keeps me from shivering. I am drawing beads of glue along the edge of slender cedar strips, bending them around station-molds that establish the tapering contours of a canoe, and stapling them onto these molds in order to clamp them together, edge to edge, while the glue dries. All year, as I have been pursuing my hikes, I have also been stealing hours to work on this wooden canoe, as a project honoring my father's memory. It's a task considerably beyond my experience or skills, and one I would have never taken on had it not been for a dream.

Last August Rita and I were taking a two-day vacation on the coast, having dropped Caleb off at his youth-orchestra camp in New Hampshire and on our way to pick up Matthew from a canoeing camp in Maine. It was a rare time to relax together, and we spent most of one day strolling along the harbor in Camden and poking around in shops. One bookstore had a large section on sailing and boat construction, and I became fascinated by the books on canoe building. The next night we were in Portland and decided to go out to dinner for our twenty-fourth anniversary. This was stretching it, since it was only August 19th and the actual date was the 30th. But we weren't likely to have another evening so spacious as the beginning of school approached, and we had heard about an elegant little restaurant in the old part of town, called Alberta's Seafood Grill. The meal was in fact wonderful, the atmosphere warm and inviting. But throughout a very happy evening tears kept rolling down my cheeks, to my total surprise. It seemed funny, really, just an overflow of love.

That night, when we returned to our motel on the outskirts of town, I had a dream as vivid as the image of a clintonia blossom beside a trail. In it, a sleek cedar-strip canoe was floating on the water. Its mellow reddish-golden color especially struck me, along with its name, the Tribute, written in calligraphic script along the right side of the bow. I walked closer to the shore by which it hung and looked down at the smaller letters of the inscription on the bow-deck. It read "JLE" and below that, "1918–94." Around these letters and numerals were wreathed the words "of the current to the source," with "source" coming right around to the circle's beginning and making one continuous phrase. I wrote this dream down in my journal and told Rita about it, realizing that it was a kind of memorial to my father, still alive in Hillhaven Convalescent but in sad decline because of the progression of his Alzheimer's. This new link between him and one of my favorite lines from "West-Running Brook" stirred me, since Dad had been much on my mind. The dream felt like an appropriate form of homage, but then it faded from my mind, like other nighttime revelations.

Two days later, having picked up Matthew, we pulled into our driveway in Bristol to find a message from my mother waiting for us. Dad had died on the evening of August 19th. Frost's poem of haunting gave me permission to believe Dad's spirit traveled to me that night in tears and a dream. But it also made me buy the book that told how such canoes were made, rig up a shop in our drafty barn, and begin to transform a long crate of wooden strips into the curved and symmetrical integrity of a hull. These thin, pliable planks, which I purchased from a marine supply company in Buffalo, have bead-and-cove edges—one convex and the other concave to hold the glue even when the strips wrap around a curve rather than joining in a plane. They make me think this evening of the pillow-and-cradle patterns of a forest floor—the juxtaposition of hummock and hole that tells the story of succession and that includes passing generations of trees in the present of a single slope.

At the farther end of North Mountain lies Bristol Pond, my favorite spot for canoeing. Building this craft, I have both remembered my father and imagined paddling the completed Tribute across the pond on a placid summer day. That would bring some closure to this year of grieving, as well as to the reading, hiking, and writing that have flowed together in this book. It would be a chance to reflect in quietness, after the effort and disorientation of the trail. But now I must bend back over the canoe's skeleton and partial hull, stretching my arms out as far as they'll go to hold a new strip of the curve firmly in place while I set a couple of staples near the craft's stern. As my stapler clacks, a sudden gust rattles the big barn doors. The kerosene heater gives a roar, bathes the canoe for a moment in its vivid glow, then dies back down.

# JULIA ALVAREZ
## (1950– )

A poet and novelist, Alvarez was born in the Dominican Republic, where she spent her childhood under the dictatorship of General Trujillo before escaping with her parents and sisters to the United States. The story of her family's adventures—a tale of exile and cunning, of sisterhood and daughterhood, of friendship and community—lay at the center of her first book, *How the García Girls Lost Their Accents* (1991), which won her a wide and deeply appreciative audience. This was followed by *In the Time of the Butterflies* (1994), which told the story of several courageous sisters who dared to oppose General Trujillo and paid dearly for their opposition to his cruel dictatorship. More recently, *Yo!* (1997) returned to the story of the García family, focusing on Yolanda García—Yo, for short—who is herself a writer.

Alvarez has gone back to material that can only be called "autobiographical" again and again, although she has preferred the filter of the fictional form. In "Picky Eater," however—which appears in her most recent collection of essays, *Something to Declare* (1998)—she writes frankly and engagingly about her issues with food, which have continued to affect her long after she left her parents' table.

## "Picky Eater"

I met my husband in my late thirties and when we were beginning to date, I was surprised by his preoccupation with food. "Can we go out to dinner?" was, I believe, the second or third sentence out of his mouth. That first date, we ate at a local restaurant, or I should say, he ate and talked, and I talked and sometimes picked at my food. "Didn't you like your stirfry?" he asked me when the waitress removed my half-eaten plate.

"Sure, it was okay," I said, surprised at this nonsequitur. We had been talking about India, where he had recently done volunteer surgery. I hadn't given the food a thought—except in ordering it. Being a picky eater, my one criterion for food was: is it something I might eat? Once it met that standard, then it was okay, nothing to think or talk too much about.

Mostly, if I was eating out, I didn't expect food to taste all that good. This was a carryover from my childhood in a big Dominican family in which the women prided themselves on the fact that nobody could put a meal on the table like they could put a meal on a table. You went out for the social purpose of seeing and being seen by your friends and neighbors, but you never went out to have a good meal. For that, you stayed home or went over to a relative's house where you could be sure that the food was going to be prepared correctly—i.e. hygienically—and taste delicious.

Perhaps this bias had to do with the fact that I grew up in the 1950s in a small underdeveloped country where there were very few tourists and, therefore, few eating establishments that catered to pleasure dining. The common *comedores* were no-nonsense, one-room eating places for workers, mostly male, who all ate the same "plate of the day," on long tables with small sinks and towels in a corner for washing their hands and toothpicks for cleaning out their teeth when they were done. Little stands on the street sold fried *pastelitos* or *frío-frío* in paper cones or chunks of *raspadura* wrapped in palm leaves, treats I was never allowed to taste.

Eating *en la calle* was strictly forbidden in my family. We came home from school at noon for the big, dinner meal. On long trips into the interior to visit Papi's family, we carried everything we might need on the way, including water. It was dangerous to eat out: you could get very sick and die from eating foods that had gone bad or been fixed by people who had diseases you could catch. In fact, the minute any of us children complained we didn't feel right, the first question asked of our nursemaids was, "Did they eat anything on the street?"

My mother and aunts were extremely careful about food preparation. Had the vegetables been properly peeled and boiled so that no *microbios* were left lodged in the skins? Was the lettuce washed in filtered water? Since electricity, and therefore refrigeration, were not dependable, was the meat fresh or had it been left to lie around? During certain seasons in the tropics, some kinds of fish carry toxins—so that had to be taken into account as well. Had the milk been pasteurized? Had tarantulas gotten into the sugar or red ants into the cocoa powder? To get a healthy meal on the table seemed to be an enterprise laden with mythic dangers—no wonder a street vendor couldn't be trusted.

In short, I cannot remember ever eating out at a restaurant before coming to live in this country. The one exception was Los Cremita, the ice cream shop an Italian family opened up near the hospital. On Sundays, after we'd accompanied him on his rounds, my father took my sisters and me to Los Cremita, where we picked out one small scoop apiece of our favorite *helado*. "Don't tell your mother," my father would say. I don't know if he was worried that my mother would accuse him of ruining our appetites before the big Sunday afternoon meal at my grandparents' house or if he was afraid she would fuss at him for exposing us to who knows what *microbios* the Italians might have put into those big vats of pistachio or coconut or mango ice cream.

But even when we ate perfectly good, perfectly healthy food at home, my sisters and I were picky eaters. I remember long post-meal scenes, sitting in front of a plate of cold food, which I had to finish. One "solution" my mother came up with was a disgusting milk drink, which she called *engrullo*, a name still synonymous in our extended family with my mother's strictness. Whatever my sisters and I left on our plates was ground up and put in a mixer with milk. This tall glass of greenish-brown liquid was then placed before us at the table. We were given a deadline, five minutes, ten minutes. (It seemed hours.) At the end of that time if we had not drunk up our *engrullos*, we were marched off to our rooms to do time until my father came home.

I have to say in my mother's defense that my sisters and I were very skinny and not always healthy. One sister had a heart ailment. Another had polio as a young child. I myself lost most of my hair at age three from a mysterious malady. The doctors finally diagnosed it as "stress." (Probably from having to drink *engrullos*!) My mother worried herself sick (literally, bad migraines) that her children would not make it through childhood. In a country where the infant mortality was shockingly high this was not a moot worry. Of course, most of these young deaths tended to be among the poor who lacked proper nutrition and medical care. Still, in my father's own family, only one of his first ten siblings survived into adulthood.

And so childhood meals at home were battlegrounds. And even if you won the dinner battle, refusing to clean your plate or drink your *engrullo*, you inevitably lost the war. When Papi came home, non-eaters got shots. This is not as sinister as it sounds: the shots, it turns out, were "vitamin shots," B12 and liver, which really were for "our own good." But to this day, every time I go to the doctor and have to have blood drawn, I feel a vague sense that I am being punished for not taking better care of myself.

Once we came to this country, the tradition of family meals stopped altogether. We were suddenly too busy to eat together as a family. Breakfasts were catch-as-catch-can before running down the six or seven blocks to school. We kept forgetting our lunches, so Mami finally gave up and doled out lunch money to buy what we wanted. What we wanted was the "junk food" we had never before been allowed to eat. My sisters and I started putting on weight. I think we all gained five or ten pounds that first year. Suddenly I had leg and thigh and arm muscles I could flex! But what good were they when there were no cousins to show them off to? As for dinner—now that Papi was working so hard and got home late at night, we couldn't have this meal together either. My sisters and I ate earlier whenever the food was done. When Papi got home, he ate alone in the kitchen, my mother standing by the stove warming up a pot of this or that for him.

In a few years, when my father's practice was doing better, he started coming home at a "decent hour." Actually, he had shifted his hours around so that, instead of staying at the office late at night, he opened at five-thirty in the morning. This way, his patients, many of them Latinos with jobs in *factorías*, could see the doctor before going to work on the first shift. Since Papi had to get up at four-thirty, so he could dress, have breakfast, and drive the half hour or so to Brooklyn, we ate dinner the minute he got home. As soon as he finished eating, my father would excuse himself, climb upstairs to the bedroom, turn on the TV, and read for a little while before falling asleep.

My mother and my sisters and I stayed behind at the table, Mami eating her Hershey bars—she'd pack in two or three a night, but then put Sweet & Low in her *cafecito!* Now that her daughters were in the full, feisty bloom of adolescent health, she no longer worried over our eating habits or got insulted if we didn't eat her cooking. She had hired a Dominican maid to do the housework, so she could spend the day helping Papi out at his *oficina*. Lunch was take-out from a little bodega down the street. It was safe to eat out now. This was America. People could be put in jail for fixing your food without a hair net or serving you something rotten that made you sick to your stomach.

The family plan had always been to go back home once the dictatorship had been toppled. But even after Trujillo's assassination in 1961, politics on the island remained so unstable that my parents decided to stay "for now." My sisters and I were shipped off to the same strict boarding school my mother had gone to where meals again became fraught with performance pressures. We ate at assigned tables, with a teacher, a senior hostess, and six other girls. The point was to practice "conversational skills" while also learning to politely eat the worst food in the world. Everything seemed boiled to bland overdoneness. And the worse part of it was that, as in childhood, we had to eat a little serving of everything, unless we had a medical excuse. My father, who was still as much of a spoiler as back in his Los Cremita days, agreed to let me fill in the infirmary form that asked if we had any special allergies or needs. I put down that I was allergic to mayonnaise, brussel sprouts, and most meats. No one, thank God, challenged me.

In college, in the height of the sixties, I finally achieved liberation from monitored eating. Students had to be on the meal plan, unless they had special dietary needs. A group of my friends applied to cook their own macrobiotic meals in a college house kitchen, and I joined them. I soon discovered vegetarianism was a picky eater's godsend. You could be fussy *and* high-minded. Most meats were on my inedible list already, and mayonnaise was out for macrobiotics who couldn't eat eggs. As for brussel sprouts, they were an establishment vegetable like parsnips or cauliflower, something our parents might eat as an accompaniment to their meat.

All through my twenties and thirties as a mostly single woman, my idea of a meal was cheese and crackers or a salad with anything else I had lying around thrown in. I don't think I ever used the oven in my many rentals except when the heat wasn't working. As for cooking, I could "fix" a meal, i.e. wash lettuce, open a can, or melt cheese on something in a frying pan, but that was about the extent of it. The transformations and alchemy recorded in cookbooks were as mysterious to me as a chemistry lab assignment. Besides, once I got a soufflé or a lasagna out of the oven, what was I supposed to do with it? Eat it all by myself? No, I'd rather take a package of crackers and a hunk of cheese with me in my knapsack to work. For an appetizer, why not a cigarette, and for dessert, some gum?

When I had friends over, a meal was never the context. Some other pretext was—listening to music, reading a new poetry book together, drinking a cup of coffee or a bottle of wine, munching on some cheese and crackers. I'd clear off the dining table, which I had been using as my desk, to hold this feast of bottles and boxes and packages and ash trays.

Had I had a family I would no doubt have learned how to cook persuasive, tasty meals my children would eat. I would have worried about nutrition. I would have learned to knit the family together with food and talk. But just for myself, I couldn't be bothered. Cooking took time. Food cost money. I was too busy running around, earning a living, moving from job to low-paying job. Sometimes I lived in boarding houses where I didn't even have access to a kitchen. I grew as thin in my twenties and thirties as I had been as a child. My mother began to worry again about my eating. Maybe I had a touch of that anorexia disease American girls were increasingly getting?

"No," I protested, shades of *engrullo* lurking in my head. I preferred to think of myself as a picky eater. But probably all these bad eating habits and attitudes are "kissing cousins." Eating is dislodged from its nurturing purpose and becomes a metaphor for some struggle or other. My own experience with food had always been fraught with performance or punishment pressures. No wonder I didn't enjoy it, didn't want to deal with it, didn't want to cook it, or even serve it. (My one waitressing job lasted less than a week. I kept forgetting what people had ordered and bringing them the wrong things.)

Of course, there was a way in which my whole apprehensive approach to food fell right in with the American obsession with diets and fear of food additives and weight gain. As a child, I had never heard of diets, except as something that people who were ill were put on. It was true that women sometimes said they were watching their figure, but it was vain and rude to stick to a diet when someone had gone to the trouble of putting some tasty dish on the table before you. The story is still told of my coquettish great-grandmother who was always watching her "little waist." She would resolve to keep a strict diet—only one meal per day, but then, approaching the table, she would invariably be tempted by an appetizing dish. "Well," she'd say, "I'm going to have lunch but I'll skip supper." At supper, she again couldn't resist what was on the table. "Well," she'd say, "I'm going to have a little supper, but I'll skip breakfast." By the time she died in her nineties, she owed hundreds upon hundreds of skipped meals.

And so, when at thirty-nine I married a doctor who was very involved with food and food preparation, I seemed to be returning to the scene of earlier emotional traumas to settle some score or exorcise some demon. A single father with two teenage daughters, my new husband had learned to cook out of necessity. Since his boyhood on a farm in Nebraska, he had always been involved in growing food, but the responsibility of nurturing his two confused, heartsick girls had turned him into a chef. Enter: one picky eater.

"What would you like to eat tonight?" my husband would ask me over the phone when he called me at lunch from his office. "I don't know," I'd say. Did I really have to make up my mind now about what I was going to eat in seven or eight hours?

With all this food planning and preparation going on around me, I started to worry that I was not pulling my share. One night, I announced that I thought we should each make dinner every other night. My husband looked worried. The one time I had invited him over to my house for dinner before we were married, I had served him a salad with bottled dressing and a side plate of fried onions and tofu squirted with chili sauce. This is a story my husband likes to tell a lot. I am always aggrieved that he forgets the dinner rolls, which I bought at the Grand Union bakery, something I would normally not do, since I much preferred crackers as "the bread" to have with my dinner.

But he liked doing the nightly cooking, he explained. It was his way to relax after a day at the office. Why not just help him out? I could do the shopping, which he didn't like to do. It turned out that he had to be very specific about what he put on the list or I would get "the wrong thing": baking powder instead of baking soda, margarine instead of butter. "You're so picky!" I would say, not always immediately aware of the irony. One stick of yellow grease was so much like another.

I also helped with making dinner, though he gave me little to do beyond washing the lettuce and keeping him company while he did the rest, that I began to suspect he didn't trust me even to help. Finally, we settled that I would be in charge of making the desserts. For months we had brownies, which were really quite good when I remembered to put the sugar in.

Meals, which had been something I did while doing something else, now took up big blocks of time, especially on Sundays when Bill's parents came over for dinner. First, we had soup, and then when we were done with the soup, several platters made the rounds, and then there was dessert. Then, coffee. During all these courses there was much talk about what we were eating and other memorable variations of what was on the table. If you were to take one of those pies statisticians use to show percentages and were to cut out a serving that would represent how much of the time we talked about food, I would say you'd have to cut yourself at least half the pie, and probably a second serving before the night was over. It took so long to eat!

True, when I was a young girl, the weekly dinners in my grandparents's house were long, lingering family affairs, but that was true only for the adults. Once we children got through the chore of finishing what was on our plates, we would be excused to go play in the garden while the grownups droned on over their everlasting courses and *cafecitos*. (No *engrullos* when we ate at somebody else's house!)

But now, I was one of those adults at the table of a family that was obviously bound together, not at the hip, but the belly. Traditionally, my husband's people have been farmers, intimately connected with food—growing it, serving it, preserving it, preparing it. As we lingered at the table, I listened, not understanding at first what the fuss was about. What was the difference been a Sungold tomato and a Big Boy? Why was sweet corn better than regular corn? What was the difference between a Yukon Gold and a baking potato. What did it mean when they said raspberries were setting on? And how come the second crop was always bigger, juicier?

Eventually, I realized that if I ate slowly and kept my ears opened, I could learn a lot. I also started to taste the food, instead of swallowing it, and slowly I developed new criteria—not just would I eat it or not. Did the flavors work together? Was the polenta bland or the bread chewy enough? As my own cooking repertoire expanded beyond brownies, I discovered the wonderful pleasure of transforming a pile of ingredients into a recipe that nurtured and sometimes delighted the people I love. It was akin to writing a poem, after all.

Now, eight years into sharing our table, my husband and I have developed a fair and equitable cooking arrangement. I am in charge of certain recipes—and not just desserts. I've even learned to cook certain meats for him and his parents, though I still don't eat them. For holidays, when the house is humming with beaters, hissing with steamers, beeping with oven timers, I feel the pulse of happiness whose center is the kitchen.

But I admit that years of picky eating don't vanish overnight. I still worry when we go out if there will be anything in the category of things-I-eat. There are still times when I come back from the kitchen and spy my husband and his family gathered at the table, talking away about the difference between this week's crust and last week's crust or how you can get the peak in those whipped potatoes or individual grains in the rice, and I wonder if I belong here. Will I ever stop feeling as if I've wandered into one of those Norman Rockwell scenes of a family sitting around a table laden with platters and pies? But each time I've put down what I had in my hands—my contribution to the feast—and looked around, I've found a place set for me at the table.

# BELL HOOKS
## (1952– )

In *Bone Black: Memories of Girlhood* (1996), hooks evinces a deep sense of her world in simple, yet poetic, language, naming the difficulties and joys of being raised black and female in the South during the fifties and early sixties. She dwells extensively on the church, and the role it played in her childhood, sometimes writing in the third person (a technique adopted by many American autobiographers, including Henry Adams and Gertrude Stein). This approach enforces a certain feeling of distance from a childhood that might otherwise appear frighteningly close. Toward the end of her memoir, hooks affirms her love for reading, which has served to help her bridge the way from childhood to adulthood: "I read poems. I write. That is my destiny." For hooks, as for Vivian Gornick and many other women, reading was intimately involved with the evolution of her identity.

Professor of English at the City College of New York, hooks has written numerous books, many of them social commentary and analysis. Among these works are *Talking Back: Thinking Feminist, Thinking Black* (1989) and *Killing Rage: Ending Racism* (1995).


## FROM *Bone Black*

Wash day is a day of hard work. The machine is old and must be filled with water from buckets. Mama does most of the work. We love to stand and watch her put the clothes through the wringer after they are rinsed in huge tin buckets of water. They are the buckets we once took baths in when we were small children living on the hill. At night in the kitchen we would take turns being washed, washing. We think having our bodies washed by someone else's hands is one of the real pleasures of life. We have to grow older and bathe alone. We do—locking ourselves in to make sure no one joins us, witnesses the experience we were once more than willing to share. Everyone is irritable on wash day, especially in winter. The damp from the water and the cold enters our bones, chilling us. Clothes must be hung on the lines before we go to school. Our hands freeze as we hang piece after piece. Our feet feel the wet in the grass seep-ing through the thin soles of our shoes. Hanging piece after piece we move in slow motion hoping that we can go to school before the basket is empty. Mama warns us that we had better hang everything, that she does not care if we are late. In summer the clean clothes hanging in the fresh air are like rows of blossoming flowers. In winter they are like dead things frozen and cold. We bring the heavy work pants into the house frozen and stand them up in the bathtub where they will slowly thaw.

Washing means ironing. We come home from school knowing that the ironing board will stand ready, that the iron will be hot. Sometimes mama will still be ironing, her face hot, her feet hurting. We will stand and watch, telling her about our day. She will tell us who will begin ironing first. We learn to iron by pressing sheets. We do not know why sheets that are not even wrinkled must be ironed. Mama says it is practice. We especially hate ironing our father's underwear and pajamas. We especially hate being told that nothing was ironed correctly, that we must do the entire basket again.

It is my turn to iron. I can do nothing right. Before I begin I am being yelled at. I hear again and again that I am crazy, that I will end up in a mental institution. This is my punishment for wanting to finish reading before doing my work, for taking too long to walk down the stairs. Mama is already threatening to smack me if I do not stop rolling my eyes and wipe that frown off my face. It is times like these that I am sorry to be alive, that I want to die. In the kitchen with my sisters, she talks on and on about how she cannot stand me, about how I will go crazy. I am warned that if I begin to cry I will be given something to cry about. The tears do not fall. They stand in my eyes like puddles. They keep me from seeing where the ironing is going. I want them to shut up. I want them to leave me alone. I shout at them Leave Me Alone! I sit the hot iron on my arm. Already someone is laughing and yelling about what the crazy fool has done to herself. Already I have begun to feel the pain of the burning flesh. They do not stop talking. They say no one will visit me in the mental hospital. Mama says it does not matter about the pain, I must finish ironing the clothes in my basket.

Miss Rhobert lives around the corner in one of the storybook houses — white white with green grass, red brick steps, and matching porch furniture. Of course she never sits on the porch as that is the kind of thing the common folk do. She is not common. She comes from a long line of folks who look white. When we were small children we thought they were the color of pigs in storybooks. We know now that they are the black landowners, business people. We know now that they stand between white folks and real black folks. Like gossip, white folks spread their messages to us through them. They hate both white folks and dark black people. They hate white folks for having what they want. They hate dark black folks for reminding the world that they are colored and thus keeping them from really getting what they want. They never pass for white. They do not want to live in white communities and be treated like second-class citizens, like poor white folks are treated. They want to live in the heart of black communities where they will be looked up to, envied, where their every move will be talked about.

Miss Rhobert is one of them. She is unmarried and getting on in age. She will never marry because no one is good enough they say. She will never marry because no one has asked her they say. She was my first grade teacher. She lives alone. She has divided her house into two flats. She lives in one. Her roomers, all single men, live in the other. They live together without really seeing one another. They may not bring their women to stay. When they are gone she must look elsewhere for comfort, protection, for knowledge that she is not alone. She suggests to my mother that I should come stay nights with her, that in exchange she will give a few dollars a week and sometimes help with the buying of school-books. Going to her house after dinner is a way to avoid conflict. She and I have little to say to one another. We will eat candy or ice cream, watch TV, and go to bed. I must sleep in the same bed with her. I hide myself in the corner of the bed near the wall and pretend I am not there. She sleeps soundly, snoring, her mouth open. When she pays me I will hand the money to mama who will determine what I need, how it will be spent. The money brings me no pleasure. I am never free to choose what to buy. When I assert my right to choose she never lets me forget.

Nights at Miss Rhobert's I learn the art of being present and not present at the same time. It is the art of being a good servant. It is knowing what it is to stay in one's place. I do not speak unless I am spoken to. I do not converse, I answer back in short sentences. When I laugh it sounds as though I am afraid. Sometimes I bring a book to read. This sign that I am not always a servant, not always in my place, leads her to make conversation. She wants to know what is being talked about at my house, who is doing what. I learn the art of avoiding answering her questions directly. When we are not watching television we play Scrabble. She likes to play for money. I do not as I am afraid to win. Since she has never learned to drive a car Miss Rhobert cannot go out at night unless someone comes for her. Sometimes, every now and then, she leaves me alone for a few minutes. The muscles in my body relax, I am no longer invisible in my chair. I am grateful for the silence. Mama decides for me that I am too old for this job. My younger sister takes my place.

When we first meet I am shy. She reminds me of the small brown bird I held in my hand days ago. We were in the backyard playing when we saw the bird on the fence. It seemed to be waiting for me. When I held it in my hand I could feel the quivering, the heartbeat. It was so alive and so delicate that I felt responsible and afraid. I put it back on the fence and waited until it flew away. To me she is that bird given human form. Miss Willie Gray is a brown-skinned woman with gray hair. She is in her nineties. She is afflicted with palsy. These are her words: Affliction makes me think of church and the Bible. She moves her arms as though they are wings continually flapping. She has learned to anticipate the trembling movement—to see it as a sign that she is still alive. The movements do not bother me. They remind me of the bird flying away. She wants to fly and cannot. We both agree that it is not a sad thing for she is able to be independent, to move around, to cook for herself, to plant a garden. She is alone, old, and happy. She tells me always, Who could ask for anything more.

They say she never married because she was too attached to her father. I believe them because she talks to me endlessly about him. She tells me how he bought the grocery store and let her work in it even though it was not considered the proper thing for a lady to do. She told me how he died and left the store to her along with money and land. She tells me that she would have given all those things away if only he could have remained alive. Her mother had died when they were still girls. She took over the running of the house. In those days she said it was a common thing for the eldest daughter to housekeep until a new wife could be found. Her father never found a new wife though he had women. She stayed to housekeep and care for him until he died. She never wanted to marry. She fascinates me because all the other independent unmarried women are schoolteachers who began work in those days when the law required them to remain single. She never tires of telling me that it is her choice to remain single and alone.

She is not always alone. I am hired to come and stay nights, to do chores in the day, to go to the store now and then. At her house I have my own bed. I can read all night long and books are in every room. We both love to lie in bed and read. She reads *True Confessions*. Although I buy them at the store I do not read them. She has a copy of Milton's *Paradise Lost* which I read again and again. Her books are all hardback. They are mainly popular novels. She no longer reads them. She tells me I can read them whenever I want. We are good company for each other. Now and then I must leave my bed to get water or medicine for her. She never goes anywhere. She stays in her yard and in her garden. She loves to walk up and down the rows of growing things. I tell her that I did this all the time when I was younger. Now I sit on the fence and watch.

They would like to put her in a home, a place where they would not have to worry about her. They say that they are worried that she might fall down and hurt herself. She says they want her house, her money. She intends to stay in her house alone until she dies. She tells me that to leave her house and go to an old folk's home would be the end. In a harsh voice she wants me to tell her why they cannot leave her in peace. I remain silent, listening, watching the flapping wings.

# LUIS J. RODRÍGUEZ
## (1954– )

This voice of protest rises from the gang-infested neighborhoods of Los Angeles, which count among the most impoverished in America. Rodríguez lived *la vida loca*, taking active part in a culture that emphasized drugs and violence; in turn, he watched as his son was drawn into the same sort of life. In the opening essay from *Always Running: La Vida Loca: Gang Days in L.A.* (1993), which follows, his sharp, polemical style of autobiography becomes apparent. "The writing first began when I was fifteen," he writes, "but the urgency of the present predicament demands that it finally see the light of day. This work is an argument for the reorganization of American society—not where a few benefit at the expense of the many, but where everyone has access to decent health care, clothing, food and housing, based on need, not whether they can afford them."

The eloquence of Rodríguez's text is both impressive and disturbing. When he writes of the death of friends, or describes the feral roving of his gang companions, he paints his accounts with quick, vivid brushstrokes.

## FROM *Always Running*

"It is the violent poetry of the times, written in the blood of youth."

—Linda Mendoza, Chicana poet from South San Gabriel

The Animal Tribe practically died with the death of one of its last presidents: John Fabela.

17-year-old John—whose girlfriend had just given birth to his infant daughter—succumbed to a shotgun blast in his living room as his younger brother watched from beneath a bed in an adjacent room. About 13 members of the Sons of Soul car club, made up of recent Mexican immigrants living in East L.A., were rounded up by the police.

By then Joaquín López was already in prison for a heroin beef. Many of the older Tribe members were also incarcerated or hard-core *tecatos*. As the Tribe's influence diminished, Lomas initiated Tribe members into the various sets based on age groupings: the Pequeños, Chicos, the Dukes and the Locos. Lomas was reorganizing and recruiting. No longer could one claim Lomas just by being there. Chicharrón invited me to get in.

"They beat on you for about three minutes—that's all," Chicharrón urged. "You get a busted lip. So what? It's worth it."

So later I decided to go to a party in the Hills, fully aware I would join a Lomas set. Like most barrio parties, it started without any hassle. *Vatos* and *rucas* filled every corner in the small house; some ventured outside, smoking or drinking. The house belonged to Nina, this extremely pretty girl whom everyone respected. Nina's mother shuffled in the kitchen, making tacos from large pots of meat and beans simmering on low flames.

The dudes were polite; dignified. *Señora* this and *Señora* that. You couldn't imagine how much danger hung on their every breath.

As the night wore on, the feel of the place transformed. The air was rife with anticipation. Talk became increasingly louder. Faces peeled into hardness. The music played oldies we all knew by heart, and *gritos* punctuated key verses. Fists smashed against the walls. Just as the food simmered to a boil, the room also bubbled and churned. Weed, pills and hard liquor passed from hand to hand. Outside, behind the house, a row of dudes shot up heroin. In the glow of the back porch light, they whispered a sea of shorn sentences.

A crew of older, mean-eyed *vatos* arrived and the younger guys stacked behind them. Nina's mother showed concern. She pulled Nina into the kitchen; I could see her talking severely to her daughter.

I didn't know these dudes. They were *veteranos* and looked up to by the homeys. They had just come out of the joint—mostly Tracy, Chino or Youth Training School, known as YTS, a prison for youth offenders. Chicharrón pressed his face close to my ear and told me their names: Ragman, Peaches, Natividad, Topo . . . and the small, muscular one with a mustache down the sides of his mouth was called Puppet.

I then recalled some of their reputations: Natividad, for example, had been shot five times and stabbed 40 times—and still lived! Peaches once used a machine gun against some dudes in a shoot-out. And Puppet had been convicted of murder at the age of 16.

"Who wants in?" Puppet later announced to a row of dark, teenaged male faces in front of him. Chicharrón whispered something in Puppet's ear. Puppet casually looked toward me. They designated me the first to get jumped.

Topo walked up to me. He was stout, dark and heavily tattooed. He placed his arm around me and then we marched toward the driveway. Chicharrón managed to yell: "Protect your head."

I assumed when I got to the driveway, a handful of dudes would encircle me, provide me a signal of sorts, and begin the initiation. Instead, without warning, Topo swung a calloused fist at my face. I went down fast. Then an onslaught of steel-tipped shoes and heels rained on my body. I thought I would be able to swing and at least hit one or two—but no way! Then I remembered Chicharrón's admonition. I pulled my arms over my head, covered it the best I could while the kicks seemed to stuff me beneath a parked car.

Finally the barrage stopped. But I didn't know exactly when. I felt hands pull me up. I looked back at everyone standing around the driveway. My right eye was almost closed. My lip felt like it stuck out a mile. My sides ached. But I had done well.

Hands came at me to congratulate. There were pats on the back. Chicharrón embraced me, causing me to wince. I was a Lomas *loco* now. Then a homegirl came up and gave me a big kiss on my inflamed lip; I wished I could have tasted it. Then other homegirls did the same. It didn't seem half-bad, this initiation. Later they invited me to pounce on the other dudes who were also jumped in, but I passed.

As the night wore on, Puppet, Ragman and Nat had the initiates pile into a pickup truck. I was already quite plastered but somehow still standing. Puppet drove the truck toward Sangra. Elation rasped in our throats.

"Fuck Sangra," one of the new dudes chimed in, and other voices followed the sentiment.

We came across a cherried-out 1952 DeSoto, with pinstripes and a metal-flake exterior. Puppet pulled the truck up to the side of it. There were four dudes inside drinking and listening to cassette tapes. We didn't know if they were Sangra or what. We followed Ragman as he approached the dudes. One of them emerged from the passenger side. He looked like a nice-enough fellow.

"Hey, we don't want no trouble," he said.

I knew they weren't Sangra. They looked like hard-working recreational lowriders out for a spin. But Ragman wouldn't have it. He punched the dude down. A couple of other guys came out of the car, and they too tried to salvage the night, tried to appeal for calm.

"Listen, man, how about a beer," one of them offered.

Nat grabbed his neck from behind and pulled him to the ground, then beat on him. Ragman looked at the other guys who were clearly scared.

"Who don' like it?" he demanded. "Who don' like it . . . you?"

Ragman hit another guy. By then the dudes in the truck had climbed out and bashed in the car, breaking windows and crunching in metal with tire irons and two-by-fours which had been piled in the back of the truck. One dude tried to run off, but somebody chased him down with a wine bottle and struck him on the head. The dude fell down and I saw the wine bottle keep coming down on him, as if it was supposed to break, but it wouldn't.

The driver of the DeSoto tried to pull out, but somebody threw a brick at his head. For a long time, I observed the beatings as if I were outside of everything, as if a moth of tainted wings floating over the steamed sidewalk. Then I felt a hand pull at my arm and I sluggishly turned toward it. Puppet looked squarely into my one opened eye. He had a rusty screwdriver in his other hand.

"Do it, man," he said. Simply that.

I clasped the screwdriver and walked up to the beaten driver in the seat whose head was bleeding. The dude looked at me through glazed eyes, horrified at my presence, at what I held in my hand, at this twisted, swollen face that came at him through the dark. *Do it!* were the last words I recalled before I plunged the screwdriver into flesh and bone, and the sky screamed.

Within a year, the local headlines' business boomed:

> "*Gang Violence: Teen Wars Bring Death To Two*"
> "*Valley Teen Gangs Flourish*"
> "*Three Wounded By School Intruders*"
> "*Youth, 17, Murdered: Victim Shot In Chest*"
> "*Five Hurt, Two Arrested In Rosemead Party Crash*"
> "*Three Still Held In Gang Deaths*"
> "*San Gabriel Teenager Shot In The Face*"
> "*Rosemead Youth Gunned Down: Murder Said Gang Related*"
> "*Shooting Victim Critical*"
> "*Fired From Car: Four Wounded By Gunshots*"
> "*Rosemead Boy, 17, Shot By Deputy, Dies*"
> "*Deputy Escapes Sniper*"
> "*Slaying Suspect Bound Over To Superior Court*"
> "*Sheriff Moving On Gangs*"

Committees, task forces, community centers, born-again storefront churches and behavior guidance counselors proliferated in response. Rosemead's South Side, South San Gabriel and San Gabriel's barrio became targets of programs, monies and studies. Local reporters drove along with law enforcement officers through Lomas and Sangra to get "the feel" of these misaligned and misunderstood communities. Gang members were interviewed and news photographers worked the Hills to depict the poverty—usually of children playing in mud next to rusted cars, trash cans and pregnant mothers peering out of makeshift sheds.

La Casa Community Center served the needs of Sangra; Bienvenidos Community Center and its John Fabela Youth Center covered Lomas; and the Zapopan Center catered to the southside of Rosemead. The centers offered dropout programs, welfare assistance, federal job placements, teen mother day care and places for young people to hang out.

The people who worked at the centers put in 80-hour weeks, covered
weekly funerals and had to enter the doors of domestic conflicts armed
with nothing but a prayer. Some were ex-gang members who ventured
back to help. Or they were the first wave of minority college students who
entered institutions of higher learning through special scholarships and
economic opportunity grants.

At La Casa and Zapopan, community activists made the payroll. The
triumvirate of community centers began to play a leading role in the
struggles which emerged out of the Mexican sections here. Besides the
gang killings, there was widespread drug use. Police beatings and killings
became prominent. And the battles in the schools for decent education
intensified. Because the three centers were dealing with similar crises,
their staffs often met together to consult on strategy.

By 1970 I felt disjointed, out of balance, tired of just acting and reacting. I wanted to flirt with depth of mind, to learn more about my world.
My society. About what to do. I became drawn to the people who came
to work at the community centers; they were learned. Full of ideas and
concepts; they were, I realized, similar to my father, this former teacher
and biologist, who once labeled all the trees and plants in the backyard
so we would know their scientific names.

Amid South San Gabriel's hottest summer, the Bienvenidos Community Center hired Chente Ramírez. His credentials included a lifetime in the White Fence barrio in East L.A.—known as the oldest "street
gang" in the country. But Chente managed to avoid gang involvement,
went to school, worked in industry, helped his father with his trucking
business and pretty much took care of his mom, six sisters and a brother
while his dad traversed the land in a tractor-trailer rig.

Chente, in his late 20s then, had already gone to a university, been a
founding member of the United Mexican American Students (UMAS),
helped organize the East L.A. school walkouts of 1968, participated in
forming MEChA (Movimiento Estudiantil Chicano de Aztlán) and the
Brown Berets. Later still he put together a number of East Los Angeles
study groups engaged in revolutionary theory. He was also a martial arts
expert.

I had certain yearnings at the time, which a lot of us had, to acquire
authority in our own lives in the face of police, joblessness and powerlessness. Las Lomas was our path to that, but I was frustrated because I
felt the violence was eating us alive.

Chente impressed me as someone I could learn from. He was calm,
but also street enough to go among all those crazy guys and know how

to handle himself. He didn't need to act bad to operate. He could be strong, intelligent, and in control. He was the kind of dude who could get the best from the system—education, karate training—without being a snitch or giving in. I wanted to be able to do this too.

I was in my mid-teens and Chente was about twelve years older. I looked up to him, but not as a big brother. He was someone who could influence me without judging me morally or telling me what to do. He was just there. He listened, and when he knew you were wrong, before he would say anything, he would get you to think.

*       *       *

The cue ball rolled across the tattered green felt and struck an odd-numbered striped ball like a firecracker, the violence sending it twirling into the corner pocket. Smoke curled through the luminance of the fluorescent light hanging by wires over the billiard table. Puppet gazed momentarily at the remaining balls which lay scattered on the playing field as he contemplated the next move. Across from him stood Toots, aware of Puppet's every gesture. Puppet placed a well-worn piece of chalk and twisted his cue stick into it for several seconds, all the time deducing the trajectory of the cue ball for his next stroke. Next to him in leather blouse and tight denim jeans stood Pila, Puppet's squeeze.

Puppet's forearms were a canvas of extremely elaborate, interwoven and delicately-pinned tattoos that danced on skin with *cholo* images, skulls, serpents and women's faces. On his neck was a stylized rendering of the words *Las Lomas*. At 20 years old, he was a *veterano* and just out of YTS.

Along with a handful of other *pintos*—like Ragman, Peaches, Natividad and Topo—Puppet ruled the 'hood with fear. Soon the *veteranos* took over the John Fabela Youth Center, along with its pool and ping pong tables.

Puppet bent low, closed an eye, and with the other followed the length of the stick, which rested on the skin between his thumb and forefinger, all the way to the cue ball.

"Eight ball in the corner pocket," he announced, as if he had sawdust in his throat.

He waited, breathing easily, then he pumped the stick, the cue ball sliding toward the side of the table, then back down in an angle and striking the eight ball into another corner pocket. The game belonged to Puppet.

Pila placed her arms around Puppet's shoulders. Toots pulled out some bills from his pocket as his *jaina*, Lourdes from Mexico, looked hard in Pila's direction.

"What you looking at, *puta tijuanera?*" Pila responded.

Lourdes walked up, placed her arms out wide and replied:

"Fock you—*quieres algo conmigo, pues aquí estoy.*"

Toots rushed up between them and pushed Lourdes back into the dark. He knew what messing with Pila meant—a rip across the belly or face. But he also knew it might involve crossing Puppet, and he wanted to avoid this more than anything.

Fuzzy then called out for other players and more bets.

Puppet looked intently at everyone, especially Toots in a corner with Lourdes. He neither disciplined nor encouraged Pila. She took care of what she had to take care of. Puppet didn't like people from Mexico anyway. For that matter, he didn't like blacks, whites or other barrios. In fact, Puppet didn't care about anybody.

*       *       *

La Casa Community Center occupied a two-story, former warehouse building with Mexican motifs on the outside, a gym and a recreation area with a single pool table. For a few weeks I took karate lessons there until I decided to leave before anyone discovered my ties to Las Lomas. Sangra members roamed in and out of the center nightly, planning battles, drug deals, or just to get high. Cokie and Dina would practically live there, along with the other girls in the flaming red hair. Sal Basuto was the community organizer, playing the role Chente had at the Bienvenidos/John Fabela Center. He walked through the T-shirted and muscular Sangra dudes, with combed-back short hair or bald heads.

"*¿Qué hubo?*" Sal greeted.

Some gave him Chicano-style handshakes while others responded with hand signs signifying Sangra. Boy, Hapo, Night Owl, Tutti and Negro were there, sort of hanging and barely acknowledging Sal's enthusiastic approach.

"Hey, homes, you got a *frajo?*" Hapo asked.

"Lung cancer kills," Sal said and handed him a cigarette.

"Don't worry," Hapo smiled. "I don't inhale."

Sal entered the pool table area, a small room which once held books and tables and a record player but which were taken during a break-in by unknown persons who also vandalized the place, tore shelving off brackets and ripped away chunks of wallboard.

Blas played a solitaire game of pool. Blas had a birth defect in which his right arm came out missing and only a rumor of fingers pressed out of his shoulder. But he trained himself to play pool with one arm and became a leading player, often beating those with two good arms.

Sal looked weary. Once, he told me he always tried to put on a face of interest. He felt a lot depended on his mood. There were days he didn't know what else to do with these young people. There were no jobs for them. The schools surrounding the barrio catered to the affluent whites who lived around Sangra, so they all dropped out. And Sangra and the police were in a constant clash.

Appropriately, the initiation for new Sangra members involved jumping a cop. Ambushing police car units in any of the narrow alleys here became a common occurrence. The city of San Gabriel had its own police force and jail house, which lay on the outskirts of the barrio. Every homeboy knew the inside of those cell walls. It was home.

Sal often returned to his cluttered office inside La Casa's main building. He would sink down in an ancient metal chair, and stare out the window at the small, well-kept homes in front of the center. He felt sorry for Sangra. They were a small barrio. The leading section, Los Diablos, had no more than 100 members. Lomas, on the other hand, had several hundred. Sangra was constantly under fire: Monte Flores, 18th Street and El Sereno were some of the other barrios at war with them—and each of them as big as Lomas. In the first year Sal worked at La Casa, he attended nine funerals of Sangra warriors.

Yet in many ways this made Sangra more vicious. Because they were small in number, they made up their strength with guts, intensity and uncompromising *locura*.

Cokie and Dina made sure the Sangra girls were intimidating and feared. The leader of Los Diablos, Chava, did the same thing with his stylized dress and ever-present small felt hat and cane. Also their style of graffiti, quite colorful and cryptic—and their ability to sneak into the Hills unnoticed and cross out Lomas *placas*—brought much ire upon them.

Sal knew one day they would pay a heavy price.

*　　*　　*

Many nights in the garage, while in the throes of sleep, I heard knocking and voices. They appeared to be woven into the dreams. But I'd wake up and realize it was no dream but Chicharrón or another homeboy or homegirl needing a place to crash, to party or just hang.

On such a night, I woke up to raps on the window. I yanked myself out of the blankets and opened the door. Santos, Daddio and Pokie, three of the Lomas crazies, were standing there.

"*Qué hubo*, homes?" I greeted.

"Chin, we need to do something tonight," Santos responded. "You with it man."

I already sensed what they meant. They wanted me to do a *jale*, a hit against Sangra. The night before Tutti from Los Diablos had gotten into a big argument with his long-time girlfriend, Cokie. In anger, Tutti drove up to Las Lomas and shot Little Man, killing him instantly. The police had already busted Tutti, but Lomas needed to exact some revenge. I knew the whole story. What I didn't know was Puppet, Ragman and the other main dudes had decided I needed to help "take care of it."

"*Orale*, let me get ready."

I put on dark clothes and my trench coat. It became a habit for me to take the trench coat whenever I did jobs like this.

We climbed over fences behind the garage and emerged onto Ramona Avenue. A car was there already. I entered, sitting in between Pokie and Little Man's brother, Beto, who had been sitting, deathly still, in the car. Santos and Daddio sat up front.

"What we got to do?" I asked.

"Look under the seats," Santos casually suggested.

I looked down with my eyes, without moving, and could see the edges of bottles and some rags. Shit, I thought, they want to firebomb a house. This meant somebody's mother, little sister or brother could be hurt or killed. But this is how things had gotten by then. Everyone was fair game in barrio wars; people's families were being hit all the time.

We cruised toward Sangra. Santos knew the police would be extra heavy the night after a shooting. But if we didn't move in a timely manner the impression would be anyone could hit us, anytime.

"Where we going?" I asked.

"We're going to Chava's *cantón*."

This was heavy. We were going after Sangra's main warrior. Who knows how they found out where his family lived, because Chava had moved in with Dina somewhere else. But the idea was to make him pay dearly, going after his mother's house, and if need be, anybody who might have the misfortune of being there.

I felt edgy, my muscles straining, my leg striking a beat against the back of the seat. I didn't want to do this. But once you're asked to do a hit, you can't refuse, can't question or even offer an excuse. Since I was easily accessible in the garage, I became a good candidate for these undertakings.

We pulled up to a quiet, suburban-looking street. Chava's family actually lived outside the barrio, in a better part of San Gabriel, pretty much like me. We parked down a ways and climbed up an embankment behind a row of houses.

Pokie brought up a bag filled with the bottles and rags. Daddio had cans of gasoline. We squatted in weeds behind a brick-fenced house with a back yard full of flowers and exotic plants, the way of many Mexican homes. A back porch had leisure chairs and gaily-painted rubber tires filled with soil and topped with purple, red and yellow petals.

It looked similar to my mother's back yard.

Santos poured gasoline into the bottles and stuffed the rags at the top, leaving a section hanging over. We each had a bottle. We were to toss them at the back porch, then run like hell to the car where Beto kept the engine running.

I didn't want to do it, but I couldn't stop. I felt trapped. I knew the only thing for me was to go through with it, and get out of there as fast as possible. I felt excitement. And an ache of grief.

A news account reported five people ran out of a house in San Gabriel after four molotov cocktails struck its back porch. Everybody got out safely, but the back of the house went up in flames and the rest of it sustained irreparable water damage from the fire hoses.

Little Man's death and the firebombing were part of a series of violent incidents between Lomas and Sangra which stretched back generations. Dudes had fathers and even grandfathers involved in the feud.

Of course, word got around about who did Chava's house. I don't know how this happened. But it soon involved my family.

By then my sister Gloria, 13 years old and a student at Garvey, looked up to me. To her, I was independent, in starched khaki pants, tattooed, with an earring in one ear before anybody did this kind of thing; always full of stories and good times. Her inexperienced mind soaked it all up.

Gloria joined a younger set of Lomas girls called United Sisters or US, and called herself Shorty. Sometimes I hung out with them, just for the kicks. I didn't see Shorty becoming a crazy Lomas girl. I saw it only as something she would get over as she matured.

One night she attended a dance at the San Gabriel Mission sponsored by Thee Prophettes, another girl's club. I didn't go, so Shorty played it smooth, hanging with her homegirls Cece and Huera from US.

Sure enough, Cokie and Dina showed up at the dance with a few Sangra girls. One of them was Spyder, who knew me from Garvey before she moved to Sangra and became one of the *locas*. When Spyder first noticed Shorty she felt a tug of recognition.

The Sangra girls gave everyone hard looks. US and Thee Prophettes kept cool, not wanting anything to undermine the benefit dance. Later that evening, though, Spyder figured out Shorty was my sister. I was "marked," meaning Sangra members were obligated to shoot Chin from Lomas. But a sister would do as well, Spyder reasoned.

Spyder relayed the information to Cokie and Dina. They had small caliber handguns. They discussed how they would corner Shorty and then let her have it, possibly in the girl's restroom.

Sometime later, my brother Joe received a phone call.

"Pick us up Joe," Shorty whispered in a frightened tone. "There's something happening here—and I'm scared."

Shorty told Joe to drive around the dance hall to a back entrance. Shorty, Cece and Huera planned to be there and get into the car. Timing was everything.

Joe didn't know what the problem might be. He got into his car and proceeded to do as Shorty asked.

He drove to the side of the dance hall where a door entrance was located, but Shorty and her friends weren't around. He waited. Suddenly the doors burst open. Shorty, Cece and Huera ran out, almost tripping as they held their heels in their hands.

"Joe, get the car going—hurry!"

"What the . . ."

But Joe couldn't get the final words out. A volley of gunfire came toward him. My sister and her friends rushed into the car, piling on top of one another. Joe pressed the accelerator, forcing the car to peel across the asphalt. Shorty didn't quite get inside but she held on as the car sped off; Cokie and Dina stood in the entranceway, and, firing from the shoulder, continued to pump .22 bullets toward the car as it vanished into the fog-drenched distance.

∗     ∗     ∗

Sheriff's helicopters were a nightly annoyance. It could have been Vietnam, only we were the enemy. They hovered above the slopes and ravines, covering the ground with circles of lights. Deputies drove by often, pushing dudes against walls, detaining them and dispersing crowds of two or more. The homeboys shot out the few lampposts to keep the place in darkness. We hid in bushes, in basements and abandoned buildings. We were pushed underground. Codes, rules and honor became meaningless.

Rapes became a common circumstance in the Hills. They began as isolated incidents, then a way of life. Some believed this ritual started with outsiders, not from within the Hills. Others said it began with one guy who happened to be crazy, but the rest followed suit as the attacks signified a distorted sense of power. One dude was said to have raped 17 girls one summer.

Enano once pulled up in a four-door green Chevy as Chicharrón and I lolled around on Teresa Avenue. He climbed out of the car, opened the back door and invited us to "get in on this." A naked girl, passed out, lay in the back seat. A black patch of pubic hair stood out on a shock of white skin which looked as if she had been immersed in flour.

"*Chale*, homes," I responded. "I ain't with it."

Chicharrón nodded the same sentiment.

Without hesitation, Enano closed the door, entered the front seat and took off, perhaps looking for somebody else to approach.

A rainy evening greeted Yuk Yuk, Fuzzy, Ernie López and me as we left a *quinceñera* dance in the Avenues, a barrio northeast of downtown Los Angeles. We jumped into Ernie's lowrider van. Paco and two girls were inside the van. Ernie put on some music which rattled the brain cells through speakers in the front and back of the van. Fuzzy and Yuk Yuk talked with the girls as I took swigs of Silver Satin wine and snorts of heroin. Mellowed and mumbling, we drove through the wet side streets toward the Hills.

The girls were loaded; incoherent and sleepy. Makeup smeared their faces. Paco groped through the blouse of one of the girls, who faintly tried to pull him off. Fuzzy held the other girl up as he smiled at Yuk Yuk and me. I nodded off, and then woke, nodded off and then woke. Soon I noticed Paco on top of the girl he had been manhandling. Her legs were spread outward, and a torn underwear twisted around an ankle. Paco's pants were below his knees and I could see his buttocks rise up and down as he thrust into her, her weak moans more from the weight of the body than anything else.

Ernie pulled up to Toll Drive. Yuk Yuk and Fuzzy pulled the other girl out and down the slope to the field. Paco kept at it with the girl in the van. I clambered out, the cold humid air jolting me to my feet. Ernie passed me the bottle of Silver Satin as he wobbled down to where Yuk Yuk and Fuzzy were already situated. I looked back. I could hear Paco coming, scratchy noises rising from his throat. The girl, who was somewhere between 12 and 14 years old, had her arms laid out over her head, her eyes closed, her mouth opened—unconscious, but as if in a silent scream.

I made it to the field and saw Yuk Yuk kissing the other girl on a section of cinder-block wall while Fuzzy opened her legs with his hand to get a better feel. Ernie looked at me and motioned me to come over. I didn't want any part of it. Something filled my throat and I puked around my shoes. Yuk Yuk by then had thrown the girl to the ground. I knew what they were going to do, and wandered off.

I walked up the slope, saw Paco pulling his pants up through the slightly-opened van doors. As before, I found myself ambling along a dirt road.

\*       \*       \*

Wilo and Payasa moved to El Monte to live with an aunt, partly to remove themselves from the violence surrounding the barrio. Their older brothers stayed and continued to carry on the fight. Glad my friends were not to be in the line of fire, I went to say goodby on the day they were leaving.

They lived on Berne Street, a section of Lomas called "Little TJ," which consisted of a road which flowed in mud on rainy days, making it difficult to get in and out. Makeshift stucco, brick and clapboard shacks clawed the hills on either side of the road.

Payasa looked different, following several months in rehab hospitals and half-way homes. Her hair was back to its normal luster, short and combed straight down instead of teased. She had on no makeup and thus seemed a stranger, although we were so close at one time, sleeping together on park benches, sniffing and groping in the tunnel or in my garage room. I no longer knew this person in front of me.

Payasa didn't smile. Yet she acknowledged me rather sweetly.

"Oh my Chin—you'll miss me?" she asked, more a statement than a question.

"Depends," I replied. "Just keep in touch."

"I'll always remember you, homes," she said and placed her hand on my face; meandering scars across her arms. "We've seen things most people never see. We've seen death. And here we are, still able to say goodby. I don't know if we deserve this."

"*Orale*, sure we deserve it. Don't ever forget that."

"I mean, we haven't done anything really decent," she said, then paused.

"You know," she continued. "I've forgotten what it is to cry. I don't know why."

"Me neither, but I know one thing, we better find out."

Wilo came by with a medium-sized bag of his belongings, but then he wasn't one for possessions.

"Hey, *ése*, what's up?" he said.

"*Aquí nomás.* You got everything?"

"You pack for where you're going, and where I'm going there's nothing to pack for."

"Are you sure you want to do this?"

"I'm sure I don't want to do this," he answered, then looked back toward his former home. "But there's nothing I can do about it. Even my *carnales* want us to leave. And I do what they say."

I helped Payasa and Wilo put their things into their father's beat-up station wagon which had a side door held on by twine and good wishes. I would miss them but it was best they leave, maybe start fresh again if this were possible.

"I owe you man," I finally said, something I never told Wilo about his role in my near-death experience. "You saved my life."

"*Chale, ése* don't put that on me," he said. "You don't owe me nothing. Just pay yourself back."

I hugged them both and proceeded down Berne Street to the nearest fields. It would be the last time I ever saw them again.

Later I found out Payasa ended up pregnant and in a prison of matrimony somewhere. But 10 days after they moved, dudes from the Monte Flores barrio would shoot and run over Wilo several times; his body discovered wedged between metal trash bins in an obscure alley. Payasa called me one day to say she hadn't heard from Wilo for a day or so. Then she called back to tell me she heard of his death while listening to the radio. Wilo was 15 years old. Payasa didn't cry.

*     *     *

Everything lost its value for me: Love, Life and Women. Death seemed the only door worth opening, the only road toward a future. We tried to enter death and emerge from it. We sought it in heroin, which bears the peace of death in life. We craved it in our pursuit of Sangra and in battles with the police. We yelled: *You can't touch this!*, but *Come kill me!* was the inner cry. In death we sought what we were groping for, without knowing it until it caressed our cheeks. It was like an extra finger in the back of our heads, pressing, gnawing, scraping. This fever overtook us, weakening and enslaving us. Death in a bottle. In spray. In the fire-eyes of a woman, stripped of soul and squeezed into the shreds of her humanity.

*     *     *

I stopped spray soon after my near-death experience. But I needed something else. At first, the dudes in the Animal Tribe used to go off somewhere and shoot up smack. At 13 years old, they shooed me away.

"This is not for you," Joaquín used to say.

Still, I fooled with all kinds of pills, with mescaline and meth. I sought the death in Silver Satin and muscatel, and then pure tequila and vodka. I snorted heroin and PCP with Payasa. By the time I turned 15, smack was everywhere. The epidemic followed a pattern in the barrio. It began with the *pachucos*. Most of the old-timers in prison, the *pachucos* of the 30s and 40s, were incarcerated because of *chiva*. Then every ten years or so a generation of ex-gang bangers became hooked. Now it was our time. Already, the older dudes in the Tribe were hypes, most of them behind bars.

Chicharrón went with me the first time I tried it. For this maiden trip, we skin-popped it in our forearms, a few "cents" worth. Lencho, who had marks up and down his arms, only gave us a taste until we could score with more money. Because Yuk Yuk turned us into a stealing organization, this became the basis for scoring heroin.

Chicharrón and I often cruised Whittier Boulevard. Every weekend, the 14-block stretch between Atlantic Boulevard and the Long Beach Freeway became the cruising capital of the world. Lowriders from every barrio in Southern California, and often from places throughout the Southwest, congregated there. Girls sat on car tops, dressed to impress, while dudes piled into dancing "shorts" as speakers blared the latest street beat. Some of the corners were taken over by different barrios. Lomas controlled the corner of Clela Avenue and the Boulevard. The lowrider club, Groupe, allowed us use of the parking lot there. In our finest *cholo* attire, we drank, laughed, and challenged. We picked up women and fought with other barrios. Sometimes we had shoot-outs with the dudes from 18th Street who controlled the corner across from us.

So on weekends, Chicharrón and I went out on excursions, looking for good times. Being out of school, and up to our eyeballs with time to kill, this also involved hitchhiking throughout East L.A. and the San Gabriel Valley and pretending to be incoming students at local high schools for a day. It proved to be easy: We told school officials we were new students and our parents would come in the next day to sign us up. Some of the schools allowed us to figure out our courses and start attending classes. We met more girls this way. We also got into fights with the local *vatos*, one time being chased by a mob of irate boyfriends in La Verne.

Soon we had girls to visit with in Pomona, Pasadena, Norwalk, in Boyle Heights, and El Monte.

So there we were, cruising the boulevard and pulling into a side street crowded with girls. We offered them booze or pills and then slid around an alley, behind a brick wall. We drank, staggered about and had a taste of some of them by pushing a finger around the crotch of their panties and into their vaginas, then continued on our way.

Around two in the morning, we passed Atlantic Boulevard when we spotted two girls sitting at a bus stop. We pulled over. Many times girls would shine us on when it got to be this late, but one of them came up to the car. She was big, but not fat, in tight jeans. She had kinky hair and *chola*-style makeup. The other girl was thinner, cute like a china doll, with short straight hair and a party dress.

"You want a ride?" I asked from my shotgun position in the car.

"Sure, you know where there's a party?" the kinky-haired one inquired.

"No, but I'm sure we can find one."

They climbed into the car, almost too easy, and we sped on looking for some "haps." The big one was named Roberta, the cute one was Xochitl, a Nahuatl name which sounded like Shoshi, so that's what we called her.

We ended up in Legg Lake along Whittier Narrows. The park was closed but we snuck in and ran around the swing area, having our own party with the pills and booze Chicharrón had left over from before. Police cruised by and we fell to the ground, quiet as the grass, until they passed by.

That night we drove Roberta and Shoshi to barrio La Rock Mara in the Maravilla Housing Projects. Roberta said she lived in one of the duplexes there with a 21-year-old sister named Frankie, which stood for Francisca. Frankie also happened to have five children. Shoshi was a runaway who stayed with them for a while. They were both 15 years old, like us.

We sat in the car until the dawn swam in orange-red colors across the horizon. I moved over to Roberta and kissed her, while Chicharrón made out with Shoshi in the front seat. After that night, Chicharrón and I practically made this our second home.

"Oh, Louie, touch me there . . . *simón*, just like that . . . ummm."

Sweat roamed down the side of my face. The car windows steamed. I broiled, as if working in a foundry, while Roberta lay there in the back seat with her blouse open and ample breasts wet with my saliva.

"Don't stop . . . ummmm, don't stop."

My tongue drew circles around her nipples, which were on a dark patch over honey-brown skin. My hands rubbed her cunt from the outside of her pants. Her hips moved in waves, pushing harder and harder into my hand. She groped for my zipper, tugged and slid it down. Her fingers kneaded the top of my penis, hard and wet with anticipation.

"*Eso, así* . . . oh baby, lick me."

Roberta pushed me up, my back arched and my head scraped the top of the car. Then she held on to my penis with both hands while her lips smothered it and her tongue lightly flickered over the tip. After a moment, she pulled at her pants, pushing them off with her hands and feet. I looked down and saw the tuft of wild hair at the crotch, her legs spread and nearing my shoulders, inviting me to enter.

She grabbed the back of my neck and then pressed me down to her. The penis sank into the bristle of pubis, then slid into the oiled vagina, covering it in flesh and juice and rhythm of pelvis. Roberta's mouth sucked at my chest, my neck and shoulders as her fingernails scraped tracks into my back. The scent from her hair and neck filled my head as I moved and quivered inside of her.

Night after night, I stayed over at Roberta's place. Because there were many children in her house, who never appeared to fall asleep, we made love in the car, beneath the staircase, or fondled in the driveway. Chicharrón and Shoshi found their own spots. At four or five in the morning, Chicharrón and I left, grabbing some *huevos rancheros* at a 24-hour Mexican restaurant on First Street.

Sometimes Fermin, Frankie's wino husband, would show up and the fights would start; the yelling and plates being tossed against a wall, and then the poor bastard being thrown out on his ass. Frankie was one tough East L.A. mama.

But other times we had to hassle with Smokey, Roberta's brother and a member of La Rock. I stayed cool with him and he pretty much left me alone. But Chicharrón and Smokey didn't get along. I believed Smokey also liked Shoshi.

One night, after Roberta and I lay back in the car seat, following a fevered bout of lovemaking, Chicharrón rapped on the car window.

"What's up homes?" I yelled out.

He opened the door. A lead pipe filled his hand.

"I'm waiting for Smokey," he said. "He's after me. You got to back me up, *ése.*"

"Ah, just leave it alone, he's only testing you," Roberta responded. "He does it to everyone—to see how tough you are."

Chicharrón didn't like being around there though. Often he took Shoshi away from there while I stayed with Roberta.

There were a few nights when I came over to see Roberta and she wasn't there.

"Man, where does she go?" I once asked Frankie.

"You don't want to know," she said.

"What do you mean, I don't want to know," I replied. "Of course I do."

"Listen, I like you Louie," Frankie confided. "So it's better you just don't ask."

But I insisted. And it was true. I shouldn't have asked.

It happened that Roberta turned tricks. This is how she could pay for staying with Frankie, and sometimes to help pay for her sister's habit. Frankie had marks on her arms—but she was careful not to get popped because she didn't want the children taken away. In fact, her husband Fermin had been an old hype who turned to the bottle. To Frankie, this was worse, and she threw him out.

A fever of emotion swept through me. The thought of Roberta selling herself to other guys for money choked on me. Frankie told me Roberta worked the Boulevard, the same place I met her.

"How come she didn't ask me for money?" I yelled. "How come she didn't even come off like a whore then?"

"Maybe she liked you from the start," Frankie submitted. "She's only a teenager, Louie. She still has feelings for men—but I don't know how long this will last."

I didn't know what to do. I wanted to rush out of there. But I felt I had to wait for Roberta to come home. I wondered if Shoshi also sold her sex and if Chicharrón knew.

"Oh, yeah, her too," Frankie said. "Not only does Chicharrón know, but he's out there pimping for her."

"Are you fucking with me!" I yelled. "How come he never told me?"

"You're a sweet dude, Louie," Frankie said, coming up to me and kissing me softly on my lips. "There's not too many of you out there. We told him not to tell you."

I started to feel tears beneath my eyes, but I wouldn't let them fall. Frankie pressed her finger on my eyelids and a drop traced down my cheek. She kissed me again. Told me how much she liked me, how she had liked me from the first day, then led me into her bedroom and closed the door.

Later that morning Smokey came by and invited me to a house across the street, situated on top of another one. We climbed a section of unkept stairs. Smokey knocked, said a few words to the door before it opened and we entered. The place had no electricity or gas. Candles were situated around a kitchen table. Hypodermic needles, spoons, matches and bags of powder were on the table. I looked around and saw about five people, including two women. They had dark circles beneath their eyes, tattoos like old *pachucas*, and collapsed veins along the inside of their arms.

Smokey was also a *tecato*, although he looked fit and muscular; if you know what you're doing you can actually live well on heroin for a while.

My head swarmed with tortuous thoughts of Roberta in somebody else's arms, but it was also my fault. I fell in love with a prostitute. Although she never asked me for money, indicating perhaps I was special, I still felt hollow inside. Smokey prepared a kit while I tightened a belt around my upper biceps. I watched the needle enter a bulging vein that Smokey brought up through the skin by slapping it with two fingers. I saw the tinge of blood enter the needle, indicating it had punctured the vein, then watched the clear liquid get pushed into the bloodstream. The sensation began like a pinhole glow at the inner pit of my stomach and then spread throughout my body. There was nothing like it, this rush, and here I was on the edges of a new fraternity which crossed barrio and sex lines, this fellowship of *la carga*, so integral to "la vida loca."

# MARY KARR

## (1954– )

A poet who teaches at Syracuse University, where she herself studied, Karr propelled herself into the front rank of American autobiographers with *The Liars' Club* (1995), a dazzling (and popular) memoir of her childhood in an East Texas oil town. The writer's training in poetry is reflected in the quality of her prose, which is peppered with rich colloquial speech and surprising images. Karr tells a wild, raucous, gritty tale of growing up in what can only be called a wildly dysfunctional family. With remarkable honesty and clear-eyed grace, she confronts poverty, ill health, and self-destructive behavior at every turn, somehow managing to be extremely funny about situations that are often wrenching and painful. As a reviewer in the *New York Times Book Review* put it, Karr's "toughness of spirit, her poetry, her language, her very voice are the agents of rebirth on this difficult, hard-earned journey."

## FROM *The Liars' Club*

When Grandma came back to our house she had ossified into something elemental and really scary. She seemed way thinner than she had been in the hospital, though perhaps not as pale. She had been fitted with an artificial leg that she strapped on every morning. It wore a sturdy black shoe that never came off. At night, she detached the leg and stood it by her bed. Once, when I passed her door on my way to the toilet, I caught sight of it standing there with no person tacked on top of it, and it was casting a long shadow into the hall that nearly reached my bare feet, so I scrambled back under the quilt with Lecia, my heart thumping, not caring whether I wet the bed that night (I did). The honeysuckle that grew up our screens made spiky wall-shadows on nights like that. Sometimes I'd hear Grandma hop down the short hall into the bathroom, her cane whacking the door molding. Lecia says that I misremember one specific sight of her standing in our doorway with that stump bluntly hanging down under her nightie, her arms spread so she could hold herself up by the doorjamb, and her hair fanned out around her face like white fire. I can see it like yesterday's breakfast, but Lecia claims it never happened.

Grandma wore very pale pink nylon pajamas with a matching robe, and her wheelchair was spookily silent in the way somebody walking never was. With Daddy's 3-In-One oil and the same maniacal patience she had brought to tatting, she kept it tuned silent on purpose. She'd upend the chair by her bed and squirt oil in all the tiny hollow places so it was nothing but glide. Then she could materialize soundlessly around a corner. She had a habit of sneaking up on Lecia and me and shouting *Aha!* as if she'd discovered us shooting up heroin with a turkey baster or eviscerating some small animal. Once she found us playing gin rummy and let out her *Aha!*, then called Mother. Grandma even watched us the whole time she was yelling as if we were going to cover up the cards before Mother got there. "Charlie Marie! Come in here and whip these children. I swear to God . . ." Mother, who never excelled as a spanker, arrived and asked some bewildered questions. Grandma gave an evangelistic-sounding lecture on the evils of gambling (and liquor, oddly enough), this despite the fact that she'd been an avid cheater at church bingo (and was, since her surgery, consuming about a case of beer every day). After a while, Mother just gave in to Grandma's rantings and went through the motions of flailing at our legs with a flyswatter till we ran into our room and slammed the door. I remember crawling up in Lecia's lap and whining about how I hadn't done anything. Lecia reasoned that we'd probably gotten away with fifty things we should have been spanked for that day, anyway, so we should just call it even.

It was sometime in August that I started walking in my sleep. Actually I did things other than just walk: I'd go squat behind the living room drapes and go to the bathroom in a pile they sometimes didn't find till the next morning. Once I wandered outside, and Daddy had to come chasing after me.

That fall my school career didn't go much better. I got suspended from my second-grade class twice, first for biting a kid named Phyllis who wasn't, to my mind, getting her scissors out fast enough to comply with the teacher, then again for breaking my plastic ruler over the head of a boy named Sammy Joe Tyler, whom I adored. A pale blue knot rose through the blond stubble of his crew cut. Both times I got sent to the principal, a handsome ex-football coach named Frank Doleman who let Lecia and me call him Uncle Frank. (Lecia and I had impressed Uncle Frank by both learning to read pretty much without instruction before we were three. Mother took us each down to his office in turn, and we each dutifully read the front page of the day's paper out loud to him, so he could be sure it wasn't just some story we'd memorized.)

He let me stay in his office playing chess all afternoon with whoever wandered in. He loved pitting me against particularly lunkheaded fifth- and sixth-grade boys who'd been sent down for paddlings they never got. He'd try to use my whipping them at chess to make them nervous about how dumb they were. "Now this little bitty old second-grader here took you clean in six plays. Don't you reckon you need to be listening to Miss Vilimez instead of cutting up?" When Mrs. Hess led me solemnly down the hall to Frank Doleman's office, I would pretend to cry, but thought instead about Brer Rabbit as he was being thrown into the briar patch where he'd been born and raised, and screaming *Please don't throw me in that briar patch!* At the end of both days, Uncle Frank drove me home himself in his white convertible, the waves of kids parting as we passed and me flapping my hand at all of them like I was Jackie Kennedy.

It was also at this time that I came to be cut out of the herd of neighborhood kids by an older boy. Before that happened there was almost something sacred about that pack of kids we got folded into. No matter how strange our family was thought to be, we blended into the tribe when we all played together. For some reasons, I always remember us running barefoot down the football field together, banking and turning in a single unit like those public-TV airplane shots of zebras in Africa.

But obviously I had some kind of fear or hurt on me that an evil boy could smell. He knew I could be drawn aside and scared or hurt a little extra. When he came for me, I went with him, and my going afterwards felt as if it had been long before plotted out by something large and invisible—God, I guess.

But before that boy singled me out, the sheer velocity of running across a wet field with other kids felt safe. There were dozens of us. We ranged in age from thirteen or fourteen for the big boys down to Babby Carter, who at two trailed behind the herd everywhere. I was seven and fit into the group about dead center, age-wise. I was small-boned and skinny, but more than able to make up for that with sheer meanness. Lecia still holds that I would have jumped a buzz saw. Daddy had instructed me in the virtue of what he called equalizers, which meant not only sticks, boards, and rocks, but having one hell of a long memory for mistreatment. So I wouldn't hesitate to sneak up blindside and bite a bigger kid who'd gotten the better of me a week before. To my knowledge, I never slouched off an ass-kicking, even the ones that made me double up and cry. It might take me a week or so, but I always came back. (To this day, I don't know whether to measure this as courage or cowardice, but it stuck. After I grew up, the only man ever to punch me found himself awakened two nights later from a dead sleep by a solid right to the jaw, after which I informed him that, should he ever wish to sleep again, he shouldn't hit me. My sister grew up with an almost insane physical bravery: once in the parking lot outside her insurance office, she brushed aside the .22 pistol of a gunman demanding her jewelry. "Fuck you," she said and opened her Mercedes while the guy ran off. The police investigator made a point of asking her what her husband did, and when she said she didn't have one, the cop said, "I bet I know why.")

In some ways, all the kids in my neighborhood were identical. Our fathers belonged to the same union. ("Oil Chemical and Atomic Workers, Local 1242" was how they answered the phone on Daddy's unit.) They punched the same clocks for almost exactly the same wage. (Our family had been considered rich because of Mother's part-time newspaper work.) Maybe one kid's daddy worked Gulf and another Texaco and another Atlantic Richfield, but it amounted to the same thing. Maybe one was a boilermaker and another controlled the flow of catalyst in a cracking unit. But they all worked turning crude oil into the various byproducts you had to memorize by weight in seventh-grade science class—kerosene, gasoline, and so on. The men all worked shift work because that paid a little better, so all of us knew how to tiptoe on days when the old man was on graveyards. The union handed out cardboard signs that ladies tacked to their doors: SHHH! SHIFT WORKERS ASLEEP. Nobody but Mother had ever been to college. (She'd attended both Texas Tech and art school.)

When the football field was cut on weekends, we'd gather hay from behind the tractor and lay it out in lines that followed the same square floor plans our fathers had unrolled on blueprints when their GI loans were approved—two bedrooms, one bath, attached garage, every one. The cut brown clover and St. Augustine grass smelled wetter and greener than any field cuttings I ever encountered in my adult elsewheres.

It's that odor that carries me to a particular cool day when I lay down within the careful lines of my own grass house. I was sure that I could feel the curve of the earth under my spine. I watched the clouds scud behind the water tower. Then I rolled over on my stomach. There were wild pepper plants that had hot little seeds you could pop between your teeth. Clover squeaked when you pulled it out of the ground, and its root was white and pulpy sweet.

Once I got stung by a bee, and this older boy I mentioned doctored me with a plaster of spit and mud till I stopped my snubbing. So I believed he liked me, and I was thirsty for liking.

On the hot days, when running was forbidden—heatstroke was always bringing little kids down—we played a game some kid invented called Torture. This sounds worse than it was. A bigger kid would herd us into the skin-tightening heat of the most miserably close spot we could find—the spidery crawl space under the Carters' back porch, say, or Tommy Sharp's old pigeon cage, or some leftover refrigerator box waiting for the garbage truck. There we'd squat into the hunched and beaten forms we

thought made us look like concentration-camp inmates. This evil boy
had a picture of Buchenwald survivors in his history book. All of us collectively studied it, memorized it. We did so not out of any tender feeling for the victims' pain or to ponder injustice, but so we could
impersonate them playing Torture. We lined up shoulder to shoulder and
thigh to thigh under the cold dull eye of this big boy's Nazi. He didn't
twist arms or squish heads or inflict wounds. He was too smart for that.
He just reigned over us while our parents called us home for lunch. We
hunkered down without moving. I imagine all those bodies when
crammed into a tight space generated temperatures well over a hundred
and twenty degrees. Blinking or whimpering wasn't permitted. We
melted into a single compliant shape. It was almost a form of meditation.
The world slowed down, and your sense of your own body got almost unbearably distinct. Sweat rivered down my rib cage. I could feel every particle of grit in the fold of my neck. The Nazi boy would menace us not
with overt cruelty but with an empty professional stare. There was no
need to switch-whip us; we didn't dare move anyway. That was the whole
game. We sat there together, radiant with misery. Eventually, of course,
some adult arm would poke into where we were hiding and signal the arrival of somebody's mom come to pull us out and drag us home for lunch
or supper.

   And it was one of these times—an evening, oddly enough—when the
arm felt around and didn't find me huddled in the corner, that all the
other kids poured out and scattered to their separate homes for supper,
so this big boy and I were left alone.

   It was going dark when he got hold of me under God knows what pretext. He took me into somebody's garage. He unbuttoned my white shirt
and told me I was getting breasts. Here's what he said: "You're getting
pretty little titties now, aren't you." I don't recall any other thing being
said. His grandparents had chipped in on braces for his snaggly teeth.
They glinted in the half dark like a robot's grillwork. He pulled off my
shorts and underwear and threw them in the corner in a ball, over where
I knew there could be spiders. He pushed down his pants and put my
hand on his thing, which was unlike any of the boys' jokes about hot dogs
and garden hoses. It was hard as wood and felt big around as my arm. He
wrapped both my hands around it, and showed me how to slide them up
and down, and it felt like a wet bone encased in something. At some
point, he tired of that. He got an empty concrete sack and laid it down
on the floor, and me down on top of that, and pumped between my legs
till he got where he was headed. I remember I kept my arms folded
across my chest, because the thing he'd said about my breasts seemed
such an obvious lie. It made me feel ashamed. I was seven and a good ten
years from anything like breasts. My school record says I weighed about

fifty pounds. Think of two good-sized Smithfield hams—that's roughly how big I was. Then think of a newly erect teenaged boy on top of that and pumping between my legs. It couldn't have taken very long.

(I picture him now reading this, and long to reach out of the page and grab ahold of his shirt front that we might together reminisce some. Hey, bucko. Probably you don't read, but you must have somebody who reads for you—your pretty wife or some old neighbor boy you still go fishing with. Where will you be when the news of this paragraph floats back to you? For some reason, I picture you changing your wife's tire. She'll mention that in some book I wrote, somebody from the neighborhood is accused of diddling me at seven. Maybe your head will click back a notch as this registers. Maybe you'll see your face's image spread across the silver hubcap as though it's been flattened by a ballpeen hammer. Probably you thought I forgot what you did, or you figured it was no big deal. I say this now across decades and thousands of miles solely to remind you of the long memory my daddy always said I had.)

When he was done with me it was full dark. I unballed my clothes and tried to brush off any insects. He helped me to pull them on and tied my Keds for me. He washed me off at the faucet that came out of the side of somebody's house. The water was warm from being in the pipe on a hot day, and my legs were still sticky after.

Our porch light was amber. The rest of the houses were dark. You could see the spotlights from the Little League park and hear the loudspeaker announcing somebody at bat. I wondered if this boy had planned to get ahold of me way in advance, if he'd picked the time when everybody would be at the game. Which was worse—if he'd only grabbed me at the opportune moment, or if he'd plotted and stalked me? I couldn't decide. I didn't want to be taken too easily, but I had been, of course. Even at seven I knew that. On the other hand, the idea that he'd consciously chosen to do this, then tracked me down like a rabbit, made me feel sick. He walked me home not saying anything, like he was doing a baby-sitting chore.

Then I was standing on my porch by myself. I could hear his tennis shoes slapping away down the street. I watched the square of his white T-shirt get smaller till it disappeared around the corner.

The honeysuckle was sickly sweet that night. I stood outside for a long time. I tried to arrange my face into nothing special having happened. There was a gray wasp nest in the corner of our porch. It had chambers like a honeycomb, each with the little worm of a baby wasp inside, sleeping. I thought sleeping that way would be good. After a while, Daddy pulled open the door and shoved the screen wide and asked me had I been at the game. "Come in, Pokey. Lemme fix you a plate," he said. I still fit under his armpit walking in. You could hear a roar from the park as somebody turned a double play or got a hit. I thought of the boy climbing the bleachers toward his admirers. I thought of all the jokes I'd heard about blow jobs and how a girl's vagina smelled like popcorn.

I looked at my father, who would have climbed straight up those bleachers and gutted this boy like a fish, and at my mother, who for some reason I imagined bursting into tears and locking herself in the bathroom over the whole thing. Grandma in her wheelchair would have said she wasn't surprised at all. Lecia was at the game, probably at the top of the bleachers combing down her bangs with a rattail comb and laughing when this boy came climbing toward her. He didn't even have to threaten me to keep quiet. I knew what I would be if I told.

# TERRY TEMPEST WILLIAMS

## (1955– )

A Mormon by heritage, Williams often writes about the sense of place in her life—a subject explored in detail in *Refuge: An Unnatural History of Family and Place* (1991), both a natural history of a particular biosphere and a deeply moving family saga. Williams learned in the spring of 1983 that her mother was dying of cancer; that same spring, Great Salt Lake began to rise to new heights, posing a genuine threat to the Bear River Migratory Bird Refuge, a remarkable region that was full of herons, owls, and snowy egrets—birds that had become important to Williams in her imaginative life.

Her first book, *Pieces of White Shell: A Journey to Navajoland* (1984), told of her experience as a teacher among the Navajo, exploring the culture and mythology of Native Americans with unusual grace and sensitivity. Although her writing has primarily centered on the West, she has also written passionately about other wild places, including the Serengeti Plain of Kenya. Her personal narratives, which frequently examine the complex interaction of mental and physical landscapes, have won a wide and sympathetic readership.

## FROM *Refuge: An Unnatural History of Family and Place*

### BURROWING OWLS

#### LAKE LEVEL: 4204.70'

Great Salt Lake is about twenty-five minutes from our home. From the mouth of Emigration Canyon where we live, I drive west past Brigham Young standing on top of "This Is the Place" monument. When I reach Foothill Drive, I turn right, pass the University of Utah and make another right, heading east until I meet South Temple, which requires a left-

657

hand turn. I arrive a few miles later at Eagle Gate, a bronze arch that spans State Street. I turn right once more. One block later, I turn left on North Temple and pass the Mormon Tabernacle on Temple Square. From here, I simply follow the gulls west, past the Salt Lake City International Airport.

Great Salt Lake: wilderness adjacent to a city; a shifting shoreline that plays havoc with highways; islands too stark, too remote to inhabit; water in the desert that no one can drink. It is the liquid lie of the West.

I recall an experiment from school: we filled a cup with water—the surface area of the contents was only a few square inches. Then we poured the same amount of water into a large, shallow dinner plate—it covered nearly a square foot. Most lakes in the world are like cups of water. Great Salt Lake, with its average depth measuring only thirteen feet, is like the dinner plate. We then added two or three tablespoons of salt to the cup of water for the right amount of salinity to complete the analogue.

The experiment continued: we let the plate and cup of water stand side by side on the window sill. As they evaporated, we watched the plate of water dry up becoming encrusted with salt long before the cup. The crystals were beautiful.

Because Great Salt Lake lies on the bottom of the Great Basin, the largest closed system in North America, it is a terminal lake with no outlet to the sea.

The water level of Great Salt Lake fluctuates wildly in response to climatic changes. The sun bears down on the lake an average of about 70 percent of the time. The water frequently reaches ninety degrees Fahrenheit, absorbing enough energy to evaporate almost four feet of water annually. If rainfall exceeds the evaporation rate, Great Salt Lake rises. If rainfall drops below the evaporation rate, the lake recedes. Add the enormous volume of stream inflow from the high Wasatch and Uinta Mountains in the east, and one begins to see a portrait of change.

Great Salt Lake is cyclic. At winter's end, the lake level rises with mountain runoff. By late spring, it begins to decline when the weather becomes hot enough that loss of water by evaporation from the surface is greater than the combined inflow from streams, ground water, and precipitation. The lake begins to rise again in the autumn, when the temperature decreases, and the loss of water by evaporation is exceeded by the inflow.

Since Captain Howard Stansbury's *Exploration and Survey of the Great Salt Lake, 1852*, the water level has varied by as much as twenty feet, altering the shoreline in some places by as much as fifteen miles. Great Salt Lake is surrounded by salt flats, sage plains, and farmland; a slight rise in the water level extends its area considerably. In the past twenty years, Great Salt Lake's surface area has fluctuated from fifteen hundred square miles to its present twenty-five hundred square miles. Great Salt Lake is now approximately the size of Delaware and Rhode Island. It has been estimated that a ten foot rise in Great Salt Lake would cover an additional two hundred forty square miles.

To understand the relationship that exists at Great Salt Lake between area and volume, imagine pouring one inch of water into the bottom of a paper cone. It doesn't take much water to raise an inch. However, if you wanted to raise the water level one inch at the top of the cone, the volume of water added would have to increase considerably. The lake bed of Great Salt Lake is cone-shaped. It takes more water to raise the lake an inch when it is at high-level, and less water to raise it in low-level years.

Natives of the Great Basin, of the Salt Lake Valley in particular, speak about Great Salt Lake in the shorthand of lake levels. For example, in 1963, Great Salt Lake retreated to its historic low of 4191′. Ten years later, Great Salt Lake reached its historic mean, 4200′—about the same level explorers John Fremont and Howard Stansbury encountered in the 1840s and 50s.

On September 18, 1982, Great Salt Lake began to rise because of a series of storms that occurred earlier in the month. The precipitation of 7.04 inches for the month (compared to an annual average of about fifteen inches from 1875 to 1982) made it the wettest September on record for Salt Lake City. The lake continued to rise for the next ten months as a result of greater-than-average snowfall during the winter and spring of 1982–83, and unseasonably cool weather (thus little evaporation) during the spring of 1983. The rise from September 18, 1982 to June 30, 1983, was 5.1′, the greatest seasonal rise ever recorded.

During these years, talk on the streets of Salt Lake City has centered around the lake: 4204′ and rising. It is no longer just a backdrop for spectacular sunsets. It is the play of urban drama. Everyone has their interests. 4211.6′ was the historic high recorded in the 1870's. City officials knew the Salt Lake City International Airport would be underwater if the Great Salt Lake rose to 4220′. Developments along the lakeshore were sunk at 4208′. Farmers whose land was being flooded in daily increments were trying desperately to dike or sell. And the Southern Pacific Railroad labors to maintain their tracks above water, twenty-four hours a day, three hundred sixty-five days a year, and has been doing so since 1959.

My interest lay at 4206′, the level which, according to my topographical map, meant the flooding of the Bear River Migratory Bird Refuge.

There are those birds you gauge your life by. The burrowing owls five miles from the entrance to the Bear River Migratory Bird Refuge are mine. Sentries. Each year, they alert me to the regularities of the land.

In spring, I find them nesting, in summer they forage with their young, and by winter they abandon the Refuge for a place more comfortable.

What is distinctive about these owls is their home. It rises from the alkaline flats like a clay-covered fist. If you were to peek inside the tightly clenched fingers, you would find a dark-holed entrance.

"*Tttss! Tttss! Tttss!*"

That is no rattlesnake. Those are the distress cries of the burrowing owl's young.

Adult burrowing owls will stand on top of the mound with their prey before them, usually small rodents, birds, or insects. The entrance is littered with bones and feathers. I recall finding a swatch of yellow feathers like a doormat across the threshold—meadowlark, maybe. These small owls pursue their prey religiously at dusk.

Burrowing owls are part of the desert community, taking advantage of the abandoned burrows of prairie dogs. Historically, bison would move across the American Plains, followed by prairie dog towns which would aerate the soil after the weight of stampeding hooves. Black-footed ferrets, rattlesnakes, and burrowing owls inhabited the edges, finding an abundant food source in the communal rodents.

With the loss of desert lands, a decline in prairie dog populations is inevitable. And so go the ferret and burrowing owl. Rattlesnakes are more adaptable.

In Utah, prairie dogs and black-footed ferrets are endangered species, with ferrets almost extinct. The burrowing owl is defined as "threatened," a political step away from endangered status. Each year, the burrowing owls near the Refuge become more blessed.

The owls had staked their territory just beyond one of the bends in the Bear River. Whenever I drove to the Bird Refuge, I stopped at their place first and sat on the edge of the road and watched. They would fly around me, their wings sometimes spanning two feet. Undulating from post to post, they would distract me from their nest. Just under a foot long, they have a body of feathers the color of wheat, balanced on two long, spindly legs. They can burn grasses with their stare. Yellow eyes magnifying light.

The protective hissing of baby burrowing owls is an adaptive memory of their close association with prairie rattlers. Snake or owl? Who wants to risk finding out.

In the summer of 1983, I worried about the burrowing owls, wondering if the rising waters of Great Salt Lake had flooded their home, too. I was relieved to find not only their mound intact, but four owlets standing on its threshold. One of the Refuge managers stopped on the road and commented on what a good year it had been for them.

"Good news," I replied. "The lake didn't take everything."

That was late August when huge concentrations of shorebirds were still feeding between submerged shadescale.

A few months later, a friend of mine, Sandy Lopez, was visiting from Oregon. We had spoken of the Bird Refuge many times. The whistling swans had arrived, and it seemed like a perfect day for the marsh.

To drive to the Bear River Migratory Bird Refuge from Salt Lake City takes a little over one hour. I have discovered the conversation that finds its way into the car often manifests itself later on the land.

We spoke of rage. Of women and landscape. How our bodies and the body of the earth have been mined.

"It has everything to do with intimacy," I said. "Men define intimacy through their bodies. It is physical. They define intimacy with the land in the same way."

"Many men have forgotten what they are connected to," my friend added. "Subjugation of women and nature may be a loss of intimacy within themselves."

She paused, then looked at me.

"Do you feel rage?"

I didn't answer for some time.

"I feel sadness. I feel powerless at times. But I'm not certain what rage really means."

Several miles passed.

"Do you?" I asked.

She looked out the window. "Yes. Perhaps your generation, one behind mine, is a step removed from the pain."

We reached the access road to the Refuge and both took out our binoculars, ready for the birds. Most of the waterfowl had migrated, but a few ruddy ducks, redheads, and shovelers remained. The marsh glistened like cut topaz.

As we turned west about five miles from the Refuge, a mile or so from the burrowing owl's mound, I began to speak of them, *Athene cunicularia*. I told Sandy about the time when my grandmother and I first discovered them. It was in 1960, the same year she gave me my Peterson's *Field Guide to Western Birds*. I know because I dated their picture. We have come back every year since to pay our respects. Generations of burrowing owls have been raised here. I turned to my friend and explained how four owlets had survived the flood.

We anticipated them.

About a half mile away, I could not see the mound. I took my foot off the gas pedal and coasted. It was though I was in unfamiliar country. The mound was gone. Erased. In its place, fifty feet back, stood a cinderblock building with a sign, CANADIAN GOOSE GUN CLUB. A new fence crushed the grasses with a handwritten note posted: KEEP OUT.

We got out of the car and walked to where the mound had been for as long as I had a memory. Gone. Not a pellet to be found.

A blue pickup pulled alongside us.

"Howdy." They tipped their ball caps. "What y'all lookin' for?"

I said nothing. Sandy said nothing. My eyes narrowed.

"We didn't kill 'em. Those boys from the highway department came and graveled the place. Two bits, they did it. I mean, you gotta admit those ground owls are messy little bastards. They'll shit all over hell if ya let 'em. And try and sleep with 'em hollering at ya all night long. They had to go. Anyway, we got bets with the county they'll pop up someplace around here next year."

The three men in the front seat looked up at us, tipped their caps again. And drove off.

Restraint is the steel partition between a rational mind and a violent one. I knew rage. It was fire in my stomach with no place to go.

I drove out to the Refuge on another day. I suppose I wanted to see the mound back in place with the family of owls bobbing on top. Of course, they were not.

I sat on the gravel and threw stones.

By chance, the same blue pickup with the same three men pulled alongside: the self-appointed proprietors of the newly erected Canadian Goose Gun Club.

"Howdy, ma'am. Still lookin' for them owls, or was it sparrows?"

One winked.

Suddenly in perfect detail, I pictured the burrowing owls' mound— that clay-covered fist rising from the alkaline flats. The exact one these beergut-over-beltbuckled men had leveled.

I walked calmly over to their truck and leaned my stomach against their door. I held up my fist a few inches from the driver's face and slowly lifted my middle finger to the sky.

"This is for you—from the owls and me."

My mother was appalled—not so much over the loss of the burrowing owls, although it saddened her, but by my behavior. Women did not deliver obscene gestures to men, regardless. She shook her head, saying she had no idea where I came from.

In Mormon culture, that is one of the things you do know—history and genealogy. I come from a family with deep roots in the American West. When the expense of outfitting several thousand immigrants to

Utah was becoming too great for the newly established church, leaders decided to furnish the pioneers with small two-wheeled carts about the size of those used by apple peddlers, which could be pulled by hand from Missouri to the Salt Lake Valley. My ancestors were part of these original "handcart companies" in the 1850s. With faith, they would endure. They came with few provisions over the twelve-hundred-mile trail. It was a small sacrifice in the name of religious freedom. Almost one hundred and fifty years later, we are still here.

I am the oldest child in our family, a daughter with three younger brothers: Steve, Dan, and Hank.

My parents, John Henry Tempest, III, and Diane Dixon Tempest, were married in the Mormon Temple in Salt Lake City on September 18, 1953. My husband, Brooke Williams, and I followed the same tradition and were married on June 2, 1975. I was nineteen years old.

Our extended family includes both maternal and paternal grandparents: Lettie Romney Dixon and Donald "Sanky" Dixon, Kathryn Blackett Tempest and John Henry Tempest, Jr.

Aunts, uncles, and cousins are many, extending familial ties all across the state of Utah. If I ever wonder who I am, I simply attend a Romney family reunion and find myself in the eyes of everyone I meet. It is comforting and disturbing, at once.

I have known five of my great-grandparents intimately. They tutored me in stories with a belief that lineage mattered. Genealogy is in our blood. As a people and as a family, we have a sense of history. And our history is tied to land.

I was raised to believe in a spirit world, that life exists before the earth and will continue to exist afterward, that each human being, bird, and bulrush, along with all other life forms had a spirit life before it came to dwell physically on the earth. Each occupied an assigned sphere of influence, each has a place and a purpose.

It made sense to a child. And if the natural world was assigned spiritual values, then those days spent in wildness were sacred. We learned at an early age that God can be found wherever you are, especially outside. Family worship was not just relegated to Sunday in a chapel.

Our weekends were spent camped alongside a small stream in the Great Basin, in the Stansbury Mountains or Deep Creeks. My father would take the boys rabbit hunting while Mother and I would sit on a log in an aspen grove and talk. She would tell me stories of how when she was a girl she would paint red lips on the trunks of trees to practice kissing. Or how she would lie in her grandmother's lucerne patch and watch clouds.

"I have never known my full capacity for solitude," she would say.

"Solitude?" I asked.

"The gift of being alone. I can never get enough."

The men would return anxious for dinner. Mother would cook over a green Coleman stove as Dad told stories from his childhood—like the time his father took away his BB gun for a year because he shot off the heads of every red tulip in his mother's garden, row after row after row. He laughed. We laughed. And then it was time to bless the food.

After supper, we would spread out our sleeping bags in a circle, heads pointing to the center like a covey of quail, and watch the Great Basin sky fill with stars. Our attachment to the land was our attachment to each other.

The days I loved most were the days at Bear River. The Bird Refuge was a sanctuary for my grandmother and me. I call her "Mimi." We would walk along the road with binoculars around our necks and simply watch birds. Hundreds of birds. Birds so exotic to a desert child it forced the imagination to be still. The imagined was real at Bear River.

I recall one bird in particular. It wore a feathered robe of cinnamon, white, and black. Its body rested on long, thin legs. Blue legs. On the edge of the marsh, it gracefully lowered its head and began sweeping the water side to side with its delicate, upturned bill.

*"Plee-ek! Plee-ek! Plee-ek!"*

Three more landed. My grandmother placed her hand gently on my shoulder and whispered, "avocets." I was nine years old.

At ten, Mimi thought I was old enough to join the Audubon Society on a special outing to the wetlands surrounding Great Salt Lake. We boarded a greyhound bus in downtown Salt Lake and drove north on U.S. Highway 91, paralleling the Wasatch Mountains on our right and Great Salt Lake on our left. Once relaxed and out of the city, we were handed an official checklist of birds at the Bear River Migratory Bird Refuge.

"All members are encouraged to take copious notes and keep scrupulous records of birds seen," proclaimed the gray-haired, ponytailed woman passing out cards.

"What do copious and scrupulous mean?" I asked my grandmother.

"It means pay attention," she said. I pulled out my notebook and drew pictures of the backs of birdwatchers' heads.

Off the highway, the bus drove through the small town of Brigham City with its sycamore-lined streets. It's like most Utah settlements with its Mormon layout: a chapel for weekly worship, a tabernacle for communal events, and a temple nearby (in this case Logan) where sacred rites are performed. Lawns are well groomed and neighborhoods are immaculate. But the banner arched over Main Street makes this town unique. In neon lights it reads, BRIGHAM CITY: GATEWAY TO THE WORLD'S

GREATEST GAME BIRD REFUGE. So welded to the local color of this community, I daresay no one sees the sign anymore, except newcomers and perhaps the birds that fly under it.

A small, elderly man with wire-rimmed glasses and a worn golf cap, stood at the front of the bus and began speaking into the handheld microphone: "Ladies and gentlemen, in approximately ten miles we will be entering the Bear River Migratory Bird Refuge, America's first waterfowl sanctuary, established by a special act of Congress on April 23, 1928."

I was confused. I thought the marsh had been created in the spirit world first and on earth second. I never made the connection that God and Congress were in cahoots. Mimi said she would explain the situation later.

The man went on to say that the Bird Refuge was located at the delta of the Bear River, which poured into the Great Salt Lake. This I understood.

"People, this bus is a clock. Eyes forward, please. Straight ahead is twelve o'clock; to the rear is six. Three o'clock is on your right. Any bird identified from this point on will be noted accordingly."

The bus became a bird dog, a labrador on wheels, which decided where high noon would be simply by pointing in that direction. What time would it be if a bird decided to fly from nine o'clock to three o'clock? Did that make the bird half past nine or quarter to three? Even more worrisome to me was the possibility of a flock of birds flying between four and five o'clock. Would you say, "Twenty birds after four? Four-thirty? Or simply move the hands of the clock forward to five? I decided not to bother my grandmother with these particulars and, instead, retreated to my unindexed field guide and turned to the color plates of ducks.

"Ibises at two o'clock!"

The brakes squeaked the bus to a halt. The doors opened like bellows and we all filed out. And there they were, dozens of white-faced glossy ibises grazing in the field. Their feathers on first glance were chestnut, but with the slightest turn they flashed irridescences of pink, purple, and green.

Another flock landed nearby. And another. And another. They coasted in diagonal lines with their heads and necks extended, their long legs trailing behind them, seeming to fall forward on hinges the second before they touched ground. By now, we must have been watching close to a hundred ibises probing the farmlands adjacent to the marsh.

Our leader told us they were eating earthworms and insects.

"Good eyes," I thought, as I could only see their decurved bills like scythes disappearing behind the grasses. I watched the wind turn each feather as the birds turned the soil.

Mimi whispered to me how ibises are the companions of gods. "Ibis escorts Thoth, the Egyptian god of wisdom and magic, who is the guardian of the Moon Gates in heaven. And there are two colors of ibis—one black and one white. The dark bird is believed to be associated with death, the white bird a celebration of birth."

I looked out over the fields of black ibis.

"When an ibis tucks its head underwing to sleep, it resembles a heart. The ibis knows empathy," my grandmother said. "Remember that, alongside the fact it eats worms."

She also told me that if I could learn a new way to tell time, I could also learn a new way to measure distance.

"The stride of an ibis was a measurement used in building the great temples of the Nile."

I sat down by the rear wheels of the bus and pondered the relationship between an ibis at Bear River and an ibis foraging on the banks of the Nile. In my young mind, it had something to do with the magic of birds, how they bridge cultures and continents with their wings, how they mediate between heaven and earth.

Back on the bus and moving, I wrote in my notebook "one hundred white-faced glossy ibises—companions of the gods."

Mimi was pleased. "We could go home now," she said. "The ibis makes the day."

But there were more birds. Many, many more. Within the next few miles, ducks, geese, and shorebirds were sighted around "the clock." The bus drove past all of them. With my arms out the window, I tried to touch the wings of avocets and stilts. I knew these birds from our private trips to the Refuge. They had become relatives.

As the black-necked stilts flew alongside the silver bus, their long legs trailed behind them like red streamers.

"*Ip-ip-ip! Ip-ip-ip!*"

Their bills were not flattened and upturned like avocets, but straight as darning needles.

The wind massaged my face. I closed my eyes and sat back in my seat.

Mimi and I got out of the bus and ate our lunch on the riverbank. Two western grebes, ruby-eyed and serpentine, fished, diving at good prospects. They surfaced with silver minnows struggling between sharp mandibles. Violet-green swallows skimmed the water for midges as a snowy egret stood on the edge of the spillway.

With a crab sandwich in one hand and binoculars in the other, Mimi explained why the Bird Refuge had in fact, been created.

"Maybe the best way to understand it," she said, "is to realize the original wetlands were recreated. It was the deterioration of the marshes at Bear River Bay that led to the establishment of a sanctuary."

"How?" I asked.

"The marshes were declining for several reasons: the diversion of water from the Bear River for irrigation, the backing-up of brine from Great Salt Lake during high-water periods, excessive hunting, and a dramatic rise in botulism, a disease known then as 'western duck disease.'

"The creation of the Bear River Migratory Bird Refuge helped to preserve the freshwater character of the marsh. Dikes were built to hold the water from the Bear River to stabilize, manage, and control water levels within the marsh. This helped to control botulism and at the same time keep out the brine. Meanwhile, the birds flourished."

After lunch, I climbed the observation tower at the Refuge headquarters. Any fear of heights I may have had moving up the endless flights of steel stairs was replaced by the bird's eye view before me. The marsh appeared as a green and blue mosaic where birds remained in a fluid landscape.

In the afternoon, we drove the twenty-two-mile loop around the Refuge. The roads capped the dikes which were bordered by deep channels of water with bulrush and teasel. We saw ruddy ducks (the man sitting behind us called them "blue bills"), shovelers, teals, and wigeons. We watched herons and egrets and rails. Red-wing blackbirds poised on cattails sang with long-billed marsh wrens as muskrats swam inside shadows created by clouds. Large families of Canada geese occupied the open water, while ravens flushed the edges for unprotected nests with eggs.

The marsh reflected health as concentric circles rippled outward from a mallard feeding "bottoms up."

By the end of the day, Mimi and I had marked sixty-seven species on our checklist, many of which I had never seen before. A short-eared owl hovered over the cattails. It was the last bird we saw as we left the Refuge.

I fell asleep on my grandmother's lap. Her strong, square hands resting on my forehead shielded the sun from my eyes. I dreamed of water and cattails and all that is hidden.

When we returned home, my family was seated around the dinner table.

"What did you see?" Mother asked. My father and three brothers looked up.

"Birds . . ." I said as I closed my eyes and stretched my arms like wings. "Hundreds of birds at the marsh."

# HILTON ALS
## (1961– )

Als has emerged in recent years as an intriguing figure on the literary scene, a regular contributor to *The New Yorker* since 1994 whose idiosyncratic explorations of gay and black identity are exuberantly on display in *The Women* (1997), his book-length meditation on self and ancestry, on writing and sexuality. As Andrea Lee said in her review of this book in the *New York Times Book Review*, *The Women* "has an almost magical cohesiveness" that is "due to the peculiar talents of the author, who combines a quirky brilliance at analytical thought with a gift for visual and psychological description worthy of a novelist." Als has also edited the catalog for a Whitney Museum of American Art exhibition entitled "Black Male: Representations of Masculinity in Contemporary American Art."

## FROM *The Women*

Until the end, my mother never discussed her way of being. She avoided explaining the impetus behind her emigration from Barbados to Manhattan. She avoided explaining that she had not been motivated by the same desire for personal gain and opportunity that drove most female immigrants. She avoided recounting the fact that she had emigrated to America to follow the man who eventually became my father, and whom she had known in his previous incarnation as her first and only husband's closest friend. She avoided explaining how she had left her husband—by whom she had two daughters—after he returned to Barbados from England and the Second World War addicted to morphine. She was silent about the fact that, having been married once, she refused to marry again. She avoided explaining that my father, who had grown up relatively rich in Barbados and whom she had known as a child, remained a child and emigrated to America with his mother and his two sisters— women whose home he never left. She never mentioned that she had been attracted to my father's beauty and wealth partially because those were two things she would never know. She never discussed how she had visited my father in his room at night, and afterward crept down the stairs stealthily to return to her own home and her six children, four of them produced by her union with my father, who remained a child. She never explained that my father never went to her; she went to him. She avoided explaining that my father, like most children, and like most men, resented his children—four girls, two boys—for not growing up quickly enough so that they would leave home and take his responsibility away with them. She avoided recounting how my father—because he was a child—tried to distance himself from his children and his resentment of them through his derisive humor, teasing them to the point of cruelty; she also avoided recounting how her children, in order to shield themselves against the spittle of his derisive humor, absented themselves in his presence and, eventually, in the presence of any form of entertainment deliberately aimed at provoking laughter. She avoided explaining that in response to this resentment, my father also vaunted his beauty and wealth over his children, as qualities they would never share. She was silent about the mysterious bond she and my father shared, a bond so deep and volatile that their children felt forever diminished by their love, and forever compelled to disrupt, disapprove, avoid, or try to become a part of the love shared between any couple (specifically men and women) since part of our birthright has been to remain children, not unlike our father. She avoided mentioning the fact that my father had other women, other families, in cities such as Miami and Boston, cities my father roamed like a bewildered child. She was silent about the fact that my father's mother and sisters told her about the other women and children my father had, probably as a test to see how much my mother could stand to hear about my father, whom his mother and sisters felt only they could understand and love, which is one reason my father remained a child. My mother avoided mentioning the fact that her mother, in Barbados, had had a child with a man other than my mother's father, and that man had been beautiful and relatively rich. She avoided explaining how her mother had thought her association with that relatively rich and beautiful man would make her beautiful and rich also. She avoided explaining how, after that had not happened for her mother, her mother became bitter about this and other things for the rest of her very long life. She avoided contradicting her mother when she said things like "Don't play in the sun. You are black enough," which is what my grandmother said to me once. She avoided explaining that she had wanted to be different from her mother. She avoided explaining that she created a position of power for herself in this common world by being a mother to children, and childlike men, as she attempted to separate from her parents and siblings by being "nice," an attitude they could never understand, since they weren't. She avoided recounting memories of her family's cruelty, one instance of their cruelty being: my mother's family sitting in a chartered bus as it rained outside on a family picnic; my mother, alone, in the rain, clean-

ing up the family picnic as my mother's aunt said, in her thick Bajun accent: "Marie is one of God's own," and the bus rocking with derisive
laughter as my heart broke, in silence. She avoided mentioning that she
saw and understood where my fascination with certain aspects of her
narrative—her emigration, her love, her kindness—would take me, a
boy of seven, or eight, or ten: to the dark crawl space behind her closet,
where I put on her hosiery one leg at a time, my heart racing, and, over
those hose, my jeans and sneakers, so that I could have her—what I so
admired and coveted—near me, always.

By now, the Negress has come to mean many things. She is perceived
less as a mind than as an emotional being. In the popular imagination,
she lives one or several cliché-ridden narratives. One narrative: she is generally colored, female, and a single mother, reduced by circumstances to
tireless depression and public "aid," working off the books in one low-
paying job after another in an attempt to support her children—children she should not have had, according to tax-paying, law-abiding
public consensus. Like my mother. Another narrative: she can be defined
as a romantic wedded to despair, since she has little time or inclination
to dissemble where she stands in America's social welfare system, which
regards her as a statistic, part of the world's rapacious silent majority.
Like my mother. Another narrative: she gives birth to children who grow
up to be lawless; she loves men who leave her for other women; she is
subject to depression and illness. Her depression is so numbing that she
rarely lets news of the outside world (television news, radio news, newspapers) enter her sphere of consciousness, since much of her time is
spent fording herself and her children against the news of emotional disaster she sees day after day in the adult faces surrounding the faces of her
children, who, in turn, look to her to make sense of it all. Like my
mother.
    What the Negress has always been: a symbol of America's by now for-
gotten strain of puritanical selflessness. The Negress is a perennial source
of "news" and interesting "copy" in the newspapers and magazines she
does not read because she is a formidable character in the internal drama
most Americans have with the issue of self-abnegation. The Negress
serves as a reminder to our sentimental nation that what its countrymen
are shaped by is a nonverbal confusion about and, ultimately, abhorrence for the good neighbor policy. Most Americans absorb the principles of the good neighbor policy through the language-based tenets of
Judaism and Christianity. These laws lead to a deep emotional confusion
about the "good" since most Americans are suspicious of language and
spend a great deal of time and energy on Entertainment and Relaxation
in an attempt to avoid its net result: Reflection. If the Negress is repre-

sented as anything in the media, it is generally as a good neighbor, staunch in her defense of the idea that being a good neighbor makes a difference in this common world. She is also this: a good neighbor uncritical of faith, even as her intellect dissects the byzantine language of the Bible, searching for a truth other than her own. Which is one reason the Negress is both abhorred and adored: for her ability to meld language with belief without becoming sarcastic. Take, for instance, this story, reported in the *New York Post:* "The Trinidad woman who lost her legs in a subway purse snatching is not looking for revenge—but she hopes her mugger becomes 'a better person' in prison. . . . Samela Thompson, 56, fell onto the tracks in the Van Wyck Boulevard station in Jamaica, Queens. . . . She was trying to jump onto the platform from an E train as she chased a homeless man who had grabbed her sister's purse. . . . The feisty mother of five's attitude is 'you have to take life as it comes.' Thompson wished [her attacker] would know God."

To women who are not Negresses—some are white—the Negress, whether she calls herself that or not, is a specter of dignity—selfless to a fault. But eventually the Negress troubles her noncolored female admirer, since the latter feels compelled to compare her privilege to what the Negress does not have—recognizable privilege—and finds herself lacking. This inversion or competitiveness among women vis-à-vis their "oppressed" stance says something about why friendships among women are rare, let alone why friendships between noncolored women and Negresses are especially so.

For years before and after her death, I referred to myself as a Negress; it was what I was conditioned to be. And yet I have come no closer to defining it. In fact, I shy away from defining it, given my mother's complex reaction to Negressity for herself and me. I have expressed my Negressity by living, fully, the prescribed life of an auntie man—what Barbadians call a faggot. Which is a form of kinship, given that my being an auntie man is based on greed for romantic love with men temperamentally not unlike the men my mother knew—that and an unremitting public "niceness." I socialized myself as an auntie man long before I committed my first act as one. I also wore my mother's and sisters' clothes when they were not home; those clothes deflected from the pressure I felt in being different from them. As a child, this difference was too much for me to take; I buried myself in their clothes, their secrets, their desires, to find myself through them. Those women "killed" me, as comedians say when they describe their power over an audience. I wanted them to kill me further by fully exploiting the attention I afforded them. But they couldn't, being women.

Being an auntie man enamored of Negressity is all I have ever known how to be. I do not know what my life would be, or if I *would* be at all, if I were any different.

To say that the public's reaction to my mother's being a Negress and my being one were similar would be egregious. My mother was a woman. Over the years in Brooklyn, she worked as a housekeeper for a relatively well-off Scotsman, as a housekeeper for a Jewish matron, in a beauty salon as a hairdresser, as an assistant in a nursery school. My mother responded to my being a Negress with pride and anger: pride in my identification with women like herself; anger that I identified with her at all. I could not help her react to any of this any differently than she did. This failure haunts me still. I have not catapulted myself past my mother's emotional existence.

Did my mother call herself a Negress as a way of ironically reconciling herself to her history as that most hated of English colonial words, which fixed her as a servant in the eyes of Britain and God? I don't think so, given that she was not especially interested in Britain or history. But "Negress" was one of the few words she took with her when she emigrated from Barbados to Manhattan. As a Negress, her passport to the world was restricted; the world has its limits. Shortly after arriving in New York in the late forties, my mother saw what her everyday life would be; being bright, a high school graduate, and practical, she looked at the world she had emigrated to, picked up her servant's cap, and began starching it with servitude. In her new country, my mother noticed that some New Yorkers retained the fantasy that in writing or speaking about the "underclass," or the "oppressed, silent" woman, or the "indomitable" stoic, they were writing about the kind of Negress she was, but they weren't. My mother was capricious in her views about most things, including race. As a West Indian who lived among other West Indians, my mother did not feel "difference"; she would not allow her feelings to be ghettoized; in her community, she was in the majority. She was capable of giving a nod toward the history of "injustice," but only if it suited her mood.

I think my mother took some pleasure in how harsh the word "Negress" seemed to the citizens in her adopted home. I have perhaps made more of the word "Negress" than my mother meant by it, but I saw and continue to see how it is used to limit and stupidly define the world certain women inhabit. I think my mother took pleasure in manipulating the guilt and embarrassment white and black Americans alike felt when she called herself a Negress, since their view of the Negress was largely sentimental, maudlin, replete with suffering. When my mother laughed in the face of their deeply presumptive view of her, one of her front teeth flashed gold.

My mother disliked the American penchant for euphemism; she was resolute in making the world confront its definition of her. This freed her mind for other things, like her endless illness, which was a protracted form of suicide. From my mother I learned the only way the Negress can own herself is through her protracted suicide; suffering from imminent death keeps people at a distance. I was so lonely knowing her; she was so busy getting to know herself through dying. When my mother became ill with one thing or another, I was eight; by the time my mother died, I was twenty-eight. When she died, I barely knew anything about her at all.

My mother killed herself systematically and not all at once. Perhaps that is because, as a Negress, she had learned stamina, a stamina that consisted of smiling and lying and maintaining the hope that everything would eventually be different, regardless of the facts. Until the end, my mother avoided the facts; she was polite. She would not die. She became ill, and for a long time, which is difficult to cope with; illness silences the well, out of respect. My mother knew that. Being somewhat generous, she acknowledged her children's helplessness in the atmosphere of her dying by allowing us to live with it so that we could see her physical dissolution (clumps of hair, one leg, a few teeth, eventually all gone) without delineating any of its mysteries. Being children, we could only see her imminent death in terms of our imminent loss; we failed to understand what her dying meant to her. She imposed her will by not telling anyone what was really "wrong"; this kept everyone poised and at her service. She would not speak of the facts contributing to her death; nor would she speak of the facts that contributed to her wish to die in the first place. She was quietly spirited, functional, and content in her depression and love; not for the world would she have forfeited the will she applied to disappearing her own body, since it took her so many years to admit to her need for attention, and being ill was one way to get it. The reasons my mother chose to disappear herself, slowly, are manifold. Perhaps she chose to destroy her body out of a profound sadness at the eventual dissolution of her thirty-year romantic relationship with my father; perhaps she chose to disappear her body out of her interest in the discipline inherent in self-abnegation. Perhaps it was both.

My mother first became ill at the end of her love affair with my father. As with most aspects of my parents' relationship, it is unclear whether or not my father dictated the course their relationship would take. The difference between my mother and the woman he became involved with after my mother was significant: she consented to live with my father whereas my mother had not. After my mother refused to marry him, my father never asked her to again. My mother encountered my father's girlfriend once, on the street. My father's new girlfriend was in the company of one of my father's sisters. My mother saw a certain resemblance between my father's new girlfriend and herself: they were both homely but spirited, like Doris Day. It was clear to my mother that his new girlfriend was capable of withstanding my father's tantrums, his compulsive childishness, and his compulsive lying. It was perhaps not as clear to my father's new girlfriend as it was to my mother that my father lied as much as he did because of his need to rebuild the world according to his specifications while being ashamed of this need. Just like a woman.

I think the resemblance my mother saw between herself and my father's new girlfriend shattered any claim to originality my mother had. And, being a woman, she chose to be critical of this similarity rather than judge my father. Shortly afterward, she was made sick by a mysterious respiratory illness. In the end, I think my mother's long and public illness was the only thing she ever felt she experienced as an accomplishment separate from other people. And it was.

When diabetes cost her one of her legs, she said, politely: Oh, I'm dying now. When they removed a gland in her neck as a test for whatever, she said, politely: Oh, I'm really dying now. When one of her kidneys failed completely and a machine functioned in its place, she was still polite. She said: Well, I'm dying. When she lost her vision in one eye, she said she was dying; eventually she could not breathe without stress, and she said she was really dying; her blood pressure was abnormally high, her teeth were bad, she could not urinate or take sugar in her tea or eat pork or remember a conversation, but she remembered these two things: that she was polite and dying.

After they cut off one of her legs for diabetes' sake, she often experienced phantom pain. The world twitched and throbbed. For my mother, experiencing physical pain became a perspective she could own. In pain, she wasn't anything but ill—not a Negress, not a mother of six, not a lover, not a patient. Pain has its own meaning. She passed life by long before she died. When she died, the things she wore in her casket—a wig made of a synthetic fiber colored brown; a white polyester shawl—didn't look as if they belonged to her at all.

# ALANE SALIERNO MASON

## (1964– )

An editor who has worked at various New York publishing houses, Mason grew up in an Italian American family in the southern part of New York State. In "Respect," a poetic evocation of an Italian American family and neighborhood, Mason writes about the conflict between independence and ethnicity—an issue commonly evoked by memoirists writing out of a particular ethnic tradition. There is often in this work a desire to escape the confines of that world, and a feeling of deep nostalgia for the enclosed (sometimes oppressive and patriarchal) world left behind. "Respect" was originally published in *Beyond the Godfather* (1997), an anthology of Italian American writing edited by A. Kenneth Giongoli and Jay Parini. The attraction to the ethnic world is obvious in "Respect," where Mason poignantly summons the ethos of her grandparents, with its delicate smells and tastes, its quiet repressions, its inherent safety and protective covering. By the end of the essay, one sees exactly how the elements of love and rage are combined.

## "Respect"

It is a love and a rage.

The love you already know about, lurking in all the clichés of ethnicity: pungent, generic. Like garlic, it stays with you.

You already know: the smell of garlic frying. On a Sunday morning, Grandmother with fleshy arms in a housedress, swaying as the kitchen cabinets open and shut, the refrigerator opens and shuts: basil, big cans of tomatoes, the golden blocky pillar of a tin of olive oil, meat for the *braciole* to spread with shortening and bread crumbs and spices, green-bean salad made on Saturday and chilled. A hard block of pale tart cheese to grate for the table. Grandfather wearing his best vest and ruby ring and cologne for the midday meal, having washed up for company after coming in from the garden with zucchini flowers to be basted in egg and bread crumbs and fried in olive oil. As each aunt and uncle, cousin and second cousin arrives, a kiss for everyone in the room. The great-uncle with the cigar, the favorite great-aunt with freckled arms, hardy as a hazelnut. Relatives from the Bronx, New City, Patterson, Saddle River, Suffern, Croton-on-Hudson, all strung like beads from the landings on Ellis Island. Wine, mixed half-and-half with sweet soda for the children. The long table with the lace tablecloth, hours later strewn with orange and apple peels and the hulls of walnuts and roasted chestnuts, to be cleared away and thrown in the fireplace before black coffee and anisette are poured.

In the summer the fruit peels and the nut hulls might be thrown in the garden. "What comes out of the ground goes back into the ground" my grandfather always says as he throws the peelings from the kitchen between the tall stakes of the tomato plants. "Nothing wasted. You get out of the ground what you put into the ground" (referring to the seedlings that sometimes sprouted from discarded peach pits), "and what comes out of the ground goes back in. Dear granddaughter, I'm telling you something very important: you get out of life what you put into it."

When he came to America, he had delivered eggs and milk, worked in a laundry and in a candy factory, become an apprentice plasterer and ultimately a building contractor, constructing and renovating churches and schools. "You got to have a good foundation," he always told me, pointing out cracked pavement a year after new road work was done, peeling paint in places where no one had bothered to scrape the old coat. "You have to take pride in your work. The problem with this country, nobody anymore takes pride in his work."

And also, "It's very important to have respect for the old people. They know something about life you don't know. Dear granddaughter, listen to what I say: you have to have respect."

II

In this brownstone neighborhood in Brooklyn, there are many old ladies, as hardy to the eye as olive trees. One of these, Mrs. Gianquito, lived on the ground floor of the building I lived in when I moved here ten years ago. She used to cry when I saw her: "*Sono sola, sola sola!*" (I'm alone, alone, alone!) Sometimes I sat beside her in the building's tiny courtyard, separated from the street by a short iron fence, keeping her company while she talked to me in an Italian I couldn't understand. Perhaps it was mostly dialect; or perhaps because I spoke a few words, she granted me perfect comprehension and spoke very rapidly. In any case, of her torrent of words I understood only *sola* and this single saying: "*Se si rispetta, si sera rispettata.*" "If you respect others, others will respect you."

My grandfather was born in Naples in 1908, and Brooklyn was the first place he lived when he came to America in 1920. He met my grand-mother when his eldest sister married a widower, also Italian, with four daughters born in America, one exactly his age. Later they lived in the Bronx, then in Italian East Harlem, and finally in upstate New York, where I was born. I moved to Brooklyn in 1987, a year after I graduated from college. My grandfather said, "I spent my life trying to get the fam-ily out of Brooklyn, and now you're going backwards, back where I started!" Now he says, "I'm going to shoot that Brooklyn Bridge!" be-cause he imagines it transporting me away from the family.

In this neighborhood of four- and five-story buildings with gardens in the front and back, there are grapevines growing on the telephone wires. My neighbor yells to her kids, "Get in hee-yah!" On Saturdays in the su-permarket, the old ladies' carts jam up against each other; they trade Italian gossip about their friends and advice about different brands. The men stand outside the bakery or in the doorways of their social clubs: The Society of Citizens of Pozzallo. The building with the ground-floor wineshop was owned by the proprietor's grandparents; his grandfather used to make wine in barrels in the backyard, he says, and when he hosed out the barrels the yard was stained purple. The grandson, in his thirties, has lived here all his life; when he decided to open the store, everyone he knew told him he could not succeed, but there has been an influx of Manhattanites into the neighborhood and the store thrives. He flirts with all the young women who go into Manhattan to work. Yet his store hasn't launched him into their world; he is still a fixture of the neighborhood. If he took the subway into Manhattan, he says, he would have to carry a gun, because of the *melanzane*: eggplants, or black peo-ple. (And perhaps the *finucchi*: fennel, or gays.)

At the neighborhood church my old landlady, Mrs. Amaroso, used to call the *cathedrale*, there is a Rosary Society, a Cabrini Club, and the Our Lady of Loreto Council Columbiettes; they sponsor card games and trips to Atlantic City and, a few times a year, accompany a statue of the Vir-gin Mary in promenade around the streets. On Good Friday the women wear black and carry candles in a funeral procession around a wax figure of the dead Christ in a glass casket. The casket is born aloft by burly dark-haired men wearing scapulars, or religious medals on long red rib-bons around their necks.

It was the smell in the bakeries that drew me here, the strong smell of childhood, sharing my grandfather's expectation of an occasion, a holi-day or Sunday company. The fresh-baked anisette biscuits and *regine* (sesame) and pignoli (pine nut) cookies, the cannoli and *sfogliatell'* and *pasticiott'*, the boxes tied with red-and-white string. These Brooklyn bak-eries even carry Manhattan Coffee Soda, the sweet, carbonated espresso in a small glass bottle with an old-fashioned yellow label. There are also half a dozen places in the neighborhood where they make homemade mozzarella, the firm strings of cheese dripping moisture. My second cousin Gina, in the Bronx, has been making it in her father's deli since she was eleven. When I was a child and my grandfather brought this kind of mozzarella home, I would eat it right from the milky wet waxed paper it was wrapped in while my grandmother made us *mozzarell' in carozz'*, in a carriage, that is, between two pieces of bread, dipped in egg and bread crumbs, then baked in the oven.

My grandfather usually buys his pastries in New Jersey, but since I've lived here I like to bring him the real thing from Brooklyn, where they're better and cheaper. Each holiday now, I can expect a call with his "order" (*roccoco* and *mustacioli* for Christmas, *sfingi* and *zeppole* for St. Joseph's Day), which I bring to him in the big white boxes tied with red-and-white string. Sometimes I will remember to ask the bakery for additional small boxes, for my grandfather always buys enough to give away. This is very important, that no visitor should leave the house empty-handed. Between my grandparents' house and my mother's, I am always carrying cheese, vegetables, fruit, half a vat of soup, half a loaf of bread. An Italian American writer once told me that his mother made him take home half an onion. "Take it, you might need it, I'm not gonna use it," she'd said.

For four of my first five years in Brooklyn, I dated an Italian American lawyer living across the street, who made *biscotti* from his grandmother's recipe and on Sundays liked to make a marinara sauce and espresso with a shot of anisette. His landlady, sitting in a chair on the building stoop, would stop me as I went in to tell me how he did his own laundry and cooking and housecleaning, that he was *un ragazzo buono, oggi e diffi-cile a trovare, un ragazzo buono*, a good boy, the kind difficult to find these days. I wanted my children to have Italian traditions, to know themselves as something other than just plain American. (There is no greater occasion—none so garlanded with expectation—as an Italian wedding.) But in the months I tried to bring myself to decide whether to marry him, or not, I often lay awake at night, alone, violently trembling with rage or sorrow.

When my old building was sold, I stayed in the neighborhood. On the old block there was a man in a wheelchair, whose friends always gathered on his stoop. When I told him I was moving a few blocks away, he said, "Eh, you're moving up. You'll find a different class of people over there."

Up in the country, when my grandfather moved house for the first time in forty years, he took with him a couple of wheelbarrows full of topsoil and several of his favorite rocks.

I, too, collect stones from many of the places I've been.

## III

On Sundays, the stairwell of my building smells of garlic frying in oil, of marinara sauce or zucchini in bread crumbs. The landlady and landlord I have had now for the past five years are not, as far as I can tell, a different class of people from those a few blocks away. Umberto immigrated in the fifties and still does not speak English well; Rosa was born in this building, where her ancient mother lived with her in the same three rooms on the ground floor till her death.

Like my grandfather, I have a sociable streak, and every few months I host an out-of-town guest or have friends over to my home to eat and talk. This is one of my great joys—or was, before Umberto started standing on the doorstep at the beginning of a dinner party, shouting "This is not a club!" and interrogating guests, male or female, about what they were doing here and how soon they were leaving.

Unlike my grandparents, who have been married for sixty-five years, I have been serially monogamous and remain unmarried. Shortly after I moved here, the Italian lawyer moved to California. When I started seeing someone else, Rosa began standing at her front window, peeking through the curtains, whenever she heard more than one set of footsteps on the stairs. Now that I have had a man in my life more seriously (truly, the most seriously) for over a year, Umberto and Rosa have become increasingly agitated. First, when Umberto saw him on the stairs, he raised the rent fifty dollars. Then Rosa started calling on the telephone. "I wanna know what's goin' on up there—that guy, he's been there for a week!" That time he'd been visiting a day or two from the distant city where he is a university professor. "It's none of your business!" I said indignantly, thinking for a moment that I was in America. Rosa shouted back, "None of my business! Every week I see a different guy. What'ya do, take every guy in the neighborhood into your bed?" That month I had had two other male visitors, both gay, who stayed in my living room one night each, and earlier that week I'd had a work-related dinner party and had asked my guests to tiptoe down the stairs when they left so as not to disturb the landlords. "The other night you had six people over," Rosa added, "and I didn't hear any of them leave. Whaddya have them all sleepin' over?"

I went downstairs to sit at her kitchen table. "Rosa, there must be some kind of misunderstanding; I'm not the person you say I am," I tried to tell her, but she insisted. "I have to worry about your reputation," she said. "Rosa," I said, "let me worry about my own reputation. I have a very good reputation."

"People around here, they talk," she said. "They ask me, what'sa matter with that girl, she's got so many boyfriends? And I says to them, I donno, they're friends of hers. But I gotta look out for your reputation and the reputation of the house!"

I explained that I had friends in Washington, in California, in North Carolina. "When they come to visit, I shouldn't offer them a place to stay? I'm a hospitable person. I'm Italian!" I tried to tell her. She said, "You wanna have foreigners? Let them find a hotel. Listen to me, you do what I say, you'll be happier. They'll respect you for it. And don't worry, you'll get married eventually, because you're good-lookin'. I'm tellin' ya, listen to me, because I'm tellin' ya for your own good: don't go with a guy just because he likes you. Make sure he has a job!" I rolled my eyes. She said, "Don't you look at me that way. I'm tellin' ya the truth!" As I left, she said, "I'm tellin' ya for your own good! My father would've killed me if I so much as looked at a boy, and I tell ya I'm glad I was brought up that way, to respect myself."

Over the years I've tried giving my landlords plants, homemade panettone and gingerbread, a bottle of anisette, a pleading letter written in Italian. I stopped having parties. I've tried to tell them I want to be left alone to live in peace, in my own way, in my own home. I've tried to rationalize: maybe there's too much noise on the stairs? Maybe they come from the mountains of Sicily and are so suspicious of strangers that they can't stand to see anyone around they don't know? Perhaps because they see me in church, because they know I have Italian blood, they think I should live exactly as they do? "A relative, once in a blue moon, it's all right," Rosa once said to me. "I don't have people over; why do you have to have people over?"

My friends say, get a lawyer to write your landlords a letter. They have no right to harass you. You're a good tenant, you're hardly ever there, you're always working; even when you're home, you're working; you're quiet; you pay your rent on time. But the law doesn't matter here, I know; it is the kitchen table that matters.

The next time my boyfriend was in town, the next time the phone rang from my landlords downstairs, I tried to be respectful. I took him to meet Rosa. We both paid our respects at the kitchen table. She asked him what his intentions were. Satisfied, she delivered her verdict: "He looks like a nice guy, an intelligent guy. If you're goin' steady, and he's the only one, it's all right. But if I see any other guys around here, I'm gonna snitch on ya! I told her she'd find someone eventually, because she's good-lookin'." I rolled my eyes again. "She doesn't believe me, but I'm tellin' her the truth!"

Then he was away for a month, then here for three days in one week; Rosa called up and said, "What's he livin' with you?"

I want to point out that I am a different class of people. I want her to understand that I am respectable, a professional, that I take pride in my work. Yet each time she calls, I shake with rage, then burst into tears. If I were a true American, wouldn't I be living someplace where no one cares what I do?

When my boyfriend and I went to pick up the dry cleaning, the lady who runs the laundromat asked me, "Who's he?" When I shyly said, "*mio amico*," she gave him a complete report: I was *una buona ragazza, educata, rispettosa, fa i fatti suoi, non riguarda nessuno* (a good girl, well-mannered, respectful, does her own thing, doesn't look at other guys). The next time I saw her, she advised me to find another man, younger, and see both of them for a while, then decide. She asked what my family thought, and I said only that my mother did not approve. I did not say that my grandparents did not know he existed, let alone that he sometimes stayed in my apartment. He is not Italian, not Catholic, divorced, sixteen years older, and has a beard. My mother says my grandfather will have a heart attack if I take him to meet them. Without my saying any of this, the laundromat woman said, "*Non odi tua mama*" (don't hate your mother); it's natural for a mother to be concerned about such things.

Then there is the man in the family-owned fruit market who flirts with me in front of his mother and brother, but when he asks me why I'm not married yet, such a *bella ragazza*, I know how to behave: flattered, embarrassed, not scornful but reserved, proper. Sometimes he tells me it's better not to get married; that's when I know he has had a fight with his wife. I don't know if he has yet spotted me with my boyfriend, or what he will say, but this is not the neighborhood to live in if you want a life protected from the eyes of strangers.

It strikes me that *rispettare*, to respect, has the same root as *aspettare*, to wait, to expect. To expect something must be to look *toward* its arrival; to respect, then, must be to look again, maybe to see the same thing from another point of view, through someone else's spectacles. When my grandfather says that this generation of today, these kids of today, have no respect, I think he is telling the truth. They are full of disregard— *riguardare* also means to look again—they look away. While the evil eye must see in one direction only. Looking at Rosa, I think I begin to understand why, in tribal cultures and small villages, people needed protection against the evil eye.

The other day, Rosa tried to raise the rent a second time in six months, and I refused. While she called me "you sonuvabitch, you *tramp*," I slammed the door in her face. I had had enough. I too was raised to respect myself.

A week before Christmas in this neighborhood, they begin selling fish for the Christmas Eve feast—the *stocca*, the *baccala*, or salt cod, the eels, the *vongole*, or clams—from the back of a truck parked near the fruit market, in front of the bank. They also do this in the south of Italy. Some mornings in summertime, when I look out my window in slanting morning light over the low buildings and see Umberto watering his fig tree in his white sleeveless undershirt and long black shorts with black knee socks and hear someone shouting in Italian in the street, I don't know what country I'm in.

## IV

You might say I have a bad case of third generation-itis. I did go to Italy to see the town my grandfather was born in. I saw the dry goods shop my great-grandmother used to run in the corner of their house, the church bell my grandfather used to ring in the dusty town with onions drying on the rooftops and horse-drawn carts returning from the fields. Somewhere near Naples my great-grandfather might be buried. The first of my ancestors to come to America, he was also the only one to set foot again on Italian soil. He did not sponsor his wife and children to follow him to this country. Eventually, they came anyway, sponsored by other, more distant relatives. "That's a mystery," my grandfather says. He tells of how, when he got off the boat in America, his father came to meet them, but he did not recognize him, did not know which man was his father. Shortly after that, his father got sick and went back to Italy to die. Or so he was told. His father had been working in a leather factory in Newark, my grandfather told me, but because of his accent, I thought he said *ladder* factory; in this way misinformation can pass through generations.

In Naples, I stayed with the daughter of my grandfather's cousin, a grade-school English teacher. When I arrived, she had already read my mail. My Italian cousins could not understand why I was quiet; they thought I was melancholy, depressed. They did not understand the meaning of privacy or solitude. And when they shouted, I couldn't understand that they were just enjoying a conversation; I thought I had made them angry. They would not let me go anywhere alone. They wanted to introduce me: "This is our cousin from America. Her mother was divorced. Do you know that in America the fathers don't come home for lunch with their families? That's why there's so much divorce."

My cousin said she could understand why I wasn't married yet: I didn't have to live with my parents, I lived alone, I had my freedom. Her husband shouted: "Are you sorry you met me? Are you sorry you have these children? What's the most important thing, love or freedom? You want freedom over love? What is freedom compared to love! Love!"

We took a picture of a distant relative to take back to my grandfather;

a stout old woman in black, she tried to pull a small boy to her, but he pulled away: he was afraid of having his picture go to America. The old woman cried, and my cousin said to me, "Is your grandfather also very emotional? Yes? You see, they are related."

My grandfather, I understand now, is an idealist of a sort. He has strong ideas about how things *should* be. He was not easy on his children and disapproved of each of their marriages (one too young, another from the wrong side of the tracks, another an artist whom he threatened to shoot), and even now, thirty and forty years later, they have not forgotten. It is a close family full of distances. Lately, when something happens that my grandfather does not understand—when the family does not all come together on a holiday, for instance, or we show up at his house at different times—he has taken to saying, "I must have been born in the wrong country."

He is susceptible to rhetoric: family values, God and country, productivity, not tax and spend. He loves politics and ran for local office three times on his own "Productivity" ticket before finally winning over those whose partisans called him "uneducated" and "a foreigner." Since Hoover was president when he became an American, he became a Republican, to express his loyalty to his new country; but his Italian best friend, a former head gardener for a big estate, is a Democrat; he is a tall, bony man with a freckled forehead, always neatly dressed in jacket and checked shirt and wide, florid tie. They are both nearly ninety, and they like to argue about things on which they don't really disagree: "If we only made a dollar, we were glad to have that dollar, as long as we had a job!" "These kids don't have respect, and nobody tells them any different, not the parents, not the Church!" My grandmother, who doesn't talk much, doesn't participate in the debate; she says her Rosary and votes as my grandfather votes. Once he complained that my grandmother never wants to have a discussion. For sixty-five years of marriage he told her how to vote; now he wants to have a discussion?

Recently, my grandfather told me about his friend who was a friend of Caruso and how Caruso was given a title by Mussolini. I said I didn't think a title from Mussolini was anything to be proud of. My grandfather said, I know, he made that mistake, making friends with Hitler. I said, even without Hitler he was a fascist, he was a bad egg. My grandfather looked confused. Hadn't he told me from childhood that Mussolini made the trains run on time, just as Marconi invented the telegraph?

I always argue. Well, not always; sometimes I boil in silence or gently demur, depending on the subject. My grandmother told me once she loves to hear me talk, I talk so nice: grammatically and with a big vocabulary. Neither does my grandfather seem to mind that I disagree with him. With me, he doesn't consider it a sign of disrespect. He always told me he wanted me to grow up to be president, though when Ferraro ran for vice president, he thought it a bad risk—what if we ended up, God forbid, with a lady president? I reminded him of his plans for me, and he laughed. "That's different," he said, and when I asked why, he answered, "Because you're my granddaughter." When he complains about this generation of today, and I try to defend us, he says, "I don't mean you. I mean the others."

My grandfather points out that it is impractical for unmarried people to live apart from their families: "two phone bills, two electrical, two water bills, heat, groceries." I say, "Grandpa, we don't pay for water in the city." He says, "The landlord pays, but you pay in the rent. You're working for the landlord."

He says, "The problem with this country is no one has time for family. It used to be, everyone came together for Sunday dinner, and they spent the day eating and talking—hours went by, the whole day! Now they eat and run, an hour and then they're off to play golf; if they give you two hours, it's a miracle!" He says, "The problem with this country is career before family. You live to work, instead of work to live!"

He says, "I want to see the mothers home with the children, the way it should be, not the child comes home and the house is empty. A man should bring home the bacon, the wife, put it in the pan"—and laughs.

He says, "I want you to know, dear granddaughter, that family is the most important thing."

V

As for the rage close to grief, you may know that too: like parsley, curly or flat, bitter, individual.

My grandmother suffers from what she calls "nervous tension." Each Christmas, before preparing the Christmas Eve feast of eels and macaroni with fish sauce and lobster, she disintegrates into days of hiccuping burps and sobs, her eyes rubbed red under her glasses, sometimes not even wearing her wig to cover the baldness caused by menopause. Her sons argue and cajole, offer to have the dinner elsewhere, at a restaurant; my grandfather refuses, says they will stay home. "Right away he steams up, gets so excited," my grandfather says; at the last minute she recovers, and the dinner is cooked. Her children say that next year they will do it differently; each year it is the same, even when they bring over the main dishes ready cooked: still the bald head with wisps of white, the red-rimmed eyes, the burping, the wishing to die; my grandfather decorates the house with blue lights and flashing multicolored rosettes still in the box; I roast the nuts, set the table, make the salad, mix the parsley, garlic, and oil into the bread crumbs to stuff the mushrooms; the dinner goes on; at the end, the table is strewn with orange and tangerine peels, the hulls of walnuts and chestnuts.

I wonder, with all the modern tools at hand, is it something in my grandmother's childhood, something about Christmas in the convent school where she and her sisters were raised by nuns? Was it that she learned to cook from her mother-in-law and not from her mother, who died so young; is it the pressure of living up to the ways of an Old Country she herself never knew? Anger at the rigidity of expectation, the tyranny of ritual, the respect for authority, the insistence that certain truths not be uttered and certain feelings not be had? Either my grandmother herself does not know or if she knows, has never told anyone. Or if she told my grandfather, for instance, he then has never told. Or if her doctor, he has only prescribed antidepressants, which she calls her "depression pills."

The past is inscrutable, but not my grandmother's radiance when, inexplicably happy again, the holidays past, she giggles and her eyes shine. In such good spirits she will sometimes sing the songs she sang with the other girls as they worked in the garment district making wedding dresses, sewing thousands of tiny beads. "I want God to keep me living to see you a beautiful bride, then he can take me," she says. "I pray God finds you a good man, a good man like your grandfather."

My grandmother loves to sew and would have liked to keep working, she once told me, but my grandfather wouldn't let her once they could get by on his earnings alone. "It wouldn't look right," she said; he wanted to appear a man of means. He once told me he wanted to make Salierno a respected name in this country, as it had been in Italy. For the same reason he came home one day, to their apartment in a building full of relatives in Italian East Harlem, to tell my grandmother he had bought a house in the country. They were moving up and out, taking his mother with them.

In the country, within twenty minutes drive (but she won't drive now, which leaves her housebound) of each of her brothers and her parents, my mother suffers, terribly, from the depression that struck each of her parents, as well as a premature decline from Parkinson's disease. Though her husband comes home at night, she is alone, alone, alone, alone! Each time I see her, she cries, "I wish you could come more often. When are you coming again? I wish you didn't have to leave!" She says, "I don't want you to have to quit your job," which means, of course, that in some part of herself she has already imagined, already wished that I will. And is it not the proper role for the only daughter of an only daughter in an Italian family to care for her parents, for the old and the sick? What about my pride in my work? Isn't family the most important thing? What's more important, freedom or love?

If I don't visit for more than three weeks, my grandfather greets me, "Hello, stranger." My grandmother counts the weeks. My friends think I visit my family often; they don't understand that my living alone, visiting only thirty-six or forty-eight hours every two or three weeks, is one version of poverty, just as it is an American form of wealth. The demands of my family are not those of a modernity so fluid it carries effortlessly along even nostalgia for the smell of the marinara sauce bubbling on the stove, the "Kiss Me, I'm Italian," the San Gennaro Festival in Little Italy—of an America where we might have the bakeries without the landlords.

Recently, when my grandparents both had the flu, I made them a big vat of chicken soup. While the soup was cooking and I sat working in the other room, I could hear my grandmother talking about me—loudly, because she'd taken out her hearing aids. "You know, Joe, I think she misses us," she shouted. "Do you hear me? I think that little child misses us. And I just have a feeling, she's going to bring us a lot of happiness one day. Yes, God is going to let us see her a beautiful bride, I just have that feeling."

In my neighborhood church in Brooklyn, its walls lined with lurid statues of bleeding saints, two teenage girls gossip in the pew, playing with a beeper, whispering loudly over the pages of a young adult novel. Three times I tell them to be quiet. Each time they ignore me. I tell them, "You may not want to be here, but that doesn't mean you have to be disruptive for people who do." They roll their eyes. These kids of today, they have no respect! My blood boils. I get steamed up right away. I have, I know, my grandfather's cardiovascular system, the same relation between blood and heart.

And some mornings, I wake up with my stomach in knots, burping like my grandmother. I have my grandmother's gut, which twists up with the knowledge that I am not, somehow, what I am wanted to be.

## VI

First the garlic, then the parsley, then the bread crumbs and oregano; the landlord's fig tree, the backyard stained with wine; grandfather without a father, grandmother without a mother; holiday dinner with red-rimmed eyes, best vest coffee soda mozzarella black coffee anisette zucchini flowers orange peels hulls of walnuts roasted chestnuts kids today without respect love rage love.

# SHERMAN ALEXIE
## (1966– )

Raised in the Pacific Northwest as a member of the Spokane/Coeur d'Alene tribe of Native American Indians, Alexie is among the most interesting younger voices to emerge in the nineties. He began his career as a poet and writer of short prose pieces, publishing such volumes as *The Business of Fancydancing: Stories and Poems* (1992) and *First Indian on the Moon* (1993), which contains the autobiographical vignette included below, while still in his twenties. An early collection of stories, *The Lone Ranger and Tonto Fistfight in Heaven* (1993) was widely acclaimed as a wryly humorous and often wrenching portrait of contemporary Native American life on the Spokane Indian Reservation.

This was followed in 1995 by *Reservation Blues*, a darkly funny novel about a Spokane Indian called Thomas Builds-the-Fire who encounters a legendary blues star and is passed his enchanted guitar. Only a year later he published *Indian Killer*, a novel about an Indian serial killer who murders whites in retribution for the injustices done to his people. Alexie joins Leslie Marmon Silko, Michael Dorris, and Louise Erdrich as one of the outstanding Native American writers to emerge in recent years.

## FROM *First Indian on the Moon*

### YEAR OF THE INDIAN
*January*

New Year's Eve, out with my girlfriend and ten other friends, everybody white except me. We were all in the pizza place in Reardan, just off the reservation, when the door opened and this Indian stranger walked in, just blasted, and sat at the counter. He gave me a nod and smiled, one Indian to another.

Then my girlfriend leaned into the middle of the table and we all leaned into the middle of the table to hear what she had to say.

"I hate Indians," she said.

Oh, my first brief love.

### February

Temperature below freezing, but the entire population of the Spokane Indian Reservation watched as Lester FallsApart stumbled out of his tin shack this morning and checked the length of his shadow.

That shadow stretched for miles down the tribal highway, ran past pine tree and Coyote Springs, right down to the very edge of the reservation where it stopped, grew darker.

Spring may never come.

### March

So many Indians in the Breakaway Bar on St. Patrick's Day, drinking green beer and talking stories.

"What you giving up for Lent this year?" Seymour asks me.

"Catholicism," I tell him.

And we laugh.

"Hey," he asks. "Did you ever hear about the guy who was half-Irish and half-Indian?"

"No," I say.

"He owned his own bar but went out of business because he was his own best customer."

And we laugh.

And I buy him another beer and then another. One, because he's Indian all the time, and two, because he's Irish today.

We've all got so many reasons, real and imagined, to drink.

### April

How would your heart change if I told you Jesus Christ had already come back for the second time and got crucified again?

He called himself Crazy Horse and never said anything about a third attempt.

### May

Today, Moses wanted to memorialize every Indian who died in war, fighting for this country and against this country during the last five hundred years, so he began the task of capturing swallows, one for each of the dead.

Moses held each swallow to his mouth and breathed out the name of a fallen Indian: man, woman, child. But those names are secret and cannot be shared with you.

Moses worked for years. After he was finished, Moses released the swallows into the air over the reservation, millions of them.

Millions.

Fly, warriors, fly.

### June

June begins and ends with a powwow and there are powwows everywhere in between.

That is how it should always be.

Arlene, my sister, she says, "Before this month is over, the best traditional dancer in the world is going to call me sweetheart."

June begins and ends with a powwow and there are powwows everywhere in between.

That is how it will always be.

### July

Fourth of July and the air is heavy with smoke and whiskey. I find Tyrone passed out in the dumpster behind the Trading Post. I reach in, slap his face a little, tug on his arms and legs.

"Hey, cuz," I say. "Wake up. Someone's going to come along and throw you away."

He doesn't move. Tyrone was my best friend in the reservation grade school. In sixth grade, he was so perfect and I was nearly as good. Once, Tyrone and I took on the rest of our class in a basketball game. Two-on-thirteen, full court, regulation time, and we beat them by twenty points. But that was a century ago. Now, Tyrone is too far gone to swat at the flies that crawl into his open mouth.

"Hey, Tyrone," I say. "Come on. Somebody's grandma is going to think you're salvageable and take you home with her."

He doesn't move at all. He is breathing, though, and I jump into the dumpster with him. I try to lift him but he's too heavy with alcohol and commodity food. I can't get any leverage.

"Hey," I yell at the Trading Post manager as he walks by. "Help me get Tyrone out of this damn thing. The garbage men might not see him in here."

"Don't worry about it," the manager says. "They stopped collecting that kind of trash a long time ago."

Listen: all I want is a little piece of independence.

### August

Sweet songs from the tribal drum and the mosquitoes, both driving me crazy in my bed when I try to sleep.

These end of summer days drag on with no measure other than Indian sweat and hot tempers. Ernie Game punched Seymour thirty-seven times the other night because it was 7:37 P.M.

This kind of heat creates that sort of twisted logic.

Ten years ago, Little Dog drowned when he passed out and fell face down into a mud puddle, probably the only mud puddle left in that year of drought. It was so strange that the tribe created a holiday for it. No one worked and no one drank in celebration. We all just sat around and laughed at the stupid wonder of it all.

And last night, after everyone had gone on home, I stood naked on my front porch and howled like an old coyote and the old coyotes, beautiful and crazy, howled right back.

### September

Working at the Laundromat seven days a week. Change for dollar bills, sweeping up stray detergent, amusing little white kids.

All for minimum wage.

It's Labor Day and I'm supposed to honor the sweat that made my sweat possible. My hands are bleached white from drop-off laundry; my feet and back ache because I'm always at attention, never use the employee's chair that sits in the back office. I'm always doing an awkward fancydance between washer and dryer.

All for minimum wage.

I punch a clock when I make promises now; I punch a clock when I tell lies. Every day I feel dirty and used. I'm a dishrag, cloth diaper, mismatched sock.

Come on in, sir, I have beautiful braids. Come on in, madam, I have granite cheekbones, and my clothes, my work clothes, my blue shirt and blue jeans, are clean, clean.

### October

In the shopping mall today, a little white boy ran up to me, shouting so loud that he attracted everybody's attention.

"Hey, mister," he yelled at me. "You're an Indian and I'm dressing up like an Indian for Halloween, too!"

There were smiles and laughter all around. I smiled and laughed a little, leaned down and whispered into the little boy's ear. His smile quickly disappeared and he ran toward his mother, crying.

The crowd circled me, accused me of child abuse, demanded apologies and explanations. But I just left before mall security could arrive to question me and before some group of rednecks could gather enough courage to jump one crazy Indian.

"Son," I whispered into that little boy's ear, "I'm just wearing my nice Indian mask today. If I take it off, you'll see the warrior that wants to cut your tongue out."

### November

Walking down the tribal highway, hungry, wondering where my family will find their food during the long winter, when a truck rolls by me, stops.

"Hey, chief," the driver asks. "Where the hell am I and how do I get out of here?"

I tell him he's on the Spokane Indian Reservation and that I'm not really sure how to get out.

"Ha, ha," he laughs. "That's a good one, chief. Now, really, how do I get out of here?"

I point down the road and tell him he just needs to follow the road he's on, stay on the pavement, don't make any turns until you cross water, then it's a left to the rest of the world.

"Thanks, chief," he yells.

As he drives away, a bag drops off the back of his truck and I run over, pick it up, and nearly cry because it's a fifty-pound bag of potatoes. Then, I do cry because it's potatoes, potatoes, potatoes.

We give thanks, Lord, for the food we're about to receive.

### December

Crazy Horse dresses up like Santa Claus for the reservation school Christmas Pageant, reads the letters of all the Indian boys and girls asking for jobs, college educations, a ticket for a Greyhound travelling back or ahead five hundred years.

Crazy Horse searches his pack but he only finds a few hard candies, an orange, and miles and miles of treaties.

Crazy Horse leaves out the back, straight into the Breakaway Bar, where he watches a holiday movie, Bing Crosby singing *White Christmas* for choirboys who go home afterward and open their presents, all finding rifles, hammers and nails to build walls.

# ELIZABETH WURTZEL

## (1967– )

Wurtzel has often been called a prodigy. Abandoned by her father, she was raised in New York City by her Orthodox Jewish mother. She attended Harvard, and published her first book, *Prozac Nation*, in 1994. In a vividly written account of the transformations wrought by this drug, she told of her struggles with depression and her subsequent discovery of Prozac. While the book was often harshly criticized in the press ("It smacks of self-pity and reeks of marketing research," said a reviewer in the *Dallas Observer*), it became a best-seller. Between 1989 and 1993, Wurtzel wrote rock criticism for both *New York Magazine* and *The New Yorker*. In 1998, she published *Bitch: In Praise of Difficult Women*, a book about famous female troublemakers from Delilah and Anne Sexton to Wurtzel herself. The following essay appeared in the anthology *Next: Young American Writers on the New Generation* (1994).

## "Parental Guidance Suggested"

It is the spring of my junior year of college, I am lying in a near-catatonic state in a mental ward, I have just been given an industrial-strength antipsychotic—the kind they give to schizophrenics—because I have not been able to stop crying and shaking and wailing for hours, and the doctor is afraid that I might, quite literally, choke on my own tears. The pill they've given me—some variation on Thorazine—has knocked me into a silent state of submission that would be perfectly blissful if only the therapist on duty would stop trying to get me to talk to her. She wants to know what's wrong; she wants to know what I am experiencing that is so potent and profound that it takes a brain-draining drug to make it go away.

I don't know, is all I keep saying. I don't know, I don't know, I don't know.

What have you lost? she asks, trying a new approach.

I know I better come up with something. I better think of an answer before they start trying out other things on me—different drugs, electroconvulsive therapy (known in the vernacular as *shock*), whatever.

I think it's got something to do with summer camp, I say.

She looks at me blankly.

It's like this, I begin: I'm from New York City, my mom is Jewish and middle class, my dad is solidly white trash, they divorced when I was two, my mom was always unemployed or marginally employed and my dad was always uninvolved or marginally involved in raising me, there was never enough money for anything, we lived in state-subsidized housing, I went to private schools on scholarships, and my childhood, as I recall it, is one big flurry of application forms for financial aid or for special rates on this thing or that thing that my mother thought I should really have because she didn't want me to be deprived of anything.

My mom really did her best.

But then, as soon as I was old enough, my mother decided that I had to go to sleep-away camp for the summers. She was overextended as a parent throughout the school year, my dad wasn't willing to take care of me, and there was nothing for a girl like me to do in New York City during the long hot summer except get into trouble with the neighborhood kids. So it was off to camp. That was that.

I went to camp for five years in a row—a different one each year, a different setup in a different rural town in the Poconos or the Catskills or the Berkshires or wherever I could enroll at a discount rate. And the funny thing is, I explain to the therapist, after my mother had sent me off to these places that I thought were so lonesome and horrible, instead of hating her for it, I just spent all summer missing her. All my waking and sleeping energy was devoted to missing this rather minimal and unstable home I came from. Starting on June 28, or whatever day it was that I got to camp, and never even achieving a brief reprieve until I'd come home on August 24 or so, I would devote myself fully to the task of getting back home. I'd spend hours each day writing my mom letters, calling her on the phone, just making sure that she'd know exactly where and when to pick me up at the bus when it was time to return. I would run to the camp's administrative offices to make sure that notices about the location of the return trip would be sent to my mother so that she'd know where to find me. I'd extract promises that she'd arrive there one or two hours early. I'd even call my dad and get him to promise to be there at least a half hour before the estimated time of arrival. I'd talk to the head counselor and express my concern that I might be put on a bus to New Jersey or Long Island and somehow end up in the wrong place and never find my way back home. I would ask other New Yorkers in my bunk if I could go home with them if my mother failed to materialize at the bus stop. I would call grandparents, aunts, uncles, and baby-sitters—always collect—to find out where they would be on August 24, just in case I had to go to one of their homes, in case my parents didn't show up to get me.

Instead of discovering the virtues of tennis and volleyball, or of braiding lanyards and weaving potholders, I would devote a full eight weeks of my summer to planning for a two-hour trip back home.

The therapist looks at me kind of strangely, as if this doesn't quite make sense, that summer camp was so long ago and I'll never have to go back again, so why is this still bothering me? There's no way, I realize, to ever make her understand that homesickness is just a state of mind for me, that I'm always missing someone or some place or something, I'm always trying to get back to some imaginary somewhere. My life has been one long longing.

And I'm sick of it. And I can't move. And I've a feeling, I tell the therapist, that I might as well lie here congealed to this hospital bed forever because there's no place in the world that's at all like a home to me and I'd rather be dead than spend another minute in this life as an emotional nomad.

A few days later, having lost all hope of anything else working, a psychiatrist gives me a prescription for a new, virtually untried antidepressant that she thinks might help. It's called fluoxetine hydrochloride, brand name Prozac. A few weeks later, I am better, much better, as I have been ever since.

But there's just one small problem. They can give me all sorts of drugs to stabilize my moods, to elevate the downs, to flatten the ups, to make me function in this world like any other normal, productive person who works, pays rent, has affairs, waters her own plants. They can make it all feel pretty much all right most of the time. But they can't do anything for the homesickness. There's no pill they can come up with that can cure the longing I feel to be in a place that feels like home. There's no cure for the strange estrangedness, and if there were, I am sure my body would resist it.

Since I first began taking Prozac, the pill has become one of the most commonly prescribed drugs in the country, with 650,000 orders filled each month. Back in 1990, the story of this wonder drug made the cover of periodicals like *Newsweek* and *New York*, while *Rolling Stone* deemed Prozac the "hot yuppie upper," and all the major network newsmagazines and daytime talk shows began to do their Prozac-saved-my-life segments. While a backlash of reports linked Prozac with incidents of suicide and murder, the many people who it relieved from symptoms of depression had nothing but praise: Cheryl Wheeler, a Nashville folkie, even wrote a song called "Is It Peace or Is It Prozac?"

Yet this is not just about Prozac: it's about the mainstreaming of mental illness—it's about the way a state of mind that was once considered tragic has become completely commonplace. Talk of depression as the mental disease of our times has been very much in the air in the last few years, to the point where it has almost become a political issue: As Hillary Rodham Clinton campaigned on behalf of what she deemed "The Politics of Meaning," it was hard not to notice that her references to a "sleeping sickness of the soul," to "alienation and despair and hopelessness," to a "crisis of meaning," and to a "spiritual vacuum" seemed to imply that the country's problems have less to do with taxes and unemployment than with the simple fact that we were in one big collective bad mood. It is almost as if, perhaps, the next time half a million people gather for a protest march in Washington it will not be for abortion rights or gay liberation but because we're all just so bummed out.

Of course, one of the striking elements of this depression outbreak is the extent to which it has gotten such a strong hold on so many young people. The Valium addicts of the fifties and sixties, the housewives reaching for their mother's little helpers, the strung-out junkies and crackheads who litter the gutters of the Bowery or the streets of Harlem or the Skid Row of any town—all these people were stereotyped as wasted, dissipated, or middle-aged. What is fascinating about depression this time around is the extent to which it is affecting those who have so much to look forward to and to hope for, who are, as one might say of a bright young thing about to make her debut into the world, so full of promise.

Recently, I was reading a magazine on an airplane, and I chanced upon an article titled "The Plot Sickens," in which a college writing instructor sees the gruesome, pessimistic nature of the work that her students produce as an indication of a wave of youth malaise like none she'd ever noticed before in twenty-one years of teaching. "To read their work, you'd think they were a generation that was starved, beaten, raped, arrested, addicted, and war-torn. Inexplicable intrusions of random tragedy break up the otherwise good life of the characters," the author writes. "The figures in their fictions are victims of hideous violence by accident; they commit crimes, but only for the hell of it; they hate, not understanding why they hate; they are loved or abused or depressed, and don't know why . . . Randomness rules."

Perhaps for the author of that article, the nature of her students' work is surprising. For me, and for everyone I know my age, it just seems normal, peculiarly ordinary. I mean: Randomness *does* rule.

A few years ago, I wrote an article about my bout with depression for *Mademoiselle*. I was rather alarmed when the piece generated more mail than anything else they'd run in several years and was somewhat heartened but also terribly saddened to see that I had touched such a raw, exposed nerve in so many young women. Shortly after the article ran, I was on the phone with my editor, and she suddenly asked, "I wonder what Prozac would do for regular people—I mean, not clinical cases like you, but just the rest of us who are normally depressed."

Once again, that word *normally* seemed to be creeping up in a place where it oughtn't be. Since when is it *normal* to be depressed? What kind of world do we live in that someone can refer to depression as a *normal* state?

Christopher Ricks once wrote an essay about the difference between "disenchanted" and "unenchanted," the former describing someone sprung by reality from an enchanted state, while the latter is a person who was never enchanted to begin with. And that's me. And that's what society's come to: the spate of depression that I have come into contact with is not among people who've been disappointed by life—it's among those who have given up on it before they've even given it a real go. So many of us who are in our twenties now were born into homes that had already fallen apart, fathers on the lam, mothers on the floor, no sense of security and safety, no sense of home at all. So we muddle through our adult lives wandering around, kind of dazed, kind of wasted, looking like lost children who are still waiting to be claimed at the security office of the shopping mall or amusement park or supermarket where our parents last lost track of us. When Sonic Youth titled its 1989 album *Daydream Nation*, I think they must have been referring to this youth cadre of the walking wounded, of people who spend so many of their waking hours lost in thought, distraction, and abstraction, trying to get a grip on the hopes—on the dreams—that they dare not have in their conscious minds. Sleep is no relief because they are always sort of asleep. All these young people are homesick and in a reverie for an enchanted place they've never known.

While I often get the sense that many older people look back on their childhoods with a sense of sorrow that they had to grow up and say goodbye to all that, most of my friends could not wait to come of age and get out of the house because the house was not a home. The lucky among us had two active, participating parents and had to spend a lot of time schlepping between two households, always lugging an overnight bag or wondering whether the black-and-white saddle shoes and box of Lego were at Mommy's or Daddy's. In my case, only my mother really cared for me, and she had a really hard time just making ends meet; she seemed forever on the verge of a nervous breakdown, so I spent much of my time just trying to keep her calm. My dad used Valium and pretty much managed to sleep through my whole childhood (when I was nine, we went to see *The Last Waltz*, he fell asleep, and we ended up sitting through the movie three times because I couldn't get him to wake up); our Saturday-afternoon visits mostly involved his putting me in front of the television set to watch "Star Trek" reruns or college basketball while he dozed off.

But these are only the incidental, aftershock effects that divorce has on children—far more terrifying is the violent rupture it creates in any young person's life because any sense of home is ripped asunder, any sense of a safe haven in a cruel world is taken away. We did not learn about bitterness and hatred on the streets (the supposed source of all terror)—we learned from watching our parents try to kill each other. We didn't learn to break promises and (marriage) vows from big bad bullies at school—we learned from watching our parents deny every word they once said to each other. And we learned from them that it is not just acceptable, but virtually normal, to realize that love does not last forever. There are certainly plenty of kids whose parents will stay together until death do they part and who haven't experienced the symptoms I've just described. But even they are affected by the divorce revolution because it colors their worldview, too. They know that their own marriages might end in divorce. They know that the family unit is not sacred, and this adds a degree of uncertainty to their own plans.

But I don't want to get too down on divorce. It has become all too facile a neoconservative impulse to blame divorce or the decline of so-called family values for all the ills of our society. Even more troubling is how easy it has become for people in my age group to blame the lack of a structured family life when they were growing up for all their problems as adults. If I allowed myself to express the full extent of the bitterness I feel toward my parents for not, shall we say, having their shit together while they were raising me, I fear that I might start to sound like an ally of Dan Quayle. And I don't want to do that. The main reason: it is precisely those family values that Dan Quayle referred to in his famous anti–Murphy Brown speech that drove my parents, and so many of my friends' parents, into marriages they were not ready for and bearing children they were not capable of properly nurturing.

It was the family imperative, the sense that life happens in a simple series of steps (something like: adolescence-college-marriage-kids) that all sane and decent people must adhere to that got our parents in trouble to begin with. Remember, the progenitors of people in my age group are not, for the most part, those freewheeling, wild baby boomers who took it upon themselves to transform our society in the late sixties and early seventies. Our parents were, on the whole, a little too old for that, they are people who were done with college and had moved on to the work world by the early sixties—several years before the campus uprisings, the antiwar activities, and the emerging sex-drugs-rock-and-roll culture had become a pervasive force. By the time the radical sixties hit our home bases, we were already born, and our parents found themselves stuck between an entrenched belief that children needed to be raised in a traditional household and a new sense that anything was possible, that the alternative lifestyle was out there for the asking. A little too old to take full advantage of the cultural revolution of the sixties, our parents just got all the fallout. Instead of waiting later to get married, our parents got divorced; instead of becoming feminists, our mothers were left as displaced homemakers. A lot of already existent unhappy situations were dissolved by people who were not quite young or free (read: childless) enough to start again. And their discontent—their stuck-ness—was played out on their children.

My parents are a perfect case in point. Lord knows what ever possessed them to get married in the first place. It probably had something to do with the fact that my mom was raised with many of her first cousins, and all of them were getting married, so it seemed like the thing to do. And from her point of view, back in the early sixties, marriage was the only way she could get out of her parents' house. She'd gone to Cornell, wanting to be an architect, but her mother told her all she could be was an architect's *secretary*, so she majored in art history with that goal in mind. She'd spent a junior year abroad at the Sorbonne and did all the studiedly adventurous things a nice Jewish girl from Long Island can do in Paris—rented a moped, wore a black cape, dated some nobleman type—but once she got out of college, she moved back home and was expected to stay there until she moved into her husband's house. (Certainly there were many bolder women who defied this expectation, who took efficiencies and railroad flats with girlfriends in safe neighborhoods in the city, who worked and dated and went to theater openings and lectures—but my mom was not one of them.) She took a job in the executive training program at Macy's, and one day while she was riding the escalator up from the main floor to the mezzanine, she passed my father, who was riding down. They got married less than a year later, even though he hadn't gone to college, had no ambition, and was considered a step down for a girl like my mom.

My parents did weird things after they got married. My dad got a job at IBM and they moved to Poughkeepsie, New York, where my mom went nuts with boredom and bought herself a pet monkey named Percy. Eventually she got pregnant with me, decided a baby was better than a monkey, and she moved down to New York City because she could not bear another day in a town that was half Vassar College, half IBM. My father followed, I was born, they fought, they were miserable, he refused to get a college degree, they fought some more, and then one day I wouldn't stop crying. My mom called my dad at work to say that if he didn't come home immediately and figure out how to get me to calm down, she was going to defenestrate me. Whatever my father did when he got to the apartment must have worked, because I'm still alive today, but I think that moment marked the end of their marriage.

This was a marriage that could have peacefully ceased to be one fine day with an understanding that it was just a mistake, they were just two foolish kids playing house. Problem was, they had a child, and for many years after they split up, I became the battlefield on which they fought through all their ideological differences. This was New York City in the late sixties, Harlem had burned down, my mom was petrified about being a single mother with a deadbeat ex-husband, so she sent me to the synagogue nursery school, thinking this would provide me with some sense of community and stability. My dad would turn up to see me about once a week, and he would talk to me about atheism and insist I eat lobster and ham and other nonkosher foods that I was taught in school were not allowed. For years, my mom was tugging toward trying to give me a solid, middle-class, traditional upbringing, while my father would tell me that I should just be an artist or a poet or live off the land, or some such thing. She was desperate to keep at least a toehold in the bourgeoisie, and he was working overtime (or actually, not *gainfully* working at all) to stay the hell out of it. Back and forth this went for years, until it felt clear that all three of us were caught mostly in the confusing cross fire of changing times, and what little foundation my parents could possibly give me was shattered and scattered by conflict.

When I was ten or eleven, I really cracked up, started hiding in the locker room at school, crying for hours, or walking around the corridors saying, *Everything is plastic, we're all gonna die anyway, so why does anything matter?* I'd read this phrase in a picture of some graffiti in a magazine article about punk rock, which I decided was definitely a great invention. When I stopped talking, stopped eating, stopped going to school, and started spending my time cutting my legs up with razor blades while listening to dumb rock music like Foreigner on a little Panasonic tape recorder, my parents agreed I needed psychiatric help. To make a very long and complicated story short, my mom found a therapist for me, my dad didn't like him and kept trying to sneak me off to others, I never got terribly effective treatment, my father refused to file an insurance claim for the psychiatrist I was seeing, and the whole scenario concluded with me as messed up as ever, but with all the adults involved suing one another. My mom sued my dad for unpaid alimony and child support, my psychiatrist sued my dad for unpaid bills, and after years of lawyers everywhere, my father finally fled to Florida when I was fourteen years old and did not turn up in my life again until my freshman year at Harvard.

By the time I actually did grow up, I was so grateful to be out of my parents' firing range and not stuck in between them or torn apart like an overstretched rubber band they each tugged at for years that my depression actually began to lift. For me, growing up was not about coming face-to-face with the cruelties of the world; it was about relief.

Obviously, divorce is inevitable and at this point there is joint custody and divorce counseling and all sorts of other things to make the process less painful for the children and for the adults. Which might mean that things are better now, although I think things must be so much worse if divorce is being normalized—because let's face it, all these strangely pieced together families of half siblings and stepparents and all that are not natural. At one time, a kid got two parents who did their best to get it right, but now, taking stepparents into account, he can have twice as many guardians—along with nannies, therapists, tutors, and whatnot—but somehow, all these people put together can't seem to raise a child decently. It's like having ninety-two channels of cable and nothing to watch.

And that was pretty much the world I grew up in—a world where nothing seemed to matter because there was no strong parental force and no reasonable parental guidance (what paleolithic era were they thinking of when they invented the PG movie rating?). And that is why an album titled *Nevermind* by an unknown band called Nirvana became one of the most popular releases of recent years: nevermind is the code word of this life, nevermind is all we ever do—we never mind that we never mind that we never mind because there is nothing left to care about.

Critics complained that archetypal twentysomething movies like *Singles* or television shows like "Melrose Place" seemed to revolve around such mundane concerns that the characters were all wandering in a haze, looking for love and approbation in every person and every crevice of a person, looking for the next small fix to make the next few days bearable—above all, they complained that none of the Jennifers and Jasons seemed able to get out of their own heads long enough to take a look at the big picture. In a *Mirabella* essay titled "Twentysomething," Walter Kirn points out how cinematic young adults have been reduced to so little. "In this twentystuff soap opera, public causes exist to be gestured at ('Think Globally, Act Locally' reads a bumper sticker), but private life is all the life there is, the world's having shrunk to the cramped dimensions of one's wacky, sad, starter apartment with its sardonic, cheap, recycled furnishings," Kirn writes. Kirn is, of course, correct and astute in his observation, but like so many commentators he is unable to understand that getting by from day to day is all you can do when simple things like lovingkindness seem to be so scarce.

This fixation on private life and personal problems is constantly being assigned to twentysomethings as some sort of character flaw and one that seems especially flagrant when you consider that young people in the six-ties were, at least in legend, in the throes of a belief that they could change the whole wide world. Of course, no one thinks that way any longer. These days, the first hard lesson you learn—most likely when you're too young to know that it's hard or that it's meant to be a lesson—is not to let it bother you too terribly much that Mommy and Daddy are trying to kill each other, that Mommy says Daddy's a jerk, and Daddy says Mommy is a hysterical bitch, or whatever. And the downward spiral of studied apathy just continues on from there: instead of learning to care about the world around us, we learn not to care about anybody. The possibility of mass movements that are antiwar or proecology are hard to organize in a country where on the simplest one-to-one level people have trouble making connections that last.

Let's translate this into more solid terms: let's consider the many things that *do* exist that we *should* care about—stuff like democracy, the envi-ronment, world peace, the future of our country. All these things are ab-stractions, pie-in-the-sky ideals, soft, slippery concepts that are hard to wrap your loving arms and loving legs around. That's not to say that no one my age cares about them—and heaven knows, when you throw us a concrete agenda like the right to abortion on demand, we can all get pretty worked up about it. But in order to have the personal strength and perseverance to see past your own most immediate needs and worry about the world as a whole, you must have a sense that your needs are being met.

Furthermore, the idea of growing up and assuming a responsible place in society is not a very happy thought to many children of divorce who have been taking care of other people since they were very young. We watched our parents get married not just twice but sometimes three or four times. And with our mothers and fathers out dating, breaking up and making up and discussing their affairs with us as if they were teenagers once again, the lines between who was the grown-up and who was the child were blurred. In an essay about *E.T.*, the sweetest, dreamiest movie of the eighties, John Podhoretz points out how this film is at its core a grim story of decaying family life. "Spielberg also touched a chord be-cause his portrait of the demands placed upon Elliott and his friends by eighties America were starkly realistic," he writes. "These are children of divorce, saddled with incompetent parents and expected in some ways to rear themselves."

It is no wonder that there are certain rather regressive and infantiliz-ing trends that are repeatedly pointed to in all the articles about people in their twenties: the first one is the habit that so many of us have of mov-ing back in with Mom and Dad—or, more likely, Mom *or* Dad—after college graduation; the second is the creation of "slacker" culture, the tendency that some people with educations and prospects have to just get dumb jobs that pay the rent—waiting tables, working the counter of a video store—and give them plenty of time to sleep, read, watch TV, see movies, smoke pot, and to just, like, hang out in amenable extended-campus towns like Austin or Berkeley or Cambridge or Seattle. Usually, when either of these lifestyle choices is discussed, the trends tend to be attributed to simple economics, to the lack of available cheap housing and the lack of employment situations with a real future. I'm not saying that monetary concerns are not factors, but I really think that a lot of this is about wanting to be a kid a little while longer because so many of us were barely able to be children when we actually were children.

I can use myself as an example here. I don't live with either of my parents—in fact, I don't even know where my dad is—and for a long time I was the popular music critic for *The New Yorker*. But I was slacking off then and I still am now. If I wanted to, I could take many more magazine assignments than I do, but I'd rather sleep. When I was doing my pop music column, I'd pull myself together and get the necessary work done for a few days each month, and then I'd spend the other twenty-seven or so days just reading and going to movies and bumming around with friends. I did precisely what I needed to do to earn my living and not a single thing more. I would regularly accept magazine assignments and then just blow them off. At one point, my boyfriend asked me if I wasn't ruining my career with my laziness. All I could say was that I didn't know and didn't care. All through college I'd been a freelance writer to earn a living, and all through high school I had odd jobs and tons of schoolwork, and a lot of emotionally taxing entanglements and crazy parents to deal with, and now that I was old enough to choose, I just wanted to hang out. I wanted to be able to run for the hills on a sunny day; I wanted to be able to kick back in the sandbox at the local playground and toss frisbees with five-year-olds and do all sorts of fun, childish things I never got to do.

So I've got the whole life cycle backwards: all grown-up and running a household at ten and all set to jump on the seesaw and slip down the sliding pond at twenty-five. And I know I'm not the only person in this predicament. How many friends have I got who have already, in their mid-twenties, decided that they want to get off this hamster wheel to nowhere? There's the woman who was a year ahead of me at school who found her job as a stylist at *Harper's Bazaar* too taxing, so now she's a *maitresse d'* at a restaurant. There was the guy who worked as a magazine researcher but decided he'd much rather be a bike messenger (given the nature of most taxi drivers in New York City, to *want* to be a bike messenger here when you could be in a cushy office must surely constitute a new form of mental illness). There is my girlhood friend Jordana who decided she didn't want to be a social worker in the child-welfare department in the Bronx any longer, who concluded that all the idealism in the world wouldn't make a difference, and instead got married and decided to become a garlic farmer in upstate New York. There's Ben, a college classmate of mine who gave up the publishing fast track to work at a Mexican restaurant where his proudest accomplishment has been establishing a Jimi Hendrix brunch every Sunday.

And I know it is tempting to say this is just a bit of Ivy League lassitude, some form of slumming through our twenties before we get on an executive track in our thirties. But it's not just rich children of privilege who have surrendered the ticket before takeoff. There are working-class versions of the same phenomenon—in fact, I think it's become pretty clear that in every stratum there are some people on the fast track, many more on the slow track, and many many more on no track at all.

When I first got out of school, I lived in the far reaches of the East Village, which is supposed to be some kind of grungy epicenter of cool, but is really just a mess. Because I didn't ever have a normal work schedule, I'd spend a good deal of time in cafes or sitting in Tompkins Square Park, and I got to know a lot of my fellow Alphabet City residents who, no matter what the gentrification reports have claimed, were definitely not yuppies. Mostly they were a cohort of young people hanging on to the fringes of the Lower East Side, working as bartenders or waiters or in pet stores or in beauty salons to support a lifestyle with no apparent objectives. When I would meet them at the Life Cafe or Bandito's or King Tut's Wawa Hut, I discovered that the tacky-artsy kids with dyed black hair and do-rags and all sorts of body piercings are not, for the most part, aspiring artists—at best, some of the girls want to design oversize rhinestone earrings or clothing made with lots of leather and lamé. They've got the trappings—the untidy, unheated apartments, the *outré* dress code, the tendency to shoot heroin—of the previous generations of creative souls and Communists who lived in the Village, but they are not *committed* people. They've come to New York from the Everglades, the Appalachians, the Midwest, the Ozarks, the Black Hills, the small towns in Pennsylvania, and the suburbs outside of Chicago, but none of them seems to have gotten an education beyond high school, and none of them seems to be aspiring to anything more than living day-to-day. They don't think of themselves as bohemian and it's unclear whether they think at all. They don't read newspapers or watch CNN, they don't vote, they don't even *rock* the vote, and if anyone were to tell them that they are part of some twentysomething youth culture *thang*, they'd be truly amazed.

Don't get me wrong—in many ways I think it's just great that a visible group of young people is refusing to do things the normal, expected way. And I would never argue on behalf of conventional careerism—I don't think the nine-to-five world is good for many smart, creative people. Certainly, it is tempting to see the slacker culture as a boon compared to the go-go blind ambition of the eighties. But one thing that can be said in behalf of the investment bankers and corporate kids who made lots of money in the last decade; at least they had a certain spark, a desire, a dream—at least they approached life with faith and gusto and a plan to relish the benefits. These days, the slacker kids just draw a blank. And this abandoning of the straight-and-narrow path is not some sixties-style attempt at nonconformity, it is not about a search for greater spiritual truths, it is not about getting back to nature or basics or anything like that—in fact, as far as I can tell it's about one simple thing: fatigue.

How on earth are we ever going to run the world and behave like responsible adults when we're all just so tired?

Despite the exhaustion, I still think that adulthood has been a lot better for me than growing up was. And I believe the task of a lifetime for my generation will be to reinvent the family unit in a way that works and endures. Perhaps critics will say, *Those twentysomethings, all they ever worry about is their private lives*, but I for one believe our private lives deserve some thoughtful attention. If anyone had bothered to give our development as human beings some constructive thought while we were still young enough to receive the benefits passively, we wouldn't have to think about our personal lives so damn much now.

I have heard it said that in our modern world, twelve-step fellowships have become a substitute for family, that the rooms of alcoholics and junkies offering each other support in church basements and community centers is the closest thing anyone has to a familial setup. I have also heard that the neo-Nazi kids in modern Germany, the inner-city youth who join gangs in Los Angeles like the Bloods and the Crips, the homeboys hanging out on the corner—all these movements and loosely bound organizations are about young people trying to find a place in this world to call home, trying to find people in this world to call family. The interesting thing about the attraction of something like AA is that an organization like that involves such a large group of people—not just a few random friends but a big collection of helpful people. And I think we all need some version of that. In the worst moments of my depression, I used to wish I were a drug addict—I used to think it would be so nice if it were simply a matter of getting heroin or alcohol out of my life—because then I could walk into a meeting of fellow sufferers and feel that I'd arrived home at last.

But I'd hate to think that I'd have to become a junkie in order to find my place in this world. And I don't think that is the case. In fact, I think one of the ways many of us twentysomethings have come to deal with our rootlessness has been by turning friends into family. For those of us without addictions, those of us who are just run-of-the-mill parasites on society, our alliances are all that's left. For many of my friends, the world feels like one big orphanage—we're so far from our families, or without families at all, or without families that are able to serve a familial role, and here we get thrown into this lot of life together. Of course, some pundits make fun of us for turning friends and ex-lovers into pseudo-family members, but I believe this is an arrangement that actually works. (Besides, if anyone has a better idea, I'm glad to listen. Joining the Moonies, hooking up with the Branch Davidians, or running off to Esalen are *not* acceptable substitutes.)

And obviously, the theme of friends-as-family seems to resonate in the media a great deal: whether it's in the Banana Republic advertising campaign that pictures several versions of "Your Chosen Family," or it's in the United Colors of Benetton billboards and print ads that try to depict an international loving brotherhood of all races and nations. It's in MTV's attempt at *cinema vérité* with "The Real World," a series that shows a group of young people living in a loft together and puttering their way through the tribulations of everyday; and it's in the way the typical television drama or sitcom of today is likely to revolve around the odd connections and acquaintances made by single people or one-parent families in their apartment complex or subdivision, not on the freestanding biological family that was the center of almost every show thirty years ago. It's in all the press that surrounded the Clinton-Gore bus campaign that attempted to portray the two candidate couples—Al and Tipper and Bill and Hillary—as a little fun-loving family on a perpetual double date rolling its way across the country; and it was in Clinton's beckoning speech at the Democratic convention, in which he invited everyone out there to "join our family." All these examples just amount to a manipulation of Americans' simplest desire to imagine the possibility of home, and yet even as I know my emotions are being toyed with, I still appreciate all these public attempts to define family as something that's got nothing to do with blood.

All my friends, inadequately parented as we seem to have been, spend as much time looking after one another as we do just hanging out and having fun.

I recently spent a three-day weekend in Vermont with a man I was dating—who happens to be an alcoholic and going through a divorce—along with his father and his six-year-old daughter. As one can imagine, the pastoral promise of a few days in the country was frequently disturbed by his wife calling and the two of them having screaming fights for hours, or by his daughter getting hysterical because her parents were splitting up, or by his father not knowing how to handle the oddity of the four of us away together on this farm. The drama I experienced that weekend involved some terrain that was a little too familiar—this poor little girl reminded me so much of myself at her age—but on the whole it was a pleasant enough weekend.

Just the same, it was a great relief to walk into my living room on Monday night and see a bunch of my friends sitting on the sofas and wing chairs, waiting for me to return, wanting me to know that they were worried about me. I'm not kidding myself—I think they were mostly at my house to just kick back and watch the Knicks-Bulls game—but all of them seemed to know where I'd been, whom I'd been with, what the circumstances were, and I felt a comfort and security about myself and my world that I had never ever experienced the whole time I was growing up. I hate to think of what I'd do if I didn't have such patient and forbearing friends, if I didn't have people so willing to see me through years of crises, years of crying on the kitchen floor and running out of parties in tears and screaming for no apparent reason and calling in the middle of the night and everything else that comes with depression. Insofar as I'm now able to get work done, to make attempts at having relationships, to live a life that is fruitful and productive at all, I attribute it completely to the friends that I have turned into my family.

And if anyone finds that pathetic, I don't care. I don't want to spend another minute of my life supine and suffering in a hospital bed, praying to God for any form of relief he can give to a mind—not even a body—in terrible pain. I don't ever want to endure another morning of the orderlies coming in at 7:00 to take a blood sample and take my temperature because that is the routine in a health-care facility—even though the only thing that's wrong with me is in my head. I don't want to roam the streets at all hours of the day and night, feeling crazy from the heat in the middle of January, running like hell from the voices in my head. I don't want to live life as a sicko. And the friendships I have developed as an adult are probably the only thing standing between me and Bellevue. More to the point, they are the only thing standing between me and suicide. The hole in my heart that was left by a grievous lack of family connections has in some ways been patched over, if not altogether filled, by a sense of family I've found in the last few years.

But I must say, I'm sure my friends and I often seem like these sad lost people who are scared to grow up. I sometimes worry that the clinginess of our relationships is kind of a sorry thing, that we often seem to be holding on tight because of the depth of our desperation and need—and perhaps this just isn't healthy. We often spend time together in large groups of people, and I keep thinking we all really should be out on dates in couples, but it doesn't seem as though any of us is quite ready even to think about getting into deeply committed relationships. I have plenty of friends who have been going out with the same person for years, but none of them is showing signs of heading to the altar. We're all just much too frightened.

And it is this nervousness, this lack of trust, that makes this generation seem ineffectual to many older people on so many fronts.

But we are trying our best to take care of one another. And it is my hope that when we finally do have kids of our own, the sense of community we have created for ourselves will be passed along to them. I hope my children know that their father and I are not the only adults in their lives who can be counted on—I hope they feel that Christine, Jason, Mark, Larissa, Tom, Heather, Ronnie, and Sharon are as much a part of their family as they are part of mine. I hope my friends' children will play with my kids, and I hope they all grow up understanding that they too can choose families of their own. I hope they don't ever think that their world and their expectations are limited by two people who just happen to be their parents, and might do some really stupid, silly things along the way.

These days we all sit around, drinking Rolling Rock and smoking pot late into the night as if we were still in our college dormitory rooms, and sometimes we talk about how it will be to have kids someday. And we all say the same thing: we can't wait to bring children into the world and do everything right that our parents did wrong. Of course, I suspect that our parents had the same idea themselves, and look where it got them.

But still, I've got to believe I can do better. I've already brought up myself, so surely I ought to be able to raise someone else.

I think.

# PERMISSIONS